The American Critical Archives is a series of reference books that provide representative selections of contemporary reviews of the main works of major American authors. Specifically, each volume contains both full reviews and excerpts from reviews that appeared in newspapers and weekly and monthly periodicals generally within a few months of the publication of the work concerned. There is an introductory historical overview by the volume editor, as well as checklists of additional reviews located but not quoted.

This book reprints contemporaneous reviews of Ellen Glasgow's books as those reviews were published from 1897 through 1943. Originally printed in newspapers and other periodicals in the United States and in Great Britain, they tell the story of Glasgow's critical reception during her long and productive career. Nineteen novels, as well as a volume of poetry, one of short stories, and one of criticism, were published during her lifetime. Her first book, published anonymously in 1897, elicited much attention when it was revealed that the author was a young Richmond woman. By the time of the 1943 publication of her volume of literary criticism, *A Certain Measure*, she was a much respected and much honored author—winner of a Pulitzer Prize, a Howells Medal, and other awards.

AMERICAN CRITICAL ARCHIVES 3
Ellen Glasgow: The Contemporary Reviews

The American Critical Archives

GENERAL EDITOR: M. Thomas Inge, Randolph-Macon College

1. *Emerson and Thoreau: The Contemporary Reviews*, edited by Joel Myerson
2. *Edith Wharton: The Contemporary Reviews*, edited by James W. Tuttleton, Kristin O. Lauer, and Margaret P. Murray
3. *Ellen Glasgow: The Contemporary Reviews*, edited by Dorothy M. Scura

Ellen Glasgow

The Contemporary Reviews

Edited by
Dorothy M. Scura
University of Tennessee, Knoxville

Published by the Press Syndicate of the University of Cambridge
The Pitt Building, Trumpington Street, Cambridge CB2 1RP
40 West 20th Street, New York, NY 10011–4211, USA
10 Stamford Road, Oakleigh, Victoria 3166, Australia

© Cambridge University Press 1992

First published 1992

Printed in the United States of America

Library of Congress Cataloging-in-Publication Data
Ellen Glasgow: the contemporary reviews /edited by Dorothy M. Scura.
p.   cm.—(American critical archives)
Includes index.
ISBN 0-521-39040-0
1. Glasgow, Ellen Anderson Gholson, 1873–1945—Criticism and interpretation.   I. Scura, Dorothy McInnis.   II. Series.
PS3513. L34Z6544   1992
813'.52—dc20   91-42851
                             CIP
A catalog record for this book is available from the British Library

ISBN 0-521-39040-0 hardback

This book is for the memory of three men who encouraged and supported me in my work: J. Edgar McInnis, 1905–1985, my father; George W. Scura, 1924–1981, my husband; Lewis G. Leary, 1906–1990, my mentor.

Contents

Series Editor's Preface	page ix
Preface	xi
Acknowledgments	xii
Introduction	xv
The Descendant (1897)	1
Phases of an Inferior Planet (1898)	15
The Voice of the People (1900)	33
The Battle-Ground (1902)	51
The Freeman and Other Poems (1902)	69
The Deliverance (1904)	77
The Wheel of Life (1906)	97
The Ancient Law (1908)	117
The Romance of a Plain Man (1909)	131
The Miller of Old Church (1911)	145
Virginia (1913)	155
Life and Gabriella (1916)	173
The Builders (1919)	189
One Man in His Time (1922)	207
The Shadowy Third and Other Stories (1923)	225
Barren Ground (1925)	237
The Romantic Comedians (1926)	271
They Stooped to Folly (1929)	293
The Sheltered Life (1932)	321
The Old Dominion Edition of the Works of Ellen Glasgow (1929–33)	353
Vein of Iron (1935)	367
The Virginia Edition of the Works of Ellen Glasgow (1938)	399
In This Our Life (1941)	411
A Certain Measure (1943)	443
Index	477

Series Editor's Preface

The American Critical Archives series documents a part of a writer's career that is usually difficult to examine, that is, the immediate response to each work as it was made public on the part of reviewers in contemporary newspapers and journals. Although it would not be feasible to reprint every review, each volume in the series reprints a selection of reviews designed to provide the reader with a proportionate sense of the critical response, whether it was positive, negative, or mixed. Checklists of other known reviews are also included to complete the documentary record and allow access for those who wish to do further reading and research.

The editor of each volume has provided an introduction that surveys the career of the author in the context of the contemporary critical response. Ideally, the introduction will inform the reader in brief of what is to be learned by a reading of the full volume. The reader then can go as deeply as necessary in terms of the kind of information desired—be it about a single work, a period in the author's life, or the author's entire career. The intent is to provide quick and easy access to the material for students, scholars, librarians, and general readers.

When completed, the American Critical Archives should constitute a comprehensive history of critical practice in America, and in some cases England, as the writers' careers were in progress. The volumes open a window on the patterns and forces that have shaped the history of American writing and the reputations of the writers. These are primary documents in the literary and cultural life of the nation.

M. THOMAS INGE

Preface

This volume reprints reviews of Ellen Glasgow's books as those reviews were published during her lifetime. Reviews not printed in full or in part are listed at the end of each section. If printed reviews have excisions, the missing parts are indicated by ellipses, in the case of a brief deletion, or by [. . .], in the case of a lengthier deletion. If a review covers more than one book, the part of the review that focuses on Ellen Glasgow's work is reprinted with no indication of deletion.

In general, the reviews have been reprinted as they appeared originally. Typographical errors have been silently corrected; book titles and characters' names are consistently spelled correctly; book titles are consistently italicized.

Every effort has been made to be as comprehensive as possible in collecting reviews. Although the reviews reprinted include ones from newspapers and journals in the United States and in Great Britain, not all of the contemporaneous reviews of Glasgow's work are reprinted or listed in this volume. Many that do appear here come from major newspapers and journals, and it is hoped that they provide a representative sampling of the variety of critical responses printed in Glasgow's lifetime.

Acknowledgments

In studying the critical reception of Ellen Glasgow, one begins with the work of William W. Kelly—his 1957 dissertation for Duke University, "Struggle for Recognition: A Study of the Literary Reputation of Ellen Glasgow," and his 1964 volume *Ellen Glasgow: A Bibliography*, edited by Oliver Steele and published by the University Press of Virginia. I am most grateful to him for his work. Also very helpful is the secondary bibliography printed in Edgar MacDonald and Tonette Bond Inge's *Ellen Glasgow: A Reference Guide*, published in 1986 by G. K. Hall.

In the years I have worked on this project, three graduate students have provided valuable assistance—Rebecca Wall, Carla McDonough, and Margaret Bauer. For their diligence, I thank all three of these young scholars. And I am most grateful to my secretary Margaret Goergen, who assisted me with typing, permissions, and a multitude of other details.

The staffs of several libraries have been cooperative and helpful: the Alderman Library at the University of Virginia, the Richmond Public Library, the Richmond Newspapers Library, the Virginia Commonwealth University Interlibrary Loan Department, the University of Tennessee Interlibrary Loan Department. To all of the workers in those libraries who assisted me, especially to Edmund Berkeley, Jr., Michael Plunkett, and William S. Simpson, Jr., I extend my appreciation.

For support in obtaining permissions to reprint reviews, I acknowledge the John C. Hodges Better English Fund in the English Department of the University of Tennessee. For collegial support of this project, I thank Maggie O'Connor and Tom Inge.

Perhaps my greatest debt is to the newspapers, journals, and authors who have granted permission to reprint their reviews in this volume. I am sincerely grateful to each of them.

Acknowledgment is made to the newspapers, journals, and individuals listed below for permission to reprint reviews. Francis X. Connolly, "Insipid Liberalism Challenged in Great Prose," reprinted with permission of America Press, Inc., © 1941 All Rights Reserved. "New Novel by Ellen Glasgow Is Worth While"; R.E.S., "Sex, Marriage and Blueblood"; Emily Clark, "Emily Clark Finds a Charm in Miss Glasgow's Stories"; Emily Clark, "Glasgow Novel of Virginia Poor Whites: A Triumphant Experiment"; Gerald W. Johnson, review of *The Romantic Comedians*; Gerald W. Johnson, "Ellen Glasgow's Mailed Fist Inside a White Kid Glove"; Gerald W. Johnson, "Ex Libris"; Gerald W. Johnson, "World of Women" reprinted from *The Baltimore Sun*, © 1919, 1922, 1923, 1925, 1926, 1929, 1932, 1935. "The Benefit of Malice"; Lee E. Cannon, "Unending Quest"; Lee E. Cannon, "Harvest of the Years" published originally in the *Christian Century*. "Miss Glasgow Turns Out Another Splendid Novel," originally published in *The Plain Dealer*. Review of *The Builders*, reprinted with permission, from the Columbus, Ohio, *Dispatch*. Roland Nelson Harmon, "Fool's Paradise"; Edward Skillin, Jr., "*In This Our Life*," reprinted with permission of *Commonweal*. John Chamberlain, review of *Vein of Iron*, reprinted with permission from *Current History* magazine. James Sibley Watson, Jr., review of *The Builders* printed in *Dial*, permission granted by Literary Executor of the Estate of Dr. James Sibley Watson, Jr. The Sigma Foundation, Inc. "An Inconoclastic Hero"; "Strength Gone Astray"; "Ellen Glasgow: Her New and Striking Novel, *The Voice of the People*"; "*The Voice of the People*"; "Miss Glasgow's *The Battle-Ground*"; "Some Recent Verse"; Mrs. M. Gordon Pryor, "First Novel of 1904"; M. Gordon Pryor Rice, "The First Important Novel of 1906"; Issac F. Marcosson, "A Virginia Valjean"; "Class and Caste in Old Virginia"; "*The Miller of Old Church*"; "Miss Glasgow's Strongest Book"; L[ouise] M[aunsell] F[ield], "*Virginia*: Miss Glasgow's Portrait of a Last Century Type"; "The Hundred Best Books of the Year"; "Humor and Pathos in a Woman's Life"; "Ellen Glasgow, Works of Fiction by Many Well-known Novelists Among the Important Books Published This Week"; "*The Shadowy Third*"; Joseph Collins, "Gentlemen, the Ladies!"; H. I. Brock, "Southern Romance Is Dead"; Joseph Collins, "Ellen Glasgow's New Novel a Tragedy of Old Age"; Percy Hutchison, "Wit and Wisdom in a New Novel by Ellen Glasgow"; J. Donald Adams, "Ellen Glasgow's Finest Novel"; J. Donald Adams, "A New Novel by Ellen Glasgow"; J. Donald Adams, "The Novels of Ellen Glasgow"; Charles Poore, "Books of the Times"; J. Donald Adams, "A New Novel by Ellen Glasgow"; John Chamberlain, "Books of the Times"; Hamilton Basso, "Ellen Glasgow's Literary Credo," Copyright © 1897/98/1900/1900/02/02/04/06/08/09/11/11/13/13/16/19/23/23/25/26/29/32/35/38/41/41/43/43 by The New York Times Company, reprinted by permission. Malcolm Cowley, review of *The Builders*; Carl Van Doren, "*Barren Ground*"; Robert Herrick, "*The Romantic Comedians*"; Louise Bogan, review of *They Stooped to Folly*; Clifton Fadiman, "Ellen Glasgow's South"; Stark Young, "Deep South Notes, VI: At Sheltered Valley"; Stark Young, "Prefaces to Distinction"; Stark Young, "Ellen Glasgow's New Book"; Robert Cantwell, "A Season's Run"; Malcolm Cowley, "Miss Glasgow's 'Purgatorio'"; Stark Young, "Beautiful Apologia," originally published in *The New Republic*. Clifton Fadiman, review of *Vein of Iron*, copyright © 1935, 1963 by Clifton Fadiman, review originally appeared in *The New Yorker*; Clifton Fadiman, review of *In This Our Life*, copyright © 1941,

1969 by Clifton Fadiman, review originally appeared in *The New Yorker*; Clifton Fadiman, review of *A Certain Measure*, copyright © 1943, 1971 by Clifton Fadiman, review originally appeared in *The New Yorker*; review of *Barren Ground*, reprinted by permission, © 1932, 1960 The New Yorker Magazine, Inc.; [Harry Esty Dounce], "A Really Fine Novel by Ellen Glasgow," reprinted by permission, © 1932, 1960 The New Yorker Magazine, Inc.; A[gnes W.] S[mith], "A Study in Scarlet," reprinted by permission, © 1932, 1960 the New Yorker Magazine, Inc.; R[obert] M. Coates, review of *The Sheltered Life*, reprinted by permission, © 1932, 1960 The New Yorker Magazine, Inc. "The New South"; review of *The Builders*; Emily Clark, "*The Sheltered Life*—Ellen Glasgow's New High in Brilliance and Satire," reprinted with permission from *The Philadelphia Inquirer*. H. W. Boynton, "Back to the Soil"; W. T. S[cott], "Ellen Glasgow Surveys Her Virginian Novels"; originally published in the *Providence Journal*. "'Realism Has Crossed the Potomac' by Ferry"; "Perennial Husband"; "Stoopers to Folly"; "Womanhood Affronted"; "Retreat to the Hills"; "Blood and Irony"; copyright 1925, 1926, 1929, 1932, 1935, 1941 Time Inc., reprinted by permission. J. M. Lalley, "Posting the Books," © *The Washington Post*, reprinted with permission.

Introduction

To read the reviews reprinted in this volume is to trace the story of the critical response to Ellen Glasgow's work in journals and in newspapers from the publication of *The Descendant*, her first novel, in 1897 to the publication of *A Certain Measure*, a volume of criticism, in 1943. Between 1897 and 1943, she published nineteen novels, a volume of poems, a volume of short stories, and a collection of prefaces to thirteen of her novels. Two collected editions of her work also appeared in those years: *The Old Dominion Edition of the Works of Ellen Glasgow* (1929-33) and *The Virginia Edition of the Works of Ellen Glasgow* (1938). Other works, not included in this volume, were published posthumously: her autobiography, *The Woman Within* (1954); a selection of her letters, edited by Blair Rouse (1958); a collection of short stories, edited by Richard Meeker (1963); and a novella, *Beyond Defeat*, edited by Luther Gore (1966). Recently, Julius Raper has collected other unpublished material, including essays and interviews, in *Ellen Glasgow's Reasonable Doubts* (1988).

Glasgow was born 22 April 1873, eight years after the close of the Civil War, and she died 21 November 1945, three months after the close of World War II. When her first novel was published, in 1897, Queen Victoria was on the throne in England and William McKinley was in the White House; when her last work was published, in 1943, King George VI occupied the throne and Franklin D. Roosevelt the White House. In the first decade of her writing career, authors such as Thomas Nelson Page, Stephen Crane, Theodore Dreiser, and Edith Wharton were publishing books. By the second decade of her career, 1907-14, Gertrude Stein, Willa Cather, Ezra Pound, Robert Frost, and T.S. Eliot were publishing prose and poetry. When she published *Barren Ground*, in 1925, the literary scene included Sinclair Lewis, Ernest Hemingway, F. Scott Fitzgerald, Thomas Wolfe, and William Faulkner. The year of publication of *In This Our Life*, her last novel, 1941, is also the year of Eudora Welty's debut with *A Curtain of Green*. Glasgow's literary career, therefore, spans the time from Thomas Nelson Page to Eudora Welty.

Because her literary career was a long one and her publications were substantial, the story told by the reviews collected in this volume is lengthy. Her two earliest novels showed promise but were heavily influenced by her reading in science and philosophy. She improved in her art when she abandoned

New York City as a setting and came home to Virginia for her third novel, but she did not actually end her apprenticeship until her tenth novel, *Virginia*, in which she not only used Virginian materials but also made a woman the protagonist for the first time.

Glasgow's best work was published between 1925 and 1932, when she was in her fifties, and she experienced seven miraculous years artistically with the publication of *Barren Ground*, *The Romantic Comedians*, *They Stooped to Folly*, and *The Sheltered Life*, her masterpiece. If the shape of her writing career was plotted, the line would move upward steadily with a few valleys and a few peaks for almost three decades and then ascend dramatically for seven years, dropping slightly for the last two novels, *Vein of Iron* and *In This Our Life*. With the publication of her last book, *A Certain Measure*, in 1943, her career reached its apex. It is, in fact, a most interesting career, with growth and change and recognition present for forty-five years but with the best work and the great honors coming to the mature artist. From 1925 onward, Glasgow was consistently reviewed by important critics in the major journals and newspapers. Many honors were bestowed on her late in her career.

Perhaps the lateness of all those honors contributed strongly to Glasgow's feeling that she was neglected, misunderstood, and ignored during most of her career. Certainly, the record of reviews of her books shows that she was from the very beginning taken seriously by critics and that her books were widely recognized by reviewers. She felt, however, that her work was not appropriately appreciated while that of other writers, less able than she, was acknowledged and honored more.[1]

Glasgow was extremely sensitive to criticism, and she believed ferociously in her work. As a result of these feelings, she took an active interest late in her career in the critical reception of her books. She has, in fact, been accused of cultivating reviewers of importance and of mercilessly manipulating the reviews of her work. James Branch Cabell reports in *As I Remember It* that she invited to her beautiful home in Richmond anyone who was in a position to review books, and seductively played Circe, turning the critic into her press agent (228–30). Too, her volume of letters reveals her cultivating and sometimes instructing such people as J. Donald Adams, Henry Seidel Canby, Allen Tate, Carl Van Vechten, Howard Mumford Jones, Stark Young, and Irita Van Doren. Frequently she befriended wives of powerful men—Bessie Zaban Jones, Sara Haardt (wife of H. L. Mencken), Signe Toksvig (wife of Francis Hackett). In *The Woman Within* she lists her New York friends, and they are all people involved in the reviewing of books—Van Doren, Young, Adams, the Canbys, the Van Wyck Brookses, the Joneses, the Herschel Brickells, the Van Vechtens, and the Menckens.[2] Certainly all of this evidence raises the question of how much influence Glasgow exerted on her late critical reception.

In addition to providing much material for the study of Glasgow's early critical response, the reviews in this book tell stories about the changing fashions in reviewing, the reception of a woman author in the first half of the twentieth century, the comparative responses from journals with various political leanings. And these reviews furnish part of the material for a comparative study of the critical response to three important women authors publishing during these years—Glasgow, Edith Wharton, and Willa Cather. Although a number of stories are embedded in these texts, this introduction will focus on Ellen Glasgow's early critical response.

"Not a Trace of the Feminine Hand": Ellen Glasgow's Auspicious Literary Debut

In the context of Glasgow's view that she was not treated well by critics during the first thirty-five years of her career, it is interesting to go back and look at the critical reception of her first six books. What we find is that from the very beginning she was reviewed seriously and thoughtfully in major newspapers and literary journals. Many critics read her work carefully and offered criticism that might have been helpful to the young writer. On the other hand, many of them encouraged Glasgow in her own attempt—conscious or unconscious—to write like a man, praising her "masculine force and vigour" (*Bookman*, May 1897) from the first. In a 1900 review of *The Voice of the People*, Issac F. Marcosson succinctly states the view expressed by other critics of each of her novels when he observes that her work shows "not a trace of the feminine hand."

Glasgow's first novel, *The Descendant*, was published anonymously in March 1897, one month before her twenty-fourth birthday. It tells the story of Michael Akersheim, an illegitimate child from the white underclass in Virginia, who becomes an advocate of social reform and moves to New York City, where he eventually edits a socialist publication, *The Iconoclast*. Michael has a love affair with Rachel Gavin, a painter, but eventually falls in love with a more conventional woman. He murders an associate from *The Iconoclast*, serves eight years in prison, and dies in Rachel's arms.

The publication of this book was an auspicious debut for the young author. Laurence Hutton, in an April review in *Harper's Magazine*, calls the novel a "very strong, and a very unusual, piece of fiction." He describes the story as "exciting," "rarely dull," "well considered," and "well handled." "And the reading world," he explains, "will wonder who the unknown author can be."

Some readers thought the author might be Harold Frederic, author of *The Damnation of Theron Ware*, and at least two of the earliest reviewers refer to the author as "he." One, the reviewer for the Boston *Evening Transcript*, begins by saying that the novel "is unquestionably a strong book, but the strength is that of bitter aloes." After praising the "color and passion," "the acute character study and careful description," and the sparkling epigrams, the reviewer criticizes the book's "dominant note" which is "cynically bitter":

"Not that the author has made it so intentionally" the writer explains; "one rather obtains the impression that he would willingly have had it otherwise, but that he is overpowered by his motive." For this reviewer the book is "sad reading."

Many reviewers describe the book in terms that are clearly masculine. The *Chap-Book* says it is "forcefully written"; the *New York Times Saturday Review of Books and Art* observes its "uncommon vigor"; *Bookman* notes its "masculine force and vigour in characterisation"; *Literary World* says it is "virile and vigorous"; the *Critic* calls it a "strong book" and compares reading it to "being out in a tornado."

When the news breaks that this powerful and somber book has been written by a young Richmond woman—always referred to as a "girl" in the reviews—Clarence Wellford in *Harper's Bazar* writes about Glasgow's "keen brown eyes and chestnut hair" as well as her dainty hands and feet. He compares her to George Eliot, Olive Schreiner, and Emily Brontë. The tone of many of the reviews changes as reviewers focus on their curiosity at a young Richmond woman's writing this gloomy and philosophical book.

The most important of the reviews is the one by Hamlin Garland published in *Bookbuyer* in August 1897. Garland praises the book extravagantly and—echoing Emerson's words about Whitman—observes, "It is evident that in Ellen Glasgow American fiction has acquired a novelist worthy the most cordial greeting."[3]

Glasgow's second novel, *Phases of an Inferior Planet*, published in the fall of 1898, a year and a half after *The Descendant*, did not elicit the kind of review written by Garland about the first one. *Phases* tells the story of Mariana Musin, a modestly talented singer from the South, who comes to New York and marries an agnostic biologist, Anthony Algarcife. Mariana leaves Anthony for a singing tour, they are divorced, and eventually he becomes a famous Episcopal priest, although privately he is an unbeliever. Mariana and Michael are reconciled at the end, before she dies. Anthony is saved from suicide by a summons to speak to striking workers.

There is much negative criticism of *Phases*. The *Dial* remarks on the "strange title," the meaning of which is unclear; the Brooklyn *Daily Eagle* refers to the title as "a somewhat infelicitous caption. . . . too bookish . . . scarcely definitive." The darkness of the book is observed by many reviewers: John Kendrick Bangs, in *Harper's*, advises that pessimistic readers "will enjoy the somewhat despondent note which it has been given to Miss Glasgow's lyre to sound forth." The Boston *Independent* complains that the plot has "no light or joy" and sees the novel as "sodden with hopelessness all the way through."

Critics complain of more than the bleakness of the philosophy. One observes that the book is "about three times too long" (*Athenæum*); another, that its plot is "melodramatic" (*Literary World*); Droch, in *Life*, says it needs an infusion of humor; the Brooklyn *Daily Eagle* suggests the novel shows more knowledge of books than of human nature; and the *Nation* sums up the book's effect by claiming that it is "shallow science, shallow art, and shallow feeling."

The reviews, of course, are not wholly negative. A number of critics remark that the novel shows strength, power, and promise. The Richmond *Times* review, a reprint of the one in the Boston *Evening Transcript*, is a mixed response that compares the work to Thomas Hardy's. And in what is surely meant to be a compliment and was doubtless taken as one by the young writer, the reviewer quotes "one of our best masters of prose" as saying of Miss Glasgow that here is "one woman writing like a man in a nation of men writing like a woman."

With her third novel, *The Voice of the People*, published in April 1900, approximately a year and a half after *Phases*, Glasgow abandons New York City as a setting and comes home to Virginia. Set in Kingsborough, a town based on Williamsburg, the novel features a protagonist from the white underclass. Nicholas Burr rises to become governor of Virginia and is killed in the denouement as he tries to prevent the lynching of a black man. For the first time Glasgow has placed her novel in a setting she knows well.

Reviewers agree that with this novel Glasgow has regained her position as a promising novelist after the critical debacle that followed *Phases*. On April 21 the reviewer for the *New York Times Saturday Review of Books and Art* writes that *The Descendant* had "proclaimed the advent of a new and vivid pen," but *Phases* had proved a "disappointment," and "the reader greatly feared that the author's genius was about to flash in the pan." This reviewer finds the new novel to be a story of "compelling interest," "sometimes sparkling and sometimes sombre," "irradiated with humor." The review closes by calling the work a "genuine contribution to both literature and life."

There are negative comments among the mostly positive reviews. A number of reviewers find the book too long, among them those for the *Spectator* and *Academy*. The reviewer for the British journal *Academy* churlishly berates Glasgow for the length of the novel and for her "triviality of observation." "Miss Glasgow's faculty of observation," the reviewer continues,

> needs discipline. It is too busy, too fussy, and a great deal too fanciful—fanciful where it should be imaginative. She often does not observe the right *kind* of thing. She trifles, and gives rein to mere fancy. And gradually she passes into a condition, a mood, which, without conscious intent, twists and contorts life into something untruthfully pretty—something emasculate and feebly emotional.

All this sounds as if the reviewer actually wants to say that Glasgow is writing like—a woman.

For her fourth book, *The Battle-Ground* (1902), Glasgow chose to write a historical romance, her first work in this popular genre. The book tells the story of two aristocratic Virginia families, the Lightfoots and the Amblers, including the love story of Dan Montjoy, grandson of Major Lightfoot and Betty Ambler, daughter of Governor Ambler. The spirited Betty Ambler is perhaps the most appealing of all of Glasgow's heroines. The tale begins years before the Civil War, at the well-ordered plantations Uplands and Chericoke, and ends with the broken and exhausted Dan, after the war, united with his gallant and indomitable wife, Betty.

The reviews are generally positive. *Athenæum* calls Glasgow's account "reminiscent of the late Stephen Crane's vividly impressionistic work" in *The Red Badge of Courage*. Hamilton Mabie, in *Outlook*, says, "She writes simply and truly," terms her characters "human and well rounded out," her humor "natural and unforced." William Payne, in the *Dial*, raves that this is "one of the best novels of the South during the period which precedes and includes the Civil War that has ever been written," and he says that "the war itself is excellently done."

The Louisville *Courier-Journal* calls the 29-year-old Glasgow "one of the foremost women writers of her country." And reviewers continue to praise her masculine abilities. The *Spectator* observes, "The picture of the war drawn by the author would be remarkable in any case, and is especially so as coming from a woman's pen." *Book News* comments on the "virility and mastery of stroke in Miss Glasgow's novels which make one almost forget that their author is a woman, so masculine do her works appear at times."

The Battle-Ground is well received, and although it is written in a popular genre, reviewers take the work seriously. *Current Literature*, for example, calls it "a historical novel in which character takes the place of claptrap melodrama" and says the story "shall appeal to the intellect and to the emotions, rather than merely to the nerves." Glasgow placed this novel first in her social history of Virginia because it told a story of the years 1850–65. She explains in *A Certain Measure* that in *The Battle-Ground* she "tried to portray the last stand in Virginia of the aristocratic tradition."[4] "For Virginia, in that disastrous illusion," she observes, "the Confederacy was the expiring gesture of chivalry" (25).

In 1902, Glasgow publishes not only her Civil War novel but also her only volume of poetry, *The Freeman and Other Poems*. The Book is not widely reviewed and does not sell well. The Boston *Evening Transcript* points out that "Miss Glasgow's thoughts ... dwell frequently and strongly upon ethical problems," and her verse "is both genuine poetry and sterling truth." The *New York Times Saturday Review of Books and Art* notices "in these poems ... their virile, and militant, though somewhat sombre strain." The *World's Work* observes that the poems "present some of the darker aspects of life ... with daring and vigor." In a brief but scathing review, the *Nation* charges that "Byronic fever" is prevalent in the poems and observes that Glasgow's novels show "so much more maturity of judgment as to make it a pity that her fifty pages of verse, full of flashes of power, should be almost wholly painful, even to ghastliness." Perhaps such a review discouraged Glasgow; in any case, she would publish no more volumes of poetry. *The Freeman* serves as little more than a footnote to her career.

Her next novel, however, *The Deliverance*, published in 1904, is well received and sells well, earning second place on the year's list of best-sellers.[5] Set in the tobacco country of Virginia in the years 1878–90, again the plot involves two families, the Fletchers and the Blakes. The Blakes, having lost their plantation and most of their land to their former overseer Fletcher, now live in a small house. The Blake matriarch is blind, and her children have conspired—at great personal cost—to keep from her the news of the fall of the Confederacy. Nor does she know that the family no longer has an estate. The plot tells a story of revenge, with Christopher Blake seeking to corrupt Fletcher's grandson. It ends happily, however, with the reconciliation of the two families in the planned marriage of Christopher and Maria, Fletcher's granddaughter.

The book receives positive reviews; a number of them could be classified as rave reviews. One dissenter is the reviewer for the *Times Literary Supplement*, who calls the book a failure, and a number of reviewers find Mrs. Blake not a credible character. The *New York Times Saturday Review of Books and Art*, in a generally positive review, questions that Mrs. Blake could be deceived for so many years. Eleanor Hoyt, in *Lamp*, proposes that "Mrs. Blake's deception staggers even willing credulity." William Payne, in the *Dial*, concurs with that opinion, as does the reviewer for *Everybody's Magazine*. This criticism would apparently still rankle Glasgow more than three decades later, and in an essay included in *A Certain Measure*, she would persuasively defend the character of Mrs. Blake, explaining that this character has symbolic meaning and represents "Virginia and the entire South, unaware of the changes about them, clinging, with passionate fidelity, to the ceremonial forms of tradition" (27).

A number of reviewers find much to praise in *The Deliverance*. The Louisville *Courier-Journal* terms the novel "mighty in proportion, great in promise, magnificent in the fulfillment." Archibald Henderson, writing in the *Sewanee Review*, calls the novel her "most distinguished piece of work" and praises Glasgow for combining a "Southern instinct for feeling" with a "Northern passion for ethics." Henderson's praise ultimately echoes the view of many critics of Glasgow's earlier novels: "The book betrays the strong, sure grasp of genuine literary craftsmanship, the keen power of clear and epic visualization, the reach and mastery of a tremendous moral, ethical, and social problem. The masculinity and stark power of its appeal grip and hold you to the end." Also echoing earlier reviewers who have praised her "masculine" gifts is Edwin Clark Marsh, in *Bookman*, who observes that "she has a style that at times is distinctly virile, and a gift of generalisation that is rare in women."

The story of the critical response to her first six books shows that Glasgow's work—with the exception of her second novel and her book of poetry—was well received. Her first novel was reviewed seriously and attracted attention when she was revealed as the author only after publication. The second novel was clearly a disappointment to reviewers, but the next three were widely reviewed in journals and in newspapers across the United States, as well as in England. Although her work did receive negative criticism, Glasgow earned much praise for her fiction. Her claims of neglect and misunderstanding are not based on the critical response to her early work.

An obvious leitmotiv in these early responses is the observation that Glasgow produced surprisingly strong and virile fiction. Those reviewers who praised her work by suggesting that she wrote like a male author may have postponed Glasgow's achievement of her own voice in fiction, which enabled her to write her best novels—each of which shows more than a trace of the feminine hand.

"Trespassing upon an Alien Field": Three Poorly Received Novels, 1906–1909

With her first five novels, Ellen Glasgow built a solid reputation, but beginning in 1906 with *The Wheel of Life*, she published three novels that did not add to the luster of her critical reputation. Some critics believe that the end of her most meaningful love affair, in 1906, led to heartbreak and depression that affected her work. She tells in *The Woman Within* about this romance with a married man who, according to Glasgow, died in 1906. [6]

Whatever the reasons may have been for a drop in quality of her fiction, it is clear from the reviews that her work between 1906 and 1909 was not well received. In a negative evaluation of *The Wheel of Life*, the reviewer for *Literary Digest* criticizes Glasgow for an "imperfect assimilation" of the New York atmosphere that is the setting of the novel. He goes on to explain that the novel is not up to her usual standard and to suggest that "this seems largely due to her trespassing upon an alien field." William Payne, in the *Dial*, makes a similar observation when he remarks that Glasgow should not have deserted her "native heath." In choosing New York City as the setting of her sixth novel, Glasgow repeats the choice she had made with her first two novels. She would set no more novels outside her native Virginia except for *Life and Gabriella* in 1916 and a part of *Barren Ground* in 1925. While writing *Life and Gabriella*, she would actually be living in New York City, and she would do her usual research on locale and have a better knowledge of the place than she had when she wrote *The Wheel of Life*.

Wheel is a novel of manners and includes a large number of characters, six of whom play important roles. Some are sophisticated New Yorkers, happiness hunters; others are transplanted Southerners. The novel features psychological approaches to characterization, and it also carries a heavy weight of philosophy.

The House of Mirth, by Edith Wharton, had been published several months before *Wheel*, and comparison of the two works is undertaken in many reviews. When the novels are viewed retrospectively, there is no question that Wharton's book is superior, but Glasgow's friend Louise Collier Willcox compares the novels in a glowing appraisal for the *North American Review*. She comments that Glasgow's novel is "the work of a genius" and Wharton's "the output of an artist." Other reviewers are not so balanced in their comparisons.

Although there are other positive reviews, negative ones outnumber them. The reviewer for the Richmond *Times-Dispatch*, for example, predicts that the book is "almost certain to be a disappointment" to Glasgow's admirers, criticizes the number of characters with no single one taking a "commanding place in her scheme," and considers the author "ill-advised in forsaking the Virginian background" so effective in other books. Other reviewers complain that male characters are not believable, that the book lacks humor, that Glasgow's use of psychology is intrusive, that the style is pretentious, that the book is too long, and that it is simply not interesting. In advising Glasgow not to "go further in this direction," *Outlook* seems to be saying what others are implying. Not since *Phases of an Inferior Planet* has Glasgow received such a negative response to a novel

Two years later, in 1908, Glasgow's seventh novel, *The Ancient Law*, is published with a reception that again includes many negative reviews. The main character is Daniel Ordway, a man who goes to prison and then builds a new life with a new name, only to return to prison for a crime he did not commit. The book is dark, philosophy-laden, and seems to portray the purifying effects of suffering. Set in Virginia, the novel's "alien field" is Glasgow's attempt to tell the story largely from the point of view of Ordway, "a very ordinary person, if he is a person at all," according to H. W. Boynton in *Bookman*. The Boston *Evening Transcript* observes that Ordway is "never for a moment a convincing character," and the *Nation* points out that he is "commented upon rather than presented."

Other "alien fields" for Glasgow in this novel are both sentimentality and melodrama. The *Nation* terms the work "crude melodrama," and William Payne, in the *Dial*, comments on the melodrama at the end of the novel. The British *Saturday Review* claims, "The story is founded on a basis of false sentiment and false psychology and is constructed throughout on sentimental sensational lines."

Some positive views of the novel are expressed. Issac Marcosson, in the *New York Times Saturday Review of Books*, calls it "a novel of dignity and of distinction." Louise Collier Willcox again writes a positive review for the *North American Review*, and Edwin Mims praises the book highly in the

South Atlantic Quarterly: "Glasgow shows that she is a thinker as well as an artist. She has humor and pathos, and rare insight into human nature. She has distinction of style, too." Most reviewers, however, would have agreed with H. W. Boynton in *Bookman*; he calls the novel "a mediocre affair at best."

Glasgow's next novel, *The Romance of a Plain Man*, is published in 1909—again to negative reviews. In this tale of the rise of a poor boy to the presidency of a railroad, Glasgow chooses—for the first and only time—to make the narrator a man, Ben Starr, the "plain man" of the title. The "alien field" in this novel is the male consciousness, which reviewers criticize in scathing terms. Francis Hackett of the Chicago *Evening Post* calls the novel an "amateur romance" and explains that the narrator, a man of affairs, talks "in the pretty idiom of a southern lady." Edwin Francis Edgett, in the Boston *Evening Transcript*, observes that "Benjamin Starr is created in woman's image" and that the author "is not able to discern how a man can feel and behave." The reviewer for the *New York Times Saturday Review of Books* says the "narrating hero . . . is never quite convincing."

Several reviewers compare *Plain Man* to Mary Johnston's *Lewis Rand*, published in 1908. The *Nation* points out that there are "startlingly frequent points of similarity," and the *Independent* says both Glasgow and Johnston "are a trifle too much inclined to intimate the peacock tails of their own excellent pedigrees in fiction." H. L. Mencken deals Glasgow the unkindest cut of all: "Miss Johnston's volume is a work of art, while Miss Glasgow's is not."

Some reviews were positive, but the response to this novel could not have cheered Ellen Glasgow. The years between 1906 and 1909 mark the low point in the critical reception of her work. Glasgow included none of the three novels published in those years in the eight-volume *Old Dominion Edition* (1929–33) of her works and included only *The Romance of a Plain Man* in the twelve-volume *Virginia Edition* (1938).

"The Feminist Note": Glasgow Writes Women, 1911–1923

Two of the five Glasgow novels published between 1911 and 1923 feature protagonists who are women—for the first time. And each of the other three novels includes important and interesting female characters. Her volume of short stories, published in 1923, includes sensitive portrayals of important women characters. A focus on women characters is a significant development in Glasgow's work because it allows her both to move beyond the need to write like a man and to acknowledge in her art the importance of women. Responding favorably to her 1913 novel *Virginia*, the reviewer for *Athenæum* remarks that "the Feminist note . . . is commendably mellow throughout."

The "Feminist note" is sounded in all of the work published during this period.

The Miller of Old Church, published in 1911, has a complex plot involving two families: the Gays, enervated aristocrats, and the Revercombs, members of the emerging middle class. Abel Revercomb is the miller of the title, but the novel includes a gallery of women characters: Molly Merryweather, the spirited heroine, who is illegitimate but also part Gay; Angela Gay, a protected and genteel lady; Kesiah Gay, a talented artist condemned by homely looks; and Blossom Revercomb and Judy Hatch, both doomed by love. Glasgow pursues her theme of the rise of the middle class, but she also focuses on the position of women.

Some reviewers note the interesting treatment of women in the novel. The *Nation* points out: "No one has heretofore let in the cold clear light of common sense upon the status of the Southern woman under the old regime." And the *Independent* notes: "It may be suspected that Ellen Glasgow is a bit heterodox as to both Calvinism and 'the womanly woman.'"

The book receives positive reviews in the Richmond *Times-Dispatch*, *Bookman*, *New York Times Saturday Review of Books*, *Nation*, *North American Review*, and *Athenæum*; *The Miller of Old Church* is called "a capital piece of work" and "her best book up to the present time." She is compared to Thomas Hardy, and her "epic method" is praised. Dissenters criticize the plot and the characters, and H. L. Mencken claims he cannot even read the book and quotes other reviewers. Although the critical response is not wholly positive for this novel, it receives a much better reception than the three that preceded it.

Virginia (1913) is Glasgow's tenth novel. Her finest thus far, it is also her first with a woman protagonist. The title of the book suggests the main character, Virginia Pendleton Treadwell, but it also suggests the state, as well as a state of mind. Set in the period 1884–1912, the novel tells the story of a beautiful young woman—the perfect Southern lady—who marries a playwright. She focuses her energies on her children, and she plays the complete martyr in her family life. Her husband eventually finds success on the New York stage, falls in love with an actress, and divorces Virginia, leaving her bereft and alone in her forties.

The critical reception for this novel is mostly positive, the best reception since that for *The Deliverance* in 1904. The *New York Times Book Review* calls *Virginia* Glasgow's "most mature and significant" book and compares her to Jane Austen. Lewis Parke Chamberlayne, in the *Sewanee Review*, points out that the novel gives "a picture of the ideals of a whole people reflected in one woman's life." Chamberlayne terms the work a "noble tragedy" and points out that it is a "most important contribution to the vigorous feminist movement now in progress in the South." *Book News Monthly* calls it a "remarkable book, alight with life and compelling in its truth."

Two of the negative responses are registered by Edwin Francis Edgett in the Boston *Evening Transcript*, who criticizes the "archaic theme," and the *Literary Digest*, whose reviewer considers the work an "involved and depressing tale." Other critics complain that the book is too long and lacks humor. There are a number of negative responses, and the book does not sell well, but it is the work that marks the end of Ellen Glasgow's long literary apprenticeship.

Life and Gabriella, published in 1916, also features a woman protagonist, but this woman is very different from Virginia Pendleton Treadwell. Gabriella Carr is, according to Glasgow, a woman who departs completely from the great Victorian tradition, "the symbol of an advancing economic order."[7] Gabriella, the daughter of an impoverished widow, takes a job in a department store in Richmond. She falls in love with wealthy George Fowler and marries him, and they move to New York City. George, a failure as a husband, keeps a mistress, and Gabriella divorces him. To support her two children, she works for a dressmaker, and she is so successful that she buys the business from the owner. At the end of the book she plans to marry a man from the West, Ben O'Hara. Set in the years 1894 to 1912, this novel has a protagonist who does daring things for the time, including finding her own successful career. While writing *Life and Gabriella*, Glasgow lives in New York City, and this is the only novel she will actually have written outside of Virginia. Although the work is not as fine a novel as *Virginia*, it sells well, achieving fifth place on the best-seller list.

Life and Gabriella receives favorable, if not enthusiastic, reviews. The *New York Times Review of Books* is positive about the novel, calling it "exceedingly well written." The New York *Tribune* terms Glasgow a feminist writer and says she has produced "another readable and extremely well written novel." Emilie Blackmore Stapp, in the Des Moines *Capital*, points out that Glasgow "reflects the feminist awakening by the economic success accorded her heroine." The *Nation* is negative—accusing Glasgow of verbosity and of using "repetitions and reassurances." Edward E. Hale in the *Dial* is also negative, but H. L. Mencken, in giving this book faint praise, writes for Glasgow a better review than he has thus far. He accuses her of sentimentality but calls her "much above the average woman novelist in America."

The Builders, published in 1919, focuses on the time period of World War I. The novel has three main characters: the Blackburns—David and Angelica—and Caroline Meade, a nurse who comes to work for the Blackburns to care for their invalid daughter. The most interesting character is Angelica, a duplicitous and manipulative woman. David is involved in politics, and the novel is full of his pontificating and theorizing. Caroline is attractive and idealistic. Although she and David care for each other, they eventually renounce their love. The novel serves as a vehicle for Glasgow's expression of her ideas about the war and about the political situation in the

United States. It is heavily influenced by her fiancé at the time she was writing the novel, Henry Anderson, a successful Richmond lawyer.[8]

The critical response is surprisingly positive, given the present view of the work as a failure. Reviewers praise the characterization of Angelica: The New York *Herald* says, "the delineation of Angelica Blackburn is the real triumph of *The Builders*"; Jay Hubbell, in the Dallas *News*, calls Angelica "the most interesting character in the novel"; and the Salt Lake City *Herald* finds Angelica "one of the best studies of a woman" Glasgow has written. Other positive reviews appear in the Boston *Evening Transcript*, Philadelphia *Press*, St. Louis *Globe Democrat*, and Baltimore *Sun*. Negative reviews of the book comment on the amount of theorizing and point out that the book is "over solemn" and superficial. The *Knickerbocker Press*, in a fairly positive review, expresses the book's weakness well, observing that Glasgow is carried away by her concern with the problems in America and that, in her desire to find a solution, "she has sacrificed her story in a good cause."

Three years later, Glasgow publishes her thirteenth novel, *One Man in His Time* (1922). The "one man" is Gideon Vetch, who rises from life in a circus tent to the governorship of Virginia, only to be killed accidentally at the scene of a strike. Because he is a progressive politician, this novel is reminiscent of *The Builders*; it is also reminiscent of the earlier *Voice of the People*. As do the other novels written in this period, this one has interesting women characters—Patty Vetch, the governor's daughter, and Corinna Page, one of Glasgow's most attractive heroines.

One Man in His Time receives better reviews than might be expected for a novel Glasgow would choose not to include in either of her collected editions or to mention in *The Woman Within*, her autobiography, or in *A Certain Measure*. The *Literary Digest*, Louisville *Courier-Journal*, and Philadelphia *Evening Ledger* award the novel good reviews. British journals are more positive than American ones, with the London *Morning Post*, *Bookman*, London *Daily News*, and Yorkshire *Post* all praising the book.

The Shadowy Third and Other Stories, Glasgow's only collection of short stories published in her lifetime, comes out in 1923 (published in England under the title *Dare's Gift and Other Stories*). Of the seven stories in the book, four are ghost stories and three focus on an abstract moral problem. Included is the much anthologized "Jordan's End," which features the strong and tragic Judith Jordan, who prefigures Dorinda Oakley in *Barren Ground*.

All of the reviews for this volume are favorable, both those in the United States and those in England. Glasgow's friend the neurologist Joseph Collins seems prescient when he writes in the *New York Times Book Review*, "She has never done anything that better entitles her to be called artist than 'Dare's Gift.' From consideration of her last volume we readily convince ourselves that she has not yet done her best work."

"Her Best Work":
The Miraculous Years, 1925–1932

In 1925, when she was fifty-two years old, Ellen Glasgow published the first of four novels that constitute her very best work. *Barren Ground* is a long, somber novel that tells the story of Dorinda Oakley from age twenty to age fifty. Glasgow explains in *A Certain Measure* that Dorinda "exists wherever a human being has learned to live without joy, wherever the spirit of fortitude has triumphed over the sense of futility. The book is hers, and all minor themes, episodes, and impressions are blended with the one dominant meaning that character is fate" (154).

Barren Ground is told from Dorinda Oakley's point of view. The young daughter of a poor farm family with worn-out land, Dorinda is jilted by her lover. She flees to New York City, but ultimately returns home to Virginia. Beginning with borrowed money, she directs her energies to the land, redeems her father's farm, increases her holdings, and becomes a successful farmer and landowner. Glasgow explains in *A Certain Measure* that she had determined that "for once, in Southern fiction, the betrayed woman would become the victor instead of the victim" (160).

The critical reception of *Barren Ground* is overwhelmingly positive. Joseph Collins, in the New York *Sun*, calls it "her masterpiece"; Edwin Francis Edgett, in the Boston *Evening Transcript*, terms it "an epic story"; Cameron Rogers, in *World's Work*, says it is "her most distinguished" novel; the reviewer for the *Times Literary Supplement* regards it as "an unusually impressive and fine book." Archibald Henderson, in the *Saturday Review of Literature*, compares Glasgow to Hardy and to Zola and says, "Surely *Barren Ground* is a great novel—great in austerity, great in art, great in humanity." And Stuart Sherman, writing in *New York Herald Tribune Books*, gives her perhaps the finest comprehensive review she would ever receive. He explains, "She treats provincial life from a rational point of view; that is, without sentimentality, without prejudice, with sympathy, understanding, passion and poetic insight, yet critically and with a surgical use of satire."[9]

Glasgow's fellow writer from Richmond James Branch Cabell reviews *Barren Ground* for the *Nation* and mentions for the first time in print that her work portrays "all social and economic Virginia since the War Between the States." Glasgow may have later adopted this idea and claimed she had this plan all along. Critics have debated which of the two writers actually first formulated the idea.[10]

H. I. Brock writes a savagely negative review for the *New York Times Book Review*. The *New Yorker*, *Time*, and *Smart Set* also print negative reviews. The reviewer for the *New Yorker* claims to be "bored to misery" by the book, and H. L. Mencken, giving his usually negative response to Glasgow, charges in *Smart Set* that the novel "is boldly imagined and competently planned. But it is not moving." Negative reviews, however, constitute a small minority in the reception of this book.

Glasgow considered *Barren Ground* her favorite book, and some critics agree that it is her best, although others prefer *The Sheltered Life*. Although reviewed positively, *Barren Ground* was not a popular book, perhaps because of its somber tone. Glasgow must have felt great disappointment at her lack of recognition at the time. Edith Wharton and Willa Cather had certainly been regarded as Glasgow's competitors for many years. Wharton had won the Pulitzer Prize in 1921 for *The Age of Innocence*, one of that author's finest novels and published during a period when Glasgow's books were among her weakest. Cather had won the Pulitzer in 1923 for a book that is not among her best, *One of Ours*. Then, when *Barren Ground* was published in 1925, Glasgow's most important book up to that time, the American novel celebrated a banner year. Among the works published almost simultaneously were John Dos Passos's *Manhattan Transfer*, Theodore Dreiser's *American Tragedy*, F. Scott Fitzgerald's *Great Gatsby*, and Sinclair Lewis's *Arrowsmith*. The Pulitzer was awarded to Lewis. It was not the last time Glasgow would be passed over for this prize.

Beginning in 1926, Glasgow published three novels of manners—*The Romantic Comedians, They Stooped to Folly* (1929), and *The Sheltered Life* (1932). *The Romantic Comedians* offers a dramatic change of pace and tone when compared with *Barren Ground*. Whereas the earlier novel is a serious treatment of character, the later one is a witty and ironic comedy that focuses on society. According to Glasgow, *The Romantic Comedians* is a "tragicomedy of a happiness-hunter."[11] She seems to have followed the advice of James Branch Cabell and others to concentrate on her comic talents. In addition, she follows the advice of book reviewers for almost three decades and produces a novel shorter than her usual ones.

The elderly, widowed Judge Gamaliel Bland Honeywell is the "happiness-hunter," who seeks pleasure after his wife's death not by marrying the lovely Amanda Lightfoot, who has loved him for almost four decades, but by marrying the 23-year-old Annabel Upchurch. The spry judge is exhausted after a three-month European honeymoon followed by the attempt to keep up with his young wife, who delights in parties and social events at home in Queenborough. Eventually Annabel falls in love with a young architect and deserts the judge, but his wandering eye still does not find Amanda. It lights, instead, on an attractive nurse in his hospital room. This comic novel was written easily and quickly in one year; Glasgow explains in *A Certain Measure* that Judge Honeywell's "biography bubbled over with an effortless joy" (211).

Mostly positive reviews greet *The Romantic Comedians*. Gerald W. Johnson, in the Baltimore *Evening Sun*, calls it "almost a novelists' novel" and terms it "high comedy, the sort that walks delicately upon the verge of tears." Ellen

Duvall, in the *Atlantic Monthly*, says the novel appeals to the intellect, not the heart, and compares the work to George Meredith's. A number of reviewers comment on Glasgow's wit. Among them are Christopher Morley, in the *Saturday Review of Literature*, who calls the novel a "really witty book"; Mary Ross, in the *Nation*, who terms it a "wise and witty book"; and Carl Van Vechten, in the New York *Herald Tribune*, who observes that the novel is "witty, wise, and delicious." Harry Esty Dounce, in the *New Yorker*, confesses that although he called *Barren Ground* "tiresome," he finds this novel "worth dozens of . . . *Barren Ground*."

Time pronounces Glasgow "too merciless to make her Judge bearable" and considers the book overwritten. Frederick P. Mayer, writing in the *Virginia Quarterly Review*, admits the book has "flashes of genius," but calls the plot wooden and the characterization stiff. Objections are few, however, and the novel not only receives excellent reviews but is a Book-of-the-Month Club selection and sells very well.

Glasgow's next novel of manners, *They Stooped to Folly*, is published in 1929. Glasgow would later explain that this story was inspired by "the almost forgotten myth of the 'ruined' woman," but in writing the novel, she widened her scope, and the novel changed from her originally planned "satire" to a "serious study, with ironic overtones . . . of contemporary society."[12]

The novel features three women of different generations, each of whom has "stooped to folly." Aunt Agatha, a flower of the Victorian age, suffers a lifetime sentence for a youthful indiscretion; she is banished to the third-story back bedroom, and she finds solace in banana sundæs and romantic movies. Mrs. Dalrymple, a product of the gay nineties, is a fallen woman who has had two husbands and countless lovers. Milly Burden, who has a love affair during World War I, learns that "being ruined is a state of mind."[13] Many more characters—both men and women—are satirized in this comic tale, which takes place in the short time of six months in Queenborough.

They Stooped to Folly receives many favorable reviews, but some critics find Glasgow's wit too harsh and her dislike of her characters reprehensible. John Hervey, in the *Saturday Review of Literature*, excoriates Glasgow: "With a pen like that of Suetonius, pitilessly barbed, each [character] in turn is flayed alive and placed quivering before us." He claims Glasgow has "not betrayed a spark of genuine sympathy for a single one" of the protagonists. Even a reviewer who likes the book, Percy Hutchison of the *New York Times Book Review*, comments: "Her caustic burns just a bit too deep, her rapier comes too near the slice of a saber; for it has, besides the sharp point, the cutting edge which that weapon should not possess."

Most reviewers, however, are enthusiastic about the book. In the Baltimore *Evening Sun*, Gerald W. Johnson offers high praise: "Ellen Glasgow in her latest novel has adopted the practice of Anatole France. She is wrapping dynamite in curl-papers. *They Stooped to Folly* is witty, amusing, light as thistledown in appearance, but under the surface it is as grim and ruthless as a prohibition agent raiding the Y.M.C.A." Amy Loveman, in the *Saturday Review of Literature*, calls Glasgow "perhaps the leading woman novelist of America" and adds that no male novelist "surpasses her in the beautiful precision of a style which conceals its artistry under its art." In *New York Herald Tribune Books*, Isabel Paterson suggests that without Glasgow "it is easily credible that [the Southern Literary Renaissance] would not have occurred in her time."

The Sheltered Life, Glasgow's third novel of manners, and perhaps her finest novel, is published in 1932. Set in Queenborough in the years 1910–17, before World War I, this story presents a darker view of society than is depicted in the two novels that preceded it. Glasgow again demonstrates her gifted use of irony and wit, but *The Sheltered Life* is ultimately a tragedy as well as a dark comedy.

Part I of the novel is primarily seen from the point of view of 9-year-old Jenny Blair Archbald, a bright and adventurous young girl. Part II takes place seven years later and is wholly in the consciousness of 84-year-old General David Archbald. The action of Part III is viewed through the eyes of several figures. At the center of the novel are the Archbalds' neighbors the Birdsongs: Eva, a fabled beauty who has shaped her life to conform to the myth of the ideal woman, is struggling to maintain appearances in a troubled marriage to George, a weak but charming philanderer. The action moves inevitably to the tragic outcome when Eva finally expresses her repressed rage and shoots her husband. Jenny Blair, who has contributed to this drama, is immediately consoled by her grandfather, and the tragic act is called an accident to shelter her from the truth.

Glasgow's subtle description of George's murder at the denouement of the novel is misunderstood by some readers. The reviewer for the Denver *Post*, for example, thinks George Birdsong has committed suicide. Glasgow would explain later, in a letter to Van Wyck Brooks, that she added three words— "She killed him"—to subsequent editions in order to make it clear that Eva shot George. [14]

Among all the positive reviews of *The Sheltered Life*, one negative one stands out. Clifton Fadiman, casting a decidedly minority vote, attacks the novel in the *New Republic*: "There is nothing here . . . which retains freshness or vitality for us today." Stark Young writes a second, wholly laudatory, review for the *New Republic*, plainly designed to counter Fadiman's views. In a letter to Allen Tate, Glasgow explains that Fadiman, whom she calls a communist, wrote the only "disagreeable" review of the book and that Young's review "expressed perfectly what I had had in mind. I had asked him to do it from that angle."[15]

This tale seems to confirm the idea that Glasgow mercilessly manipulated reviews of her novels. In this case, however, she had another justification for objecting to Fadiman as a reviewer. Fadiman was an employee of Simon and Schuster, and in reviewing *The Sheltered Life*, he was attacking a book published by his firm's competitor Doubleday, Doran. The literary editor of the Pittsburgh *Sun-Telegraph*, George Seibel, wrote in protest to Page Cooper at Doubleday, Doran, objecting to a "rival publisher" reviewing Glasgow.[16]

Mary Ellen Chase, in the *Atlantic Monthly*, calls the novel Glasgow's "best work," and reviewers for the Chicago *Herald-Examiner* and Newark *News* judge the book a "masterpiece." Major reviews in the Chicago *Daily Tribune* (by Fanny Butcher), *Saturday Review of Literature* (by Henry Seidel Canby), *New York Times Book Review* (by J. Donald Adams), and *Nation* (by Dorothy Van Doren) heap praise on the novel. Fanny Butcher, for example, says the book is "rich in satirical humor" but, "when the delicious petals of the artichoke are peeled away, bristly with tragedy at its core." And in a well-written and intelligent review, E. K. Brown, writing in the *Canadian Forum*, says the novel "is good because of the visibility and human complexity of at least six characters, the simple naturalness of the story, the bittersweet elegance of the style and, above all, the delicate humanization of a social idea, the idea expressed in the title."

With *The Sheltered Life* Ellen Glasgow reaches the high point in her career for the critical reception of a novel. The novel also sells widely, attaining fifth place on best-seller lists for the year. But Glasgow is dealt a bitter disappointment when T.S. Stribling's *The Store* is awarded the Pulitzer Prize and she is—again—overlooked. Newspaper articles criticize the prize committee for its decision, and her friends, including Allen Tate and James Branch Cabell, express outrage that she did not receive the award.[17]

Crowning Glasgow's achievement during these productive years is the publication by Doubleday, Doran of the *Old Dominion Edition* of eight of her novels. She has done some rewriting and pruning of the texts and has written a brief introduction for each volume. *They Stooped to Folly* is printed in 1929, and three more volumes are added in 1930: *The Battle-Ground*, *The Deliverance*, and *Virginia*. The eight-volume set is completed in 1933 with the publication of *The Voice of the People*, *The Miller of Old Church*, *Barren Ground*, and *The Romantic Comedians*.

James Branch Cabell, reviewing the first four novels for *New York Herald Tribune Books* in 1930, writes about the "belatedness" of the author's "general recognition as the foremost woman novelist of America" and dates the beginning of her serious recognition to 1925 and *Barren Ground*. Cabell's thesis in this essay in that Glasgow's novels provide "a complete natural history of the Southern gentlewoman, with every attendant feature of her lair and general habitat most accurately rendered." He discusses various women characters in her works, pointing out that they are "predestined victims of male chivalry."

Three years later all eight volumes are reviewed by Stark Young in the *New Republic*, James Southall Wilson in the *Virginia Quarterly Review*, and H. L.

Mencken in *Smart Set*. Young focuses on the prefaces to the novels and says these "revelations and comments, hesitant and brief, always distinguished, will be, I suppose, the best comment on the novels of Ellen Glasgow." Wilson writes a graceful essay praising Glasgow, observing that she has steadily improved in her art, and predicting that her work will endure. Mencken writes a restrained essay, giving Glasgow his most positive review thus far. He ends by observing, "Not many of her rivals . . . have brought [to novel writing] so ingenious and so civilized a mind."

"A Stately and Imposing Talent": Her Last Works, 1935–1943

In 1935 and 1941, Glasgow, now in her sixties, publishes her last two novels, *Vein of Iron* and *In This Our Life*. In addition, Scribner's brings out in 1938 a handsome, twelve-volume collected edition of her novels, the *Virginia Edition*, for which she has written new prefaces. In 1943, Harcourt Brace publishes those twelve prefaces plus the preface to *In This Our Life* in a volume entitled *A Certain Measure*. The work published in her lifetime is now complete—nineteen novels, one volume of poetry, one of short stories, one of criticism, and two collected editions. It is an impressive body of work, published over almost a half century. And finally the honors are bestowed: honorary degrees from Duke University and the University of Richmond in 1938 and from the College of William and Mary in 1939; membership in the American Academy of Arts and Letters in 1938; the Howells Medal (awarded every five years) from the Academy of Arts and Letters in 1940 for achievement in the writing of fiction; recognition by the *Saturday Review of Literature* in 1941 for "Distinguished Service to American Literature"; and—at last—the long-awaited Pulitzer Prize in 1942. She has become, as Margaret Halsey writes in a review of her last book for the New York *Patriot and Morning Advertiser*, "a stately and imposing talent."

For her eighteenth novel Glasgow has abandoned the happiness hunters of Queenborough and chosen a family of Scottish Presbyterians in Rockbridge County, Virginia. The novel is set in the first third of the twentieth century and begins in 1910, when Ada Fincastle is ten years old. This novel focuses on Ada, a heroine with a vein of iron, reminiscent of Dorinda Oakley. Ada's father is a defrocked Presbyterian minister and a philosopher; her great love is Ralph McBride, a man without Ada's strength of character. The tale is told from multiple points of view, and the plot is complex and includes many characters. The action moves from Ironside to Queenborough, covers family history retrospectively, and continues through World War I and the Great Depression.

Positive reviews in the major journals greet this novel: James Boyd's in the *Saturday Review of Literature*, Fanny Butcher's in the Chicago *Daily Tribune*,

J. Donald Adams's in the *New York Times Book Review*, Stark Young's in the *New Republic*. Heywood Broun, in the New York *World-Telegram*, calls it her "best novel" and praises the account of Ada's grandmother assisting at the birth of Ada's illegitimate child: "These particular pages are as eloquent and moving as anything in modern fiction." Clifton Fadiman, in the *New Yorker*, praises the book but says he prefers the author "in her vein of irony rather than her vein of iron" Gerald W. Johnson, in the Baltimore *Evening Sun*, discusses Glasgow's strengths and weaknesses. He criticizes her male characters, saying she paints only "the more contemptible varieties of the male half of the human race," but he observes that her "gallery of women . . . deserves unstinted praise."

Two reviews are as negative as any Glasgow ever received. Bernard Smith of *New Masses* admits he has never been south of Washington, D.C., and then he excoriates Glasgow's style, imagination, characters, and story. He closes his review by observing that Glasgow is old and then adding cruel and patronizing words: "She has failed utterly, but let us respect her attempt." In a negative response for the *Southern Review*, Randall Jarrell writes that Glasgow's description of John Fincastle as a philosopher is not convincing, her style is commonplace, and she is "full of prejudice and presupposition." Nevertheless, he grants that the book "has considerable power." These negative reviews come from both ends of the political spectrum—a leftist journal, on the one hand, and a conservative Southern journal edited by Cleanth Brooks and Robert Penn Warren, on the other.

With only a few exceptions, however, *Vein of Iron* receives favorable reviews. The novel is chosen by the Book-of-the-Month Club and reaches second place in best-seller lists for the year. It sells more copies than any of Glasgow's books since *The Deliverance* in 1904.[18]

The *Virginia Edition* of Ellen Glasgow's novels is published in 1938 in a limited edition of 810 signed copies. In a brief review, the Richmond *News Leader* calls the prefaces written especially for this edition "superb." Howard Mumford Jones, in a lengthy review for *New York Herald Tribune Books*, proposes that the prefaces "are likely to be the most important pronouncements upon novel writing since Conrad and Henry James." Jones discusses her novels, pointing out that Glasgow is "haunted by heredity." He says that her work presents "a feminine reading of life." Henry Seidel Canby, in the *Saturday Review of Literature*, calls the prefaces an "invaluable critique upon the art of fiction." He says Glasgow is "our best contemporary master of the tragic drama of significant manners." J. Donald Adams, in the *New York Times Book Review*, praises the prefaces and calls Glasgow's work "likely to be one of the most enduring achievements in American fiction." Jones and Canby call for her to recieve the Pulitzer Prize, and Adams hopes she will win a Nobel Prize.

Glasgow's successful manipulation of a reviewer is revealed in letters to

Mrs. Howard Mumford Jones about a review of the *Virginia Edition* for *New York Herald Tribune Books*. Glasgow writes Mrs. Jones in April 1938, explaining that she wishes to be "judged" by the works in the *Virginia Edition*. Then she writes Mrs. Jones in May, telling her that she would like Howard Mumford Jones to review the books, if he will do so with the appropriate "sympathy and understanding." In addition, Glasgow points out that the reviewer will receive a complete set "of this really lovely edition."[19] Jones does, indeed, write a positive review for *New York Herald Tribune Books*—just as Glasgow has suggested he should—and it is clear that Glasgow has exerted influence on the review.

In This Our Life, Glasgow's last novel, is published in 1941, having been written during years when Glasgow suffered poor health. After her first heart attack in 1939, her writing was limited, and she had a difficult time completing the novel.

Set in the period 1938–9, the novel deals with problems of modern life by focusing on the Timberlake family. The central characters are Asa Timberlake, the middle-aged father who seems to be the author's spokesperson, and his daughter Roy, another of Glasgow's strong young women of good character. Lavinia is Asa's neurotic wife, and Stanley is Roy's wicked sister. The plot is complex, and a subplot involves a young, ambitious black man who is wrongly accused of a crime committed by Stanley.

Reviewers seem to be aware that this will be Glasgow's last novel. They are generous, and she is treated in most cases as the person of "stately and imposing talent" described by Margaret Halsey in her review. Favorable reviews by important critics appear in the major journals and newspapers: by Howard Mumford Jones in the *Saturday Review of Literature*, Louis Kronenberger in the *Nation*, J. Donald Adams in the *New York Times Book Review*, James Southall Wilson in the *Virginia Quarterly Review*, Edwin Mims in the Nashville *Banner*, Fanny Butcher in the Chicago *Tribune*, Edwin Muir in the *Listener*. Some reviewers complain about her pessimism. As Clifton Fadiman puts it in the *New Yorker*, she is "rather hard on the young folks." Most reviewers, however, praise *In This Our Life*.

The Pulitzer Committee finally awards Glasgow the coveted prize for fiction in 1942, a fitting acknowledgment of her last work of fiction. The award is presented on the occasion of the publication of *In This Our Life*, but the committee makes the award for all of her work.

Glasgow's last publication in her lifetime, *A Certain Measure*, is published in 1943 by Harcourt, Brace. Its thirteen essays include the twelve prefaces written for volumes in the *Virginia Edition*, as well as an additional one for *In This Our Life*.

She receives much adulation, but one review, published in the New York *Evening Post*, stings her and affects her friendship with her Richmond friend James Branch Cabell. In a rather puzzling and snide review, Cabell compares

Glasgow to Edward Gibbon, pointing out that their initials are the same and that he regards all of Glasgow's work as "history of the first quality." He calls *A Certain Measure* "the best of her books." Much would be written about the consequent quarrel, and it may be that Cabell was motivated by Glasgow's failure to acknowledge publicly his help with *In This Our Life* and *A Certain Measure* when she was ill, or he may have envied Glasgow's great success in recent years. At any rate, the old friends would be reconciled before Glasgow's death in 1945. [20]

Many of the reviews of *A Certain Measure* are encomiums on all of her work. Major reviewers provide an overwhelmingly positive critical response. Her literary essays are called an "intellectual biography," and she is compared to Henry James by a number of reviewers. Extremely favorable reviews appear in the *New York Times Book Review* (by Hamilton Basso), *Saturday Review of Literature* (by Howard Mumford Jones), *Nation* (by Joseph Wood Krutch), *New Republic* (by Stark Young), and New York *Mirror* (by Benjamin De Casseres). Basso, offering perhaps typical adulation, explains, "Writing of the craft of fiction, she has written a notable essay on the craft of life. It is a privilege to be able to salute her in her own time." In a review for the Richmond *News Leader*, Jack Kilpatrick writes, "Miss Glasgow's *A Certain Measure* will stand as a solid achievement to end her career. For sheer perfection in writing, few books will ever equal it."

And so Ellen Glasgow—old and full of honors—closes her writing career with *A Certain Measure*, although she will continue to write, working on a novella, *Beyond Defeat*, a sequel to *In This Our Life*, and her autobiography, *The Woman Within*, both of which will be published posthumously. When she began her career at the end of the nineteenth century, she was precociously young, lacked formal education, and consciously rejected popular forms of the day—the romance novel and the adventure novel. In a literary sense, she was alone in Richmond without mentors; so she taught herself to write by studying Flaubert, Maupassant, Tolstoy, and Chekhov.

For half a century she wrote her books, producing one approximately every two years. She left "a series of novels which composes, in the more freely interpretative form of fiction, a social history of Virginia" from 1850 to 1939. Dominant themes in this chronicle are "the stubborn retreat of an agrarian culture before the conquests of an industrial revolution, and the slow and steady rise of the lower middle class" in the South. She applied "blood and irony" to her vision of the Old Dominion.[21] And she left a solid shelf of books, a handful of which deserve to survive—among them, *Virginia*, *Barren Ground*, *The Romantic Comedians*, and *The Sheltered Life*. She also added a number of heroines to the gallery of memorable women in American fiction—Betty Ambler, Virginia Pendleton Treadwell, Dorinda Oakley, Eva Birdsong, Ada Fincastle.

This volume of contemporaneous reviews of Glasgow's books depicts her critical reception in her own time. Its story is just part of the larger story of Glasgow's career, the heart of which is, of course, her fiction.

Notes

1 See, for example, W. W. Kelly, *Ellen Glasgow: A Bibliography* (Charlottesville: University Press of Virginia, 1964), xxiii–xxiv, and James Branch Cabell, *As I Remember It* (New York: McBride, 1955), 224. (Subsequent page references to this volume are given in parentheses.)
2 Ellen Glasgow, *The Woman Within* (New York: Harcourt, Brace, 1954), 273.
3 W. W. Kelly, in "Struggle for Recognition: A Study of the Literary Reputation of Ellen Glasgow," Ph.D. diss., Duke University, 1957, pp. 15–17, suggests that Garland could have been an important mentor for Glasgow, but they met twice after this review was printed and apparently were not compatible. They were hindered in discussion by Glasgow's growing deafness.
4 Ellen Glasgow, *A Certain Measure* (New York: Harcourt, Brace, 1943), 13. (Subsequent page references to this volume are given in parentheses.)
5 Information in this introduction about Glasgow's novels as best-sellers is in Alice Payne Hackett and James Henry Burke, *Eighty Years of Best Sellers: 1895–1975* (New York: R. R. Bowker, 1977).
6 Glasgow details this romance and her heartbreak afterward on pages 153–68.
7 Glasgow, *A Certain Measure*, 97.
8 See E. Stanly Godbold, Jr., *Ellen Glasgow and The Woman Within* (Baton Rouge: Louisiana State University Press, 1972), 116–18, 123, and Linda W. Wagner, *Ellen Glasgow: Beyond Convention* (Austin: University of Texas Press, 1982), 59–66.
9 Kelly points out in "Struggle" (pp. 220–2) that Sherman showed great understanding of Glasgow's work in this review and made sensible criticisms of her faults. According to Kelly, Sherman might "have become the most influential critic of her career," but he died in 1926.
10 See Daniel Patterson, "Ellen Glasgow's Plan for a Social History of Virginia," *Modern Fiction Studies* 5 (Winter 1959–60), 353–60, and Edgar E. MacDonald, "The Glasgow–Cabell Entente," *American Literature* 41 (March 1969), 76–91.
11 Glasgow, *A Certain Measure*, 211.
12 Ibid., 234, 237.
13 Ibid., 243.
14 Blair Rouse, ed., *Letters of Ellen Glasgow* (New York: Harcourt, Brace, 1958), 262. See also Kelly, *Ellen Glasgow*, 79.
15 Rouse, *Letters*, 123.
16 Kelly, "Struggle," 277.
17 See Lewis Gannett, "Books and Things," New York *Herald Tribune*, 5 May 1933, p. 13. See also Rouse, *Letters*, 135, 139–40. In a letter dated 5 May 1933, Cabell wrote, "I did not think it possible for the Pulitzer Prize committees to excel their past records in criminal idiocy, but I admit they really have done it. The one consolation is that the novel award was absurd on every conceivable account: there can be no question of rivalry but merely the question why you should have been thus flagrantly cheated of your plain due" (James Branch Cabell Collection, Clifton Waller Barrett Library, University of Virginia Library).
18 Kelly, "Struggle," 309.
19 Rouse, *Letters*, 235, 238–40.

20 See MacDonald, "The Glasgow-Cabell Entente"; Edgar MacDonald, "The Final Word," *Ellen Glasgow Newsletter*, 26 (Spring 1991), 2–7; and Dorothy Scura, "Two Letters: Glasgow and Cabell," *Ellen Glasgow Newsletter*, 26 (Spring 1991), 7–10.
21 Quotations in this paragraph are from Glasgow, *A Certain Measure*, 3, 75, 28.

THE DESCENDANT

THE DESCENDANT

A Novel

"*Man is not above Nature, but in Nature*"
                                    HAECKEL

NEW YORK
HARPER & BROTHERS PUBLISHERS
1897

Outlook, 55 (27 March 1897), 855

From [Harper & Brothers] comes *The Descendant*, an anonymous novel of the strenuous kind which exhibits untrained force. There is passionate intensity in the story of the despised illegitimate boy who becomes a fierce Socialist editor, a misanthrope, and a misogynist; his failure to carry out his theories in his personal life, his imprisonment for manslaughter, and his death in the home of the one woman who has loved him and whom he has ill-treated, make a gloomy, painful tale, but one written with considerable power.

Laurence Hutton, "Literary Notes," *Harper's Magazine*, 94 (April 1897), 549

A very strong, and a very unusual, piece of fiction is *The Descendant*, by an author who chooses to remain anonymous. The hero is an Ishmaelite who began life by cursing and hating everybody, from his father, whom he called a villain, to his mother, whom he called a fool. His hand was against every man, and every man's hand was against him. He hurled defiance at law and order, until he was brought to order by the power of the law. As a journalist and a writer upon *The Iconoclast*, he had much of the power of Ibsen, and all Ibsen's audacity. He left nothing unassailed. He had a genius for upsetting and destroying. His lecture upon "Social Lies" set society ablaze. "Life is an apple," he cried, when he was twenty-six. "It has three stages: first, the rind, which is sour—cynicism; next, the pulp, which is sweet—optimism; and third, the core, which is rotten—pessimism. Well," he added, "I've tried the first. I skipped the second; and I'm pretty well into the third." He certainly skipped the second, and before he consumed his apple he existed entirely upon the core. Across his path, and into his life, came a woman quite as well and as powerfully drawn as he is. A wholesome young person, as her creator describes her, with a well-regulated nervous system and great power of self-absorption. When she expended herself she expended herself utterly. There was no half measure in her concentration. Her work demanded her time, and she yielded it; it demanded her vitality, and she yielded that as well. She was a woman both strong and tender, a woman in the beginning of her career as innocent and as impulsive as a child. The story of their association, a delicate subject, is handled with great delicacy. They were both the victims of adverse circumstances, and, perhaps, the fault was not altogether their own. They were both Descendants. And the laws of heredity cannot always be broken.

It is a tragic tale in which there is nothing light or humorous. It preaches degeneration as strongly as Nordau did; and it preaches despair. It is a deep study of the sad and serious sides of human affairs. As a story it is exciting, and it is what is called "thought-compelling." It is rarely dull. It is well considered, and it is well handled. It is bound to create no little comment. And the reading world will wonder who the unknown author can be.

"By the Great Unknown," Chap-Book, 6 (1 April 1897), 403–4

Centuries ago, William Camden found "what's bred in the bone will never out of the flesh," a fact sufficiently obvious to the multitude from the beginning to have passed into a proverb. Nowadays, men devote volumes to plethoric proof of it, and call it "working out a problem in heredity." Such was the purpose of the anonymous author of *The Descendant*. The title indicates it, and the headings of the four divisions of the work approve it. Its motto is Haeckel's "Man is not above Nature, but in Nature." The first of its books bears the legend, *Omne vivum ex ovo*, it ends with Dead Sea apples, Schopenhauer and Ibsen are served between, its Nietzsche-like protagonist flavors it throughout; yet man is left a free moral agent, and the essential sweetness of life remains unimpugned at its close.

The hero, Michael Akershem, was born out of wedlock—his father being a villain and his mother a fool, as he himself abruptly characterizes them. The mother, a woman of the fields, dies, the father remains undisclosed, and the child is taken by a neighboring farmer. When the story opens he is a swineherd; but he grows up a scholar, an innate longing for knowledge seeming to commingle with an understanding that it affords an escape from odious surroundings. In the first flush of youth Akershem leaves his birthplace in Virginia and goes to New York, where he soon becomes editor of *The Iconoclast*, an Ishmaelitish journal devoted to the justification of its name at the expense of existing social conditions. He achieves something better than mere notoriety by the force of his writings; he loves and is loved by a young artist from the South, whom he treats much as his father treated his mother. He is taken to task for it by his best friend and early patron; he kills a devoted admirer when frenzied with the rebuke, and serves his term in the state's prison. Eventually, he comes back to die in the arms of his first love—an ending wholly conventional to a story in many respects remarkable.

While the book is forcefully written, disclosing a hand skillful in the treatment, and a perception discriminating in the choice of materials, the chief character is elusive and self-contradictory. He is the slave of heredity and of environment in unstable equilibrium,—like the rest of us,—which leaves proof of his creator's theme unpleasantly suspended. The love affair is charmingly told, but it lacks coherence and probability. Akershem perpetually sways between that hatred for society, for which both his birth and early training are responsible, and the desire of civilized man to establish a home, due both to nature and his surroundings. And in the final catastrophe there is nothing of inherence or imminence but the mere frenzy of a mind over-wrought by a conscience arbitrarily developed. And the arbitrariness so apparent in this is to be noted in a score of minor details.

All that the author has done by the intrusion of a point of view is to confuse a character in which the results of instinct and example are too perfectly intertwined to be quite true, when considered either as philosophy, nature, or art. Yet, *The Descendant* presents phases of modern thought rarely dealt with in fiction, is both able and daring in its treatment of them, and is readable and worthy of reading.

"An Iconoclastic Hero," *New York Times Saturday Review of Books and Art*, 17 April 1897, p. 7

You scent catastrophe in *The Descendant*. There is going to be human smash-up, and on the first page you note that the victim must be Michael Akershem. Michael is of a dubious lineage. His youth is unhappy. He feeds the swine. The better portion in him finds some slight chance when he meets a kind-hearted minister. There is awakened in him a thirst for knowledge. He picks up an education as he can, then gets somehow or other to civilization and New York, and at first he starves.

Michael's opportunity, a risky one, comes at last. There is a newspaper written for demagogues, and at heart a savage is a natural demagogue, and of that kind is the man of *The Descendant*. In time Michael becomes the brains of *The Iconoclast*, and the mission of this sheet and of its editor is to fight everything and everybody.

Rachel Gavin, a Southern girl, an art student, is far too good for Michael, but the two fall in love and live together. Then Michael meets another young person, Anna Allard, who is honesty and purity combined, who sees no reason why she should not follow the "conventional" laws which govern this world. She is no new woman. Anna might have loved Michael, but his wildness affrights her.

There is a loud-mouthed blatherskite, Kyle, who is in *The Iconoclast* office. It may be Anna Allard who has brought about in the journalistic Ishmael a change of heart, for Michael begins to question the wild theories he has advanced in his paper. In a quarrel with Kyle, Akershem kills him. Then Michael very properly goes to prison. When he regains his liberty his strength has left him—he has consumption. His condition is pitiful. He finds Rachel once more. "You are so steadfast," he said, and she kissed him, for he knew he was forgiven. Then came back some little of his fearless spirit, and he gasped: "Give me half a chance and I will be even with the world at last." But upon his lips was set the blood-red seal of fate. Michael died then, but what did Michael mean by being "even with [the] world at last"?

The anonymous author of *The Descendant* has uncommon vigor and feels the dramatic situation. If the story is a painful one, such was the intention of the author. We are not always to be amused, and supposably it is not a necessity for novel readers to be always laughing. Novels which are "hard packed" when treating of social conditions, as of human sufferings, to be impressive want a return at times to natural, commonplace conditions; then the contrasts become the stronger. Schopenhauer and Ibsen are unwholesome sources to drink from.

Bookman, 5 (May 1897), 368–70

The identification of the author of *The Descendant* with Miss Ellen Glasgow will come as a surprise to those who have read the book. Not since Miss Katharine Pearson Woods published her first story, *Metzerott Shoemaker*, about eight years ago, in the same manner, have we had in this country an anonymous novel which by its masculine force and vigour in characterisation, and in its treatment of certain phases of life, was so deceptive as to the sex of its author. In both cases we can trace back some of the influences that operated in producing such striking and remarkable effects in these initial performances to heredity and education. Miss Glasgow was born in Richmond, Va., just twenty-two years ago. She is sprung from an old and prominent Virginian family, and is of Scotch-Irish descent. During the last six years she has pursued the study of physical science and political economy with unremitting ardour, and her familiars in the book-world are Spencer, Darwin, Haeckel, Huxley, Romanes, Mill, Bagehot, Clifford, and Weissmann. This has given her imaginative work a scientific basis, and has developed her poetic sense of things into a concreteness of form that rarely is found in the work of women. George Eliot is the grand exception, and it is this tendency in Miss Glasgow which presumably has caused some of her loving friends to advertise her rashly in the same category. She will be wise not to heed such indiscriminate praise, but to be faithful to her own ideal. There is sufficient power and originality together with a love of beauty in her first book to lift it above the ordinary, and to make us look forward with eagerness for her next work in fiction. It is certainly difficult to explain the marked sympathy with the mystery of pain and the tragedy of failure in the work of one so young and adolescent. Such deep sympathy comes from intuition rather than from knowledge, and betokens the possession of that high order of mind which we call genius, but which often lacks staying power. If Miss Glasgow will nurse her powers carefully and work conscientiously, without haste or pressure from without, we shall hope for something from her pen which may justify the unusual promise of *The Descendant*. But if publishers and editors constrain her, she is lost.

Boston *Evening Transcript*, 1 May 1897, p. 20

The new anonymous book, *The Descendant*, is unquestionably a strong book, but the strength is that of bitter aloes. It is full of color and passion, acute character study and careful description, and sparkles with epigram. But it is not pleasant as a whole, in spite of certain passages here and there delightful in themselves, for the dominant note is cynically bitter. Not that the author has made it so intentionally; one rather obtains the impression that he would willingly have had it otherwise, but that he is overpowered by his motive. The central figure, Akershem, is the child of shame, and is reared in an atmosphere of sordid toil. Escaping from this at nineteen, embittered against the world thus early, he presently becomes the editor of a socialist paper in New York, and further we need not pursue his history here, beyond saying that it is of absorbing interest. Carefully studied as this character is, the author has not succeeded in making it fully consistent. A man of his stamp would not have wavered as did Akershem in the crisis of his life. His life was a protest against social laws and customs, and any deference to them is more or less out of character. It is nevertheless a very true touch which makes this scoffer at marriage so bitterly resent the fact of his own illegitimacy. Like many another bitter enemy of society, Akershem finds himself unable to contend successfully against it. What he does not see, however, is that he and those like him are but beating their heads against the wall. He cannot realize that society is stronger than the individual; that no successful revolt is possible in which society itself does not take part. But the Akershems do not perceive this, and it is this imperfect vision of theirs that makes such a book as *The Descendant* sad reading.

Literary World, 28 (15 May 1897), 164

Whatever faults may be urged against this novel by an anonymous author, lack of strength is not among them. The book is distinctly, almost audaciously, virile and vigorous. It is a study of heredity, exemplified in the career of a fatherless and friendless boy of nameless parentage, who escapes from the bondage of a small Virginia village, and gradually makes a mark in New York as the editor of an iconoclastic newspaper. It is also a study—a terribly distinct one—in selfishness. Michael Akersham, stung and maddened by his own disappointments and annoyances, flings himself upon the social order and does his best to destroy it; but he has scarcely a throb of personal sympathy for the down-trodden and suffering folk whose cause he is avowedly espousing. He excites and exasperates them into fierce resistance to their real and imaginary wrongs—to hate capital, law, the marriage tie, and restraint of every kind; but to go among them, to personally interest himself in them, would never have occurred to him as possible, so, as the "gift" without the giver is bare, his efforts recoil in himself, and his selfishness poisons all that might have been sweet to him, and life is a failure, and the tale and the moral of the tale are alike lamentable. For love is the one sweet drop in the world's cup, and without it the draught is bitter indeed.

William Morton Payne, "Recent Fiction," *Dial*, 22 (16 May 1897), 310–11

The anonymous author of *The Descendant* is unduly oppressed with the doctrine of heredity. His thesis seems to be that the invidious bar of birth lies athwart the best intentions and the most resolute character, shaping the life in spite of itself. This thesis is worked out in the character of a man whose childhood has been hopelessly embittered by the slurs cast upon it on account of illegitimacy, who leaves his country home for the city, who throws his whole energy into journalism of a radically socialistic and destructive type, who wins only to scorn the love of the woman who might have saved him, and whose maturer realization of the folly of his course results only in a fit of passion that makes him a murderer and lands him in a felon's cell. The book is undeniably strong, and rises to the height of genuine passion in its climacteric scenes; but it is crude in the working-out of many of its episodes, and is rather suggestive of future possibilities than the earnest of achieved mastery.

"The Descendant," *Critic*, n.s. 27 (22 May 1897), 352–3

This is a strong book, and, like most strong books, it is not continuously agreeable. If you enjoy the sensation of being out in a tornado, beaten and buffeted and driven on by wind and rain, then you will enjoy the maelstrom of emotions and experiences in which the characters of this novel move and have their being; but if you like to be aware subconsciously of the snap of the hearth-fire, the bubbling of the kettle and the purring of the kitten as you read, you may be sure that it is not a book for you. It is a study of the evolution of character in contact with life in some of its bitterest aspects....

If Hall Caine had written this novel, the world would have said that it was one of his most powerful stories, and much more coherent and artistic than anything he had previously done. Whether the world will be prepared to accord an equal measure of appreciation to an anonymous American author remains to be seen. The writer is evidently a woman. This is made manifest, not by any absence of virility, but by the presence of certain delicacies of insight, such as no man could be expected to exhibit. The book is very brilliantly written, but it is a testimony to its engrossing human interest that the reader can absorb page after page of shrewd and epigrammatic observations and hardly be aware of it. Such a book deserves success—and this one, we believe, has won it.

Clarence Wellford, "The Author of *The Descendant*," *Harper's Bazar*, 30 (5 June 1897), 458

There was a gasp of amazement when Miss Ellen Glasgow walked out of my study the other day, and I turned to the remaining callers and said, "That young girl wrote *The Descendant*."

"Wrote *The Descendant*!" some one exclaimed. "Why, she looks as if she had spent her life dancing the german!"

Never did appearance so belie a person's occupation. This bright-looking young girl, with keen brown eyes and chestnut hair and the very daintiest of hands and feet, after one winter of dancing, renounced society for her own chosen pursuits.

No one knew she wrote, for she is both reserved and sensitive, and although she has been given to literary composition ever since she could hold a pencil, nothing had ever been shown to the world, except a short story called "A Woman of To-morrow," until *The Descendant* appeared. Only since her novel's success has she taken the members of her own family into her confidence and showed the reams of written paper that testify to her youthful apprenticeship. There are odd bits of poetry—scrawled when the little hand was hardly steady enough to form the letters and when spelling was evidently still an uncertain science—short stories, sketches, and whole novels. But editors' offices were never besieged by these manuscripts; they were laid away where she kept her private papers; and her career is perhaps unrivalled, certainly enviable, in that she has so far been asked to publish more than she was willing to.

Miss Glasgow is self-tutored, and independent as a thinker. She did not go to school as a child, because physical frailty forbade, and with but a little teaching from older sisters she conquered the usual beaten path of education alone and unaided.

As a little child she was an omnivorous reader, devouring, at ten years old, all of Scott's novels, Hugo's *Les Misérables*, and any book with a story to it that she could lay hands on. Fortunately she belonged to a bookish family, so that her opportunities were many. By the time she was sixteen years old her mind seemed to have found its natural bent, and since then her studies have been wholly scientific and political.

With a rigid thoroughness and a complete self-absorption rare among women, she has followed in the steps of Spencer's *Synthetic Philosophy*, and has studied the works of Darwin, Mill, Huxley, Haeckel, Lubbock, Lyell, Romanes, Moleschott, Weissmann, Laing, and Grant Allen.

History and natural law are Miss Glasgow's studies, and man's real life, development or failure, is what she cares to write about. The romantic does not especially appeal to her, and the unreal, the sham poetic, she spurns; but there is no actual suffering of man or brute, no innate, insuperable weakness, no tragic combination of forces or circumstances under which man is downtrodden, for which she has not keen insight and a broad, tender sympathy which remind one of George Eliot. Her love of animals, her especial cherishings of forlorn dogs and sickly kittens, make one think, too, of what George Eliot writes of her own preference for friendless curs.

In the reviews of *The Descendant* Miss Glasgow's work has been frequently compared with *The African Farm*. It must have been the forceful writing and intensity of emotion in both books which suggested the resemblance, for the former writer does not share Miss Schreiner's love of the allegorical and supernatural. I find in the whole field of English literature but one writer who might be thought of as Miss Glasgow's prototype, and that is Emily Brontë. The "Last Lines," "The Old Stoic," and the stanzas beginning,

Often rebuked, yet always back
    returning
To those first feelings that were born
    with me,

might have come from Miss Glasgow's pen; there is in both these women somewhat of the same intellectual courage, singleness of purpose, and "more than manlike strength."

Just about in the centre of Richmond, on the very corner where the streets are divided into east and west, stands the old gray Colonial house where this young writer lives and works. It is a large, roomy house, and four daughters live at home. The fact of Miss Ellen Glasgow's writing was a secret, so that she had no study of her own. *The Descendant* was written in her bedroom and in the family sitting-room, and as the author pathetically relates, "I had to stop a dozen times in Michael's most exciting predicaments to see whether a certain flower looked better on the left or the right side of a hat."

The first deliberate acknowledgment of *The Descendant*'s success was that the author's father assigned a small quiet room on the second floor for the future work to be done in. Here, under the window, stands the writing-desk, and on either side along the wall are bookcases full of scientific books and works on political economy, and the walls are literally covered with beautiful photographs brought home from England last summer.

Not long ago Miss Glasgow and two intimate friends sat up until long after midnight in this little study while the author read aloud her beautiful poem "In a Buddhist Temple," and after that numbers of short poems that have been accumulating for years were then heard for the first time.

"I know I am not a poet," Miss Glasgow says. "This is only a way of giving vent to the emotion of the moment." But some of these short poems are flawless, and all are forceful and spontaneous, seeming to be, as she says, "as easy as to feel." Well, art is but expression, and the seal of genius is that expression should be as natural as living or thinking.

One criticism of the book that came as a great surprise to the author was that it was "sombre throughout." She had expected possible misunderstanding and disapproval of certain phases of it, and she was not astonished that the political economy was attacked; but she said very plaintively, "I did not know it was all sombre; I thought the conversations were rather light, even bright at times." But Miss Glasgow's outlook upon life is naturally a serious and grave one, and she does not wholly realize how deep the imprint upon the book was.

The editor of a Western daily paper made a severe attack upon the book upon the grounds that a "copy of Weissmann's *Heredity* lay upon the floor" in Akershem's room, and yet the author apparently believed in the transmission of acquired traits. Whether the book's being upon the floor was taken as a sign that it was the basis of the work, or whether the editor felt that no one having once read Weissmann could side with the more conservative scientists, was not explained. The author has been accused of being imbued with Schopenhauer, whom she knew not at all except from one or two casual essays. Indeed she has never concerned herself with speculative thought at all; but when she writes of tested science and verified history she feels the ground fairly firm under her feet.

One lady wrote from England to know why the hero had blinking eyes. I questioned the author seriously, for I too thought this a defect; but she answered, "Michael had blinking eyes; I could not help it; I have to write of my people as they are."

Miss Glasgow is now at work upon another novel of broader scope than *The Descendant*. The hero is a young scientist and the heroine a most vivid and bewitching personality, with less of genius than Rachel Gavin had, but with more vivacity and more varied talents.

Miss Glasgow has very remarkable ability, and great achievements lie before her. Those who know her best are certain that she is not a one-book author, and that *The Descendant* is only a first indication of her capacity. She is now only twenty-two years old, and her interest in study and mental energy insure a future of brilliant results. The first book excited unusual comment and controversy, and the fact that it did so is proof that it was thought-challenging. Perhaps the new book will solve some of the riddles its predecessor left unanswered.

Her care in writing, her felicity of expression, and the equipment she brings to her work, prepare us to expect much from one who has already made so favorable a beginning.

Independent, 49 (29 July 1897), 980

This is the story of miseries manifold. From its opening chapter the reader feels the inevitable outcome to be sodden tragedy. An illegitimate son of a rustic Virginia woman is the hero. His unfortunate origin stamps itself in his character. He goes to New York and becomes a socialist, lives in defiance of law with a young woman while editing a socialist newspaper. Falls in love with a girl in good standing in society, commits murder, goes to the penitentiary for eight years, comes out a wreck, and dies miserably. The book is vigorously written, with considerable show of dramatic power; but it leaves a nausea in the mind, and one feels the need of a liberal tonic. If it was written for a moral purpose it is a failure.

Hamlin Garland, "*The Descendant* and Its Author," *Book Buyer*, 15 (August 1897), 45–6

It is scarcely four months since the anonymous publication of *The Descendant*, and already it has sold two editions and its author's name is demanded with unusual insistence, and Miss Ellen Glasgow seems likely to be a much discussed personality. It happened that, when I took up the book soon after its publication, I was already aware that it was the work of a young Southern girl and that it was a first book. I read it at a sitting, which I do not often do, and in the forenoon, when I should have been at my own work. Such was the interest of the book.

The narrative itself interested me less than the method and the characterizations which gave a clue to the thought and purposes of the writer. It started out to tell the story of a poor white boy, "the offspring of a harlot," as a neighbor brutally characterized him. Michael Akersham was an Ishmaelite from the start. The first part of the book was taken up with his growth to young manhood in Virginia, and his meager education; and in all this, curiously enough, I felt a marked unreality, as though the writer had not sufficient knowledge at first hand—notwithstanding her Southern birth. The boy was real enough, but the surroundings seemed shadowy and sometimes artificial.

The second part took Michael to New York city to try his fortune. Here again I felt the lack of significant details. Sometimes the happenings were forced or illogical. There was a certain uncertainty. The boy did things and moved among things which never seemed quite as actual as himself. They were like a very good stage setting—but still a setting. But when Michael Akershem, successful and self-confident as editor of *The Iconoclast*, met Rachel Gavin in the cafe, there was an end of question. I took off my hat. The author had found herself. The early life of the Ishmaelite reformer was too difficult for her, but the story of Rachel's love and Michael's conquest came within the scope of the writer's intuition. Her forte was disclosed—she had the genius which delights to deal with spiritual combats.

Up to this point the story had been a strenuous and somewhat artificial narrative of Michael Akershem, without humor and with little drama. Humor and self-analysis entered with Driscoll. Drama began with Rachel and Semple. The narrative became a novel, bold, fearless, and unconventional, dealing with emotions and concepts with which the youth of this day are characteristically concerned. Rachel's fear of the bondage of marriage, Akershem's assaults on society while slowly yielding to the charm of the regular, the settled, and the tranquil, expressed through Mrs. Semple and Miss Allard, struck me as great conceptions, and they were worked out with great skill and self-restraint.

Knowing the youth of the writer, I was profoundly impressed with her imaginative power. Her very lack of experience, her ignorance of New York city, forced a wonderful display of intuitive conception. She showed herself capable of making the reader forget her sex and her youth while delineating scenes which belong exclusively to the world of men; as, for example, the scene where Michael in a German saloon gets a frank opinion of the merits of his work as a writer of reform articles. Others equally good are the various conferences in the office of *The Iconoclast*. Her men were men. Semple, Driscoll, the fanatical Kyle, were all capitally done. Their talk was candid, full of character, and very masculine.

But it was in her delineation of Rachel's restless soul, vibrating between love of love and love of art, in her analysis of Michael's "reversal" to the norm, and in Rachel's strenuous, even desperate support of her lover's theories after they were no longer vital to him—it was in the dramatization of these inner struggles and defeats that the author rose to the full stature of the novelist. She lost every tone of the novice, and spoke with the certainty and precision of genius.

It is evident that in Ellen Glasgow American fiction has acquired a novelist worthy the most cordial greeting. Her training has been peculiar. Since her early childhood she has been an eager reader of the boldest scientific treatises of the world. She has an intimate knowledge of Spencer, Darwin, Huxley, Haeckel, and other evolutionist leaders. She is intellectually akin to the most powerful artists of her day. She loves the clash of opinion, the war of creeds, the drama of the intolerant. Her wide reading in science, united to her woman's insight and scientifico-emotional interpretation of life is sure to produce the most singular and original results.

Where she is weak she will grow strong by the study of men and localities. Her diction, which is a happy adoption and adaptation of the scientific phraseology, is already distinctive, individual, and powerful, but with further study it will become still more flexible and exact (it is a little vague at present), and will lend itself with superb results to the expression of the most elusive and unusual mental moods.

The Descendant has grave faults, but keeping in mind that it is a first book, written by a girl of twenty-three years of age, it must be admitted that the friends of Miss Glasgow are justified in the most extravagant hopes of her future work. She is a soul of deep earnestness, a writer not disposed to dodge, or pander to weak readers—a woman with something to say, and the will and the skill to say it well.

She has what might be called the intellectual imagination, and loves to concern herself with characters who think out the problems of the day, and yet she has the self-restraint of the artist. She lets her characters work out their problems. Where she moralizes she is neither offensive nor tedious, but in her best moments she ceases even to comment upon her characters.

The principal thing to be observed is that, in a time of lath swords and tin armor, here is a young girl who sets herself to the difficult task of dealing with the life of a man "whose hand is against organized society," and whose brilliant and splendid powers seem to produce only evil while he strives with his whole will to reform and to purify. That she has been only partly successful in this great work is not to be wondered at. The courage of the attempt was superb, the achievement is worthy [of] generous praise, and entitles the author to very high rank among the novelists of America. I consider *The Descendant* one of the most remarkable first books produced within the last ten years.

Louisville *Courier-Journal*, 29 August 1897, sec. 4, p. 2

When, several months ago, *The Descendant* was published anonymously by the Harpers, it was speedily recognized as a novel of force and originality. Indeed, so shrewd was the knowledge of human nature and of varied phases of life displayed in it that even the most discerning reader could hardly have suspected it to be the work of a young woman in the early twenties. Now that the authorship is known, Miss Ellen Glasgow takes her place among the most interesting and promising of the younger American authors. A Richmond girl, with very little literary training beyond that acquired through her own extensive reading, largely devoted, moreover, to the scientific writers, Miss Glasgow has displayed in *The Descendant* a power of utilizing in fiction some of the most vital social problems of the century, expressing them through striking types of character and genuinely dramatic situations. At a time when so many writers are turning to the romantic periods of history, Miss Glasgow has shown how rich the present-day life in this country is in material for the novelist.

Checklist of Additional Reviews

Christine Terhune Herrick, "The Author of *The Descendant*," *Critic*, n.s. 27 (5 June 1897), 383.

Richmond *Dispatch*, 13 June 1897, p. 2 (reprinted from ibid.).

Book Buyer, 14 (July 1897), 564–5.

"A Brilliant New Novelist," *Literary Digest*, 15 (24 July 1897), 371.

PHASES OF AN INFERIOR PLANET

Phases of an Inferior Planet

By ELLEN GLASGOW

Author of "The Descendant"

HARPER & BROTHERS PUBLISHERS
NEW YORK AND LONDON
1898

William Morton Payne, "Recent Fiction," *Dial*, 25 (16 September 1898), 172

Miss Ellen Glasgow, whose strong novel, *The Descendant*, attracted much attention a year or so ago, has published a second story with the strange title, *Phases of an Inferior Planet*. What this means we hardly venture to say. Mercury and Venus are the only inferior planets known to astronomy, and Miss Glasgow's story is distinctly one of this mundane sphere. Probably the title aims to suggest the faultiness of earthly existence, an impression fortified by perusal of the novel, which tells us of human lives turned awry in the most perverse fashion. We can hardly wax sympathetic over a hero who learns nothing more from suffering than to make his career a living lie, and the heroine, winsome as she is in the earlier chapters, loses hold upon our interest when she deserts her husband for a life of ease such as he is unable to secure for her. The book has alternations of vivacity and sombre strength that make it undeniably interesting, but seems to be based upon no controlling idea except that of two mismated people, and the wretchedness that invades the life of husband and wife when neither of them can possibly understand the temperament of the other.

"Strength Gone Astray," *New York Times Saturday Review of Books and Art*, 17 September 1898, p. 617

Rather more than a year ago *The Descendant*, appearing anonymously, gave a new sensation to the jaded novel-reading public. The plot was original and dramatic; the characters were charged with vitality; the style, sometimes crude and uneven, was striking in its picturesqueness and power. The modest, unheralded volume was a literary event. The author had struck a new and strong note in fiction. *The Descendant* was unique in its daring, its virility, its "iridescence," to use one of the author's favorite words. Since the scene was laid in what may be called Bohemian New York, conjecture was disposed to ascribe its authorship to some young journalist or artist, or, perhaps, to some student of science familiar with the ways of the "Quartier Latin" of the metropolis. When the writer was revealed as a young girl, a Virginian, born and bred in what is, perhaps, the most sheltered and conservative society in the world, the astonished reader could find no parallel for her achievement, save in those marvelous stories that began to steal out of Haworth parsonage half a century ago.

It is natural that a second book should have been eagerly expected; natural, too, perhaps inevitable, that the second book should not satisfy expectation. Yet, after all due allowance has been made for the recoil from extravagant hope, we must confess that *Phases of an Inferior Planet* is distinctly a disappointment.

The very titles of the two stories indicate the difference between them. *The*

Descendant is simple, direct, suggestive; *Phases of an Inferior Planet* is vague, strained, far-fetched. The divergence runs throughout the volume. In *Phases of an Inferior Planet* there is none of the spontaneousness of *The Descendant*. The style has lost its chariot wheels and moves heavily. The author falls sometimes into the vice of "fine writing," notably in the opening pages. Some sentences remind one of Mme. d'Arblay's Johnsonese. The writer is hardened by her scientific knowledge, which produces the impression of "intellectual fat, rather than intellectual muscle and sinew." She sometimes lapses into an exploitation of her learning that cannot fail to carry her older readers back to the days of the ponderous pedantries of *Macaria* and *St. Elmo*.

Like its predecessor, *Phases of an Inferior Planet* belongs to the world of Bohemia. It is to be doubted whether even in that world womanly purity is compatible with the absolute and unprotected liberty of Miss Glasgow's young girls. We receive certain situations with the same incredulity with which we hear of the doings of Glory Quayle. The hero, Anthony Algarcife, is as perplexing as his name. His creator apparently believes in him; she does not intend to represent him sinking like another Tito into depths of infamy. Yet what is one to say of a pronounced unbeliever becoming a priest of a ritualistic Church? One can fancy a man taking holy orders in all sincerity of purpose, and afterward drifting into skepticism and lacking the moral strength to break his bonds—a Robert Elsmere without the courage of his convictions. But what man with a shred of honor, with a ray of decency, would deliberately enter a life in which he knows every word and every deed must be a lie? And what man would accentuate the lie by writing with equal power anonymous articles against Christianity and signed articles in her defense? This might well be an episode in the dual life of Dr. Jekyll and Mr. Hyde. In real life, often as the impossible becomes the actual, we may safely say of this history, "Impossible!" And yet it is apparent that the author intends Algarcife to be, upon the whole, a noble character and to enlist the sympathies of the reader.

There is, nevertheless, much to admire in *Phases of an Inferior Planet*. Were it the author's first story, it would be pronounced, with all its faults, a book of great power and promise. But because it is strength gone astray, because it shows decadence instead of progress, we take alarm at the tendencies that may prove fatal. The characters are shown with a firm hand, the dialogue is brilliant, the situations are effective. As in *The Descendant*, the story is full of verve and daring. The insight of genius is shown in the portrayal of the young mother with her newly born child and over the cradle of her dead. The truth and tenderness of the delineation are perfect. Not less admirably drawn is the picture of poverty in the great city, that hardest of all poverty, the poverty of the sensitive and cultured, and the revolt of a luxurious nature against its sordid conditions.

We find, too, as in its predecessor, wonderful flashes of wit and wisdom, searchlights turned upon the weaknesses and the deep places of human nature. It is sacrilege to say so, and we rather expect the sky to fall upon us, but if certain of Miss Glasgow's gems of condensed philosophy were shaken together with an equal number of George Eliot's, we think that only an expert could unerringly asort them.

Mrs. Browning said of *Jane Eyre* that it possesses "qualities half savage and half free-thinking." This may more truly be said of both of Miss Glasgow's stories. Especially of *Phases of an Inferior Planet* may we add Mrs. Browning's criticism of a greater novel: "Very clever, very effective; but cruel to human nature. A painful book, and not the pain that purifies and exalts. Partial truths, after all, and those not wholesome."

Miss Glasgow has shown that she can feel finely and portray tenderly the elemental and eternal whole truths of life. Should she renounce what is bizarre and strained, high achievement is possible to her. But in the path that is tempting her, there are rocks ahead, and the road is strewn with the bones of other travelers. As she stands at the parting of the ways, the critic feels an imperious call to speak a word of warning, although, like the most of its kind, that word is pretty sure to be a "warning of Cassandra."

John Kendrick Bangs, "Literary Notes," *Harper's Magazine*, 97 (October 1898), 627–8

Those who take up Miss Glasgow's latest study of real life, *Phases of an Inferior Planet*, with the idea in mind that they are to read of something appertaining to astronomy, will be surprised and possibly disappointed. They will learn, after they have read a few pages, that the inferior planet referred to is the curious little ball upon which they are themselves eking out an existence, and that the phases thereof of which Miss Glasgow treats are on its darker side. If they are of a pessimistic turn they will enjoy the somewhat despondent note which it has been given to Miss Glasgow's lyre to sound forth. If they rejoice in a vivid picture of an alleged bohemianism struggling for existence in the midst of an advanced philistinism, they will find here very much the sort of thing they desire.

Whatever may be thought of the necessity for the presentation of this sort of story, it cannot well be denied that Miss Glasgow reproduces life. All through her book one can see the hurry and worry of a great city. One can almost hear the noisy clangor of the cable-cars. One can breathe in the oppressive air of a city of a lung-power somewhat in advance of its ozone supply, and one can wonder how anything so hopelessly unhappy could have inspired a novel containing so much that is provocative of pleasurable emotion. When, a year ago, *The Descendant* was published, its authorship was attributed by many to old and experienced pens. When it was learned that it was the first published work of a hitherto unknown author, great things were prophesied for the writer. As yet these great things are unfulfilled, but it must be admitted that *Phases of an Inferior Planet* at least sustains the immediately earned reputation of the author of *The Descendant*, and shows the same genius for the presentation of a real picture, the same effective characterization of the minor actors in the tragedy, the same tendency toward the melodramatic in the drawing of the principals, and, worthiest to be commended, the same occasional flashes of the kind of epigram that sticks to the reader's remembrance.

Droch [Robert Bridges], "Bohemianism on an Inferior Planet," *Life*, 32 (13 October 1898), 286–7

So far as one can figure it out, most of the trouble in that intense novel, *Phases of an Inferior Planet* (Harper), was due to the unfortunate circumstance that the heroine's stepmother persisted in having "cabbage one day and onions the next." Such things must be expected on an inferior planet like the world, where "time and chance happeneth to them all." If it had not been for the cabbage and onions, the beautiful *Mariana* would not have precipitated herself into the arms of the gloomy agnostic, *Algarcife*. Now, a student of science, especially a gloomy one, is apt to be a poor hand at making a living; and the day came when *Mariana* would not have turned up her nose at cabbage. So she ran away to be a comic opera singer, and eventually married an Englishman. The skeptical *Algarcife* swallowed his convictions and became a high-church priest. The financial circumstances of both professions are likely to be easy, if not opulent—so that in worldly comfort both prospered. Of course, having once been in love, fine raiment and rich vestments did not bring happiness to them—and the second phase of the book reveals eight or nine kinds of misery, terminating in pneumonia. Having run the gauntlet from cabbage to pneumonia, the author kindly averts an almost inevitable suicide in the very last paragraph.

Miss Glasgow also reveals some belated signs of the "Trilby" influence. It is probable that she is very fond of the "Bohemianism" of the earlier chapters. Artists, journalists and cynics who congregate in studios or at table d'hôtes to fling epigrams at each other are supposed to be fascinating in books. They are real wicked in hurling reckless and cynical phrases at conventional things. Indeed, they spend most of their time making phrases. How they have an opportunity for serious work at their professions is always a marvel. They would rather talk sententiously about "life" than do an honest day's work.

It is rather surprising, therefore, to find that in the second part of the book most of the "Bohemians" have prospered amazingly. They are still cynics, but they are well dressed and well fed. They have their sorrows, though—most of them expressed in very high-sounding phrases. *Algarcife*, for instance, looks back on the time he had spent without *Mariana* as "a colorless stretch of undifferentiated days."

All of the fine phrases are not wasted on "life." Broadway at night comes in for a special assortment of its own. It is a wonderful scene, for there "the aberrant shadows of the passers-by met and mingled one into another. A phantasmagoric procession took place upon the sidewalk"—which is indisputable evidence that Tammany was in power and everything was "wide-open." Under the severe reign of Captain Chapman it would not have been possible for "the ethereal accompaniment of the physical substance of a Wall Street plutocrat to glide sedately after that of a bedizened daughter of the people." This general demoralization affects the higher walks of art, and the handsome young dramatic critic of the story, we are told, "regarded life as a gigantic jag, facing failure with facetiousness and gout with inconsequence."

In short, the deduction is inevitable that Bohemia in New York needs a strong infusion of plain, ordinary good humor.

It is probable that the wine served with table d'hôte dinners has at last got on the nerves of the Bohemians, and real art and real literature are in danger of extinction. When that time arrives this will, indeed, be an "inferior planet."

Independent, 50 (20 October 1898), 1127–8

In speaking of this novel it is difficult to say why the uppermost thought is that the characters are drawn from literature and not from life, yet the impression comes almost in the outset and deepens on to the end. It is not that Miss Glasgow fails in intensity of expression and vividness of characterization; her pages do not lack earnestness and fire; the trouble seems to be in what painters understand by "composition"; the story is without impressiveness, as a whole, much as some of the scenes have of somewhat gloomy attractiveness. A young girl, whose father is poor and has a second wife, is pursuing the study of vocal music and having her voice trained in New York with a view to a public career as a singer. She has for next room neighbor a young man who makes a precarious living by writing. He has been a divinity student but is now an agnostic. Presently the girl's father notifies her that he is entirely unable to keep up her scant allowance any longer and that she must come home, whereupon she weeps and wails, then rushes with the letter to the young man's room, and as they are already madly in love with each other, he begs her to marry him. She consents; the step is taken; and so begins a miserable married life which is sketched forcibly and with apparent delight in its hopelessness. After a year or two of wretchedness and the death of a child, the wife leaves her husband and goes upon the stage to sing her way to fame and fortune. Abroad, after the usual divorce, she has a brilliant career and marries a titled man, and through his family gets a large estate. Then she comes back to New York and finds out that her first husband has returned to the priesthood. There is a reconciliation, but too late; she dies of pneumonia. With such a plot there could be no light or joy in the story. It is, indeed, sodden with hopelessness all the way through, and its end leaves not a glimmer of pleasure by which to think back over a long and dreary yet not unfascinating perusal.

T.P., "An American Tragedy," London *Weekly Sun and Sunday Sun*, 23 October 1898, p. 1

Last year a considerable sensation was created in literary circles in America by the publication of a book called *The Descendant*. It was original, audacious, pessimistic.... It was evidently the book of a young writer; but though the world was prepared for that, it was not prepared to find that the writer was a girl, who could not be supposed to have known much of the world or of life from practical experience. The name was kept from the public; it is now revealed; for the title page of the book before me contains the name of Miss Glasgow as its author; and Miss Glasgow, if I mistake not, was the author of *The Descendant*.

The present book is an advance on the first; and yet it has a number of faults. There is plenty of vigour, there is passion; there is true insight into life's tragedies and depths; very often there is extremely keen and subtle observation, and as will be seen there are passages of real literary beauty. But, on the other hand, there is the sense of effort, almost of pretence. Miss Glasgow, until she is carried away by her subject, often dreads simplicity of expression; she must put things, even the simplest, in an unusual way. Very often her language is scarcely English at all. Take the very title of the book, *Phases of an Inferior Planet*. Are there no pretence and a want of lucidity in these words? It is Miss Glasgow's way of saying "Phases of human life in New York," a form of expression that is not so striking nor so far-fetched; but that at least says what it means, and says it so that everybody can understand.

[...]

And when you have seen by such passages [a scene between Mariana and Anthony] what fine talent there is in this young girl, go on to the passages in which she strikes a deeper note, and has to describe the miseries and the conflicts that poverty, suffering, and misunderstanding bring to those two people. I am outrunning my space, and can not quote any more.

There is a baby, a delicate little thing, that becomes ill from the stifling city air; that wants the breezes of the sea shore; and that cannot get them because the father has not the money to send the child there, though the poor fellow is working fifteen hours a day. There are other passages which any living author might be proud to have written. The girl, who wrote it, has done a fine thing in this novel; she will do even finer by and by.

Athenæum [England], 112 (29 October 1898), 605

Mariana, the heroine of the story, is "elusive" and "absorbent," and has many strange qualities, of which endurance is not one, for she parts with her husband mainly on the ground that her neighbours devour fried cabbage. She has harmonious lines, in spite of her irregular nose and her long chin, so an artist made a poster of her upon their first acquaintance. Her profession was singing, which she came to New York to prosecute. In the curious society of the Gotham House, where Mr. Paul the pessimist, Mr. Nevins the artist, and others of her admirers dwell together, she meets her literary lover, Algarcife. Once in love, he finds many feelings revived which have been subdued so long that their expression is very difficult. Their married life is disastrously broken by poverty and the death of the child, and Mariana leaves her husband to despair, which somehow ends in the agnostic becoming a Ritualist priest. The transition is accounted for by the necessity of working on philanthropic lines for work's sake; but it is as little convincing as Mariana's neurotic incompetence or the late reconciliation. There is merit in the story, and some of the minor characters are deftly handled, but it is about three times too long.

Literary World, 29 (29 October 1898), 353–4

This second work, by the author of *The Descendant*, Miss Glasgow, exhibits much of the quality of its predecessor, the bitterness, the vigor, the revolt against precedents and conventional usage, the almost savage portrayal of passion. The heroine is a highly Bohemian and attractively anemic young woman from the South, who is trying to build up her voice to the standard of the German opera. The hero is a hard-working, coffee-drinking young man, who, while laboring at a "History of Man with Special Application of the Science of Ontogeny," supports himself by lecturing before classes of young ladies at a girls' school. The two meet at "The Gotham," a shabby apartment house. They love and marry. A child is born, the young wife's health breaks down under the strain of care and poverty, the baby dies, and a little later, worn out with the sordid monotony of their lives, she leaves her husband and goes on the stage as a singer at concert halls, ignoring his passionate protests. Here the real interest of the novel ceases. Her return as the wife of an Englishman (to find the divorced first husband an Anglican priest), their meeting, the renewal of attraction between them, the finale—all strike us as melodramatic and devoid of sincerity. There is something tawdry and unreal about the situation, which mars the real merit of the first half of the story.

"Praise for Miss Ellen Glasgow's New Novel: *Phases of an Inferior Planet*," Richmond *Times*, 13 November 1898, p. 19 (largely reprinted from Boston *Evening Transcript*, 5 October 1898, sec. 1, p. 7)

For about one month Miss Ellen Glasgow's latest novel *Phases of an Inferior Planet*— has been "upon the market." The high praise bestowed upon it by the English press as well as that of this country, would seem to confirm the judgment of those critics of her earlier novel *The Descendant* who pronounced it indicative of reserve power that might, if it chose, make the public later listen with an intent ear.

The following is from the *Transcript*, of Boston, which is a discriminating journal not certainly open to the charge of being "afflicted with the fatal disease of admiration."

Somewhat more than a year ago an anonymous novel appeared, entitled *The Descendant*, and bearing the imprint of Messrs. Harper & Brothers on the title page. The book received much more than the usual attention accorded a first novel from an unknown hand. When the third edition appeared, signed Ellen Glasgow, the literary reviews were much concerned with details of the life and characteristics of this new author, whose work, whatever else it might be, was not commonplace.

The authentic data seemed finally to be that Miss Glasgow was then twenty-two years old, of a well-known Virginian family, of good, old Scotch-Presbyterian stock, of a reserved and retiring disposition and of studious and scientific habits of thought. Last November a poem by Miss Glasgow, entitled "The Freeman," with the motto "Hope is a slave; despair is a Freeman," appeared in the *Atlantic Monthly*, and called forth wide comment. It was a poem to set beside Emily Bronte's "Old Stoic" and Mr. Henley's incomparable

"Out of the night that covers me."

This month Messrs. Harper & Brothers issue a new novel by Miss Glasgow, with the somewhat puzzling title *Phases of an Inferior Planet*. The planet turns out to be this earth as we know it, and the phases sufficiently interesting.

Prague is evidently the capital of Miss Glasgow's imagination, and the glamour of Bohemia is over it all. The story deals with that large element of brainworkers in New York, who ogle fame in the far distance and divert themselves as best they may on short rations for the present.

It is said that Mr. Max Beerbohm is lamenting as one of the most grievous signs of the times the fact that there is no campaign of ridicule and satire against the young genius of today. And when one considers the general output in fiction one is inclined to share the grievance. We have dallied much of late along the primrose path of cheap romance and adventurous activity in fiction. We have seen a great deal of rehabilitating of Colonial days where the figures and thoughts of to-day masquerade in ancestral costumes and forced archaisms. We have made much of such books as may be read without too strenuous an effort and thrown aside without painfully deep impressions. About a year ago the whole United States went quite wild with enthusiasm—or so our literary journals led us to believe—over the mild and flabby moralizings of a Kentuckian Sir Galahad who heroically married his landlady's daughter, because he had—he hardly knew how—inadvertently asked her, while he left the woman he loved and who loved him to eke out a lame, one-sided existence as best she might.

In the thick of such fiction it was interesting to hear one of our best masters of prose greeting Miss Glasgow as "one woman writing like a man in a nation of men writing like a woman."

Miss Glasgow's work is individual. It falls in with no prevailing fashion, and if one wished to place her it would be most easily done by saying "here is one of spiritual kin to Thomas Hardy." For there is in both writers somewhat the same note of fatality; the same sense of the inevitable pathos of life at cross-purposes; the same questioning of the power of the will and the plasticity of circumstances.

"I should like to feel," says the heroine to the husband whose life she has maimed. "I should like to feel that you see it was not my fault—that I was not to blame—that you forgive me for what you have suffered."

But he looked ahead into the blue-gray distance and was silent.

"Tell me that I was not to blame," she said again.

He turned to her.

"It was as much your fault," he said slowly, "as it is the fault of that feather that the wind is blowing it into that lake. What are you that you should conquer the wind?"

What is man that he should master heredity and temperament? Will a few years of living in a universe with which we make such slow acquaintance serve to unforge the fetters of centuries of deeds behind us?

Hardy points these same questions when he leaves the obscure Jude to die alone, lacking all final aid as he starts on that great passage from time into eternity. Hopeless questions, perhaps, but at any rate a relief from too blind and flimsy an optimism.

Miss Glasgow's moral questions then are vital, and however little we may fall in with her solution of them, they are interesting and worthy of note. Here is a wife whose charming vivacity and artistic temperament has won our sympathy, deserting the husband whom she loves because she cannot forego luxury, and a man who has held our admiration, living a daily lie. The one succumbing to the ignorant impulses prompted by a swift, mobile, unreflecting nature, the other, to that satanic subtlety which is incapable of any real conviction. Miss Glasgow's chief aversion we should take to be the mistaking of conventionalities for moralities, and her intensest sympathies to be with individual freedom of thought and act. Again, Miss Glasgow holds in common with Hardy, with perhaps all writers who have learned the lesson France is teaching the literary world of to-day, the sense of the picturesque value of ugliness. She does not shirk or overlook the hideous, the sordid and the shabby; she is not mercilessly negligent, even to the commonplace in character, nor does failure appall her. Perhaps this young author bears in mind that line of the great ethical teacher of this century: "Most failure is most progress."

The book opens in New York City at the closing of a long, rainy day and the author gives well the effect of the place and the hour—the vague, indistinct outlines in the half-light, the gloom, the mystery, the shadows and the electric lights flickering like feeble stars through the great, gray veil of mist. The scenery of a great town is as full of infinite variety as sea and sky, mountain and plain or stretch of meadow and woodland and not so hackneyed, and Miss Glasgow's atmospheric effects are fine and full of promise for even better things in her later work.

It is evident that the perfectly beautiful heroine has had her day and ceased to be quite as much as the very ugly, pale-faced small women, who throve under the patronage of the Brontë girls. Miss Glasgow offers us a heroine with a sallow skin, a nimbus of dry-brown hair and eyes that differ from the hair in tone but not in color. Yet she is full of an illusive charm, of a subtle and swift vivacity that fill the place of physical perfection. One involuntarily harks back to Meredith's Carinthia, that boldly-hazarded creation, with her face like a mountain-crag, and its constant volte-face from noble beauty to simple ugliness.

There is little or no direct ethical teaching in Miss Glasgow's work. Geo. Eliot gave us moral and philosophic maxims enough for a generation of time and men; Miss Glasgow gives only epigrams and cynicisms. Her intense sympathy with the infinite pathos of suffering and ignorance one feels rather than reads.

Miss Glasgow's style in the first book was remarkably fluent and sure; the present work shows steady development. Her vocabulary has still an odd predominance of scientific words, almost as figures of speech and an almost total absence of those vague and abstract terms to which no definite image attaches. The syntax is clear, terse and exact, though rarely fastidious and the gloom of the whole book is lightened by the author's ready wit and sane sense of humor.

"Ellen Glasgow's *Phases of an Inferior Planet*," Brooklyn *Daily Eagle*, 13 November 1898, p. 18

Miss Ellen Glasgow, whose first novel, *The Descendant*, published a year and a half ago, attracted such wide attention when it came anonymously from the press of the Harpers, has brought out her second story through the same publishers, under the title, *Phases of an Inferior Planet*. When the identity of the author of *The Descendant* was revealed and it was found that she was a young Southern woman, whose years still counted her in the early twenties, the wonder grew that so young a writer was able to produce a work of such unquestioned power, and there was great interest manifested as to her second story, upon which it was then stated she was engaged. Naturally the literary world was curious to see whether Miss Glasgow would repeat her first success. The fact that she is a Virginian by birth and lineage classes her with that group of writers of the "New South" whose brilliant achievements have added a fresh luster to American literature. And yet she is very different from any one of them.

It is inevitable that this second story should be judged to a greater or less degree by the standards set in *The Descendant*, although it is an entirely different work. But Miss Glasgow has not yet published a sufficient amount for her work to be judged by its general average. At the outset let it be said, without reference to whatever faults may inhere to this book, that it gives no sign of failure. The author's unusual power is as evident in *Phases of an Inferior Planet* as it was in her first novel, which, it will be recalled, was a study in heredity. This book is nowhere an echo of that work save that the leading characters show the influence in their development of inherited environment. It is modeled upon entirely different lines. It is not worth while, as a rule, to cavil at an author's choice of title; still, one cannot help feeling that in this instance *Phases of an Inferior Planet* is a somewhat infelicitous caption. It is too bookish, is scarcely definitive, and might have been more direct and striking.

[. . .]

We said at the outset that Miss Glasgow's wonderful powers were fully evidenced in this story. There are also apparent the faults which are inevitable to this stage of her literary development. Her story shows more of that knowledge of human life which is a part of the lore of books than of that deeper knowledge which comes from the great book of human nature. Her intuitions are seldom wrong, however, and that other knowledge will come in time if eyes are open. Much of the dialogue, particularly in the earlier portions of the story, is stagy and unnatural, yet, while her characters talk stiltedly, there is a keenness of analysis, a vividness of portrayal, a sureness of touch that would be surprising even in an author of twice her years and experience. It should be noted, however, that as the action of the story proceeds the posing of the characters becomes more unconscious and natural. The dramatic power and intensity of the narrative is progressive from the first page to the last, and in the second part especially it holds your attention in a steadfast grip. Of the two principal characters in the book it is probable that the reader will be most attracted by Anthony. Most writers would have made his cession to ritualism a conversion, and thereby forever ruined the interest in his character. Miss Glasgow is too original to have made this error. By holding him still in the bonds of scientific doubt and making his apparent faith a realism of humanitarian effort and sanitation the unity and natural sequence of his development is maintained. While Mariana is genuine she is neither admirable nor lovable, but one feels a profound pity for one so self cheated of happiness. Here, also, the author avoided a pitfall which would have trapped most writers. Mariana's innate purity of character is maintained throughout. Anthony's surroundings as rector of Father Speares' church remind one of John Storm in Hall Caine's *Christian*, but he is a much more picturesque and attractive character. He is reasonable and not hysterical like John Storm.

From beginning to end Miss Glasgow's pages sparkle with wit and epigram. When Mariana says that she had as soon wear wooden shoes as eat with a pewter fork one sees at a glance the revolt of her artistic temperament as the galling restraints of poverty. There is a world of truth, also, in the sentence, "for a fool may jog shoulder to shoulder with a comfortable sinner, but it takes a philosopher to support an unmitigated saint." As one becomes absorbed in the story these scintillations appear more spontaneous than in the earlier pages. The author's viewpoint shows that she is a student of the philosophy of Mill and Spencer and Haeckel; her method illustrates the application of the modern scientific spirit to fiction. It is a source of profound satisfaction to rise from the perusal of this story and feel that this young author's strength gives every proof of being a continuing quantity. Her vision of life and of the human soul will broaden as the years come and experience ripens. Not long after she came before the public some one likened her to Charlotte Brontë; Miss Glasgow is no more Charlotte Brontë than she is George Eliot, and yet there is something about her which suggests both, but it is suggestion and not resemblance. Fortunately for herself and for us she is an American young woman of undoubted genius and rare promise, who has given us a second novel that well sustains the prophecy of success which her first published work warranted. We are content with that.

Academy, 55 (19 November 1898), 290

This is a New York story of Bohemian art life. The chief fault is that the author has so passionately concentrated herself on the two leading characters that the minor figures are carelessly imagined, and drawn without force or originality. But it will be read for its extraordinary and pitiless analysis of a very woman of the time. The effect achieved is one of unrelieved misery. For ourselves, we say frankly—and it is a tribute, in a way, to the writer's power—that we regret having opened it, so painful was the depression it left behind. The life of everyone is, in large measure, a struggle against pessimism and melancholy, and contains sorrow enough, without calling in this ill-omened prophet to destroy the last germ of hope. For that is the conclusion of the whole matter. Mariana passes through all the deep experiences of life, and finds nothing but illusion. She wins such a love as might be thought to redeem any existence from despair, yet it leads but to deeper sorrows. Motherhood yields no consolation. "It seemed inexplicable to her that women went on travailing and giving birth. That a woman who had once known the agony of maternity should consent to bear a second, a third, or a fourth child struck her as ridiculous. She closed her eyes and laughed." The experienced novel-reader needs no telling that a story written in this temper ends in death; but how that gloomy consummation is reached we leave the explorer to discover. The hero is left in despair—he is a "Father," but an atheist. He has uncorked a bottle of poison, when a knock comes to the door:

> He replaced the stopper, still holding the phial in his hand. For a moment the heavy silence hung oppressively, and then he answered: "What is it?" His voice sounded lifeless, like that of one awakening from heavy sleep or a trance.
> "You are there? Come quickly. The men at the Beasley Rolling Mills have gone on strike. A policeman was shot and several of the strikers wounded. You are wanted to speak to them."
> "To speak to them?"
> "I have a cab. You may prevent bloodshed. Come."
> Father Algarcife returned the phial to its drawer, withdrew the key from the lock, and rose. He opened the door and faced the messenger. His words came thickly:
> "There is no time to lose," he said. "I am ready."

With this message, and the moral underlying it, the book abruptly ends. It is not to be disputed that Ellen Glasgow has obtained a brilliant success, if her aim was to impress the miserable doctrine that life is not worth living. Were such a mournful philosophy well founded, its dissemination could only end in discouragement and decay. But her insight is not equal to her powers of observation. The best of her work is largely made up of externals, and the reader cannot help feeling at the salient points in the career of her hero and heroine that there must have been in their lives much more than comes within her ken. Every thinker has moments of despair, but none has attained real greatness who has cast the shadow of these over all life. "We bid you to hope" was the final message of the greatest writer of this century, and one cannot help thinking that the latter-day lady novelist would not be so gloomy and pessimistic if she would ponder the grounds on which that message was based. At all events, of all the "isms" in the category—realism and sensationalism included—we are inclined to think this "ism" of blank misery by far the most pernicious.

Critic, n.s. 30 (December 1898), 512–13

Youth, like murder, will out. The author of *The Descendant*, who triumphantly overcame in that strong if gloomy story the literary disadvantages of being in the very early twenties, has yielded to the inevitable and written another novel which it is impossible not to call "young." . . .

Miss Glasgow has great force and facility of expression and the power of making vivid such characters as she fully comprehends, but she does not know several fundamental rules of the game of novel-writing. One of these rules—it was formulated by the Society for the Prevention of Cruelty to Readers—forbids a writer to inflict unhappiness upon his creations unless it can be justified by the demands of the plot, or shown to serve some defensible ethical or artistic end. Another rule forbids novels to be as chaotic and irrational as life itself. For we endure an appearance of malignity and lack of design in life which we decline to tolerate in literature. Perhaps this is because the last chapter has not yet been written in the book of existence and we cherish the secret hope that it will satisfy the normal thirst for a happy ending, explaining and justifying what has gone before. At all events the fact remains that Providence has privileges which lesser creators may not safely imitate. The supremacy of "time and chance" in human life may serve as an individual creed now and again, but it does not make an adequate underpinning for a novel of any weight. Also, hysteria is not strength, and the effect of deep passion is not produced by dwelling upon the minutiæ of its strenuous moods.

These and other unwritten laws are broken in the making of *Phases of an Inferior Planet*, but although the force which has gone into the book may be misdirected, this does not affect the writer's power and promise, which are great, even if her work is still painfully far from the ripeness and symmetry which we may hope she is presently to attain.

Literature, 3 (3 December 1898), 524–5

Phases of an Inferior Planet, by Ellen Glasgow, is very emotional, unconventional, and uncomfortable. The scene is laid in New York, chiefly in a boarding-house, where a group of young men and young women lead a more or less Bohemian existence, the heroine being of the serpent type, "as elusive as thistledown whipped-up with snow," smiling a "radiating, indescribable smile, which dawned gradually from within deepening until it burst into pervasive wealth of charm." The book is hardly likely to appeal to the ordinary healthy English reader.

"Recent Fiction," *Nation*, 67 (15 December 1898), 451–2

We find *Phases of an Inferior Planet* inferior even to the Planet, which is Earth, and of which to some extent it is. It deals with a heroine who is sorely in need of juvenile discipline, and with a hero for whom a bad habit of writing essays on both sides of a question in college days made it possible that he should become, first a scientist, then an agnostic priest in a ritualistic church where there is a stained-glass window of a smiling Christ in a purple robe. The novelist has undoubtedly thought deeply on many phases of life; but with much that is real there is a mass of shallow science, shallow art, and shallow feeling. What she has treated with thoroughness is the detail of the heroine's life. No woman but one ever had so much printed about her. Indeed, from the internal evidence afforded by that which constitutes the sincerest flattery, we hazard a guess that the author of this novel had read and admires *The Beth Book* [by Sarah Grand].

Bookman, 8 (January 1899), 493

A novel without a central idea is like a wheel without a hub, its direction is uncertain and it hardly arrives. The author of *The Descendant* apparently recognised this all-important fact, since that story is bound to its motive with iron bands. So firmly indeed is it rivetted to evolution, that a semi-scientific importance increases the grim power of the work. It is, therefore, with surprise as well as disappointment that her new book is found lacking in concentration, and even in distinctness of purpose. It is hardly more than an inarticulate moan at the pain of living, the old groan over old miseries and sins that has been uttered since the beginning of the world, and that will be heard to the end of time. This new moan over the old misery does nothing to make it less. Such black books inveighing hopelessly against despair can only increase the world-pain. It is hard to find any excuse for their making. They are not literature in its higher sense. They are too bitter and gloomy to interest the young, who hardly understand, they repel the mature, who already understand too well. And yet aside from its depressing, unwholesome effect, the book can scarcely be characterised as actually harmful, except in two respects. The wife who deserts her husband solely because of the poverty for which he is not to blame cannot be accepted as the adorable creature the author believes her to be without blunting the moral sense. The deserted husband who turns to the Church as a means of livelihood, and who poses as a saint because it pays, cannot be admired, as the author admires him, without profanation of holy things. The only resemblance between this new book and the earlier work of the author, which gave such brilliant promise, may be found in the epi-grammatical character of the style and the detached bits which flash from many pages.

Bookman [London], 15 (January 1899), 121

This is one of the exasperatingly clever, exasperatingly incapable books, which are produced so frequently to-day. There is no grip of life in it, and there is intellect in abundance. The writer has a sense of style, and she descends to bunkum. She has shrewdness, and she lets her characters take her in. She has humour, but it is of a truant fickle quality. The story told baldly is rather sordid. A luxury-loving girl, who mistakes herself for a genius, marries a very poor man of science. Privations make her miserable, and him too, for her sake. So she leaves him; and her art—she is a singer—gives her opportunities for becoming very rich. Meanwhile her husband, who is, and continues to be, a freethinker, gives up science, and becomes a highly successful Ritualist priest. Do not ask us why. It seems so natural to Miss Glasgow that she does not think it worth while to explain. After many years the erring wife returns, and says she has never loved but him. With some decency he repulses her at first, then succumbs to her fascinations, and only her death saves his cutting his pastorship and running off with her to the sunny south. The story is aimless nonsense. But in the detail there is a surprising amount of ability. The writer has a real power of sketching a character in a word or two, as here, for example. "Miss Ramsey belonged to that numerous army of women who fulfil life as they fulfil an appointment at the dentist's—with a desperate sense of duty and shaken nerves." And there is an inimitable glimpse of the heroine in her frivolous moods. She has aspirations towards seriousness sometimes, and from her husband's bookshelves she takes Mill for perusal. He is much satisfied. But, "I haven't gone beyond the first page yet," returned Mariana,... "There was something in the first page about 'a web of muslin,' and, somehow, it suggested to me the idea of making that bonnet. Odd, wasn't it? And I am so glad I read it, for I am sure I should never have thought of the bonnet otherwise—and it *is* becoming."

"But you like Mill?"

"Oh, yes," said Mariana, "I find him very suggestive"!

"A Group of Recent Novels," *Atlantic Monthly*, 83 (February 1899), 284–5

Miss Ellen Glasgow's *Phases of an Inferior Planet* suggests the aspects of life from the window of a New York elevated car. The clatter and roar of city sounds form the dreary undertone of this entire story of two unhappy lives. That a girl with a passion for music and a genius for sensation of every keen variety should have met and married a man of extraordinary development, almost wholly mental, was sufficient to bring tragedy to each of them. Their union has given Miss Glasgow the opportunity of drawing not only the life they both lived, but also a vivid picture of the Bohemian New York in which they found themselves and each other. They and their fellow occupants of a cheap apartment house, the whole sordid background for the tragic birth and death of their child, and their own bitter separation are depicted with convincing skill in the first Phase of the narrative. The exceptional success of the detached husband as the rector of a church with a name impossible for an Anglican parish contributes to the second Phase of the story something less of reality; for it is difficult to conceive that the reverend father could have wrought such clerical wonders with a head so little aided by his heart. But in this Phase the reunion of man and wife is the real thing, and it is vigorously brought about by the author. That its final outward achievement is frustrated by the woman's dying and the man's becoming a suicide, by intention if not in act, may be regarded merely as a bit of the general evidence that destiny is too much both for Miss Glasgow and for her creations. The book, if you will, is a morbid anatomy of the spirit,—an anatomy of the morbid spirit may define it more truly,—and those who care not for such undertakings may well abstain from it. Yet it possesses the distinction of dealing bravely with actual life, although in unlovely manifestations, and therefore of affecting the reader very much as such life might move the observer to sympathy or repulsion. The story, moreover, in spite of a tendency at times to sacrifice too much to the sententious and epigrammatic, is excellently told, without too many traces of the influence of "favorite authors." It bears out the promise of the writer's first attempt in *The Descendant*, and it makes promises of its own for further interpretations of the modern.

Checklist of Additional Reviews

"The Story of Anthony and Mariana," Louisville *Courier-Journal*, 1 October 1898, sec. 1, p. 7.

"A New Novel by the Author of *The Descendant*," Boston *Evening Transcript*, 5 October 1898, p. 15.

Outlook, 60 (8 October 1898), 395.

THE VOICE OF THE PEOPLE

The Voice of the People

By

Ellen Glasgow

NEW YORK
DOUBLEDAY, PAGE & CO.
1900

E.A.U.V., "Miss Glasgow's New Novel," Baltimore *News*, 13 April 1900, p. 6

[...]

... The novel has some striking and dramatic qualities, and holds the attention by the intensity of its spirit in spite of a great deal of detail—detail, however, which in great part rounds out the work as a picture of modern Southern life. *The Voice of the People* is marked with true distinction and that feeling for the pains and perplexities of life, which are so much the inspiration of the modern novelist. Miss Glasgow has evidently outlived the morbidity and theatric ideas that showed themselves in *Phases of an Inferior Planet* and, though in a lesser degree, in *The Descendant*, and with the present strong and not unwholesome romance to her account, there is every reason to believe that her pen may be depended on for work which will be an important contribution to our latter-day American fiction.

"Miss Ellen Glasgow's New Book Entitled *The Voice of the People*," Richmond *Times*, 15 April 1900, p. 8

[...]

To Virginians the book will prove of special interest on account of its local color. No one who has ever visited Williamsburg will fail to recognize it under the name of Kingsborough with its colleges, William and Mary, and its insane asylum. Well described, too, are the old overgrown church yard and the wide, dusty "Duke of Gloucester" Street. Most happy is the author's characterization of it as a village that "dozed through the present to dream of the past and found the future a nightmare." Very true to life are the descriptions of Capitol Square at Richmond, the Governor's Mansion, the scenes on Franklin and Main Streets, and the lobby of the Capitol during a session of the Legislature, with the men lounging against the iron railing around the Statue of Washington.

If there are faults in the book, they are that the political scenes and the negro dialect are somewhat exaggerated, while rather improbable is the relation between the hero and heroine, in view of the great difference in their social position.

As a whole, the book is a fine piece of work, written in strong, vivid style, and holding the reader's interest throughout.

I. F. Marcosson, "*The Voice of the People*, Ellen Glasgow's Notable Book of Southern Social and Political Life," Louisville *Courier-Journal*, 21 April 1900, sec. 1, p. 8

To Virginia, the cradle of American romance, there has come a new distinction as worthy in its bestowal as was that other virtue of being the mother of States. The spirit of maternity is still alive and to the glories of the old Dominion there is now added the honor of being the parent of a new and virile force in American literature. To have produced almost within a year the ripened work of Mary Johnston and Ellen Glasgow is her triumph. And yet Virginia is no stranger to triumph; she has ever been the proud boast of the sisterhood of the Union. There is magic in her name; she is steeped in the romance of an imperishable past and rich in the memory of a great regime. Her daughters have been first in war and first in peace; the inspiration of high deeds and the preservers of a noble race. And as they have ornamented life so do they now grace and dignify literature.

With her latest book, *The Voice of the People*, Miss Glasgow places herself in the front rank of American writers and shows herself worthy of a place among those greatly gifted. She has produced a book glowing with life and fragrant with sentiment. It is a masterly study of social and political conditions and reveals the young Virginia girl as the herald of a great new democracy. Something in the sweeping truth of the narrative, in the enthralling earnestness of the motive almost disarms criticism. There is not a trace of the feminine hand. With remarkable force, vigor and color, the story is sustained from beginning to end. It is truly an astonishing performance marking a great step in the art of a writer who must henceforth be reckoned as a genuine factor in our fiction.

Miss Glasgow's book is a romance of Virginia. Ordinarily this very simple statement would be sufficient to quicken the memory of an imposing past and conjure up a rare procession of stately figures linked with the tenderest of love stories. It is no shattering of sentimentalities that has been wrought in this book even if it is a story of the new Virginia. Time has not stood still in the Dominion any more than it has in Tennessee, Maryland or Louisiana, where a great new social democracy has risen out of the ashes of the civil war. Its voice is the voice of the people, and while the common people may be considered an uncertain and sometimes ungrateful abstraction, the fact remains that out of its tangled mass there is evolved the mighty structure of our national life that to-day knows no caste. The splendid representative of that life is the hero of Miss Glasgow's book, and it is a figure of magnetic force as much a Virginian for Virginians as was that proud ancestor of his who knew the magnificence of aristocracy.

One of the first values of Miss Glasgow's book is at once apparent. It is practically the same social aspect exploited by Harrison Robertson in his fine new book, *Red Blood and Blue*. His "locale" is Tennessee, but there is perhaps a keener contrast in the life of Virginia only in the fact that the social life of Virginia was more extensive. Like Mr. Robertson, Miss Glasgow presents a logical, intelligent treatment of the new South that confronts us in all its phases of reawakened life and altered social conditions as naturally as that familiar picture of the old estate of luxurious ease in the good old days. Miss Glasgow combines a fine reverence for that departed splendor with a keen, discriminating knowledge of the needs and the advantages of the present.

The Voice of the People begins in Kingsborough, a drowsy old town of sleepy ease "that dozed through the present to dream of the past," whose boast was "that she had been and was not." It is a place where the very air is charged with the memory of old loves and old lives, and where the echo of the past can almost be heard. Then the scene shifts to Richmond, the battle ground of thrilling ambitions, and where amid historic scenes destinies are shaped and lives made and marred.

[. . .]

There is so much to be said about *The Voice of the People*; the accuracy of its picture of life; its intimate knowledge of the modern political machine; its fine fabric of human nature and its sustained record of dramatic events. There must be a word about this woman's style. No living American writer save James Lane Allen has arranged a book in such glorious description. The very thrill of nature is in her pen and she flashes across the sight the vast almost nameless beauty of the Virginia landscape, "the landscape of a country where each ragged inch of ground wears its strange distinctive charm; where each rotting 'worm fence' guards a peculiar beauty for those who know it." All the seasons are on her palette, every divine touch of the glowing sunset, every tint of the uplifting dawn. She puts almost the breath of life into her exquisite pictures and one can well nigh feel the caress of lilacs and roses and the sweet soft air heavy with the fragrance of rare old gardens. . . .

Miss Glasgow has come nearer the great American novel than any writer of recent years, for her story embodies so many of those characteristic elements of our varied and fascinating national life. One closes her book with a strange mingling of regret and joy, the haunting remembrance of a splendid story well told, the recollection of the tragedy which dimmed its close. Real people have lived and loved and they are the sort to enter the chamber of memory and there to stay.

"Ellen Glasgow: Her New and Striking Novel, *The Voice of the People*," *New York Times Book Review*, 21 April 1900, p. 259

It is not a little remarkable that within a few months two novels full of the stress and strain of life should have come from what Mr. Henry James is pleased to call "the land of the relaxed," and each from the pen of a young woman not yet in the maturity of her power. *To Have and to Hold* belongs to historic, *The Voice of the People* to contemporary, fiction. The former deals with the doughty deeds of the brave days of old, the latter with the social and political conditions of the present. One is built upon history, the other holds material for history building. Differing widely in their general trend, they are alike in originality, virility, distinction of style. Virginia has long been conspicuous for her pride of ancestry. Boasting now of Thomas Nelson Page, of Amélie Rives, of Mary Johnston, of Ellen Glasgow, and of many other less known but successful writers, she may indulge an equal pride in her living children.

[. . .]

The Voice of the People is a story of compelling interest. Sometimes sparkling and sometimes sombre, there is not a dull page in the book. It is so irradiated with humor, so filled with genial characters and pleasant, homely happenings, that the tension of a strenuous plot is constantly relieved. The hero is so truly great and we love him so much that we cannot forgive him for not being just a little more lovable. We wish he had been more sparing of "the universal adjective," and we find his implacable spirit toward the man who, not from malice, but from cowardly weakness, had blighted his life, a jarring note. To hesitate when his broken enemy lay in his power should have been impossible to Nicholas Burr. Very touching and tender are the relations between him and the toilworn, querulous, sympathetic stepmother, Marthy Burr. There is something of Tolstoy's magic in the way this illiterate woman is made to take hold of one's heart strings. The old Judge, "from his classic head to his ill-fitting boots," is one of the noblest of Virginia gentlemen; Gen. Battle, a Colonel during the war, but "raised to the rank of General by the unanimous voice of his neighbors upon his return home," is not less fine after his own fashion. His whimsical denunciation of his negro dependents and his shame-faced and open-handed ministry to their needs are capitally depicted. Miss Glasgow's children are very real in their winsomeness and their unconscious cruelty, genuine children, not grown-ups masquerading. The negroes are simply perfect, not to be exceeded in lifelikeness by those of Mr. Harris himself. None of the women are as lofty in soul and as richly endowed as the Rachel of *The Descendant*. They are high-bred, fascinating Southern women, belles before marriage, loyal wives, and devoted mothers thereafter. These are not the women given to heroics and to introspections, not the women to figure in the triplicate tragedy so dear to the modern novelist; but they are the women who make life wholesome and happy, in whom the hearts of their husbands do safely trust, and whose children rise up and call them blessed.

With some glimpses of Richmond in its political and uniquely delightful social aspect, the chief theatre of the story is ancient and historic Williamsburg, thinly veiled under the name of Kingsborough. The dreamy old town with its quaint customs makes a restfully sweet picture; while in sharp contrast the lobby of the Richmond Capitol with its circle of spittoons around Houdon's statue of Washington, and its group of tobacco-ejecting statesmen, is as present to sight and smell as the corridor of Maslooa's Russian prison. The line of cleavage between the poor and the impoverished whites, the subtle law of "like unto like," which impels the reluctant feet of the well-born maiden to the mate of her circumstance rather than of her soul, the married serenity existing just because of the absence of fervid emotion and exacting love, the power of baby fingers to press from a true woman's heart all thought of passion for any other than the father of her child, these things Miss Glasgow portrays with unerring insight and conclusive art. She has done well, too, in that *The Voice of the People* is not a sex-novel, but observes the values and proportions of real life. Carlyle was certainly in acid and dyspeptic mood when he called "the whole concern of love a beggarly futility," but he was right in declaring it "altogether false and damnable" to represent "the thing people call love as spreading itself over our whole existence and constituting the one grand interest of it," instead of being "but one thing to be attended to among many infinitely more important things." Miss Glasgow gives due weight to the influence of love, but she puts it into right relations with life as a whole. Miss Chris, busy and helpful, was "happy for forty years with a broken heart"; Nicholas, full of personal ambitions and of large interests, often forgets the love of his youth for months at a time; and Eugenia, recognizing the mistake of her girlhood and the limitations of her marriage, can yet feel sure that she will go on "happily, neither regretting nor despairing, but filled to the finger tips with the cheerful energy of a busy life." All this is as it should be, natural and sane. There really are in this great world of ours other things than the relations of men and women, and it is good to find more than one recent novel joining the revolt against "the sex-conscious school in fiction." . . .

Without doubt one might find flaws in *The Voice of the People*. The author lingers rather too long over the early years of her leading characters. Her hero is in spots hard, of a temperament too suggestive of the more pardonably brutal *Descendant*. The mistake which shattered the romance of Burr's life seems, after all, absurdly ineffectual, though that may have been with intention, since the "little rift" had shown itself before the catastrophe in the lovers' fatal difference of caste. But it is more pleasant to rejoice in a novel of very rare and high qualities, charming as a story, valuable as a study of character and conditions, and, read between the lines, vital with sincere and noble purpose, a genuine contribution to both literature and life.

M.F.J., "Miss Glasgow's Novel of Virginia To-Day," *Book Buyer*, 20 (May 1900), 318–20

In the present flood of historical fiction we are tempted to forget that historical romances are not the only kind, nor, for that matter, the most important kind, of novels. The higher artistic achievement, and surely the more difficult, is the novel that deals successfully with the great forces of contemporaneous life; for in such a novel something more complex and of deeper human interest must be presented than a series of adventures in a proper historical setting.

A very wholesome reminder of this more earnest and (to thoughtful readers) more interesting kind of fiction is given by Miss Glasgow's new story. The career of this young writer, who gave evidence of very unusual power in her first book, *The Descendant*, has been watched with keen interest. Her second book, *Phases of an Inferior Planet*, showed the same kind of vigor and originality, but the choice of the subject was unfortunate. But *The Voice of the People* is a strong, free, and wholesome piece of work as regards both subject and treatment. It is a book that will give great pleasure and make a deep impression.

The story tells the career of a postbellum man of very humble origin, who grew up amid the most aristocratic surroundings in Virginia. The social classes, yet separated by the wide chasm of the old order of life, give room for the highest dramatic effects. The two worlds, the shiftless poor-white class, and the somewhat antiquated but proud and powerful class of the gentry, are faithfully presented to the reader, side by side. The progress of the hero out of one class into the other—in so far as he really succeeded in entering this other and upper world—is the story; and there is no more real or heroic struggle in any human society than the struggle of such a man against such conditions. The gentleness of the gentility, along with its remorseless unconscious cruelty, is memorably typified in the characters of an ex-Confederate General and the women of his household, and in the unyielding and sombre dignity of a widow of another soldier; the conquering power of modern democracy and the great will and strong character of an ambitious man, are shown victoriously in the career of the hero; and the mass of Virginian humankind, who are neither aristocrats nor "poor-whites," are exemplified in a number of subordinate characters. The book presents a witty, incisive, sympathetic and convincing picture, such as can nowhere else be found, of all grades of present Southern life—well-balanced, wholesome, uncompromising and true in every detail.

Nor is the story subordinate to the picture of society; for the strong action of social forces gives the narrative a stirring and exciting character. It would be hard to find a more active or in many periods of his life a more exciting career than the struggle of Nicholas Burr from the barren home of his childhood, and its hopeless and repressing atmosphere, through repeated triumphs over a narrow view of public or private duty, to his honorably won distinction as Governor of Virginia. He became a power in public life because he was "the man with a conscience" in politics. And his tragic death, while doing his duty in resisting a mob, was a melancholy but a triumphant end of a noble career.

The quality that distinguishes the book and sets it apart from and far above the ordinary novel is the earnestness of the author in the practice of her art. She is writing to entertain her readers, as all novelists must do; but she is writing also for a higher purpose, and she produces a correspondingly lasting effect. To call a novel "philosophical" unfortunately suggests dullness; and there is not a dull page in this book. But it is a serious and thoughtful piece of work, as far removed from the mere novel of adventure on one side, as from the psychological novel on the other side. It is written in the key in which the greatest fiction is written—the study of life in its normal development and in its interesting phases.

Incidentally the descriptive passages are of uncommon interest. The scene of the first half of the novel is laid at "Kingsborough," which anyone who knows Virginia will at once recognize as Williamsburg, the seat of William and Mary College, where the hero received his academic training. The rest of the action takes place in Richmond. In every part of the story the reader breathes the social and political atmosphere of the South. Not a peculiarity of the people escapes the keen observation nor the accurate description of the author. Kingsborough "dozed through the present to dream of the past, and found the future a nightmare." Its "proudest boast was that it had been and was not," that it had "once been a chartered city," and yet now only the charter is left. "On the wide, restless globe, there is, perhaps, no village of three streets, no settlement that has been made by man, so utterly the cradle of quiescence." The vivid descriptions of the hero put him before the reader as clearly as a portrait. His father was a "hairy, ominous, uncouth" man. The son was homely with the ugliness that attracts. There was a "furrow that cleft the forehead like a scar." "His appearance suggested the battle-grounds of nature—high places, or the breadth of the open fields." In the house of his aristocratic patron he "was an alien—an anachronism—the intrusion of the hopelessly modern into the helplessly past."

The book is full of epigrams. Although epigrams and descriptions do not divert the reader from the march of the story towards the tragic climax, he closes the novel with the certainty that he has read the most sympathetic and accurate description of life in the South of the present generation that has yet been published.

American Monthly Review of Reviews, 21 (May 1900), 634

Miss Ellen Glasgow has done two worthy things in a very worthy way in her novel, *The Voice of the People*. She has painted the best picture of Southern life we have ever seen in a work of fiction and she has made about the large figure of Nick Burr an impressive study of social problems in the South. At first glance, no class of people in any community would seem to possess less of the picturesque and fewer possibilities for the novelist than the class of folks in the South known by the darkies as "po' white trash." They have neither the grace of living of the higher classes nor the dramatic vices and engaging simplicity of the mountain people.

Miss Glasgow has selected a hero from a family which, in its ineffectiveness and ignorance, makes a typical specimen of the class we have referred to. In the story we have on the one hand this Nick Burr, the rufus-headed son of the people, and on the other hand the aristocratic, if seedy, old town of Kingsborough. This young Nick Burr is a boy of character, with a capacity for taking infinite pains. He makes his way into the homes of some of the aristocratic folks of Kingsborough, and even makes the daughter of one of the proudest families fall in love with him. A tragic incident brings his greater pride into opposition to her and separates them forever, Nick Burr going on to win a great career for himself in politics in the character of "the man with a conscience."

The engaging absurdities, the largehearted goodness and the graces of real Southern gentle-folk have never been better portrayed than by Miss Glasgow's pen in this book. The old stock characters,— the gallant and courteous judge, the loud-swearing but tender-hearted general, the lovely and coquettish Southern maiden, the austere widow-lady who has never surrendered, the old darkies, and all, take on new life from Miss Glasgow's inspiration. Her darkies, Delphy and Uncle Ish, are not to be questioned.

Miss Glasgow comes to her fundamental understanding of the old *régime* in Virginia life by birthright, for she is the descendant of a long line of notable Virginians. The "Kingsborough" of the novel is the town of Williamsburg. One of Miss Glasgow's forefathers was president of King's College in colonial times, and other of her ancestors were early residents of "Kingsborough."

New Orleans *Daily Picayune*, 6 May 1900, sec. 3, p. 8

In this fine story Miss Glasgow has chosen a new field—the period just after reconstruction times in Virginia, when life was still close enough to the civil war and its memories to have them as a background and to a certain extent as vital influences. The hero is a strong man without social standing, a son of the soil, a man who comes from the neglected, forgotten and inefficient class known as "poor whites." But being a man of great force of character and much charm of manner, he succeeds against great odds politically, at least. In his less definite social success the author emphasizes her revelation of the great principles of the society she describes. Social forces and political methods as they were in the Virginia of those days run through the whole story. The close is a great tragedy, and yet an inevitable one.

The subordinate characters are all well drawn and contribute to the completeness of the pictures. There is a loud-talking but soft-hearted old Confederate general, and his kinswoman, an elderly spinster, comes to his house to spend the night, and remains twenty years. There is a haughty and unbending southern widow, who keeps a boarding-house in a condescending manner, and never leaves off her mourning, and a striking episode in which Judge Lynch and his impromptu court occupy a central position.

Independent, 52 (24 May 1900), 1267

In some of its lines Ellen Glasgow's new story commands immediate and unqualified praise. While it is not especially notable as literature, and while the opening chapters lack magnetic attractiveness, there soon sets in a current of strenuous and interesting life which flows forcefully on to the somewhat tragic end. It is a story of Virginia life since the war, a story of political ambition, love, rivalry, victory and downfall. Many of the scenes are brilliantly effective, and the air of Virginia circulates freely between them.

Nation, 70 (24 May 1900), 402

Miss Glasgow's novel presents a comprehensive picture of Virginia in the years following the Reconstruction. First there is life in Kingsborough, an old town whose "proudest boast was that she had been and was not"—her people "a people without a present." Then the scene shifts to Richmond's fashionable society and the very pulse of the machine politic. There is a closely observant treatment of all classes—the negro, the poor white, the aristocrat. There are, moreover, divers well-drawn types in character, as well as in class, familiar, yet individual: a blustering ex-General, fierce in fight and fiercely hospitable in peace; a war widow wearing a Confederate button, and saying, "The women of the South have never surrendered"; the patrician Judge; the young girl in whom pride of race is stronger than self; Uncles and Aunties and pickaninnies, and the white-trash farmer, scorned by black and white alike. Out of this last unheroic class the author has evoked her hero, and the novel is a history of his struggles, failures, and successes, with the inevitable clash of races at the last. It is a faithful panorama of Southern life and character, and could have been written only by one reading deeply into the region and the epoch. Robert Louis Stevenson somewhere remarks that "a man who knew how to omit would make an Iliad of a daily paper." The talent for omission is the one chiefly missed in Miss Glasgow's work. Especially in the realm of landscape does commission run wild. The most thrilling moments of the story are hyphenated by purple patches of scenery. Every emotion has its landed estate, and it is the weary reader who pays the tax. This lack of proportion is surprising in a writer who describes with delicious humor the florid oratory of a Southern political convention.

"Novel Notes," *Bookman*, 11 (June 1900), 397–8

After producing two indoor books of rather oppressive atmosphere, the author now presents an outdoor book wide open to the sun and the clouds. *The Descendant* and *Phases of an Inferior Planet* deal almost exclusively with morbid physical and social conditions, and follow the psychological into the painful. This new work, *The Voice of the People*, may also be described as psychological, but its psychology is of an entirely different and much more admirable kind. It is a study of the natural and the normal, and the result is more convincing than the outcome of those earlier studies of the unnatural and the abnormal.

The story grows out of the soil of old Virginia, springing from deep-buried roots stirred by the ploughshare of the South's new civilisation. The author knows its old civilisation as well as its new, and her work is as true to one as to the other. Nicholas Burr, the son of the soil, "who walked rough-shod where his abilities led him, among men who were his superiors only in the accident of a better birthright," is not truer to his time and his type than is Judge Bassett, who "from his classic head to his ill-fitting boots upheld the traditions of his office and his race." Of the women, Marthy Burr and Mrs. Webb offer the most striking contrast, representing from first to last the extremes of the social poles. They are much less modern than the men, belonging to the old order when the iron barriers of caste still held fast within and without, and no Southerner might hope to reach higher than his father stood. To Mrs. Burr—as much as to Mrs. Webb—it seemed, therefore, a miraculous, an utterly incredible thing, that her humbly born stepson could ever become learned and strong enough to break all barriers and cast them out of his way. The character of Nicholas Burr is drawn with much skill and considerable power. The little aristocrat who loves him, and is beloved by him, describes him well when she says he is "clear as the sun and terrible as an army with banners." The steady progress of this Lincoln-like son of the people from the plough to the Governor's chair of the proudest State in the Union, makes a good story, not strictly new, perhaps, but one that always appeals and which is this time unusually well told. There may be criticisms that the cause of the quarrel which separates the lovers also lacks freshness, but the admirable working out of the dénouement must make up for any such shortcoming.

In a word, it is a quiet story, notwithstanding its tragic end; never rising to great heights, it never falls to the commonplace, and it is throughout a well-written book of evenly sustained interest, and seems likely to win popular favour. At all events, the author is to be congratulated upon having passed with this new work from the pent-up hot-house of her earlier work into a far wider and more wholesome field.

"Fiction," *New York Tribune Illustrated Supplement*, 10 June 1900, p. 11

It is now some three years since Miss Ellen Glasgow made her first appearance as a writer with *The Descendant*, a novel crude in treatment, but with some originality and with suggestions of talent. It was followed about a year later by *Phases of* an *Inferior Planet*, which dealt with Bohemian life in New York. This began well, but deepened into sensationalism, and lacked authority in the handling of the material used. In her latest book, *The Voice of the People*, Miss Glasgow has her abilities more in hand. Studying the conditions of life in the South developed by the Civil War, she is plainly at home with her subject, and her work shows gains in sureness and vigor. Her hero, a young Southerner with a genius for politics who rises from the masses, falls in love with a girl of higher station. The resulting complications are worked out with marked fidelity to the truth, with considerable insight. The author falters here and there, notably in her treatment of the man. She permits him to say things obviously out of harmony with his character. But as a whole, her presentation of two interesting types is uncommonly good. She sees clearly into political conditions, and, in spite of a certain fondness for melodrama, she leaves a persuasive impression. Miss Glasgow appears to write with ease, but her style is injured by a constant straining after effect.

"The Voice of the People," New York Times Saturday Review of Books and Art, 16 June 1900, p. 408

The fact that this story is already in its twelfth thousand is an evidence that it possesses the charms necessary to lasting success. Its author will be remembered as the author of *The Descendant*. She has now written a very strong and vivid story of life in Virginia after the war of the rebellion. It is a thoroughly dramatic story, in which the love interest is absorbing and the character-drawing of the kind that pleases all readers. The reader will find food for thought, as well as an interesting narrative, in the delineation of the sharp conflict which the hero wages from his inferior station against the rigidly exclusive aristocratic prejudice of his neighbors. The book shows a decided advance over the same author's previous works. It will prove to be one of the most satisfactory books for Summer reading. The author's name is already well known, and this book will add to its celebrity.

William Morton Payne, "Recent Fiction," *Dial*, 29 (1 July 1900), 23–4

It is with modern rather than with colonial Virginia that *The Voice of the People*, by Miss Ellen Glasgow, is concerned. This is Miss Glasgow's third novel, and it is thus far distinctly her best. Beginning with a charming description of an old Virginian town, which has been left sidetracked in the march of modern civilization, and is none the less interesting for that, we are at once introduced to the hero, an unprepossessing child of humble parentage, who has the intellectual instinct, and who is determined to raise himself above the level of his surroundings. The book is essentially the story of this child's career, as he painfully acquires an education, becomes a successful lawyer, enters politics, and is chosen Governor of the Commonwealth. He illustrates that type of American manhood of which Lincoln is the great historical exemplar, and of which Mr. Ford's Peter Stirling is a striking example in fiction, the type of sturdy honesty and downright manliness which our country is still capable of illustrating from time to time, and without which our prospects would indeed be hopeless. There are numerous minor characters in this book, carefully studied and agreeably diversified, who add materially to the interest, but the figure of Nicholas Burr rises predominant above them all, and it is with his personal fortunes that we have chiefly to do. In the end, the story rises to the height of tragedy, and the hero, now Governor of the State, sacrifices his life in defending the honor of the Commonwealth. A negro has been guilty of a nameless crime, and a lynching party has been organized. The governor comes unexpectedly upon the scene of action, opposes the lawless fury of the mob, and, before he has been recognized, is mortally wounded by a shot. "And he died for a damned brute," is the comment of a bystander when the sobered mob learns what it has done. But even in the most brutish of that mob there must have been some dim recognition, in the lesson thus sharply brought home to them, of the shame of their assault upon the majesty of law, and of the noble cause for which their victim had given his life. Shocking as was the murder, it was less shocking and less permanently demoralizing than the success of their lawless undertaking would have been. In describing this scene, the author rises to the true dignity of the situation, and leaves a deep impression upon the minds of her readers. We have to thank her for a strong book, and for a message of practical idealism which cannot be weighed too seriously.

Academy, 59 (14 July 1900), 34

A story of American life by the author of *Phases of an Inferior Planet*. We watch the hero's career from farmer's boy to judge. "There ar'n't nothin' in peanut-raisin'" is Nick Burr's early conviction; he accounted a judge's career "cleaner work." The story is a strong commentary on the lynching practices which are the disgrace of certain States of America.

"Novels of the Week," *Spectator* [England], 85 (28 July 1900), 117

It seems an ungrateful thing to criticise an interesting book for being too long, but it is almost inevitable in the case of Mrs. [sic] Glasgow's new story, *The Voice of the People*. The book does not want shortening at the end, but a little compression at the beginning would be a decided improvement. Although the opening picture of life in a country town in Virginia—the story is American—is picturesque enough with its sleepiness, its negroes, and its Southern charm, still the author gives us at first no central figures on which to hang our interest. The man and woman on whom the story of the book is to hang are in the beginning only children, and the reader's interest is not sufficiently aroused by what is really merely a *mise-en-scène*. After reading the rest of the book, it would be worth while to re-read the opening and there study the beginnings and surroundings of the clever characters in whom the author has interested us in the later part of her book. But as it is, the first two books of the five into which the novel is divided are tedious. The fault, however, argues a painstaking quality in the author with which the reviewer should be the last to quarrel, and by its very nature shows that there is good stuff in the novel. From Book III onwards all tediousness entirely disappears, and the story becomes thoroughly interesting. Nick Burr, the self-made man, is a fine creation, and his love idyll with Eugenia is painted with a delicacy of imagination which makes the reader grieve for its sudden ending. It is very like life for a charming woman to decline "on a lower range of feeling," and to be quite satisfied with an intolerable "bounder" like the fascinating Dudley Webb for a husband, after having in girlhood been loved by a man like Nick Burr. Still, though lifelike, Eugenia's conduct is unideal, and she herself is sufficiently living to make the reader regret the fate with which she is quite content. Readers who like a good long novel, and are interested by the study of America, will very much enjoy *The Voice of the People*.

Athenæum [England], 2 (11 August 1900), 179

The Voice of the People is by a comparatively new writer. The trend and matter of the actual story are not of any particularly notable nor distinctive kind. They deal with the career of an ambitious high-souled rustic—a boy who from nothing reaches a position of importance in his native state. The hopes, despairs, successes and failures, and other vicissitudes that meet him on his path, are described with some vividness. But there is more than this to attract the reader, and more especially those with a liking for tales of the Southern American states. These latter are a happy hunting ground for clever novelists across the Atlantic. Since *The Open Question* and a book by Mrs. Burnett we do not remember any story with so fine a Southern setting and background for character as this. Where it is not plot and incident it is a series of bright, soft pictures of nature itself, of luxuriant gardens, and of people instinct with droll or lovable peculiarities. The life of the old Virginian landowners, the negro servants, their quaint ways, their outspoken freedom of speech, yet exceeding loyalty to Marse' This or Mis' That, are individually as well as traditionally excellent. One feels the genuine human nature of old General Battle, who keeps open house of a ruined and ruinous kind, also the sister who takes the reins of government, and the charming little daughter. Aunt Verbeny, Uncle Ish, Delphy, and her meek son-in-law Mose are also admirable. So is the household of Judge Bassett, and so, in another way, are the hardworking family of the ambitious "poor-white" hero, the farmstead, and the harsh, yet kind stepmother, and her chronic "neuralgy." All these persons, places, and things are excellent, because beneath the impressionist touch of Miss Glasgow there is a solid hold on average human nature. We perceive this in many matters, in the relations between the general and his daughter, and in a sense of an underlying unforced pathos in passing people and inanimate objects around them. The group of happy irresponsible children is charmingly drawn. Then there are the sayings and doings of the black people, often comical to a high degree. Indeed, Uncle Ish, his dignified, almost injured attitude towards the kind human ravens who supply his daily bread, is most amusing. The story is divided into books. We prefer the earlier parts, but the interest is on the whole well maintained.

Academy, 59 (18 August 1900), 133-4

Phases of an Inferior Planet was a clever book, and this book is both clever and very ambitious—as every novel must be ambitious which pretends to embrace the whole life of a man from the cradle to the grave. The fault of *The Voice of the People* is that it is too long. We do not mean that its length is excessive in any absolute sense, nor that the author digresses unduly from the theme which she has set herself; nor do we mean that the book is dull; it never is dull. We mean that much of it is unimportant and inessential. In the pretty and diverting scenes of white and black life at sleepy Kingsborough, the home of Nick Burr, that born lawyer and politician and State Governor, this triviality of observation is especially felt. It has a weakening effect on the story as a whole. The original projective force of an author is strictly limited by nature, and if the author tries to spread that force over too large an area, the result must be, in a measure, to render it futile. Miss Glasgow's faculty of observation needs discipline. It is too busy, too fussy, and a great deal too fanciful—fanciful where it should be imaginative. She often does not observe the right *kind* of thing. She trifles, and gives rein to mere fancy. And gradually she passes into a condition, a mood, which, without conscious intent, twists and contorts life into something untruthfully pretty—something emasculate and feebly emotional. When her hero and heroine approach the passionate climax of their lives, this is what occurs, according to Miss Glasgow:

> Then, by a curious emotional phenomenon, she seemed to be suddenly invested with the glory of the sunset. The goldenrod burned at her feet and on her bosom, and her fervent blood leaped to her face....

This may be truth, but it is truth falsified, scarcely recognisable beneath its envelope of fanciful and *quasi*-maudlin "intensity." We insist on this aspect of Miss Glasgow's novel, because it is characteristic of much modern fiction. The writers of such fiction should undergo a course of Balzac. In many respects *The Voice of the People* is admirable. The style is generally distinguished, and the dialogue, though too plentiful, is life-like and effective. The sketches of negro character are excellent. Miss Glasgow has a wide knowledge of life and manners; the novel seems to be her true vocation, and one is bound to accord to her that serious consideration which is only accorded to a serious artist.

R.W.V., "Ellen Glasgow," *Book News Monthly*, 19 (September 1900), 1-2

In 1897 Harper and Brothers published a novel called *The Descendant*: it had had but little preliminary advertising and yet so true is it that a strong book will command attention, this story written by a girl not twenty-two years old was immediately taken up by the leading reviewers in the country, some of whom said it was morbid, some simply stated that it was interesting, but none "damned it by no mention," or pronounced it weak. Naturally there was much speculation as to the authorship, most of the critics claiming it was the work of a man, *one* going so far as to recognize the author of the

Damnation of Theron Ware, but so reticent was the writer that even the members of her own family were kept in the dark until the book was ready for publication. . . .

Ellen Glasgow has written three books which have been published—*The Descendant*, 1897—*Phases of an Inferior Planet*, 1898—and last and best, *The Voice of the People*. Kingsborough, the principal scene of this novel, "once a chartered city," is easily recognized as Williamsburg—and Miss Glasgow knows well and loves better the Kingsborough of her own time; indeed she has intimately acquainted herself with the surrounding country and woodlands. Her happy childhood was largely spent out of doors in the open country and in forests thick and silent as those of Kingsborough. It may almost be said that she looked into her heart to write the first three-fifths of her novel. "Battle Hall," under another name and in a neighborhood not immeasurably distant, is the more modern half of a large rambling house which was at one time her home, and the darkies at the "quarters" are none of them absolute strangers. Her literary methods are failures of effort if they do not make for truth and accuracy. Though she does not consider her book a political novel, the personal career of her hero made it necessary that she should make an exhaustive and often exhausting study of political ways and means. As early as 1897, when the book was only in mind, she drove more than twenty miles over the mountains in August weather to sit two days and nights in a Democratic Convention, which was convened to nominate a Governor. Through friendly influence she was smuggled in at the stage door of the Opera House which was the Convention Hall, and sat upon the stage surrounded by kinsmen delegates, herself and her companion the only women in the building.

The list of the Southern novelists grows longer day by day—so far the writers of the "New South," who have been heard, have had interesting things to say—it has been the matter more than the manner which has attracted. Miss Glasgow has combined both of these qualities to a remarkable extent in her latest novel, and she has been universally accorded a seat on the front row in the great American School of Fiction.

Atlantic Monthly, 86 (September 1900), 416–18

The title of our next book, *The Voice of the People*, would seem to suggest that we are still in the region of types, tendencies, and social problems. Yet except for its underlying thoughtfulness, and for the condemnation implied rather than pronounced, in the closing chapters of some of our prevalent political methods,—the latest work of Miss Glasgow has little in common with *Unleavened Bread* [by Robert Grant]. For this is a true romance, a simple, and wholly probable, yet admirably wrought and deeply affecting story. It actually essays, for a wonder in any novel of the year 1900, to portray a grand passion; the tyrannous and consuming passion of a great man of low origin for a bright, alluring, but, as the event proves, quite ordinary woman in a rank of life above his own. *The Voice of the People* comes to us from the latitude whence we get all our best imaginative work in these days, the region along Mason and Dixon's happily obliterated line,—the most hotly contested and grievously devastated battleground of the great civil war. Surely there must have lurked in the ashes of that burning—*tot funera!*—a wonderful enrichment of soul and enlargement of vision for the generation that was to grow up there after the fight was lost and won! The best of the apologues they bring us are so broadly based upon the final certainties of life and morals, so clear of all bookish affectation and sophistication, so lightly encumbered by material flummery! Not that the optic nerve is by any means "starved" in Ellen Glasgow's tale. The scenery of her drama is always vividly present to the writer's mind, and she manages with a few strokes of a skillful brush to make it equally clear to the reader. Strictly speaking, there is too much landscape in the book; yet it is hard to quarrel with pictures where the color is as discreetly and delicately applied as in this of the old shire town of Kingsborough in Virginia, where the action of the piece begins and ends. . . .

The period of twenty years or so covered by the story embraces the youth and early maturity of the first generation born and bred in Virginia after Lee's surrender, and comes up with the present time. The survivals from the ante-bellum era,—testy old General Battle, the judge who "had not spoken an uncivil word" since the close of the civil war, and who "from having been, in his youth, one of the hopes of his state, had become in its age one of her consolations"; the stately widow of a fallen Confederate warrior, Mrs. Dudley Webb, impenitent and inscrutable; and all the foolish, fond old negroes, whose wool is white, and their elementary speech racy with memories of "dem good old slavin' times,"—each one of these obsolescent types is tenderly and reverentially depicted; their personal oddities and anachronisms hit off with wistful, caressing, half-unwilling wit. But if the writer's heart is in the past, her faith, albeit stripped of illusions and forlorn, is fixed upon the future. The long and groveling agony of the poor white trash, from which her hero springs, is portrayed both with unflinching realism and unfailing sympathy; all the harsh contrasts of the situation softened, and its more cruel aspects half disguised by the curiously pensive and subdued but all-pervading humor which plays over the surface of the narrative like the ruddy twinkle of veiled sunshine upon still waters in a smoky autumn day. The career of the protagonist, Nicholas Burr, is at once a triumph and a tragedy. The lady-love who had fired and fed his young ambition, and who had promised in the ardor of one exalted hour to wait for his victory, forsakes him in the moment of ordeal for a man of her own caste; yet he is governor of the Old Dominion when he meets his untimely end. The lesser actors in the history all fall back before the catastrophe arrives, leaving the rugged figure of the hero outlined in lonely grandeur upon the steps of Kingsborough court house, where he dies by the shot of a fellow townsman, in the vain attempt to defend from the violence of an infuriated crowd the criminal confined within.

A faint reminiscence of the end of Beauchamp's Career is almost the only suggestion of direct influence by any other author which occurs in *The Voice of the People*. The work is not quite a masterpiece, but its noble and impressive dénouement makes it one not easy to forget.

Bookman [London], 19 (October 1900), 29

The North may have the greatest output of books—we are referring to the United States—and perhaps the North has given to the world the most lasting literature. But about the books raised in the South there is something their northern rivals cannot rival, cannot even reach. They have charm, a mellow old-world charm that captures and does not let go its hold. Something of this peculiar attraction, best seen in the books of Mr. Cable's earlier days, can be felt in *The Voice of the People*. A sleepy old Virginian town, groups of old-world characters, quaint and individual, but with their idiosyncrasies softened and toned by high-bred courtesy and by a sunny clime, are described in a very leisurely fashion. We linger willingly among them. Miss Glasgow is a writer of exceptional power. She knows human nature, and while here she dwells by preference among the more amiable specimens of it, she does not shirk sterner realities. Indeed the story of her central character is so full of pain that we somewhat resent her inexorable treatment of him; at least, we resent her indulgent feelings to Eugenia, the prosperous young woman, who wounded Nicholas sorely, married his rival, and took his tragic death a little too placidly in the end. Among these comfortable, charming folks the personality and career of Nicholas have an added pathos. The hard-used struggler, with the strong will, the clear brain, the inexorable conscience, and the heart that is always unsatisfied, is a hero after a real pattern, made living and near to us by Miss Glasgow's power; of so much interest, indeed, that when he falls, killed in a sorry scuffle, defending a rascal, we think it almost well, life not being inclined to give him much delight. Virginia, with its slow, sleepy ways, its chivalrous instincts, its cautious venturing into the world of progress, and its fine-mannered, restrained regret for the days that are past, lives again in these pages. Yet the centre of it is an eager, forward spirit made for battle, who gets all the fighting he wants in his resolve to cleanse the politics of his state and his time.

Checklist of Additional Reviews

"Miss Ellen Glasgow's New Novel," Brooklyn *Daily Eagle*, 14 April 1900, p. 7.

"*The Voice of the People* by Ellen Glasgow," *New York Times Saturday Review of Books and Art*, 14 April 1900, p. 249.

"Library Table: Glimpses of New Books," *Current Literature*, 28 (June 1900), 355–6 (reprint of part of *New York Times Book Review*, 21 April 1900).

"*The Voice of the People*," Boston *Evening Transcript*, 9 May 1900, p. 12.

Benjamin W. Wells, "Southern Literature of the Year," *Forum*, 29 (June 1900), 501–12.

St. James Gazette [England], 30 July 1900.

"Current Fiction," *Saturday Review* [London], 90 (11 August 1900), 180.

"New Writer," *Bookman* [London], September 1900, 167–8.

"Some English Views of *The Voice of the People*," *Literary Digest*, 21 (29 September 1900), 370–1.

"Three Novelists of Sincerity and Charm," *World's Work*, 5 (November 1902), 2791–2.

THE BATTLE-GROUND

The Battle-Ground
By
Ellen Glasgow

ILLUSTRATED BY
W. J. BAER AND W GRANVILLE SMITH

NEW YORK
DOUBLEDAY, PAGE & CO.
1902

"*The Battle-Ground*: Ellen Glasgow's New Story of Life in Virginia," Louisville *Courier-Journal*, 29 March 1902, sec. 1, p. 5

Virginia's place in the statehood of letters is a proud one. Her very name is one to conjure with. Out of that gallant array of soldiers and statesmen, fair women and brave men who have made the history of the Old Dominion, the historian in fiction has seen rich and fascinating material. And back of these people is a record fairly aglow with the passion of great emotions and tender with the pathos of magnificent conflict. It is a story splendid with incident from that early day when the Puritan and Cavalier mingled on her shores through the long and turbulent years to the present.

The historian of that colonial day is Mary Johnston, who has caught all the fine romance of the cavalier day. But it has remained for Ellen Glasgow to be the best depicter of the dramatic period, the reconstruction, when the great State, torn by war, rallied for new life and new hope. In *The Voice of the People* Miss Glasgow presented a masterly story of the new and altered conditions which grew out of the war. It was a remarkable achievement in fiction, the first fulfillment of a golden promise held out by her two earlier books.

When it was announced that Miss Glasgow had taken the Civil War period as the time of her fourth book, a wide interest was aroused. Herself a careful student of Virginia history, it was conceded that here would be a book of rare value.

To a large degree *The Battle-Ground*, which is the title of the new book, meets these expectations. It is a striking and forceful presentation of antebellum as well as bellum days; it is an admirably written and consistently developed story, but it falls short of *The Voice of the People* in scope and brilliancy, and yet this does not mean that *The Battle-Ground* is a disappointment. Miss Glasgow is too careful an artist, too keen a student of conditions and, above all, too clever a story teller to fail in her work.

Miss Glasgow begins her story some years before the Civil War and continues through the conflict to peace. The average reader has learned to shun war stories. They have reached the flood stage. But there are all sorts of war stories. *The Red Badge of Courage* was the story of a lifetime. All stories of war are not reeking with blood. After all it is a matter of treatment of incident and in this Miss Glasgow has shown herself to be an artist. There is little of the roar of battle in this book despite its title. Rather is it a story of cause and effect.

Charmingly does the story begin—the rich, pleasant valley brooding with the peace of summer and fragrant with the violet and the lilac. Miss Glasgow introduces her leading characters when they are children and the reader follows them to eventful manhood and womanhood. In *The Voice of the People* one man of superb character dominated. In *The Battle-Ground* it is a woman who leads. It is a story of two sisters, each lovely and radiant, each destined to win men's hearts, and to know the bitterness as well as the triumph of love. These women are the daughters of an ex-Governor, a stately gentleman of the old school, steeped in the traditions of his great State and loyal to them. His neighbor is a proverbial Virginia gentleman, a Major who has lived and loved. The Major has a grandson, the child of a beautiful daughter who ran away one Christmas eve with a worthless wretch. It is natural to suppose that this grandson should fall in love with one of the sisters, and he does. Between these two people the chief interest of the story lies. The boy is hot blooded, impulsive, hasty, and he is not an ideal lover, and the consequence is that the course of the love is not altogether smooth. The boy goes to war and lays his sacrifice on the altar of the stern god of battles. The father of his sweetheart likewise goes to war and is killed.

Miss Glasgow has wisely avoided much of the incident and carnage of wars. There is enough to impress the reader with the horror of it; there is all the story of martial display, and there is all the infinite pathos of the Lost Cause and the return of the shattered, but proud, hosts in glory.

Miss Glasgow is at all times a graceful and vigorous writer and a review of her new book would surely not be complete without something from her. Here is her fine description of the battle:

> Behind him and beside him row after row of gray men looked from the shadow—the very hill seemed rising to his support, and it was almost gayly, as the dead fighters lived again, that he went straight onward over the enemy's field. He saw the golden dust float nearer up the slope, saw the brave flags unfurling to the breeze—saw at last man after man emerge from the yellow cloud.
>
> As he bent to fire, the fury of the game swept over him and aroused the sleeping brute within him. All the primeval instincts, throttled by the restraint of centuries—the instinct of blood guiltiness, of hot pursuit, of the fierce exhilaration of the chase, of the death grapple with a resisting foe—these awoke suddenly to life and turned the battle scarlet to his eyes.

The Battle-Ground must inevitably be compared with *The Voice of the People*. Nowhere in this new story will be found a characterization to rank with that of Nick Burr. There is no incident equal to his magnificent struggle for success. The characters of *The Battle-Ground* are admirably grouped; the hot-headed Mountjoy, the radiant and loving Betty, the beautiful Virginia; Gov. Ambler, grave, stately and courteous, and the dear old Major, the type of the old Virginia gentleman. All through this book is that gentle and gracious courtesy which is the heritage of the true Virginian. There seem to be no lay figures in this book. There is action for every one.

But the fact remains that Miss Glasgow is a better historian of the Revolution than of the Civil War. Her style is at all times good. One catches the tender glow of the fair Virginia skies, and she knows the values and the beauties of romantic old gardens. All her people live and breathe. They are never puppets. *The Battle-Ground* is a finished and artistic production; it is serious and thoughtful. If it does not surpass its predecessors, surely it impresses the fact that Miss Glasgow is one of the foremost women writers of her country, and it is a genuine pleasure to commend her work.

G.A., "The Leopard's Spots and The Battle-Ground Are Out: Southern Books by Southern Authors Lead American Literature," Richmond Times, 30 March 1902, p. 20

Now on sale at the book stores Miss Glasgow's latest effort has been received with enthusiasm by her home people and The Battle-Ground is well worthy of the praise that is being showered upon it. It is a vigorous and delightful story, much stronger and more mature in finish than even her very successful Voice of the People.

The Battle-Ground deals with Virginia home life immediately before and during the Confederate War, and the dramatic pictures of that bloody struggle during which this state was the debatable ground are heightened in effect by the fascinating background of old-fashioned culture and refinement which crested among our antebellum gentlefolk.

[...]

The book is rich in local color and vibrant with the moods of home, the humor of the plantation, the passion and pathos of war. It is one of the most human and illuminating pictures of these terrible times that has ever been written.

Nation, 74 (10 April 1902), 294

Miss Glasgow's books improve with each deeper plunge into the past and into the South. Her story of Reconstruction was better than her novel of New-York, and best of the three is The Battle-Ground, which shuns even small towns, and tells of Virginia before and during the civil war. Two or three of the portraits are masterly. Of these are the heroine, Betty, and the two old men, the Governor and the Major. Secondary, but as lifelike, are the studies of the mountaineer known as "Pinetop"; the faithful old slave, "Big Abel," who follows his young master to the war; Aunt Molly, reading The Mysteries of Udolpho in bed, a tall silver candlestick standing on her breast; Aunt Lydia tending her old garden, and liking apple-toddy, though she regarded the taste "as an indelicate one, and would as soon have admitted, before gentlemen, a liking for cabbage." As to the young hero, his attractiveness is more insisted on than patent. However, if not a very positive character himself, he is the cause of much excellent characterization in others, being the chief object of much and varied loving, petting, and cursing. The South—say rather the Virginia—of a generation ago has found a most sympathetic reproduction, with its neighborhood amenities and the manners of an age of chivalry. The women (always excepting the spicy Betty) are an irresistible compound of the seraphic and the silly; the men roystering, tender-hearted, elegant, readers of Horace and Addison, but none the wiser for it; vehement declaimers upon the rights and duties of gentlemen. What is a gentleman, by the way? As many different things, seemingly, as there are communities and professions. Major Lightfoot's creed declared, "There's no man alive that shall question the divine right of slavery in my presence; but—but it is an institution for gentlemen, and you, sir [to a nobody white who had struck his slave] are a damned scoundrel." When he finds his grandson, as he thinks, fickle, he roars, "Would you trifle with a lady from your own State, sir?" And his reproach to the hotheaded youth for duelling in a chivalrous cause is that he has "tried to murder a Virginia gentleman for the sake of a barroom hussy." The old Major, indeed, is a very fine example of a local product. With the Governor, the strictly Virginian idea is enlarged to a wider patriotism. Incurring his friend the Major's unrestrained wrath, the Governor sadly hopes to save the Union, not as one who loves his State less, but his country more.

Coming to the second generation, we find Dan Montjoy, in the stress of camp life, forming a warm friendship with a despised mountaineer as they fight side by side, the young patrician for the right to hold slaves, the other to "keep Virginia." The war half of the book is vivid; moving, as always, is the story of the beardless boys who made up the army of the South, especially the followers of Gen. Lee, their justly adored "Marse Robert." The writer writes whereof she evidently knows. But intimacy has not dulled her perception. She takes heed of tragic and humorous as one who writes from without, though she has seen from within. We must except the natural scenery, which looms too large. At times, like that in *Parsifal*, it sustains the entire action while the figures are stationary.

"Miss Glasgow's *The Battle-Ground*," *New York Times Saturday Review of Books*, 19 April 1902, p. 266

There is no lack of variety in *The Battle-Ground*. It is at once a tender romance of constant love, a living picture of a society that is no more, and a drama of war. As a romance it is full of interest, and it has the rare charm of a most satisfactory heroine, one whom to know in real life would be a liberal education in womanly virtues. Blithe, honest, and kind; endowed with humor and with the grace of unselfishness, Miss Glasgow's "Betty" torments neither herself nor her lover, as is the approved fashion of heroines; but in the times that try men's souls makes life less difficult for her little world, and, rising above her own shadows, "makes a sunshine in a shady place" for all around her—bird and beast, gentle and simple. Since young people will read romances, they cannot read one more wholesome and helpful than that contained in *The Battle-Ground*.

But even ignoring the love story, one finds *The Battle-Ground* full of interest and illumination. A generous half of its pages portrays society in Virginia during the decade immediately preceding the great cataclysm of 1861. The author has selected the life of a large plantation as most characteristic, and has painted with skillful and rapid touch its simple stateliness, its almost feudal chivalry, its boundless hospitality, its grave responsibility. It was a society not given to introspection or to problems; it was high-minded, honorable, happy as few others have been, its feet serenely planted upon a firm faith in its superiority to any other society upon earth, a faith which, carrying its corollary of noblesse oblige, went far toward its own fulfilling.

This vanished social life blooms again upon the pages of *The Battle-Ground* with a wonderful glow and fragrance. Miss Glasgow ranks with Mr. Page as a painter and an interpreter of the Old South—that South too sure of itself to condescend to explain itself.

Along with this simple, high-bred aristocracy Miss Glasgow shows the free negro and the poor white, unfortunates both, ground between the upper and the nether millstones, despised alike by slaveholder and slave. She shows, too, in the person of old Rainy-Day Jones the creature loathed and ostracized by Southern society—the man reputedly cruel to his slaves. In one swift sentence of scorn she voices the sentiment of the Old South, "There's no man alive that shall question the divine right of slavery in my presence, but—but, it is an institution for gentlemen, and you, Sir, are a damned scoundrel." "An institution for gentlemen"—into these four words Miss Glasgow has compacted the apologia of the South.

She has omitted nothing from her picture, not even the serious New England tutor, "unduly weighed down by responsibility for the souls of his fellows," gravely "discussing schemes for the uplifting of the negroes," and even daring to hand old Rainy-Day himself a pamphlet on "The Duties of the Slaveholder"—a sketch full of humorous sympathy. As the war cloud draws nearer the author depicts the varying tempers with which it was faced. There is the "fire-eating" secessionist burning with impatience for Virginia to throw herself into the fray; there is the man like Robert E. Lee, clinging to the Union to the last, resisting secession until there came the alternative of fighting the South or fighting with the South. Miss Glasgow admirably reveals the complex passions and conflicting loyalties of that dread "hush before the storm." The sentiment that finally swept away all divergence of opinion she comprehends no less clearly. The hardy mountaineer Pinetop (one of the best characters of the book) expresses the feeling of the poorer whites in his comments upon his first battle.

> I ain't got much of a stomach for a fight myself. You see, I ain't never fought anythin' bigger'n a skunk until to-day; and when I stood out thar with them bullets sizzlin' like fryin' pans round my head, I kind of says to myself: "Look here, what's all this fuss about anyhow? If these here folks have come arter the niggers, let 'em take 'em off and welcome. I ain't never owned a nigger in my life, and, what's more, I ain't never seen one that's worth owning. Let 'em take 'em and welcome," that's what I said. Bless your life, as I stood out thar I didn't see how I was goin' to fire my musket, till all of a jiffy a thought jest jumped into my head and sent me bangin' down that hill. "Them folks have set thar feet on ole Virginny," was what I thought. "They've set thar feet on ole Virginny, and they've got to take 'em off damn quick." I've got a powerful fancy for old Virginny, and they ain't goin' to project with her dust, if I can stand between.

In different fashion is voiced the feeling of the gentleman who "fought hard against secession until it came," and, who fell wearing the gray:

> He loved the Union, and he had

given it the best years of his life. I think if he ever felt any bitterness toward any one, it was for the man or men who brought us into this; and at last he used to leave the room because he could not speak of them without anger. He threw all his strength against the tide, yet when it rushed on in spite of him, he knew where his duty guided him, and he followed it, as always, like a pleasure.... He always felt that he was fighting for a hopeless cause, and he loved it more for the very pity of its weakness.

And widely differing from both these spirits is shown the light-hearted way in which "merry gentlemen went to war," as to a tourney, fearful only that the fight would be over before they could reach the firing line; objecting not at all to danger or death, but to having their "elbows jagged by the poor white trash" while they did battle for their country. "Clean out the camp!" exclaims one in anger at the order. "Does he think my grandmother was a chambermaid?"

The disillusioning, the sufferings, the privations of the four years of civil strife are given in almost relentless detail. Miss Glasgow has written a poetic tale of young love, but there have been others as admirable; she has wonderfully well portrayed Southern society, but there, too, she has her compeers, fit though few; but as a story of the civil war *The Battle-Ground* stands alone. The grim humor that never left the ragged, starving Confederate soldier, the irrepressible gayety of heart of the negroes—and Miss Glasgow's negroes are as perfect as Mr. Harris's—relieve a recital which would else be almost unbearable in its tragedy. Nor does the author forget to show "how nobly natures form" in this stern school, nor to give some of the many instances of delicate kindness from victors toward vanquished, for which history finds few parallels.

The most unsympathetic reader will find his eyes grow dim over "The Hour of Defeat." One feels, perhaps for the first time, what Appomattox meant to the people of the South.

"General Gossip of Authors and Writers," *Current Literature*, 32 (May 1902), 625

Miss Ellen Glasgow has done several remarkable things in her latest book. She has written a historical novel in which character takes the place of claptrap melodrama. She has given us a story without a villain. She has dared, in the face of a popular cry for swashbuckling, to write that which shall appeal to the intellect and to the emotions, rather than merely to the nerves. She has made her hero go through an entire war of four years, made him fight in the ranks, made him endure the carnage and din of battle honestly and manfully, and made him issue from a conflict with no chevrons on his coat sleeve, a plain private just as when he entered, but a man every inch of him. All of which, as stated at the beginning, is quite remarkable.

The Battle-Ground is, in the first place, a story of the Civil War; but in the second and greater place, it is a beautiful study of Southern life and Southern character. Even the reader most jaded by the all-pervasive and clashy popular historical novel need have no fear in taking up this book. From cover to cover there is not a single duel, not a single intrigue, not a single touch of melodrama. There is no straining nor forcing of the interest, yet there is plenty to hold and many things to grip the attention. Rarely during the last ten years has there appeared a book with a historical background that is at once so real, so simple and so dramatic. It is in a way a lesson that should be studied by our so-called popular novelists.

Book News, 20 (May 1902), 685–6

There is a virility and mastery of stroke in Miss Glasgow's novels which make one almost forget that their author is a woman, so masculine do her works appear at times. In *The Battle-Ground*, she has undoubtedly accomplished her most significant achievement. In Virginia from immediately before the war to the final fall of the Confederacy, Miss Glasgow has placed a story at once tender, romantic and real.

The time is not well chosen. So many tales have been surrounded by that selfsame background, so many tales have taken their coloring from that period, that the deeply inspiring and thrilling spirit of the conflict has to some extent lost its potency and the picture no longer calls forth the deep admiration and interest which once made a book founded upon its scenes so greatly favored and demanded. But despite the ill-selected period, despite the fact that Miss Glasgow's attempts at dramatic and vivid portrayal of battles and her efforts at tragic climax are for the most part, ineffectual, the picture that she has drawn of Virginia itself, with its quaint and old-time aristocracy, the cleverness with which she has introduced so many different and realistic characters, and the skill with which she has woven a charming little love story into its midst, make it a work replete with human interest and with the varied emotions of life.

The people captivate us, what matter if we do have, now and then, to skip a wearisome description or to pass lightly over a vain striving for effect? Miss Glasgow is an optimist, and we see her at her best in the quick, bright touches of wit that are scattered like sunbeams through her chapters. In the earlier portions of the work, wherein she touches the lighter situations and scenes of the romance her writing is a sparkling, spontaneous flow that dances merrily across the pages and sometimes fairly bubbles over in the exuberance of its joy. But in the later chapters, when she leaves the social life of the Old Dominion and turns to the bloody scenes of war, Miss Glasgow seems to realize her insufficiency in imparting force and vigor to the picture and makes a manifest effort to overcome her weakness. In consequence, while the portrayal of events in that serious "time" are strong in comparison to many another modern writer, even among men, yet if we place them side by side with some of the more masterful portrayals we soon realize their lack of the fullest power and become painfully aware of a missing naturalness and ease of manner. Notwithstanding, the book is one of the most enlightening works that have yet appeared dealing with that particular time, while its excellent literary finish and all-pervading charm render it a story well worthy of perusal and of appreciation.

Carl Hovey, "Ellen Glasgow's *The Battle-Ground*," *Bookman*, 15 (May 1902), 258–9

Of the many novels dealing with the period of the Civil War that have been written during the last few years, only two or three, at most, really represented what the people living through this acute and momentous condition of things were feeling and experiencing. In some books of this class we had merely a love-story, with a lurid setting for its scenes; a kind of campaigner's diary, setting forth with sincere interest intricate military movements, the whole breathing of "villainous saltpetre," was offered in others; and, again, we had attempts, praiseworthy, but uninspired, to reproduce some great fragment of the drama, with portraits of Lincoln, Grant, Lee, Stonewall Jackson, drawn to the life. Nearly all proved unsatisfactory because of the failure to relate simply and faithfully the experience of some one person, or group of persons, when the war came, and strangely altered the ordinary aspect of life.

In reading *The Battle-Ground*, one observes, almost from the beginning, that here is something new and different from the common run of novels, fire-eating, ponderous, or simply mediocre, as the case may be, dealing with the same general subject. Things and characters are brought in simply and naturally, without that familiar, ominous rasp of the author's pen down the pages of half a dozen chapters, to put the reader into the proper attitude toward the events and scenes to come. Without affectation or flourish, Miss Glasgow introduces us at once to the life of a typical neighbourhood of Virginia gentlemen and ladies, with their beautiful plantation homes, the high-living notions and refinement, some time in the years just preceding the war. One thing happens after another with as much apparent lack of continuity as in real life, and the development of the story makes its way by means of just the causes and consequences that are found in real life. The result is that Miss Glasgow's delicate and discriminating powers of observation and of expression finally work in us a sense of novel and enlightening experience; we know what happened at Chericoke, where the master of Uplands, Major Lightfoot, Betty, Dan, Champe, not to mention Big Abel, Rainy-Day Jones, and all the other interesting personages of the countryside, lived and flourished, quite as well as though we had seen the events take place; and we know these people, too, quite as familiarly and comprehensively as we know our own near neighbours and friends.

This is remarkable; the book is remarkable, both for its pervading charm and for its essential truth in detail. It has the defect of diffuseness; hardly any other fault, on the whole; although it must be said that the portion of the novel relating how the "merry gentlemen" fought on the battlefield, and how they bore the hardships of the campaign, is not so interesting as that devoted to the doings at Chericoke; because there is too much of it.

[. . .]

But it will do this excellent novel nothing but disservice to quote passages from it at random; it is a book to be read as a whole, and to be enjoyed by almost every one, because of its sincerity and charm.

Boston *Evening Transcript*, 14 May 1902, p. 18

Two storybook girls of the South who are pretty sure to win their way into the affections of a majority of readers are those that figure in a fine new Southern story by Ellen Glasgow. As the title hints, *The Battle-Ground* is not so much the story of the great conflict between North and South as it is the story of how the fine, old Virginian home life and neighborhood spirit was disturbed and broken by that bloody struggle. It makes the reader intimately alive to the terrible uncertainty and woe of the days when with the State as debatable ground and their men fighting or wounded perhaps not a day's ride distant, remnants of families did their woeful best to keep their old places in safety while sending what aid they could to the dear ones in the actual conflict. Yet all these dramatic pictures are heightened in effect by the fascinating background of old-fashioned culture and refinement which existed among the gentlefolk "befo' the wah."

This is not a typical Southern war story; it has an individuality of its own; it looks at the war from behind, from the inside, and perhaps the majority of readers will find rather more than the usual interest in it for this reason alone. But the two girls—the one all dash and fire—"des an out'n out firebran'" as Uncle Shadrach said—and the other gentle and frail and sensitive, but with good stuff in her, too—are as charming types of Southern "belles" as have ever been portrayed in fiction; and the masterful delineation of character both of white master and black slave vies in interest with the delightful humor which keeps cropping out all through the book.

As for the depiction of scenes directly associated with the battlefield, perhaps one of the most human and illuminating pictures of those terrible times that has ever been painted in words is that of Richmond, while the cannon are booming at Seven Pines and the wounded are streaming into the city over the Williamsburg road until warehouses and public halls are crowded like hospitals. No such scenes as that are familiar to people who knew only the North in war time.

Altogether Miss Glasgow has written a vigorous and charming story, stronger, perhaps, than her other well-known book, *The Voice of the People*. Its readers are fortunate, too, in illustrations by such men as W. Granville Smith and W.J. Baer, for their drawings are thoroughly in sympathy with the text. . . .

Independent, 54 (22 May 1902), 1251

It has been a long time since we have read a more striking novel of the Civil War than this; it is interesting and thoroughly beautiful; it is as readable as *The Crisis*, and it is, in addition, a work of art. The story is a picture of Virginia life before and during the great struggle; it is a picture drawn with loving faithfulness and with real charm. Its characters are all people who live and move, its scenes are many of them delightful. The author has humor and a sense of the picturesque; she has also tenderness and an artistic sense. There are very few false touches in the book. *The Battle-Ground* is, in brief, a picture of two Virginia families and of the love of two Virginia maidens. Half of the book deals with a period before the war and the rest with the great contest. The hero is a private in the army of Lee, and many of the descriptions of his experiences are really fine. The account of the broken and beaten army at the end particularly so. This is not saying that *The Battle-Ground* is a great picture of the Civil War, for it is not that. The author's imagination has not been equal to this high and tragic theme—one feels the lack of an uplifting inspiration, feels that the story often fails to rise to the heights, to be equal to the subject. But nevertheless it is in every way a readable and creditable piece of work, a piece of work that one would be glad to see go far.

Hamilton Wright Mabie, "The Fiction of the Season," *Outlook*, 71 (24 May 1902), 212–14

It has been a special pleasure to watch Miss Ellen Glasgow's literary career because she has avoided the three pitfalls which have entrapped so many of the younger writers of fiction—rapidity in production, eagerness to gain by factitious flurries of popular taste, and tendencies toward morbid psychology. Miss Glasgow's new book, *The Battle-Ground*, is the third she has written within a period of five years, while in the same time Mr. Crockett has put forth fifteen. There is no trace in any of Miss Glasgow's stories of the hasty, helter-skelter work of the producer of "pot-boilers." She writes simply and truly; her characters are human and well rounded out; her humor is natural and unforced. From the opening scene of *The Battle-Ground* the reader feels that he has been introduced into a company of people of individuality, living in a little Southern town which is distinct from every other, although it is at the same time typical. A more charming and agreeable picture of Virginia life just before the Civil War and at its outbreak has never appeared than that in the first half of this novel. The war scenes which follow bring the tragic side of life into prominence, and here too the note rings true; there is no cheap melodrama, no grandiloquence, no sentimentality. The events and people speak for themselves, and the author's knowledge of war conditions, although of necessity second hand, is intimate and thorough. At least half a dozen of the characters stand out as distinct human entities; Betty is a delightfully vivacious Virginian damsel; her lover Dan, despite one or two apparent discrepancies of character, is manly and true-hearted, while even better than these central actors are the irascible Major and his dame and the devoted slave Big Abel. In negro dialect, by the way, Miss Glasgow may rank with Mr. Page and Mr. Harris—and this is the highest praise possible. There is not a sign of sectional rancor about this book; it is cheerful, wholesome, and forceful.

William Morton Payne, "Recent Fiction," *Dial*, 32 (1 June 1902), 385

The Battle-Ground is the fourth novel of Miss Ellen Glasgow, and is much the best of the four. Indeed, it seems to us one of the best novels of the South during the period which precedes and includes the Civil War that has ever been written. The generous qualities and the amiable weaknesses that make the Virginia life of a generation ago so charming to us in the retrospect are pictured with sympathetic insight, and the horrors of internecine conflict are softened into pathetic outline by the art of the writer. The broad hospitality, the essential refinement, the semi-feudal social organization, and the high-minded idealism of the Old Dominion in ante-bellum days, are now vanished forever from our civilization, or exist in out-of-the-way regions as faint simulacra of a past that now seems as old as the Flood. We have organized our life upon a more rational basis, perhaps, but much has been lost that may never be regained, and one sometimes wonders if the change has been altogether for the better. This book might have been called *The Making of a Man*, for that is what provides its main interest, and we care more for the development of the hero's character under the stress of sternly adverse circumstance than we do for the picturesque accessories of the narrative. The war itself is excellently done, but even more excellent is the art with which its reactions upon the several leading characters are set forth. Such books as this help us to respect the Southern standpoint, and help also to wipe away the last lingering traces of Northern resentment.

"American Fiction," London *Sunday Times*, 8 June 1902, p. 2

Today we get here almost as much American fiction as English, fiction which follows, perhaps, a pronounced school of its own. That is to say, the best American fiction is, for the moment, more or less of one type, while in England our best writers are known each by his own style. In *The Battle-Ground* Miss Ellen Glasgow gives an exceedingly good example of the story which most often comes to us from America, one which tells of the doings of brave men and fair women, of hasty tempers and warm-hearted repentance, of stately hospitality and contented slaves. The time is the War of Secession, and the scene is Virginia. There is something generous and happy in the pictures of Uplands and Chericoke, the homes of the two families who supply heroes and heroines for the romance, and they tend to make more visible the justification of the view of those who upheld slavery. Major and Mrs. Lightfoot are splendid pictures of sturdy, high-bred, self-willed people, and it is little to be wondered at that their daughter, forbidden her lover, runs away with him, or that the grandson, coming of so quick-tempered and generous a stock, quarrels with his grandfather. The courteous, refined Governor Ambler is also a pleasant picture; indeed, his whole household is like a painting on porcelain. Mrs. Ambler is so sweet and dainty, the aunts so fragile, such delicate pictures in their "filmy ruffles" and laces, and Virginia and Betty such beauties, the former with her dove-like eyes and pretty manners, and the latter with her sunny aureole of hair and beautiful smile, that the feeling it all awakens is of decided unreality. This is the fault of the book; that, apart from Betty and Mrs. Lightfoot, the women are but delicately-tinted pictures very pleasant to look at, but far more rare than the author allows. However, the story is packed with incident, will raise both smiles and tears, and is thoroughly interesting.

Spectator [England], 88 (14 June 1902), 922

Miss Glasgow in her new novel follows her previous plan of introducing us to hero and heroine during their childhood. This time, however, the beginning of the book does not lag so much as it did in *The Voice of the People*, and though the second half is again immeasurably superior to the first, the reader is sufficiently interested by the picturesque charm with which he is entertained before the real action of the book begins. Virginia is again the scene of the novel, and the tragedy of the Southern side of the war is its subject. War is always tragic, and little as we sympathise with the spirit of the South, it is impossible to help pitying her sorrows. The picture of war drawn by the author would be remarkable in any case, and is especially so as coming from a woman's pen. We are all familiar at this moment with graphic pictures of warfare, and it is curious to note how accurately Miss Glasgow has caught the dominant note of weariness so characteristic of modern campaigns. In spite of the difference of weapons and "technique" between the American War and our Boer War, in reading Miss Glasgow's book it is the likeness both in spirit and in deed which strikes one. Both were fights *à outrance*, and in both cases the higher ideal won. In both cases the winning side was fighting for liberty, and again in both cases it was not its own liberty which was in question. Perhaps had the plot hatched only the other day in Pretoria remained undiscovered, the most tragic scene of all might have had its terrible counterpart. Miss Glasgow has again been most successful in her portrait of her heroine. Betty is a charming creature. She is delightful in all her moods, from her childhood, when on her sister taking the brownest "waffle" while she is saying grace she bursts out, "Well, the Lord oughtn't to have let her take it just as I was thanking Him for it," up to the time when, grown to womanhood, she keeps her home from utter ruin by her exertions. Altogether this is a book which should not be missed, though people who dislike a minutely realistic account of the horrors of war may find it a little too much for their nerves.

Academy and Literature, 63 (28 June 1902), 14

The war between North and South is not an original subject for a novel. In *The Battle-Ground*, however, it is treated so freshly as to make us forget how often we have had to read about it before. The hero, for one thing, is not an abolitionist who loves the daughter of a slave-owner; nor are our sympathies ranged, as a matter of course, on the side of the slaves. Indeed, there is a wholesome impartiality about the book which is generally absent from this sort of story, and which perhaps owes its existence to the author's sense of humour. One of the best instances of this humour occurs in a delightful conversation between a faithful old nigger and his master, who has just been thrown into a frenzy by the remarks of an abolitionist neighbour:—

> "They say I've no right to you, Congo,—bless my soul, and you were born on my own land!" "Go 'way, Ole Marster, who gwine min' w'at dey say?" returned Congo soothingly.... The Major wiped his eyes on the end of the neckerchief as he tied it about his throat. "But if they elect their President, he may send down an army to free you," he went on, with something like a sob of anger.... "Lawd, Lawd, sah," said Congo, ... "Did you ever heah tell er sech doin's! ...

Don' you min', Ole Marster, we'll des loose de dawgs on 'em, dat's w'at we'll do!"

A writer who can infuse humour into the slave question certainly deserves our gratitude; but Miss Glasgow does not keep hers only for politics. It is absent from hardly a page of the first part of the book, which deals with the childhood of most of the characters in it; and it is always the right sort of humour—the kind that never lets us forget the pathos that is lurking beneath, even when we are reading of the little girl who "hates boys" and yet resents being made to "sit against the wall" at a party, while her pretty sister is dancing. Her Uncle Bill dries her tears for her with an unexpected offer of fifty cents:—

"I reckon fifty cents will make up for any boy, eh?" Betty lay still and looked up from the floor, "I—I reckon a dollar m-i-g-h-t," she gasped.

But humour is not the only quality to be found in *The Battle-Ground*. There is excellent character-drawing, plenty of genuine human feeling, and a really fine description of a battle. The story itself rattles along without halting and is well worth reading to the end.

Athenæum [England], 1 (28 June 1902), 812

Upon the cover of this well-upholstered volume (it contains over five hundred closely printed pages) a young woman with hair of the favoured ruddy shade looks out at one from a sort of medallion, which rather suggests the scrap-album. Within, however, one finds no traces of scissors and paste, but an adequately drawn picture of life in old Virginia at the time of the war of secession. Needless to say, Ellen Glasgow writes on the side—if not of the angels—of the cavaliers and romance, of the slave-holding aristocracy of the South. But she is not at all concerned with special pleading or argument, but simply with the affairs of a very charming group of wealthy Virginians, for whom the holding of slaves was an ordinance of nature, and the war a long, sad tale of destruction, outrage, and calamity. The second half of the story deals exclusively with the war, and is reminiscent of the late Stephen Crane's vividly impressionistic work. For us, fresh from the sounds of rejoicing over the declaration of peace in South Africa, there is peculiar interest in a narrative dealing as realistically as this with the horrors of a campaign waged in open field and wood, hill and valley, through weary months and years. There are chapters, too, which have a Dickensian charm in their description of old-time Virginian festivities, and over the whole lies a glamour of real romance. A very creditable piece of work, this novel lacks only the creative originality which belongs to greatness.

"A Fine Novel," *British Weekly*, 10 July 1902, p. 300

The Battle-Ground is Virginia, the lovely and well-loved State in which so many homesteads rich in memories were devastated by the American civil war. The choice of this title seems to indicate that the author has found the chief interest of her story in that most calamitous period. And the campaigns, as seen from the private's point of view, with all their blood, rags, and starvation, were probably never better described. It is not the crash of contending armies, not the numberless deeds of gallantry daily performed, on which the gaze is here fixed, but the long-drawn suffering and long-defered hope of those who confidently followed Lee and Jackson through years of hunger, disease, and wounds. The picture is one to make the heart wildly beat, and at times stand still; and ever out of all the pandemonium spring the inalienable virtues of man and woman—endurance, self-sacrifice, courage, love. Wonderfully coloured as this picture is, it is the beauty of the old Virginian breed, that marvelous fineness and nobility of spirit, coupled with physical beauty and perfectness of courtesy, which shows the Anglo-Saxon at his and her very best. It is this that forms the charm of the book. Let it be understood that this is no ordinary novel to read and throw away with the hours spent on it, but a book full of beauty, tenderness, pathos, and humour: a book which produces an atmosphere which it is life to breathe, and which inevitably draws us back to it to enjoy its purity again, and which introduces us to a heroine that more than satisfies the expectation produced by the exquisite face that invites us from the outside cover.

"Notes on New Novels," *Illustrated London News*, 12 July 1902, p. 64

Miss Ellen Glasgow's new story, *The Battle-Ground*, is stirring in every sense of the word, and likely to be popular. The cheap cynicism and the laboured epigram which disfigure so much promising work nowadays find no place in her pages: Miss Glasgow's grasp of character and her sane and wholesome way of looking at life lead her safely past these pitfalls. Her story is of Virginia in the troublous days preceding the abolition of slavery, and Miss Glasgow is not so much concerned to discriminate between abstract right and wrong, represented by North and South, as to present a faithful picture of the situation as it affected the characters in her story, and in this, doubtless, she has done wisely. To many persons, of whom the present writer is one, negro dialect is a stumbling-block and a hindrance to the full enjoyment of any book. The story under notice is no exception; but it is only just to add that when the phonetic eccentricities have been patiently mastered, one is rewarded on occasion by examples of shrewd and pawky humour. We do not intend to tell Miss Glasgow's story, but we may add that, contrary to custom, her hero is on the losing side, and comes back to Betty without laurels of any kind; and yet he is, in truth, a conqueror, and those who would read the riddle should also read Miss Glasgow's fine story.

Critic, n.s. 41 (September 1902), 279

Evidently, Miss Glasgow is still experimenting with an interesting talent, whose early manifestations were brilliantly disturbing. *The Battle-Ground* is a story of the South before and during the war. It contains some very pretty pictures of life in old Virginia homes; two sweet heroines, one of whom is strong as well, and some delightful gentlemen of the old school. But in achieving restraint and sanity, the author has lost the brilliance of manner and the vividness of phrase that made her work most attractive and promising in spite of its obvious faults. Her early books were visualized with almost startling distinctness, and left on the reader's mind a definite and deeply-etched picture. In the present volume the edge of the etching-tool seems blunted. The book is simply a war-time story, like many others. In spite of its subject it does not "take hold."

Checklist of Additional Reviews

Book Buyer, series 3, 24 (May 1902), 318.

Hamilton W. Mabie, "A Charming Virginia Novel," *Ladies' Home Journal*, 19 (June 1902), 17.

"Notes on Novels," *Academy and Literature*, 63 (7 June 1902), 574.

"Two Romances of the South," *Literary Digest*, 24 (14 June 1902), 815–16.

Saturday Review [London], 19 July 1902, 91.

"Six Months of American Literature," *Saturday Review* [London], 94 (3 August 1902), 274.

THE FREEMAN AND OTHER POEMS

THE FREEMAN
AND OTHER POEMS
BY
ELLEN GLASGOW

NEW YORK
DOUBLEDAY, PAGE & CO.
MCMII

"Ellen Glasgow's Poems," Boston *Evening Transcript*, 10 September 1902, p. 12

Some of the poems contributed by Ellen Glasgow to the *Atlantic Monthly* and other magazines have been made into a book by Doubleday, Page & Co. It is printed at the De Vinne Press, is bound in board covers with paper label, and bears for title *The Freeman and Other Poems*. Miss Glasgow's work as poet really preceded her labors as novelist, and the poems in this little volume exhibit not a little of the imagination and vigor of thought which have made *The Voice of the People* and *The Battle-Ground* distinctive among fiction of its kind. Miss Glasgow's thoughts as expressed in verse dwell frequently and strongly upon ethical problems, upon the relations of man to man, upon human justice, and it is fortunate that she has the facility to turn these subjects into verse which is both genuine poetry and sterling truth. Her satiric powers and a grim humor more than once illumine what would otherwise be dark and disagreeable. In the brief compass of eight lines, she thus characterizes fame:

In life he lived among them and they cast
   Him stones for bread.
He that was mightiest of them all had not
   Whereon to lay his head.

In death, where flaming poppies fired
   the dust,
They brought a laurel wreath:
Honour to ashes on the coffin lid!
   Fame to the skull beneath!

Upon other themes more near to our daily life Miss Glasgow writes with equal force and like temperamental vigor. The following is a poem entitled "Reunion":

Ah, hold me fast! What of the day?
   I care not if the sun be dead,
Nor if the stars be gold or gray.
   Nay, though the rising moon be red,
     Our dawn is here, our night is past,
     The world may fade—but hold me
       here!

Ah, hold me fast! What of the years?
   I care not if our youth be fled.
Nor that our drink be blood and tears,
   And bitterness our daily bread.
   Nay, though the flames of hell be
     cast—
   They light thy face—ah, hold me
     fast!

The poems in Miss Glasgow's little volume are few in number, yet they are of exceptional importance. Each one of them is filled with meaning, and they express moods which find their reflection in the mind of the reader. They are, in short, genuine poetry.

"Some Recent Verse," *New York Times Saturday Review of Books and Art*, 20 September 1902, p. 639

Ellen Glasgow's thin volume of verse, printed by the De Vinne Press, comes robed in elegant simplicity; or, one might almost say, in Quaker splendor. A single poem, no better nor longer than the others, gives the book its title, while its bold, black type seems grateful and inviting to the eye. In this cool and sober grayness we should suspect that serious thinking, at least, with fluent art, might find its fit environment. And, what is noticeable in these poems is their virile, and militant, though somewhat sombre strain. In some of the lyrics there are thoughts plain spoken and daring, making a truly vigorous "criticism of life." A stringent message inspires them all, and in the following is a pleasingly recorded possible experience:

Love has passed along the way—
   Lo! the doors have opened wide,
Hands have beckoned him to stay,
   Hearts have fluttered to his side.
Let him loiter as he may,
Love has passed along the way.

Ah, what means the vacant room?
   Ashes where the flames were red?
What the shudder in the gloom?
   What the corpse upon the bed?
Break my heart as best it may,
Love has passed along the way.

A particularly even merit is a characteristic of these poems, so that quotation cannot be made on any sharp line of preference. A certain sureness of touch, however, will perhaps be illustrated by this soliloquy of "The Mountain Pine":

Around me in the void of night there
   moves
   The struggle of uncreate worlds to be,
The stars are not the stars, I hear afar
   The planets' minstrelsy.

For me there is no time, no space, no
   depth,
   No love, no hate, no passionate
     despair.
I face my destiny—to what has been
   And will be, I am heir.

The vulture sails below me, and across
   Immeasurable spaces tempests roll.
Decay cannot unmake me, I am part
   Of an eternal whole.

Nation, 75 (9 October 1902), 290

The tendency to exuberance and cheap tragical utterance which has been so long charged upon the poets of our Southern States—a more prolonged prevalence of the Byronic fever—finds full expression in the thin volume, *The Freeman and Other Poems,* by Ellen (Anderson Gholson) Glasgow. Some of the prose writings of this young author, especially some with a philanthropic aim, have shown so much more maturity of judgment as to make it a pity that her fifty pages of verse, full of flashes of power, should be almost wholly painful, even to ghastliness, and should seem to be mainly based on the theory attributed to the Deity at the close of one of the most tragic of them, "The Earth is Hell." For this reason we prefer to choose one of the briefest and certainly the calmest among them (p. 18):

COWARD MEMORY

A street half flecked with shade and
   sun,
   A last year's leaf along it blown,
A gray wall where green lichens run;
   Like water falling on dry stone,
A robin's ripe notes dropping one by
   one.

Sad sun and shade and sadness over all
   The distance blended into solemn hues,
On the warm air suspended as a pall
   The sweetness dying violets diffuse,
While from a single tree the ashen elm-
   flowers fall.

At the street's sudden end a shining
   square,
   The sunny threshold of an open door,

Thick with the dust of an untrodden
   stair
That leads beyond me to the upper
   floor—
Then memory halts—it dares not enter
   there.

"Miss Glasgow's Novels and Poems," *World's Work*, 5 (November 1902), 2791–2

Miss Glasgow's latest book is a volume of verse, *The Freeman and Other Poems*; a slender book, but individual in thought and expression. Most of these poems are in the mood of her earlier work. They present some of the darker aspects of life, and present them with daring and vigor. There is an almost uncompromising effort to face the worst and to interpret it with relentless frankness and with a fine philosophic courage. Whether this attitude represents a mood or a conviction—perhaps both—it is certain that in this book, as in her prose, there is freedom from the commonplace and an original power. Observe the quality of the following:

The trumpet of the Judgment shook the
   night,
   Dust quickened and was flesh; grave
      clothes were shed;
With moaning of strong travail and
   lament,
   The sea gave up her dead.

One, rising from a rotting tomb, beheld
   The heavens unfold beneath Jehovah's
      breath.
"Great God," he cried, "with Thine
   eternity,
   Couldst Thou not leave me Death?"

"Poems by Ellen Glasgow," Boston *Evening Transcript*, 22 December 1902, p. 10

... Doubtless "The Freeman" and the little volume which takes its name from Miss Glasgow's first poem, might have fallen as still-born from the press as Francis Thompson's intricately wrought and delicate songs or Henley's strong, impassioned protests, had the volume not been signed by the name of a well-known novelist. Miss Glasgow's first two novels showed her a clever and virile psychologist; her second two novels, *The Voice of the People* and *The Battle-Ground*, proved her a faithful historian and acute observer.

Close upon the heels of *The Battle-Ground*, Messrs. Doubleday, Page & Co. brought out Miss Glasgow's volume of verse. The volume is small but has all the external attractions of hand-made paper, the exquisite type of the De Vinne press and very artistic binding. It is strange to be able to say of any volume of verse that not a poem in it is commonplace and but one is reminiscent. The general tone and atmosphere is one more widely felt and understood today, than ever before, since Nietzsche has become the exponent of the *Uebermensch*. It is the utterance of the man who above all virtues prizes courage and who has the courage of his faith, his acts, aye, even his sins; who stands before his Creator giving account of himself and demanding an account in return; who holds himself above Fate itself.

Then he stood up and trod to dust
Fear and desire, mistrust and trust,
   And dreams of bitter sleep and sweet
   And bound for sandals on his feet
Knowledge and patience of what must
   And what things may be, in the heat

And cold of years that rot and rust
    And alter; and his spirit's meat
Was freedom, and his staff was wrought
    Of strength and his cloak woven of
        thought.

This is the same man whom Nietzsche called Zarathustra and of whom Henley said he is the master of his fate, the captain of his soul. He speaks throughout Miss Glasgow's volume:

Let me but learn to smile—
    Let me face lightly any blow that falls;
Bear bravely with my bondage all the
        while
    And hug my freedom within prison
        walls.

Thus when the end draws near,
    With lifted head, let me the potion
        quaff.
And so—as one who never learned to
        fear—
    Pass on to meet thy judgment with a
        laugh.

"The Freeman," which appeared first in the *Atlantic Monthly*, strikes the same note:

The clankless chains that bound me I
        have rent;
    No more a slave to hope I cringe or
        cry;
Captives to fate, men rear their prison
        walls
    But free am I.

I tread where arrows press upon my
        path.
    I smile to see the danger and the dart;
My breast is bared to meet the slings of
        hate,
    But not my heart.

I face the thunder and I face the rain,
    I lift my head, defiance far I fling—
My feet are set; I face the autumn as
    I face the spring.

But perhaps the most keen and cutting, as well as final utterance of this mood is given in "The True Comedian," concise enough to be given in full:

What if the road is rough, the dart
    Of mischance levelled at thy breast?
Beyond the shudder and the smart
    Canst thou not see the jest?

What if the arrow in the sling
    Was tipped with poison ere it flew?
Since thine the heart and thine the sting,
    Be thine the laughter, too.

Canst thou not read the wit that lies
    Beneath the bold burlesque of fate?
Or art thou sick of parodies
    Who playest with love and hate?

What, take the stage again and grasp
    The comedy of self-control?
Nay, better stand aside to grasp
    The humour of the whole.

Oddly enough, though the volume is a woman's and a very young woman's, the theme of love may be said to have been not touched upon at all. To be sure one poem is called "Love Has Passed Along the Way," but the theme is sorrow, not love and "The Suppliant" and "Reunion" are addressed in both cases to the great Creator of all, demanding compensation for this "sorry scheme of things entire."

Sympathy with all forms of half development and inefficiency, with all victims of injustice and cruelty, nature's no less than man's finds powerful expression in the poems entitled: "Aridity," "Justice," "Fame," "A Vision of Hell," and "To my Dog." A great yearning for the Sage's tolerance and gentleness and revolt from the dire and futile worry of the Western nations comes out in "The Sage," "The

Mountain Pine," "To a Strange God," and "A Creed."

In truth that falsehood cannot span,
  In the majestic march of laws
That weed and flower and worm and man
    Result from one Supernal Cause,
In doubts that dare and faiths that cleave,
      Lord, I believe.

One cannot turn from these poems without attempting to convey some impression of Miss Glasgow's masterly handling of the uncanny. "The Shadow" and "Death-in-Life" have the very thrill and shudder of Poe, but perhaps even more mystically suggestive and alarming than any of the others is "Coward Memory."

A street half flecked with shade and sun,
  A last year's leaf along it blown,
A grey wall where green lichens run;
  Like water falling on dry stone,
A robin's ripe notes dropping, one by one.

Sad sun and shade and sadness over all,
  The distance blended into solemn hues,
On the warm air suspended as a pall
  The sweetness dying violets diffuse,
While from a single tree the ashen elm flowers fall.

At a street's sudden end a shining square,
  The sunny threshold of an open door,
Thick with the dust of an untrodden stair
  That leads beyond me to the upper floor—
Then memory halts—it dares not enter there.

The whole volume is one to note not only as a subjective utterance of a very objective novelist but as a powerful and fine expression of a widely spread and markedly modern trend of thought.

Critic, 42 (January 1903), 89

The seriousness, the definiteness, the austerity, the intensity that characterize Miss Glasgow's novels are likewise noticeable in her verse, and while there may be a lack of flexibility and melody there is no lack of power. We have been particularly impressed by the two poems "Resurrection" and "Justice."

Checklist of Additional Reviews

Book Buyer, 25 (December 1902), 430-1.
Chicago *Record-Herald*, 28 November 1903, p. 9.

THE DELIVERANCE

The Deliverance

ELLEN GLASGOW
A Romance of the Virginia Tobacco Fields·
With Illustrations by
Frank E Schoonover

New York
Doubleday Page & Co
1904

"Miss Glasgow's New Book," Louisville *Courier-Journal*, 16 January 1904, sec. 1, p. 5

The usual quiet after the fall output of notable books has at last been broken. Like a great thunder storm on a peaceful summer day comes Miss Glasgow's *The Deliverance*, mighty in proportion, great in promise, magnificent in the fulfillment. Several years ago *The Voice of the People* and *The Battle-Ground* predicted better things to follow, and better things have followed. *The Deliverance* is a story of the tobacco fields of Virginia twenty years after the war. The reader at once feels grateful that the time is not during the war. Christopher Blake is the hero; by birth a gentleman, by fate a toiler in the tobacco fields. Several years before the story opens he is robbed of his birthright by his father's former overseer, Fletcher, who is now owner of Blake Hall. Within sight of his ancestral home, Christopher lives on a miserable patch of land with his sisters, his uncle and blind mother.

This mother, a belle and beauty of her day, is one of the most original characters in fiction. By her children's love she is shielded from every sorrow. Her blindness enables them to deceive her absolutely. She is still mistress of Blake Hall, still mistress of 400 slaves. She knows nothing of the poverty, her children's daily fight. In her world there is no hatred, no ruined young lives, no wrong. Miss Glasgow treats this unusual situation with a quiet dignity that makes the tragedy more intense. But in Christopher's world, hatred of Fletcher and an ever burning desire for revenge are the ruling passions.

By deliberately ruining Fletcher's grandson he gets revenge; by loving Fletcher's granddaughter he learns remorse. Through love the animal becomes a man, the man a hero. The climax is thrilling and unexpected.

Maria Fletcher is an admirable heroine, commanding at once pity and affection. The reader finds it hard to understand her ready forgiveness when her lover tells of his deliberate ruin of her only brother. Could any woman at once understand such an injury done an innocent child, flesh of her flesh, blood of her blood? That is the question. Miss Glasgow's treatment according to her views is broad and noble, but is it true to life?

The Deliverance is one of the finest pieces of fiction from a woman's pen published in many a day. Original in plot and conception, strong in its powerful characterizations, wonderful in its sustained interest, its tragedy, its spontaneous bits of humor, it is undoubtedly a book which should have everlasting life. The colored illustrations are by Schoonover.

"Miss Glasgow's New Book, *The Deliverance*, Is One of Her Best Productions and Will Be Popular," Richmond *Times-Dispatch*, 17 January 1904, p. 6

Readers of Miss Glasgow's latest book will be impressed, first of all, by the sincerity of the work she has done in it. She has made use of no adventitious aids in her localization or her characterization. The scene of her novel is laid in a rural

Virginia neighborhood, remote from the comparative bustle and stir of Virginia city life. Its advantages and disadvantages are dealt with most impartially and yet—so faithfully and fully have the flavor and color of Virginia localism, provincialism, narrowness, caste ideas, prejudices, traditions, standards of honor or call them all by any other name at will, been infused into its pages, that an almost perfect piece of realism is the result.

Especially in regard to the Virginia tobacco field does Miss Glasgow prove her literary methods to be most careful and accurate. The history of the cultivation and the dissemination of the weed is the history of the State since the days when tobacco grew strong and tall in the streets of Jamestown, down to the present. Miss Glasgow might have her interest in the great staple by heredity, for one can look up from what she writes and almost breathe the pungent odor which is borne on the August breezes from the yellowing green growth of the tobacco planter's domain. In all stages of the crop on which she had based her romance, from its planting to its curing, she displays a knowledge of detail and minutiæ, which one is persuaded must come from personal knowledge and observation. . . .

The Deliverance is begun, continued and almost ended in shadow. Not until the very last does the cloud lift and a glimpse of happiness, like sunshine, illumine the atmosphere. For Miss Glasgow has not compromised or extenuated or bent circumstances to her liking, or thrown over them the rosy glamour of imagination. Life, and strong life at that, life strong enough to break down and oversway the tyranny of the old and to fulfill the mission of the new, stirs the leaves of a book, which because of the freedom given as the meed of a great love is called *The Deliverance.*

"Books of the Day," Boston *Evening Transcript*, 20 January 1904, p. 16

It is no small undertaking to write such a novel as *The Deliverance*, and it is therefore with more than ordinary pleasure that we are able to give Miss Glasgow the highest praise for so remarkable a literary achievement. The story is artistically conceived and eloquently narrated, its plot and its characters, its scenes and its dramatic episodes being vivid and faithful transcripts from life itself. Its hero is the heir to a great Virginia estate, which, through the misfortunes of the Civil War and the ill luck of bad management, has fallen into the hands of its former overseer. Its heroine is the granddaughter of that vulgar and newly-rich planter, popularly known throughout the surrounding country as Bill Fletcher, and it is through her influence and his love for her that the hero finally works out his deliverance from the spirit of vengeance against the Fletchers, which for years has dominated his entire life. Purposely dragging Fletcher's idolized grandson down into the mire, his revenge finally recoils upon his own head when the planter is murdered in a fit of momentary passion by the whiskey-sodden youth. In years gone by this would have seemed to Christopher Blake a fitting culmination to his carefully prepared scheme of vengeance, but the spirit of Maria Fletcher had gained such control over him that he shielded the lad, took the curse upon his own shoulders and suffered the term of imprisonment awarded by the law. This story is told with an unusual comprehensiveness of view and exceptional dramatic power, its author's ability being especially shown in the acute sense of proportion which enables her to disregard unessential details and to concentrate her attention upon the things which make for the development of Christopher Blake's character.

But *The Deliverance* is not altogether sombre. In fact, it is thoroughly rich in genuine humor of the most pungent sort. The hero's mother, a doughty old lady who possesses an indomitable spirit in spite of decrepitude and blindness, is kept in ignorance of the fall in the family fortunes, and she lives in the past with a cheery wisdom and a practical worldliness which is infectious. "I have never slouched in my life," she remarked, "and I do not care to fall into the habit in my seventieth year. When my last hour comes, I hope, at least, to meet my God in the attitude becoming a lady, and in my day it would have been considered the height of impropriety to loll in a chair or even to rock in the presence of gentlemen. Your Great-aunt Susannah, one of the most modest women of her time, has often told me that once, having unfortunately crossed her knees in the parlor, after supper, she suffered untold tortures from 'budges' for three mortal hours, rather than to be seen to do anything so indelicate as to uncross them. Well, Well! ladies were ladies in those days, and now Lila tells me it is quite customary for them to sit like men. My blindness has spared me many painful sights, I haven't a doubt."

Humor of this sort is both frequent and natural throughout the pages of *The Deliverance*, and in it as well as in the entire story itself, Miss Glasgow makes it plain that she has studied deep into the inmost secrets of human nature. Once in a while she lets her pen run away with her thoughts, especially in the emphasis which she is constantly placing upon her hero's manly figure and upon her heroine's exquisitely feminine beauty. When she says that "bewildered, flushed, and trembling," the beautiful Maria lay upon the breast of the gigantic Christopher, "while their lips clung together," the reader may be able to recall many a similar scene in the pages of more than one sensational novel. These, however, are minor flaws. The picture of life among the tobacco fields of Virginia affords a fitting background to the story, but neither its time nor its place is in any wise essential. It is a story of world-wide motive and emotion, and its scenes might be laid with equal truth among the hills of New England. In that case, it might lose a little of its picturesqueness, especially to those readers to whom the plantations of Virginia are strange and interesting ground, but it would lose not a whit of its dramatic power and its clear-sighted truth. This indeed, is Miss Glasgow's greatest achievement in the writing of *The Deliverance*.

Mrs. M. Gordon Pryor Rice, "First Novel of 1904: *The Deliverance*, Ellen Glasgow's Story of the Virginia Tobacco Fields," *New York Times Saturday Review of Books*, 23 January 1904, pp. 49–50

Like Mr. Allen's story of the hemp fields of Kentucky [*The Reign of Law*: *A Tale of the Kentucky Hemp Fields*], and Mr. Norris's unfinished trilogy of the wheat [including *The Octopus* and *The Pit*], Miss Glasgow's romance is pervaded by the influence of a plant—that mysterious weed of good and evil which, according to

Indian legend, sprang from the touch of the Great Spirit upon the answering earth. The tobacco crop is an insistent factor in a tale of intense human interest, a tale sombre and strong, but with beams of delightful humor shining everywhere through the clouds, and closing with the lift and irradiation of the great Deliverance.

A novel's chief end is to be interesting, and this end *The Deliverance* perfectly fulfills. Every one of its generous allowance of pages holds the reader with an ever tightening grip, and it leaves him full of eager inward questioning in regard to that fateful "Day After," which our fiction so seldom permits us to see. We forget that we are reading a book; the people have taken possession of us. With an anguish of suspense we follow the drama of a soul, and watch the powers of good and evil as they struggle for dominion over it. These are early days for calm criticism— it has all been too vital, too real. We cannot yet, "see the wood for the trees"; we cannot hold the book at arm's length and view it in proper perspective.

Perhaps because we are a little ashamed of our obsession we are glad to carp at a few circumstances of the plot that give pause to our credulity. We cannot think otherwise than that the fair world of illusion created for the sightless woman would have crumbled at a touch many years before the two decades of tender deception were rounded. The web of fancy spun by Dickens' little toymaker for his blind daughter seemed always one of Dickens' sentimental impossibilities, but it was as nothing compared with the unreal world in the midst of which Mrs. Blake sat, blind and motionless, for not only were all the facts of her environment imaginary, but history itself was invented for her behoof....

[...]

But though we find thus much of fault with the construction of the plot, from first to last the handling is masterly. Nothing is fumbled, nothing blurred. All is coherent, firm, spacious. The characters are alive to their finger tips. Whether simple, tender, humorous, or fierce, the dialogue is always natural, always in keeping with the speakers, never infected with the microbe of mere cleverness. There is a delightful play of humor, but nobody hurls epigrams or scintillates; yet few novels can furnish a longer array of pregnant sayings, racy, wise, ethically inspiring.

[...]

"I do not want to write literature; I want to write life," declared Frank Norris. In *The Deliverance* Miss Glasgow has written both, though, to her praise be it said, we almost forget the literature in the absorbing interest of the life, the unerring artistry of word and phrase in the truth of the "human document." It is a book of large vision, of wide horizons; one worthy to be held high above the rushing torrent of "popular fiction" that so soon plunges into oblivion.

"A New Field in Southern Fiction," New York *Post*, 23 January 1904, p. 7

[...]

Considered simply as a story, the book is delightfully interesting, and it contains more distinct systems of philosophy than ever appeared before in a Southern novel. Each character is a commentator on affairs in general from his point of view. The resignation gospel of the old soldier, Tucker Corbin, stretches across the horizon of the tale like the evening afterglow of a fierce summer day. The ethics of class and caste, expounded with a grand dame's unscrupulous wit by Madam Blake, swing airily like rich faded tapestries in manners. Even the little barnyard henwomen of the lower class peck virtuously at the riddle, with smart, cackling phrases, and every man upon the scene finds time to deliver his scriptures upon marriage, and his conjectures upon the greatest of all uncertainties—woman.

But the central figure in the book is that of young Christopher Blake. With the temperament and tastes of a reckless, and somewhat profligate ancestry, he is driven by poverty into the tobacco fields at the age of ten, and kept there until the struggle with alien forces awakens in him a sense of resentment and humiliation. Men whose fathers own slaves and ride horseback are never on intimate terms of agricultural friendship with nature. From being the roadway beneath their feet, the earth becomes the fickle mistress of their fortunes, and they resent her inanimate tyranny. Thus, Christopher Blake declared his antagonism to the earth and his hatred of Fletcher, while honor compelled him to serve both. He had a Promethean rage against fate that made the language of his heart a sort of eloquent blasphemy.

But having bound him in mutinous slavery to the situation, the author makes a significant distinction between what a man thinks and what he is. Christopher is not consumed by his evil passions, nor in the end brutalized, as one might expect. He outgrows defeat, survives shame, and steadies himself on the edge of crime with a supreme renunciation. It is the battle courage of the cavalier changed to moral energy.

One other feature of this excellent book claims attention. Every novel has its occupation, its pastime. In the historical romance, it is duelling; in the society novel, it is the making of a scandal; as in every tale of peaceful English life it is the drinking of tea. Before this time, in every Virginia story, it has been horseback riding, but in *The Deliverance* it is the farming of tobacco. This is a new departure in Southern fiction. Much has been written in a sentimental way about the cotton and tobacco plantations, but until now neither the one nor the other has been dramatized as Frank Norris dramatized the Western wheat plains. Now Miss Glasgow has caught the keynote of the earth's surrender and the green spirit of life that leaps from her bosom challenges the imagination.

Baltimore *Sun*, 28 January 1904, p. 8

This is one of the strongest novels of the recent months. It is a work of which its author may well be proud, for in it she has surpassed her former successes. In character drawing she has given us evidence of a master hand, and in the incidents of the story she has with abundant and faithful local color drawn for us types of Southern life. They have never before been so skillfully depicted. Here we have a novel of the South that holds up the mirror to nature in a manner to call forth the highest praise. It does so in such wise that the Southerner cannot take exception to some of the harsh lines of its pictures nor the Northerner fret at imputations he by nature resents. In fact, speaking of the man of the North, he is not in the novel. We are freed—Praise the Lord—from the eternal lover from the North who wins the Southern girl against her principles and prejudices. We are freed—praise the Lord—from the eternal "It might have been," and we are given pictures of the Southerners and of the South without foreign admixture and without appeal to sectional prejudice. The story is of the latter days of Reconstruction. It is of the days when the people who had been ruined by the War saw their homes and their lands in the possession of those who a few years before had been enemies or servants. The story is concerned with the fortunes of the Blakes and the Fletchers. The Blakes, for three centuries lords of the soil, and the Fletchers, for a score of years their servants and the head of the Fletchers their overseer.... *The Deliverance* will stand as one of the best novels upon Southern life and *the* novel of the tobacco country. If we mistake not it will be regarded as one of the best books of the present year, and this without regard to the scene of its story or of the time in which it is laid.

Eleanor Hoyt, "Ellen Glasgow Again," *Lamp*, 28 (February 1904), 70

The Deliverance, Ellen Glasgow's new novel, deserves first place among the January novels, and would win consideration in any month of the year. Miss Glasgow gained recognition with her first novel; and, with each subsequent book, has made a distinct step forward. She is one of the young women who write, not because they have nothing else to do, but because they have something to say, and she says the something with decided force and brilliancy. Her work is full of flaws, open to criticism, but it is never commonplace, never lacking in originality and power.

This is true of *The Deliverance*, as of the novels that preceded it, but there will be many to claim that here Miss Glasgow has failed to forge ahead, that the new book does not surpass, does not even equal, *The Battle-Ground* in matter and technique.

It is a story of hate and love and class prejudice, in the tobacco district of Virginia, and the hate motif is handled with power and dramatic effect. It is grim, convincing, throbbing with real feeling; but with the introduction of the love motif the story loosens its grip. One can hardly blame the author. Anticlimax was perhaps inevitable, and the love story is cleverly worked out, but the fact remains that the last half of the book has not the absorbing interest of the first half, is, in a measure, disappointing.

Miss Glasgow has drawn a number of the characters with unerring and logical skill, has set shrewd humor beside her pathos and her tragedy. Occasionally folk are dragged into the story by the heels in order to furnish this lighter element, and it is doubtful whether the vulgarity of Sol Peterkin or the morality of Mrs. Spade adds to the book. One feels that much matter included in the novel might have been omitted without loss, that there is non-essential repetition of theme, that various happenings are totally inconsequent. The twenty-year deception of Mrs. Blake staggers even willing credulity, as one thinks of the necessary changes in family life which even a blind invalid must have noted, of the separation from the old friends and intimates, of the social isolation of the family. The revelation made by Fletcher to the old lady, holding possibilities of vital tragedy, falls flat and trickles into inconsequence.

All of which but brings one back to the original proposition. It is easy to pick flaws in the work, to grumble about this chapter and that, but the novel is far above the ordinary and well worth the reading.

"A Moral Dénouement and Good Art," *Literary Digest*, 28 (6 February 1904), 187

Miss Glasgow has added another laurel to a chaplet already sufficient to satisfy an ambitious writer. She again demonstrates that she belongs to the new novelists of the South who blend somewhat of the tougher fiber of the North with the emollient charm of their own latitudes.

The Deliverance concerns itself with the evolution of a young Virginian, Christopher Blake. A wrong inflicted upon his family had sown in his mind as a boy of tender years a sense of injustice which ripened into vindictiveness that dominates his very life. What affected this ruling passion and what was its outcome is the theme Miss Glasgow handles here with masculine mastery and feminine sensibility. With unfaltering strength, that makes *The Deliverance* a substantial work of fiction, there are literary grace, striking invention, and individuality. More than this, there is excellent character-drawing. Mrs. Blake and Maria Fletcher, two strongly depicted personalities, lodge firmly in the memory....

There are two things especially to be remarked about this novel. As in two recent novels, Mrs. Wharton's *Sanctuary* and *Petronilla Heroven*, by Una L. Silberrad, both of which are exquisite literature, so in this vivid tale of Miss Glasgow there is a strong uplift in the morality enforced in working out the motif. This is notably remarkable in *Petronilla Heroven* and *The Deliverance*, because it is almost identical. There is the same passion for revenge in a strong and otherwise beautiful character, which, through the influence of another, is transformed into a more exalted feeling. It proves what should be an agreeable truth to sane and earnest minds: that the strength and color and interest of characters and of a story, so far from being diminished, may all be notably enhanced by having rectitude triumph over a fascinating passion which is wrong, despite its potent appeal to sympathy.

"A Story of Southern Hatred and Love," *New York Tribune Sunday Illustrated Supplement*, 7 February 1904, p. 12

The author of *The Deliverance* gives her reader a pleasant surprise. Here is a story of life in modern Virginia, and, be it said with deep appreciation, there is not a single battle scene in it. For sounds of war, for portraits of two gallant young fellows, one fighting for the North, the other for the South, and both adoring the same girl, we look as a matter of course. Forthwith Miss Glasgow proceeds to show that she is, after all, capable of rising above routine. We are really grateful to her, for of late years the "Southern romance" of the sort which we have just indicated has become something like a plague. Every novelist treating of the South in the 60's seems to have felt it incumbent upon him to babble sentimentally of fearful and wonderful "types of chivalry," of beautiful but strangely idiotic heroines, and of utterly priggish heroes. *The Deliverance* has been written along different lines. It is tinctured, to be sure, with a little of the old superstition. We are vouchsafed glimpses of certain Southern types which for the life of us we cannot find at all plausible. But the central situation is an altogether credible and interesting one. It implicates a broken-down family whose possessions have been acquired through fraud by a coarse scoundrel who formerly occupied a dependent position on the estate. The Blakes live in the humblest circumstances, while "Bill" Fletcher, their despoiler, lords it over their ancestral acres. The oldest member of the fallen clan is a blind and aged woman whose misfortunes are kept from her by her devoted children. One of the latter, Christopher Blake, is the hero of the tale, a huge young man whose good breeding has not saved him from the coarsening of nature that follows on long brooding over thoughts of revenge. Blake is resolved to "pay off" the debt of hatred that he owes to Fletcher, and the book is concerned chiefly with events that flow from his uncompromising attitude toward his enemy.

The story is admirably told. Miss Glasgow has realized some if not all of her characters; those which are of most importance in the action of the novel are clearly and consistently drawn. The fact is that the pale colors in which the subsidiary figures are sketched do not much matter. They cannot diminish our interest in young Blake and the Fletchers. The hero's rage comes to the surface on the slightest provocation, and while his behavior sometimes has a brutality about it, calculated to make the reader wince, it is made to seem, on the whole, very human. He sinks deeper and deeper into black moods, and allows himself to do unworthy things, but for these he atones in a fashion that may not be wholly convincing from an ethical point of view, but which indubitably serves to round out the narrative as the novel reader with a romantic turn of mind would want it to be rounded out.

Outlook, 76 (13 February 1904), 395–7

[. . .]

It is not difficult to find defects in Miss Glasgow's story; but there is so much power and promise, such passion and vitality, in it, that it is to be counted one of the real achievements in recent fiction; a novel singularly vivid in its picture of tragic social transition, singularly powerful in its frank, bold, vigorous handling of those phases of experience which a good many American novelists have evaded or failed to discern. Miss Glasgow has still something to learn as an artist, but she is very richly endowed with the qualities of the true novelist: feeling for life, the dramatic sense, the power and the courage of passion.

William Morton Payne, "Recent Fiction," *Dial*, 36 (16 February 1904), 118–19

Place aux dames! The most important books of fiction in our present selection are Mrs. Wharton's *Sanctuary* and Miss Glasgow's *The Deliverance*. Each of these novels is, in its own peculiar fashion, a masterpiece of conscientious workmanship, vivid in its portrayal of a half-tragic situation, and powerful in its appeal to our human sympathies. Aside from their common quality of successful performance, the two books stand far apart from one another. *Sanctuary* is no more than a novelette, hardly more than a short story, while *The Deliverance* is a full-grown work of fiction, spanning many years of suffering and unachieved purpose, and provided with a great multiplicity of incident and detail. But both are works of art in a highly satisfactory sense....

The Deliverance is the most important book thus far written by Miss Glasgow. It makes clear the fact that this novelist has "come to stay," and that her work may be expected to go on broadening and deepening with the years. The scene of the story is Virginia, and the period is that covered by the past quarter-century. Tobacco provides its harmony with a sort of *basso ostinato* very much as hemp performs a similar function in one of the novels of Mr. James Lane Allen. We are conscious of its presence everywhere as the groundwork of the structure, and made to realize that the entire scheme of life portrayed by the novelist rests upon that foundation. If this be a borrowing of Mr. Allen's idea, it is made quite legitimate by the original treatment it receives. More questionable, however, is the use of Malory at a certain point in the narrative, for Miss Glasgow takes the very passage introduced with such striking effect in *The Choir Invisible*, and turns it to exactly the same emotional effect. One feature of *The Deliverance* is ingeniously contrived, but remains absolutely unconvincing. Old Mrs. Blake has been blind since the middle of the Civil War, her family has lost its fortune, and moved from a colonial mansion to an humble cottage; yet through all these vicissitudes she has been made to believe that nothing is changed, that she still owns her hundreds of slaves, that the Confederacy has triumphed, and the South become a nation. This situation passes the bounds of all possible credulity, and, however tempting it was to the author, should not have been woven as it is into the very structure of her fabric. The love interest of the story is provided by Christopher Blake, the dispossessed inheritor of the plantation, and Maria Fletcher, the granddaughter of the rascal who has come into its ownership by fraud upon his former employer. The boy grows up to hate the Fletchers with all the passion of a strong and primitive nature; the girl grows up in ignorance alike of the history of her grandfather's fortune and of the feelings that rankle in the breast of the seeming peasant who is her neighbor. When they are first thrown together in their early adult years, each is instinctively attracted to the other, while assuming the mask of hatred or scorn. Not for many years is this instinctive feeling to ripen, and in the meanwhile Christopher goes on nursing his hate and planning revenge, while Maria contracts a loveless marriage and disappears from the scene for a long time. It is by means of this leisurely development that the author achieves her largest effects. We know that the outcome is inevitable, but we approach it with such deliberation that all the subtle psychological processes of the years find room for analysis and exposition, and the figures of both characters become very completely human. The book has many minor features and characters deserving of warm praise; we have not space even for their mention, but trust that we have said enough to send our readers to one of the strongest and most vital productions of recent years.

"Fiction,"
Book News Monthly, 22 February 1904, 718–19

Miss Glasgow's tendency to write morbidly is less perceptible in this, her latest novel. Not that *The Deliverance* is marked by happy optimism, that were hoping for too much, but there are here and there bright streams of sunlight glowing through the darknesses and in the conclusion one feels less the sorrow for what might have been than the joy for what ultimately was.

The Deliverance depicts a great soul struggle. It has to do with one of those old Southern feuds, so common to the period of the Reconstruction and so deplorably bitter. It was a mighty injustice that was done to a proud old family and out of it sprang the same old overwhelming thirst for revenge.

Miss Glasgow gives a vivid picture of the tobacco land and the tobacco planter. Her descriptions are vigorous, her characters have at once both diversity and reality. The grand old mother, blind but haughty, living in that atmosphere maintained only by careful lying, living there and recounting her girlhood triumphs—happy in the midst of sordidness because it was unknown—protected lovingly lest the truth should come out and the shock should kill, as it finally did—oh, the infinite pathos of it all, more poignant, too, that the self-sacrifice entailed lacks all the more beautiful phases of self-sacrifice. Cynthia gave up her life, but was it a grand giving? No such nobility of soul emanated from her as that which enfolds and enhances Maria.

The whole tells the story of over twenty years' living tragedy. The deliverance was love—love that brought remorse and killed that hunger for a vengeance dark and terrifying. And yet the revenge was accomplished and the partial price paid before the joys of love and possession could be experienced. After all it was Fate!

Miss Glasgow has accomplished in *The Deliverance* her strongest novel. It bears the aspect of a story well-constructed and well executed. It has invention, it has atmosphere, it has characters true to the life, it presents a whole stageful of people who work out its magnificent lesson. Sometimes it touches just a little too strongly the minor keys of melancholy, but the variety born of introducing higher, lighter notes is not missing.

Independent, 56 (25 February 1904), 442–3

The contention of some that *The Deliverance* is not equal to Miss Glasgow's other novels is a criticism that may be sustained so far as the story goes; for she is too much interested in the development of individual characters to fit the different elements together in a swiftly moving action. But this is a fault easily forgiven when we consider that each person's life portrayed is a complete drama in itself. Besides, this representation is not far from the truth of things. No community life is so co-ordinate, so compact, as to make a good play if it were actually dramatized. In this novel the one common element of interest is the tobacco fields. These are like green inland seas across which the wind sends a thousand leaf waves. And soon or late every character in the book is drawn into some sort of contrast with this emerald surface, either scenic or dramatic.

Eckert Goodman, "The Novel of the Month: Miss Glasgow's *The Deliverance*," *Current Literature*, 36 (March 1904), 315–16

The name of Miss Glasgow's book fits it in a way not intended by the author. This book is a deliverance from the inane historical hodge-podges with which we have been deluged; it is a deliverance from the graceful innocuous story, the mere time-killer; a deliverance from all the cheap slovenly written books which have turned the publishers' presses these many days. Here is a story to which criticism may be applied and upon which the reviewer need not expatiate in vague complimentary terms. It is distinctly a "big" book, a book which may be considered in the light of the best that constitutes literature.

For Miss Glasgow has dared to do more than merely tell a story that would appeal to the popular taste of the moment. She has written not for the present time alone, but we think for a permanent place in our literature. Out of a small theme she has drawn pictures and philosophy which place her in the class of such a writer as even George Eliot.

We have had many books upon the Civil War; but none which have so brought out certain things about that war as has this book, which is not based on the war at all, and which is a story of present-day Virginia. For in the two families, Fletcher and Blake, you see in no unmistakable way some curious reverses that war brought. At the beginning, old Bill Fletcher was nothing but a coarse-mannered man, a surly overseer upon the Blake estate. The close of the war found this crude individual master of Blake Hall and of practically all the estate, the Blakes living upon a small strip of ground in the center of the immense tract that had been theirs, living pitiably poor, their fine aristocratic hands hardened and calloused by work. Yet neither time nor condition can change blood. The Blake, poor and reduced to menial labor, still remained the Blake— the fine, splendid, aristocratic Blake. The Fletcher, turned wealthy, still remained the Fletcher, coarse, brutal, vulgar. Herein Miss Glasgow has not only shown a picture of political change, but has combined it with subtle psychology of character.

When we come to the story itself, the matter is not so easy to handle. But, put brutally, it is the story of great elemental passion, of a "grudge"—the grudge between young Christopher Blake and old Bill Fletcher, a grudge founded upon the very dubious way by which Fletcher has gotten possession of the Blake property....

And that brings us to Miss Glasgow's study of character. There is no woman writer of to-day who can surpass her portrayal, not only of her principal characters but of every character. Take young Christopher—a subtle problem he offers. A man, at bottom a gentleman, with the blood of generations of gentlemen in his veins. For a time he is so mastered by passion that he becomes the elemental savage. Then comes the esthetic into his life again, through love, love for the person whom he should have hated—Fletcher's granddaughter, sister of the man whom he has ruined; and the gentleman awakes in him again. There is in him something of the French aristocrat of the Revolution who went to the guillotine reciting a sonnet; something too of the downright manhood which characterized a Nathan Hale and the best heroes of real American life—when he stands up before his judge and answers that he alone is guilty of Fletcher's murder. It is the hero without heroics. For the study of a complex nature of living truth this character of Christopher stands quite alone in recent fiction. Of course the objection might be raised, and obviously comes first to the reader's mind, that no one with the training or instincts of a gentleman could have stooped to so degrading a revenge. Yet hate is a powerful thing, and passion is dangerous. The disintegration of the character of Othello, for instance, is absolutely true, though told in bare outline it might prove questionable. So granting Miss Glasgow's premise, you see the truth of her portrayal....

It will not do to take up every character: but one, and that a minor character and one not inherent in the story, should be mentioned as showing Miss Glasgow's skill. The character is Tucker, the poor cripple—a hero of the Civil War, whose return for his gallant service and best effort was helplessness and the defeat of the cause for which he fought.

Miss Glasgow has done something really worth while in this story of *The Deliverance*. She has used fine restraint in the evolution of her recital. She has made plot subservient to motiving character. She has given a full, well-rounded, definite picture. And she has placed herself well in the front rank of modern novelists....

Edwin Clark Marsh, "The Epic Novel and Some Recent Books," *Bookman*, 19 (March 1904), 43–5

What Mrs. Stowe did for the South of antebellum days, from a frankly abolitionist standpoint, a good many recent writers have tried to do for the Reconstruction period, from the standpoint of the Southerner; and none has come nearer to achievement than Miss Ellen Glasgow, in *The Deliverance*. In the subtitle Miss Glasgow defines her story quite simply, as a "romance of the Virginia tobacco fields"; but it was heralded and put forth as something considerably more ambitious, a comprehensive picture of the South, bridging over the years from the Civil War down to the present day. Looked at from this point of view, *The Deliverance* loses more than it gains. It is unquestionably a strong piece of work, one of this season's books which will deservedly attract a good deal of serious attention; but it will be ranked higher in the scale by those who take it simply as an earnest, thoughtful story, taken straight from life, than by those who try to find in it an epitome of the whole New South. And yet, from a critical standpoint, the latter is the more interesting view to take, because it helps us to see by what a very narrow margin the author missed doing something very much bigger than she has done. Miss Glasgow possesses the requisite qualifications for the handling of big themes. She has a style that at times is distinctly virile, and a gift of generalisation that is rare in women. One does not need to have first-hand knowledge of present-day Virginia in order to feel that the social and economic conditions that she pictures are absolutely true, and that they are not merely local or exceptional, but that they are prevailing conditions. When stated in general terms, the theme of *The Deliverance* seems one well adapted to a broad, impressionistic, epic treatment. There is, in the foreground, the typical case, a proud old Virginia family, impoverished by the war; the estate passed into other hands; even the birthright of education and refinement and social prestige slipping from the grasp of the younger generation. And behind all this is the suggestion of a bigger theme,—a whole social structure shaken to its foundations, an entire people struggling to adapt themselves to new conditions. And all these changes of fortune, both general and particular, the downfall of a family, the passing of the old régime, are bound into one single, comprehensive whole, by a bold, dramatic device which, if not wholly new in fiction, is none the less a stroke of genius in its present application. It is nothing less than the introduction of one character who, through all the changes and privations of the vanquished South, continues tranquilly to live in imagination the old life of antebellum days....

These are the strong features of *The Deliverance*, and one feels that a little more concentration, a little more insistence upon them would have made it the big symbolic story that it just fails to be. What Miss Glasgow herself seems to have been chiefly interested in is the romance between young Blake and the granddaughter of his bitterest enemy, his father's former steward. It is an intimate personal drama, a peculiar case of warped conscience, in which a man's love for an innocent girl does not prevent him from planning the ruin of that girl's brother, when by doing so he can strike a deadly blow at his enemy's pride. But all this takes us out of the realm of what is big and typical and symbolic; it constantly focuses our attention upon individual interests and exceptional conditions. And over and over again, just as the vista seems to widen out, and we get a glimpse of a bigger, broader South, beyond the boundaries of the ubiquitous tobacco fields, the horizon relentlessly shuts in again, and focuses our thoughts once more upon the troubled conscience of a young man who by no stretch of the imagination can be regarded as a symbol of the New South.

Academy and Literature, 66 (12 March 1904), 273

In this romance of the Virginian tobacco fields we welcome an unusual and remarkable novel, which will add fresh laurels to Miss Glasgow's fame. There is a breadth of treatment, a skillful handling of great natural emotions, an all-pervading atmosphere, which mark out this novel from most of its fellows. It is a story of natural animal instincts, of hate and love, of revenge and remorse, which, passing through the refining fire of sorrow and self-sacrifices, are finally subdued unto the life of the spirit. The entire action of the story takes place in a little village in Virginia some thirty years after slavery was abolished. Christopher Blake, a young giant of the soil, is the rightful but defrauded owner of Blake Hall, where his ancestors had gallantly if recklessly lived for two hundred years. His birthright has been taken from him by his father's one-time overseer, who took advantage of the Blake prodigality and heedlessness to ruin the family and send them forth homeless and penniless. Christopher Blake, his blind mother and two sisters, are living in a mere hovel when the story opens. The overseer, who has been in possession of Blake Hall for some twenty years, has a grandson and granddaughter. Christopher attempts to pay back his debt of revenge by ruining the grandson. The story of Christopher's inevitable but fiercely fought-against love for Maria, the granddaughter, is a fine piece of writing. All the minor characters in the book are careful, vivid studies, especially that of the blind mother, who is never told of their change of fortunes, and whose injunction to her son on her death bed is "Remember to be a gentleman, and you will find that that embraces all morality and a good deal of religion." Altogether a book instinct with life, not paper-and-ink life, but real life; the characters live and breathe, hate and love with an unforgettable intensity and truth.

Nation, 78 (24 March 1904), 234–5

[...]

Tobacco is a leading character in the story. We see the Virginians looking to it for their daily bread as for their daily work; we follow it as a crop and as a motive; we see Virginia methods of two hundred years ago still applied to the processes of the planting and the harvest; we see the human struggle surging round it as it always surges round the mainstay of material life, whatever that may be. Whatever glamour tobacco can borrow from sunrise and moonlight is here with all the dignity that labor's hard hand can bring. Not as poison, luxury, or comfort does it win a thought, but as life or death. Instinctively Millet's pictures come to the mind's eye as one follows the struggle of man with Nature. With its many interests, black, white, human, inanimate, ethical, social, psychologic, *The Deliverance* offers richness and variety. The writing is almost wholly good, the reading often so, however one may protest against improbabilities, or however weary one may have become of decayed Southern gentility.

Spectator [England], 92 (2 April 1904), 539

This "romance of the Virginian tobacco-fields" is an effective piece of work, though there are, it seems to us, some flaws in it. We do not quite see, for instance, how the wise and serene Maria of the latter part of the story can be the same person as the Maria, who is not specially wise or serene, of the former. But about Christopher Blake, a Virginian aristocrat, who has to pay for the omissions and commissions of many generations of easy-going ancestors, there can be no mistake. Few more striking figures have been drawn in American fiction. Nor could we have anything more genuinely pathetic than the old mother, still surrounded with the fiction of a splendour that had passed away. What a scene is that when, in her last hours, she takes a stately farewell—she is blind, it must be remembered—of a household which had ceased to exist. And then there is poor Cynthia, so used to lying—she had had to keep up her mother's delusions—that she was fairly lost when the necessity had ceased. *The Deliverance* is a fine story.

Times Literary Supplement [England], 15 April 1904, p. 116

Miss Ellen Glasgow's book *The Deliverance*, a Romance of the Virginia Tobacco Fields, is remarkable in several ways, and not less for its weak points than for its strong. The strong points are easily defined. Here is a book of 543 pages, crowded with characters of varying importance, which nevertheless maintains its balance and concentration to the end. Miss Glasgow, in fact, knows better than to aim at too many effects. She has one contrast foremost in her mind, the contrast between the old aristocracy reigning before the Civil War and the new democracy that succeeded it, usurping its position indeed, but not filling its place; and to this contrast she devotes herself. High mettle, faultless breeding, and valiant carelessness on one side, coarse fibre, vulgarity, and solid purpose on the other—it is a contrast with great possibilities. Mrs. Blake, the old society queen, living on in dreamland and nursed with filial lies, and Fletcher, the brutal usurping overseer, exemplify it in the first generation, where it is palpable in every line. Miss Glasgow's purpose, however, goes deeper than this. She follows it into the next generation and the next, where the lineaments begin to blend and the ironies creep in. Christopher Blake, a gentleman by birth, is a *terræ filius* by profession and necessity; Maria Fletcher, a labourer by descent, has the nerve and breeding of the Blakes. Out of the first two strands, now crossing and twisting into a web of little ironies, Miss Glasgow weaves a story which as we have said, she carries firmly and consistently to its accomplishment. There is no doubt of her capacity, her zeal, and careful workmanship. Not less clear is it, on the other hand (and this brings us to her weak points, less easy to define), that, despite her qualities, she has written nothing that rises above—shall we say sound intention and good technique? Where her effort at pathos or passion is greatest, it leaves you critical, unsatisfied; not once in all these pages, for all their conscientious workmanship, do you catch the glamour and fearfulness and exhilaration of romance. It is a melancholy confession to make, for the defect, if it exists, is usually incurable. So many people, worthy of all esteem, know and attempt what ought to be romance, so few achieve what is. Miss Glasgow takes human nature on a large scale; primitive emotions, "laws of being"—human nakedness, in fact—these things, on one side, are her *forte*. On the other side, too, she knows of philosophy and resignation and sweet content. But the two sides have no connexion, no necessary link; they are not body and spirit, they are rough wood and veneer; the milder world is artificial, it seems, and simply superimposed on that of human nakedness. Somewhere, in fact, her insight fails, and hence the failure of this book. Perhaps in future books she will develop what she now lacks; if conscientious work can do it, she certainly will. Unfortunately, conscientious work cannot do everything.

"Novel Notes," *Bookman* [London], 26 (April 1904), 27

This is a romance of the Virginian tobacco fields, a story of a great wrong and of a slowly matured vengeance that accomplishes itself, at last, when the man who shaped it has ceased to desire its fulfilment. Christopher Blake was cheated out of his inheritance by Bill Fletcher, who had formerly been his father's overseer, so that he and his mother and sisters are reduced to living on a small farm on the estate that had been presented by the father to Tucker Corbin, an old soldier who was wounded in the Civil War, and who has now returned the gift to his benefactor's family. Here Mrs. Blake, the mother, who has gone blind, keeps up something of state amidst her children and a few negro servants, in pathetic ignorance of the ruin that has come upon her. Meanwhile, Christopher devotes himself to the degradation of young Will Fletcher, old Fletcher's grandson and heir, in whom the old man takes an especial pride. Under Christopher's subtle tuition he develops into a confirmed and besotted drunkard, and marrying in defiance of his grandsire's orders is disinherited, and practically turned adrift. Then, for love of Will's sister Christopher regrets the mischief he has wrought, and sets himself to remedy it, and when, in the heat of a quarrel, Will strikes the old man down and kills him, Christopher helps him to escape, and resolutely takes the crime upon himself. The story has many finely dramatic situations, and is written picturesquely, and with an intimate knowledge of the country and the life it portrays.

"Books," *Everybody's Magazine,* 10 (May 1904), 721

The first novel of 1904 was *The Deliverance,* by Ellen Glasgow; and unless the year is distinguished by exceptionally good work, *The Deliverance* will remain its first novel. The book is an exceedingly neat, strong piece of work. It has an unusually close attachment to the *locale* of its events; one sees the actual soil of these Virginia tobacco-fields thrusting up in the landscape, and feels its influence working throughout the book; the characters are made by it. It was fine dramatic sense that made the hero suffer before the world as well as in his own soul for his part in the downfall of Will Fletcher. It seems improbable, however, that old lady Blake could have been kept for thirty years ignorant of the family misfortunes, even though blind; and some element of comedy to offset the severe seriousness of the tale would lighten the story, yet not retard its progress. As a whole, however, the book is so good that these half-hearted objections are unimportant. One of the best things about it is, that it does not try to exploit after-the-war conditions.

H. W. Preston, "A Few Spring Novels," *Atlantic Monthly,* 93 (June 1904), 852–4

Out of a score or more of smartly attired volumes the most important among the native American products is the *Deliverance,* by Miss Ellen Glasgow,—and even this is hardly up to the high level of the author's previous work. It is neither as broad and sane, nor as masterly in its grasp of complex and chaotic social conditions, as *The Voice of the People;* nor has it all the solemn unity and concentrated pathos of *The Battle-Ground.* Nevertheless, it is a searching and a striking book; and, like its predecessors, it is especially interesting for the strong light it sheds on what, after a lapse of forty years, is only now beginning dimly to be perceived as one of the most momentous consequences to our whole country of the war of secession,—the death, namely, and by violence,—or, at least, the mortal hurt,—of a comparatively ripe white civilization in the Southern United States.

[. . .]

The plan of reprisals over which Christopher Blake brooded throughout his growing years was a ruthless, not to say a revolting one. How he achieved his grim purpose, and then, when suddenly awakened to a sense of its moral enormity, what he voluntarily underwent by way of expiation, may best be read in the book itself. The title of the tale foreshadows a hopeful conclusion, and we gladly accept its augury. Nevertheless, it is, as I have said, the haunting thought of a civilization untimely slain, which *The Deliverance,* no less than *The Battle-Ground,* leaves uppermost in our minds.

Athenæum [England], 2 (13 August 1904), 201–2

This is an American novel of the better sort. Its great merit is that (to quote the heading of one of the chapters) it treats "of human nature in the raw state." The principal character is the son of an impoverished old Virginian family with traditions of grandeur and idleness which have made its members unable to face the new conditions of life after the abolition of slavery. Family pride, hatred of the new man who has bought the old acres, and the revengeful feeling which the uneducated are apt to cherish, are all thoroughly well realized and presented. The writer has also lavished her undoubted talent upon another object, one which a woman is peculiarly able to deal with satisfactorily, the devotion of a daughter to a duty which to some extent she constructs for herself, and which enables her to revel, as women will, in secret misery and silent self-immolation. There is nothing morbid, however, in the writer's method of dealing with this trait of character. Her book evinces a clear perception of the persons and circumstances which she has set before her, and she reveals, as if unconsciously, the natural taste of an artist.

Archibald Henderson, "Recent Novels of Note," *Sewanee Review*, 12 (October 1904), 462–4

It has been said more than once that the literature of the South in the United States reveals remarkable sensitiveness to feeling and sentiment, but exhibits no masterly grasp of mental and moral problems. In dealing with fundamental phases of nature and of life, the Southern writer passes out of the realm of thought into the realm of feeling. The dictum that the South has not produced the great thinkers, the great moralists, the great ethical teachers of American literature and American life has become almost a banality of criticism. How often is heard the statement, however false, that the Southern artist has not the seer's vision, does not "see life steadily and see it whole"! For the Southern writer, according to this narrow and partial estimate, the vision in the magic glass of art is not of intellect, moral inspiration, and breadth of view. Instead, there appear the prismatic and irradiant images of passionate feeling and subtle sympathy with nature.

Miss Glasgow's *The Deliverance* is notable and important in the literature not only of to-day but of the decade, chiefly because it is a marvelous composite of the Southern instinct for feeling and the Northern passion for ethics. In this fact lie the supreme distinction and the artistic significance of Miss Glasgow's latest and most distinguished piece of work.

In this novel is seen, on the one hand, the most delicate sympathy with the moods of nature, the sensitiveness of feeling which stoops even to deception for the larger sake of sparing human suffering, the expansiveness of poetic and imaginative insight which always projects man against the background of a primeval and life-infusing nature. The smell of virgin soil, the aroma of the fields, the air of wide expanses hang about its backgrounds and vistas. It conveys a sense of extent, an impression of spaciousness. The genius of the author suggests wide horizons of hope, great reaches of passion. In this way the poetic instinct of the South has spoken.

On the other hand, the moral problem is the central fire of the story, and this central fire slowly expands and well-nigh envelops the whole scene. The evolution of the young aristocrat through suffering, the exfoliation of moral consciousness through the vitalizing power of a generous and whole-hearted love, the expansion of moral vision through manly renunciation and truly heroic self-sacrifice—this tells the story in its ethical import and individual significance. These are largely the qualities of the literature of the North—the emphasis upon thought, the primal, quintessential stress of conscience, the ultimate triumph of right over wrong.

In *The Deliverance* these traits of South and North blend in a wonderfully consistent and satisfying picture—a picture instinct with feeling, passion, nature; animate with morality, conscientiousness, and ethical finality. We are called to witness not the staggering feat of the evolution of moral consciousness in a single night, but the leisurely exposition of human character and its final evolution into shapes of eternal verity. The book betrays the strong, sure grasp of genuine literary craftsmanship, the keen power of clear and epic visualization, the reach and mastery of a tremendous moral, ethical, and social problem. The masculinity and stark power of its appeal grip and hold you to the end.

Under foot is the virgin soil, all about you is heard the rustle of the green tobacco plants, and across the farm, set in the peace and quietness of nature, surge in devilish deliberation the malignant and destructive passions of racial hatred and individual animosity. The primitive, the elemental passions are at large, and slowly, surely, inevitably they work toward a climax, the fulfilling of the law of ungovernable hatred, which is ruin, murder, and sudden death.

But at the heart of this hatred dwells also the purifying, regenerative power of a noble and unselfish love. In the pitting of these two overmastering forces against each other lies the fundamental interest of the story. In the deliverance of a great soul from the obsession of an ingrained, fostered, and fiercely burning hatred through the instrumentality of a pure and exalted love consists the moral import of this dramatic recital of human frailty and human struggle.

Of the new novelists of the New South, Miss Glasgow stands preëminent as the artist who has blended, in a firmly motived, consistently wrought, and powerfully imagined story, the emollient charm and graceful romance of the South with the more rigid self-examination and moral introspectiveness of the North.

Checklist of Additional Reviews

"The Saving of Christopher Blake, Knight of Soil and Field," *How to Know the Books*, 2 (February 1904), 13–14.

"The First Novel of the New Year," *Town Topics*, 4 February 1904.

Louise Collier Willcox, "Ellen Glasgow: One of the Rising Novelists of America," Boston *Evening Transcript*, 17 February 1904, sec. 2, p. 17.

"The First Novels of 1904," *Review of Reviews and World's Work*, 29 (March 1904), 380.

Carolyn Shipman, "Books Reviewed—Fact and Fiction," *Critic*, 44 (April 1904), 375–7.

John Raper Ormond, "Some Recent Products of the New School of Southern Fiction," *South Atlantic Quarterly*, 3 (July 1904), 285–9.

THE WHEEL OF LIFE

The Wheel of Life

By
ELLEN GLASGOW

New York
Doubleday, Page & Company
1906

"The Latest Books Under Brief Review," Richmond *Times-Dispatch*, 20 January 1906, p. 4

Finished and carefully elaborated as it is in style and manner, *The Wheel of Life* is almost certain to be a disappointment to many of the admirers of Miss Ellen Glasgow. In one or two ways, none the less, it shows a higher development than any of her previous books. For one thing, it shows a little too plainly, it is true, her recognition of the fact that the novel of plot, however excellent, must always stand for a lower type than the novel of character. It shows further a gain in sureness of touch, in accuracy and ease of expression, in the deft turning of a phrase; and exhibits, to a greater degree than she has yet exhibited, qualities of observation and insight, and a laudable desire to grapple with some of the more lasting and fundamental problems of living.

These highly desirable gifts, had their possessor given them a chance for really effective display, might have wrought a result in which we could find little to criticize. But it is just here that Miss Glasgow has allowed her achievement to fall short of her abilities. To begin with, she has carried her disregard for the demands of plot to the point of not having any at all. This, in itself, might have been no fair criticism upon a novel with the purpose and intended scope of this one. Great novels have been written with no specific plot, and the greatest, it may be, will always rather ignore this element. But Miss Glasgow has not brought to her work the transcendent abilities which alone could make the "story" features superfluous. She lacks as yet, it would seem, the constructive powers and the wide grasp necessary to make the novel of pure character unfailingly interesting. In addition, she has handicapped herself with several sets of characters, none of whom occupies a commanding place in her scheme, and some of whom might have been dispensed with to probable advantage.

Perry and Gerty Bridewell, Arnold Kemper and Laura, Adams and Connie, are, for at least a large part of the book, accorded the center of the stage in turn with the utmost impartiality. One never loses one's instinct for locating precisely the hero and heroine of every book, and in this case is likely to lay down the volume in bewilderment as to who is designed for these roles here. From the several strands which the author has alternately woven, Adams' story no doubt emerges most nearly to a leading place; and certainly Adams' character has been drawn with the most care and pain. Miss Glasgow's conception and intentions here are alike admirable. In the kind, quiet, faithful, selfless editor of the *International Review*, she has sought to give us a man who found the secret of life in renunciation, to whom the yielding of all selfish desires and ambitions, come in time to be a joy not wholly passive. There is, obviously, a great truth here, and it is regrettable that Adams is so delineated as to be on the whole unconvincing, and certainly not particularly attractive. He elicits, unhappily, the reader's pity, rather than his sympathy and admiration. His unresisting smile and ready acceptance of much of the worst that life can hold for any man, fail to command the tributes so evidently due them.

Laura, who "wrote vague beautiful verse that nobody ever read," starts well, but rather loses her individuality as the story progresses. Her demeanor in the matter of Madame Alta's letter to Arnold Kemper, then Laura's betrothed, comes distinctly as a jar. And she steadily fails to see how utterly impossible was her idea of marrying Kemper, though even Kemper was troubled by his occasional doubts on that score. Kemper is half animal, half masterful man, big, sensual, full of desires, and for the most part, strong enough to fill them. He is easily the most vivid character in the book, and the most real. He wholly obliterates the identity of Perry Bridewell, who, being described as like Kemper in many ways, remaining through the book like an indeterminate shadow of him.

In the earlier stages, one is constantly likely to get the two mixed. Gerty Bridewell is well-done, but the genuine skill expended upon her is made unavailing through her complete insulation, from whatever action the story affords. However definite her personality may be, the reader simply does not get interested in her. Trent, the play-writing young Virginian, is another whose connection with the theme in hand is so uncertain as to make one wonder why he was introduced at all. And the same might be said of most of the subsidiary characters, designed types though they are like the "conventual" Angela, and the flute-playing Uncle Percival.

No doubt Miss Glasgow has been ill-advised in forsaking the Virginian background which has lent distinctiveness to her earlier work, for the most conventional but doubtless, less familiar atmosphere of metropolitan life. This, however, we would be willing to submit to her own discretion. Our criticism on her book is not based on any such consideration as this. *The Wheel of Life*, it seems to us, contains the novel's cardinal defect. It does not hold the reader's interest. The change from the novel of plot to the novel of character is a great one, involving new methods and different endowment, and Miss Glasgow's psychological mastery is not yet sufficiently developed to make the new plan effective. Her insight and art, increasingly, as this book exhibits them, are not now great enough to enchain the reader's attention to a long novel devoid of progressive action and even of a single dominating life-story. With more fully developed powers or, more simply, with a more liberal injection of plot, she has shown in *The Wheel of Life* that she may some day make a new and triumphant success in a higher field than she has hitherto attempted.

M. Gordon Pryor Rice, "The First Important Novel of 1906," *New York Times Saturday Review of Books*, 20 January 1906, p. 32

The first important novel of 1904 was *The Deliverance*, Miss Glasgow's strong story of the tobacco fields of Virginia. She begins 1906 with a novel of equal power and of even larger grasp. She has shifted her scene from the lonely plantation to the jostling metropolis, and her dramatis personæ belong to that gilded circle which seems just now peculiarly alluring to writers of fiction.

For this reason it is impossible to avoid a momentary comparison of *The Wheel of Life* with *The House of Mirth*, with the result, however, of an instant and striking contrast of impression. Although each of Mrs. Wharton's characters is a vital personality, it is as a portrayal of a certain segment of society that the book, for the present at least, makes its strongest mark, and arouses widest interest and discussion; whereas in Miss Glasgow's story one thinks entirely of the individuals, whose social setting appears as an atmosphere simply. While Mrs. Wharton's wonderfully imagined heroine is the child of her conditions, Miss Glasgow's is so aloof from hers that she might almost as well have had any other environment. Laura Wilde is a young poet who "lived buried away in Gramercy Park and wrote vague, beautiful verse that nobody ever read." She is the centre of a group of relatives, eccentric enough to have stepped out of one of Miss Brown's or Miss Wilkins' New England villages.

[...]

The three women represent as many types: Gerty a mondaine of the better sort, abiding, it is true, in the perilous House of Mirth, but holding her silken skirts above the soil of scandal, and underneath a mocking mask keeping a pinioned soul; Connie Adams, a silly moth, fluttering in endless gayeties outside the more exclusive circles, passing from imprudence into recklessness until she became "one of the very best of the impossibilities"; and the cloistral Laura, not only a genius, but a consummate flower of womanhood. Of the men, Perry Bridewell and Arnold Kemper are not unlike—pleasure-seeking men of the clubs, of feminine conquests, of racing automobiles, and all the costly toys wherewith the rich cheat ennui. Bridewell is not much more than a well-groomed, handsome body; Kemper is Bridewell with intellect added. Adams, on the contrary, is the absorbed man of letters, editor of *The International Review*, caring for no pleasure outside his work.

[...]

After all, however, when the book has been closed, and we can give the true perspective to persons and circumstance, we perceive that Roger Adams holds "the point of sight." Around him as its soul and centre is the story written. Indeed, if we mistake not, he is its raison d'etre. Gerty's character is indurated by her tragedy, Laura's crushed for a time by hers; but Adams, to whom comes the ghastliest catastrophe of wedded life, rises above it glorified. Through an absolute elimination of the personal factor he attains that holiness which is "an infinite compassion for others," that greatness which "takes the common things of life and walks truly among them," that happiness which "is a great love and much service."

In drawing the character of Adams, and, in depicting the relations between him and his degraded wife, Miss Glasgow set herself no easy task, and therein she has achieved a triumph. She belongs to the few writers who succeed in representing goodness as not only the right and beautiful thing, but the strongest and manliest thing. She has done her best work in her portrayal of Roger Adams. As she traces the steps which led to his complete renunciation of self; as she shows his attitude of perfect pity and tenderness toward the wife who has so cruelly wronged him, her method reminds us again and again of the simple, convincing directness of Tolstoi, as he points the path which led Nekhtudoff to "Resurrection."

[...]

As in its preceding novels, we have in *The Wheel of Life* color, humor, the light touch and go of clever talk glancing about the surface of things, characters that live, romance vibrant with passion—all that goes to make up the human drama, whether it be played upon a sumptuous social stage or in the homely neighborhood where a boy eats out his heart as he toils in the Virginia tobacco field. For the interest of this drama the story will be widely read for the strength and charm we have learned to take for granted in

Miss Glasgow's work. But its reach is greater than that of its predecessors; its author has gone down into the deep places, and the distinction, the lift that is all its own is that in the last analysis it is the Apotheosis of Goodness.

George Seibel, "Miss Glasgow's New Novel," Pittsburgh *Gazette*, 20 January 1906, p. 7

The important event of the week, of course, is the publication of Ellen Glasgow's *Wheel of Life*, which is reviewed below. It is not very likely that this novel will take its place among the "six best sellers"—it isn't built that way, but it is the maturest and profoundest work Miss Glasgow has yet done, and challenges comparison with the best of Mrs. Wharton.

[...]

The old Greek tragedians made men see the futility of life, the inexorable destiny. Alan, like Prometheus was chained upon a rock, rent by vultures, and though his agony was old as memory, it was new with every dawn. Something of this tragic depth is in Ellen Glasgow's new book—it is shadowed forth by the title, for *The Wheel of Life* is that endlessly revolving engine of torture upon which the human race is fastened by the irony of fate.

[...]

This novel puts Miss Glasgow level with Mrs. Wharton. While not as firm in its technique as *The House of Mirth*, it goes far deeper. While not as dramatic as *The Valley of Decision*, it is more poignant and vital. This is all the more gratifying since in her two previous novels, *The Battle-Ground* and *The Deliverance*, Miss Glasgow's development seemed to have been arrested, the fine promise of her earlier work dispelled. But *The Wheel of Life* is an achievement. It puts again before us, in a modern phase, with motor cars and prima-donnas, 'twixt Union square and Gramercy park, the problem as old as Aeschylus and Job, Fate or free will? The triumph of personality or the remorseless mills of God? Do we fall as a stone falls, because it must; or do we soar as a bird soars, because it would? Like all the tragic poets from the hero of Marathon and Salamis to Ibsen and Hauptmann, Miss Glasgow gives no direct answer.

Washington *Evening Star*, 20 January 1906, sec. 2, p. 2

Miss Glasgow departs from her former field, in which she succeeded so emphatically as the teller of dramatic tales of the southland. She ventures into the uncertain currents of social psychology, into the mælstrom of New York life. This is unfortunate, for she fails to carry with her into this new region the quality of personal authority which gave *The Deliverance* and *The Battle-Ground* their great charm. In *The Wheel of Life* she tells a story of domestic unhappiness and of tangled love affairs, intensely subjective in treatment and devoid of the brisk action which has heretofore characterized Miss Glasgow's fiction....

Miss Glasgow shows signs now and then of an over development of style. She indulges in long passages of mental communings which call for a strain of attention to unravel. Occasionally she draws too heavily upon her adjectives....

It is to be hoped that Miss Glasgow will return to her first line of work. It is more characteristic and yields more interesting results.

"Miss Glasgow's New Novel," Springfield [Massachusetts] *Sun Republican*, 21 January 1906, p. 23

Miss Ellen Glasgow seems to make rather a specialty of bringing the new year in with a new novel. *The Wheel of Life*, published yesterday by Doubleday, Page & Co., may not be literally the first novel of 1906, but it may be taken as a convenient starting point for the new season. Miss Glasgow has earned a prominent place among the younger writers by the unfailing seriousness of her purpose, by her most laudable ambition for "the big thing," and *The Battle-Ground* with its fine picture of the desolate land and the vague terror of the distant guns, justly won for her a wider public than her earlier novels had commanded. *The Wheel of Life* is a book of a very different sort, and it may as well be owned at once that it is not so interesting. That the material is not intrinsically so good perhaps even the author will admit.

It is to be noted that in her work she has followed two quite different lines, both of which are suggested in her first book, *The Descendant*. This she published anonymously eight years ago, when she was but 23, and its crude vigor roused much curiosity. Some wild guesses as to its authorship were made, various veterans being credited with it. The *Republican*'s shot was so lucky as to bring a query as to how the secret had been betrayed, but it was only internal evidence that showed the hand of a woman, young, a novice, a southerner, who had been in New York, but did not know it, who had read much and was interested in the arts. Since then she has alternated between the soil and the city, between subjects that call for a bold style and those that require a finer brush. She does the big things best; her hand has not yet the delicacy needed for the finer touches. It is not simply a matter of taste; in a picture of one genre strokes will answer which in another give a sense of glaring unreality. It is perhaps in the matter of reality that Miss Glasgow is weakest: she leans to bizarre and exceptional types and has not quite the plausibility needed to carry them off. One too often comes upon a piece of dialogue which, if not demonstrably false, has at any rate the effect of provoking doubt, which is almost as bad. One gets but scantily the spontaneous conviction that these are real people speaking in their natural voices.

In the present case the effect of this blemish is enhanced by unfortunate construction. The interest of the book does not center easily; the reader is not inducted insensibly to the exact place where he is meant to stand. Even the "wheel of life" must have a center: the novelist has unhappily contrived to keep us spinning round on the periphery. First the emphasis is thrown on Gerty Bridewell and her husband, lazy, good-natured, self-indulgent people, taken as types of materialistic New York. But they are not to be important figures, and neither is the young playwright, St. George Trent, who is presently introduced. The drama as it finally shapes itself has for the center of its web the poet, Laura Wilde, who is presented from an outside point of view, which does not carry the sympathies far. She lives in Gramercy park, in a family of eccentrics, an uncle 80 years old who plays the flute, a secluded aunt who had made a false step in youth and shut herself up ever since to her melancholy and repentance, other uncles and aunts, more lucky but equally queer. This menagerie somehow fails to produce the effect which alone could justify it; too much is made of it or not enough. As it stands it is simply an incongruous note; it belongs in some other book.

Laura, in whose poetical genius it is not quite easy, on the evidence presented, to believe, has four suitors—Mr. Wilberforce, who is rich, 60, and harmless; Trent, who is too young, and two who count. In Arnold Kemper we come to a variant of that type of brutal masculine force to which Miss Glasgow, like some other novelists of her sex, is rather addicted—prognathous jaw, wicked life, and all that. He drives fast automobiles; he has divorced his wife to marry the grand opera star, Jennie Alta, and then changed his mind. In Roger Adams we have another type of force, a bony, consumptive, masterful editor, married, to be sure, to a shallow woman, who uses cocaine, but the cocaine solves that difficulty. Others the novelist has not been so lucky with; the spokes of the wheel radiate too distractingly from the center in Gramercy park. Art should simplify life, instead of further confusing it. There is too much detail—in the wrong places; the accents seldom fall right. The reader is left with the dissatisfied feeling that he has been left to wander pretty much at random through scenes not remarkable enough in the detail to make up for the facts in the perspective. There are interesting qualities in Miss Glasgow's work; she has vigor and a personality. She is not yet master of her craft, and she has not yet learned to see life quite as it is, but something better than she has yet done is to be expected from her.

"Miss Glasgow's Story of New York," New York *Evening Post*, 27 January 1906, p. 6

For once, Miss Glasgow has deserted the South, which she knows so well, and set the scene of her new novel in New York. The persons in the drama are men and women of to-day, moving in circles of refinement and culture. Such problems as most of them feel called upon to face are of the sort which tens of thousands of New Yorkers are facing and solving every day, each in the manner which seems best to him. Only, in the big city there are a few who are willing to face the larger problems which are worked out with fear and trembling by Laura Wilde and Roger Adams in The Wheel of Life.

Some idea of the intention of the work may be gained by referring to the headings into which it is divided. Like the wheel of the prophet's vision, it has four faces: Impulse, Illusion, Disenchantment, and Reconciliation. The whole purpose of the book is to emphasize the fact that for all of those who have seen only the first three of these faces, there remains the fourth, which is more beautiful even than the second.

Roger Adams, the hero of a story in which, to quote the title of the first chapter, "the romantic hero is conspicuous by his absence," has wrung his heroism, his human fellowship, and his sense of humor from acute physical suffering, long endured. But suffering still more acute is brought to him by the actions of his wife. It becomes necessary even for him to extend the boundaries of his philosophy.

He is not a church-goer; in the eyes of many he would scarcely be considered a Christian. But now, in this hour of necessity, comes the message: "Seek ye first the kingdom of God, and his righteousness." How he accepts the loving command, and how in the end the happiness and other things apparently relinquished are added unto him is a story too long to tell here.

Through experiences leading even into the valley of deepest humiliation, Laura Wilde, the undoubted heroine of the novel, comes also to a state of understanding and reconciliation.

The Wheel of Life is not without flaws as a novel, but it is the best work of an author, all of whose books have compelled attention. If some of the secondary characters appear to be as unnecessary as they are unconvincing; if the rare descents from high comedy to low are not always accomplished without sacrifice, the principals are very real and the important scenes are admirably conceived and worked out. There can be little doubt that it will be one of the most important works of fiction of the year.

"Ellen Glasgow's New Novel of Society," Philadelphia *Press*, 28 January 1906, p. 4

Ellen Glasgow adopts the "grand style" in her latest novel, *The Wheel of Life*. Commonplace ideas are expressed in redundant periods. Where three adjectives may be employed, the author cannot content herself with two; where two are possible a single adjective is out of the question. Worst of all, these redundant adjectives are invariably obvious. For instance, to speak of an atmosphere as "conventual" necessarily carries the idea of stillness and quietude; but Miss Glasgow must write of the "quiet conventual atmosphere." Superfluous adjectives and adverbs help to build up the periods which are expected to impress readers with the literary brilliancy of *The Wheel of Life*. The truth is that a liberal use of the blue pencil to give crispness to the style would have greatly improved what is in some respects an exceptionally meritorious novel. This would also have remedied some of the vagueness of diction, due to paying less attention to the meaning than to the elaboration of the mass of periods.

Miss Glasgow forsakes the South and its sociological problems for the tempting field offered by New York. The story is about misleading impulses and tarnished illusions, about the deification of clay and inevitable disenchantment with its humiliations. Her first few pages introducing a young married woman of gay proclivities are likely to provide irreverent joy. Gerty Bridewell, awakened by the light, stifles a yawn with her pillow, and remembers that she was very unhappy when she went to bed. The object of her unhappiness is her husband, but both he and her unhappiness "were of less disturbing importance to her than the fact that she must get up and stand for three minutes under the shower bath in her dressing room." The "discreet and confidential smile" of Gerty's maid draws from her "a protesting frown of irritation." She cannot get up until she has had her coffee. As a matter of fact, she lingers on her downy couch until the afternoon.

Gerty is vain: "Her eyes followed the woman across the room and through the door, and then, turning instinctively to the broad mirror above her dressing table, hung critically upon the brilliant red and white reflection in the glass. It was her comforting assurance that every woman looked her best in bed; and as she lay now, following the lines of her charming figure beneath the satin coverlet, she found herself wondering, not without resentment, why the possession of a beauty so conspicuous should afford her only a slight and temporary satisfaction." Fie, fie! Must these mysteries be exposed by a sister of the red-haired beauty? Must not feminine frailty in the person of a frivolous woman in bed be preserved from the ribaldry of cynical man? Gerty married the richest man she knew; but luxury did not bring happiness. He is large, florid and impressive. When he enters from his dressing room to speak to his wife, he settles "his ample, carefully groomed body in his clothes with a comfortable shake." Good heavens! The well groomed man who could settle his body into his clothes with a comfortable shake needs to change both his tailor and his valet.

The reader encounters an oddly assorted group of people in the book. Laura Wilde, a lady with a "Creole voice" who writes poetry, is the heroine. She comes of an eccentric family. Some of the best character portrayal in the book is that which concerns Laura's people. A third woman among the characters is Connie Coles, who likewise writes poetry. In fact, there is a hazy literary atmosphere to the book. The hero, who is admittedly not a romantic figure, edits a review. He is Roger Adams, a "gaunt, scholarly-looking man of forty years, with broad, singularly bony shoulders, an expression of kindly humor, and a plain, strong face upon which suffering had left its indelible suggestion of defeated physical purpose." Possibly the "indelible suggestion of defeated physical purpose" can be clearly realized by the reader; but the reviewer is fain to confess that he does not know what the expression means.

Miss Glasgow has chosen a large canvas. She has a strong imagination and much literary force in spite of the redundancies noted; but her capacity for the revelation of character is greatly superior to her constructive ability. In the present book the social situation involves on the one hand an unfortunate marriage by Adams. He prevents Gerty Bridewell from compromising herself with a man who subsequently wins away the hero's wife, no other than Connie Coles. She becomes wretched, drinks brandy and dies in a hospital. On the other hand, Laura Wilde, a creature of impulses and enthusiasms, becomes infatuated with Arnold Kemper, a divorced man of forty, assiduous in the pursuit of pleasure through devious ways. A few days before the marriage Laura encounters a certain operatic soprano to whom Kemper has been devoted and with whom his name has been publicly associated. The interview results in the sudden disappearance of Laura, who wanders away and is lost for several days. Eventually, it is Adams to whom she sends a message concerning her whereabouts.

A long siege of illness is before Laura, but the predestined end is foreshadowed. Adams loved her and she was for him all the time. Miss Glasgow has done much more convincing work than is to be found in *The Wheel of Life*. She is dealing with people and conditions that are not so familiar to her as those in the South. She does not offer a transcript of her life as observed by her. The characters and their ways are people of her imagination and she cannot make them seem real. It is a long novel, sadly inflated, and the dialogue is frequently theatrical. The characters pose continuously while they are talking and never seem to be at their ease or at rest.

Baltimore *Sun*, 31 January 1906, p. 11

The Voice of the People, The Battle-Ground, The Deliverance have we read and found good. *The Descendant* and *Phases of an Inferior Planet* were not to our mind worth the reading, and yet all are from the pen of Ellen Glasgow, the author of *The Wheel of Life*, itself one of the most effective novels that have been published within a twelvemonth. It is effective, but with an effectiveness that is repellant. With sex novels and problem novels the public have been well-nigh surfeited and the public mind has not by them been elevated nor the public conscience made more tender. But the present fashion in literature is of the sort that panders to the weaknesses of readers, and authors with an eye to fashion and the results of successful work in the prevailing mode have hastened to supply the public with the literary viands in demand. The movement has brought to the front a few strong novels; for example, *The House of Mirth* and *The Wheel of Life*. But it has also produced a flood of worthless books of instant popularity and immediate death; for example, *The One Woman* and *Baccarat*. *The Wheel of Life* is a novel whose complex plot is treated in a masterly manner. Its field of action is New York, its time the present and its characters men and women that you know; that is, whose replicas you know. The story is one of hearts—of mismatched hearts, we might say—of women who flutter moth-like at the burning tapers of passion and with singed wings retreat in pain; of men who dominate by the force of mentality or else to whom the physical gives the power of control. In a strange tangle are the loves of the men and women of this novel; the characters juggle with truth and virtue, they blind themselves—consciously blind themselves—to right. They do these things and yet avoid the consequences that seem inevitable. Herein lies the falsity of the whole conception of our author—that is, the seeming lack of appreciation of the certain consequences that attend certain acts. But there is another weakness that we had not expected in the work of so talented a writer. That is the crass sentimentality of the concluding chapter. The author indulges herself. She does so at the expense of truth. She preaches to us at an inopportune time—her plan is one out of date, her method is one out of harmony with the rest of her work. We sum up by saying of *The Wheel of Life* that by it—when we eliminate its last chapter, or even when we consider it—Miss Glasgow has established her right to a place with our leading fictionists.

Independent, 60 (1 February 1906), 284–5

"Life," to our young women novelists, seems to be a sorry business. Characters admirable and detestable alike are bound to *The Wheel of Life* in Ellen Glasgow's latest novel, and the public is invited to watch their tortured forms. As in *The House of Mirth*, the New York smart set provides the victims and the torture. Miss Glasgow's stories of her native South were better, and the little group of Southerners—introduced, by the way, as a sort of "aside" to the main speech of the plot—are decidedly the best thing in it. The Southern mother transplanted to a New York apartment with her old bits of china and endless knitting work, is a rare study, fit to put beside Jane Austen's best.

[...]
The dear, lonely lady counts up the people that she "might speak to on the street" and found but "five, including the doctor, the butcher's boy and the woman who came to scrub." Such work as this portrait of a lady seems to us wasted upon the annals of a fast and vulgar crew of fashionable folk, whose only avowed object in life is to get the most possible pleasure out of it. That the pursuit of pleasure for its own sake is a ghastly and hideous mistake is the moral taught by this somber story. We are unwilling witnesses at the death of several souls and the birth of others, and which is the more painful of the two it would be hard to say. Perhaps the echoes of old loves and sins never sounded more harshly thru the strains of a pure love-idyl than in the crucial chapter of Laura's heart-history; but the suffering seems so useless and so hopeless, as the wheel of life turns now up, now down, with its living burden, and we sigh, as often before, for some fresh, sweet and happy presentment of the actual joy of living.

"Some Recent Popular Novels: Ideas, Ideals, and Idols," San Francisco *Argonaut*, 3 February 1906, p. 907

Miss Ellen Glasgow is barely over thirty years of age; and yet she has written *The Wheel of Life*. No one who has not read the book can fully understand the significance of the two statements. It is useless to meditate on the personal element in this new volume, except to remark, quite politely, that Miss Glasgow takes a very sound position, where women are expected to be illogical. *The Wheel of Life* is the story of a woman of ideas and ideals and—men. True, there is only one man throughout the greater part of the book. But he is, through the woman's eye, manifold, varying, and it is almost a sense of shame in polyandry that causes her to give him up. There are other persons, cleverly drawn, and kept in their proper and subordinate place. Miss Glasgow is an optimist. Laura's soul is not broken on the "wheel of life."

This remarkable novel deserves consideration apart from its form and content and interest. It is really an approach by Miss Glasgow to masculine art—inspiration carried to completion. One may criticise her style, resent her constant qualification of the verbs "to say," "to smile," and "to address." Yet it has its effect. The style is culminative and, however rough the method, it is powerful. As remarked above, the author is young. What will she do when she has matured her art? Certainly she will not say such things as this: "... all the harm on earth comes from women telling men the truth. It is the woman who tells the truth who becomes—a door-mat." She will be too wise to lay the emphasis of an epigram on what is not worth disputing.

"Books of the Day," *Reader*, 7 (March 1906), 448–9

There are suggestive evidences that our novelists are breaking away from the narrow confines of recent years wherein all love and adventure and the very universe itself have been considered solely with reference to two certain people inevitably placed toward each other in the position of lovers. The drama of two will always possess a peculiar strength by reason of its unity, and a peculiar fascination because of its intensity, but it is only in the drama of many characters that we feel the flux of life in its fullness; it is then that we most completely lose ourselves and so yield highest tribute to the writer's art. Such a drama is *The House of Mirth*, and so, likewise, is Miss Ellen Glasgow's latest story, *The Wheel of Life*. That the two books may fairly be compared in several ways is, in itself, a marked compliment to Miss Glasgow, for *The House of Mirth* almost deserves to be called the American *Vanity Fair*. *The Wheel of Life* and *The House of Mirth* are both reflections of fashionable life in New York, each with a young and unusual woman as the central figure. In each the garishness of a life in which show and sham are main factors, is artistically pictured, and with complete unanimity of verdict, though with the essential and permeating difference in manner that Mrs. Wharton's story is remorselessly finished, absolutely cruel in its perfection, while Miss Glasgow's betrays a very human desire for the conciliatory ending. But *The Wheel of Life* is by no means provocative only of comparisons; it has a very decided absolute value, being indeed one of the most virile of recent novels. The author's manner has for some time been established as quite her own. She has full, rich powers of expression. She might even be called a phrase-maker, if the term be understood without the burden of reproach that it has unjustly been forced to convey: where would our literature be if it were not for fine and beautiful phrases! Miss Glasgow's warm, vital and decisive imagination has minted things worth remembering. Her sentences are well ordered, even cadenced, though one must record with regret that in one or two instances she has fallen into the foolish cant of the day in using such expressions as "He went white." Old-fashioned readers, being accustomed to think that people "go" to places, not colors, resent the intrusion of this modern flippancy into a book of such repose and such elevated purpose. Miss Glasgow has given us one of the loveliest of heroines, and by such delicate touches that we are scarcely aware by what means and at what moment she becomes completely alive to us. The description given to her when she is first introduced, though suggestive, is brief, but it is supplemented by the remark of first one of *Laura's* friends and then another, until her completed portrait, in rarest beauty, hangs before us. One man is certain that her eyes are bottomless depths; another says that her "soul burns like a golden flame within her;" a third declares that "she lives in a little hanging-garden of the imagination;" a fourth pronounces her "a precious first edition, not to be handed out to the crowd." *Laura* is a poet, but she is a woman, too, and the woman side of her is the one that most nearly touches our sympathies. If she loses, through contact with the world, something of that conventual purity that in the beginning of the story sets her as a lily apart, she gains more than an equivalent in human warmth and womanly wisdom. There are four distinct groups of characters in this novel of Thackeray spaciousness: *Laura's* eccentric family, with the passionately penitent aunt and the little old wizened flute-playing uncle, as the most interesting members, illustrating Miss Glasgow's fine sympathy for the portraying of human nature somewhat awry; there is *Trent*, his charming silver-haired mother and pretty, feminine *Christina Coles*; there are the *Adamses*, husband and wife, enduring each other, and there are the *Bridewells*, husband and wife, each trying to outwit the other. All of these groups are faithfully and well wrought, and each adds its increment of genuine substance to the sum total effect of an admirable book.

William Morton Payne, "Recent Fiction," *Dial*, 40 (1 March 1906), 156

We are not altogether satisfied that Miss Glasgow should again have deserted her native heath (if a Virginia plantation may be thus designated) for the allurements of the metropolis and its so-called "society." As we said of *The House of Mirth*, it is next to impossible to make a story of human interest out of the vapid and insolent life of the idle rich, and even the delicate art of Mrs. Wharton was balked in the effort. Now Miss Glasgow's art, although possibly stronger, is less delicate, and by so much she has been even less sucessful than the writer with whose latest work *The Wheel of Life* is brought into inevitable comparison. We may say in behalf of the newer novel that it offers us at least one fine character in the person of its hero, who is in "society" but not of it, and another of strong but elusive charm in the person of the woman poet whose apparition haunts many of the pages. But as compared with *The Deliverance* for example, this work is an inferior production.

"A Grab at Metropolitan Color," *Literary Digest*, 32 (31 March 1906), 491–2

Miss Glasgow has so firmly established herself in the world of English letters that she need fear no detractor but herself. One inevitable consequence of such attainment is that, like all successful artists, she will be judged with her most excellent work as standard. Thus appraised, she is "broken" upon *The Wheel of Life*, her latest novel. The reason is not far to seek. *The Descendant*, another premier work of hers, was a full-blooded ebullition of scenes, characters, and potentialities which she had absorbed into her soul from her native South. In *The Wheel of Life*, seeking new worlds to conquer, she sets her field of action in the garish atmosphere of New York "society." It is as if she had wandered through the doleful corridors of *The House of Mirth* and, with an exultant gasp something like Correggio's "Anch' Io son pittore" as he gazed for the first time upon Rafaelle's canvas, had called on the Tragic Muse to sound chords on Gotham's raucous harp. It is a clever attempt at New York "atmosphere," but an imperfect assimilation of it.

This is the smallest defect in *The Wheel of Life*, however, and not by this has Miss Glasgow been frustrated. Her failure, judged by her own standard, is that which usually attends the artist who is not so much dominated by his *motif* as he is concerned in achieving a *tour de force* by clever manipulation of his material. She seeks to flog her *Wheel of Life* into briskness as the spring urchin whips his hoop. It has strength, earnestness, and conscientiousness, but the strength is that of the resolute craftsman; the interest is in the style and the promise of fitting fulfilment, which is not satisfied; the conscientiousness is only in doing her best in an ambitious effort at literary grafting.

True, the merit is hers of falling "*magnis ex ausis.*" In these days of cocky maunderings about pseudo-ideals in the field of the human, the esthetic, and the ethical, it is to her credit to have 'dreamed right' in as noble an ideal of a man as Roger Adams, and to have essayed courageously the task of making him wallow through life's quagmires to the attainment of God as the crowning consummation of personal development. But the pity is that such righteous and heroic manliness eventuates so wanly! Laura Wilde is also largely a made character. The weird environment of her Gramercy Park home and its odd human remnants is bizarre rather than justificative of her bent.

The Wheel of Life is a museum of "types." Terry Bridewell and Arnold Kemper are almost twins, the "beefiness" of Perry only veiled by a trifle more distinction and aim in Arnold. Gertie Bridewell is the most convincingly human thing in the book and with a genuine appeal.

Several of the characters simply walk across the stage and are only slightly contributory to the action. The young Virginian, who has come to New York with a play (which, of course, is accepted) and whose eyes "run entirely to sparkle," just as Mrs. Payne's diamonds have a habit of "winking," is somewhat irrelevant. The young woman who can't write but is so convinced that she can as to starve in the attempt, seems introduced only to mate her pleasantly with the aforesaid dramatist. *The Wheel of Life* is not up to Miss Glasgow's level, but this seems largely due to her trespassing upon an alien field. . . .

"A Group of Novels," *Outlook*, 82 (31 March 1906), 756

In such a story as Miss Ellen Glasgow's *The Wheel of Life* there is no lack of tragedy of a pitiful kind, but the tragedy involves growth rather than waste, and out of the chaos of weak wills, self-indulgence, poverty of interests, and empty frivolity something definite and significant in character emerges. The people in this very seriously conceived drama of spiritual growth belong to the so-called "fast set," so mercilessly studied in *The House of Mirth*. Miss Glasgow, like Mrs. Wharton, has made New York the background of her novel, but every large city and many small cities furnish the same conditions on a smaller scale and produce the same types of character. A vein of Orientalism, suggested by the title, runs through this novel, which deals, in its largest aspects, with the early illusions, the pain of education, and that enlightenment which involves, not rejection of the order of life, but acceptance of a spiritual scale of values and the subordination of the lesser to the greater. Through the four stages of impulse, illusion, disenchantment, and reconciliation the two chief actors move to a tempered happiness which is the fulfillment of a moral process and the justification of its inexorable and penetrating discipline. This interior movement does not obscure the exterior dramatic action of the novel, though it is occasionally overemphasized by too much definition. There are broader contrasts of character than in *The House of Mirth*, though not quite the same sureness of touch, the same sense of intimacy with the most elusive aspects of a well-defined though loosely ordered social group. Frivolity and vice are relieved by the play of light from the finer virtues across the picture, and the studies of character are done with the most delicate fidelity. The style shows a marked change, and approaches more closely the analytic and subtle selective process of those sophisticated writers who reflect a dominant, though, it may be suspected, not the deepest, mood of the period. It is to be hoped that Miss Glasgow will not go further in this direction.

"New Novels," *Athenæum* [England], 1 (7 April 1906), 416

There is no question as to the cleverness of Miss Glasgow; the very texture of her writing discovers that to an experienced eye. But she has a psychological fluency which is almost alarming. She will take you through the whole course of a character's thoughts, meditations, and reminiscences, between breakfast eggs, in a dozen pages, and you will be convinced that she is right. But at the same time you would rather have been spared them; for, frankly, you see no necessity for the intrusion. Psychology for the sake of psychology seems to appeal to the author. The average level of the tale is extra-ordinarily high, but it does not rise to anything that matters very much anywhere. And it has the feminine vice of heroizing. Most of Miss Glasgow's men are of sound human flesh, particularly the sensual Bridewell and his cousin; but the author must have a hero marked out for the post from the outset. And thus we are introduced to the hardworking, good-hearted Adams, whose noble character shines in a naughty world. Adams, alas! is not of human blood. But the women of the tale are excellent. So far as the structure of the novel goes, its main fault is that it is concerned with the fortunes of various groups of people, and is thus somewhat formless. But that charge could be levelled against a much greater work—*Middlemarch*.

Olivia Howard Dunbar, "Readable but Crude," *Critic*, 48 (May 1906), 435

Is Miss Glasgow's study of contemporary New York life as profoundly symbolic, after all, as her title would imply? It is a readable story, containing frequent paragraphs of observation for which "clever" is precisely the appropriate adjective; and, technically considered, the narrative is well-ordered and symmetrical. But it cannot be discovered that either Miss Glasgow's method or her point of view is strikingly new, a point that would doubtless escape comment if the book did not flaunt an implication of self-conscious novelty. But, apart from its lack of vital significance, what one most seriously misses in the story is a richness of texture and a perception, on the author's part, of the luminous contrasts of life, such qualities, in short, as made Miss Sinclair's *The Divine Fire* a memorable novel. Miss Glasgow has not seen deeply nor interpreted richly; her book is, frankly speaking, crude.

[...]

... Laura Wilde, the heroine, who escapes marrying the object of her ephemeral passion, is a poet; but will perhaps appear to have a less complex nature than has usually been attributed to her living counterparts. Her physical appearance is dwelt on to redundancy, and it is perhaps in contrast with her smile, holding "all the mystery of flame and of shadow," "her skin, which was like porcelain touched by a flame," her "illusion of mystery," that her actions appear strangely normal, if not actually commonplace. As often happens in the work of writers who fall short of genius, the minor characters have most of truth and suggestiveness. Gerty Bridewell, for instance, who pretends to no intrinsic interest of character, is a successfully sardonic little study. "Why, for instance," this luxuriously miserable young woman asks herself, "when she had been wretched with but one man on the box, should the addition of a second livery fail to produce in her the contentment of which she had often dreamed while she disconsolately regarded a single pair of shoulders?" It is a pity that Miss Glasgow's humor does not shine forth more abundantly; her work needs it. The book is a sincere and intelligent effort to approach the realities; yet after reading it one is obliged to admit that more than one obstinate veil still lies between.

the business man in New York. The hero of *The Wheel of Life*, however, is not a business man, but an idle man about town,—that is, if the man who during the course of the novel acts as lover to the heroine can be called the hero. The man who ultimately marries the heroine, and who is cast in a far more heroic mould, is a literary man, and Miss Glasgow's study of him is finely contrasted with that of the worldly lover, Arnold Kemper. Laura Wilde, the heroine, belongs to the literary section of the book, and the way in which she unwillingly but completely succumbs to the fascination which Kemper exercises over her is cleverly shown by the author. The novel is a study of manners, and is extremely clever, very subtle, and slightly disagreeable. Miss Glasgow's talent is well displayed in the book, but we cannot help liking her work better when she is dealing with scenes of action, as in *The Battle-Ground*. In the present novel she does not seem so much at her ease, and the detailed analysis of character on which the success of the book depends is perhaps a little too much laboured to be quite successful.

Spectator [England], 5 May 1906, 718

It cannot be said that Miss Glasgow's accounts of society in New York give her readers a very pleasant impression of the social conditions of that city. A society which is semi-literary, semi-wordly, seldom shows an agreeable aspect in fiction, and London society from Miss Glasgow's point of view would probably be even less agreeable than New York. Perhaps, though, the Wall Street atmosphere is more absorbing on the other side of the Atlantic; and English people certainly imagine that there is no class among them which takes such an exclusive interest in stocks and shares, and in nothing else, as does

Saturday Review [London], 101 (19 May 1906), 625

Like most feminine writers, Miss Glasgow is chiefly concerned with the problems of sex, and with the mutual attitude of men and women. There is much that is original and thoughtful in her studies of the various couples whose loves and antipathies fill the book, but she is too fond of discussion. She is overflowing with ideas but they are not all valuable and her perpetual gushing eloquence seems out of proportion to the importance of the incidents. The women characters are remarkably well drawn, the men are less successful—they are so very literary and introspective in their conversation.

Louise Collier Willcox, "The Content of the Modern Novel," *North American Review*, 182 (June 1906), 919–29

... This year, the two best novels were written by women and by American women. *The Wheel of Life* and *The House of Mirth* stand first and have other points of similarity beside the identical number of syllables in their titles and their authors' names. Both Miss Glasgow and Mrs. Wharton have chosen to set up a spiritual and an intellectual value against a background of sordid animalism. Both books deal with New York and with a set of people whose interests and occupations it is unhappily all too easy to know. Miss Glasgow's is a work almost primitive in its vigor and strength, the work of a genius. Mrs. Wharton's is a work still-pulsed, restrained, curiously impersonal, the output of an artist. The large play of life, the quick pulse and rush of emotion make Miss Glasgow's book all quiveringly alive, while Mrs. Wharton's is a carefully veiled, fatally truthful picture. These two authors represent the difference between the overwhelming impulse of genius, hewing its own way with an elemental force, and that of a highly wrought culture, conscious of its means and austerely selecting its effects. In structure, too, there is a great difference to be noted. Miss Glasgow's novel is more "enveloped," as the sculptors say. The framework is entirely hidden; the covering is large and irregular as life itself; the sweep of the rhythmic ebb and flow is so long that the little events come and pass, apparently, without relation to total impression, and without blending into the significance of the whole. This is like life and it gives us the feeling of life, its largeness and variety, its capriciousness and lack of selection.

[...]

... Wharton's great gifts as a novelist are style, first and foremost, then clever manipulation of plot and unwavering truth of vision. Miss Glasgow's are force, characterization and profound insight into human experience.

Erskine Steele, "Fiction and Social Ethics," *South Atlantic Quarterly*, 5 (July 1906), 257–60

[...]

It is not then a matter for surprise that Miss Glasgow, with such diversity of talents, should have abandoned the somewhat circumscribed field of her former novels, and boldly stepped forth into a more cosmopolitan area. And yet in deserting a field in which her pre-eminence was quite generally acknowledged for one alien and untried, she has undertaken a dubious hazard of new fortunes. Massively rounded by its masculinity of touch, focussed again and again to brilliant points, Miss Glasgow's latest book is lacking in one indispensable quality. Lack of intimate familiarity with the life with which it deals may perhaps explain its failure as a social document of convincing veracity. One may readily accept Miss Glasgow's conclusions; it would be difficult to justify what an impressionist would call the "values" in her picture. Her contrasts lack nothing in sharpness; but her effects of light and shade were secured from the wrong point of view.

And yet, despite this secret sense of disappointment, one finds in this novel much that is sane, mature, and solid. Informed with the modern spirit, it echoes with reverberations of Ibsen, of Maeterlinck, of Shaw. It is, *comme toujours*, an affair of the "eternal triangle"—a pagan devotee of the senses, a worshipper at the shrine of the buried temple of the soul, and a fair idealist ardently cruising, like an Argonaut, in search of the Golden Fleece of life. A dreamer of dreams, seeing life through the "haze of a golden temperament," Laura Wilde is a poetess by default: her poetry is but the translation of her desire for the joy of living. Thrilled through by the magnetic personality of that devotee of dalliance, Arnold Kemper, she flings aside her poetry in exchange for the fullness of life. Like Domini Enfilden in *The Garden of Allah*, she wishes to live and to live more abundantly—"to be, to know, to feel, . . . to go through everything, to turn every page, to experience all that can be experienced upon the earth." Prevising neither the illusion of desire nor the disenchantment of passion, she all too readily surrenders to the bold challenge of the male antagonist in the eternal duel of sex. Like Dick Dudgeon in accomplishing the fulfillment of the law of his own nature, Kemper lives upon the surface of life with no more serious passion than "to live in pleasure and to let live in pleasantness." Instead of following Ibsen's injunction to achieve one's destiny in developing one's individuality, Kemper cleaves to the Rabelaisian motto of *l'homme moyen sensual*: "*Fais ce que tu veux.*" With defiant cynicism, he struggles after the illusion of a happiness which has no part in any possession nor in any object; and self-pityingly fights against the conviction of his own spiritual and moral bankruptcy. The coming of satiety was a rift in his lute, and discounted his pagan view: "'Men were not born monogamous'—it was a favorite jest of his, for he was inclined to throw upon nature the full burden of her responsibility." In striking contrast to Kemper stands Roger Adams, filled with a sense of the secret beauty of the inner life, and secure from the shocks of external fatality in the conviction that all life is forfeiture. With the mystic stoicism of a Maeterlinck, Adams has learned that one must be broken upon the wheel of life and feel the pangs of death before he can attain a philosophic attitude of wise-hearted, broad-visioned tolerance. Only then may one perhaps hope to pluck here and there, in stillness and almost in terror, a few stray flowers of happiness. The radical distinction separating him eternally from Kemper is found in these words: "Too much Nature he (Adams) had learned during those months of mental apathy is in its way quite as destructive as too little—there must be a soul in desire to keep it alive, he understood at last, or the perishing body of it will decay for lack of a vital flame in the very hour of its fulfilment." Only just in time does Laura awake to a consciousness of the satyr in her hero, and bravely take the long straight road of forfeiture and self-denial. And in the end, one surmises, she unites with Roger Adams, in spirit and in the faith that it is not so much what we think, or even what we do, but what we are that eternally matters.

Thus, the book closes, not on an unresolved cadence, but on a positive note, an affirmative chord. Throughout the story, we see the characters sharply silhouetted against the garish background of a fickle, heartless, empty cosmopolitan life of social frivolity. Perry Bridewell, imperfectly monogamous by instinct, was "by nature designed for a lover, and it seemed, broadly viewed, the merest accident of circumstance that he should tend toward variety rather than toward specialization." And there is Gerty, his wife, like Isabel Carnaby, failing to win happiness in the empty life of society, yet pathetically conscious of her inability to be happy without it. True at heart to her fickle, epicurean husband, whom she loves with the ferocity of a wounded animal, she condescends "to lie and cheat and backbite—and strangle her little soul within her"—to please her husband, whose amusement, paradoxically enough, is built on her long boredom. And even at times she has gleams of insight into the life of the soul and vague, unsatisfied longings for an existence she lacks the strength to live. Beyond Kemper, Bridewell, Gerty, Connie Adams, and Brady stretch a vast concourse of feverish pleasure-seekers, starved souls futilely searching for the oasis of happiness upon the arid plains of amusement and frivolity. Seeking happiness above all things, for that very reason they never overtake it. Conversation is surcease from boredom—they talk to fill up the blanks of life. And in this hopeless disillusionment, they are all struggling for forgetfulness—summoning every anodyne—religion, dissipation, morphia—to intoxicate themselves into "forgetting that life is life."

[...]

Checklist of Additional Reviews

F. Dana Reed, "Miss Ellen Glasgow's New Novel; E.P. Oppenheim's Latest Romance," Brooklyn *Daily Eagle*, 20 January 1906, sec. 2, p. 4.

"Miss Glasgow's New Novel," Louisville *Courier-Journal*, 27 January 1906, sec. 1, p. 5.

Hartford *Daily Courant*, 17 February 1906, p. 18.

Mary Moss, "Miss Glasgow's *The Wheel of Life*," *Bookman* 23 (March 1906), 91–3.

"Recent Fiction and the Critics," *Current Literature*, 40 (March 1906), 338.

Boston *Evening Transcript*, 7 March 1906, p. 18.

Alice M. Tyler, *Book News Monthly*, 24 April 1906, 570–1.

"Love Stories," *American Monthly Review of Reviews*, 33 (June 1906), 758.

"Books of the Month," *Appleton's Booklovers Magazine*, June 1906, 855–6.

New York Times Saturday Review of Books, 16 June 1906, p. 384.

THE ANCIENT LAW

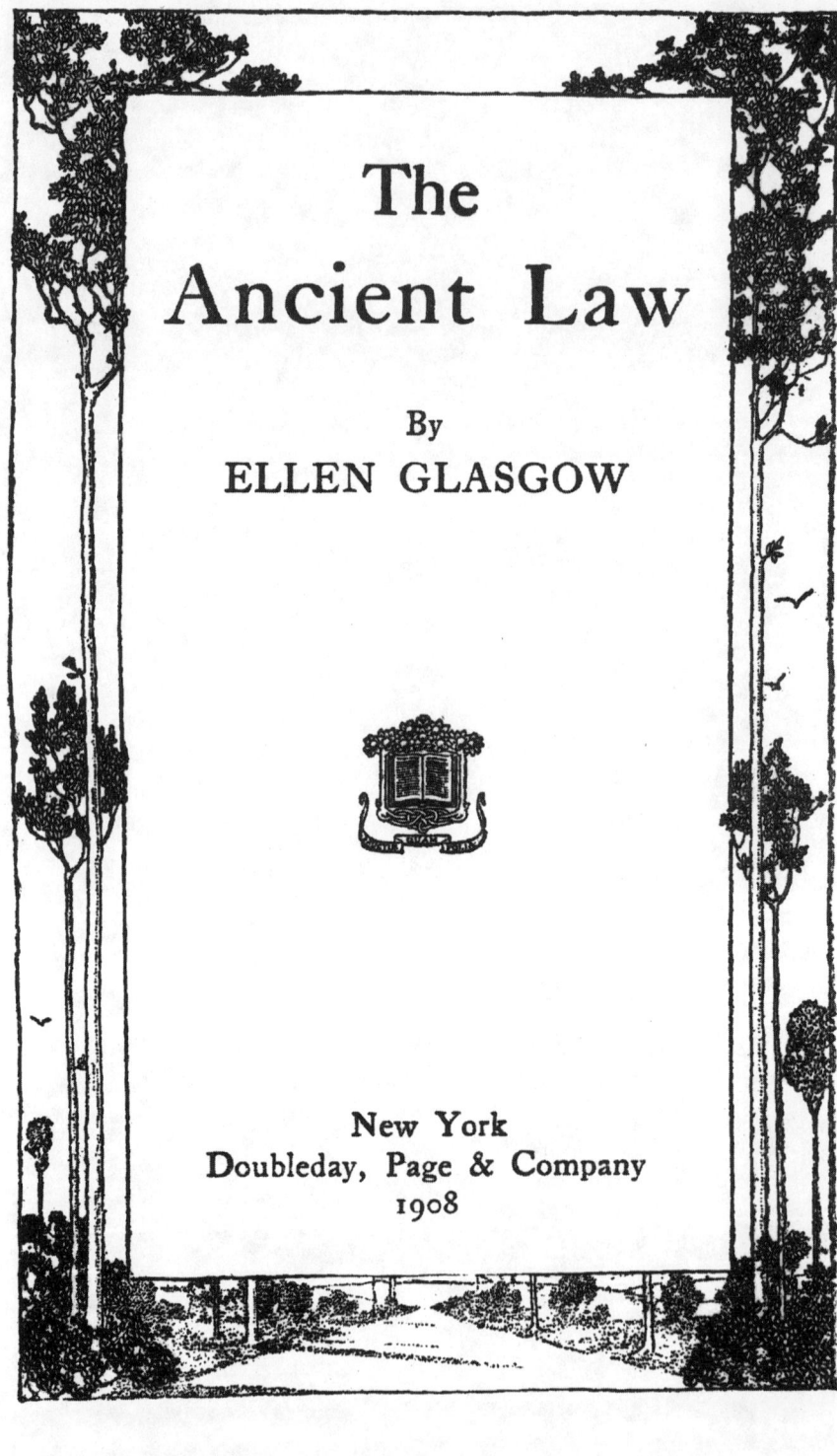

The Ancient Law

By
ELLEN GLASGOW

New York
Doubleday, Page & Company
1908

Issac F. Marcosson, "A Virginia Valjean," *New York Times Saturday Review of Books,* 1 February 1908, pp. 53–4

Between the novelization of bridge whist in the north and the commercialization of race prejudice in the South, all for best-selling purposes, the element of character in fiction has been having something of a struggle for existence. There are occasional evidences, however, that Strenuosity and Timeliness have not yet been permanently installed as dictators, particularly when a new novel by Miss Ellen Glasgow comes along. Her latest story is of such distinguished qualities as to make its consideration not only a matter of personal pleasure, but an occasion for the renewal of faith in a genuine literary artist.

To have watched the growth of Miss Glasgow's art has been to measure a steadily increasing purpose to do large and worthy things, not only in those conventional externals which comprise the mere forms of fiction, but in those larger and more enduring phases, one of which may be summed up as the philosophy of the work. In *The Ancient Law* Miss Glasgow presents a Virginia Jean Valjean, a man intensely human in his frailties, yet winning in his regeneration. It is a long, weary, beaten road that he travels, and he is but the concrete embodiment of a world-old tragedy and a world-old problem which has survived crumbling ages. What makes him distinct among many of his brothers is an all-encompassing vision that comprehends both the Letter and the Spirit of the Law that enchains him. Herein is the keynote of an absorbing and convincing story.

There is much cause for gratification in the fact that in this new book Miss Glasgow is once more amid the scenes of her most vital work. Again the Virginia fields beckon, and the varied, intimate life of the "small town" passes in picturesque panorama. Here, too, is merciful emancipation from the thrall of sectional dispute, because Miss Glasgow, like all other sane students of life, whether for fiction or other purposes, long ago realized that even in a Virginia story the civil war may be forgotten for a moment and that human nature, like art, has no section. Invariably strong in the characterization of her men, in creating Daniel Ordway she has added a compelling portrait to a gallery of fine figures which began with Nick Burr in *The Voice of the People*. It is a group of men, each of whom stands for the working out of a strong passion, be it hatred, revolt, revenge, or real love. It is not by masterful powers, however, that Ordway dominates, but rather by a marvelous sense of humanity. . . .

In a sense *The Ancient Law* is primarily the study of the development of one man, and Miss Glasgow has done nothing finer, deeper, or truer than her picture of the evolution of his character. There is about it none of the tumult of stirring spectacle. Rather is it invested with the larger dignity of high service. A great heart finds itself through denial and suffering, and the journey of the spirit toward its triumphant regeneration is heightened by the consciousness of a greater love. Through disillusion and sacrifice, the hero reared the structure of his soul. Yet the book is not a vitalized sermon. . . .

Such a story can only be serious, yet its seriousness is lighted by humor at once fresh and appealing. Miss Glasgow's books are never without a character whose observations are sure to lend zest and fill in the dark backgrounds with occasional gleams. In *The Ancient Law* there is a verbose and angular person, not far removed from the familiar "poor white" of so many Southern towns. You recall her with a smile.

The Ancient Law is an important book, not only because it is a distinct advance in the work of an author who ranks with the best of our women novelists, but also because it has the qualities of high endeavor and worthy purpose. It is a book calculated to make you pause in the survey of rapid-fire fiction and realize that here is the real note of study, of character, and of observation. It is indeed a novel of dignity and of distinction.

F. Dana Reed, "Miss Glasgow's *The Ancient Law*: A Novel of Unusual Quality," Brooklyn *Daily Eagle*, 8 February 1908, p. 5

Miss Ellen Glasgow's new novel, *The Ancient Law*, just published, presents in a striking degree the qualities of moral earnestness and sincerity which are characteristic of her fiction. Like its immediate predecessor, *The Wheel of Life*, published two years ago, *The Ancient Law*, is a study in character, rather than a novel of incident or adventure. Even the thread of a love motive which runs through the tale, is shadowy and from the viewpoint of the romance writer, ends nowhere. It is rather a phase of the evolution of character which is the novel's theme than a dominant influence in the narrative. And yet "the ancient law" is the law of love, only in this instance it is love sublimated and refined from all materialistic quality, become wholly spiritual, and dominated by the passion for self-sacrifice. Miss Glasgow has given her readers a story with an unusual plot—unusual in the fashion in which results are worked out from the primary conditions. . . .

[. . .]

The defect of *The Ancient Law*, structurally considered, and from the usual fictional viewpoint, is, that it ends in the air. Ordway is left recovering from an illness; there is before him the vision of a life of self-sacrifice. He is going forward along the same lines; that is all. There could be no other ending without resort to the stage machinery of the average fiction writer, and Miss Glasgow is too much of an artist, too loyal to her ideals for such a finale. The unhasting novel reader—the one who reads not for sensation, but for the keen delight which is found in superb artistry and delicate craftsmanship, will understand, and will not cavil because there is no dramatic "curtain" to the story.

The Ancient Law is a further step in advance upon Miss Glasgow's previous work. It is notable how this young woman has steadily progressed with each succeeding novel, until she has reached a point that places her in the very front rank of American novelists. More and more does she depend upon the literary quality and artistic strength of her work for its interest. Strong, delicate, finished, inspiring, always with its atmosphere of hope and belief, her work makes an appeal that is always forceful and always heeded.

"Ellen Glasgow's Latest Novel,"
Louisville *Courier-Journal*, 8 February 1908, sec. 1, p. 5

This story is full of both force and tenderness. It has the best of themes—the surrender of personal joy and happiness, the leading of an unselfish life in order to atone for a wrong done society and the individual. An eye for an eye is the old law, but in almost all human instances when the offender has given the eye and so has paid his debt the world at large continues to exact payment.

[. . .]

The story is one of surprising unity in the manner of its telling. The development of the theme, the careful characterizations, the contrasts give a reflection of real life. But it has a singular, inexplicable quality. There is every reason why the character of Daniel should be one of the most appealing in fiction, but it nowhere excites the deepest feelings. He is a brave, strong man, he rises to heights, he is the incarnation of sacrifice, yet one's emotions are never deeply stirred by his woes. Perhaps humility comes too easy to him; perhaps he goes out of his way to be too good, but somehow his sorrows excite neither the pity nor the sympathy of the reader; they appeal to the intellect alone.

Another fault lies in the ending. Everything in the whole book points to tragedy, but things are manipulated so that the hero instead of dying goes back to the home of his choice to start his model mills, schools and factories surrounded by friends who know his past, but are still friends.

As a whole the book shows much that is unusually good. Miss Glasgow has put poetry, the ideal, in her treatment. These people of hers who have seen the vision are the best of teachers, for they reconcile one to much that is cruel and hard in real life. Her text that happiness can be found only in surrendering all hopes of it is exemplified in various characters. In many respects she is a remarkable writer and it would not be surprising if in her future work she were to develop sufficiently to rank with the few great writers of fiction that this country has brought forth.

Nation, 86 (13 February 1908), 152–3

Miss Glasgow writes, as always, with fluency, gravity, and a species of *empressement* which may go a long way toward achieving the effects of depth and subtlety. Her books are, we gather from the triumphant bulletins of her publishers, widely read, in the main we must suppose, by a class which does not read very much, and is guided to its few choices by the conversational clue. Her work is planned upon a generous scale. There are four books and forty chapters in *The Ancient Law*, and they cover some five hundred pages—quite the old three-decker plan. After going over it all, one may find oneself speculating as to whether the cargo is worth the carriage. Superficially the book is of the right kind. The theme is older than Jean Valjean: What shall the convict do with himself when, with the best will in the world, he finds himself outside the bars? One Daniel Ordway goes wrong on the stock exchange, and, after five years' imprisonment, is to face the world again. . . . Ordway himself, to be sure, with all the author's deliberateness of portraiture, is a person commented upon rather than presented. Our first impression of him is promising, but after the opening scene it wanes steadily in distinctness. We do not live with him through his experiences; we do not feel the charm and power in the man which are said to work such wonders in that stubborn rural community. But some of the minor scenes and characters have life; above all the gracious and strong figure of Emily Brooke, the beautiful girl who falls innocently in love with our jail bird. As he has a wife who has failed and repudiated him in his need, this, according to the code, should not have been allowed to happen; but the relation which develops between them keeps itself within the prescribed bounds. One would like to have parted with them both at the moment when, after the full revelation of his past, she professes her unalterable faith in him. But here begins the anticlimax, and the story sinks through chapters of crude melodrama whither we shall not follow it.

"The Ancient Law," Boston *Evening Transcript*, 19 February 1908, p. 18

Regeneration is Miss Glasgow's theme in *The Ancient Law*, and placing her hero and the subordinate characters in the midst of an atmosphere that is redolent of the Virginia soil, she expands her story so that it covers year after year of evolutionary progress. Her scenes are two Virginian towns, to the first of which at the outset of the story comes the hero out of a Northern prison in search of work. The other town is his birthplace, where dwell the family, including father, wife and child, that he has disgraced by transgressing the laws of the society and the financial world of New York wherein he had ruled to the time of his downfall. At Tappahannock he finds employment as bookkeeper and factotum in a tobacco warehouse, rises in the esteem of his fellow-townsmen through the manliness and goodness of heart that lead him to be the Good Samaritan of the place, is proposed for the office of mayor, and after three years of honorable living thinks himself compelled to flee when, to save a girl from ruin he is obliged to confess his prison record. Going to Botetourt, his birthplace, in time to be present at his father's funeral, he lives there in the midst of a depressing and disheartening environment, his uncle being upright but cold-hearted, his wife, who had deserted him in his hour of need, repellent and unsympathetic, and his daughter frivolous and disobedient.

But Daniel Ordway is able to endure everything and to see but little of the selfishness of others through the merit of his own unselfishness. He comes into contact with an impoverished Virginian family, he grows to love—and he does not fall in love with, in the conventional sense of the phrase—the sturdy woman who supports her lazy brother, and he everywhere makes the world better by his presence. But he is never for a moment a convincing character or a type of the strong manhood that Miss Glasgow endeavors to make him. If he were, he would see more clearly his wife's indefensible attitude towards him; he would not live beneath the same roof with her and ruffle her irrational contempt uncomplainingly; he would teach her the lessons that he taught others for their and his own good. As a matter of fact, he is the strong man made weak by adversity, and although his misfortune has regenerated his soul, it has also weakened his self-confidence. He is too humble and too willing to be a victim of circumstances. The end of the story is chaos, and after an attack of brain fever we leave him to suffering under the delusion that he has a message for the world, "for all places where there were men and women working and suffering and going into prison and coming out." What his fate is to be, Miss Glasgow leaves her readers to decide for themselves.

Independent, 64 (27 February 1908), 469–70

Since Miss Glasgow's new novel is so radically different from those she has already published, some reference to them is necessary in order to prove the contrast. She was recognized several years ago as one of the popular novelists, and few of her discerning critics expected her to become anything better. Until the appearance of this last book her stories have been marked by the peculiar weaknesses to be observed in plays, fiction and all forms of art produced merely to please the imagination of the populace—a crude, bedlam faculty that should be disciplined, not humored. The scenes were always laid in Virginia, and to lay the scenes of a story in Virginia, if you know *how*, is to give it a sort of romantic diploma at the start with the cavalier seal upon it. Then it was her custom to spend a chapter in hanging family portraits and in discussing the hero's pedigree until the reader was properly humbled (for, mark you, the average reader still likes to be humbled by his author, and to feel that he is receiving confidences about grander folk). Having effaced the reader, she would begin the story. And we all remember what the character of the story was—always a decayed gentility struggling to rise again. Nothing could be more futile. That kind of gentility never rises again except it is lost in the blood of the common people, as the kernel of corn must fall into the earth and die before it shall live again. And that was the tragedy of Miss Glasgow's stories which neither she nor her readers seemed to recognize. She went on writing them with that dramatic sentimentality which appealed so strongly to the invincible ignorance of her Northern readers concerning the South, and no less flatteringly to the equally invincible pride of her Southern admirers. Also her novels were moral....

Now, these are some of the reasons for Miss Glasgow's success; also they show why many believed she would never do anything better.

But Ellen Glasgow has ascended. She has omitted the family portraits and most of the pedigrees in her new story and made ready for a long, wide sweep of the wings. She has not parted company with the populace. She has simply assumed a nobler attitude to it. Her telepathy is no longer with the past or with some small sectional sense of the present, but it is with the Spirit of Time, not of the times. We make too much of the yawping spirit of the times, a little distracted bird of the mortal mind. And this accounts in part for the ephemeral character of modern fiction. She has founded her story upon the ancient law of self-sacrifice, rather than upon some sentimentality of abnegation. Hugo could have written it better, but Miss Glasgow could not.

... Miss Glasgow has a literary style that is grave and glowing, like the fine plain frame of a grand picture. There is a sort of integrity in her choice of words, a freshness and a charm, as if she had cultivated a vocabulary somewhere in the open air and sunshine among the Virginia lilacs. There is suffering, to be sure—that suffering which comes from perfect comprehension of misfortune, but the reader is not harrowed because the man is so sublimely equal to the situation, so intelligently able to forgive his enemies, so logical rather than morbid in working out his sacrifice according to law rather than sentiment. And his liberation at last is worthy of the ideal upon which the story is founded.

"Comment on Current Books," *Outlook*, 88 (29 February 1908), 511–12

From Ellen Glasgow we may always expect thoroughly well written fiction, with accurate rendering of Southern color and atmosphere, and also with a definite ethical and social purpose. *The Ancient Law* is essentially a sad story, and one could wish the bright spots picturing Virginian life and humor a little more frequent, but the book is not in its essence either pessimistic or depressing. The "ancient law" that evil will have its inevitable consequences, despite repentance and reparation, follows Daniel Ordway implacably. He has forged to save his fortune, and has served a term in prison; when he is free he begins a humble life in a little Virginia town under a new name, and unknown to all. But he is so helpful, brave, and unselfish, and so makes himself the champion of the poor and the oppressed, that "Ten Commandments Smith," as he is called, is loved by all good citizens, and remains so even when his past is dragged into light.... There is sympathetic and delicate working out of character throughout, and the book is eminently dignified and worthy. In its nature it is less entertaining than other novels by Miss Glasgow, but it is a fine piece of literary work notwithstanding.

Louise Collier Willcox, *North American Review*, 187 (March 1908), 445–7

...It is the inner life of Daniel Ordway that Miss Glasgow presents us, his struggles, his sufferings, his days of discouragement, his reactions in the teeth of calamity, his silent ponderings and inner growth, his progressive power of renunciation, and, finally, out of these, the enlarging of consciousness, the flowering of the fruits of the spirit.

When we recall that Miss Glasgow, with seven largely constructed novels behind her, is still on the earthward side of thirty-five, and when we see how steadily and surely her art has grown from *The Descendant* to *The Ancient Law*, we realize that we have a born novelist to cope with; not, as one might have feared from the emotional intensity of *The Descendant* and *Phases of an Inferior Planet*, merely a writer of one strong imaginative impulse, like Olive Schreiner, or a cultured craftsman looking about for a story to tell, like Mrs. Wharton. Miss Glasgow is a storyteller, first and foremost, with a keen insight into life; a mind still plastic, broadening and growing in ability to note the detail of life and to fathom meanings and relations and weave them into a whole.

[...]

There are many fine and haunting passages, and among them the first and last chapters stand out as being not only, in themselves, beautiful, but as sounding the key-note of the spiritual portent of the book and summing up the lesson of Daniel Ordway's life....

H. W. Boynton, "Ellen Glasgow's *The Ancient Law*," *Bookman*, 27 (March 1908), 59–60

The present reviewer may as well admit that this is the first of Miss Glasgow's books which it has actually befallen him to read. . . . To judge by the present story Miss Glasgow is the type of author who is taken seriously by a great many persons who ought to know better. No observer whose business it is to follow the whole main stream of contemporary fiction in England and America and who is able to take it seriously can help being a little disappointed, even aggrieved, at the blandness with which the ordinary compatriot of the better class is wont to accept as representative or extraordinary what is mere pretentious commonplace. *The Ancient Law* is better in workmanship than the average American novel, but it is a mediocre affair at best.

No better theme could be asked for than the theme of the reformed jail-bird. Daniel Ordway is a Wall Street broker who in the middle of a successful career uses other people's money for speculation, is caught and sent to prison for five years. . . . We are told a good many things about his nobility, his self-sacrifice, his commanding power, but they do not persuade us that he is anything but a very ordinary person, if he is a person at all. What is really wanting is a sense of humour, which is, strange as it may seem, the last thing demanded of its novelists by our public. We may be thankful for the lack of funny business in Miss Glasgow's book, but we have still to regret its lack of proportion, of perspective, of that indefinable circumambient atmosphere, of insight and sympathy with which true humour surrounds its material.

William Morton Payne, "Recent Fiction," *Dial*, 44 (1 March 1908), 134–5

Miss Glasgow's latest novel has both dignity and charm, although certain almost melodramatic happenings, huddled into the closing chapters, do not seem quite in keeping with the sincerity and restraint of what has gone before. *The Ancient Law* is the title of the book, and its theme is the inevitable consequence of sin. . . . The later chapters of the story have a sort of Jean Valjean pathos that works powerfully upon the reader's feelings. The end is rather inconclusive, but falls just short of tragedy, for it leaves the hero with the prospect of a return to the little town in which his new life began, and of a peaceful rounding out of a destiny that had once seemed hopelessly shattered.

"New Novels," *Athenæum* [England], 28 March 1908, 380

The culminating point of this thoughtful story may be termed an ethical development. We are introduced to the central figure newly released from a term of imprisonment for misappropriation; a period of self-abnegation in personal social service follows, spent partly in a primitive tobacco-raising corner of Virginia, and partly by the side of, but not in association with, his own family circle. Finally he is seen voluntarily taking upon himself the burden of sins which have already made their mark on the second generation.

The story maintains its hold to the end, mainly because the less self-conscious world to which the erstwhile prisoner returns is peopled by real men and women—clear-cut, convincing studies of sturdy Virginians. So excellent are these that an even greater measure of success might reasonably have been expected in the hero. As it is, his very perfection is wearisome; his introspective habit, and his much-used "radiant smile," are apt to cloy; and moreover one is conscious throughout of the sex of his creator. In spite of these drawbacks the book is well worth reading.

nal into the man known as "Ten Commandments Smith." The portion of the story that deals with the little town of Tappahannock is the most interesting, Ordway's doings when he rejoins his wife and children being narrated in a more conventional spirit. His daughter Alice is, it may be hoped, an almost impossibly irresponsible figure. When, however, she commits forgery, it does not seem to occur to Daniel that heredity has anything to do with her action. The picture of Daniel's wife, Lydia, is one of the most successful in the book, and the author very cleverly makes the reader feel how extraordinarily irritating can be the conduct of a woman known to her circle as a kind of saint. Miss Ellen Glasgow's books are always distinguished by the bestowal of unstinted labour on her writing, and *The Ancient Law* is no exception to the rule.

Spectator [England], 100 (28 March 1908), 505

—Though written in a different vein from some of Miss Glasgow's other books, none the less this story furnishes very excellent reading. The hero of the novel, which is of American origin, is a man released from a term of penal servitude for misappropriation of trust funds. Daniel Ordway has sinned more through weakness than through deliberate vice, and has derived enormous moral benefit from his punishment. In fact, "Daniel Smith," as he calls himself, is a totally different person from the Daniel Ordway who was condemned to imprisonment. So different is he, indeed, from the man of the ante-punishment days, of whom the author allows us glimpses, that the reader is inclined to doubt the possibility of any such transformation as that of the careless young crimi-

Edwin Mims, "The Ancient Law," *South Atlantic Quarterly*, 7 (April 1908), 200–1

While Miss Glasgow's latest novel has a large human value that makes it truly cosmopolitan and universal, the setting is distinctively Southern. Readers who were disappointed in *The Wheel of Life* and who explained their disappointment by the fact that the author had written about New York rather than Virginia, will rejoice that in *The Ancient Law* she returns to the land and people that she knows best. The Southern background is not emphasized nearly so much as in her earlier works, but it is all the more effective because the art of suggestion is brought into play. The crude factory village contrasts vividly with the dilapidated and yet picturesque old Southern home where the Brookes live. Mr. Beverly Brooke, pompous in his poverty, is a fine type of the run-down gentry, while his sister, who carries about with her the atmosphere of old libraries and is the incarnation of Southern refinement, is alert and vigorous, eager to seize new opportunities of service. "Was it some temperamental disgust for the hereditary idleness which had spurred her on to take issue with the worn-out traditions of her ancestors and to place herself among the labouring rather than the leisure class?" She is the spirit of the future rising amid the decaying sentiment of the past. Daniel Ordway, who is likewise a descendant of Virginia aristocrats and has served seven years in a prison, struggles toward the same ideals of service in the village which he enters as an unknown workman. In two years' time he aroused and vitalized the community. Tappahannock is the child of his brain. He is, therefore, a type of the Southerner of a new era struggling in a constructive way to bring into being a new democracy.

In this, as in all her other novels, Miss Glasgow shows that she is a thinker as well as an artist. She has humor and pathos, and rare insight into human nature. She has distinction of style, too. But in dealing with the Southern situation—always artistically—, she is in striking contrast with those Southern story-writers and novelists who write as if, with the decline of the Old South, the richest elements in Southern life passed away. In all her novels there is a suggestion of the glory of a new era, distinguished by the ideals of service and genuine democracy. From this standpoint her novels have a large social value.

J. B. Kerfoot, "The Latest Books," *Life*, 51 (16 April 1908), 412

On the outside cover of Ellen Glasgow's novel, *The Ancient Law*, it is set down that Miss Glasgow's work "shows a moral earnestness that causes it to tower" ... etc. It seems to us that, without quite realizing it, the writer of that sentence has stumbled on a diagnosis. Moral earnestness is invaluable, but it is strong medicine. One-fortieth of a grain of it in an adult novel is a powerful tonic. But an overdose is dangerous and "causing one to tower" is a septic symptom. *The Ancient Law* is a story of the south, and traces the self-rehabilitation of an ex-convict of good family. It is full of human touches and human beings. In spots it is positively self-forgetful. But as a whole it is nothing because it insists upon "towering."

"Fiction," *Academy*, 74 (9 May 1908), 767

It is some considerable time since America—that land of strange surprises—has furnished us with a genuinely finer novel than *The Ancient Law*, by Ellen Glasgow. The book is one of those rare exercises in the art of fiction-writing that deserve to be dignified by the term "a work." The theme of the book is expounded in the large manner that is now so seldom met. The chronicle of Daniel Ordway is related, as all tragic history should be related, with a calm, almost literal, simplicity that at times through its very subject-matter is tinged with an unhappy splendour. The story is really the biography of Daniel Ordway from the time he leaves prison. His after-life is minutely described in all its many varied phases, and we learn in graduating periods, from a slow but precise undertone that runs like a thread of silver fire through the gloomy texture of the entire history, the growth and expression of the man's expanding spirit. Every character in the book is etched with a sure hand that has mastered technique and the relative values of light and shade. Banks, "the impossible"; Baxter, the benevolent tobacco merchant; Milly Trend; Lydia, Daniel's wife, who lives in an atmosphere of anæmic sainthood; Alice, Daniel's prodigal daughter; Beverly, the inconsequent relic of the old Southern aristocracy; and lastly, the woman who loved Daniel and was beloved by him, are all portraits in Miss Glasgow's picture-gallery that stand out with a boldness of outline that is astonishingly life-like. There is little in the book that is dramatic, and nothing that can be called theatrical. The story might easily have degenerated into a sequence of cheap situations and tawdry climaxes. It offers very obvious temptations for an author to produce meretricious effects, but all these Miss Glasgow has avoided with a restraint that is as commendable as it is rare. She has preferred to tell her story of Daniel Ordway with a serene disregard for melodrama or sentimentalism. Yet all the thought in the book is expressed through feeling, and the clear, sonorous prose that rolls out this history of courageous enterprises, immutable sufferings, and the consolation to be found in moments of transient compensation, carries in its burden a depth of emotion that is beyond the compass of shrill or exclamatory expression. Miss Glasgow knows her America well, but for the most part the America to be discovered in *The Ancient Law* is not the habitation of *Tammany*, or the *Great Trusts*, or the *Jungle*. It is old Southern America, beaten, impoverished, and wellnigh forgotten, but touched with the dignity of defeat and a pathos irresistibly associated with the crumbling dissolution of any State or human community that has been driven into the backwaters of the world. Such a background, breathing the autumnal spirit of decay, makes an admirable—it would seem an inevitable—setting for Miss Glasgow's powerful and very actual story.

Saturday Review [London], 13 June 1908, 760

It is only in novels that the gentleman convict, upon his release, starts out penniless to tramp in search of work. In real life the fraudulent trustee (the type of criminal chosen by Miss Glasgow as her hero) usually retires comfortably on the money settled on his wife, or is provided for abroad by his friends. Miss Glasgow is apparently under the impression that she has chosen the least reprehensible form of crime to fulfil the purpose of her story, and that the ruin of trusting clients is a comparatively pardonable offence. Daniel Ordway is a truly sentimental hero, his prison experience converts him into a general philanthropist with a ready tear of sympathy, a simple boyish smile, and a perfect passion for self-sacrifice. There may be gambling dishonest stockbrokers who are capable of such striking reformation, but we find it difficult to accept Daniel Ordway as a recognisable type. Fortunately for his schemes of charity, he has the singular good fortune to find work at once, and later on to be reinstated in his old home with plenty of funds at his disposal. We are not told that he tried to do anything for his unfortunate clients, but he makes a great sensation by buying some cotton-mills at a time of strike, and winning enormous popularity with the hands. The story is founded on a basis of false sentiment and false psychology, and is constructed throughout on sentimental sensational lines. The style is emotionally fluent and verbose, and the characterisation conventional and not always convincing. Were it not that the scene is laid in Virginia and that there are pleasant descriptions of country life conveying a certain freshness of atmosphere, the book would be more tiresome than it is, and the absurdity of Ordway's career more apparent.

Checklist of Additional Reviews

"Fiction," *Booklist*, 4 February 1908, p. 52.

Times Literary Supplement [England], 27 February 1908, p. 71.

Norma Bright Carson, "Three Novels of Unusual Interest," *Book News Monthly*, 26 (April 1908), 623.

Saturday Review [London], 105 (4 April 1908), 449.

"Literary News and Criticism," New York *Daily Tribune*, 11 April 1908, p. 5.

"Romances of the Heart," *American Monthly Review of Reviews*, 37 (June 1908), 761.

New York Times Saturday Review of Books, 13 June 1908, p. 338.

THE ROMANCE OF A PLAIN MAN

THE ROMANCE OF A PLAIN MAN

BY

ELLEN GLASGOW

AUTHOR OF "THE DELIVERANCE," "THE
VOICE OF THE PEOPLE," ETC.

New York
THE MACMILLAN COMPANY
1909

Francis Hackett, "Amateur Romance," Chicago *Evening Post*, 14 May 1909

It is known to many tramps that within a forty-mile radius of Chicago there are still to be found farmhouses absolutely innocent of modern improvements, preserving primitive, insanitary and uncomfortable conditions with pioneer fidelity. To compare Miss Glasgow's amateur romance to one of these establishments would be violent, but her determined adherence to the ancient coincidences and still more ancient sentimentalisms of yesteryear shocks one into realizing that ideas are slow to permeate, that the contrast between Cook County and McHenry is nothing to the contrast between Shaw and Glasgow. Miss Glasgow does not write primitive, uncomfortable or insanitary romance if she is to be compared with Miss Amelia Barr or Miss Braddon. But in an era when Mr. Wells has published *Kipps* and *Tono-Bungay*, and Mr. Galsworthy has written *Fraternity*, the survival of tales like the present one is precisely as astounding as the survival of a certain paleozoic hotel in the village of Wauconda.

Miss Glasgow has to be acquitted of any serious study of her art. She has written novels in the past, but she still has an amateur idea of fiction form. Otherwise she would never have attempted to make this romance the autobiography of a railroad president. Narrative in the first person presents uncommon difficulties, but Miss Glasgow has audaciously taken romance to mean license, and from the start expects us to resign to the convention that a man of affairs would talk in the pretty idiom of a southern lady. The schoolmaster would dwell upon this atrocity, but there are others, so we pass immediately on.

If Miss Glasgow fails to identify her story with the person who tells it, she cannot be accused of wandering very far from his biography. Her book does sketch in half a dozen stock Virginia types, but it is above everything a love story—and it begins in red-shoed infancy. The pleasant sensual domestic life of humble people in the poorer part of Richmond is described for a time, and Miss Glasgow is genuinely sympathetic to humble folk, even to their corn bread and fragrant bacon—a tantalizing book for a hungry man to read. But the absorption of a fair woman in a strong man, and his unswerving devotion to her, give the romance its principle.

Old-fashioned belief in love at first sight is necessary to the enjoyment of such a romance. It may be preposterous that, after thirty years, a railroad president should recount every glance and thrill of his first meeting with the lady of his heart, he being then at the touching age of 5—or is it 3? But the novelist may be allowed to arrange definitely that this child shall move straight toward a single love and a single ambition, and if these directions be granted, the pure Arthurian devotion of Ben to Sally, Miss Glasgow's leading characters, may be accepted also as a further mystic obligation of romance.

[...]

It is not quite for itself that we have analyzed this amiable, conventional, superficial novel. It is mainly to show that because an author is popular, and a publisher reputable, it is not safe to assume that a book is important. There are readers who will enjoy Miss Glasgow's *Plain Man* with all the spirit in life. This, however, is no proof that the book is not comparatively worthless. In romance one inveterately expects either a persuasive manner in doing over the old situations, or a fresh and adroit plot. Miss Glasgow's manner, fluent and graceful, is yet far from redeeming her stale ideas and rusty machinations. Her pleasantries are often mere sentimental strictures on newer social ideals, such as woman's suffrage, and nowhere does she indicate that she is more than half sophisticated.

To this it may be answered that no one wants anything better than the strong, clean, courageous and truthful American; and that newfangled psychology, fretful and agnostic, has no place in romance and could not be applied to the actual romantic characters who have built up the new South, made their country and their womenkind happier.

It is true that a particular type exists in America, manly, simple, efficient, humorous and self-contained, who has little in common with the more or less neurotic modernist. This is the type, individualist and self-confident, who honeycombed the commandment, "Thou shalt not steal," and thought he was merely driving bargains. If Miss Glasgow had painted in Ben's character as any artist who knew Ben should paint it in, then the American gallery would have a new, veritable portrait. But unfortunately the sentimentalist and moralizer outdid the artist, and the woman of femininities outran the woman of ideas. And so we have another book to discredit the real romance of American life, of moral life everywhere.

As one of the most conspicuous woman novelists in the country, Miss Glasgow might have been assumed to take fiction seriously, to be scrupulous especially in its technique, however vague and tender-minded in her philosophy. But it needs no practitioner to find her wanting in the results of that simple self-criticism without which no one should pretend to be a writer. Her performance has passages of great charm. As a whole it is abominably lax and diffuse. She has taken 464 pages to tell a story of minor incident and scant originality. Such economy of grey matter is to be deplored, even if her present novel pretends to less import than others she has more strenuously considered.

Richmond *Times-Dispatch*, 16 May 1909, sec. B, p. 4

There was some doubt, even in the minds of Virginia readers, as to where the scenes described in Miss Glasgow's *Ancient Law* were enacted, that is, in precisely what section of the State. This doubt cannot exist in regard to *The Romance of a Plain Man*, which is throughout a Richmond story, about Richmond people in the postbellum commercial and financial renaissance.

In regard to its purpose and meaning, its strength and its weakness, a novel should be judged by itself, without relation to other works by the same author that have preceded or may follow it. Such a test is comparatively easy regarding Miss Glasgow's latest book, because in many respects it differs from anything she has hitherto written.

"The Plain Man," whom she has named Ben Starr, tells his own romance, which is begun on Church Hill and finished on Franklin Street in one of the ancestral mansions belonging to old Richmond that is fast being swallowed up by the swift progression of the city in twentieth century days. St. John's Church and churchyard and the venerable Adams home, on Church Hill, are among the localities with which the narrator has well remembered associations. . . .

It has been said that Ben Starr is still living in Richmond. If this is true the question of his identity will be one of burning interest. Miss Glasgow has drawn against his dominant personality Sally Mickleborough's character with a sure, cunning, and an exquisite skill. . . .

As Ben Starr unfolds his romance he reveals himself to be a man not only plain, but rough sometimes, and forgetful to the end of little things, a man who appears too essentially big-natured to consider them. Because he is barred by birth from taking his place as one of the old aristocratic circle of Richmond, because a kinship with his family and his past stands between him and the social world in which his wife moves so gracefully and graciously, he makes the mistake of trying to amass wealth and honors, instead of increasing his knowledge of the finer beauties of life, the things that cannot be grasped in the hands. . . .

Her remarkable power of individualization in character delineation, of investing even homely incidents and sordid surroundings with a vividness that impresses them strongly on the mind, has never been more apparent than in this, Miss Glasgow's first distinctive Richmond novel, which must additionally take rank, not because it belongs exclusively to any one place or to any special environment, but because it is as comprehensive as humanity, and as broadly real.

E[dwin] F[rancis] E[dgett], "The Romance of a Plain Man," Boston *Evening Transcript*, 26 May 1909, sec. 2, p. 22

From poverty to affluence, from boyhood to manhood, we follow Benjamin Starr as he tells his own story of his experiences in youth, in business, in love, in society. He comes of an inferior grade of white ancestry in the city of Richmond, but he emerges therefrom to marry a descendant of the Blands and the Fairfaxes, and to rub elbows with many members of the first families of Virginia. His success in business is no less than his triumphs in love, and under the tutelage of General Bolingbroke, president of the Great South Midland & Atlantic Railroad, he rises to a high position in the Southern financial world. He loses one fortune, is obliged to worry along thereafter on a pittance of $6000 a year, which is eventually raised to $10,000, until he again becomes rich beyond the dreams of avarice. Never for a moment, however, does the hero forget, or allow us to forget, that he has risen out of little things into great, that he comes of a socially despised parentage, that he was born his wife's inferior, and that he is a stranger in a strange land that only his superior business skill and his wealth have enabled him to enter.

In brief, Benjamin Starr's story is not merely *The Romance of a Plain Man*. It is *The Autobiography of a Snob*. Any youth of his persistence, any man of his great power and skill, would have outgrown his inferior beginnings so far that they would have remained in the background, and not in the forefront of his thoughts. . . .

It is to be feared that Benjamin Starr is created in woman's image, in the image of a novelist who, no matter how great her knowledge and technical skill, is not able to discern how a man can feel and behave in all circumstances. This mood of Benjamin Starr's might be plausible if it were occasional or transitory, but it is unfortunately perpetual.

However interesting Miss Glasgow's new novel may be, and it is certainly not without emphatic qualities that raise it above the average of the day, it lacks convincing power because of its persistent vein of extravagance and hyperbole. In everything, in the beauty of Benjamin Starr's wife, in the business ability of Benjamin Starr—of which we have no other evidence than his own word—in the high scorn of the maiden Blands against the poor white trash who dares to marry their niece, in the profligacy of General Bolingbroke, in the social qualities of his nephew, we see nothing but the strenuous attempt of a novelist to lay as much stress as possible upon every moment of her story. Miss Glasgow's heroine is, moreover, a woman of violent extremes, although she never goes to the one extreme of disloyalty to her husband, despite the fact that its opportunities are constantly thrown in her way. And Benjamin Starr is a man of extraordinary complacency, even though he may feel that his own social delinquencies necessitate the attendance upon his wife of a cavalier born to her own station.

But Benjamin Starr is nothing if not a hero in his own and his creator's eyes, whatever he may be in ours. Rarely do we read a novel in which so much is claimed and so little proved. This, perhaps, is the fault of the autobiographical method of telling a story. It is certainly the fault of Miss Glasgow's method. Benjamin Starr may have been all that he claims for himself, but he is certainly one thing more—a snob. It is of course needless to say to those who know Miss Glasgow's style that the story reads fluently and agreeably, and that it brings us into the delightful charm of the Southern atmosphere.

Philip Tillinghast, "The Cost of Technique in Fiction," *Forum*, 41 (June 1909), 616–17

The relation between happiness and money is also a leading motive in Ellen Glasgow's new volume, *The Romance of a Plain Man*. Perhaps the simplest as well as the shortest way to define this book is to say that it belongs in the same general class with Professor Robert Herrick's admirable *Memoir of an American Citizen*; for both these books are written in the first person, both of them depict the efforts by which a self-made man has worked his way up from a friendless and obscure boyhood to the eventual triumph of achieved ambition—whether this ambition happens to be a seat in the United States Senate or the offer of the presidency of a railway. The chief difference between the two books is that of environment. Professor Herrick's book deals with the Chicago stockyards, and all the attendant unsavory conditions of business dishonesty and political trickery. Miss Glasgow's book depicts life no more profoundly, it is true, but at least on a higher level both morally and socially. An atmosphere of old-fashioned Southern courtesy and breeding, of Southern standards of duty and honor pervades this book, as in a measure it pervades all of Miss Glasgow's books—but in none of the others to quite the same degree of perfection, quite the same attainment of delicate and subtle values. The main narrative quite lives up to the title. It is essentially the plain story of a plain man; a man who, because of his humble and rather vulgar origin, cannot understand the finer feelings of those more gently born. At heart, he has the right instincts.... The ultimate lesson Miss Glasgow would teach seems to be this: that because he was a plain man, Ben Starr's self-education was necessarily slow; that because the obvious difference between himself and the men in Sally Bland's own class was money and position and education he made the natural mistake of thinking that the attainment and possession of these things was the one thing essential to success and happiness; and the last and most important lesson he had to learn was that the essential thing did not lie in these achievements but behind them—it lay in the power to mould his own character until he was capable of attaining his goal; but that having attained it, he might, and under the specific conditions of the story, actually did, better secure his wife's happiness and at the same time prove himself a bigger and finer man by missing his opportunity and deliberately sacrificing the ambition of a lifetime.

"The New South in Fiction," *Outlook*, 92 (5 June 1909), 309

The New South, which more and more defines itself in terms of industrial progress and prosperity, is fast finding interpretation in Southern fiction. The career of the man of the new age, who is often self-made, is being dramatized with increasing sympathy and discernment.... In Miss Glasgow's latest story, *The Romance of a Plain Man* ..., the self-made Southern man of to-day is carefully drawn. By force of ability and indomitable will, the hero of this tale ascends from the position of a delivery boy for a grocer to that of an influential captain of industry.

His chief adventure, and the great romance of his life, is his love for a Southern girl of the old order; a beautiful, high-minded, high-bred, and devoted woman, to whom wealth is a matter of indifference, but to whom love is everything. The story of the winning of this girl in the face of the opposition of her family brings out the chasm between the old and the new order; between the aristocrat, with generations of breeding behind him, and the self-made democrat who never quite rids himself of the consciousness of the social superiority of the people for whose narrowness and snobbishness he has genuine contempt. He adores his wife, but he makes the mistake so many American men make of supposing that he can express his adoration by lavishing every kind of comfort and luxury on his home. To do this he unconsciously isolates himself from a woman who cares nothing for her luxuries, but passionately yearns for a constant expression of affection. The story turns at the very edge of tragedy and becomes once more a romance. It is a significant contribution to the literary interpretation of the new order in the South.

"Literary Notes and Criticism," New York *Daily Tribune*, 12 June 1909, p. 8

Miss Glasgow's new novel has nothing whatever sensational about it, yet it very soon gives the reader something like a shock. It is a shock of surprise. If there is one convention more than another cultivated by the writers of Southern stories it is that which identifies the hero with "Southern chivalry" and all the familiar properties of romance which go with it. Miss Glasgow has had the courage to seek her hero in the stratum of that "pore white trash" which is supposed, in fiction, if anywhere, to be quite impossible. The experiment is obviously dangerous, but it has proved successful in this case, and perhaps the more successful because the author is rigorously true to her idea where she must have been sorely tempted to do it violence. Indeed, her motive threatens to get out of hand almost at the outset, the earlier developments of Ben Starr's character rather straining credulity; but Miss Glasgow's good sense regains control before it is too late, and the closing chapters of her story are the most convincing of all. They are very lifelike where the first part of the book suggests things invented instead of things seen.

[...]

The man who neglects his wife in the pursuit of worldly gain is no new figure. The novelists have long wreaked their will upon him. But in this instance it is not mere sordidness that causes trouble. On the contrary, Starr is profoundly loyal to his Sally, and if his struggle for wealth is partly one of ambition it is still more inspired by a desire to surround her with luxuries. His fault lies deeper. It is to be traced to the "pore white trash" from which he sprang. It spells want of quick perception, of sensitiveness, such as you get not from heart alone but from breeding. When this hero's eyes are opened at last he touches the key to his problem in these words: "I am yours, such as I am. Plain I shall always be—plain and rough sometimes, *and forgetful to the end of the little things*—but the big things are there, as you know, Sally, as you know." The italics are ours. It is in Starr's delay in apprehending the importance of the little things that the "pore white trash" comes out, and it is in that that he is very human and interesting. Miss Glasgow has contrived, in other words, to do the thing which your novelist must always find so difficult: to make thoroughly sympathetic a man who is not only imperfect but deficient just where one does not like to have the hero of a novel fall short. The title of this book is well chosen. It is indeed the romance of a plain man that Miss Glasgow recites, and she has invested it with homely truth.

"Class and Caste in Old Virginia,"
New York Times Saturday Review of Books, 26 June 1909, p. 402

If in some century yet to come a dweller from the shores of Baffin's Bay or the Antarctic Continent, seeking for information about manners and customs in the great American Republic, should chance upon Ellen Glasgow's novel *The Romance of a Plain Man*, he would derive from it some curious ideas. He would be convinced by its perusal, for instance, that American life was firmly established upon lines of class; that nothing but the most heroic effort made it possible for a lad of the lower classes to make his way into affluence; that although he might become very rich and attain a position of great financial power, his wealth would not open for him the exclusive gates of society, that although he might marry within those gates the other people who dwelt therein would never recognize him as an equal and he would never outgrow his conviction of his own inferiority.

Possibly all these things are true, just as Miss Glasgow depicts them, in the region where the scene of her story is laid—Richmond, Va., during the last two decades of the nineteenth century. Unless there is proof to the contrary, the novelist must always be supposed to be familiar with the conditions of which he writes, and by the same token must he always be granted his point of view. Nevertheless, it is a pity that a novelist of Miss Glasgow's gifts should select a theme, no matter how true it may be locally, so at variance with our National spirit and so impossible in any other locality. For the spirit of caste dominates the whole story, and is, in fact, the central inspiration out of which it seems to grow.

[...]

Miss Glasgow, as always, has a story to tell, and knows how to tell it. She writes with a fine reserve and with a sure instinct for the dramatic situation and the telling phrase. The story has a leisurely movement that allows her opportunity to disclose remarkable powers of observation and description. The scenes pass vividly before the reader's eyes, and the serious quality of the story holds his attention from the start. With the exception of the narrating hero, who, perhaps, because in some respects he is so untrue to life elsewhere in this country, is never quite convincing, the characters stand out very clearly. In particular, that of Gen. Bolingbroke, the hero's friend and adviser, is a very lifelike creation.

"New Books Reviewed," *North American Review*, 190 (July 1909), 118

Miss Ellen Glasgow is undoubtedly one of the most capable of our present-day story-tellers, and in her recent novel she has turned back to her happy hunting-grounds, the Virginia of the Reconstruction. Her last two novels, *The Wheel of Life* and *The Ancient Law*, proved to those who cared that she was a serious and a philosophical novelist; but the large novel-reading public takes its novels as it would champagne at dinner or an opiate at night, and doubtless the present story will serve better for light diversion. The picture of Richmond and Richmond society is photographic, and many of the characters are easy for those who know the environment well to identify. The struggle of the hero to raise himself from the obscurest of human fates to prominence in the social and financial worlds is the theme of the tale, and a charming little love idyl stretching from childhood through married life is enwoven in it. *The Descendant* and *The Voice of the People* both deal with the same general theme, but setting and characters show how wide a range of human knowledge Miss Glasgow has.

Sally Mickleborough is the regular Southern type of heroine, pretty, proud, high-spirited, unbroken and unbreakable by Fate. She loves and marries the plain man, and during his reverses she is his mainstay and strength; in his prosperity, however, his pre-occupation with business strains the relation between them, and the tale is of married love perfected through much pain. We predict an immediate popularity for Miss Glasgow's latest romance, though no one who knows aught of the real value of books could say that in any way it reached the heights of her *Ancient Law* and *Wheel of Life*.

"Current Fiction," *Nation*, 89 (8 July 1909), 37

The story of this book needs a special charm to make one overlook its triteness—to forget would be impossible. In brief, it is the rise of a man who works up from absolute destitution to spectacular wealth, and marries a girl of refinement and high social position. Her family in outraged pride disown her, and her husband, pursuing the Business to the neglect of the Dream, drives her in loneliness to lean almost to scandal on the tender consideration of a rejected but constant lover. The husband is ruined, and falls ill; Sally does fine laundering to maintain the family, and there is a brief interlude devoted to the Dream. But with Ben's returning to strength, the Business regains the ascendancy, and he recovers his fortune only to find at last that he has tried Sally's faithful heart too far and that her sweet and dutiful affection can never be rekindled even by the sacrifice of his ultimate ambition, which, knowing this, he makes silently, in expiation, not in hope.

As with the greater number of Miss Glasgow's books, the plot is only a thread whereon are held up for our delectation single characters as carefully and intricately cut as Chinese beads. There is a fine distinction in the brief but suggestive picture of the hero's mother; in the more exhaustive presentation of the General, the "gay old bird," all whose faults cannot wholly belittle his inner greatness; and of those two gentle daughters of Pooh Bah, the conservative Miss Mitty and the radical Miss Matoaca, united only by sisterly love and "family pride." Miss Matoaca indeed impinges sensibly upon the issues of to-day. As she marches with her suffragist banner, "her eyes on the sky and her feet in the dust," one is reminded of modern instances of the pathetic incongruity of the real with the ideal; while in the General's naive outburst, "I tell you there's not a woman alive that ain't happier with a bad husband than with none at all. What business has a lady got with a view anyway?"—one catches the crude essence of the spirit that, homeopathically, to be sure, is still prescribed for the health of the body social. The plain man himself is so living and human that one involuntarily compares him with other figures of fiction. The story as a whole has a haunting flavor of *Lewis Rand*, and readers of the two books will find it an interesting diversion to note the startlingly frequent points of similarity. The resemblance, however, is kept well this side of the danger-line by the subtle individuality of the writer, which invests the most hackneyed themes with a touch of her own originality.

"Miss Glasgow's Novel," Louisville *Courier-Journal*, 10 July 1909, sec. 1, p. 5

Introducing a hero in his childhood and following him along the road to manhood, especially if that road be steep and rough, is a good, old-fashioned way of engaging the reader's sympathy which has hardly been improved upon since the advent of David Copperfield. Miss Glasgow has drawn an endearing picture of the childhood of Ben Starr and Sally Mickleborough....

[...]

The thought recurs that Miss Glasgow, fashioning women after conventional types, finds the pattern too small for her liking and adds to each some larger trait from a storehouse of her own. Sally must be a humanitarian as well as a spoiled beauty, and Miss Matoaca, encased in a shell of Southern tradition and caste pride, must work for the emancipation of women. The humane note is sounded again in the mentioning of thirsty dogs following the water cart through the dusty street, in the love of dear old Dr. Theophilus for his dog, and in the pensioning of Sally's old mare. Pity and courage are the keynotes of the book.

H. L. Mencken, "Novels and Other Books—Chiefly Bad," *Smart Set*, 28 (August 1909), 153

The latest work of Ellen Glasgow's, *The Romance of a Plain Man*, must inevitably invite comparison with Mary Johnston's *Lewis Rand*, for both deal with the excessively snobbish aristocracy of Richmond, and each has for its hero a common man who woos and wins a fair daughter of that aristocracy, and then finds, to his sorrow, that even such a feat cannot transform a commoner into a patrician. The comparison of one book with the other need not proceed further. They have little in common save the theme, for Miss Johnston's volume is a work of art, while Miss Glasgow's is not.

The hero of this story is a prodigious scion of Richmond's poor white trash—a boy who senses the subtle difference between "who" and "whom" at the age of five (see page 38, line 12) and who rises, before he is thirty, to the rank and dignity of a captain of finance. In his nonage the little daughter of a proud old Virginia house laughs at him and calls him common; in his manhood he marries her, though without any actual notion of revenge. It is the conflict between the patrician poise and dignity of the wife and the plebeian running amuck of the husband that makes the drama. He is capable of loving her, but he can never quite understand her. He believes at the start that the difference in rank which separates them is a mere convention; that so soon as he learns how to enter a room without falling over the rugs he will be her equal. But, like Lewis Rand, he finds out in the end that it takes more than a belt to make an earl of a dustman.

The idea at the bottom of Miss Glasgow's story is a good one, and the general plan of it is sound. But more than once the details are incredible. In one place, for example, she shows us the alert and resourceful Ben Starr reduced of a sudden to such abject poverty that his wife is forced to take in washing. That a man of his reputation should have no friends willing, and even eager, to help him in his need seems entirely impossible. To accept the situation we must consider him as a being *in vacuo*. Again, the relatives of Ben, and particularly his brother, are not convincing figures. Miss Glasgow's best portraits, indeed, are those of her aristocratic characters. No doubt this is because the Richmond that she knows best is the Richmond that they people.

Saturday Review [London], 108 (7 August 1909), 173

The atmosphere of the life of the old landed gentry in Virginia remains mysterious to the self-made man of business whose autobiography is given in this story. Had the book been merely the presentment of his career from errand-boy to millionaire, it would have possessed little interest. But Ben Starr, son of a working mason, is deeply impressed in childhood by a pretty little girl who, when they first met, would not play with "a common boy," and from the first makes up his mind not to stay common. (O democracy!) He so far succeeds in his aim that the girl of good family marries him in spite of the horror of her relatives. Then follows a mode of life not unfamiliar to students of America—the husband absorbed in business in order that his wife may live in luxury. But since Mrs. Starr was not a society leader of New York, but a gentlewoman of the South with certain ideals, she found life unsatisfactory, for all its pleasures, when her husband allowed finance to absorb his soul. This is a fine novel, written with delicacy, and it is a good thing to be reminded that though the South was conquered, Richmond has not yet been annexed by Washington.

Spectator [England], 103 (14 August 1909), 245

Although Miss Glasgow brings her usual high ability to the task which she has set herself, yet novels in which the hero is autobiographer are never entirely satisfactory when the author is a woman. It is impossible to keep the feminine standpoint from occasionally appearing in a nominally masculine narrative. In the present novel Miss Glasgow tells the story of a small boy born in the Southern States of America very shortly after the war. He is the son of a stonecutter, and early makes up his mind to rise in life and become worthy of the affections of the very delightful little girl on whom he has set his heart. The story of his gradual advance to the highest position in the business world is well told, yet the reader will feel that Miss Glasgow is really more at home in describing the mental attitude of the heroine, Sally Mickleborough, before and after her marriage to Ben Starr, the "plain man" of the title. The curious emptiness of the position of the rich American woman has never been more tellingly emphasised than in this story, though the narrator, who is, of course, Ben Starr himself, does not seem conscious of the extraordinary vacuity of the life which he describes the charming Sally as leading. Unless an American woman of means has the good fortune to lose all her money, and is therefore obliged to busy herself with the physical details of life, she appears to have no function in life except the dismal one of providing herself with perpetual amusement. No wonder an energetic person like Sally Mickleborough finds this extremely monotonous, and welcomes the change of fortune which for a brief period causes her to set her shoulder to the wheel and maintain her husband and child. The book is an interesting specimen of the business novel, and is of a type which is very popular with authors at the present moment.

"Novels for Summer Holidays," *Independent*, 67 (19 August 1909), 423

If you are an aristocrat, born and bred, you cannot do better than choose Ellen Glasgow's new novel, *The Romance of a Plain Man*. If not, it is best to avoid it. The author dramatizes in a perfectly truthful manner the difference between the temperament of an aristocrat and the character of a "plain man"—and there you have really what she is driving at in part. The aristocrat may not have a character worth mentioning, but he is bound to have temperament, while the "plain man" may have an excellent character, but his temperament, if he has any temperament, may be a very egregious disqualification. In this story the difference between the two is highly complimentary to the "plain man," and by no means disfiguring to the aristocrat, but we advise against the "plain man's" choosing it for his vacation story, because the book contains the most odious and exasperating comparison made between different classes, not in society, where kinds are sadly mixed on account of dollar marks, but in nature. The fact is that Miss Glasgow has evidently attempted to do the thing that Miss Johnston attempted earlier in the year in her novel, *Lewis Rand.* Each story depends for interest upon the varying pedigrees of the characters represented. Mary Johnston showed the power, ambition and unscrupulousness of Lewis Rand, and proved the tempered steel of a patrician woman in the loyalty and integrity of his wife, Jacqueline. Ellen Glasgow proves many of the same conclusions in her story, except that the "plain man" is a nobler man, and Sally, the patrician wife, is a finer, clearer, flamelike creature, in spite of the fact that Mary Johnston knows how to decorate a woman with sweeter, fairer words. And for excellence of interpretation it is a draw between these two Virginia authors, both of whom are a trifle too much inclined to intimate the peacock tails of their own excellent pedigrees in fiction. It is a vulgarity peculiar to aristocrats.

"English and American Fiction," *Atlantic Monthly*, 104 (November 1909), 682

From the South, which has had, perhaps, more than its share of people writing with artistic intent, comes *The Romance of a Plain Man,* by Ellen Glasgow, whose work is always seriously done and to be taken seriously. The fact that the theme of this latest study of causes and results in human life is less tremendous than some of the earlier ones she has treated, does not detract from its interest; and the development of the "poor white" lad, who, through sheer force of mind and of character, wins a place among the old families of Virginia, has the charm that the story of the self-made man has always had for the American. The earlier part of the book is worked out with much significant realism of detail; the latter part is more commonplace. In sketching the background of stately Southern custom and old-fashioned types of character, the author has attempted to bring out the real values of the life she is describing, with its poverty and its pride; and the story forms a fine contrast to the imitation-English type of Southern novel.

Checklist of Additional Reviews

Booklist, 5 (June 1909), 187.
Planet [London], 10 (5 June 1909), p. 31.
"Summer Reading Books," *New York Times Saturday Review of Books,* 12 June 1909, p. 374.

Book News Monthly, 27 (July 1909), 864–5.
Literary Digest, 39 (17 July 1909), 102.
Frederic Tabor Cooper, "Representative American Storytellers," *Bookman*, 29 (August 1909), 618.
Current Literature, 47 (October 1909), 460–1.
"A Few of the Season's Novels," *Review of Reviews and World's Work*, 40 (November 1909), 635–6.

THE MILLER OF OLD CHURCH

The Miller of Old Church

by Ellen Glasgow

Garden City, New York
Doubleday, Page & Company
1911

"Among the Books," Richmond *Times-Dispatch*, 5 June 1911, p. 5

[...]

The Miller of Old Church is strong in its realism, like all of Miss Glasgow's work, and broad in its grasp. It is far more than a Virginia classic, for its divining touch in relation to life indicates the motive power by which all humanity is swayed. In the purpose and consistency of its portrayal it resembles the *Deliverance* more nearly than any of her other previous books.

[...]

"*The Miller of Old Church*," *New York Times Saturday Review of Books*, 11 June 1911, p. 372

Miss Glasgow long ago proved herself to be not only a novelist whose books are interesting enough to attract at once a wide circle of readers, but also one worthy to be counted in that small group of contemporary American fictionists whose work really counts and is likely to last longer than her own generation. In her new book she has added another to her graphic pictures of Southern life and Southern people. Its scene is laid in Virginia in the period following the civil war, when the bonds that held together the older social organization were breaking under the stress of change and readjustment, and in the unaccustomed equality of opportunities those who formerly would have had but little chance were acquiring wealth and political power. Abel Revercomb is "the miller" of the story and he is one of the most outstanding and interesting of all the many Southern plain-folk characters Miss Glasgow has pictured so vividly. The book tells his love story, the romance of a man who comes into a finer and nobler soul inheritance by the purifying power of the love he thinks he has abandoned.

"Miss Glasgow's New Study of Virginian Life," New York *Daily Tribune*, 25 June 1911, sec. 2, p. 6

Miss Glasgow long ago won her place among the contemporary American novelists that are worth while—their number is not a large one. In this latest book of hers, however, there is a new note of maturity, a new assurance of purpose and of employment of technique toward its accomplishment. The author's own clear analysis of the homely wisdom of her Virginian rustics, old and young, may too closely reveal itself in the directness of the talk in which they express it; her heroine may at times too keenly dissect her own character for a girl in her remote and primitive walk of life, but the story and its protagonists gain by this decidedly "literary" touch, and so does the reader. The old order that has changed in Virginia still survives in these pages sufficiently to give background to the new that ousted rather than succeeded it. The plot is strongly planned. Beginning with a tragedy enacted long ago, it ends with a repetition of the dark deed in a younger generation, linking present to past in a vicious circle of unrestrained hereditary impulse. This return to the beginning of a story at its close is often more dramatic than is the far commoner method of making the end the beginning of a new situation. It certainly is so in this case. A capital piece of work.

Frederic Tabor Cooper, "The Newest Problems and Some Recent Books," *Bookman*, 33 (July 1911), 531–2

An excellent illustration of a comparatively new problem which in reality is as old as civilisation is offered by Ellen Glasgow's latest novel, *The Miller of Old Church*. It is new to this extent, that the specific conditions which determine the separate details of its episodes are of recent origin, forming a definite stage in the slow transition of southern social life that began with the reconstruction period after the war and is not yet ended. But in all its essentials Miss Glasgow's theme is nothing more nor less than that of the universal and inevitable struggle of the lower classes to rise and the jealousy of caste that would hold them back—and it is precisely the universality of the theme, studied under vividly local conditions that gives to Miss Glasgow's book a large part of its vital and compelling interest. The central human story of *The Miller of Old Church* has to do with the complex fortunes of Molly Merryweather, the illegitimate daughter of Janet Merryweather and Jonathan Gay, both of whom have died many years before the opening of the story.

Janet Merryweather belonged to that humble and despised division of the white race in the South whom even the negroes felt at liberty to look down upon; Jonathan Gay, on the contrary, was of the aristocracy; the Gays were easily the social leaders of the community....

[...]

... So much of the plot it has seemed necessary to tell in detail, carefully omitting all the numerous secondary plots, the complex interwoven threads that make this story a richly embroidered piece of living tapestry. Considered as a story dealing with the intimate concerns of a group of people whom we grow to love in a very personal way on account of their stirling merits or rare whimsicalities, the real interest of the book lies a good deal less in the plot structure than in the fine portraiture of character—in which respect it is far richer than any of Miss Glasgow's earlier works. For that reason it is unfortunate that it should be necessary to put so much stress in a review upon the plot itself. But it is necessary and for the following reasons: here, as in all her books, Miss Glasgow has developed finely and powerfully the epic method. In the broadest sense, this story is not so much the history of Molly Merryweather as it is the story of the New South. In the character of Angela, for instance, we have personified the survival of the old time Southern aristocracy, with its pride and its traditions—a survival that seems with each year to approach extinction and yet clings to life with the amazing tenacity of chronic invalidism. In the older Jonathan, we have the bygone type of the reckless, devil-may-care, hot blooded Southerner who at any cost would maintain his family pride; and in the younger Jonathan and Abel Revercomb we have typified the new aristocracy already beginning to yield to the encroachment of the new triumphant democracy. And lastly, in Molly Merryweather herself, we have, if we read Miss Glasgow's thought aright, the future solution of the social problem. In her origin and in her nature Molly represents a compromise between the upper class and the lower, combining the better qualities of each; furthermore, she typifies a social intermingling which in its origin was a disgrace but which to-day, owing to changed conditions, has come to be accepted. And even her marriage has its symbolic significance. Even had he lived she would not have married Jonathan, the last representative of an effete code of living; she would inevitably have taken the miller—because the younger society of the New South is destined more and more to draw fresh strength from the sturdy ranks of the rising democracy. This apparently is what Miss Glasgow set herself to say and she has said it with a courage, a clearness and a strength of conviction that makes it easily her best book up to the present time.

Literary Digest, 43 (1 July 1911), 26

A book by Ellen Glasgow is always read with expectant interest, but this youngest of her literary children is a bit of a disappointment. There is the usual Virginia atmosphere and the natives, drawn with a power that no one questions, but the characters seem artificial; they do not ring true. There is lacking somewhere—and it is hard to say just where—that originality of theme, that vigor, strength, and convincing quality usually so prominent in Miss Glasgow's work. Miller Abel Revercomb is strong, manly, and consistent, and his absorbing love story with the lights and shadows of his pursuit of pretty, flirtatious Molly Merryweather, is very engrossing, but the situations that should be dramatic seem trite—the villain not quite villainous enough and the good, almost too good. The real Glasgow touch is recognized in the scenes at the inn—"Bottom's Ordinary"—where the natives meet to "cuss and discuss" the village and its inhabitants, but, outside of that, it is just a conventional love story, delayed by man's selfish passion and complicated by the erratic vagaries of feminine fancy. The book will be, undoubtedly, popular, but we can not see that it adds any glory to Miss Glasgow's reputation.

"Miss Glasgow's Strongest Book," *New York Times Saturday Review of Books*, 2 July 1911, p. 414

Among American novelists of the present time there is none who excels Ellen Glasgow in portrayal of character and in rich humanity of background. In these qualities she is close akin to the methods of English novelists and the best traditions of English fiction. It is curious to note how much more closely the best of our Southern novelists follow those methods and those traditions than do the authors of the North and the West. With these, action, plot and incident are the factors which they handle best and their stories are full of the rush and roar of contemporary life. But with most of those of Southern origin the interest centres in the people of the story rather than in its plot and movement. This is particularly true of *The Miller of Old Church*, which is another of Miss Glasgow's quiet,

"Current Fiction," *Nation*, 93 (13 July 1911), 33–4

intimate studies of a corner of Virginian life.

The scene is an out-of-the-way bit of countryside, and the people in it, of their several social grades, are endeavoring to adjust themselves to the new economic conditions of the South, the reapportionment of the land, the upspringing of a new democracy, the energies and ambitions of those whose ancestors were of less account than the negro slaves. There is one big estate, owned by almost the only aristocratic family of the region. Twenty years before its bachelor proprietor had been found dead, but whether by suicide or murder is a question still debated with warmth.

[...]

One doubts, somewhat, the very general mother-wit and piquancy of expression with which Miss Glasgow endows all her rustic characters. They, too, are suggestive of the English traditions in fiction, and especially of the Victorian novelists. But, even while doubting, one enjoys the rustics....

Miss Glasgow develops a quite striking facility for making neat, terse turns of phrase. Of Jonathan Gay's character she says that it "consisted less in a body of organized tendencies than in a procession of impulses," and of his mother that "she had surrendered all rights in order to grasp more effectively at all privileges."

On the whole, the book is, perhaps, the strongest and truest of all the half dozen or more that Miss Glasgow has written, close, deft, and even in its construction, and at once subtle and strong in its portrayal of character.

In Miss Glasgow's forward-looking thought the vigorous life of the New South is reflected. She relegates the negro to the background, where he appears merely as an indispensable feature of the picturesque Virginia landscape, and consigns the "dilapidated aristocrat" to a place of secondary importance. Most of her people are of the self-respecting agricultural class that has arisen out of the ignominious "pore white trash" of antebellum days. This has been a movement actually spectacular in its swiftness and its promise; and, by conveying a sense of the larger romance, Miss Glasgow amply compensates for a plot of somewhat conventional design. In the relations of the two households, the Gays and the Revercombs, the condescensions on the one hand, the hostility on the other, we read the whole story of antagonism between the families of the plantation owner and the small farmer. One is tempted to expatiate at length on the typal perfections of the Revercomb group, covering in four generations the whole psychology and most of the history of their entire class—the patiently tended grandparents, childishly greedy and quarrelsome in their dotage; the mother, harsh and devoted; the silent Abner, meeting depredations upon his womankind with summary vengeance; Archie, lazy ranger with dog and gun; and, lastly, the stalwart miller, embodying all the crude virtues of his class, its vigor, its energy, its independence, its intolerant idealism, its powers of resistance and endurance.

No less admirable is the portrayal of the cultivated Gays, survivors of a social order whose standards no longer prevail. No one has heretofore let in the clear cold light of common sense upon the status of the Southern woman under the old regime, and surely no one but a modern artist could have painted the slow martyrdom of poor Miss Kesiah, to whom nature had denied both beauty and "the liver of a lady" ("the difference between the liver of a lady and that of another person was that one required no exercise and the other did"), and whose artistic predilections had been sternly repressed as unbecoming in "a Virginia lady."

William Morton Payne, "Recent Fiction," *Dial*, 51 (16 July 1911), 51

The other woman novelist of Virginia [in addition to Mary Johnston] who has won a high place as a novelist during the last few years is Miss Ellen Glasgow, and her *Miller of Old Church* is a work that shows no signs of slackening power. It is a real novel, thereby standing in sharp contrast to *The Long Roll*, and is less affected by a social or political interest than its predecessors. It is true that the hero is represented as an embodiment of the new type of energy that is overcoming the long paralysis of Southern industry, and that he figures as a radical speaker at public meetings, but it is chiefly as an individual that he interests us—alternately attracting and repelling—and it is his love affair with the flirtatious Molly that provides the substance of the plot.... A great many pages of the book are filled with rustic talk, of the kind that is both shrewd and quaint, clearly studied from the life, but rather wearisome in more than limited doses. Most of it may be skipped without any loss to the story.

"New Books Reviewed," *North American Review*, 194 (August 1911), 302–3

Among the established novelists of our country Ellen Glasgow easily stands in front rank. None of the modern inducements to gain popularity by lowering her own fine standard of what the novel is and should be have corrupted her. Her work has been astonishingly steady and serious and each new novel has shown in some way an advance upon the earlier work; a new beauty of style, a wider philosophy, a saner grasp of living, or a profounder knowledge of the human heart.

In *The Miller of Old Church* we note two sources of strength and charm. First a more fluid and easy narrative. There is never a sense that invention has run short and been forced. The narrative moves simply, but surely and inevitably; characters are true to themselves and show temperamental integrity, and the knowledge of humanity is surer, deeper than ever before.

There is no exaggeration in saying that what Thomas Hardy has done for the folk of the south of England Ellen Glasgow has done for Virginia. She is steeped not only in the soil and landscape,—other writers have matched her here,—but in the humanity that grows on that soil.

We have a wonderful picture-gallery in *The Miller of Old Church*, and to begin with the very first there stands Adam Doolittle, a worthy study to set beside Hardy's "Sammy Blare" or "Granfer Cantle." ...

[...]

... The main story is concerned with the love of Molly Merryweather and Abel Revercombe, but the background of humanity in which the two chief actors are set is so fascinating as to lure one over and over again to the minor figures. For the first time we feel that an American novelist may come who shall stand equal to Hardy. Miss Glasgow has a like eye for landscape, a deep sense of the interplay of soil, climate, and character, as deep a probe for the human heart.... Miss Glasgow began as a novelist with the publication of *The Descendant* before her twenty-first year. She has progressed steadily, producing a novel each second or third year. We feel that in this, her ninth book, she shows herself a worthy successor to Thomas Hardy, as able and as profound in her own field as he was in his.

Outlook, 98 (19 August 1911), 894

Miss Ellen Glasgow's novels always combine an attractive rendering of character with a background of social problem. In *The Miller of Old Church* one feels that Miss Glasgow is more successful in the first element than in the second. Her men and women are delightfully introduced; their by-play of talk, their emotions, and their mutual relations are admirably presented. But the plot does not develop very strongly, and there is a lack of clearness in the working out of the author's purpose. This is to show the conflict in the New South between the old and aristocratic strain and the rough and practical rising generation, which may have grown out of the "poor white" class, but has come into independent and vigorous existence. Criticism aside, the book is thoroughly readable, is one of the best of this summer's novels, and has already interested and entertained a very large number of lovers of fiction.

Boston *Evening Transcript*, 30 August 1911, p. 18

[...]
Such a plot [featuring an aristocratic suitor and a plebeian suitor vying for a girl of humble birth] is the rightful property of anyone who wishes to use it. Only the reader has the right to ask that it shall be served in some rather new fashion. In *The Miller of Old Church* we find some variations from the old theme. The love making difficulties are not confined to the usual "triangle" of two men and a woman—there is, indeed, a quadrangle, perhaps even a pentagon of lovers, whose joys and sorrows are fierce and in some cases, tragic. The author's hand is sure in the delineation of Virginian scenery and character, and yet so delicate in its touch that many passages have much romantic beauty. Yet the reader cannot escape the feeling that the book is in many respects mechanical. It was not so much a tale that must be told, as a book that has got to be turned out. It does not live strongly and it will not survive.

"Fashions in Fiction," *Independent*, 71 (7 September 1911), 541–2

The Miller of Old Church is to-day's educated and ambitious variant of the Virginia "poor white." One of the sons of the generation molded by antebellum conditions, he lives among its still numerous survivors, of them and yet above them. Upon the whole, the best things in the book are of his elders. The shrewd wit and philosophy of their moral and religious disputations really attract more than the triple—or quadruple—love affair unfolding among their children and aristocratic neighbors. But it is the most aristocratic of the neighbors, a middle-aged and very typical Southern lady, who achieves the tragedy of two generations thru that form of goodness in whose delicate presence the immoralities of society are forbidden mention, and whose combination of frail health and hard and narrow purity two men fear to face with confession and restitution for their wrongdoing. It may be suspected that Ellen Glasgow is a bit heterodox as to both Calvinism and "the womanly woman."

Athenæum [England], 2 (23 September 1911), 353

A sturdy representative of the labouring classes in Virginia, the miller—a man of character and ambition, generous and impulsive—makes a fine figure round which to group the young men and maidens, the old men and matrons, whose lives Miss Glasgow skilfully portrays.

The miller loves a winsome maid who loves not matrimony. Pique and pity lead him to the altar with a plain-visaged soul devoted in secret to the village parson; the miller's sister succumbs to the fascinations of a local magnate, whose passion for her wanes, and is transferred to the witching maid, who eventually, like some humanized will-o'-the-wisp, learns the secret of her heart and marries the now widowed miller. These pranks of Cupid are obviously slight enough material. It is not, however, on plot or incident, or even theme, that Miss Glasgow's success as a writer depends, but on her sanity of outlook, her humanity, and above all on the delicious sense of humour, which enables her to excel in pen-portraits of the very old or the very young.

H. L. Mencken, "An Overdose of Novels," *Smart Set*, 35 (December 1911), 155

There are novels that I simply cannot read, trying my honest darndest. Of such sort, for example, are the compositions of Eden Phillpotts.... To the tomes of the lugubrious Phillpotts now add *The Miller of Old Church*, by Ellen Glasgow. The majority of American reviewers have cast their votes for it enthusiastically. One of them calls it "Miss Glasgow's strongest book"; another says that it proves beyond a doubt that "her hand is sure"; a third maintains that it is the best Southern novel written in ten years; a fourth compares it to the works of the great Victorians. I wish I could join in this chorus, but I could not do so without gross deception, for the good reason that I have been unable, after earnest effort, to read the story. I have tried and tried and tried. But I can't. I don't know why. Prejudice? I think not. Temporary insanity? Perhaps. But whatever the cause, the obstructive fact remains. So I pass on to you the kind words said of the tale by those who have read it and enjoyed it.

Checklist of Additional Reviews

Charlotte [North Carolina] *Daily Observer*, 6 August 1911, p. 14.
Booklist, 8 (September 1911), 36.
Current Literature, 51 (September 1911), 338–9.
Times Literary Supplement [England], 28 September 1911, p. 348.

VIRGINIA

VIRGINIA

By
ELLEN GLASGOW

GARDEN CITY   NEW YORK
DOUBLEDAY, PAGE & COMPANY
MCMXIII

Virginia Woodward Cloud, "*Virginia* Novel by Ellen Glasgow," Baltimore *News*, 19 April 1913, p. 5

That which Miss Johnston has done for Virginia in her novels of its historical periods, Miss Glasgow has done in another, and even a more potent way, in her novels of its local life, placed at the time of, and since, the Civil War. These have been written with a serious art which has identified her with the few who have preserved the impressions of a rapidly changing and exceptionally significant period in the South.

Miss Glasgow is eminently strong in portraiture, and *Virginia* is at start a study of character, environment, and of the primitive life in a Virginia town during the eighties. But, while the majority of novels present to us life at a suspended moment of crisis or climax, with character at high or low ebb, photographed momentarily, we have it here as transitional, moving onward, with all its subtle change, which is the evidence of a finer and more delicate art.

Virginia, a Southern girl, in 1884, is not the overwritten and overemphasized coquette, besieged with suitors, and engaged to half a dozen, the latter is a type. Virginia is the individual—a product of good inheritances and traditions, too well accustomed to them to overvalue them. Normal, lovely, receptive, ready for the best in life, she innocently marries her "first love"—an enthusiastic young playwright, who means well but has not matured. Virginia's traditions of wifehood and motherhood are too strong for her pliable, sweet soul; she slips down a pitiful, helpless sacrifice, still conscious "that her own dreams were larger than the actualities around her," and unconsciously into the pathos of resignation. For Oliver "is a Treadwell, who always get what they want."

Virginia's mother is one of those ladies afflicted with the "divine evasion which only sees what it wants to see," and the whole pathetic, resigned existence of Virginia, its endurance and devotion, is portrayed mercilessly and sincerely step by step to the inevitable change on Oliver's part and the climax of separation. "For what good will it do?" says Virginia wisely, "to hold him when he wants to be free? It is not the law—it is life."

And "I can't go on!" cries Oliver, on the eve of separation; "a generation ago I suppose we might have done it, but we've lost grip, lost endurance." Here is an idea for the divorce problematists. Has the generation "lost grip"? It is easy to say that Olivers, writing plays, should not marry. Girls in the eighties were not enlightened as to the pliability of him who already is "married to his art." As a novel *Virginia* is a trifle deliberate in its approach to the main issues, and its value as a novel would seem to begin with a swifter, sweet vision of Virginia's radiant waiting girlhood, and Oliver's enthusiasm. The story opens fully with Virginia's pathetic letters home; these begin a heart-history of the deep and fervent quality, strong and delicate fiber, woven as Miss Glasgow has woven the warp and woof of character in *The Ancient Law* and *The Romance of a Plain Man*. Through it are straight thrusts, barbed with deep understanding of suffering. Miss Glasgow's is never a light art; it is wrought too surely of the creative feeling which holds and forms imaginatively the essences of life.

E[dwin] F[rancis] E[dgett], "*Virginia*, Ellen Glasgow's Story of Old Fashioned Womanhood," Boston *Evening Transcript*, 19 April 1913, sec. 3, p. 6

[. . .]

Trivialities in stories doubtless, since there are a multiplicity of trivialities in life, have their place in the novelist's scheme of things, but *Virginia* unfortunately overflows with trivialities that can have no possible human interest. First of all the trivialities of Virginia's mental attitude, interesting at first, become wearisome upon constant repetition; while the trivialities of household life and nursery cares, the insistence upon infantile illnesses and other details of the sick room, the anticipations of birth and the preparations for weddings and funerals seem more suitable for the old-fashioned days of Mrs. Southworth and Mrs. Holmes than to these twentieth-century days of novel writing. Perhaps it is necessary to inform us that "Miss Willy and I spent all yesterday running blue ribbons in her underclothes, and though we began before breakfast, we had to sit up till twelve o'clock so as to get through in time to begin on the trunks this morning." This is a not unfair example of Miss Glasgow's unconscious humor. When she attempts it in reality we are told about a "supercilious mulatto butler who wore immaculate shirt fronts, but whom she suspected of being untidy beneath his magnificent exterior," or of an old sinner whose terror of death had become so acute that after every attack of dyspepsia he sent a check to a missionary society.

To put the matter as briefly and as tenderly as possible, Miss Glasgow has been overwhelmed by an archaic theme. She has made nothing new of it. She has filled it with types, and not with characters, and the best that can be said of Virginia is that she is gentle and pretty, of Oliver that he is agreeable and likable, and of all the others that we have met them too often to make any specific mention of them necessary. Its commonplaces of thought and expression are so frequent as to defy quotation, and its grasp upon life is feeble. Miss Glasgow deals with truths in her novel, but they are the utmost commonplaces of truth.

"The Wrongs of Woman," New York *Sun*, 19 April 1913, p. 8

In *Virginia*, Ellen Glasgow has written a "powerful" book, a demonstration of the way woman is abused by man, that rouses indignation more effectively than any plea for the suffrage can. For more than 500 pages she tortures a poor girl with Indian savagery, showing, if anything, that self-sacrifice and love are fatal mistakes. To make the matter certain she repeats the story in the case of a mother and daughter. Wherever a faint gleam of happiness appears it is overshadowed by impending disaster; every woman is abused and every man is ignoble, save one boy. The scene is placed in the South and the heroine is made a Southern woman, but that is immaterial, for she exists in every community North and West just as well.

A charming, lovable, well bred young girl, with little education and no knowledge of the world outside, falls in love with a flighty, wrongheaded, selfish youth, with half baked ideas from ill-digested reading, and literary aspirations. Through the interference of well meaning friends they are brought together and marry. She is the daughter of a very poor clergyman; he is even more impecunious. Yet to marry her he takes up a commercial position, which he holds for several years. This period and his conduct during it, which we infer was exemplary, the author passes over in silence. The pretty descriptions of the young girl's love dreams, whatever might be joyful at that time, are cast into the background by the grim story of her mother's slaving to make both ends meet, to maintain her gentility and to do service to her husband and daughter. No cruel detail of her loving self-sacrifice is spared, and we cannot but resent the ease with which the amiable rector accepts it and the hardships which the daughter perceives but is too inexperienced to put a stop to. It is a forecast of her own fate.

The first years of married life are described in letters by the wife. She devotes herself to her husband's comfort; then come children one after another and she slaves for them. She has no sympathy for or understanding of her husband's intellectual pursuits. When she returns home, and the author takes up the narrative again herself, she fusses over the children, she nags her husband about them; she neglects her personal appearance for their sake, and drops away from her friends. She is just as lovable as ever but she has placed her whole happiness in caring for others. Her husband begins to turn away from her. In describing this stage the author makes light of the woman's happiness; she criticizes her as strangers might, noting her faded appearance, her shabbiness, the things she misses.

Then come years of financial prosperity and the culmination of the tragedy. Her husband writes plays which meet with popular success; after a while he falls in love with another woman and leaves her. She makes no fight, for women of her stamp do not fight, but her futile attempts to ward off the blow are pitiful. Her daughters have been educated and tolerate and half despise their mother. She is left alone after loving and sacrificing herself all her life, but the author has mercy at the last moment and allows her son to come to his mother's relief.

There are other people in this long story who are hardly more cheerful. A mean rich man, who bullies his wife and leaves her without money, and who refuses to let his daughter go to college out of sheer spitefulness; a stolid young man, who is middle-aged before he discovers that he loves the girl he has kept waiting for years; a boarding house keeper who supports a drunken husband. It is a world where every woman suffers and every man is vile. If the author is making a plea in behalf of her sex no fault can be found with her presentation of facts, but if this is only a story it is not exactly exhilarating. It is conceivable that a less dismal point of view might have brought out pleasing compensations in the lives we are made to deplore, and even that a word in defence of the man's side might not be out of place occasionally.

The book is well written. Those who like to have their feelings harrowed may gratify their taste fully. We fear that women will keep on sacrificing themselves, however, notwithstanding the warning the author gives them.

L[ouise] M[aunsell] F[ield], "*Virginia*: Miss Glasgow's Portrait of a Last Century Type," New York *Times*, 20 April 1913, p. 244

Since the publication of her first book, *The Descendant*, some years ago, Miss Glasgow has written several interesting novels, but never one so broad in sympathy, so mature in artistry, and so significant as is this story of *Virginia*.

It is the straightforward account of a woman's life from her "flushed and expectant" early twenties until middle age. Born at the close of the civil war, and living always in the little Virginia town of Dinwiddie, nothing very extraordinary ever happens to her; only the great, well-nigh universal experiences, like love and marriage and motherhood. Allowing for the enormous differences in temperament and point of view, this novel reminds the reader of *Une Vie*. Both produce the same feeling of being in absolute accordance with the facts; one does not question the details of Virginia's history any more than one questions those of de Maupassant's famous Jeanne. Thus they were, and thus the author has reported them.

A difficult task indeed it would be to find anything more pathetic than the letters Virginia writes to her mother after her marriage. The radiant happiness, the perfect trust that the present joy will never fade—and the unconscious revelation of path-paving for certain woe in the future. Faithful to her training, to her ideals of wifely duty and self-sacrifice, and by that very fidelity slowly but surely weakening, not only her own hold upon the man she adored, but also his moral fibre.

And yet she is the very flower of her type—gentle, exquisite, loving, with courage to endure if not to fight. A perfect Southern gentlewoman of the last century, when:

> To go through life perpetually submitting her opinions was, in the eyes of her parents and her teacher, the divinely appointed task of woman.

That Virginia might find this submission easy her education "was founded upon the simple theory that the less a girl knew about life the better prepared she would be to contend with it." This was the sort of teaching Virginia's lovely mother had received, as did all the "ladies" of her generation, and she passed it on to her daughter, never doubting its efficacy and wisdom. With it went sweetness, dignity, delicate reticence, and a conviction that a woman's whole existence must not merely centre in husband and children, but be limited to them and their desires. Time spent upon reading instead of household matters seemed time wasted to both mother and daughter. Emotions, affections, must be developed to the uttermost, but intelligence was no part of the equipment of a truly womanly woman and so Virginia failed her husband in his hour of need simply because she did not and could not understand.

The background against which Miss Glasgow has drawn the lovely and lovable figure of Virginia is as real as Virginia herself. Every person who enters her life is as genuine a flesh-and-blood individual as are those we pass every day upon the street; only we know these imaginative acquaintances far better than our everyday ones. Susan Treadwell, Virginia's loyal friend and in many ways her direct antithesis, is one of whom we would like to hear more. One feels quite sure that though she refused to submit to the generally accepted theories of the time by "slaving" for her husband and children, but kept her mind alert and found a place for herself outside as well as inside her home, that when her daughters grew up they not only loved her but found her interesting.

Oliver, Virginia's husband, who was born twenty years too soon, is in some ways a more pathetic, if infinitely less appealing, figure than even Mrs. Pendleton herself. Her possibilities were never thwarted, while he became small who might have been great. We could pity him for this failure were it not for his power of escaping the consequences of his acts through the Treadwell gift of concentration joined to an optimistic ability for self-deceit almost equaling Virginia's own.

During the years covered by Virginia's life the position of women changed more than it had done in several previous centuries. And it is this tremendous difference between the girl of the eighties and the girl of to-day which the author has transferred from life to the pages of her novel; never slurring nor overemphasizing what she puts before us clearly as only an artist can. In the story of this one woman's life is concentrated the very essence of that old order which passeth its beauty, and its tragedies. Virginia embodies an ideal that enthralled the imagination of men and women alike for numberless generations; an ideal whose virtues the world has always acknowledged, whose limitations it is only now beginning to recognize.

"On the Reviewer's Table," Richmond *Times-Dispatch*, 27 April 1913, p. 11

The oft-quoted saying that "a rose by any other name would smell as sweet," is not a saying to be accepted. The name of Miss Glasgow's book, *Virginia*, links it at once with the interest of her statespeople and proves to others that, though written elsewhere, its characters and its atmosphere are unmistakably Virginian.

Miss Glasgow has not only been happy in naming her novel. Her choice of the figure in her frontispiece is exquisite. It harmonizes in every respect with what the reader conceives the young girl, about whom romantic situations and many lovers center, must be. And the climax is reached in the dedication, in which *Virginia* becomes a memorial to a rarely beloved sister of the authoress, Mrs. Cary Glasgow McCormick....

The keynote of the book is sounded in the beginning, when the figures of Susan Treadwell and Virginia Pendleton invest the garden walks with grace and youth, for it is written of Virginia that, "by her eyes and by an old-world charm of personality which she exhaled like a perfume, it was easy to discern that she embodied the feminine ideal of the ages. To look at her was to think inevitably of love. For that end, obedient to the powers of life, the centuries had formed and colored her, as they had formed and colored the wild rose with its whirl of delicate petals...."

The expectancy and the hope of youth, then, fill the pages of the first book—there are three in all—of Miss Glasgow's novel. These and the old churches and homes of Petersburg. If Miss Glasgow has one predominant merit as an author, it is her ability to visualize for her readers whatever she writes about. All the little details which bring out the historic points of such a town as Petersburg, the contrast between its past, present and future, are wrought upon with infinite nicety and care, until the atmosphere in which characters move, the influences that have shaped them, the forces that urge them forward are plainly blended into a whole that is a natural outcome, an inevitable result.

It seems that the fulfillment of her destiny when Virginia Pendleton, lovely beyond expression, surrenders at the approach of a lover "exalted by the consciousness that he was following the lead of the more spiritual part of his nature—for the line of least resistance was so overgrown with exquisite impressions that he no longer recognized it...."

The first chapters of book second then present a picture of Virginia Pendleton as a bride, describe her wedding to Oliver Treadwell, Susan's cousin, and her departure for a small West Virginia town, where Oliver buries his ambition as a writer of plays in a business struggle to support his wife and family. But between husband and wife as the years passed on "companionship of a mental sort was lacking, yet so reverently had the wife accepted marriage that she would have been astonished at the suggestion that a love which could survive the shocks of tragedy might at last fade away from a gradual decline of interest." ...

Book third interests the reader in Susan Treadwell's happy marriage to a good, commonplace man, and in the tragedy and separation between Oliver and Virginia Treadwell. The wife had given herself too unreservedly in marriage. In wifehood and motherhood, she had forgotten to be alluring, she had slighted her beauty, and the husband, an indifferent father, but a Treadwell, got the thing he wanted most in the end.

Virginia Pendleton Treadwell was not adored by her daughters as she should have been. They had preferences for the active rather than the passive side of experience. And while the husband "had moved with the world, she who was confirmed in the traditions of another age, had never altered in spirit since that ecstatic moment when he had first loved her. The needs and desires of the man were different. And resurgent youth in him was again demanding youth." The daughters partook of their father's spirit, but there was a son and, when the mother faced long, empty years, feeling that she had outlived her usefulness, her need for love was answered by a telegram from the boy, which said: "Dearest mother, I am coming home to you."

The bare outline of the novel conveys no just idea of its strength and its power, of the vividness with which the Petersburg community is sketched in, of the charm of home life at the rectory and of duty as exemplified by Gabriel Pendleton among his Petersburg parishioners. The chief lesson among many others that the book teaches is that every woman should preserve her personality and guard her youth and the charm of it. The woman of the next generation will be wiser because less given to self-effacement than Virginia Pendleton, of Petersburg, in the 80's.

Miss Glasgow has been a recent visitor to her native city and to Norfolk, where she was a guest of Judge and Mrs. Louise Collier Willcox, and spoke with great effectiveness in behalf of suffrage. The appearance of her book has been greeted with enthusiasm which must deepen with its reading and the discussion it will naturally arouse. Different personages in it will be identified and different localities—the homes, the churches, the members of the Treadwell and Pendleton families. Almost a reader will inhale the fragrance of flowering almond and lily of the valley while bending over the pages of Virginia; almost will a hand be stretched out to pluck a red and white rose from the tangled gardens surrounding old houses such as those lived in by the Pendletons, the Treadwells and Miss Priscilla Batte. In short *Virginia* will make an irresistible appeal to the imaginations and hearts of Miss Glasgow's townspeople, statespeople and countrypeople.

Book News Monthly, 31 (May 1913), 694

Miss Glasgow has written the strongest piece of fiction that has appeared since last fall. Nothing that the English novelists have done can equal it, and Mrs. Ward's latest novel is scarcely more than trash beside it. *Virginia* is the last word in the novel writer's art, and Miss Glasgow, by virtue of it, takes her place with the few masters of whom America can boast.

The progress of woman provides Miss Glasgow's theme. Her heroine portrays the old-fashioned woman left in the lurch by the long strides of the new-fashioned times. The tragedy of a woman who sacrifices sex in vain—this is Virginia.

The belle of an old Virginia town, lovely as a May morning in the blooming Southland, Jenny Pendleton falls in love with Oliver Treadwell. Oliver had lived abroad, had gained a broader vision. He desired to write plays, but the desire for Virginia proved the stronger desire of the two, and so he settled down to a business he hated, and they were married. But they did not live happily ever after.

The babies came and Virginia proved a wonderful mother. She discovered in herself a perfect passion for motherhood. And as Virginia become more and more absorbed in her children, Oliver became more and more absorbed in his ambition.

Then failure came, and Virginia could sympathize only in part—she was so busy with the children. Oliver grew bitter, self-centered, he worked desperately, relinquished his ideals and won. There followed days when money came easily—but love was gone.

Oliver had never thought to look upon Virginia with indifference. Virginia had never thought to fail Oliver in his moment of supreme need. But both had done what they had not expected to do.

In Miss Glasgow's interpretation we read the fate of a woman who is made the slave of a system—a social system that is supremely moral, supremely correct in form, but that lacks all provision for change or progress or the necessities for readjustment. And yet Virginia is so lovable that we instinctively blame Oliver, but Oliver is not justly to be blamed. He, too, becomes a victim of the system, and is powerless.

The story of Virginia leaves one sad. But its significance becomes a matter for rejoicing. Lovely women they were, given us the old South, but the new South tramples down the system and woman becomes an emancipated creature. We may sigh for the Virginia that will be no more. We realize, however, that life moves onward, and we must move with it. Wonderful as she was, Virginia was not adaptable. She became impotent.

There may be those who will read a triumph in that last message, sent Virginia from her son, but most of us will sigh and wish that Virginia had consented to be a little more modern.

It is a remarkable book, alight with life and compelling in its truth. Every reader will love Virginia.

"A Novel of Changing Ways," Springfield [Massachusetts] *Republican*, 18 May 1913, p. 35

[...]
    The story is distressingly realistic, and a sad fatality seems to attend the characters that most appeal to the reader's sympathy. Mrs. Treadway dies of a broken spirit not long after the death of her husband, and Virginia has as the reward of her wifely devotion and faithful motherhood the loss of her husband and the pitying love of her daughters, finding solace in her last days in her son Harry. The book is the realistic picture of the contrast between the old ideals of the South and those of the present time, those of the past yielding of necessity to those of the newer life and beliefs. And though one is rather saddened by the fate of Virginia herself, there is a feeling that her daughters, brought up in the fashion of to-day will find broader happiness, and, although not less loyal to husband and family than their mother, will nevertheless retain their own individuality as their mother was incapable of doing.

Nation, 96 (22 May 1913), 524–5

Miss Glasgow's moralizing is of the scientific sort. Mr. Bennett, in his "Five Towns," is not more alive than she to the historical aspects of personality. Indeed, she pushes the mode a point further, and seems rather to resemble the botanist who writes the history of a particular region's flora. As his pages explain the succession of varying growths in the same location, and the relentless supplanting of one botanical species by another, so hers account for the rise of new social types and the dying out of old ones on Virginia soil. In *The Miller of Old Church* a vigorous new type of rural manhood was springing up in the place of the old landed aristocracy. In *Virginia* a belated specimen of the old-fashioned Southern lady lingers on into the era of feminine self-assertion—the fine flower of a vanished social order, by a miracle of spiritual force sustaining itself in a hopelessly altered habitat, only to fade at last among the encroaching ranks of a lustier, more aggressive womanhood, unregarded except by an affectionate son. Her daughters are modernly self-sufficient. Her husband, who belongs as completely to the future as she to the past, finds himself at forty-seven still a young man and very much at home in the intellectual atmosphere of the day. An unappreciated playwright in his twenties, he is now a popular one. Then he had adored his gentle, uncritical wife, now he discards her for the actress who has shared his success. If the reader were to trust his own impressions, he might conclude that he was witnessing a martyrdom. But Miss Glasgow betrays none of the natural indignation of the martyrologist. Does Virginia's suffering wring your heart? It is the pain of extinction in a vanishing type. Only at the last she halts a little, torn between recognition of her subject's essential beauty and the determination to justify its fate, and her study of a social type, like Mr. Galsworthy's in *The Country House*, becomes, in effect, the reverently executed portrait of a lady....

Isa Carrington Cabell, "Womanly Submission—On Literary Thin Ice—A Violent Propagandist," *Bellman*, 24 May 1913, p. 665

Ellen Glasgow is a very wary weaver of the romance with a purpose. For more than a hundred pages her *Virginia* is just a sweet and fragrant story of young girlhood, set in a fitting frame: an old Virginia town, immediately after the Civil War, in a community never very rich or prodigal but peopled with temperate, pious gentlefolk, who had their own ways, their own code of manners and conduct, and who believed in the Bible and the "Lost Cause" and the superiority of the male over the female.

Virginia bloomed, *spirituelle* and fine, in a gray rectory, with a soldier-priest for a father and a beautiful, worn, tired housewife for [a] mother. Some women are a sacrifice to their families. Mrs. Pendleton was more,—she was a burnt offering. However, the lilies bloomed, the lilacs sent forth their perfume, blue was the sky and the peach blossoms glowed against the old wall. And Virginia's hands were kept soft and white, while her mother's were red and tortured out of shape by work. Neither she nor her spruce little warrior-father asked any questions about how both ends were made to meet, and the girl, young and charming, brimmed over with the joy of life. But of that complex maze she knew nothing, except to be submissive and unquestioning and perfectly ignorant; to believe that all happens for the best and that a woman must love God and her husband and obey them.

To this code she subscribed loyally when she fell in love. With exquisite delicacy her soul opened to Oliver Treadwell's touch, but with this yielding the intellect had nothing to do. She loved, she gave him her faith. But that she should have given him the companionship of the mind was not taught by that fine gentlewoman, her mother, nor that good soul, her teacher, who took to educating her friends' children because she had lost her money and teaching was a genteel way of earning a livelihood.

Oliver Treadwell was an advance on his people and his time. He had "knocked about a bit" in Australia and the Continent, and had strange, disturbing ideas about religion and social reform. But Virginia's mother, anxious for her child's happiness, hoped for the best. She was to be to him wife, mother and handmaiden all in one and would win him back to the old faiths. That it was as much a man's business to save his own soul as it was a woman's was not according to the catechism of the day. By a queer reversion of the Miltonic theory, with exactly the same result, Virginia was not to see God in him, but he was to find God in her and do as he felt like doing in the meantime.

So out into the wilderness they went to make their fortune,—Oliver ambitious, thwarted, held down by the sweet and appealing figure of doglike submission which crouched at his feet. Like Locke, Miss Glasgow deals with the essentials, not the accidents of life, and like Darwin, she gives the facts, but lets the student draw his own conclusions from a mass of detail.

Here lies Miss Glasgow's art: not to drive home the argument, but to make the reader the juror and the judge. One would not call this sort of treatment a brilliant feat of intellectual analysis, for brilliancy means a certain hard brightness, and Virginia is an Andrea del Sarto

Madonna, seen through a luminous veil. But it is penetrating analysis that never yields to the temptation to uncover the skeleton beneath. Sweet, fair, ideally faithful creature,—we lay her away, the gentle Virginia, in the past to which she belongs. Her day is done; she may live in the one child who holds for her something more than a half-contemptuous affection, but it is a projected life. Only as we close the book do we realize that in this pathetic figure we see the embodied mistakes and tragedies of a civilization.

"Among the New Novels," Outlook, 104 (31 May 1913), 260

Miss Ellen Glasgow's novels of Southern life are always carefully and conscientiously written. She takes her men and women seriously, working out their development under the stress of life with fine appreciation of effect and cause. *Virginia* has less of local color and of action than her novel last preceding, *The Miller of Old Church*. It is indeed essentially sad in its picture of a sweet and faithful wife mated to a self-centered man. The record of her disillusionment and final abandonment for a brilliant young woman is told with absolute fidelity to human nature, but while it stirs the sympathy and is pathetic in a true sense, it does also leave a feeling of depression. In short, the book lacks what Miss Glasgow has usually not ignored, the contrast of humor and quick movement to offset the essentially tragical theme. It is a sincere piece of work, but not an inspiring one.

"New Books Reviewed," *North American Review*, 197 (June 1913), 856–7

We have said elsewhere of this book: In this great realistic novel, a woman's heart, at the mercy of a system and a tradition, reflects the entire history of a people. It is not only a personal history; it is the "new history which in its amplest meaning includes every trace and vestige of everything that man has thought and done." We have here the history which is conscious that the tiniest stirrings of emotion, the surprises, the set convictions of the obscurest individual are a legitimate part of the structure of life and go to the making of a civilization. As Arnold Bennett has immortalized the "Five Towns," so Ellen Glasgow has caught and set in lasting mold the civilization of a certain period in Virginia.

A great realistic novel; this phrase gives the key-note to any criticism that can be made of *Virginia*. "Great fiction," its author says elsewhere, "is neither more nor less than great truth-telling." To hold up the mirror of life, to see the figures there reflected without distorting glamour, or subjective breathings, and then to give honest report of what is seen; this is to be the great writer of fiction.

The state of Virginia, so long a picturesque survival into a new age, has suffered no little from the sentimental tenderness of her historians. It is human, probably, to regard the past through a softening haze that blurs outlines and modifies ugliness. It is the greatest of Miss Glasgow's achievements that she has always been able to see with precision, and the value of her novels lies in their untrammelled sincerity. She knows her own land from beginning to end; she has watched its development; she has noted those who are at ease in their environment, those who have rebelled and by rebellion made the entering-wedge for progress. Virginia, in this case, however, is not the name of a country, but of a woman; a typical woman of her locality and her time, the early eighties. She is a woman who has never questioned the traditions in which she was bred and whose reading and experiences have given her no glimpses into a wider or more varied life. Virginia is beautiful, gentle, self-sacrificing. She felt ardently, but she neither thought nor read. Indeed, it was a part of the very tradition in which she was reared that reading was a luxury for the idle, only to be indulged in as one would in dancing. Education was not so much a mental preparation for acquiring an understanding of life as a moral training for self-sacrifice; for this, according to tradition, was the sole object of a woman's life. Before marriage, beauty and joyousness and freedom from care were but the duteous means of attracting a husband, but after marriage one became a slave to that convention which regards the continuance of life as its sole object. Not that life should gain in value and worth, but that it should go on, was the objective-point of woman's creation; and to this theory Virginia devoted herself instinctively.

"Your first duty now," was her mother's parting admonition to her after her marriage, "is to your husband. His will must be yours now, and wherever your ideas cross, it is your duty to give up, darling. It is the woman's part to sacrifice herself." And so with outworn traditions, sheltered by a fallacious view of life, Virginia falls in love, marries, bears children, suffers the pangs and knows the rewards of motherhood, and learns that the fruits of renunciation are more renunciations. She flings away her youth, her beauty, her part in the outside world in the service of wifehood and motherhood, only to find in the end that the world has moved on without her; that as she gave up, others fulfilled their lives and that fate demands more of us than mere renunciation. It demands the will-to-live, to create, to add to the fullness of consciousness and being.

If the first book in this novel is idyllic, the last one is poignantly and unrelentingly austere. The great chapter in the first book is "White Magic," a chapter which in poetic loveliness may be set beside the famous nineteenth chapter of *Richard Feverel*. The great chapter in the end is "Bitterness." With the truth of the historian and psychologist, to whom nothing so much matters as fact, Ellen Glasgow preserves a complete fidelity to life. What was lovely and exquisite in her heroine remains so to the last. Virginia trained in gentleness and self-restraint retains these virtues to the last. She accepts, almost unconsciously, the slow withdrawal of personalities that comes between her husband and herself without recriminations or scenes or quarrels, but only with the slowly divergent interests, till there is nothing of soul that one can give the other; so that when the physical bond is broken the partners wake suddenly to find that nothing is left.

It is a profound tragedy that Miss Glasgow depicts, and in these days, when traditions are breaking up and ties are loosening, her tale carries a fine moral.

The English of this book is faithful to the coloring of the author's spirit. Unforced and unadorned except where the subject is of itself poetic, it is throughout of a classic purity. There is not a trace of the modern mixing up of the parts of speech, or of modish defacements of the language. As far as language goes it might have been written in the days of Addison himself.

Indeed from many points of view, Ellen Glasgow's work bears the imprint of permanency. She has never courted public favor; she has never written a "best-seller" for applause or money; but like Hardy, like Meredith, like John Galsworthy, she does the work to the highest reach of her capacity and leaves the results to Life. But her books are more likely than any other American novels of this day to find a place on the ultimate and permanent shelves of literature.

Athenæum [England], 1 (7 June 1913), 620

There is something fine and touching in this story. It is in the first place concerned with marital relations which are sufficiently rare to be interesting, yet sufficiently common to be recognized as veracious. It is also written with that apparently simple ease and fluency which belongs to the good story-teller. Each character stands out, and each—faults and foibles notwithstanding—seems to be realized and understood.

No maiden could fulfil better the ideals almost universally associated with "true womanliness" than Virginia. Her education "was founded on the simple theory that, the less a girl knew about life, the better prepared she would be to contend with it." Out of her love, her self-abnegation, and her intellectual limitations comes—naturally and inevitably—a slow-growing crescendo of misery. This might presage strident developments and a boastful comparison of the new with the old, but the Feminist note, without which no harmony is complete nowadays, is commendably mellow throughout. . . .

Frederic Tabor Cooper, "Inconclusiveness and Some Recent Novels," *Bookman*, 37 (July 1913), 536–7

It is pleasant to be able to begin the present survey of the month's fiction with a volume in which the above-mentioned shortcomings are so conspicuously absent as in *Virginia*, by Ellen Glasgow. One of the leading qualities of Miss Glasgow's work is her sureness of touch. She not only knows precisely what she is trying to say, but she also quite unerringly says it, with just the right inflexion, just the suitable variation in emphasis needed to carry, to any reader of discrimination, the full measure of her meaning. It is this fact which explains why her novels are at one and the same time preëminently local and as wide as humanity itself. She knows her people and her locality with an assured knowledge as welcome as it is rare; but this knowledge is not given forth again until it has passed through the crucible of a keen and alert intelligence and become transmitted into symbols of big, basic truths. In after years, *Virginia* will be remembered as a transition work in Miss Glasgow's literary development. As compared with her previous volumes, it is surprisingly simple in the economy of its structure, its theme and its cast of characters. Indeed, it might almost be defined as an intimate study of just one woman, the Virginia of the title. She represents the type of Southern gentlewoman of the generation immediately following the Civil War, when changed conditions had not yet begun to make inroads upon time-honoured traditions. She is the type resulting from centuries of masculine assumption that woman's whole duty is to be gracious and charming, to preside over her household, train her children, accept the homage of her male friends and relatives as her just prerogative, and diffuse an atmosphere of generous hospitality, a lingering impression of low, sweet laughter and soft-spoken words. Virginia is of the period when women still accepted as a matter of course the necessity of living up to the ideal that masculine egotism prescribed for them; and being by nature a born wife and mother, she does not rebel as a more modern woman would have done, when her illusions are one by one rent to tatters, but can still wear the mask of outward serenity, when in the course of years her heartache over the infidelities of an errant husband is replaced by similar pangs on behalf of her children. In all of this the picture is Southern to the last degree; it glows softly, with a sense of the mellow warmth of glad sunshine, the redolence of exotic blossoms, the tender witchery of youth and beauty. Yet at the same time it sums up in the heart throbs of just one woman a problem as old as motherhood and as wide as civilisation: how shall a woman share herself between husband and children? How shall she do her duty as a mother and yet not awaken a jealous resentment on the part of the man who has hitherto held first place? Above all, how is she to learn that the daily joys and sorrows of childhood do not necessarily have the supreme interest for the father that they have for her, and that a nightly chronicle of such household details begets weariness and satiety? Such is the wider significance of *Virginia*; and it is conveyed with a wise understanding of masculine selfishness and feminine shortness of sight that awaken an answering throb of contagious sympathy. *Virginia* is a picture painted on a more modest canvas than such volumes as The Battle-Ground and The Deliver-*ance*; it lacks something of the robust vigour of the author's earlier manner. But on the other hand, it shows a gain in subtle shadings and delicate intuitions; in short, it represents a new and welcome phase in an author whose rare volumes it would be hard to await with patience, if it were not for the fact that their long delay testifies to the faithful workmanship and careful polishing that make them the finished product that they are.

H. L. Mencken, "Various Bad Novels," *Smart Set*, 40 (July 1913), 153–60

And now, to make an end of the novels, brief mention for five of finer metal—not masterpieces, nor even secure second-raters, but things infinitely above the vapid stuff I have been leading you through.... *Virginia* would be better if it had either more or less to do with Virginians. As it is, the author's portrayal of their peculiarities is incommoded by the story of Jinny Pendleton's adventures with her very un-Virginian husband, who deserts her for an actress, and the story of those adventures is made a bit unreal by its background. But the book is well written, as novels go in our fair land, and some of its minor characters are fragrant.

South Atlantic Quarterly, 12 (July 1913), 287

Ellen Glasgow's latest novel *Virginia* deserves a place of distinction among recent works of fiction. It is both personal history and the history of civilization. Personally it is the story of husband and wife who grow apart: the development of the mental life of a talented man and of the heart life of a self-sacrificing woman. In a wider view we have here pictured the influence of changing times and social demands upon the sphere of woman; the faithful, devoted, home-centered wife and mother of the old school is contrasted with the "new woman" aspiring to compete with men on equal terms in every field of political, professional and intellectual life. More than this Miss Glasgow's book is an intimate picture of the people and life of a Virginia town, portraying with sure touch the typical human units who compose the social structure, and revealing in many a striking sentence an insight into their deepest convictions and emotions. Such work as this adds greatly to our admiration for one of the most serious writers in the field of American fiction.

have little in common with the old idea that a mother should give her children all her time and attention. It seems strange to find that made an issue in the present volume, but there it is. You find it hard to decide how much to pity and how much to censure Virginia for the deplorable conditions that finally existed, when a lifelong devotion to home and family was rewarded by desertion and a breaking heart. Miss Glasgow's style is thorough and sincere, her diction good, and her character-drawing very complete, but she leaves too little to the imagination by analyzing all emotions and thoughts down to the finest point, even dissecting and explaining every little detail that might influence an action. As a development of type the book is notable, but it is monotonous and lacking in interesting and stimulating thought. The characters are consistent if monotonous and fate seems inexorable, but tho it may be impossible, this book seems to prove that one can be too good.

"Review of New Books," *Literary Digest*, 47 (6 September 1913), 388

When we recall this author's, *The Voice of the People* and its big message and appeal, we can not realize that the same writer produced this involved and depressing tale. In all the scenes depicted and among all the characters, lovable and otherwise, Virginia Pendleton moves on to an inevitable fate. With her usual power, Miss Glasgow makes us feel the force of inheritance and tradition over this beautiful daughter of the Dinwiddie pastor, but it seems as tho both atmosphere and plot could have been developed in less than five hundred pages. Modern standards

Lewis Parke Chamberlayne, *"Virginia," Sewanee Review*, 21 (October 1913), 500–3

Miss Glasgow's latest novel, as the symbolism of its title suggests, is a picture of the ideals of a whole people reflected in one woman's life. It is a gloomy picture, as most of her portraits of life in Virginia are, and opinions will vary greatly as to its justice. Notwithstanding that, the power of the book is undeniable. That the author herself is a Virginian and lays her scene in a definite city and at a specified date,—challenging by a hundred touches of careful description of locality and minute analysis of custom, the sharp criticism of her fellow Virginians,—may not be important to the mere novel reader, but must give the book an unusual historical value. For quite apart from the literary distinction of the novel, it contains that rare and valuable thing which Miss Glasgow has offered before; it is a true, but never so convincingly a serious, criticism of the South from the inside.

Of laudation from within—of what the author calls "the endless worship of a single moment in history"—and of indiscriminate condemnation from without, the South has had more than enough, while the benefits of honest self-criticism, like this, are just beginning. Under such circumstances, it is natural that the early examples of this criticism, such as *Nicholas Worth* and the present book, should err on the side of severity. Indeed, Miss Glasgow's novel, which is a most important contribution to the vigorous feminist movement now in progress in the South, is less a criticism of the old-fashioned feminine ideals in Virginia than an indictment of them, an indictment that will seem to conservative people harsh, sweeping, and bitterly unjust. To those Southerners, on the contrary, who hope for radical change, the book is to be recommended as one of startling modernness and extraordinary timeliness in this year of the restoration of the South in national authority after fifty years of exclusion....

Against such a background, sketched with infinite loving detail, the character of the heroine, her parents, her husband and children, and her friends, all stand out with the clearness of life. Compared with these perfectly real people, the characters of Miss Glasgow's former novels are book-figures. Some readers may find the first chapters overloaded with analysis of character, and too sparing in the delineation of character through dialogue. The last two-thirds of the book, however, grow steadily in power as the story is unrolled of a good woman's married life and its gradual wreck. Here every trait of character brought out in the earlier chapters, every weakness fostered and cultivated by Virginia's false and superficial education, is shown working out to its irresistible conclusion. In the last chapters the sociology and history, the didacticism and bitterness fall away, and the reader loses himself, because the writer lost herself before him in the pitifulness of one poor human life. If tragic power is truly measured by its effect in purging with pity and terror, Miss Glasgow has written in Virginia a noble tragedy.

"The Hundred Best Books of the Year," *New York Times Book Review*, 30 November 1913, p. 665

The old order changeth, and Miss Glasgow's new novel reveals the tragedy of the woman who, essentially of the outgrown time, endeavors to bring its ideals over into the later generation. From the time of the appearance of her first book, *The Descendant*, Ellen Glasgow has been recognized as one of the most capable of the present-day American novelists. With each succeeding story she has grown in knowledge of human nature, in understanding of her time, and in the skill with which she uses her medium of expression. So one is not disappointed in finding her latest book the most mature and significant, as well as the broadest in sympathy and the most skillful in treatment of all her product.

It is the straightforward account of one woman's life, a woman brought up under the old idea and according to the old method, "founded upon the simple theory that the less a girl knew about life the better she would be prepared to contend with it." She is a lovely and lovable figure—gentle, exquisite, able to endure with fortitude. When she marries she is faithful to her ideals of wifely duty and self-sacrifice, and by reason of them and that very fidelity she undermines what should have been some of the best and strongest traits in her husband's character and acts as a weakening force upon his moral fibre. And, finally, in the hour of need, because self-effacement has atrophied her own powers and contributed to the failure of his, disaster comes upon them.

The book is a noteworthy and significant study of our own times, done with an art that in its neatness and fineness is more like that of Jane Austen than is usual in modern writers. During the years covered by Virginia's life the position of women changed more than it had done in several previous centuries. And this tremendous difference between the girl of the eighties and the girl of to-day Miss Glasgow has transferred to her pages with all the clarity and fidelity of the artist that she is.

Checklist of Additional Reviews

Times Literary Supplement [England], 15 May 1913, p. 214.
Booklist, 9 (June 1913), 454.
Review of Reviews and World's Work, 47 (13 June 1913), 762.
Spectator [England], 110 (28 June 1913), 1122.
Current Opinion, 55 (July 1913), 50–1.
"Recent Reflections of a Novel-Reader," *Atlantic Monthly*, 112 (November 1913), 690.

LIFE AND GABRIELLA

LIFE AND GABRIELLA

THE STORY OF A WOMAN'S COURAGE

BY
ELLEN GLASGOW

FRONTISPIECE
BY
C. ALLAN GILBERT

GARDEN CITY   NEW YORK
DOUBLEDAY, PAGE & COMPANY
1916

Mary Katherine Reely, "Excellent Novels of Married Life Problems," *Publishers' Weekly*, 89 (15 January 1916), 187–8

Henry Sydnor Harrison in one of his novels has said that there is nothing more remarkable in the present day than the "revolt against chivalry's old home and seat." That this revolt is serious on the part of the South's leading novelists at least is certain, as books by Mr. Harrison himself, Mr. Johnston, and Miss Ellen Glasgow go to show. This is Miss Glasgow's second novel on the theme. The first was *Virginia*, published three years ago.

Gabriella Mary of this story is not at all a radical revolutionist, although she is the antithesis of the gentle Virginia. Indeed to the end of her career, or for so much of it as we are permitted to follow, she is never quite free from the traditions to which she was bred. The characteristic thing about Gabriella is that she refuses to be a victim. Gabriella's mother, eking out a limited income with gentle needlework and reverencing the imaginary figure that in the sixteen years of her widowhood had been built up as the memory of her husband, is a victim. Her sister Jane, married to charming and faithless Charley Gracey, is a victim:

> "Poor Jane Gracey," as she was generally called, had wasted the last ten years in a futile effort to hide the fact of an unfortunate marriage beneath an excessively cheerful manner. . . .

It is with this none too happy example before her that the young Gabriella declares that she can manage her own life. She begins to do so by entering the millinery department at Brandywine & Plummer's to learn how to earn a living. This she does in the face of the protests of her mother, Jane, Cousin Pussy, and the rest. If Gabriella must earn money why not do so in a ladylike way, in her own home, making button holes or crocheting lamp shades!

But Gabriella's first lesson in life's school is not to be learned through Brandywine & Plummer. Her business career is cut short—and in the immemorial manner. No delicately bred maiden of the old South, brought up to look upon marriage as a career, ever gave up her independence more joyously than does Gabriella at the first call of love.

Of her marriage nothing need be said here, save that, like other marriages insecurely based on sudden passion, it comes to wreck, and from the wreck Gabriella learns her lesson:

> . . . She saw her mother, worn to a shadow by the unnecessary deaths she had died, by the useless crucifixions she had endured; she saw Jane, haggard, wan, with her sweetness turning to bitterness because it was wasted; and again she found herself asking for balance, moderation, restraint.

And now that the test had come, Gabriella refused to be a victim. "You can't be a victim unless you give in," she said, and she would not give in. With a living to earn for herself and her two children, she picks up the broken pieces, and, remembering her early experience with Brandywine & Plummer, takes to dressmaking and millinery. At thirty-eight she is a successful New York business woman, manager, as she said she would be, of her own career.

But Life—which can be a humorist at times—has something more in store for Gabriella. It throws Ben O'Hara in her way:

> "Yes, he is good looking," she admitted, reluctantly. "There is no question about that, and he has personality, too—of a kind." His hat was in his hand—a soft hat of greenish-gray felt—and her eye rested for a moment on his uncovered head with its thick waves of red hair, a little disordered as if a high wind had roughened them. "If he only had breeding or education, he might be really worthwhile," she added almost approvingly.

For Gabriella is of the old South, and this man, with whom—for all her thirty-eight years and her position as the mother of two grown children—she is falling in love, isn't a "gentleman" as the old South would understand the word; in the sense in which Charley Gracey, her brother-in-law, and George Fowler, her husband, had been gentlemen!

For it is in her hero—he is the book's hero, although he does not appear till near the end of it—that the author voices her revolt against the old ideal of chivalry, putting in its place the newer ideal that women are beginning to desire, and that Gabriella, for all the persistence of inherent traditions, is wise enough to recognize as desirable.

The story lacks the intensity of the novel preceding it, and the sense of inevitability that pervaded *Virginia* is lacking too. Perhaps it is unfair to attempt comparisons with still earlier books by the author without a careful re-reading, but if memory serves, there is less firmness in the handling of character than in those first books. The author here is using types that suit her purpose.

But as a novel to be read for enjoyment, *Life and Gabriella* is to be preferred to its immediate predecessor. Humor has more place in it, and through all its course, from 1895 onward, it offers an illuminating commentary on contemporary tendencies.

It is a novel of manners and customs rather than of character. Since Gabriella's business is dressmaking, clothes are given much attention, and it is well in this day when we-don't-know-what-the-world-is-coming-to with-women-dressing-the-way-they-do to have the true modesty and delicacy of the wasp-waisted nineties held up to impartial view.

"Humor and Pathos in a Woman's Life," *New York Times Review of Books*, 16 January 1916, sec. 5, p. 1

With the publication of *Virginia* Miss Glasgow established her right to a place in the front line of contemporary novelists. And this new book, *Life and Gabriella*, makes yet more unassailable the position she won then—nearly three years ago. For Miss Glasgow is not a writer who turns out a book every six months. Her work is done carefully, with much thought and artistic conscientiousness, and shows that maturity and finish, that total absence of the slurred or the slipshod, which is sometimes associated with English rather than American writers. Her latest novel is not only a worthy successor to *Virginia*, but somewhat resembles it in its general structure. Like *Virginia*, it is the story of a woman's life from youth to middle age, beginning when she is about

20, and carrying her through love and marriage, disillusionment, pain and joy. It is very unlike *Virginia* in its incidents, and yet more unlike in its heroine, a woman of an altogether different type from that gentle, exquisite embodiment of an outworn ideal.

Gabriella Mary Carr was even as a child "the sort you could count on." Her mother a "weak person of excellent ancestry," who had been left a penniless widow when Gabriella was little more than a baby, and her elder sister, Jane, still a child—was constitutionally gentle, timid, dependent and futile, while Jane, who had married "a reforming rake" and spent ten years trying, ostrich-like, to conceal the unhappiness of which every one was perfectly well aware, was a person of the plaintive, saintly, nagging sort with "a natural tendency to clinging sweetness" who would certainly have driven almost any man to drink. When the book opens Jane has just left her husband for the third time in twelve months, and is in a state of angelic collapse very trying to the indignant and energetic Gabriella, who declares: "But one can always do something if it's only to scream"—a speech which gives a very good indication of her character. It is courage which is Gabriella's most pronounced trait; her tendency is always to resist misfortune, not supinely to resign herself to it; "to do something" herself, not to sit with folded hands waiting for some one to do something for her. And this courage of hers is indomitable. Of course there are moments, hours even, when it seems to fail her, for her life is by no means an easy one, and she has difficulties and disappointments to meet that might well have daunted a woman less strong of heart and soul. But Gabriella fights her battles with magnificent bravery; "she wanted knowledge now, not faith; truth, not illusion," and she firmly believed: "I have a right to be happy, but it depends on myself."

The development of this character is the theme of Miss Glasgow's novel—its growth and testing and discipline. When we leave Gabriella she is a woman 38 years old, who has left behind her the illusions and traditions and conventions that were her heritage, whose "will to grow, to strive and to conquer" has risen supreme and vanquished "the empty rules of the past." She is young, too, able to adventure and to enjoy, realizing that "the true middle-age is not a period of years, but a condition of soul." All this is not easily achieved; Miss Glasgow writes of things as they are, and Gabriella's spiritual success, like her material, is the result of hard work and constant effort. She has a natural gift, enthusiasm, good health, innate optimism and self-confidence, but ten years lie between the fifteen-dollars-a-week assistant at Mme. Dinard's and the capable head of a large and fashionable establishment. And even at the end, although she is happy, one of life's victors, we know that she is bound to have a good deal of trouble with Fanny, that perfect example of a certain type of modern young girl. Although Gabriella was born and brought up in Richmond, most of the action of the book takes place in New York. It is to New York that Gabriella comes with her young husband, George Fowler, whose good looks and charm had always enabled him to take what he wanted and made it possible for him to win from Gabriella a love which was almost worship. To her he was the incarnation of romance and adventure. "His physical power over her was complete," but through her character there ran a vein of iron which even passion could not destroy. The story of this early love of Gabriella's and the threatened disaster that Miss Glasgow never pretends to conceal from the reader is exquisitely portrayed. Were George a little less well drawn the whole would fail, but he, with his stupidity, his inarticulateness, his selfishness and his wonderful physical charm is a real person and one whose attraction for Gabriella it is easily possible to understand.

Two other men play important parts in Gabriella's story: Arthur Peyton, gentle, good, perfectly mannered, with his "philosophy of hesitation ... his deeply rooted distrust of happiness," and buoyant, red-haired Ben O'Hara, a man "bigger than any attributes," a born fighter, truthful, generous, sincere, brave, kind and tolerant; but crude, altogether lacking in moderation and restraint. His is an exceptionally interesting personality, vivid, full of color, almost aggressively alive. And the many minor characters are scarcely less well drawn; there is hardly one of them who does not tempt to comment and quotation, from Cousin Pussy to Mme. Dinard, who had been "born O'Grady and married to a Schwartz," from the shrewd little old spinster seamstress, Miss Polly, to Mrs. Fowler, Gabriella's resolutely cheerful mother-in-law. The entire Fowler household, indeed, is typical. There, as in Gabriella's own home, the perpetual striving "to keep up an appearance" absorbed the mistress's energy to such an extent that little or none was left for other things. The dinner parties, after each of which "the family lived on scraps—for days," the absence of ready money, the refusal to spend a penny on anything that did not show—all this is descriptive of many a ménage. But excellently as it is done it fades into insignificance when compared with the subtlety and finesse shown in the sketch of Gabriella's married life. The truth is never shirked, it is all made perfectly clear and plain, but without a touch of coarseness or any of the repulsive details upon which many so-called realists seemingly love to dwell. Each scene of Gabriella's changing fortunes is depicted with the same sure, graphic touch; the little home in Richmond, Brandywine & Plummer's "dry goods store," where she got her first bit of business experience, the Fowlers' establishment in Fifty-seventh Street, Mme. Dinard's smart shop where all was glitter and show on the outside and slipshod, unsystematic methods underneath; the apartment just off Columbus Avenue and the house in London Terrace—all these represent the outward aspects of a life which was exceptional only in a spiritual sense. Few of the external events of Gabriella's life were unusual; it was she herself who was very far out of the ordinary, and transformed external happenings by the power of her personality.

For it all goes back to that—to Gabriella herself, the finest, most lovable and thoroughly worth-while heroine it has been our good fortune to meet in many a long day. A real flesh-and-blood woman, not perfect by any means, making mistakes, learning many an enforced lesson, but always normal, optimistic, true and dependable as steel. The book is exceedingly well written; it has humor and pathos, reality, an exceptional insight into character, and a brave and inspiring philosophy of life. It sets a very high standard for the novels of 1916; those that measure up to it will be notable ones indeed.

New York *Tribune*, 22 January 1916, pp. 8–9

Miss Glasgow is always at her best when writing of her own people. She knows and understands and loves them, yet never allows her sympathy to tinge her interpretation of them. Her books form a link between the vanished South, the period of transition from the Surrender to the end of the last century, and the present phase of its progress, its ever more complete merging with the general life of the nation. In the North, in the metropolis of the country, she is less securely at home. There her characters remain Southerners in a strange and not altogether sympathetic environment. This may be taken as a felicitous realistic touch, no doubt, but of necessity it keeps the storm on the surface of things. Miss Glasgow is never more sectional than when the scene of her story shifts to New York.

In this new novel of hers, dealing with the latest phase of the changing South and with a Southern woman's fortunes in New York, she gives first place to the New Woman, still struggling down there with the last aggressive survival of traditions and conventions which in the North have already vanished or been put on the defensive. In *Virginia* she pictured for us the life and submergence of a woman who submitted to these conservative influences, who sacrificed herself in the service of her children according to the precepts of the old dispensation. The heroine of *Life and Gabriella* revolts and escapes. It is through marriage and divorce that her indomitable spirit wins its way to economic independence as the head of a Fifth Avenue dress-making and millinery establishment. It is through mere chance that, when she is thirty-seven, another man fills the emotional void which her children, at the threshold of youth, no longer can keep warm for her. Thus the story resolves itself into still another study of the modern woman and marriage, a study not of the subtler perplexities of its negative disillusions, of waning affections, exhausted interests and an aimless, empty prospect, but of primitive causes: neglect, brutality, infidelity and desertion. As Gabriella's mother says, the members of the family marry badly. There is sister Jane, who leaves her husband after every one of his infidelities, only to forgive him. She finds the reward of her Griselda spirit in a calm, prosperous middle-age.

Miss Glasgow has never written better pages than those of the earlier part of this book, in which she depicts the life, the men and women, the viewpoints and opinions of the generation of Southerners which formed the link between the Old South and the first phase of the New, immediately after the Civil War. These Virginians are types, but they are presented with a touch so sure and yet so delicate that they never cease to be individuals. Gabriella's New York, whither her love match brings her, is sufficient unto Miss Glasgow's purpose. It is composed of conventional details, readily recognizable, made familiar by many novelists, but, if the picture means little more than a background to the author's New York readers, it will, no doubt, have more significance for those at a distance, and Miss Glasgow's audience is nation-wide. As for her theories of marriage, they leave the problem very much where it was before. Man is on trial again, and once more is found wanting. It is, at least, one side of the question, which presents so many aspects. The economic independence hammered out by Gabriella by hard work and ability is an exceptional case. Where one succeeds a thousand fail. We hear far too little in our feministic fiction of these failures, of underpaid drudgery wearily carried on until energies begin to lag and earning power dwindles with the passing of the years. Gabriella finds true love and a millionaire, and that too, is of fiction rather than of life. It is characteristic of the optimism of the feminist writers that, while man sees the dire necessity of old age pensions, they blithely insist upon the economic independence of their sex—its right to work—as the solution of another and still more serious problem—marriage—instead of as a grave problem in itself. But, though Miss Glasgow does not probe deeply, she has given us another readable and extremely well written novel. It is, we are now told, the second volume of a trilogy. The first, *Virginia*, dealt with the old-fashioned woman and her submission to shibboleths. *Life and Gabriella* presents the insurgent who fearlessly cuts the Gordian knot. The story still to come will present the woman who faces the world with the weapons of subtlety.

"Miss Glasgow's Novel," Chicago *Tribune*, 29 January 1916, p. 8

... Ellen Glasgow is one of the most cultivated and devoted of the present day novelists, and in her latest volume, *Life and Gabriella*, she has confronted a question of the greatest significance to women, the question of divorce. It has not been her policy to advise the clinging together of men and women who have ceased to care for each other and whose lives are being dragged down by their association. Instead, her arguments are all for the dissolution of homes from which ... love and fidelity has departed.

Miss Glasgow is a southerner, and she understands, as few northern women can, the aversion to divorce, amounting to an obsession, which prevails there in certain communities. A woman who breaks through the course of an unhappy or degrading married life is regarded as lacking in womanliness and religion, and if the circumstances are so appalling that her "act" is approved of, she is expected to keep herself in the background the rest of her life and to "feel her position" with all the poignancy that her own conscientiousness and public sentiment can inflict upon her....

This brief outline of the story gives no indication of the engaging and sympathetic manner with which Miss Glasgow has presented her tale. She has understanding of women and understanding of the prejudices and convictions by which they move. Her style is firm and vigorous, totally free of sentimentalism, touched with a virile humor, and supported by strong common sense. She does not idealize, and she does not distort. Her vision is clear, her judgment sound, and the methods by which she intrigues the interest are legitimate from a literary standpoint.

Salt Lake City *Herald*, 30 January 1916, p. 17

[...]

Except as the intimate study of a woman's heart and mind must always be more or less complex, *Life and Garbriella* is a simple story. It moves smoothly and naturally. Its leading incidents are vital and decisive without being sensational. Its adherence to the truth and the possibilities of life is among its most admirable and impressive qualities.

Miss Glasgow, telling this story, lingers just long enough in her own south to give us very faithful and moving portraitures of Gabriella's mother, of Cousin Jimmy and Cousin Pussy, and of the gentle lover Arthur Peyton, who could neither hold our heroine nor grow up to the new times.

Emilie Blackmore Stapp, "Miss Glasgow Offers Another Southern Story of Rare Charm," Des Moines *Capital*, 16 February 1916, p. 9

Ellen Glasgow is a thoughtful observer of life and its problems and her books are not of the hurried, feverish "best seller" type, but are more purposeful and marked by a deeper note of sincerity. *Virginia*, which was published three years ago, won for Miss Glasgow a place among the foremost of our American novelists. In *Life and Gabriella*, her latest book, she reflects the feminist awakening by the economic success accorded her heroine.

[...]

Life and Gabriella is a story that is told with many deft touches, its humor and its pathos cleverly contrasted, its characters human and convincing. Naturally it is Gabriella's development on which the author centers her talent and as a study of woman's growth thru a period of changing fortunes she has given us a splendid and graphically true picture. Gabriella believed "I've a right to be happy, but it depends on myself." Miss Glasgow has written a novel that is a worthy successor of *Virginia*, and one that will arouse admiration and comment among more thoughtful fiction readers.

Gordon Ray Young, "Good Fiction and Other Books," Los Angeles *Times*, 6 February 1916, sec. 3, p. 22

In this hurlyburly world there be lady-novelists and women writers. We admit that it is our own and an arbitrary classification, extemporized to get Ellen Anderson Glasgow, Mary S. Watts, Edith Wharton and one or two more into a class by themselves. They are not lady novelists.

Ellen Glasgow remains on the energetic side of middle age with perhaps more really good novels to her credit than any other American woman. It may not wisely be said that she has written the "best." Among truly fine workmen there is no "best"—each has points of individual excellence. Mrs. Wharton, for instance, has no equal when polishing a cynicism with vitriol; she is unsqueamish as a surgeon and with a hand as steady.

[...]

Throughout, the novel is excellently sustained; with pleasing dexterity the author keeps in touch with all persons in the story though always developing it from Gabriella's viewpoint. It is a story without raveled threads, or hasty patching—a fine piece of well-rounded workmanship showing a woman of lovely character and good courage making, despite many adverse circumstances and hard difficulties, her life much as she wants it to be.

Nation, 102 (17 February 1916), 197

This romancer, who has written so many books and acquired an audience so considerable in numbers, has reason to suppose that her method of story-telling is satisfactory to that audience. Doubtless she finds profit in being verbose, being obvious, dealing much in repetitions and reassurances. Having once revealed to us that Gabriella has a vein of iron in her nature, she finds that it is safer to remind us of the fact every few pages, lest, in our dazed stupidity of the novel-soaked, we let the fact slip our minds. If we find Gabriella on page 280 "patiently stitching bias velvet bands on the brim of a straw hat," we may rest assured that we shall find her on page 307 "patiently stitching flat garlands of flowers" on the brim of another hat. If we hear once that Gabriella has a favorite child, but does not know it herself, we hear it a dozen times. These are the methods by which one approaches children, theatre audiences, and a vast and enthusiastic section of the reading public. Gabriella is a poor-genteel maiden of Virginia, who jilts a rather useless Southern young gentleman, marries a very worthless Northern one, and after much tribulation is divorced. She becomes a successful New York milliner, and keeps assuring herself that she is dead to love. But she cherishes an ideal sentiment for the useless Southern gentleman, no longer young but still faithful; and, somewhat later, really comes to love an O'Hara, a self-made man, but one of nature's noblemen.

"A Good Book Is the Precious Life-Blood of a Master Spirit," Baltimore *Evening Sun*, 26 February 1916, p. 6

On the whole, the absolutely essential and vital necessity in a hero or heroine of fiction is that they be interesting. They may be saint or sinner, wise or foolish, but their personality and their doings must hold the attention of the reader and make him eager to pursue their acquaintance and follow their careers. When a character in fiction fails to interest subsequent proceedings cease to stimulate the imagination and the annal of their days becomes as unexciting as the log of a ship that is becalmed.

That is what is the matter with the second half of Miss Ellen Glasgow's *Life and Gabriella*. No one will dispute that the distinguished Southern authoress has drawn a realistic picture of "life," but after she becomes a wage-earning woman in New York Gabriella seems to lose her identity as the spirited girl who held her own as a Virginia belle in spite of poverty, and becomes a sort of wooden image totally lacking in personal magnetism.

The novel is called in its subtitle "The Story of a Woman's Courage," and is sharply divided into Book I, "The Age of Faith," and Book II, "The Age of Knowledge." The vignette in color, by C. Allen Gilbert, is so charming as to explain fully Gabriella's fascination for the sterner sex and why George Fowler fell in love with her at first sight. It is a beautifully written story; its literary quality enthralls and its pictures of Southern life and the Carr family of Richmond (ancient of lineage but fallen in fortune) are painted with wonderful knowledge of time, place and people. Miss Glasgow grasps with rare acumen the mental attitude of the Southern gentlewoman whose fortunes may have suffered but who continues to enjoy the same social estate that was hers when she lived in luxury and dispensed hospitality in a gracious manner. She also grasps the wider, more practical outlook of the rising generation in the Southland. In the youthful Gabriella is personified the newly awakened spirit of feminine independence in the Southland, that rather than be a burden to kindred is eager to put the hand to the commercial plow, and that neither falters nor looks back.

Gabriella, in her Southern environment, is a beautiful and glowing creation, a rose of the new rather than the old regime, but a lovable, strong creature, adorably girlish, impulsive and generous of heart. The love of Juliet of Verona for the stranger Romeo is scarcely more delicately and tenderly pictured than the infatuation of this Virginia heroine of fiction for the magnetic man who suddenly came from the North to disturb the still waters of her maiden soul.

Other characters are no less skillfully portrayed. The passive yet immovable resistance of Mrs. Carr to her daughter's advanced ideas, the tearful Jane and incorrigible Charlie, the youthful but sincere lover of the South, the impetuous but fickle wooer of the North, the kindly relatives who strive to make the road of poverty as easy for feminine weakness as they can. All these leading and minor characters are the creations of a writer of rare discernment and strength of pen. The contrast between poverty with sincerity of soul in the girl's home city with poverty screened behind seeming affluence and false standards in the metropolis of New York is keenly drawn. The Fowler family also are distinctive and interesting types,
but when love goes out of Gabriella's life the light of her personality suddenly vanishes also. She becomes a successful wage-earner, nothing more. In the end the authoress makes the inartistic blunder of permitting her heroine to find love for the second time in marriage with a worthy but uncultured man. One whose birthplace was a cellar, whose parents were laborers, whose home was the street, whose scant knowledge was self-acquired. Gabriella was not even driven to his arms through the grateful love sometimes awakened by benefactions. She had achieved financial success, but felt the heart hunger inseparable from any lonely life. She married a man whom chance threw in her way.

Samuel Merwin, in *The Honey Bee*, has made his heroine truer to her own character than is Miss Glasgow's Gabriella. His wage-earning woman, with far less ancestry or culture behind her than Gabriella Carr, is a woman of even greater courage and far truer to feminine instincts. She earned a livelihood and battled triumphantly with self. Even when, intensely lonely, she would have accepted love from a less cultured man than he who had been her inspiration, she could not bring herself to do so. Perhaps what is wrong with Miss Glasgow's book is its too great length, for it is decidedly too long, since it outlasts its interest; and the fact is that the authoress has not wholly grasped what commercial life is and its possible effect upon a woman's character. Given a woman of Gabriella's type, her personality should have become intensified rather than stultified.

"A Dauntless Lady," *Independent*, 85 (28 February 1916), 316

In *Life and Gabriella*, by Ellen Glasgow, there is a duel between the two, and, at first, Life appears to have conquered the bright, spirited girl. But Gabriella has courage as well as spirit and the gift of doing one thing well, which is the best gift the fairies can bring to the cradle of any child. Miss Glasgow contrasts Richmond in the middle nineties and its spare and Spartan living, with New York in its growing extravagance. The effort of the less opulent people in both cities to keep up appearances is a sordid struggle to which she does full justice. Gabriella's escape into the business world, and her career as a successful woman of affairs, add the romance of trade to the story of social and domestic complications. The heroine who can throw aside her home worries by a plunge into practical finance, is happier than the lady of older fiction who could only sit by the fire and weep—and she is more interesting.

Florence Finch Kelly, "Some Novels of the Month: *Life and Gabriella*," *Bookman*, 43 (March 1916), 80–2

The very attractive heroine of Miss Glasgow's new novel is the converse of the Virginia with whom her last story dealt. Comparison of her with the heroines respectively of Mr. Webster's *The Real Adventure* and Mr. Hughes's *Clipped Wings* is interesting as showing steps of the journey upon which the woman of to-day has set her feet. The distance measured between the two women of Miss Glasgow's successive novels is very considerable. In an interview the novelist lately said that originally her plan was to write three feminine biographies that would show the relations of individuals to the facts of their lives and the way in which they react to the situations which their lives evolve. "Virginia," she said, "was the passive and helpless victim of the ideal of feminine self-sacrifice. The circumstances of her life first moulded and then dominated her. Gabriella is the product of the same school, but instead of being used by circumstances, she uses them to create her own destiny." Miss Glasgow added the interesting information that, if she decides to write the third book in a trilogy of American womanhood it will deal with "a woman who faces her world with the weapons of indirect influence or subtlety."

In part, as between Gabriella and Virginia, the contrasting ways in which they face life is, as their author points out, a matter of temperament. But the difference is also due in part to the differences in the times. Would Gabriella have had enough "courage" for a "story" to be written about it if she had been born twenty years earlier? We first see her, in her young womanhood, in her Richmond home, striving to help her mother make both ends of the meagre family income meet while they grip the faded ends and shreds of the gentility which had once been theirs. Already she shows the ability, the energy, the common sense which are, not very much later, to enable her to rescue her life from defeat and disaster. Most admirable is the art with which Miss Glasgow catches the social atmosphere and puts it, living and colourful, into these pages. She has never done finer, truer work than these delicate, firm strokes with which she paints the life of Gabriella and her family and friends, with humour and pathos and sympathy and with such vitality and vivacity in the manner of the telling as make it all entertaining....

Edward E. Hale, "Recent Fiction," *Dial*, 60 (16 March 1916), 280–2

[...]

Miss Glasgow is a bit more definite [than May Sinclair in *The Belfry*]. We should find it hard to say whether she had first in mind Gabriella or the idea that Gabriella finally gained from her experience of life. We rather think the latter. *Virginia*, a few years ago, was the story of a woman whose life appeared a failure because it had been too definitely moulded by old ideas, settled by forces that were no longer effective in the world to-day. Virginia was true to the conventions of a passing era, and could not really live on into the new atmosphere of a changing world. Gabriella is a different woman. She is a product of the same era, is born and brought up in the same conventions, but she gets away from them or (more exactly) is gotten away from them and forced to live in new conditions and keep alive in new currents of existence.

Whatever be the fact of creation, the result in impression seems clear enough. We feel the thing that Gabriella does more distinctly than we feel Gabriella herself. She is a Southern girl, living in "reduced circumstances" in Richmond, taken from the South to New York by an emotional marriage and stranded there to make her own way in the world. She makes her way, makes a life for herself as a modern business woman, looks out successfully for herself and successfully brings up her children. Accompanied all along by a vague dream of past idealism, she finally attains a surer reality and a more logical reward. The idea seems the main thing, and hence there is a certain hardness of touch in the presentation of character. All this may be in keeping: Miss Polly says of Gabriella that there was always a hard streak somewhere down in her, and that she got no softer; and she says herself that if she had been "soft" she would have long been broken. But it is not really a question of hardness of character or hardness of touch. It is rather a question of whether we have here a generalization from life or a rendering of a bit of life itself. With Miss Sinclair, as has been said, we have a rendering of an impression so vivid that the generalization (left to us if we choose) is not always to be got at. With Miss Glasgow we never miss the idea: we always feel clearly that women like men must make their own lives (whether as dress-makers or otherwise), and not drift along as chance and men may will or allow. We always have that, but we rather miss the effective reality that we should like to have too. It is not that Miss Glasgow lacks the ability to describe—to present people or situations; she has a considerable gift in such things. One feels rather that one is following a preconceived idea rather than being shown some of the strangely complex workings of the human spirit.

L.C., "Modified Feminism," *New Republic*, 6 (18 March 1916), 194

Miss Ellen Glasgow is the most reasonable of women, as well as the most conscientious of novelists. Most writers, even the ablest, are afflicted with a betraying bias toward the special predicament of one sex or the other, which makes unlocking their inventions with the Freudian key a game belittling to their perception. But it is impossible to convict Miss Glasgow of absurdity or malice or want of humor. If Gabriella represents Miss Glasgow's dream of womanhood—and one may be quite certain that she does—it is a commonsense dream. Gabriella is without any of the adventitious aids; she hasn't beauty or talent or fortunate circumstances to lean on. Hers is a logical success, and a moderate one. For Miss Glasgow wants us to see how far courage can go toward carrying a woman of good instincts safely over the jumps of contemporary life, but she doesn't want us to see it going farther than it can; she refuses to victimize us. And so Gabriella is just a nice girl with courage added; with, indeed, as deep-lying a conviction as Miss Glasgow's own that life is what you make it, coupled with a steady determination to make it worth while.

All the differences between Gabriella and her mother, who was a southern woman of the admirably helpless sort, and her sister Jane, who made marriage an exercise in forgiving her irresponsible husband, take their origin in Gabriella's courage. Gabriella is outraged by Jane's acquiescence. The spectacle of her sister's histrionic capacity, which made the unfaithfulness of Charles the occasion of concealing, in a pageant of moral superiority, her complete economic dependence on him, stirs Gabriella to conquer her world. Gabriella hadn't the spectator's detachment with which to see, any more than she had Miss Glasgow's instinct and skill to render, the comedy in which the contest of Charles and Jane was so rich. She saw only the moral and she had to act. With a fine ruthlessness she broke through the convention of gentility in which she had been brought up and landed squarely on her own feet in Brandywine & Plummer's millinery department.

Nevertheless, Gabriella was a woman. She fell romantically in love with George. She was agreed with him, Miss Glasgow writes, "that the object of their marriage was to make George happy." But a daily experience of George's futility cured Gabriella of this woman's weakness. When George was unfaithful Gabriella no longer loved him, and she had no more stomach for compromise in her own case than she had had in Jane's. She set resolutely and at once about the task of making a living for herself and the children. She managed it from the first, though narrowly, and thereafter steadily gained in her power to bend life to her purpose. It was the triumph of the whole woman, when, at thirty-eight, securely in charge of a Fifth Avenue shop, she escaped the last remnant of snobbery and married O'Hara, who was neither cultivated in the northern sense nor gentlemanly in the southern sense, but who had a tempered soul, like her own.

Passion after adolescence is the one danger which Miss Glasgow has not permitted Gabriella, the one jump she does not have to take. What would have happened if some time in those ten years of going on and up Gabriella had met a man and a circumstance which had turned all her courage against her determination to manage life? Miss Glasgow leads us firmly away from this consideration.

Life and Gabriella is a sound novel, the work of a writer who knows her task and does it. But it has, of course, the defect as well as the advantage of the sturdy intelligence which produced it. Dealing always with the very stuff of woman's modern adventure, it is not adventurous. Miss Glasgow leans backward in her rectitude. She is so determined not to play life up that she gives us, often, the effect of playing it down.

H. L. Mencken, "The Publishers Begin Their Spring Drive," *Smart Set*, 48 (April 1916), 150–6

Another fair flower of fancy is Ellen Glasgow's *Life and Gabriella*, the story of a Southern girl's revolt against the superstition, incapacity and general dunderheadedness of the South, and of her struggle for existence in New York. Warring upon Southern sentimentalism, Miss Glasgow here reveals it; the ultimate solution of Gabriella Carr's problem is love; the curtain comes down upon an amorous surrender, with the future serene. But the downright maudlin is very skillfully avoided, and if the book had no other virtue it would at least deserve praise for its pitiless picture of Gabriella's mother, a genuine Southern mush-worshipper. Miss Glasgow is much above the average woman novelist in America; she has sound and honest work to her credit; she belongs to that slender rank which includes Mrs. Watts and Miss Cather.

Times Literary Supplement [England], 22 June 1916, p. 299

A good example of the careful, assured study of social life and character which marks this American novelist's work. It gives the centre of the stage to the daughter of humble gentlefolk in a Southern town—the question, by the way, of gentility and who is or is not a "lady" is seldom absent for very long from these pages. Her sister's unhappy marriage helps to determine Gabriella to earn her own living, which takes us away to New York and millinery. But she, too, makes an unhappy marriage, which ends in divorce; and the novel includes both her business career and her love affairs. She is a little bit over-masterful and superior. It seems to fit in with the rest of her that "if there was anything on earth she disliked it was a comic song"—though the singer who evoked this "impatient" reflection was the chivalric hero with whom she ultimately found happiness.

Saturday Review [London], 122 (26 August 1916), 205

Nine books by Ellen Glasgow figure opposite the title-page, but not the one we remember, *Phases of an Inferior Planet*. Perhaps, in accordance with a stupid fashion, that book had one title in the United States and another in this country. Anyway, since 1898 the author has made a great advance, and has added to the arresting quality of her work considerable skill in craftsmanship. Gabriella is a fine character, and her refusal to be victimised by life, however heavily she was handicapped, is attractively portrayed. But she always had something on her side, as she was no doll type sinking to a peroxide blonde, but a brunette whose appearance improved up to the age of thirty-eight. Her marriage and the break-up of the home which supported her sensual, good-looking husband left her with two children. Their nurture proved her sustaining interest in New York, and in her home in Richmond she had been the one member of the family who did not sentimentalise. It would not be fair to reveal how she finally found happiness after steady and lonely work in the great city. Several minor characters are notably effective, especially the business woman clinging to the remains of youth who runs a large dressmaking establishment. Here, as elsewhere in American fiction, we notice an attempt to idealise the uneducated pioneer who rises out of the gutter to create railways and build towns. The attempt does not quite come off, we think; but, perhaps, that is not the author's fault. She has a good idea of character, which is the main business of the serious novelist.

Checklist of Additional Reviews

"New Fiction," New York *Post*, January 1916.

E[dwin] F[rancis] E[dgett], "A Virginia Girl's Contact With Life," Boston *Evening Transcript*, 19 January 1916, p. 26.

Brooklyn *Daily Eagle*, 29 January 1916, p. 4.

Springfield [Massachusetts] *Republican*, 30 January 1916, p. 15.

Louisville *Courier-Journal*, 31 January 1916, sec. 1, p. 6.

Wisconsin Library Bulletin, 12 (February 1916), 90.

Charlotte *Daily Observer*, 13 February 1916, p. 28.

Booklist, 12 (March 1916), 289.

"The Newest Fiction," *Review of Reviews and World's Work*, 53 (March 1916), 377–8.

Carnegie Library of Pittsburgh *Monthly Bulletin*, 21 March 1916, 133.

Athenæum [England], 1 (July 1916), 336.

Spectator [England], 117 (19 August 1916), 217.

Wilson Follett, "Sentimentalist, Satirist, and Realist," *Atlantic Monthly*, 118 (October 1916), 501.

THE BUILDERS

THE BUILDERS

BY
ELLEN GLASGOW

GARDEN CITY   NEW YORK
DOUBLEDAY, PAGE & COMPANY
1919

V.P., Boston *Transcript*, 1 November 1919

To show that the time has passed for the south to harbor her sectional differences and to vote solidly for one party, regardless of the platform of either side and the characters of the men seeking office, is the purpose of *The Builders*, a new novel by Ellen Glasgow, of Richmond. In her clear and forceful story the author pleads for a united Americanism and a doing away of party limitations that the country may develop along lines most essential permanently to overcome the acute problems now confronting it. Miss Glasgow has placed the action in her own city in that restless period when the world was wondering whether or not America would enter the war and through the first year of her participation in the struggle. The characters are portrayed vividly and each is representative of a phase of society.

David Blackburn, the central figure, is a man governed by high principles and a wide and lofty vision of the needs of his country. He has made his fortune in industry and is respected and understood by the better element of his employees. His friends like him well enough, but having the grave misfortune to be a Republican, he is looked on always with suspicion, for it is never forgotten that he stands for the party which liberated the negroes and sanctioned the terrors of reconstruction. Blackburn is the embodiment of a fine man warped by an unfortunate marriage and he is often victimized by unsavory stories concerning his treatment of his wife. Angelica Blackburn is a great beauty, but the author has made her all that is selfish and cruel, caring nothing for the feelings of her fellows, yet donning the becoming cloak of pity for a suffering world. She is of the type whose war work was generally a means for self-glorification, but her utter paucity of character is artfully covered by a cloying sweetness.

Into their home comes Caroline Meade, high bred, spirited, womanly—and poverty-stricken. She is a trained nurse engaged to care for Letty, the prim, delicate little daughter, who is the idol of her father. There is a touching scene in which the nurse saves the life of the child in circumstances serving to make the mother appear peculiarly callous. Notwithstanding the sacrifice of the former, she is compelled soon to leave the house, for Angelica becomes jealous, regardless of her own indiscretions. Blackburn goes to France and Caroline turns to her profession while Angelica, who leaves home the same day as Caroline, stays in Chicago, only to reappear when the man has reason to think she may have gone out of his life forever and he is looking forward to a brighter future with Caroline, whom he has loved silently from the first. Just before returning from Europe he writes a stirring letter to the girl, who has meant so much to himself and his small daughter, in which he voices all his sentiments for the future welfare of the country, for he has warned her that his communications will be totally impersonal.

It is evident that Miss Glasgow regards the day of the selfish, ultra pleasure-loving woman as done, and in her place must rise the strong, intelligent, self-sacrificing individual to whom the happiness and well being of others are of greater import than the trivial things of the moment. It is not on territorial expansion, but on the development of moral fiber that America must depend if she would fulfill her opportunities, thinks the author, who carries the same spirit into her treatment of capital and labor. While she believes the indolent and trouble-making workers should be cast out, she is equally harsh toward the patronizing attitude of the wealthy, especially the women, who would preach thrift and dole out baskets of provisions to the poor, yet grudge an extra penny. In its ending, the story is unsatisfactory from the viewpoint of the novel, for the reader is left in grave doubt as to what solution David and Caroline reach, but this fails to detract from the main point of the book, which is intended as an inspiration and a warning.

Like most current writers, the author is seeking to help reconstruct the country by pointing the way, and it is toward the individual men and women of the south that she is looking with expectant eyes to help in the righting of present-day wrongs. Miss Glasgow has relieved all suggestion of somberness by the introduction of her inimitable character sketches, principally, in the persons of Mrs. Timberlake, the housekeeper who said little but saw much, and Mammy Riah, the old negro. Well known Virginia names are adhered to with the utmost accuracy and each is given its careful placing. The voume is not only interesting as a contribution to Virginia literature, but is a wholly delightful novel written in the author's best style.

"The New South," Philadelphia *Press*, 1 November 1919

This is a new Ellen Glasgow, even as it is a new South. Miss Glasgow's habit has been to interpret her own beloved section of the country in terms familiar to those who have known the South, of post–Civil War days, the first period of reconstruction through which these United States passed. Now, with a fresh point of view born of the events of the past few years, Miss Glasgow shows the South of Virginia and the Carolinas as it passed through the agonies of political rebirth in the year preceding the re-election of President Wilson.

Against a background of domestic drama, the problems of which arise out of the mating of a woman of the old South with a man who stands for political progress and so is deemed by many of his friends and neighbors to be a traitor to the traditions amid which he was born, the author draws a picture of the forces and counter forces urging to a new era. These are the builders of the new democracy, the constructive agencies, which, realizing that between the North and the South there can only be unity and harmony since a greater foe from the outside is about to step in, seeking the humiliation of both, are ready to lay aside prejudice and historical bondages and lend themselves to the readjustments necessary in an entirely experimental situation.

The deep interest of the story revolves around the characters of the man and wife whose relations to each other give the general theme, and of the few members of their household who are most closely associated with them and who inevitably take sides with one or the other. The real heroine of the story is a nurse, a girl of good family, who is engaged to look after the young daughter of the pair. The influence of this girl in the house becomes the predominating factor in the whole situation, and her individual romance engrosses the reader's attention.

Miss Glasgow handles the plot with the agility of a master. Her character development is smooth and convincing. She shows an artist's deftness in distributing her passages of political philosophy, so that David Blackburn's thought processes end before they have a chance to become tiresome, and a frivolous conversation is interpolated, or the picture of social life, light and bright and sometimes scintillating, alternates with the dark scenes of personal antagonism that lead up to the two or three really dramatic moments of the book.

The big test of the novelist is the ability to grow with the times. Miss Glasgow has demonstrated that she has that ability. American to the core, she studies her country's development with a singularly passionate intensity and translates it into romance after the fashion of the artist who is so sure of his medium that its mechanical necessities are wholly lost sight of in the purely spontaneous expression of his inspiration.

Jane Frances Winn, St. Louis *Globe Democrat*, 1 November 1919

It is three years since Miss Glasgow wrote a book, but this one was well worth waiting for. It is a story of the new South, that is trying to get away from the ideas that were all right, perhaps, in the old South, but out of date in this era of progress. David Blackburn shocked the men of the old South because he dared to be something else than a Democrat. His wife was a beautiful, selfish woman, who always put every one else in the wrong who might in any way oppose her wishes. She was catty, but with such velvet claws that only those who knew her well could understand that she was anything but a suffering angel. Caroline Meade, a trained nurse, came to the home prejudiced against Blackburn, but it did not take her long to see who was the real martyr of the family. To accomplish her own ends Mrs. Blackburn would not have hesitated to sacrifice the reputation of her nurse, if the war had not intervened and made a victim of the man whom she wanted to marry if she could obtain a divorce from her husband. Blackburn let her come back to her old home, he and Caroline willingly sacrificing the love that had grown up between them, and in reviewing his reasons he said his year of loneliness in France had taught him the value of sacrifice. The responsibility for American ideals, he said, "is yours and mine. It belongs to the individual American, and it cannot be laid on the peace table, or turned over to the President. There was never a leader, yet, that was great enough to make a great nation."

In regard to parties Blackburn voiced the sentiment of many of his Southern friends and scandalized others. "The demand now is for men," he said. "We need men who will construct ideas, not copy them. We need men strong enough to break up the solid South and the solid North, and pour them together into the life of the nation. We want a patriotism that will overflow party lines, and put the good of the country before the good of a section." Blackburn is one of the best, if not the very best of Miss Glasgow's characters, and in a way the book is a daring one for a Southern woman to write.

"Ellen Glasgow, Works of Fiction by Many Well-known Novelists Among the Important Books Published This Week," *New York Times Review of Books*, 2 November 1919, p. 609

It is not Ellen Glasgow's custom to turn out a novel every six months or so, and an interval of no less than three years has intervened between the publication of *Life and Gabriella* and the appearance of this latest novel, *The Builders*. As might be expected, *The Builders*, though by no means a war book, is very emphatically a war-time story—which is what every novel must be that is not purely fantastic nor concerned with a period more or less apart in thought and feeling as in time from the present day. The war has an effect upon the external activities, upon the minds and upon the destinies of all the more important characters. For one or two, it opens a way of escape from situations which have become intolerable, and, at the very last, it is his conviction of the personal responsibility resting upon every American to render America worthy of the dead who died "believing in America" which helps Blackburn to make his great decision and his great sacrifice.

The book, however, is essentially a character novel; not for a moment does it depend upon plot for any of its interest. In fact, by the end of the first chapter the general outline of the "story" and its two possible endings are perfectly clear to any experienced and discerning reader. But this does not mean that the novel is uninteresting; on the contrary, it holds one's attention firmly, save, perhaps, toward the close, where there is rather more theorizing than seems necessary, and the book drags a trifle in consequence, besides suffering from the temporary loss of its most interesting personality. Though the plot is both familiar and obvious, there is so much cleverness and skill and ingenuity shown in its handling, and one in particular of the characters is so very well drawn, that the question of what is going to happen next is none the less absorbing because the general outline of the plot is evident. This particular character, the one whose devices and manipulations and manoeuvres are of such interest, is not the heroine. Caroline Meade, but Anna Jeannette—who preferred to be and usually was called Angelica—Blackburn, the wife of David Blackburn, who had made a fortune by discovering "some new cheap process" in the manufacture of steel. To attempt to describe Angelica would be to spoil her and to rob the reader of the opportunity to follow Miss Glasgow's gradual and subtle revelation of her character, a character deftly presented in its every aspect and phase. Drawn at full length, with an abundance of exquisite and carefully wrought detail, hers is a portrait which, in its completeness, its admirable rounding out, is worthy to stand beside any other in Miss Glasgow's gallery—that of the lovely and unforgettable Virginia always excepted. She dominates the novel, and when toward the end her actual presence is withdrawn—though never the influence of her personality—the lack of her is keenly felt.

We see Angelica Blackburn, as we do all the characters and all the events of the book, through the eyes of Caroline Meade, a heroine very closely akin to the conquering Gabriella. So entirely is the reader's knowledge bounded by that of Caroline, that the story might almost have been related by her in the first person. She is a woman 32 years old, fine and strong and lovable, who has fought her way through tragedy and emerged therefrom with a hard-won cheerfulness and a philosophy of life partly expressed in the phrase, "People can't hurt you unless you let them," before the book opens. She is a Virginian, well born, well bred and poor, one of the four daughters of an incurably optimistic mother, whose own hard life had not abated her courage one jot. After the terrible thing happened which laid Caroline's happiness in ruins at her feet, she had become a trained nurse, and it is while she is at home on a brief vacation that the story opens with the coming of a letter offering her a position in the house of David and Angelica Blackburn, whose one little daughter, Letty, a very delicate child, has some sort of spinal trouble and is in need of the most skillful and faithful sort of care. Caroline accepts the offer, and her experiences at Briarlay, the Blackburns' splendid place just outside of Richmond, occupy all but a comparatively small portion of the book.

It is in the early Autumn of 1916 that Caroline goes to Briarlay. The national election was approaching when "both parties avoided the direct issue, and sought by compromise and concession to secure the support of the non-American groups." But there were Americans who had realized from the very beginning that this was in very truth "America's war," and David Blackburn was one of them. He was, too, one of those Virginians who believed that "the urgent need in America was for unity," that because of this need sectional boundaries must be forgotten and the "solid South" become a thing of the past. These political views of his brought him some friends and many enemies, but they are not very closely interwoven with the fabric of the story until the end is in sight, when his viewpoint and his ideals become predominating factors, and show a good deal of clear and conscientious thinking on the part of the author—and yet, perhaps because one feels that he is to a very great extent Miss Glasgow's mouthpiece, he is the least real and the least human among the varied personalities of a book in which nearly all the characters are very real and very much alive.

There is indeed scarcely one of them who does not deserve comment, from the bluntly honest Mrs. Timberlake, whose shrewd remarks do so much for the enlivening of the story, to that shallow yet charming little gossip, Daisy Colfax. As for the style, those who are familiar with Miss Glasgow's work do not need to be told of the sheer beauty of her writing. Many of the descriptions in this latest novel—descriptions never permitted to become overlong—are especially sure and fine. There is one of an October afternoon at Briarlay when "all the noise and movement of life seemed hushed and waiting while nature drifted slowly into the long sleep of Winter," which is among the many one would like to quote in full. *The Builders* is a shorter and a smaller novel than either *Virginia* or *Life and Gabriella*. It has less of variety, less of scope. It is confined far more closely within bounds both of time and space and locality; no one of the characters is, like Virginia herself, at once an individual and the perfect embodiment of an ideal and of a type, nor do we follow the development of any one of them as we did that of Gabriella. We meet them when they are already full grown; what they were at the beginning of the story, that they essentially are at the end, despite the broader acceptance of sacrifice they have learned from the war. But though not so big a book as either of its two predecessors, *The Builders* is an interesting one, full of a splendid courage, a high and fine idealism. There is a spiritual victory won against heavy odds, and this, the supreme force of the free and courageous spirit, is the note which rings through the book again and yet again, and culminates in its plea of individual responsibility for the maintenance of those ideals which are at once the meaning and the soul of America.

Philadelphia *Inquirer*, 4 November 1919

A new novel from the pen of Ellen Glasgow is always welcome, and *The Builders* is all the more so since some three years have passed since her last was published. This new story, of course, deals with Virginia and Virginians, but is quite different from all of her other stories. The main character is a trained nurse, who comes of an ancient and impoverished family, and who enters the home of a rich manufacturer, one of the new generation of business men, to nurse his invalid daughter. The rich man himself is also prominent, though not in a romantic way. It is evident that the author uses him to set forth the changed social and political conditions in the South, since this strong man has the courage of his convictions and is not afraid to desert to the Republican Party on occasion. He is for war and hence voted against Wilson three years ago. It must be admitted that in a sketchy sort of way this is a good revelation of the new South, and one can only lament that Miss Glasgow did not give us more of the man who, after all, should be the main figure in the book aside from the nurse. He doesn't quite hold that position, and mainly because the author has introduced so many delightful characters of interest that he is rather befogged. The story is one which will interest all admirers of this gifted woman.

Times Literary Supplement [England], 6 November 1919, p. 633

American politics bulk largely in this novel. David Blackburn, a Virginian who, brought up as a Democrat, has gone over to the Republican Party, expounds his views about the development and destiny of America at considerable length, particularly in a letter of over 3,000 words written from France, after the United States entered the war, to Caroline Meade, who had come into his house to nurse his ailing child. In his wife Miss Glasgow presents an extraordinarily skilful and subtle study of a woman whose reputation for sweetness of disposition and devotion to good works is, except with a discerning few, such that Angelica seems the only possible name for her, who yet is mean and stingy, and who, while utterly selfish and consistently given to the pursuit of her private ends, has the faculty of always appearing to be in the right and of putting everybody else in the wrong, her husband included. Still, whether right was not really on her side when she wanted him to dismiss Caroline Meade is a question on which at least a difference of opinion is possible.

Boston *Herald*, 8 November 1919

Given a nurse, strong of character, fine of spirit, lovable and brave, in a household of wealth where there is a husband, a leader in business and an idealist in politics, and a beautiful wife who hypnotizes herself and her friends into the belief that she has married beneath herself and that she is a martyr to neglect and even abuse. The situation is familiar enough; the plot can hardly baffle the reader; the outcome, or, rather, the alternative between two outcomes, is apparent from the first. But in the hands of Ellen Glasgow, who develops her characters so deftly and subtly and who writes with a charm so exceptional, the situation has great possibilities. Miss Glasgow has made the most of them in *The Builders*, and her book, the first since her widely popular *Life and Gabriella* of three years ago, is to be reckoned one of the notable novels of the year.

Of course, it is a Virginian story. Rather, it is less of a story than a character study and a political discussion with the scene laid in Virginia. The time is the early fall of 1916, just before the presidential election, and the problems of America's responsibility and of Wilson's policy or lack of policy are prominent in the background. We gather that Miss Glasgow was far from enraptured by the he-kept-us-out-of-war slogan that won Mr. Wilson the votes of western women and the presidency that fall. She obviously puts in the mouth of David Blackburn her views of a southern Americanism that is casting off the shackling traditions of Democratic ancestry.

Though the story is not told in the first person we get it all as Caroline Meade, the nurse, sees it. Caroline, rallying from a love tragedy, had become the support of her mother and sister—a family with abundant pride and courage as compensation for a lingering after-the-war poverty. She goes to the splendid place of the Blackburns as nurse or companion for their little daughter Letty. She goes believing the hard stories she has heard of David Blackburn and full of sympathy for his wife. The revelation of David Blackburn at his real worth, with his splendid courage and his capacity for sacrifice, and of his wife in all the unlovely attributes of her selfishness and pettiness of spirit constitute the heart of the novel.

There is an interesting group of secondary characters: Mary Blackburn; Roane Fitzhugh, the dissipated brother of Mrs. Blackburn; Alan Wythe, the lover of Mary, but infatuated with Mrs. Blackburn; Mrs. Timberlake, the housekeeper, with a shrewd philosophy; Daisy Colfax, shallow and gossipy, but likable, and the political friends and enemies whom David Blackburn made. The character on whom Miss Glasgow lavishes her skill, until it is drawn before us with a marvellous perfection of detail, an exquisite nicety of finish, is Mrs. Blackburn. She is a character certain to win a permanent place in the memory though hardly in the affections of the reader.

If the novel lacks the popular happy ending it comes so near to it that it seems to Caroline, looking at dusk across the rose garden, that "beyond the meadow and the river, light was shining on the far horizon." And the book from cover to cover carries the story of the inevitable triumph of the courageous spirit and a plea for the ideals that are the hope of the American people.

"Ellen Glasgow Returns with *The Builders*," Salt Lake City *Herald*, 16 November 1919

Ellen Glasgow, whose *Life and Gabriella* made such a furore among fiction lovers of this nation, has writtem still another book which is distinctly off the beaten trail of story writing. It is entitled *The Builders*, and is a picture of American life in the last two years, dealing in part with the political problems directly before us and showing the effect of the war on a man intensely patriotic from boyhood and yet who had been rather a spectator than a participant in the public life of his Virginia home.

The heroine of *The Builders* is one of the best studies of a woman Miss Glasgow has ever given us—a woman who always appears right and is always wrong—the wife and handicap of a man who always appears wrong and is always right. One of Angelica's circle once said of her that "she kept her figure by climbing over every charity in town."

This is the first novel from Miss Glasgow for three years. The result is a book of wide interest and strong appeal from one of the foremost literary workmen writing in America. Those who have read *Virginia* and *Life and Gabriella*, knowing Miss Glasgow's later work, will surely have the keenest pleasure in her latest novel.

"New Virginians," New York *Herald*, 16 November 1919

In *The Builders* Miss Ellen Glasgow has done two good things; she has written an interesting story and she has drawn two excellent characters, one of whom might, like Selma White in *Unleavened Bread*, serve as a type of the class she represents. The scene of the story is laid in and around Richmond, and the hero, David Blackburn, unlike the majority of Virginians, claims no relationship with General Robert E. Lee, but frankly acknowledges his humble origin. He has made much money but has nothing of the upstart about him; on the contrary, he is a man of intelligence, patriotism, and great force of character. His prevailing desire is to break down the sectional feeling that has always pervaded Virginia, to get away from the idea of the solid South, so dear to many of her politicians, and to awaken in her citizens the larger and nobler idea of America as a whole, and to encourage the growth of a national, instead of a provincial spirit. The period of the story is just before the election that placed Woodrow Wilson for the second time in the Presidential chair, and Blackburn creates a veritable furore among his friends by proposing to vote the Republican ticket—a thing almost unheard of in a man of his position. Miss Glasgow has strong views on the subject of America's future, the line to be taken up after peace is settled, and her firm conviction is that our duty lies rather in the development of moral fibre than in national expansion. Through the mouth of David Blackburn she sets before us the highest standards of individual character as the real remedy for political evils. The other notable character in the book is Angelica Blackburn, David's wife—beautiful, delicate and sweet in manner; commanding the admiration and sympathy of every one whom she meets, but, in reality, thin of nature, bent on securing her own ends and utterly unscrupulous as to the means she employs.

Her little girl is an invalid, and the story is concerned with Caroline Meade, a fine woman who comes to live with the Blackburns in her capacity of trained nurse. At first she is completely fascinated by Angelica, but later on she begins to see what lies under that lovely exterior. Caroline has had an unhappy love affair, but the book ends with a suggestion that happiness is to be hers after all, while the delineation of Angelica Blackburn is the real triumph of *The Builders*.

Albany [New York] *Knickerbocker Press,* 16 November 1919

This is a very thoughtful and well-written novel. The plot of Miss Glasgow's story is simple and familiar, and she seems to have taken special pains to avoid the sensational tricks with which an inferior writer would have endeavored to conceal the fact. Caroline Meade, a southern woman, thirty-two years old, of good family but poor, goes to nurse the invalid child of the Blackburns, wealthy Virginians, at their beautiful home near Richmond. Caroline is a capable, courageous woman who has suffered much and in suffering has learned her full strength and fortified herself anew to face life. Her character is admirably drawn by Miss Glasgow. But even more interesting is the portrait of Mrs. Blackburn, known as "Angelica." She is almost a new type of the "abused" and "neglected" wife, to whose story, according to her version of it, there is never more than one side. Angelica is really the heroine of *The Builders*, and not Caroline, as the reader at first supposes. David Blackburn is hardly as convincing as the women. He is somewhat overweighted by his political perplexities. In the end they are resolved into an idealism that enables him to play the man. But the process by which he finds himself is rather long drawn out. Miss Glasgow has been carried away by her realization of the problems with which America is at present confronted, and by her anxiety to suggest some practical solution of the political deadlock. She has sacrificed her story in a good cause. But here we are—finding fault with a novel that every friend of American fiction should welcome. We sadly need books of such solid worth as *The Builders*.

S. Morgan-Powell, "Miss Glasgow's Notable Novel," Montreal *Star,* 22 November 1919

The name of Ellen Glasgow is synonymous with all that is sanest and finest in current American literature. She is an author who never falters in her ideals. She does not write prolifically, but whenever she gives us a new story, it is a literary event. She has not published anything since *Life and Gabriella* charmed a continent three years ago. Her new novel, *The Builders*, is a book of serious intent, upon the writing of which it is clear that she has expended a great deal of time and thought. It is, moreover, in a sense Miss Glasgow's contribution to the general discussion of the problems that are facing the American nation today. It breathes a very clear and definite philosophy, and it preaches a very courageous and noble optimism in the face of suffering and sacrifice.

There is little that is subtle about the plot itself. Miss Glasgow understands better than most American novelists how to tell a story simply,—how to let the story tell itself, as it were. She locates her characters in the South....

A brief outline of the story conveys little indeed of the manner of its telling. Miss Glasgow is an artist in words, and she knows so well how to color a phrase with thought, until it seems as if nobody could have said quite the same thing in quite the same way. There is a charm about her style that grows upon me, and it is never other than interesting. She is one of those who do not know how to write uninterestingly, and although there is a good deal of political matter in this book, it never palls upon the reader.

There is not the wit in *The Builders* that was so marked and so delightful a characteristic of *Life and Gabriella*, nor does the later book sparkle with the scintillant gaiety that made the earlier novel so popular. But there is in *The Builders* serious purpose, lofty idealism, and a splendidly courageous outlook upon life.

This is revealed not only in Miss Glasgow's philosophical reflections, but also in the qualities with which she invests those characters in *The Builders* who appeal most strongly to our sympathies and command our admiration. Characterization is something of unusual subtlety in Miss Glasgow's hands, and in this respect *The Builders* will compare with the very best work she had previously done.

While the method is subtle, the result is a clarity as refreshing as it is rare. Miss Glasgow knows when to indulge in fullness of detail and when to stop. There are times when she gives such a wealth of minutiae that you begin to think she is too analytical, but you soon discover there is a reason for the analysis.

Perhaps the most beautiful feature of the whole book is the manner in which Miss Glasgow conveys to her readers a full realization of the spiritual victory won in the face of overwhelming odds. There are very few authors in America today who could have achieved such a triumph of vision clearly defined.

The book may stand as a notable achievement. It cannot fail to add to Miss Glasgow's reputation, which is already solidly established. If there were more writers like her in the world, it would be a better place to live in.

Jay B. Hubbell, "Ellen Glasgow as a Literary Pioneer," Dallas *News*, 23 November 1919, pp. 1–4, 9

[...]

The Builders is a story of Virginia today. It does not deal with the traditional Virginia of Colonels, languishing beauties and mint juleps, but with the Virginia that went into the war against Germany, the Virginia of prohibition—save the mark!—and the Virginia of industrial problems. The hero, David Blackburn, is one of Miss Glasgow's strong, rough-hewn men. He is a thinker who wishes to see Virginia play a leading part in a great age. Dissatisfied with the political situation in the Solid South, he attempts to play an independent part in politics in the spirit of the statesmen of the Revolution. He welcomes the war with Germany as a great opportunity for both his State and himself. He is in the best sense of the word a builder—hence the title of the novel.

Though not a war story, *The Builders* gives as fine a picture of how the recent war came to Virginia as her *Battle-Ground* does for the Civil War. She does not disguise the blindness, the endless platitudes, the hysteria which prevailed on the momentous occasion; but at the same time she recaptures something of the lift, the inspiration of that great event. Incidentally, Miss Glasgow makes excellent use of the war as a means of bringing her story to a satisfactory conclusion.

The ostensible heroine of the novel, Caroline Meade, is a trained nurse of 32. She bears a closer resemblance to Balzac's "woman of 30" than to the average insipid heroine of American fiction. She is closely akin to the courageous Gabriella. The most interesting character in the novel, however, is Angelica Blackburn, David's wife. She, too, resembles some of Miss Glasgow's earlier characters, notably Gabriella's sister, Jane. Angelica is universally believed to be the victim of an unfortunate marriage. When Caroline goes to the Blackburn home to take charge of their little girl, Letty, she at once takes sides with Mrs. Blackburn against her husband. Gradually, however, she comes to know the truth. Angelica is, in the eyes of almost all, the most perfect, the sweetest, the most refined woman in the world. In reality she is utterly selfish. The novel is, so far as it pertains to her, a study in hypocrisy. Angelica recalls the Rosamond Vincy of George Eliot's *Middlemarch*, but she is unique. There is nobody quite like her in the fiction that we have read. Miss Glasgow has perhaps not made her character altogether convincing, but the gradual revealing of Angelica's true nature is handled with wonderful subtlety and skill.

The Builders is not for those who wish to amuse themselves with an empty story. It is, like all of Miss Glasgow's stories, a serious study. Her interest is in character rather than plot, but in spite of this the novel is eminently readable. Apart from occasional moralizings in the vein of Tolstoi, there is hardly a dull page in it. The novel is shorter than most of her novels, and it drags less than some of her longer stories, *Life and Gabriella*, for instance.

The Builders is perhaps not so good a novel as *The Deliverance* or *Life and Gabriella*, but it sustains well the author's reputation.

"*The Builders*, Ellen Glasgow," Los Angeles *Times*, 23 November 1919, sec. 3, p. 34

Ellen Glasgow's new novel, *The Builders*, like Alice Brown's *The Black Drop*, Alexander Black's *The Great Desire*, and other recent American fiction, is concerned with the reactions produced by the war on American life and character. Like the others mentioned, it is the doubtful period before our entrance into the war that focuses our attention.

Yet neither *The Builders* nor the other novels mentioned can be called in any sense war novels. But since they are novels of American contemporary life, the characters and the story are inevitably affected by the great struggle of humanity in the war.

Ellen Glasgow, with the ex-post-facto wisdom of other astute Americans, is firmly convinced that the United States should have gone into the war as early as 1916, if not earlier. In the character of David Blackburn, a successful manufacturer of the new South, we see the thoughtful, eager advocate of war against Germany from the moment the *Lusitania* was sunk. Convinced that his country's honor is at stake, he is ready for any sacrifice in what he believes is a righteous and regenerating cause

[...]

In places the story drags because of the prominence the author gives to David's long speeches and long letters setting forth his very admirable views as to the duty and destiny of his State and of the nation. Nevertheless, the story is vastly interesting, though its appeal is neither so elemental nor so universal as that in the earlier novels of Miss Glasgow.

Two or three years ago Miss Glasgow explained that she planned to write three feminine biographies that would show the relations of individuals to the facts of their lives and the way in which they react to the situations which their lives evolve.

According to the author, Virginia was the passive and helpless victim of the ideal of feminine self-sacrifice. The circumstances of her life first molded her and then dominated her. Gabriella was the product of the same school, but instead of being used by circumstances she used them to create and shape her own destiny.

This is the long promised third book in the trilogy of American womanhood, dealing, in the words of the author, "with a woman who faces her world with the weapons of indirect influences or subtlety."

Angelica does this to perfection, but she lacks the greatness of Virginia and of Gabriella, because she is too thoroughgoing in her subtle deviltry to be typical.

[James Sibley Watson, Jr.], *Dial*, 67 (29 November 1919), 498

The Builders, by Ellen Glasgow ..., has for its chief character a woman who always appears right and is always wrong, who "keeps her figure by climbing over every charity in town." For background Miss Glasgow has dragged in the war, the old South and the New, Reform, and other forces, of which it seems she understands only the externals. She skates brilliantly on thin ice over deep waters; she is a very good novelist of the third order.

Chicago *Continent*, 4 December 1919

Miss Glasgow's new novel is poignant but not too pleasant. With unforgettable vividness we are given the story of a pampered and very beautiful southern woman who always appears to be in the right (though she never is) and are shown the suffering she causes her husband and all other worthwhile innocent persons whose lives touch hers. The flux and bigness of American life in war time is found in the background of this book, together with the cry for cleaner politics, constructive patriotism and for a fairer democracy. *The Builders* shows us the author's portraitive skill and is permeated with her fine and serious realism, a realism that interprets as well as depicts.

"New Novel by Ellen Glasgow Is Worth While," Baltimore *Sun*, 6 December 1919, p. 6

In a novel by Ellen Glasgow the reader is assured of a worth-while story and earnest literary endeavor, for Miss Glasgow does not write lightly, and she writes with purpose and upon the problems of the hour.

Her latest book, *The Builders*, is a study of the mental attitude of Virginians immediately preceding and during the first few months of the great war. It is also an attempt to outline the political policy that will cause the American people to cast aside partisan feeling that has separated

North and South since the war between the States and weld all sections of the commonwealth into a nation of complete unity and concentrated purpose.

She casts the scenes of the story on an impoverished Southern plantation, such as may still be found in sections of Virginia, and in Richmond—always the throbbing political heart of the Old Dominion State. She describes the home life of Virginians of the old regime and current social life of Richmond, with which she is so happily familiar, but essentially the purpose of the story is to set forth Virginia's present duty to State, country and world as consequence of the world war.

A political story of today, it is also a love story of the present, and the two most colorful characters are a professional nurse, who has sought relief from memories of an unhappy romance in a life of ministry, and a man who, descending from a war-impoverished family of gentle blood, had to fight poverty in his youth and finally amassed a fortune. A man deeply interested in political affairs, but of independent and advanced ideas among conservative Southern contemporaries.

The woman enters the palatial country home of the financier in professional capacity as nurse for the man's delicate little daughter. Strangely enough one can never meet a heroine of fiction who assumes this semi-business, semi-family relation to an employer without recalling Charlotte Brontë and *Jane Eyre* and in Miss Glasgow's grouping of characters there is suggestion of that masterpiece of English fiction. There is a master both austere and kindly, a wife who is abnormal, a child who clings lovingly to the spirited young woman who is more companion than nurse. There is even the friendly housekeeper who, like Mrs. Fairfax, is distantly connected with the family, and almost the master's first acquaintance with the nurse is meeting her unexpectedly at play with her young charge. But beyond these points of resemblance the stories have no likeness one to the other and Miss Glasgow's romance is a very tender and unconscious one, a story that holds the interest intensely absorbed and that is fine and beautiful in its ideals....

Columbus [Ohio] *Dispatch*, 7 December 1919

This is the first book from Miss Glasgow's pen in three years. Set in southern Virginia, with the flavor of the old South's charm still lurking about it, the story deals with the evolution of American life in its entirety during the last two years, leading finally straight to the political problems now before us. Through its pages moves the figure of one of the most arresting heroines Miss Glasgow has ever drawn, a woman who contrives always to appear right and is in fact pretty nearly always wrong—a woman of whom one of her intimates remarked that she "kept her figure by climbing over every charity in town."

The chief protagonist of the book, though, is not Angelica but the husband whom she retards and handicaps. Intensely patriotic from boyhood, this man has still remained a spectator rather than a participant in the public life of his Virginia home. In the quickening of the general conscience about him, and his own gradual growth in vision and spirit, the story of the man and the story of awakened America are subtly, dramatically blended.

This new book of hers is painted on a wider canvas than she has ever employed before. It more than lives up to the standard she has set. Whereas formerly she has been called first and foremost the novelist of Southern reconstruction, it seems likely she will hereafter be known as the novelist of American reconstruction.

H. W. Boynton, "Two 'Latest Efforts,'" *Weekly Review*, 2 (10 January 1920), 36

Miss Glasgow is a novelist who has won popularity without letting herself be drawn into hasty production. Like Winston Churchill, she takes two or three years to the writing of a novel—perhaps again like Mr. Churchill she is a trifle too solemn over the business. The effort of the storymaker sensibly overweighs the impulse of the story-teller. But *The Builders* is less heavy-handed than its predecessors. Its action is more compact and its dialogue shows less tendency to run to seed. Brave Caroline is something more than a replica of the conventional romantic heroine. Angelica is a mollusc-wife none too delicately drawn, but "with a difference." And the other women, Matty Timberlake the dragon of beneficence, and Mary Blackburn the Amazon in love, are excellent variations from the familiar types. But the three men of the story are hardly more than capable "parts." The Allan who is so easily lured from his Mary by the first deliberate glance of a siren, the handsome wastrel Roane who, a perfect Southern gentleman, insults women with so much charm and such comfortable impunity, are figures of "the screen." As for David Blackburn, who, hopelessly wedded to the mollusc-siren, is the natural heaven-born mate for brave Caroline, few masculine observers will have much patience with him. To his glory the ancient chord of honor, duty, and Southern chivalry is twanged without mercy. The weak point about the story is that its effectiveness all hangs on our acceptance of Angelica. Unless we believe in her supreme beauty and charm, unless we come directly under her spell, the rest is naught. Literature is full of ruthless and irresistible sirens; what one of them but Shakespeare's Cleopatra has really held us in her hands? There is little subtlety in this Angelica's speech or action, and for her physical subtlety we have only her author's word. Why should we believe that not only the Davids and the Carolines, but all of Richmond (including the Blackburn family doctor) could ever have been befooled by her? . . .

M[alcolm] C[owley], *New Republic*, 21 (18 February 1920), 364, 366

Curiously enough the heroine of *The Builders* revolts like Medora [in Eden Phillpotts's *Storm in a Teacup*] against the tedious goodness of her husband. Angelica, however, is unhealthier than Mrs. Dingle [of *Storm in a Teacup*]; she is a beautiful, pale creature, growing daily more neurotic and vindictive. There is another woman also; a colorless nurse whom Miss Glasgow elects to be heroine of her tale and who declines the office with little grace. The author fails again when she tries to crowd into the narrow compass of her story the War, Reconstruction, and half a dozen other processes of which she seems to understand only the external features. Miss Glasgow skims brilliantly over the surface of event and character, her sallies never penetrate very deeply. Pale and shadowy as Angelica seems; as little as the reader or Miss Glasgow herself understands her motives, she remains the only three-dimensional figure.

Checklist of Additional Reviews

"American Spirit in War Shown in Two Big Novels; Other Readable Tales," Brooklyn *Eagle*, 1 November 1919.

"Brilliant Character Drawing in Ellen Glasgow's War-Period Novel," Philadelphia *North American*, 1 November 1919, p. 16.

New York *World*, 2 November 1919.

St Louis *Republic*, 10 November 1919.

"New Novel by Ellen Glasgow," Cincinnati *Times-Star*, 12 November 1919.

"Ellen Glasgow's New Novel," St. Louis *Post-Dispatch*, 15 November 1919.

R.T.H., "Miss Glasgow Writing Again," Springfield [Massachusetts] *Union*, 16 November 1919.

Pittsburgh *Dispatch*, 16 November 1919.

"Ellen Glasgow's *The Builders* Gripping Novel," Boston, *Traveller*, 19 November 1919, p. 10.

Athenæum [England], 2 (21 November 1919), 1242.

Elia W. Peattie, "Literary Reviews," Chicago *Daily Tribune*, 22 November 1919, p. 10.

"Optimistic Note Sounded," Cincinnati *Enquirer*, 22 November 1919.

"Life in Modern Virginia," Philadelphia *Public Ledger*, 22 November 1919.

Detroit *Free Press*, 23 November 1919.

Houston *Post*, 23 November 1919.

Booklist, 16 (December 1919), 91–2.

F.A.G., "Virginia and Ellen Glasgow," Boston *Evening Transcript*, 6 December 1919, sec. 3, p. 10.

"Political Idealist with Flighty Wife," Springfield [Massachusetts] *Republican*, 7 December 1919, p. 15.

"All-American Novels," *Outlook*, 123 (17 December 1919), 514.

Louise Collier Willcox, "Ellen Glasgow's New Novel," *Bookman*, February 1920, 616–17.

ONE MAN IN HIS TIME

ONE MAN IN HIS TIME

BY
ELLEN GLASGOW

"One man in his time plays many parts."

GARDEN CITY, NEW YORK, TORONTO
DOUBLEDAY, PAGE & COMPANY
1922

Hunter Stagg,
"The Virginia Scene,"
New York *Tribune*,
21 May 1922, sec. 5, p. 6

As Carl Van Doren points out in his new book, *Contemporary American Novelists*, Ellen Glasgow is the one Southern writer who, beginning as a local colorist, with narratives of the Civil War and Reconstruction times, has yet "emerged from the level established by the majority," and ranged herself with fresher literary models and ideals.

She has accomplished the feat of remaining as faithful to her background as any Thomas Nelson Page, while steadily acquiring toward it an attitude shrewdly critical. Thus, in her later novels, pre-eminently in *Virginia*, she paints with warmth and fullness the atmospheric conventions and still active traditions of her scene, but plays the bitter lights of irony and glamourless pathos upon the people who confront life with only such defenses as those conventions and traditions can supply.

Having already developed from a local colorist into a type of ironist, much needed in the South, Miss Glasgow sounds in her latest novel, *One Man in His Time*, still another note, of which the chances are equal that it represents yet another milestone in her development or merely a passing phase. In either case the note is less one of literary than personal reaction. Her sanely critical records of the conflict between the old and the new always displayed a trust, unusual in a Virginia writer, in the new.

To her handling of the same conflict she now brings a touch of weariness. The old things Miss Glasgow still loves, but, it seems, retrospectively, and the characters representing them, the old majors or colonels, the faded belles, the courtly darkies and all the rest of the familiar figures, she handles still tenderly, but with a touch of impatience. She is evidently tired, not indeed of them, but of writing about them. They are in her book obviously for no other reason than that they were necessary to throw into relief the character in which she is most interested.

This character is a man born and reared in a circus tent, a man ignorant but full of force and potential greatness, who, just prior to the story's opening, has been made Governor of Virginia, defeating a man of culture and of secure antecedents. It is a significant fact in the plan of the book that the election of Gideon Vetch had been managed none too honestly, for through him Miss Glasgow symbolizes the real drama of her book, the drama of "Democracy at work, clumsy, unwieldy, incredibly stupid and yet all the time growing into something infinitely fine"—and great enough to disown the corruption without which it could not have won a hearing.

Another character in whom Miss Glasgow seemed, for a time, particularly interested is the sister of the rather colorless young man who supplies the plot by falling in love with the Governor's uncultivated daughter and standing with reluctant feet where the brook of tradition and the river of democracy meet. Stephen Culpeper's young sister is a type of flapper hardly touched upon in fiction, as most of the younger writers to whom the subject seems given ever persist in regarding all flappers, from whatever walk of life, as one dissolutely cheap type, of which one representative is as indistinguishable from another as would be, truly, their clothes if you saw only the design and never the varying quality of the cloth. Miss Glasgow might find a good subject for her next novel in Mary Byrd Culpeper, in whom is merged the old-time "Virginia beauty" and the modern flapper, without violence to either species.

Although *One Man in His Time* does suffer a little from the mood of impatience, in which it was apparently written, from the fact that the caress which Miss Glasgow bestows upon her conventional figures might easily have become the shove which would precipitate them from her stage forever, one cannot regret that impatience. Why, indeed, should Miss Glasgow not shove such figures off her stage? There is in Virginia now plenty of material to be treated independently of the past, plenty of elements and moving forces which, though new, have already acquired sufficient velocity not to need, in fictional treatment, a background of contrasting tradition to push off from.

E[dwin] F[rancis] E[dgett], "*One Man in His Time*: Ellen Glasgow Depicts Our Social Changes," Boston *Evening Transcript*, 31 May 1922, sec. 3, p. 6

Virginia is again Miss Glasgow's scene, and Virginians her characters, but they might as well be Massachusetts and Massachusetts people. Her theme is the old order against the new, the aristocracy which has come out of the early days of the English pioneers in conflict with a son of the people who, by a trick of the political fates, has become the governor of the State. In consequence, we may read in her pages what the one class thinks of the other, their contrasts forming a series of more or less argumentative interludes in the course of a story that in itself is old fashioned enough to have the roots of its plot deep down in the fertile sensational soil of a family mystery that involves the antecedents and origin of the heroine.

In such a story as this a member of the old order invariably falls in love with a member of the new. Miss Glasgow therefore is true to type and a follower of tradition when she asks us to accompany her along the rough road of the wooing of Stephen Culpeper and Patty Vetch. The two names in themselves reveal their respective patrician and plebeian heritage. At the outset we vision both as typical members of their classes, and from the beginning we foresee the difficulties that are to arise through their first accidental meeting....

Almost against his will Stephen Culpeper made acquaintance with Patty Vetch; almost against his will he fell in love with her; almost against his will they fall into each other's arms at the end of the story. It takes a long time and many pages and much ink and type to reach this foregone conclusion, to tell this very old story over again. Miss Glasgow has followed the lines of least resistance, and has given her readers a little of almost everything in the way of psychology, sociology, politics, religion and ethics. She should be thanked, however, for not forgetting to tell her story in a manner that discloses her as more expert in the matter of style than as a maker of plots or the writer of an enlightening novel on the ways and manners of this changing world.

"Political Arena Forms Background for New Novel," Baltimore *News*, 3 June 1922, p. 7

Ellen Glasgow likes the public arena, the political flavor. She is keenly interested in observing the effect of political power upon a man, and she delights in contrasting the actual with the imagined results of our system of government. It does not seem likely to her that America will grow greater or become more worth while by leaning on its traditions and depending on the rule of thumb. The conservatives are not the people who count. Yet nothing could be more sane and balanced and free from the bawlings of the radical than the philosophy of this writer. She has an extraordinary devotion to seeing both sides, to presenting both sides, and there is nothing from which she turns with such decision as from the panacea....

And Darrow takes Stephen, the rich young man, to the slums of his city, shows him the poor living in poverty and facing worse poverty; tells him that the slum is owned by Stephen's father, and then, when the boy, for he is not much more, sickens at the realization, he counsels him not to lose his balance. "That's life," he says, "yes, but it ain't the whole of life. Those folks we've been to see have had their good times like the rest of us, only we saw 'em just now when they were in the midst of a bad time. Life ain't confined to a ditch any more than it is to a lilypond." And then he goes on to relate how a cousin of Stephen's, a delightful woman called Corinna, who was confronted with the same situation, set to work and improved the property she owned, put up model flats with gardens, and charged the same rental as before the war. With the result that her tenants moved out into hovels and tenements and sublet the fine new places to more fastidious lodgers.

The Governor to whom Darrow alludes has been elected in Virginia on a wave of popular frenzy. He is a man of the people. He began as a circus performer, and comes to the head of his party, the Independents, through the sheer force of personality and faculty for leadership. Naturally he is anathema to the whole army of the privileged classes. They have to endure him, but they can at least ignore him socially and also ignore his young daughter, Patty, a vivid, fierce, clever, sensitive girl, who resents this attitude and fights it with a gallantry and a sober sense that is at once delightful and astonishing.

She has the alert adaptability that distinguishes the American woman who is evolving from one social grade to another, doing it definitely and with a purpose, but she is a fresh, ingenuous thing too, sweet to know and worth the knowing. Miss Glasgow has done a fine thing in this portrait, and another fine thing in Stephen, who comes from the side of tradition, birth, ease and who meets Patty on her upward climb, a climb that will never make her what his mother, his sisters, the girl chosen for him to marry are, but that will develop her to the finest limit of her nature—a nature far richer than the paler, securer products of generations of training, who have left the keen savors of life untasted and have themselves lost savor.

There is a good deal of plot to the book, a well managed and satisfactory plot that makes the story interesting aside from its value as a document of human experience in an environment that touches us all closely. Patty is more of a mystery than at first appears. But she is herself and that is what matters. There are other women in the book, each a carefully drawn and living character; Corinna is exquisite, the perfect flower of her caste, but utterly human, too—the sort of woman whom once known you will not willingly relinquish. She remains a part of your memory, a friend you love.

Of course, it is the Governor himself who is the chief figure. Miss Glasgow makes you aware of him even as she makes the people of her story aware of him; he gradually develops to your perception and he ends by being truly the powerful, unusual and lovable man she wishes you to see. His end is ironic. The book is, for that matter, an ironic book. The very tenderness and sympathy Miss Glasgow feels toward life must find relief in irony or her fine balance would be lost.

R.E.S., "Sex, Marriage and Blueblood," Baltimore *Evening Sun*, 24 June 1922, p. 6

One Man in His Time is a curious anomaly. It has all the earmarks of an old-fashioned dime novel—the young hero, of age-old aristocracy (F.F.V.); the heroine, not only born of the people, but wretchedly so, as well; her demagogic virile foster-father; her threatening lover—all involved in a series of melodramatic incidents, and yet it manages to be a convincing story, full of dignity, with characters that are extraordinarily well portrayed. Miss Glasgow has demonstrated the perfection that blue blood and tradition can produce in the person of Corinna Page, whose fineness and intelligence have combined to give her a true vision and an appreciation of value, stripped of the accepted outer manifestations, which, she was taught, were necessary.

The book contains much concerning the contrast between the prosperous and the poor, but it never descends to the soft sentimentality so often met with.

Henry Seidel Canby, "A Changing Order," New York *Evening Post Literary Review*, 1 July 1922, p. 771

In a recently published collection of literary estimates Mr. Carl Van Doren observes of Miss Glasgow, whom he credits with at least one book "unexpectedly full and civilized, packed with observation, tinctured with omen and irony," that she "emerges considerably—though not immensely—above the deadly levels of fiction." In this latest novel from her pen Miss Glasgow still rises above the "deadly levels," but unfortunately not far enough above them to command more than passing notice. That "critical attitude towards the conventions of her locality," which Mr. Van Doren signalled out as one of the qualities that lent distinction to her work, is still in evidence, but it has a false emphasis, a slant towards the stereotyped, that gives her tale a distorted perspective. Miss Glasgow, striving for realism, still romanticizes; she sees her Virginians as a people who no longer live in a backwater of civilization, and at the same time she presents her Virginia in the utmost orthodoxy of tradition. She takes a man who has passed through the blazing revelation of war and who has been brought to the verge of physical and mental prostration by the experience, and shows him the prey of inhibitions and narrowness that in view of his battle days anything short of the conventions of Virginia fiction must long since have demolished. She is up to the moment in her portrayal of the flapper and woefully behind the times, and, we are sure, behind Virginia, in her discussion of democracy. She is intent on displaying the personality and struggles of a man of the people who attains to the purple—since the Governorship, which hitherto had been the perquisite of the F.F.V.'s, must be so regarded—and is diverted by her desire to write a love story, or, rather, two love stories. In short, she is constantly pulled in two directions, with the result that her novel falls by the wayside as a work of art.

It is, however, interesting enough as a story, though its incident is at times hackneyed, and on more than one occasion melodramatic. Reduced to the barest outline, it is the tale of the efforts of Gideon Vetch, a man sprung from humble beginnings as a circus rider, who, through sheer force and magnetism of personality, has risen to the Governorship of Virginia, to carry out his projects for social betterment in the face of the distrust of the aristocrats and the wiles of the politicians, and of the attempt of his daughter to force social recognition from a hostile and supercilious society. In Patty Vetch's pathetic desire for happiness, in her affection for the Virginia belle of ripe experience and undiminished charms, who takes her in hand, introduces her and befriends her, and leaves her finally in the arms of the nerve-racked, irresolute, and caste-ridden Stephen Culpeper, as much as in the story of her father's career, lies the interest of the tale. It is interspersed with theatrical incident—the introduction of a mysterious woman whose identity is explained under tragic circumstances, the renunciation of the man she loves by one woman to another who no longer holds his affections, the providential disaster that brings the lovers together in the end—incident and expedient that have been worn threadbare by use. Moreover, the philosophizing on social and economic matters that Miss Glasgow now and again introduces into it has a familiar and oft-repeated ring....

Miss Glasgow has it in her to do better work than this book.

"The Old Order Changes in Virginia," *Literary Digest*, 74 (15 July 1922), 46–8

Picture to yourself one of the proudest, one of the oldest, one of the most conservative of the States confronted by the fact that, owing largely to the negligence of its better-born voters, it has elected to the important position of Governor of Virginia a man not only entirely self-made but, if rumor be correct, one who was born in a circus tent, and who represents in his politics that nightmare of conservatism, the Labor Party.

The scene of this story is laid in Richmond, the subject that strife between the old and the new, progress and prejudice, which has at last reached the South and which threatens to demolish in its advancing tide so much that is beautiful. Gideon Vetch is Governor of Virginia—a man without any pretense to the gentle breeding so highly prized by his fellow-townsmen, scornfully called a demagog by some, but possessing a certain personality whose charm is felt by the more fair-minded of his opponents. His daughter Patty is what might be expected. Pretty, vivacious and uncultivated, she too has charm, and no one perceives it more clearly than Stephen Culpeper, whose birth, breeding and education have all tended to make him regard such girls as Patty Vetch as quite outside the pale of consideration. Add to these three a fourth in the person of Corinna Page, a widow of forty-eight, whose beauty and charm have suffered nothing from advancing years and you have the chief characters in Miss Ellen Glasgow's new novel, *One Man in His Time*....

Stephen Culpeper has returned from the war, a good deal shaken nervously by his experience, a condition which takes the form of a depression that sees little to hope for in the political condition of the country, a profound discontent with matters as they stand, a feeling of entire inability to better things, and no desire to try. The conservatism in which he has been reared oppresses him even to a sense of physical suffocation, and altho he does not know it his mental attitude is ready for readjustment.

Just at this time he encounters Gideon Vetch and his daughter, and for the first time in his life finds himself in social contact with a man of undeniable ability who has risen to the highest position in the State, owing absolutely nothing to either birth or breeding. Like many another well-born man, Culpeper had not taken the trouble to vote, much less to inform himself concerning the man who was subsequently elected, and that such a man should have attained the governorship of his State is gall and bitterness to him. Patty Vetch he had seen at a charity ball where he and his set had, with refined cruelty, merely left her alone, but when he encounters her the next day, under circumstances which compel him to render her a service, he becomes aware of her intense vitality, her honesty and her charm. He sees her fairly often and always with increasing interest, and before long realizes that without her life will have no flavor. Then ensues a fierce struggle between his breeding and his affection, the past and the present, and it seems almost impossible for him to break with the traditions of his upbringing and obey the call of his heart. His father is a man whose final argument against any innovation is to ask what General Lee would have thought of it, and his mother is even more unyielding in her conservatism. The only help he gets is from Corinna Page, a woman who, unknown to her friends, has gone through something of the same experience and whose spirit has rebelled in secret against the hampering opinions and conventions of her class.

Well, the story ends satisfactorily, which is what most readers demand. The descriptions of Richmond, the fine old houses, the old furniture and silver, and the leisurely way of life there have great charm; it is the life to which the author was brought up and she knows whereof she writes. But she recognizes with a clearness not usual in her sex, that the old order changes and she is not sure that it is for the worse. Gideon Vetch is well drawn—the man whose ability triumphs over his lack of education and whose real love of his fellow-men, combined with a sense of justice, gives him a charm which is felt even by his opponents. Stephen Culpeper stands out clearly as the inheritor of old customs and traditions and his father is well done, as is the latter's crony, General Powhatan Plummer, "a tiresome, gregarious soul, habitually untidy, creased and rumpled, who was always thirsty."

Miss Glasgow's women are likewise convincing; Stephen's mother, blind to anything outside her own experience; his sisters, variations of the type of modern girl, and Margaret Blair, the woman Stephen's mother wants him to marry, the fine flower of Southern birth and breeding, who nevertheless oppresses Stephen mentally and physically—all these contribute to the interest of a book which, unlike the modern novel of "reactions," "complexes" and "psycho-analysis," has not a tiresome page in it.

Louisville *Courier-Journal*, 23 July 1922, sec. 3, p. 8

There is so much of the energy of living, of the fiber of life itself, in Ellen Glasgow's latest novel, *One Man in His Time*, that one would be tempted to pronounce it her best production, if she had not written so many strong books to claim almost an equal right. Although the story centers around Gideon Vetch, the newly elected Independent Governor of Virginia, he dominates its action without appearing too frequently on the scene—an effect very cleverly managed. The personality that engrosses the reader is that of Corinna Page, the enchanting, romantic, beauty who has a genius for humanity, but has never been able to command the love she feels herself capable of returning. Corinna is a type of purely Southern social life—edging middle age, with all the tolerance of experience and all the ardor of a nature that has never known, in their fullness, any of the realities of life. She is a remarkable study, among the many striking women of American fiction. She influences the career of Gideon Vetch, without ever closely touching his orbit, and the tragic ending of that career leaves her with only a deathless, imperishable memory.

Patty Vetch plays "ingenue" charmingly to Corinna's "lead," and the novel is so harmoniously constructed that the two women complement and supplement each other at every turn. Although supposedly political in its subject, one feels that this aspect of the book is rather skirted than directly faced; is dealt with more by implication than actuality. As a picture of Southern life it is authentic and beautiful, each character standing out with all the effect of a portrait on familiar background. It is a book likely to be largely read, although it may not make a sensation in the literary world.

Times Literary Supplement [England], 27 July 1922, p. 494

Miss Ellen Glasgow draws in this tale a quietly effective picture of the disturbance produced in the highly conservative and traditional society of Virginia after the war by the election of a Governor who is looked upon as a demagogue and is credited, on not very sufficient evidence, with having secured his election by means of more or less discreditable bargains with his supporters. He is rather a fine figure, drawn with skill and restraint; and his vigorous and idealistic temperament is effectively contrasted with a number of hostile types, which vary from the rabid octogenarian general to the Judge whose conservatism is no more than a matter of habit, common to the class to which he belongs. The element of local politics, which might make such a tale difficult of comprehension by English readers, is cleverly kept in the background, without making us conscious of any lack of necessary detail.

"To-day's Story: Tradition,"
London *Morning Post*, 29 July 1922, p. 5

Ideas arising from character and the larger environment of the world are contained in Miss Ellen Glasgow's story, *One Man in His Time*. There is the temptation to indulge in superlatives when writing of it, both conception and execution show so fine an artistry. The situations ring true, the people seem real; and Gideon Vetch—the one man in his time—has a frank nobility. His death becomes him better even than his life. The author restates the old conflict between conservative tradition and the spirit that refuses to be shackled by the past. The fight is waged in Washington; the time, after the war.

The strength and beauty of the story lie in the lights and shades of thought and emotion that glint and darken every page. The blending is as natural as the changing tones of running water. The irony, joy, tragedy, and the greatness of life flash like jewels in the stream of life.

"American Politics,"
Sussex [England] *Daily News*, 22 August 1922

As a picture of political conflict in America after the war *One Man in His Time*, by Ellen Glasgow, bears the impress, to an English reader, of being carefully and dispassionately observed. It is certainly beautifully written. In this country we some times hear rather slighting references to "the American language," but it would be a good thing for our populace if all, or even a fair proportion, of our own novelists wrote the perfect English of which Miss Glasgow is master. Her very able novel is probably too much concerned with politics to meet with "best-selling" success in this country, though one can understand that in the States it must be of absorbing interest. It should be read by English people who wish to realize very graphically what is going on "over there." According to Miss Glasgow they don't seem greatly to concern themselves about British politics. Theirs is peculiarly their own, and evidently they want no outside ideals. The love interest is considerable, and the two heroines, young and middle-aged, are drawn with exquisite skill and sympathy. If the book has an artistic fault it is that the characters are too much given to discussing each other. The effect would be finer if their minds and emotions were brought out more dramatically. But *One Man in His Time* is a remarkable novel, and it is quite delightful to reflect that an American author can shew us how to write our mother tongue with such rare form and purity of style.

Walter Jerrold,
"Six at Seven-and-Six,"
Bookman [London], 62 (September 1922), 258

The second book [after Dorothy Canfield's *Bent Twig*] that I take up is also of American origin. *One Man in His Time*, by Ellen Glasgow, which is described as a novel of courage, shares with Miss Canfield's work the distinction of being a carefully planned story, well told both in its characterisation and in its literary style.

It would perhaps appear invidious to classify any half-dozen novels taken more or less at random from among the season's output, and yet—without any attempt to place the six in any order of merit—I cannot help saying that it is the two stories by American authors—and both those authors women—that have the most sterling qualities of excellence, of true thought and deep emotion. Miss Ellen Glasgow's book has for central figure a forceful, democratic idealist who has progressed from being a figure in a circus to being Governor of Virginia; for sentimental interest the central figure is that Governor's daughter Patty. The interplay of the old Virginian feelings of aristocracy with the new manifestations of democracy is admirably presented through a number of characters, each of whom is memorable, and so skilfully does the author present her materials that diverse as may be the views of the different protagonists, all claim something of our genuine sympathy. In such a novel as this we may well feel that we have knowledge of the best in certain sections of American life and thought at the present time; it is at once absorbingly interesting as a story and illuminating and suggestive as a presentation of current history in the form of fiction.

Gerald Gould, *Saturday Review* [London], 2 September 1922, 355

Miss Glasgow deals with up-to-date politics in Virginia—the clash of a somewhat faded aristocracy with a somewhat raw democracy. She, too, uses a device which, unlike marriage, would be more legitimate if it were less usual—she gives her most commanding and intriguing character a midway position, with the power to sway things this way or that, and then, in the upshot, conveys him to triumph by having him assassinated. These things do happen: but Miss Glasgow does not convince us that this thing did happen. Politics, however, are but the flavouring to her feast. She studies human relationships with an air of criticism, of allowance; she is very clever—more than clever, subtle; but there is a consciousness, I could almost say a condescension, in the manner. We do not get her story direct: we are kept in our place, and *told* the story. Because, with all her competence, Miss Glasgow is less extraordinarily competent than Mrs. Wharton, and yet not unlike her in method, we can perhaps in her get clear what in *The Glimpses of the Moon* was itself no more than a glimpse. There is humanity in both writers: but it is consciously intellectualized, and never so much so as in their rare crudities.

Ralph Wright, "Women in Love," London *Daily News*, 8 September 1922

After these two books [*The Rustle of Silk* by Cosmo Hamilton and *Water and Wine* by Adrian Heard], *One Man in His Time* is a healthy book indeed. It is not a great novel, but it is written with observation and restraint. Its manner may perhaps, like its politics, be a little old-fashioned. Its heroine is rather sketchy, and its hero, her father by adoption, is rather too vague a humanitarian in politics to convince us that he is so great a man as we are meant to believe. But these are small points. What the book succeeds in best is in giving us the dry and gentlemanly atmosphere of upper class Virginian society.

    This alone has a distinct fascination, all the more so because the author holds the balance of her sympathies between the old regime and the new spirit that is coming in after the war, so evenly and so fair-mindedly. Actually it is unfair to talk of either heroine or hero in the story; Miss Glasgow's method is too detached for that. Her characters on the whole are ordinary characters, and it is in the delineation of the most ordinary characters that she succeeds best. Certainly one of the chief pleasures in reading the book—and it is a pleasure to read it—is the author's knowledge of women in love. There are four or five women in love in this book, and not one of them is a stock character or goes about her love affairs in any but an individual and convincing manner. Their manner of being in love is a part of their manner of living, and that is all. But when one compares it with most people's psychology of the subject one realizes that it is a great deal. Miss Glasgow, in fact, has humour and she has restraint; the setting for her story is charming and her characters are genuine; and, lastly, she writes in grave, decent English that is a pleasure to read. We cannot, after all, ask much more than that.

Mary Agnes Hamilton, "Book Reviews," *Time and Tide* [England], 15 September 1922, pp. 881–2

Every now and then, one comes upon a bit of craftsmanship that sets one puzzling over the whole question of what is genius: not because the work in question possesses it, but because it is so brilliant an example of what it is not. I use the word brilliant advisedly; the ordinary work, whether in the medium of fiction, drama, verse, sets one no such questions; sets one, indeed, very few questions of any sort, beyond that very distressing and, at times, acutely troubling one, as to whether this talk about Art is not, after all, great nonsense; whether the mass of printed stuff is not so blandly innocent of quality that the best thing that could happen would be that it should be forcibly stopped for a period of at least a year. No; the question of what is genius occurs to one with sharpness only on encountering work that, having many arresting qualities, nevertheless seems to be most easily, if not mostly fairly characterised as being without illumination, power to make the thing presented incandescent, and to light up from it the reflecting mind of the percipient. It is something, to use an Irishism, whose significance one notes from its absence. Such a feeling about a book is, indirectly, a tribute to the work that makes one feel it; the salute may be back-handed, but, nevertheless, it is authentic so far as it goes.

    Assuredly, I make it, in all genuineness, to Miss Ellen Glasgow's novel. It is so good that I shall certainly read anything else of hers I come across; so good that I feel ashamed by the admission that until I read *One Man in His Time* her name was to me only a name. It is so no longer; I now intend, very definitely, to read *Deliverance, The Builders, Life and Gabriella*, and all the other novels of hers on which I can lay hands. For not only is *One Man in His Time* a novel so good as to have set me seriously puzzling as to why it is not even better; there is behind it, expressed through it, an interesting mind—and that is by no means always the case, even with excellent novels. This story has the interest of being thoroughly well told, about interesting and attractive people, and concerned, *au fond*, with interesting aspects of, angels to, life.

The scene of the story is set in Virginia—I gather that Miss Glasgow generally locates her tales in that fascinating State—where the notorious Gideon Vetch has, to the horror of all the well-bred, nice, reactionary old families, suddenly, on a wave of popular feeling created by his oratory (or, if not by that, the nice people cannot think how), been elected Governor. Gideon is said to have come out of a circus; anyhow, he is an apparition that horrifies them. He horrifies Stephen Culpeper, whose idol, politically, is handsome, upright, high principled, dry-souled John Benham; just as his scarlet frocked daughter Patty horrifies the young ladies—and Stephen, too, at first. Gradually Stephen begins to see something else, a process in which he is notably assisted by Mrs. Corinna Page, one of the most entirely delightful women one has met in a book for a great while. Corinna, though nearly fifty, is still lovely; one believes in that loveliness: more, one sees it; she has good sense, and charm, and courage; and though life has never given her quite what she wanted, she bears it no grudge; she is big enough to know that the real cause is something in herself; something which she has not got, and something that Gideon Vetch has; which is, in fact, his secret.

With Vetch, Miss Glasgow has been successful, in proportion to her reticence about him. She has very cleverly avoided the pitfalls of trying to make him too clear; clearer than he was to any of the people who came in contact with him, and who remained, whether they loved or hated him, very much in the dark as to what precisely it was he stood for. He is a man with an "idea"; a man, too, for whom the translation of an idea is not words but action. Some notion of the quality of Miss Glasgow's writing, and of the nature of her book, may perhaps be given by quoting a passage. Stephen Culpeper is being taken by the old mason, Darrow, to see a part of the town, where he has lived always, to him quite unknown. He subsequently discovers that some of the worst slums he sees are owned by his family—a family, by the way, quite admirably sketched; the portrait of his mother is, in its way, a masterpiece. As they drive down, they talk of Vetch. Darrow asks Stephen what he thinks of the Governor. Stephen replies that he hardly knows, but he thinks he is honest.

"He is more than honest," rejoined the other quietly. "He is human. He understands. He belongs to us...."

"I suppose he stands for a great deal?"

"A man stands only for what he is, not for an inch more, not for an inch less. The trouble with all the leaders we've had in the past was that their thought outstripped their characters. They believed more than they were, and they broke down under it. I've watched them come and go."

"You think that Vetch is a great leader?"

"I think he is a great leader, but I don't mean that I think he will ever lead us anywhere...."

There is perhaps a significance in that the section selected is one of argument rather than of direct description. Miss Glasgow is, throughout, a little too apt to show one what one is to see, instead of leaving one to see it. There is a passage near the end, where Stephen explains to Corinna, that strikes one as one reads as definitely wrongly keyed. Stephen is pointing out things one is beginning to feel for oneself, and his pointing weakens their impression; moreover, one feels that the thoughts expressed are not so much his as Corinna's or the author's. With Corinna one never has this intercepted feeling; she glows with life, always.

"A Novel of Courage," Shanghai *Times*, 17 September 1922

Miss Ellen Glasgow has done much admirable work, but in several respects she has done nothing better than this. The sole defect of the book is not of a kind common in fiction, or indeed in any department of literature, to wit, a plethora of idea and emotion which results on the part of the reader in a congestion of idea and feeling. There is in this one book the stuff, actual and potential, of at least half a dozen novels. An entire book might have been made out of the political interests which centre about Gideon Vetch, the man born in a circus tent who becomes Governor of Virginia, the great hearted, great brained exponent of democracy who falls a victim to his own clear sight and inflexible honesty. Novelists much less leisurely in their method than Miss Glasgow's compatriot, Henry James, would have beaten out the sentimental life of Corinna Page into a full-length volume; and another novel might easily have been provided by the metamorphosis of Stephen Culpeper from a hidebound, rather priggish aristocrat into a thinking and feeling man. Miss Glasgow's prodigality is the reader's gain. The matter and the message of her book are both excellent, and its style is worthy of them.

"A Noble Novel: Ellen Glasgow Writes Validly and Vividly About Changing South," Philadelphia *Evening Ledger*, 19 September 1922

A noble novel is Ellen Glasgow's *One Man in His Time*. It has largeness of conception, correctness of perspective, fineness of contour and depth and richness of coloring. *One Man in His Time* in its range and contacts with life, in its sheer beauty of substance and style, deserves an enormous success. And even if it is overshadowed by much touted and more or less meretricious "best sellers," such a quantitative test cannot diminish its merits, for it has quality.

It is a book which adds even to Miss Glasgow's hard and well won reputation as a novelist, already deservedly high. Yet this work is not of the "precious" sort appealing to cultists and culturines. It is not "specialized" in any sense. The man in the street, the tired business man, the average gentle reader can follow it with zest and enjoyment, can get much out of it simply as a story, while the well read are bound to find it valid and vital and a presentation of life.

Miss Glasgow writes again in the large sense about the South, which she knows so well, and in a more special way about Virginia, and Richmond, capital of the Confederacy and the last citadel of the old landed aristocracy of Dixie. As a member of the old aristocracy, but with the liberalizing leaven of deep interest in moral and social problems, Miss Glasgow is well fitted to set forth both the society and the politics of the time and place.

And with certain modifications, her story of the rise of the man of the people to high office has applicability to other sections of the country and other strata of our nationalism.

The motif of the story is the struggle that is now going on, perhaps more intensively and intensely in the South than elsewhere in this country, between the old and the new. The Governor, who is the central figure of the story, shares in interest only with the delightful grand lady of the old regime who is yet up to date in mind and heart. He is called a demagogue by his enemies. He is a magnetic, self-made reformer—he started life in a circus and battled his way to the Capitol, bringing along his vivid young daughter, a brave little warrior herself who fights to understand the niceties and amenities of a world which is new to her and to be a recognized participant in its doings. Then there is the young scion of the old stock who is in love with this alluring Patty, a well-drawn figure of the young man, restless and discontented after the turmoil of the war and its quickening impulses. Miss Glasgow has a number of other figures in her gallery, some toryistic and some radical, who touch life very closely.

Out of their lives she weaves a novel that is fine and rich. It has both breadth and bottom.

Northern Whig [Northern Ireland], 30 September 1922

What strikes one most forcibly in reading Miss Ellen Glasgow's *One Man in His Time*—the scene of which is laid in Virginia after the great war—is the similarity between our own present-day problems and those with which our American kinsmen are grappling. Unemployment, housing, the conflicts of capital and labour, the movement for the "nationalisation" of the means of production and distribution—they are all live questions in America, as they are with us. And there, as here, men and women are mainly influenced in their attitude towards them by their early associations, modified more or less in proportion to the amount of external influence that has been brought to bear on them. The central figure in the story is Gideon Vetch, who has been elected Governor of Virginia on a split vote. His views are what members of the older parties in the United States call "Radical," but he is a humanist rather than a politician, and soon quarrels with the wire-pullers and agitators who "ran" him for the governorship. Miss Glasgow leaves us in doubt—perhaps intentionally—as to his capacity for constructive work, not at all in doubt with regard to the essential nobility of his character. Yet we feel, when he falls a few months after his election to a chance bullet in a disturbance arising out of a threatened strike which he was trying to avert, that possibly the tragedy of his death prevented his career ending in a far more lamentable manner. The rest of the characters are almost exclusively drawn from the class which is naturally hostile to the Governor. How the best of them—including Corinna, who is much more the heroine of the story than the Governor's pretty adopted daughter—are alternately attracted and repelled by him until the stronger attractive force wins is described with convincing art. This admirably written novel, with its strikingly contrasted but always perfectly natural characters, its quiet sincerity and freedom from exaggeration, deserves to rank with the best that have come to us from America in recent years.

Englishman [India], 9 October 1922

Miss Ellen Glasgow, in her latest novel, turns once more to Virginia, and gives a picture of the spirit of the old world of America groping its way through the mists and fens that are the aftermath of the war. One feels at once that this is the real America. Where home life, national pride, and a recognition of the burden of the world's problems, are acting upon and moulding the minds and thoughts of her citizens. A story with such a theme is essentially political, but the struggle in public affairs as represented by the rise of Gideon Vetch to the position of Governor, and the substitution of strong-purposed aspirations for the untroubled order of things that had preceded the war, is reflected in Stephen Culpeper, a young man whose ideals have fallen away in face of the war and its revelations. The rise and fall of Gideon Vetch, and the triumph of his fall, is an old tale, and there are many Culpepers amongst us to-day, but Miss Glasgow has told her story with a charm that strengthens the appeal for what may seem—to Englishmen at least—a measure of social reform that has passed discussion. Beneath the story of modern politics and modern aspirations lies the romance of Corinna Page, and in her treatment of the problems that confront the world one finds, if not a solution, certainly an attitude more helpful and more constructive than the setting up of a Gideon Vetch or the dethroning of a Culpeper. All the characters that come into the book, and there are many of them, are truly and carefully drawn, and Miss Glasgow has revealed again the undoubted qualities of her technique, that virtue so sadly lacking in the novelist of to-day.

Carl Van Doren, "The Roving Critic," *Nation*, 115 (11 October 1922), 377

... I wish the hero of *One Man in His Time*, by Ellen Glasgow, could have had a little more of this instinct [of Heywood Broun in *Pieces of Hate*] for the personal. Instead, he helps to prove that it is difficult for even so intelligent a novelist as Miss Glasgow to make drama out of the career of a politician whose largest passion seems to be that of sticking to the middle of the road, too friendly neither to right nor to left, neither to old nor to new. The course of politics, like the course of life in general, is indeed a compromise; but time effects the compromise, not the actors, who themselves when they are most important are almost sure to be so devoted to one idea or one program that they expect the earth to falter and the heavens to fall if one item of their aspiration goes amiss. Yet if Gideon Vetch, governor of Virginia, does not convince me, the more conservative Virginians of the story do. The melodrama of the plot hurts a charming piece of local color which contains many significant comments upon the mood and temper of the times.

"A Rare Woman's Book," Yorkshire [England] *Post*, 18 October 1922

To encounter one of Miss Glasgow's books amongst the mass of incredibly silly and sentimental fiction generally characteristic of the woman novelist of to-day, is a rarely refreshing experience. For Miss Glasgow has a measure of understanding of life which fathers a capacity to write about it in good English, and because of the possession of these two primary but unwonted qualifications of the novelist has earned a meed of gratitude from the disillusioned reviewer. *One Man in His Time* is a story of the conflict of ideals and personalities in Virginia after the war. The State has elected a Labour man as its Governor for the first time in its Conservative history; and for its background the book presents the clash of old and new political faiths as wondered over by Stephen, seeker after reality, and Corinna, eternal spectator of life's drama. These two are tossed about between their perception of the humanity and idealism for which Gideon Vetch, the Governor, stands, and the aristocratic tradition which goes deeper than their blood. To them the struggle, like so many struggles, resolves itself into the division between the romantic and the realistic temperament; between the mind which accepts with fine irony things as they are, and the mind that all aglow sees them as they ought to be. The action of the story is interwoven. Stephen loves Patty, the Governor's adopted daughter, not only because she is Patty, but because she represents courage, and the risk of the unknown. Yet because of his dual personality he holds back from marriage because of this risk. Corinna, after her unhappy marriage, thinks she has discovered romance in the love of John Benham, chief protagonist of the old political school, till there comes to her another and weaker woman who needs him more. And so she sends him back to her. But the factor most significant of the quality of this worthy novel, with its acute analysis of motive and character, are the flashes of insight which light up for us stray fragments of the tremendous design into which life is welded....

Checklist of Additional Reviews

Hunter Stagg, "Books of the Month," *Reviewer*, 3 (May 1922), 477–80.

Louise Maunsell Field, "Ellen Glasgow on the Modern Spirit," *New York Times Book Review and Magazine*, 28 May 1922, pp. 2, 26.

Publishers' Weekly, 101 (3 June 1922), 1639.

"Virginia Politics Hold Stage in Able Novel by Ellen Glasgow," El Paso *Times*, 4 June 1922.

W.G. Vorpe, "Novel That Discusses Life, but Is Not Too 'Modern,'" Cleveland *Plain Dealer*, 24 June 1922.

Booklist, 18 (July 1922), 366.

Wisconsin Library Bulletin, 18 (July 1922), 186.

R.W.N., "Benet, Singmaster and Ellen Glasgow," Springfield [Massachusetts] *Republican*, 9 July 1922, p. 1a.

"Ellen Glasgow Writes Again," Greensboro *Daily News*, 6 August 1922, sec. 7, p. 4.

"Some Recent Additions," *Open Shelf*, 19 August 1922, p. 50.

London *Daily Telegraph*, 25 August 1922.

Rochester [New York] *Chronicle Democrat*, 27 August 1922.

Truth [England], 30 August 1922.

"Latest Novel Is a Marked Success," Little Rock *Gazette*, 10 September 1922.

Pasadena *Star News*, 11 September 1922.

"The Literary Show," *Town Topics* (New York), 14 September 1922.

"A Romance of Virginia," Madras *Mail*, 22 September 1922.
"Old and New in Conflict in *One Man in His Time*," Philadelphia *Record*, 24 September 1922.
Tid Bits [England], 11 October 1922.
Lady [England], 12 October 1922.

THE SHADOWY THIRD AND OTHER STORIES
(Published in England as *Dare's Gift and Other Stories*)

THE SHADOWY THIRD
AND OTHER STORIES

BY
ELLEN GLASGOW

FRONTISPIECE
BY
ELENORE PLAISTED ABBOTT

GARDEN CITY   NEW YORK
DOUBLEDAY, PAGE & COMPANY
1923

"The Shadowy Third," *New York Times Book Review*, 28 October 1923, sec. 3, p. 16

In these days when perturbed spirits refuse to rest, when they obey that impulse for self-expression even to the point of saying it with flowers, it is pleasant to come upon such well-behaved and considerate spooks as those who people the principal stories of Ellen Glasgow's *The Shadowy Third*. But be it understood that Miss Glasgow refrains from adventuring deliberately into the pseudo-scientific side of psychic phenomena. She merely adopts the device—and in her hands it becomes a highly effective one—of making the dead who continue to live in the memory assume at times a visual form. Miss Glasgow accomplishes the transition so smoothly, and blends the natural with the unnatural so skillfully, that her tales lack entirely the self-consciousness and patent artificiality that one invariably associates with the ghost story. Indeed, the atmosphere and mood in "Whispering Leaves," for instance, or in "The Past" places the reader in such a receptive state of mind that he accepts the shifting of the image from the mental membrane to the retina as nothing glaringly untoward or even very much out of the way.

"The Shadowy Third" possesses all the well-rounded attributes of the deliberate "plot" story, and the interest centres upon machinations that are of the earthy rather than upon the ethereal visitor. "Whispering Leaves," on the other hand, shows Miss Glasgow's method developed to its nth power. Here the natural and the unnatural actually seem to merge. The incident has to do with an imaginative and highly sensitive child. Death deprived him in infancy of his mother's care, and death again, just before the story opens, took from him the negro "mammy" who had filled successfully the mother's place. But so potent is the memory of the old negress in the lad's mind that it is to him as if she really lived, and he feels at all times conscious of her continued care and solicitude. The tale culminates in the assumption that this continued watchfulness from beyond actually saves the boy's life. Proof of the method's success lies in the reader's ready reaction, "Well, why not?"

Not all of Miss Glasgow's stories, by any means, deal with the supernatural. She gives her readers a varied assortment. One, for instance, "A Point in Morals," propounds and proceeds to do its best to solve, the original problem, whether or not, in any circumstances, the saving of a human life may become positively immoral. Another, "Jordan's End," has to do with the attitude toward inherited insanity. But all have at least one point in common. They deal with life at great moments. For Miss Glasgow's characters there is no even tenor. They have no life as calm and unworried members of society. Whether they are "shadowy thirds" who have carried into the next world the traits and feelings that have got the better of them in this, and are obliged to "work them off somewhere," or whether they are flesh and blood mortals tearing at the mesh of circumstances that has caught them, their life's spark burns before us always at white heat. *The Shadowy Third* remains in the memory as a collection of "high moments."

Rebecca Lowrie, "Good Short Stories," *New York Evening Post Literary Review*, 17 November 1923, p. 256

Four of the seven stories in Miss Glasgow's book deal with psychic phenomena. They are extraordinarily fine in construction and in craftsmanship. They are ghost stories which give the ghost the benefit of a doubt, and the atmosphere is so skilfully contrived that the spirit children who play in gardens seem as real to the reader as they do to the highly sensitized characters to whom they appear in the stories.

The first, from which the collection takes its name, is an excellent tale on several counts. As a ghost story it has credibility blended with horror. The quaint figure of the child whose death has left a vast fortune to her mother dances through the halls of the old mansion, unseen except by the young nurse and her patient, the child's mother, who is a "mental case." As a mystery story it presents crime and the retribution of crime in a fresh and absorbing way.

"Whispering Leaves" displays the same faultless technique. It is the story of little Pell and Mammy Rhody, who had promised the child's dying mother that she would never let him out of her sight. She kept her promise to the dead as long as she lived. She died; but the boy Pell insisted that she was there, playing with him just as she used to do. The darkies believed that the woods were full of the ghosts of Mammy Rhody's pets. Into this atmosphere of whispering leaves and superstitious negroes comes a young woman from the North. She, like the boy, sees the old woman, tall and straight as an Indian, with her face framed in a red turban, as brown and wrinkled as a November leaf. Here, as in "The Shadowy Third," this figure comes from the hinterland of reality to play a part in a strange but actual drama.

In "Dare's Gift" it is not a spirit who haunts a house but the spirit of the house itself which drives its inmates to commit inexplicable deeds.

The last three stories, "A Point in Morals," "The Difference," and "Jordan's End," are less effective than the others, but they are nevertheless interesting and finely done. "A Point in Morals" is the story of a conscientious murderer. "The Difference" presents one of the quaint situations which are apt to arise in the happiest of marriages. "Jordan's End" is a heart-breaking picture of hereditary insanity.

Algernon Blackwood and Henry James have used the method which makes Miss Glasgow's book so arresting. It is at the same time an entirely individual volume, beautiful in its form, without waste of words, carelessness of phrase, or ill-considered characterization.

Emily Clark, "Emily Clark Finds a Charm in Miss Glasgow's Stories," Baltimore *Evening Sun*, 17 November 1923, p. 8

A group of short stories by Miss Ellen Glasgow will no doubt be a surprise even to many of those who have followed her career most closely. Although "The Shadowy Third," the story which gives the book its name, and the other stories have appeared at different times in *Harper's* and other magazines, the intervals between have been so long that Miss Glasgow has never been regarded as a magazine writer.

More notable than her appearance as a short-story writer is the nature of the stories themselves. For each is a separate adventure in mysticism: ghost stories, in fact, though not alarming ghost stories. There is a sort of occult story which does not terrify, and Miss Glasgow's, like a collection of recent stories by Miss May Sinclair, belong to that class.

While the unknown quantity in human existence has always fascinated Miss Glasgow, it has never entered, even indirectly, into her novels, where facts, often hard facts, which can be seen, heard and touched, are her preoccupation. Normal psychology, normal conditions and normal emotions govern the men and women in these books.

One of them especially, *Virginia*, is as realistic as any product of the Middle West, a truth which Mr. Mencken, apparently, has failed to realize, for he is still clamoring for a box of brass tacks from the South—brass tacks, he specifies, and no nonsense about it. Virginia, of course, cannot, with the best intentions on the part of its inhabitants, be made to appear like the great, ubiquitous Middle West, for the excellent and joyous reason that it is not the Middle West. And an ancient deserted house on the James river, no matter how unalluring in some of its aspects, is in other phases slightly romantic in spite of itself, with no assistance from any author.

It is such a house that Miss Glasgow describes in "Dare's Gift." So inevitable the name seems that it is hard to believe there is no house in Virginia which really claims it. The modern condition which she describes here is the product of an incident of the War Between the States, and the unreasoning, fine frenzy of the South—especially the women of the South—in the last days of the Confederacy is recreated without sentimentality. Miss Glasgow, it should be remembered, sometimes irritated and baffled her own State with her early books because she regarded it in the light of reason. This reason has not failed her, but sympathy, too, has never failed, for she knows her people too thoroughly to remain aloof from them. The stories concerned with Virginia are the best in the book because of this, but each story, in its own way, is extremely well done.

Miss Glasgow is more novelist than short-story writer, and she will always be, but she has here maintained the atmosphere which she successfully created in her Virginia novels.

Hunter Stagg, "*The Shadowy Third*," New York *Tribune*, 18 November 1923, sec. 9, p. 23

It is an odd coincidence that two of the foremost women novelists of England and America should bring out during the same season—indeed, within a few weeks of each other—collections of stories dealing with the supernatural. But it is even more curious that, although as unlike in most respects as books by Ellen Glasgow and May Sinclair would naturally be, the stories in these new volumes show an almost exact duplication of attitude toward ghostly appearances—that new attitude which is the result, one supposes, of the rapid democratizing of ghosts by spiritualism, and which is tending toward the complete elimination of the element of terror and mystery from the literature of spiritual visitations and the placing of them on the plane of the altogether natural, like, though not nearly so unpleasant, as one's cousins from the country.

Miss Glasgow is more thoroughgoing in her embracement of this attitude than Miss Sinclair, and a significant feature of the new order of things is that so far from being astonished at the rising of an apparition, the people in ultra-modern ghost stories are rarely even put out by the circumstance of being haunted. And as for the reader—well, the ghost story of the day might be read with impunity by any one in any deserted house at midnight on Halloween. For the literature of the supernatural seems quite able to do without the thrill of apprehension which it was formerly required to convey, and the pleasingly chill ripple down the cowering spine has been expelled from the list of necessary effects. Gone is the dread clank of invisible chains, vanished the soul shivering glance from unforgiving spectral eyes. Silent is the shrieking banshee, and sepulchral moans from the secret closet. A thing of the past is the sudden extinguishing of the lone candle, the paralyzing touch of the clammy hand in darkened corridors, and done away with entirely are the lurking, ever fraught shadows. The modern ghost story occurs in the bright light of the sun and the electric bulb, and the brighter glare of science and metaphysics—and (this is the strange part) without any appreciable diminution of the fascination which ghost stories always have exercised over even the most skeptical.

And this, too, notwithstanding the fact that nowadays the motives of the returning spirit are generally of the most beneficent, that the modern spook comes not back on mischief bent, but, generally either to console those whom their departure has plunged into despair or to satisfy their own curiosity about conditions the proper investigation of which in the flesh has been more or less rudely interrupted. In *The Shadowy Third* there is one story, "Dare's Gift," in which the supernatural is not represented by a ghost at all: one finds instead a house haunted by an idea, the corroding idea of a black treachery once conceived and executed there, which swamps and demoralizes all who afterward dwell within the circle of its influence. For, it is said, "The house remembered," though others forgot.

But there are "regular" ghosts aplenty, too—one of a dead wife sitting always, with considerable dramatic effect, between the husband and his second wife, seen by both without either ever betraying their vision to the other. To this not altogether original situation Miss Glasgow gives an unusual turn, and she also put an original quality into the tale of a pathetic child ghost that, murdered by its stepfather, is tied to earth by the plight of its mother. Then, in "Whispering Leaves," one of the best pieces of writing Miss Glasgow has ever done, there is the ghost of an old colored mammy, faithful even after death to the charge laid upon her to protect always the orphaned son of her former mistress. Each of these stories is contrived with grace and ease and related with that smoothness which is a mark of Miss Glasgow's prose and reduces to a minimum the effort of reading; but in the last mentioned a beauty of sentiment and feeling is achieved which almost makes one forget the skill with which the author has skirted the thin ice that, of necessity, abounds in all ghost stories. Having eschewed the accepted design of a smoke screen of weirdness and fear, Miss Glasgow gets over this thin ice by leaving it a matter of choice with the reader whether or no the apparitions are merely the projection into momentary visibility of forms that have continued to live vividly in the memory of those left behind.

Well, one may nourish an undiminished affection for such excruciating tales as Bulwer Lytton's "The Haunted and the Haunters," Poe's "The Black Cat," Marian Crawford's "The Screaming Skull" and that terrific account, by whom I do not remember, of the mummied hand that scurried horribly up and down the curtains and along moldings and throttled men in their sleep. They were good tales, and are no less good now. But although it is now more fashionable to turn the supernatural into the natural, there is ample evidence in *The Shadowy Third* that the ghost story is still a power and that the alteration of its charm is one of quality and not of degree.

Diana Warwick, "Life and Letters," *Life*, 82 (29 November 1923), 20

The Shadowy Third, by Ellen Glasgow..., is a book of grand, creepy stories. Not the kind that leaves you a little reluctant to turn out the bed light after finishing it. The phantoms which flit through two or three of the tales are not gruesome. In fact, there isn't a ghost in the book whom you would object to meeting socially. Those dealing with an evil influence, hereditary insanity and whether or not the saving of a life might in certain circumstances be immoral are pleasantly shivery, and there is one in which a vamp is foiled with no demands upon the supernatural or sinister.

The attempt of mystery writers to appear plausible amuses me. The formula varies so slightly. There is the old "I know this seems incredible. In fact, in the light of after years, I am inclined to think it was an optical illusion." And "I don't in the least pretend to know how or why this thing happened. I know only that it happened." And "I am beginning to wonder myself if the thing actually occurred." Well, all these old friends are in *The Shadowy Third*. But Miss Glasgow marches right along after starting out with "I had no sooner entered the house than I knew something was wrong." I may be introducing an adjectival novelty, but somehow narration never seems quite so narrative as it does in mystery stories.

There is one wise crack at the smart young people of to-day which ought to be mentioned: "It is a generation which has grasped everything except personal responsibility."

"Ellen Glasgow's Tales of the Occult Are Thrillingly Interesting," Greensboro *Daily News*, 16 December 1923, sec. 3, p. 10

Miss Glasgow's new book is a collection of short stories so interesting that the reader loses no time, after reading the first—which gives the book its title—in going on to the next and the next until he finds himself finishing the seventh and last. Each story is in itself complete, but the seven are gathered together quite evidently because they all bear on the supposed fact that there is some great force operating in the world around us which none of us has come to understand; which none of us can deny; which none of us can prove, and which therefore takes on for many people the nature of the supernatural, while others maintain that it is as much a natural law as any other. Miss Glasgow here presents her own belief that this power works through the fact that ideas once definitely and strikingly resolved into action do not die, but manifest themselves as still living long after the individual who put his own compelling idea into vivid action has ceased to live, and generally with the visible manifestation occurring in the place where the idea became, as it were, vitalized. For instance, in one of the stories, Miss Glasgow tells of a girl, living at the time of the Civil War in Virginia. Her soul was permeated with patriotic loyalty to the south, but she loved a northern officer. It came about that he, a prisoner of war at the time, escaped and took refuge in her home. The Confederates sought him there but agreed not to search the house, feeling sure of the patriotism that abounded there. They marched away, but the girl called them back, crying that she must betray the man she loved. He was promptly led out and shot at the back of her house. She heard the soldiers fire, and then, having spent herself completely, she suffered a collapse, after which her mind was never clear again. She lived on—forgetting, but, as the author says, "the house did not forget." And within its walls there lived on and on that idea of betrayal. Each family that came to live there felt the force of this thought which had been given life through that one tragic moment which long before had caused a girl to cease to live. One by one each of these families came under the influence of that idea, succumbing at last to its power, and in turn betraying a trust.

So, in each story, we have some apparently supernatural happening, caused as the author sees it by this continuance of an idea, given shape and form by certain individuals' great moments of self-sacrifice, of the glimpse they may have caught of the greatness of love, or of hate, causing perhaps some tragic deed. The individual dies; the ideal lives, and in its manifestations creates for those of us who venture into its trysting place, a sense of a pervading presence, or a belief in a haunted house, or in visitations from the spirit of someone no longer on earth.

In *The Shadowy Third*, most of the tales are drawn from legends and ghost stories of the more remote regions of Virginia; but, though Miss Glasgow is, as always, prone to lean toward Virginia as a background, her subject here is one of well-nigh universal interest. There is, in these days, a great company of people who seek to know the truth. Most of them believe that they see some glimpse of the meaning of this apparently supernatural power and draw close enough to it to use it here and there, and surely the combined efforts of these people will some day solve the mystery—for a mystery it still is—which some seek to understand; some fear; but all find deeply interesting. Therefore, it becomes tautological to say that almost every reader, no matter what his own convictions along this line may be, will find it well worth while to read *The Shadowy Third*.

Joseph Collins, "Gentlemen, The Ladies!" *New York Times Book Review*, 23 December 1923, pp. 10, 23

[...]

The Shadowy Third, Miss Glasgow's last book, is quite different from its predecessors. She has gone from the world of reality into the realm of unreality, from observation and description of the natural to consideration and depiction of the supernatural. And it is accomplished naturally, adroitly, simply and convincingly. The titular story, one of crime and retribution, is revealed by suggestion rather than by direct statement. The atmosphere chants the dirge. "Dare's Gift," particularly the second part, shows Miss Glasgow's finest craftsmanship. It has an epic sweep and comprehensiveness that make it a great story. It shows that Miss Glasgow has always in mind that a tale must have a dual theme; a human story and a great problem. She has never done anything that better entitles her to be called artist than "Dare's Gift." From consideration of her last volume we readily convince ourselves that she has not yet done her best work.

Louise Collier Willcox, "Ghosts and Others," Bookman, 58 (January 1924), 573–4

The first two of these volumes deal with the misty borderland beyond the activity of the bodily senses. Both Miss Glasgow and Miss [May] Sinclair [in *Uncanny Stories*] write of the disembodied life and psychological problems that reach the unexpected powers of the body and mind. I say "powers of the body," for these intuitions and instincts that reach out beyond the actual capacity of the five attacking senses more often belong to the untrained and undeveloped than to the highly educated. The colored race, subject as it is to superstition, is notably susceptible to supernatural influences; children are more susceptible than women; and women, than men. There may be a stage in training before the mind takes entire control of the nerves, when "the *whole* body thinks," and we are aware of more than a densely physical atmosphere. Miss Glasgow has four forthright ghost stories and three psychological tales. Her writing retains its customary distinction and freedom from all affectation and use of clichés; such English is a refreshment to mind and spirit, coming as it does direct through the fine tradition of Addison and Matthew Arnold, unvulgarized by current slang, unvilified by current bad grammar. An environment of long established customs, manners, and traditions has given her what few writers of the day have—both soil and atmosphere; a soil in which her roots are deeply set, and an atmosphere where she is sure of climate, vegetation, human types, manners, customs and traditions. When she writes of Virginia her touch is as sure, her tone as perfect as was George Eliot's when she wrote of mid-England or Arnold Bennett's when he describes the five towns. "Dare's Gift" as well as the grim and terrible "Jordan's End" are fine examples of this truth to place and speech. "The Difference" is a study of that disastrous breach between the concentrated feminine temperament and the more diffuse masculine instinct, and both "A Point in Morals" and "Jordan's End" deal with a nice point in morals: is it ever legitimate to take life? Incidentally it seems odd that "Jordan's End," the most powerful of these seven stories, is the only one not to have appeared first in a magazine.

"Ghostly Short Stories," Springfield [Massachusetts] *Republican*, 13 January 1924, p. 7A

"It is the high moments that make life, and the flat ones that fill the years," is the sentiment Miss Ellen Glasgow makes one of her characters express in *The Shadowy Third*, a collection of short stories, dealing with seemingly unreal manifestations. Each story takes a group of people through some adventure, which in the light of modern investigation loses its unreality, yet furnishes food for thought. A dim, shadowy, third presence is found in each of these stories, done in Miss Glasgow's most plausible manner, so that the reader involuntarily asks himself, "Could it have been?"

"Dare's Gift," *Times Literary Supplement* [England], 3 April 1924, p. 206

Apparitions, presences, and ghostly interferences with the living occupy Miss Ellen Glasgow in her new book of short stories, *Dare's Gift*; but for the most part she deals with gentle ghosts. It is scarcely in fashion for ghosts to be vindictive or alarming any more; and although a little, flitting child-ghost carelessly leaves her spirit skipping rope coiled on the stairs and so causes her step-father, through whom she has met her death, to meet his, it makes quite pretty reading. There is a reminder of Kipling's *They* in this tale of the mother and the returned child playing about the house and visible only to those who are good enough to see her. The first story is concerned with the psychic influence of a house on the inmates of another family and generation, a theme of infinite interest, although here it is handled without much subtlety and with a sort of unconcern on the part of the writer which detracts from the impression that should be made. "The Past" is an extremely good tale of the return of a first wife to destroy the happiness of the second, until by an act of clemency to the memory of the dead the second wife overcomes the obsession of the visitant and lays the soul to sleep in a quiet grave. "Whispering Leaves" is a story of Virginia and a negro mammy whose constant care is the small boy of her late mistress. A black ghost this, "but oh, her soul is white"; and when she rescues the child of her devotion from a burning house and gives him into the arms stretched out to shelter him in future, she melts like a wreath of smoke, her duty accomplished. "A Point in Morals" opens an interesting subject for discussion, and "Jordan's End" leaves a point in ethics undecided. "The Difference" again presents an unhappy wife and a husband of too great charm. No one could accuse Miss Glasgow of an overacted gaiety, but she does not harrow the reader unduly and she prefers her problems to be solved by kindness and generosity if possible. The mournful sounds of nature echo through her stories, and she lights them with an eerie and unearthly radiance, but in the end, if she can, she brings comfort alike to the unquiet ghost and haunted human being.

"Books Worth Reading," *John O' London's Weekly* [London], 26 April 1924, p. 135

"Dare's Gift" is the short story which christens this book. It deals with a conflict in a loving woman. She is forced to choose between the life of the man she loves and the safety of her country's army. A very dramatic moment results. Those who have experienced the patriotic fervour of the women of the Southern States will understand the tragic choice. Of these seven stories by Ellen Glasgow, "The Shadowy Third" is the one which most will haunt the reader's mind, but all strike a high minor note of delicate dramatic irony, all have felt the touch of an artist.

Spectator [England], 132 (24 May 1924), 846

These stories, which deal with supernatural, or rather supernormal events, differ from others of their kind inasmuch as they attempt to illustrate the effect left on material surroundings by a crisis of overpowering emotion. While the reader will find certain of the studies hard to credit—for instance, the possibility of a legacy of treachery in the story of "Dare's Gift"—the whole collection will tend to start his mind on a path of not unpleasant speculation. As usual with Miss Glasgow's work she contrives to suggest in her background much of the delicate charm of Old Virginia.

Checklist of Additional Reviews

"The Shadow World," Greensboro *Daily News*, 28 October 1923, sec. 2, p. 10.
Publishers' Weekly, 104 (3 November 1923), 1540.
Richmond *Times-Dispatch*, 18 November 1923, sec. 3, p. 7.
Outlook, 135 (19 December 1923), 690.
Ruth Snyder, New York *World*, 6 January 1924, sec. M, p. 10.
"*Dare's Gift* by Ellen Glasgow," *Referee* [England], 20 April 1924, p. 7.

BARREN GROUND

Barren Ground
by Ellen Glasgow

GROSSET & DUNLAP *Publishers*
by arrangement with Doubleday Page & Co.

Joseph Collins, "Realism in a Southern Novel," New York *Sun*, 4 April 1925, p. 7

Ellen Glasgow has been writing novels twenty-five years or thereabouts. They have earned her a distinctive and distinguished reputation in the literary world at home and abroad.

Until the advent of *Barren Ground* the summit of her progress had been testified by *Virginia*, an accurate and penetrating study of personality. Her latest book shows powers suggested but unrevealed by that or any of the others. *Barren Ground* is her masterpiece, and it will take its place with the best American fiction of this generation. Such a statement should have support beyond personal opinion. It is based upon the following facts, which I believe are incontestable: First, she has ruptured and dispelled the sentimental tradition of the South, that has made its literature with very few exceptions lifeless and artificial; second, she has set down the realities of life, and her characters are real people—they think, speak and act, live and die, love and hate, like real people; third, she has depicted a transformation of romance to reality that withstands the test of experience, and lastly, she has written an epic of the soil that compares with Knut Hamsun's *Growth of the Soil* and Alphonse de Chateaubriant's *La Briere*.

It need not be construed as disparagement of the reputation of Thomas Nelson Page, George W. Cable, and F. Hopkinson Smith to say that they adhered narrowly in their writings to the romantic tradition that all men are brave, chivalrous and polite; that all women are fair, virtuous and self-sacrificing, and that God's images in the South are classifiable into four groups—good families, good people, poor whites and negroes. Naturally, there are bad individuals in each group, but fewer proportionately in the first than in any of the others, and when a member of a "good family" goes wrong, alcohol acting through an ancestor tripped him. There are always facts to be cited that condone his offense and cushion his fall. An individual of the first group is as different from one of the second as wine from water. His blood is blue; his motives are high; his conduct is chivalric. In brief, he is a gentleman, and his wife, his sister or his daughter is a lady. He is not too proud to fight, but too proud to work. He is a patrician whose country compels him to live as a democrat, and he will go to the ordeal with raised head and smiling face as Savonarola went to the fire, only, instead of saying the words of his breviary, he shouts: "I believe in custom, tradition, family and the Episcopal Church."

Accounts of him, his environment and the medium in which he acts have made the literature of the South stilted, monotonous and inert. Miss Glasgow has blown the breath of life into the pulchritudinous manikin. She has given it reality while preserving its beauty; she has made it truthful without curbing its articulateness; she has clad it becomingly in garments harmonious with the period, and she has fed it with a mysterious gland that adds to its stature and increases its stride.

She has written the first honest, realistic novel of the South; and by so doing, she has done her bit to destroy "sectional" feeling.

No one can travel extensively through the South, as I have recently done, without realizing that a transformation little less than marvelous is going on there;

its people, its industries, its soil. Ellen Glasgow carries the New South to the baptismal font of literature.

The scene of *Barren Ground* is Pedlar's Mill, Queen Elizabeth county, Virginia, and the story is the narrative of the life of Dorinda Oakley, whose acquaintance we make when she is 20 years old. Dorinda is a full ripened human peach, borne by a frail and diseased tree. She drops and is trod upon by the hobnails in the boots of a coward and cad masquerading as a doctor and a reformer. She flees to New York and through the premature birth of her child she has a rebirth of the soul. It is the growth, direction and destiny of that soul, animating a tireless body, that constitute the core of the book. "Dorinda disliked darning, and because she disliked it, she never permitted herself to neglect it." That and the display of an inherited urge: to possess land and to increase its fertility, to make it testify opulently that for which she was created, but which had been denied her, were the motivating forces of Dorinda's life. She convinced herself before time had healed her wounds that she would avenge some of the wrongs that Dr. Jason Greylock had done her by buying in his ancestral home as soon as it reached the auctioneer's block by foreclosure. Long before the death of his dissolute father and his own degeneration brought it there, her vengefulness had been replaced by sympathy.

Miss Glasgow cannot expect that all her readers will agree with her that Dorinda acted consistently when she went over to the poorhouse and got Jason, who was in the terminal stage of tuberculosis, and brought him home and kept him there until he died. I do not think she did. It would have been in keeping with my own experience had she provided him with creature comfort, sent him to Asheville, or paid a nurse to look after him, but to do what she did was to display greater adhesion to Christ's mandates than in all the rest of her life together.

But taken as a whole, Dorinda's reactions to experience, considering her forbears, are in keeping with precedent. Women the world over sacrifice themselves for worthless parents, just as she did. Sisters slave and save to spare slacker brothers labor; wives deny themselves necessities that their husbands may have comforts, and pious mothers perjure themselves just as work bewitched Eudora did, that guilty sons shall be spared earned punishment.

Miss Glasgow is to be congratulated on bringing about Dorinda's marriage with Nathan Pedlar. Had Dorinda been of less heroic proportion, she would have married John Abner, Nathan's club-footed son, who showed sympathy and comprehension in his relations with her. The disparity of ages would not have been an insurmountable obstacle to marriage. But Nathan, a tall, lank, scraggy man who had a face like a clown with a squashed nose, and who was as full of virtue as an egg of meat, knew the lay of the cards in the matrimonial deck; he could always play a trump at will. And so they were married and lived as happily as it is healthy for any one to live.

A fairy grandmother or godmother who hovers about your cradle, who not only ministers to your needs but provides you with new appetites, is popularly believed to be a coveted ancilla of birth, a much-to-be-desired companion of formative years. Though I have many regrets, such a one is not of them. But that Aunt Mehitable Green, who had assisted at Dorinda's birth, did not assist at mine, did not guard me in my plastic years, did not berate me in my active days, and philosophize with me in my idle ones I shall never cease to regret. Aunt Mehitable could "throw spells, remove warts and make cows go dry"; she knew midwifery and medicine and she was something of a clairvoyant. She was a born doctor, for she could distinguish the patient from the disease and she knew that if she could manage the former, nature would take care of the latter.

The distinction of style which has been so characteristic of Miss Glasgow's novels, especially since *The Miller of Old Church*, is conspicuous in her last book. She knows how to touch words as a Rachmaninoff knows how to touch the keys of a piano to produce stirring, thrilling, stimulating, soothing sounds and essentially to produce harmony. She has succeeded in increasing the clarity, force and directness of the English language, and there are few writers today who display a greater mastery of it. Not that she sacrifices substance to style, for characterization is her chief possession as a writer.

Stuart P. Sherman, "The Fighting Edge of Romance," *New York Herald Tribune Books*, 9 April 1925, sec. 5, pp. 1–3

The fighting edge of romance is always reality. It is the cut and thrust of an active will amid the material circumstances of present life. Ellen Glasgow is bent on romance with blood in it; therefore she uses the fighting edge. Northern critics haven't known quite how to take her. She disappoints their settled expectations. What they expect of Southern writers is a rapt contemplation of the embossed and beribboned antique sword hilt of romance. She gives them the edge.

Yes, by all means read *Barren Ground*, if you are interested in American fiction, if you are interested in American life, if you wish the latest development of a great thesis, if you wish ripe comment on the common lot by one of the most intelligent and richly endowed novelists of our time.

"With *Barren Ground*," say the publishers, "realism at the last crosses the Potomac. The South, so familiarly pictured in fiction as a land of colonels, old mansions and delicate romances, is here shown to be a hard country peopled by farmers who live lives as real as any in our great cities or on our wide Western prairies."

Right! There is nothing essentially unreal about the farmer's life anywhere.

Obviously what the writer of that paragraph wishes to have us believe is that Ellen Glasgow is in the strictly contemporaneous larger movement of American fiction. Not the little whirl and eddy of merely fashionable writers who prove their superiority and their "sophistication" by being sick of everything, but that movement which records with stark honesty the adventures of upgirt, courageous young Americans of the middling sort wrestling with the dark angel of their destiny and murmuring between clenched teeth: "I will not let thee go till thou bless me."

Right again. *Barren Ground* is an expression of the realest thing in American life. It is an expression of the indomitable fighting spirit, the will to live, the desire to be free, the passion for progress and mastery, the determination to bite through to some faint sweetness in the fruit of life, though the fruit be only an osage orange. This is a cluster of fighting virtues which every one fit to speak of the sturdier American stock knows are in hot, eager tumult beneath the cynical and insouciant manners of the hour.

Symbols. Four years ago a writer who immensely accelerated this realistic movement began a well known novel with these words: "On a hill by the Mississippi where Chippewas camped two generations ago, a girl stood in relief against the cornflower blue of Northern sky.... She lifted her arms, she leaned back against the wind, her skirt dipped and flared, a lock blew wild. A girl on a hilltop; credulous, plastic, young; drinking the air as she longed to drink life. The eternal aching comedy of expectant youth."

Ellen Glasgow begins *Barren Ground* at almost the same point and on almost the same note. She begins thus: "A girl in an orange-colored shawl stood at the window of Pedlar's store and looked through the falling snow, at the deserted road. Though she watched there without moving, her attitude, in its stillness, gave an impression of arrested flight, as if she were running toward life."

When I read that paragraph I said: "A cordial and gallant gesture! Ellen Glasgow in Richmond, Virginia, waves a handkerchief to Sinclair Lewis in Sauk Center, Minnesota." These girls, Mr. Lewis's Carol and Miss Glasgow's Dorinda, will not be Northern and Southern much longer. Regret it if you must, they are coming together in a common spirit. They are types of that sincerity and fearlessness which Ellen Glasgow declares mark the American democratic ideal as grace and radiance marked the ideal of the old Virginian aristocracy.

For the moment I am conniving at the benignant purpose of the publicity writer who tells us that with *Barren Ground* realism "at the last" crosses the Potomac. Waiving the question, for the moment, whether realism, at this crossing, is going south or going north, I heartily applaud the recognition of Miss Glasgow as a significant leader of contemporary realism. It is absurd to think of her as essentially a writer for the South, wholesomely irritant as she doubtless is to Southern slackness and ancestor-worship. It is high time that novel readers from Maine to California should become aware that she treats provincial life from a national point of view; that is, without sentimentality, without prejudice, with sympathy, understanding, passion and poetic insight, yet critically and with a surgical use of satire. But with what a deeply reminiscent smile Miss Glasgow must view the statement that in 1925 realism crossed the Potomac. With what amusement she must regard my apparent derivation of her Dorinda's tune from the tune of Mr. Lewis's Carol. Miss Glasgow is only a young woman of fifty. She has the keenest interest in young people who are "running toward life." But so far as her main literary ideas are concerned, I suppose she has not been influenced by Mr. Lewis much more than General Robert E. Lee was influenced by General Pershing. She was a realist when some of our popular exponents of realism were in the cradle. She preceded into the field Mrs. Wharton, who is twelve years older, and Mr. Dreiser, who is three years older. Her first novel, *The Descendant*, was published in 1897, and there have been fifteen since, of which the titles, with dates of publication, are most conveniently printed in *Barren Ground*. Her democratic fighting realism is already incarnate in the little red-haired hero of *The Voice of the People*, 1900. Realism crossed the Potomac twenty-five years ago, going north!

Presently I hope we shall have a collected edition of Miss Glasgow's work, not monumental, for filling proud, idle, decorative bookshelves, but an edition supple and gracious to the hand, for reading, something in the style, perhaps, of those affable blue leather volumes in which her publishers used to give us Joseph Conrad. For this edition I would humbly petition the author to attempt a revision looking toward a 20 per cent reduction in bulk, out of a tender regard for the brevity of man's life and the artistic satisfaction of going through some passages of it swiftly—indicating rather than exhausting their interest. But, revised or unrevised, I should welcome such an edition, and whenever any Anglomaniac challenged me to name one living American novelist to compare with any one of the first twenty in his English list I should point to this edition and ask him if he had read Ellen Glasgow.

Publishers, booksellers and readers race along from season to season after the book of the week—so do reviewers. A contemporary novelist soon becomes inaccessible in his entirety. Whether his earlier books are on the way to oblivion or whether he is in purgatory on the way to becoming a standard author and a classic, one can only determine after research in the old bookshops. I have managed to assemble, and read, first editions of seven or eight of Miss Glasgow's sixteen books, including the badly named *The Voice of the People*, of which the first half is extraordinarily delicious; *The Deliverance*, 1904, a story of rising and falling families with an admirable piece of characterization in Maria; *The Wheel of Life*, 1906, a study of several types of men in New York and their ideals, with one flame-like woman; *The Miller of Old Church*, 1911, specially rich in humor; *Virginia*, 1913, a striking account of the insufficiency of the sweet self-sacrificing Southern wife; *Life and Gabriella*, 1916, a study of the woman who finds a fairly satisfactory second-best in business success; *One Man in His Time*, 1922, a portrait of a Governor of Virginia who is a self-made man.

Every so often the critics start up a discussion as to what constitutes abiding value in a novel. Mr. Swinnerton, Mr. A. B. Walkley and sundry other controversialists were waging such a discussion last summer. At the point where I looked in upon it opinion tended strongly to the orthodox conclusion that a novel may lack almost all the virtues and yet live by its characters. Some one, I think Mr. Walkley, dissented, maintaining rather that a novel lives by its characteristics—by the sum of all the qualities which the author puts into it.

That amounts, perhaps, to saying that a novel lives by, or on, the character of its author. If that appears true of a single novel, it appears more strikingly true when one reflects upon the entire work of a novelist after one is familiar with it, and his books have run together and made a little world in one's mind. For my part, at any rate, I seldom step into the world of Jane Austen or Charlotte Brontë, of Thackeray or Thomas Hardy or Conrad looking for any one in particular. I revisit these scenes because I like the weather, sunlit or stormy, because I relish a certain feeling in the air, which I know, when I analyze it, is the pervasive effect of the writer's personality.

For several days now I have been living happily in Ellen Glasgow's world. I attempt to take my satisfaction to pieces, and I find myself cataloging her abundant powers. I like her clear sense of the elemental things in human life and her sense of the profound interdependence of man and nature. She constantly delights by her talent for presenting the wonder and bloom of Virginian gardens and countryside. Go where you will in her Southern world, there is perfume in the sunlit air, hyacinths and the scent of wild grapes and microphylla roses; there is the budding sycamore and the foam of dogwood and red bud; sparrows rustle among the Virginia creepers, thrushes sing, bluebirds and red-winged blackbirds flicker over the pastures; sunsets glow behind dark pines; there is the sound of water flowing.

On her humor one could write a chapter. Her humbler characters—negroes and rustic ancient white folks, religious and irreligious, abound in sage observations and comparisons, earthy, droll, bitter or wise, between what the Baptist minister teaches them on Sunday and what they learn when they go outside the church door. The rural humorists in *The Miller of Old Church* could hold their own against any peasant group you may mention in the works of Thomas Hardy. As for wit of the more intellectual order, ironical wit, critical wit, epigrammatic wit, brilliantly serving in characterization and commentary, it plays incessantly through her books. It is a constant aspect of her thought. She conceives life as a brave comedy. I incline to think her the wittiest of living American novelists, and I am not surprised to learn that her favorite authors are Voltaire and Fielding.

Her range of successful characters is very wide. It includes all sorts of colored people, poor whites, middling whites and old Southern gentry; poor people going up and rich people coming down; farmers, millers, shopkeepers, artists, poets, lawyers, judges, politicians; children and octogenarians; sane and insane. She has a very lively sense of the power of the family, of the social group and caste, of the community, of the generation. At the same time she feels with intense sympathy the elemental needs and hungers and the ideal motives which animate individual men and women, and make them, for their hour of crowded life, flame out against the commonplace.

In all her novels one is aware of an attendant keenly observant ethical spirit. Her morality is her own, tolerant of nature, intolerant of cant and humbug, but her consciousness is as unmistakably ethical as that of George Eliot. She likes to see the wheel come full circle. She builds her stories with a view to showing Time bring in revenges.

Her style is firm, lucid and, if I were not afraid of giving offense, I should add, it has a masculine rhythm. It has wit and beauty. At its best it has a proud and impressive reserve, and goes over depths with the tension and moving stillness of deep rivers.

I have enumerated some of the talents and characteristics of Ellen Glasgow which have impressed me in reading these novels. As I turn away from the "specimens" of her qualities, which I have collected but have not space to exhibit, I ask myself wherein the abiding value of her work lies; what is the nature of the pervasive presence in her world which has rewarded me for entering it. And the reply which comes first to my lips is this: her wisdom, the breadth and justice of her vision.

But I have scarcely uttered that characterization when I recognize that, after all my enumeration of qualities, I have failed to bring out the really distinguishing marks of her individuality. I have said nothing of her dæmonic element, her iconoclasm, her affectionate derision of the old South, her tireless satire upon the self-immolating old-fashioned female with faded roses in her cheeks and dying violets in her eyes, her merciless incessant mockery at the ancient egotistical pretensions of the male sex, and, deeper than all, underlying all, the realistic drive of her nature toward the discovery of ends which shall make life for men and women, but especially for women, somehow not wholly unworthy of the candle which lights them into the long darkness.

Ellen Glasgow is passionate. With all the passionateness of her soul she hates lies, and she hates failure. If her realism has not been as popular as the romances of some of our practicing novelists it is because she is modern with a vengeance. She is a feminist with a vengeance. If you review her novels you find that for the last twenty-five years she has been subtly but steadily insisting that the average woman is a failure, and that the average woman's life is founded on a lie, a vital illusion, namely, that the sexual attraction which draws her to her man in the mating season is enough, is her supreme and sufficient affair with life. With all her humor, with all her wit and wisdom, and with all her passion, she asserts and reasserts that this is not enough. In one form of words or another, through novel after novel, runs this refrain: "There ought to be something more permanent than love for one to live by." Through novel after novel, with an insistence most abasing to masculine pride, she exhibits the evanescence of sexual passion, exhibits women of all sorts who are quite disillusioned about love, exhibits men in the humiliating and bewildering attitude of loving without return, and loving when they are loved no more.

One doesn't get all of Ellen Glasgow's qualities at their highest in *Barren Ground*, but it is an excellent example of her talent, and it contains a powerful development of her central thesis. Dorinda running toward life is embraced by it, seductively, treacherously. The terror and pathos of her disillusion are developed in pages of memorable beauty. Elsewhere Miss Glasgow has mockingly painted old maids of the Victorian mold who have sat forty years in an upper chamber pallidly worshiping their penitence and their memory of betrayal. Dorinda has the blood of Scotch-Irish ancestors in her veins. She packs up her wedding clothes. She packs away her dreams. With her young sense unimpaired that life is "precious and indescribably sad and lovely," she stiffens her soft lip and fights for a life which shall be independent of the admiration of men, fights for a successful life, as men rate success, and wins it—incidentally acquiring a husband whom she treats as a superior hired man. As her hands are very full with the management of her three large farms and dairy, he is quite useful to her.

Men who are realistic enough to admit that they could live without their wives but not without their work are likely to see in Dorinda a fine sort of heroine. Others will say: "But what did she get out of it—with her cows and her married hired man?" And I think Miss Glasgow would reply: "Romance! The fighting edge. She saved her soul, as modern women understand the soul. She made herself a character. She learned that in the end nothing lasts but courage."

Emily Clark, "Glasgow Novel of Virginia Poor Whites: A Triumphant Experiment," Baltimore *Sun*, 11 April 1925, p. 8

Ellen Glasgow's last novel before the present one was featured in headlines on one of the New York Sunday book pages as a story of "Virginia, the last stronghold of gentility." Now even that stronghold has apparently surrendered, because Miss Glasgow, the only Virginian novelist who records Virginia as it is today, has turned her eyes away from the ruling class, which is white, and the leisure class, which is black, to the lower-middle and poor-white classes, which have neither power nor leisure. No aristocrat, either white or black, is mentioned in these pages, which deal exclusively with that largest and most frequently ignored group in the State. The story is laid in one of the Virginia counties where many people are land-poor and the broomsedge smothers even the most mediocre ambitions. It begins about 1895 and ends at the present time.

Dorinda, in her orange-colored shawl, appears in the first sentence, and until the end of the book is her book, as definitely hers as *One Man in His Time* is Corinna's book. But Dorinda is more real than Corinna, with a reality so glowing that she stands out sharply from many of the recent women of fiction. She is the daughter of a woman of the small farmer, ultra-religious class and of a man who is unashamedly poor-white. And because of this she represents both an experiment and a triumph for her creator, whose greatest achievement until now, in my opinion, has been Virginia, of the book named for her. Virginia, like the other literary heroines of her State, was the result of an aristocracy so true to itself that it withstood even a poverty more cruel than that of the poor-whites. For it was poverty under compulsion to keep up appearances. Dorinda is spared this necessity, but carries an obligation equally exigent—to a person of her implacable Presbyterian heritage—to keep alive in herself and her family a spark of life, of inexorable determination not to be conquered by the limitless broomsedge, the barren ground, the atmosphere of failure surrounding her.

Sherwood Anderson and Miss Cather cannot, try as they may, accomplish the utter hopelessness with which Miss Glasgow has saturated a part of this book. For there is hope in the West, if only a subconscious hope, and poor-white Virginia is without hope, without fear, without pride, except in its infrequent Dorindas. Miss Glasgow has done what no other writer can do, for no other writer possesses her knowledge of present-day Virginia, combined with her unswerving fidelity to beautiful writing, however drab her subject may be. And her present subject is a flawless medium for her especial sort of irony, an irony which includes sympathy, skepticism and—yes—affection for what she is writing about.

Affection for the suffocating broomsedge itself, since it is a natural product of the soil of which Ellen Glasgow is as surely a part as Sheila Kaye-Smith is a part of Sussex, and to which she pays her debt in the same coin.

Barren Ground has the distinction of being a story neither of love nor of passion, with the exception of an early episode which makes its heroine able to say in the last sentence of the book: "I am thankful to have finished with all that." But this distinction is peculiarly Miss Glasgow's for she has persistently brought her readers face to face with the fact that the importance of love in the usual human life is enormously overestimated. It is, however, as the exponent of Virginia, who brings it in all its beauty, its appalling laziness and its tragedy before the other sections of this country which have had more than their share of attention, that Ellen Glasgow is uniquely important, now and in the future.

H. I. Brock, "Southern Romance Is Dead," *New York Times Book Review*, 12 April 1925, sec. 3, p. 2

Southern romance is dead. Ellen Glasgow has murdered it. Over the dead body of all that past which Thomas Nelson Page and Francis Hopkinson Smith and Mary Johnston wrapped in the mantle of fond dreams stands drearily triumphant the figure of a prosperous woman dairy farmer who made barren ground bear rich pasturage and paid the price of it in her own barren life. It is Miss Glasgow's black magic to take a girl glowing with her first love and use life to transform ardent youth and budding womanhood into that superior and sufficient mistress of Jersey herds.

Perhaps the woman is the New South which has taken the place of the Old South, no longer able to pay her way in the modern world—a world in which Main Street has moved West and grown up with skyscrapers, and even the crossroads store sells Chicago mail-order goods.

Perhaps—so a haunting suspicion will have it—Miss Glasgow has been driven to the deed she has done by the ambition to do for Virginia what Mrs. Wharton did for New England in *Ethan Frome*. In any case, the agony of tragedy is piled high. The difference is that the sacrifice of life in *Ethan Frome* is to a hard ironic fate, which is the self-denying ordinance of an iron country and an iron faith. The sacrifice of life in *Barren Ground* is to a soil which is lean with the hunger of exhaustion and must be fattened.

It may be that man was made for the soil, not the soil for man. It may be that poor land lays a spell on the dwellers upon it who impiously let it go to waste. It may be that salvation is won by fertilizer and crops of clover and cowpeas plowed under. But somehow the tragic theme suffers from such close contact with the too, too solid stuff of scientific farming. Dead loves and electric milking machines brought too near together jangle the eternal harmonies.

As a tragedy, therefore, *Ethan Frome* remains unrivaled. As a mirror of the drama of life Miss Glasgow's book is distorted by a lack of that very rudimentary sense of humor which is the saving grace of the treatment of all deeply serious subjects—the grace without which tragedy lies in peril of losing its essential solemn dignity in the incongruous grotesque. As a story of the development of a human personality under the stresses of life, *Barren Ground* carries no conviction of truth or force of inevitability. As an accumulation of incidents and episodes toward a predetermined end, the predetermination is more evident than the relation of the incidents to the arrival at the end. There is an inescapable feeling that with other incidents or with any incidents the end would have been the same, because the author had resolved to get there anyhow.

Poor Dorinda Oakley, who helped in the country store near the railway station, which offered to view little more than a tank to refill the locomotives—poor Dorinda, with her blue eyes and her black hair and her bounding youth that leaped to meet the youth of the medical young man in the buggy who had studied in New York and who stopped in the road to give her a lift as she trudged home to her hard-worked parents' dilapidated farmhouse—that poor Dorinda had never a chance. She was created for no other purpose than to become a model dairy farmer and to act as demonstrator of the gospel of scientific management in the redemption of the land that had been abandoned to elemental evil in the form of what the Virginians call "broomsedge."

Now broomsedge is indeed a pestilential form of vegetation, and the prevalence of it in a farmer's fields is a confession of neglect and failure. Miss Glasgow's descriptions of fields of this broomsedge with the wind blowing across it and the sun reddening it and the clouds graying it, are most excellent examples of word-painting. So is her portrait of young Dorinda. So is her picture of the white slope of the high road and the store and the station beside the rails running off parallel into the distance toward everything that Pedlar's Mill lacked. The recreative touch that only art can give is present in the vision which her words call up of the blond woman in the back room of the store lying so hopefully on her deathbed crocheting pink wool while her children play with paper dolls in front of the fire.

So is it, again, in the picture of life, in the weatherbeaten white farmhouse where

Dorinda's superior mother and Dorinda's inferior father and Dorinda's two brothers live and give everything they have and every daylight hour to the hopeless task of making the worn-out land furnish them a decent living. The backgrounds are extraordinarily good and true, the figures of the men and women are put in with sure strokes, the effect of lifelikeness, the feeling, the atmosphere, all are there and carry the stamp of knowledge and authenticity. If you happen to be one of those who knew that part of Virginia thirty years ago your memory of it is vividly recalled. If you do not know anything about the country from personal contact with it you must still perceive in the pictures of the landscape and the drawing of the characters that what they represent is not more fiction but a real land and a real life.

It is not exactly the Virginia you have read about in Thomas Nelson Page's *Marse Chan* and *Red Rock*; it is not in the least the Virginia you have read about in the works of Miss Glasgow's sometime rival, Miss Johnston. It is a somewhat different Virginia from that which is presented by the author of *Colonel Carter of Cartersville*. But it is the same Virginia which was represented with its sights and sounds and smells by George W. Bagby—who wrote as Moses Adams—long years ago. It is, in fact, the same Virginia which lurks behind the romantic haze of the writers we have mentioned and occasionally shows through where that haze is thinner. It has been since the war—and is still—a down-at-the-heels country, though there are parts of it where enterprising persons have managed to change all that and give it an aspect almost as well kept as commuting New England.

These are the redeemers of the soil for whom Dorinda stands—though most of them would be horrified at arriving at prosperity and apple-pie order by the road traversed by Miss Glasgow's heroine on her tortured way to that goal. Very few of them have been betrayed by a false love and providentially knocked down by a hansom cab at Fifth Avenue so that the natural consequences of that betrayal have been eliminated as an incident of the physical consequences of the collision. Very few of them have shot to kill—and fortunately missed. Very few of them have had to see a brother saved from the gallows by the perjury of a pious mother. No large number of them have married a worthy but absurd-looking husband, not for love but for prudence, and had their pride salved by having the poor chap die a hero's death in the fire. The majority have even escaped the privilege of rescuing from the poorhouse—and magnanimously caring for until his death—the drink-sodden wreck of the false lover of their youth. Yet all these things and more are a part of Dorinda's discipline as a modern business woman.

Miss Glasgow is not the first writer who has dealt with the poorer folk in the South—without representing them as aristocrats who had lost their money in the Civil War which deprived them of property rights in their black servants. There have been stories about the mountain people, there have been stories in which the so-called "po' white trash" figured. But hardly anybody has gone so sincerely about the job of sampling a backward community of ordinary mixed folk—mostly plain—in a part of the Old Dominion from which the decline of the land had removed most of the aristocratic conditions a generation before Miss Glasgow's story begins. Her picture is a picture of an essentially democratic community—such as most Virginia communities were twenty years after the surrender at Appomattox. As she says, it was democratic in spite of the frank acceptance of limitations attaching to certain kinds of people in the community. The negroes must stay within their limits; the po' whites had theirs—which both recognized and seldom transgressed.

In short, the background of Miss Glasgow's novel is a contribution of real value to the literary exhibition of American social conditions. The value of the story as a story is distinctly less. A gift of telling phrase is another part of the literary exhibit. This goes far toward making amends for the overparticularity and the overextension of the expositions of characters and of mood. Whatever the shortcomings, there is life in the book—except in the preposterous New York episode. Transfer to New York nearly always extinguishes the vitality of Southern and Western characters created by Southern and Western writers, and Miss Glasgow has not been luckier in that matter than her rivals and predecessors.

After all, when it is the flavor of the soil you are after you had best stick to the soil. While the story does stick to it, the flavor is unmistakable in *Barren Ground*.

H. W. Boynton, "Back to the Soil," Providence *Journal*, 12 April 1925, sec. G, p. 7

Ellen Glasgow's most recent novel, *Barren Ground*, is as homely, strong and colorless as the soil with which it deals. Dorinda Oakley, brought up in a remote Western farm, has a bitter disappointment during her one period of groping for romance. She tries city life for a distraction; but after a few years returns to wrest a living from the soil.

She is a strong, silent woman with great capabilities for engrossing herself in physical labor. Life for her is toil, success for her is represented in terms of harvest. She achieves none of the things in life that her young dreams told her were essentials and yet her life in its entirety leaves the impression of completeness and content. Hers is a stark story without gayety or enthusiasm; it is without romance or wordly success; but one feels that Dorinda achieved her destiny and that in her bravery and understanding somehow found the poetry of life. It is told with all the richness and breadth that Miss Glasgow has at her command and despite her lusterless theme she is never depressing; for as Dorinda herself says, "where beauty exists the understanding soul can never remain desolate."

Edwin Francis Edgett, "On the Barren Ground of Virginia," Boston *Evening Transcript*, 18 April 1925, sec. 4, p. 4

From the first page to the last, *Barren Ground* is a novel of the soil. Except for a brief interlude in New York, whither the heroine goes through absolute force of circumstance, it is utterly and undividedly a story of Virginia. As other novelists have written of Dartmoor, of Yorkshire, of Staffordshire, of rural Russia, of Canada, of New England, of the Far West, so Miss Glasgow has written of her native State, of a land that is so individual and so distinctive that her story could be told of no other place and of no other people. Other novels have dealt with the history, the romance, the gayety and the innumerable diversions of plantation life, but Miss Glasgow has a far different purpose in view, and that purpose is to show what may happen when a family with abundant land, but with no money or resources, is enthralled in the slavery of poverty. With the humor of life, except as she makes its ironies an integral part of her story, she has nothing to do.

To disclose and to emphasize all this, Miss Glasgow bids us follow a young woman from adversity to prosperity through a period of some thirty years....
[...]

Few novels have revealed the southland of Virginia so clearly as *Barren Ground*. It presents the spirit of the land, the weaknesses of its people, without censure and without commendation. The novelist portrays them exactly as they are. Were the word not so frequently over-used, it might be called an epic story. It has in it, in any event, the elements of the epic, and although it is the tale of one woman's progress it is nevertheless also a tale of her entire world—a little world in itself, but at the same time in its elements a graphic presentation of the whole of mankind.

"Miss Glasgow Turns Out Another Splendid Novel," Cleveland *Plain Dealer*, 25 April 1925, p. 9

Ellen Glasgow is one of our truly great and important novelists. Out of the crowd of stylists and modernists, jazz artists, sensationalists, exploiters of psychoanalysis and discoverers of sex, she stands forth distinguished in honesty and intelligence of style and purpose.

One can put beside her only Willa Cather and Edith Wharton—with a queer shock to discover that this trio does not include a male novelist. Dreiser and Hergesheimer, Cabell and Donn Byrne—crude Titan, color splasher, romanticist, prose poet—these are striking geniuses, but no part of the solid tradition of American and British letters. Ellen Glasgow's beauty touched realism interprets the land for us who live upon it.

Barren Ground is the story of a woman who lived in a part of Virginia described by the title. Her people were farmers, struggling unintelligently with an exhausted soil. Ripe and eager for romance, she cannot find it in her homely surroundings, but it is inevitable that the first stranger who comes along should bring it to her. Its disaster means the death of all romance to her.

"I have finished with all that," she says; and she becomes a scientific farmer, bringing fertility to her ancestral acres of barren ground.

This is the skeleton of the plot, doing no sort of justice to the story itself. It is the story of the whole life of a strong woman; it is the story of a whole section of America, of a whole generation of Americans. Her picture is full of well defined and memorable figures and touched with a melancholy beauty. It is only a mature art, exercised by years of craftsmanship, that can produce such finished work as this.

Carl Van Doren, "*Barren Ground*," *New Republic*, 42 (29 April 1925), 271

No contemporary American novelist is more intelligent than Ellen Glasgow. If she has latterly been somewhat overlooked in the press of other novelists, she owes it to a fact for which she is not to blame: the fact that early in her career she was popularly assigned to a school of fiction in which she belongs by geography but not by temperament. Even when she has touched the traditional Virginia in her stories, she has touched it, any critical eye should see, with a difference. Leaving others to be nostalgic for the lost cause, she has been the realist, the one important realist, of the new dominion. In particular, she has distanced all her rivals in her portraits of Southern women, who with her assistance have escaped from the sweet shadows thrown over them by chivalry, and have been permitted to amount to something in their own right.

Like Virginia and Gabriella, the most striking heroines hitherto created by Miss Glasgow, Dorinda in *Barren Ground* goes through love and beyond it before her story ends. Love takes her like a flame and burns her; love takes her like a whirlwind and drives her far outside her expected path. Then for three-fifths of her chronicle she builds herself up on what seemed the ruin of her life. Though she has thought she lived for love alone, she finds she has in her a certain yeomanly endurance which sends her back to become a farmer on the scene of her defeat by love. That part of her which has been consumed by her tragedy leaves her, because she lacks it, all the freer to bend her energies to the work she has chosen. Among the heroes of fiction this circumstance is common enough; among the heroines it is so rare that Dorinda stands like a tower. She never for a moment ceases to be a woman; her ambiguous costumes hide tender flesh. But she is the husband of her farm, working her creative will upon it, mastering it and cherishing it till it responds with the harvests she has desired. The process is as dramatic as a marriage.

Old Farm, to which Dorinda is thus wedded, becomes in Miss Glasgow's handling a symbol of fate and victory. At the same time, the symbolism is not carried, as it might easily have been, to the point of poetic fallacy. What this farm is, any farm in any average neighborhood might be. The region is without splendor and without miracles. No great plantation varies the monotony of plain existence. No shining adventures light up the dusty roads. The conflict is between mankind, toiling with little hope, and nature, resisting with a bored inertia. In the record of the conflict Miss Glasgow has gone so thoroughly into detail that she furnishes a valuable document upon a typical Virginia. Life there has, of course, its poetic elements. Storms descend upon it with the roar of thunder and the fury of lightning. The sun strikes across wide fields and colors gray mists. The seasons march by in diverse moods, the flowers spring in their places, the grasshoppers chant through the hot days. Some of Dorinda's neighbors are quaint and some are horrible. But on the whole the picture is drawn in the kind of honest white and black which perhaps most nearly reproduces the color of life for most men and women.

The narrative, kept so constantly in hand by a realistic conscience, recalls Miss Glasgow's admirable novel *The Miller of Old Church*, which has much the same setting as *Barren Ground*. The new book, however, in denying itself the softness which imparted to the older its special charm, is thereby made more true. Yet it must be admitted that the truthfulness of *Barren Ground* is bought at a price. Now and then the story lags under the weight of its materials. It would have been better if it had been shorter. As it stands, it tends to obscure a trait which is no less characteristic of Miss Glasgow than her austere fidelity. That trait is her dramatic passion. For all she has continued the story of Dorinda after her civil war through her reconstruction, and that without any effect of anti-climax, the chapters dealing with the unhappy love affair are the best in the book. Not only is there more heat in the subject itself, but there is more ease and flexibility in the representation of it. The end of the act seems somehow always in sight, even though surprises may be looked for. Reading these ardent chapters, a critic who has read all Miss Glasgow's novels with genuine admiration for their rounded substances may nevertheless venture the hope that she will some time give another of her qualities the rein and try a sparer plot of the difficult but rewarding length of *Ethan Frome*, *Miss Lulu Bett*, or *A Lost Lady*.

Cameron Rogers, "Realism from the Romantic South," World's Work, 50 (May 1925), 99–102

"Bare, starved, desolate, the country closed in about her." It is with this sentence that one first becomes aware of what is the dominant atmosphere in *Barren Ground*, the latest novel of Ellen Glasgow and, by virtue of its primary significance, her most distinguished. It is the first outrider of what may prove an army, the first note of a clarion hitherto unfamiliar to the South, that of realism; and a realism as austere in its dominion, as monochromatic in its insistence upon the tyranny of the soil and the dial of the seasons, as was ever the word of Hardy in *The Native*, in *Tess* or in the lamentable *Jude*. Until now the reader whose knowledge of the South has been founded and fed by the literature purporting to mirror its life, has conceived of it a landscape diametrically opposed to the somber etching that suggests itself in that sentence, a landscape of sunshine and cheer and in whose foreground lounge gentlemen of a military rank indissolubly connected with an old-world courtesy of manner and the fragrance of mint juleps. Virginia, the scene of *Barren Ground*, has been particularly connected with this picture. Virginia, where, one was wont to gather, existence hinged upon the mellow hospitality of the great houses and the quaint humor and touching devotion of Negro mammies, seemed irretrievably lost to realism and the sworn liegeman of a somewhat sugared romance. And there had been, of course, the Virginia of the Cavaliers and they, too, lived in this literature, lived and wrought of it a sort of tapestry of chivalric endeavor. But now with a gesture as definite as it is sweepingly destructive to all of this, comes *Barren Ground* with its bitter realities of poverty and toil, its plain song of frustration and defeat, and these little ikons of a prosperous ease come smashing to the ground. The Virginia of Ellen Glasgow is a sullen countryside, from whose resentful soil the Oakleys, father, mother, two sons and the daughter whose destiny it is we read of, wrench a livelihood that is in itself a mockery of life. Like the agonizing routine of Zola's peasants, that of the Oakleys is a slavery that terminates only with death, that is rendered more bearable by no single detail of felicity, no lightening of the burden. The very land is a portent of bleak futility.

[. . .]

Miss Glasgow's prose possesses that firm and solid beauty that lifts her work out of the class of the casual fiction of the day into that of such a man as Hardy, with whom she shares the definite kindredship of the great writers of realism. The heritage of *Barren Ground* promises to be greater than that of any other realistic novel of contemporary American letters, although, like all great books, its progress into its own may be but moderately swift.

New Yorker, 1 (2 May 1925), 26

Virginia, too, gives fiction one of those regions beloved of realists where the struggling farmers refuse to progress and the broomsedge 'll git ye if ye stay. Dorinda, its most struggling farmer's romantic-minded daughter, dreams of escape—until the doctor's son returns from the great city. "His betrayal of me," she is later to reflect, "was merely an incident" of his weakness. He is soon to take to drink and his unloved wife, who was forced on him, to go insane.

At the time Dorinda feels like killing him, but instead slips away to New York, where an accident relieves her of the child and provides helpful friends. When a fine fellow wants to marry her, he learns she is "through with all that"; it is converting itself into will to make a go of the home farm. While thus engaged, she does accept an amiable local character who has no erotic effect on her; apparently their marriage is nominal, though the point is left obscure. She derives satisfaction from contemptuous indifference to her betrayer, who still loves her, and from succeeding in life as he fails. At last, when she really is "through with all that" and tranquil, she is willing to save him from dying in the poorhouse.

This is Ellen Glasgow's *Barren Ground*, written with her usual conscientiousness and painstaking lucidity in the style that has won her some eminent admirers. On the strength of our outline, it might be an interesting if somewhat inclusively reminiscent novel. Perhaps to many readers it will be. We speak for but one, whom its five hundred pages of a commonplace subjective impersonation, purporting to manifest insight, bored to misery.

Addison Hibbard, "The Literary Lantern," Greensboro *Daily News*, 3 May 1925, sec. 2, p. 4

"Realism has crossed the Potomac," so runs a line in the publishers' announcement of a new novel. And for once we accept a book at the face value placed on it by its sponsors. And the book? It is Ellen Glasgow's *Barren Ground*.

Barren Ground is a story of the Virginia of the last three decades, an epic of the soil and of the struggle of the white farmer who is "land poor." But it is more than that. It is a chronicle of two generations against this environment of hopelessness and ignorance and of a girl who turns her back on romance, who proclaims in the first few pages that she is "through with all that" (the "that" being romance) and who works her way on to something stronger and more wholesome—a task in life. Here is, as the publishers say, realism; but it is in no sense pessimism or disgust with life. Here is the vigor of conception, the strength of outline, the simplicity which one has associated with George Eliot, with Knut Hamsun, with, and we are measuring our words, Thomas Hardy. As Miss Glasgow tells her story the reader is impressed by the part nature takes in the combat—a girl, alone in her vision and persistence, against a nature which runs to broomsedge, reveals its strength in the pine, and holds out a final hope in life everlasting, the three plants giving the names to the three parts of the book. Miss Glasgow's Virginia country reveals an American Egdon Heath....

Jessie Hopkins, "*Barren Ground*," *Atlanta Journal Magazine*, 3 May 1925, 20

Ellen Glasgow's *Barren Ground* is a study in the contrast of development on the one hand and of degeneration on the other. It is an epic of the barren soil of Virginia. The hard surface of the story has responded to the polish of Miss Glasgow's marvelous technique. It reflects more clearly than any of her previous stories the realism which is her metier.

Barren Ground presents Dorinda at twenty. Her imagination was tinctured by the romanticism which makes a woman fall in love with religion or an idea. And one day she found romance, not in imagination, not in the pallid fiction crushed among the tomes of her great-grandfather's library, but driving on one of the muddy roads through the broomsedge. This is when Jason Greylock enters Dorinda's life, and because Jason proved unfaithful life was eternally embittered for Dorinda and out of her bitterness came the desire to have her chance at life outside the realm of romance.

One might conclude from Miss Glasgow's stories that she has two purposes, one to create characters who can bear the burdens she puts upon them, and the other to tell the truth about their behavior. The extremely modern note in the story is Dorinda's gathering together her dynamic forces and reclaiming the barren ground of Old Farm, her ancestral home, redeeming it from the fate which the dry, pestilential broomsedge seemed to eternally threaten.

Dorinda succeeds in conquering the barren soil of her home, but she cannot apply the same determination to retrieve her own barren life, nor return to that state of love and affection which her nature so craved and which was the absorbing passion of her young life. Love came to her again in pleasant guises, but she would have none of it. Love was the only thing that made life desirable to her and love was irrevocably lost to her. To all who suggested that she take on a second romance, Dorinda smiled and her smile was pensive, ironic and infinitely wise: "I've finished with all that," she replied. "I am thankful to have finished with all that."

Barren Ground is a story of desolation. Miss Glasgow's creed in fiction is obviously that of the realist, with an occasional excursion into romanticism. But in the portrayal of the Virginia which she understands so profoundly lies the secret of her abiding charm.

James Branch Cabell, "The Last Cry of Romance," *Nation*, 6 May 1925, 521–2

This is the best of many excellent books by Ellen Glasgow. I record the statement after a lengthy and reminiscitory appraisal of the list of its fifteen predecessors. And in considering this list, I am surprised by two quite casually allied phenomena. One is the startling approach to completeness, presented by these books as a whole, of

Ellen Glasgow's portrayal of all social and economic Virginia since the War Between the States. The other is the startling announcement, upon the dust jacket of this new book, that "with *Barren Ground* realism at last crosses the Potomac."

Now, upon dust jackets, of course, wild statements appear as common as cardinal virtues in a cemetery. Yet this particular statement, when advanced, or at any rate countenanced, by the firm which for some twenty-five years has been publishing Miss Glasgow's novels, arouses the troubled suspicion that Messrs. Doubleday, Page and Company have been regarding, all the while, these books as pleasant little tales of the one sort—still to quote from this dust jacket—which, before the appearance of *Barren Ground*, had ever been written about the South, as "a land of colonels, old mansions, and delicate romance."

Eventually, however, every author, I reflect, must learn, with time and much vexation, how handily the pranks of publishers may be compared with the axiomatic peace of God. I therefore dismiss the problem tacitly. And, no matter what her publishers may assert, I reflect also, here, in these sixteen books, is Ellen Glasgow's picture of present-day Virginia; and here is the vast panorama of, upon the whole, futility. The land of Ellen Glasgow's birth and nurture, the land which she has so consummately depicted, has always been, in her interpreting, an unmistakably barren ground, howsoever pleasantly diversified in some places by the dejected relics of yesterday—"the colonels and the old mansions"—and in other places by the sort of perennial vaticinatory rose-coloring of Virginia's future which only out-and-out pessimists (I hope) would describe as "delicate romance." Meanwhile, it is plain enough that for the deciduous aristocracy of the commonwealth which most often and appallingly figures in oratory as a cornerstone and a guiding star and a cradle, Miss Glasgow has, in the double-edged phrase, "no use" except as bijouterie. The virtues, the really highbred vices, and the graces of the unhorsed Virginian Cavaliers survive a bit pathetically their heyday, and very nicely serve her turn: so, for their ornamental qualities she cherishes and at need extols them, with the peculiar and perturbing amiability of a past mistress in the art of parenthetic malice. And the one element of high-flown "romance" detectable in Ellen Glasgow's books is so far from being outmoded that it remains always, after a fashion which I shall later indicate, quite actually the *dernier cri*.

And meanwhile also, in *Barren Ground*, we have a hint of what I take to have been Miss Glasgow's philosophy, all through so many books, in regard to the best-thought-of constituents of "romance." This latest novel is the story of Dorinda Oakley, born in Virginia of the tenant farmer class, and getting, somehow, through a life in which the traditional ardors and anguishes simply do not ever ascend to their advertised poignancy. Love comes to you, and for the while it is well enough: but, to the other side—when that also comes about—being by this later Jason cast for the role of a forsaken and unwed Medea, after the customary childish souvenir of the faithless lover is already en route, proves not intolerable. You marry by and by somebody else, because you like this middle-aged Nathan Pedlar well enough; and when your husband in due season dies it makes astonishingly slight difference. Yet other wooers come, and pass out of your living, and some of them are well enough; but none of them really matters. Later you preserve from the almshouse your first collaborator in amour, who technically "ruined" you; and you permit him to die as a dependent upon your charity; and you are conscious of neither complacency nor sorrow, but merely feel, with a sort of incurious resignation, that the affair has turned out well enough.

No one of these material and "romantic" accidents, you find, at all poignantly matters. And when Dorinda Pedlar, a woman who has succeeded in life, a widely wooed but a convinced and contented widow, and an ever-busy and prosperous landholder now in her own right, stands at the side of her first lover's yet open grave, we encounter the pregnant passage which I abridge:

> Out of the whirling chaos in her mind, Jason's face emerged; and, dissolving as quickly as it had formed, it reappeared as the face of Nathan, and vanished again to assume the features of Richard Burch, of Bob Ellgood, and of every man she had ever known closely or remotely in her life. They meant nothing. They had no significance, these dissolving faces. Yet as thick and fast as dead leaves they whirled and danced there, disappearing and reassembling in the vacancy of her thoughts, as faces, ghosts, dreams, and regrets; as old vibrations that were incomplete; as unconscious impulses which had never quivered into being; as all the things that she might have known, and had never known in her life.

Now, that, the exact may protest, is here presented by Miss Glasgow, not as a philosophy, but as the Dorinda puppet's transitory state of mind. Nevertheless, you will find, I think, that a great many of Miss Glasgow's protagonists—and all her later ones, I am sure—reach very much this identical state of mind not far from the end of the particular book in which each of them figures. The things which ought, by every rule of tradition, to have mattered most poignantly have in reality meant nothing.

Not that Ellen Glasgow, any more than life, permits any person to remain in this state of mind. It is this "point" I have been approaching; it is upon this "point" I would dwell, after having found an inspection of Miss Glasgow's final paragraphs to be rather strikingly revelatory. Thus in *The Builders* Caroline Meade is left facing a peculiarly ambiguous outlook, uplifted by her perception—which the prosaic could only have interpreted, at that hour and location, as a sign of somebody's house having caught fire in Chesterfield County—that "beyond the meadows and the river light was shining on the far horizon." In *Life and Gabriella* the much battered Mrs. Fowler is joyously departing, with her most recently acquired lover, "anywhere—toward the future." In yet another book, the green grass of oncoming spring is, to I forget whom, already visible among the melting snows: elsewhere, the earth's rotation has thoughtfully provided a new day, and the beloved is coming, in the last clause of the last sentence and the sunlight of a remarkably fine dawn. Thus, in book upon book, does Ellen Glasgow—after, to phrase it mildly, evincing no parsimony in supplying her characters with trials and defeats and losses—yet end upon this note of indicating her puppets' unshaken faith in an immediately impending future wherein everything will come out rather more than all right. It is the exact and the very truthful note of what I have already alluded to as the last, and indeed the expiring, cry of romance.

Just so the Dorinda Pedlar of this most recent book eventually retains—about six pages after the depressing reflections which I have epitomized—her firm, her explicit, and her inexplicable plerophoria, that "the best of life was yet to come" and that "the understanding soul can never remain desolate" so long—one gathers from a colorful poetic passage—as the rural scenery of Virginia stays picturesque. For Miss Glasgow, you perceive, knows the bipedal fauna of her chosen hunting ground far too well either to boggle over the circumstance that they, toward fifty, do occasionally glimpse the truth as to their personal experience with "romance" or to omit recording the more generally significant fact that, having done so, they with haste and admirable good sense resort to narcotics in the form of fairy stories about tomorrow. Miss Glasgow knows that, after all imaginable trials and defeats and losses, life does, illogically and relentlessly, fill the battered human machine with fresh optimism, very much as when, at more palpable filling stations, fresh gasoline is pumped into an automobile, and the machine is thus kept going. And that Ellen Glasgow should so emphasize, at the conclusion of almost every one of her books, this especial human foible rather than others, you may, if you like, regard as her punctilious oblation before the fetish of the happy ending. But I elect to see in it only the final flick as the ironist dismisses her sport.

Hamilton Gibbs, "And Some Fell on Barren Ground," *New York Evening Post Literary Review*, 16 May 1925, p. 3

"Courage is the thing," said Barrie. "All goes if courage goes." This faith must be shared by Ellen Glasgow, for it is the outstanding quality of the cheated, buffeted, repressed girl, who, in *Barren Ground*, conquers life eventually almost in spite of herself. In no sense master of her fate, she remains doggedly the captain of her soul, and because of that captaincy fights her way through to the peace of understanding.

"With *Barren Ground*," says the jacket, "realism at last crosses the Potomac." This pontifical statement may be pregnant with meaning, may mark an epoch in American literature—although I have read stories of the Kentucky mountaineers which were starkly realistic—but to me it is of slight importance in comparison with the universal humanities within the book. If the setting had been in the north of Scotland or the south of England instead of in Virginia, it would make absolutely no difference. The courage is the thing, and the particular kind chosen by Miss Ellen Glasgow is perhaps the hardest of all—the courage that drives an individual, lonely, at odds with a humdrum environment and with herself, to triumph over despair.

The exposition of this is in terms of Dorinda Oakley's life and her gradual understanding not of what it means but of what it may mean when, well over fifty, it is suggested that she may marry again and she replies with a smile that is "pensive, ironic and infinitely wise," "Oh, I've finished with all that. I'm thankful to have finished with all that!"

[...]

Barren Ground is a book that gives most furiously to think. In its philosophy of duty, duty to oneself not less than to one's God, it is essentially Scotch, as Scotch as Dorinda's forbears who all came from across the water. From the point of technique it is most beautifully written, the chief characters drawn with untiring skill and the lesser ones sketched in with the swift strokes of an expert. Longer considerably than the average novel, it flows beneath one's eyes with that ease and satisfaction only to be enjoyed in unusually well-done work.

There is only one small bone that I would venture to pick with the author and that is her sin of omission in not showing us the girl's mind, one way or the other, before the coming of the child. That aspect of the girl's education, important as it is in its bearing upon her subsequent philosophy, is dealt with only by implication. Small bone or no, however, *Barren Ground* is a novel that I am very glad to have read.

"'Realism Has Crossed the Potomac,' by Ferry," *Time*, 5 (1 June 1925), 13

"Broomsedge," old Matthew Fairlamb used to say, "ain't jest wild stuff. It's a kind of fate." Opposed only by ignorance and indigence, it crowded Virginia farmlands, Pedlar's Mill in particular, into hopelessness. Men either subsided into ruts—like Dorinda Oakley's plodding father and slaving mother; or their lives straggled, grew weedy—like Dr. Greylock with his whiskey, yellow wench and brood of pickaninnies at dilapidated Five Oaks.

Walking early and late to work at the store in Pedlar's Mill, Dorinda wore a flame-colored shawl, bright symbol of protest. Her bee-stung mouth was another protest. Jason Greylock, rufous, crisp but unfound, came home from medical study to take care of his father. He thought he discovered his grip in Dorinda. For her, his charm, and love itself, were life's incredible increment.

Wilting suddenly before old circumstances, Jason let himself be married to Geneva Ellwood, empty heiress. Out of this irresolution came, for Geneva, insanity and suicide; for him, drink, failure, consumption.

Dorinda was first stunned by the blow, then slowly forged hard. She wandered in New York, fell (arbitrarily) into good hands, was disembarrassed of her child, went back to Pedlar's Mill with her secret intact, her spirit erect. She beat back the broomsedge, brought prosperity from barren ground. She beat back memory, married out of respect, and for convenience, gained a strong contentment without love. At 50, hale and even-minded, she had only pity left for the dying Jason. As from an eminence hard won, she saw lives as fretful incidents and watched her wide horizon for the serene sickle moons of many harvests yet to come.

Persons who pontificate on the "phases" of literature say: "Realism has crossed the Potomac." If that is so (doubtful), it did not wade, swim or fly. It was ferried. As an experiment, Dorinda is interesting enough, compelling to the mind; and the soil she is set in—Negroes, cowpeas, broomsedge—smells properly. But no amount of fertilizing will remove the agricultural tag: "Hardy Lady Farmer in the South, transplanted."

Miss Ellen Glasgow of Richmond, Va., now 51, tries not to pretend. Her materials, as early as *The Voice of the People* (1900) and *The Miller of Old Church* (1911), have been the roots and sap of human experience, treated not clinically but with a gracious hardihood. If it is in the romantic vein to regard fortitude and other sombre virtues as cultivable, Romanticist she is. But that distinction is unimportant. The great pity is that so painstaking, firm-handed a laborer has not yet the genius to discover native plants and feel them growing inevitably, of themselves.

V[irginia] T. McC[ormick], "New Books," *Catholic World*, 131 (July 1925), 568–9

In this book, as in their forerunners, Miss Glasgow has chosen Virginia as her *mise en scène*. This is a part of her sincerity as well as of her courage, for she deals with the country and the conditions that she knows best and is unafraid in her revelations. As courage is the outstanding trait of Miss Glasgow, so is it the distinguishing characteristic of Dorinda, the heroine of *Barren Ground*.

It is not to wonder on the part of critics that Miss Glasgow should go to the soil for her inspiration nor that she should choose a member of the class known as the "poor whites" in Virginia. These people are as much a part of the life of the State as Virginia, Gabriella, or the courtly old gentlemen who swept their hats before them as they saluted the ladies in the dim old streets of Virginia's old towns; they are as real as the charming woman who stands for such high ideals in *One Man in His Time*, or as Christopher Blake and his two sisters. Dorinda is as natural a product of the soil as was the Miller of Old Church.

Miss Glasgow has gone further with her creation, has seen into a more widely progressive future in this last book, and has made Dorinda not only a child of the soil but the exponent of the possibility of progress sustained by an unfaltering courage and lighted by the lamp of understanding.

It is a great book, but it is more than that; it is a readable book, a book touched by a certain universality that makes it a living thing, not an ephemeral expression of a transient emotion. It will be read and talked of by future generations, even as to-day we talk of *Tom Jones*, or *Vanity Fair*, of *The Newcomes*, and *David Copperfield*. *Barren Ground* is one of those few books in which moral truth and human passion are illuminated, and Miss Glasgow is an artist who is satisfied only when she has achieved the highest artistry of story-telling and style in writing.

H. L. Mencken, "New Fiction," *American Mercury*, 5 (July 1925), 383

Miss Glasgow's *Barren Ground* leaves me rather in doubt. It is a bold attempt to throw off the sentimentalism that has long ridden the Southern novel, and so come to a realistic dealing with the life of the Southern people, and especially with that of the inferior majority of them. Its defect lies in the fact that Miss Glasgow gives no sign of an intimate knowledge of the poor, flea-bitten yokels she sets before us. She has plainly tried to comprehend them, but she is still unable to *feel* with them. They thus become laboratory animals, and grow incomprehensible. Even Dorinda Oakley, the protagonist in the chronicle, never quite takes on the colors of life. She is real enough, at times, as the Eternal Woman, but she doesn't fit into the background of Pedlar's Mill. Her seduction by young Dr. Jason Greylock becomes a piece of stage business; her flight to New York becomes another. Altogether, a novel somehow weak in its legs. There is, in detail, excellent work in it. It is boldly imagined and competently planned. But it is not moving.

Mary B. Orvis, "Much-talked-of Novels," Indianapolis *News*, 1 July 1925, p. 24

In *Barren Ground* Ellen Glasgow has told the story of a woman's struggle with the barren soil and cramping environment of a Virginia farm. She has also told the story of an intense inner life, of a character of great natural endowments and capacities, turned away from the emotional toward the material. Ellen Glasgow's heroine, like Edna Ferber's heroine in *So Big*, wrestles with poverty and the soil; and, like Edna Ferber's heroine, she conquers both. But she conquers at a terrible cost, the cost of utter disillusionment.

Her philosophy is summed up as she returns from her mother's funeral: "The permanence of material things, the inexorable triumph of fact over emotion, appeared to be the only reality. These things had been ageless when her mother was young; they would still be ageless when she herself had become an old woman. Over the immutable landscape human lives drifted and vanished like shadows."

The novel is fascinating to those who are interested in the study of character as it is affected by heredity, environment and the events of life. The story of how the romantic, dreaming, pitifully eager young girl suddenly is transfigured by the miracle of meeting a pleasant, intelligent, good-looking young man from the city is poignantly told, as is the heart-breaking disillusionment that follows. It is the old story of betrayal, given a special significance as it dominates the life of this girl. The dreaming daughter of a religiously fanatical mother, dominated by a morbid revulsion against the physical aspects of love, growing out of her experience, turns her back on marriage, though several opportunities come to her. When she finally does marry, at thirty-eight, she chooses Nathan, her neighbor, who is humble and ugly, and she prays that she may remember his goodness and forget his absurdity. In his fatal humility he accepts her tolerance. In the depiction of this phase of her life, as in the others, the author maintains the powerful objectivity that we think of as belonging only to European writers. She writes faithfully of a woman with iron in her soul, of a character that, by reason of its hardness, must be distasteful to her.

If faithfulness to her characters, a sweeping imagination, emotional intensity and great beauty of expression make for artistic work, then Ellen Glasgow has given us an artistic novel. Much has been made of the fact that this story deals realistically with a phase of Virginia life that has heretofore been overlooked, and perhaps it has a certain value from this standpoint. But its real claim to greatness would seem to lie in the insight with which tremendous changes in a character are developed, and in the exquisite imagery and beauty of innumerable passages which lift the work into the realm of poetry.

Glasgow [Scotland] *Herald*, 2 July 1925, p. 4

One of Miss Glasgow's best novels, written with spirit and with a thorough grasp of her subject. It is the story of a young, ardent girl who grasps eagerly and ignorantly at the wonders of first love, only to find the romance turned to dust and ashes. Disillusioned and embittered, she directs all her energies to work; heart and brain become crystallised into a fierce weapon against failure. Thus armed, she fights magnificently, and in the end attains victory in that peace which is life's best substitute for happiness. There is an unconscious pathos in the strong Dorinda that makes this story a curious mixture of hopefulness and of tragedy. The persistence with which the existence of her recalcitrant lover runs through even her later life like a dark thread adds to the poignancy of her detached and hidden nature and to the sombre and yet dramatic atmosphere of the whole book. Miss Glasgow reveals great insight, sympathy, and wisdom in this book, and a wonderful understanding of those who love and hate the soil by which they live or die. Her descriptions of farm life in Virginia are splendidly vivid, and all the characters—from Nathan Pedlar, misunderstood "visionary" and farmer, to Fluvanna, the loyal negress—have a real and glowing identity. An exceedingly fine novel.

Gladys Wright Wood, "Due Honors," Waco *News*, 5 July 1925, p. 4

Signal triumph in what has been several times attempted with lesser success, investing the land and elements with human characteristics, and portraying them as a titanic force against which the human protagonist pits her efforts, is only one of the dove-tailing excellencies of *Barren Ground*, last and best of Ellen Glasgow's novels, published this year by Doubleday, Page and company.

To enumerate: She creates a world, supported by a substantial and deeply-rooted philosophy, in which her characters speak and move and feel—and work. So vivid is her world that the reader to return to his own must extricate himself with a mental shake. One comes from a period with *Barren Ground*—and it takes several considerable "periods" to glean it—with the same sense of having lived intimately in another world as possesses him on coming from a darkened theatre into the everyday business of the street.

Again, the deep realism that is one of her established claims to superlative craftsmanship, has swept away with finality the superficial, stratified photography of a school of professed realists that peopled the Virginias with julep-consuming, regal-mustached cu'n'ls. Her realism is earthly, as her people are; her depreciating houses outnumber the stately-columned colonial mansions of the entrenched southern school probably 50 to one; her characters are indigenous to the soil.

Observer [England], 5 July 1925, p. 4

There is something about the soil—the actual ground—and its conquest by human toil, that seems to ennoble a story. Miss Ellen Glasgow has never, to our thinking, written a book so nearly great as this account of a splendid, unconquerable young woman who will not let herself be crushed by betrayal. It is true that a sadness, a sense of futility, pursues Dorinda at the height of her success. She has had to harden herself against disappointed love, to hold up her head against shame and humiliation. She has missed the softness of life and the sweetness. Still, there is something so fine, so heartening, in her struggle with the barren acres of her father's neglected land, and in her achievement of its redemption all but single-handed, that the book does not altogether leave a painful impression of frustration, but one of courage and of life. It is admirably written and difficult to forget. The scene is, of course, America; but the appeal is universal. Everywhere there is good red earth, and the red blood in the veins of youth, for conquering.

"Ellen Glasgow's New Novel,"
East Anglian *Daily Times* [England], 6 July 1925, p. 7

Those who are familiar with this author's style will not require any further commendation of this new story than the statement that it is worthy of the writer's reputation. The scene is a thinly-settled part of Virginia, the time is the 'nineties of the last century, and the characters are a group of denizens of the district of Pedlar's Mill. The characterisation is admirable throughout, but the figure of Dorinda Oakley dominates the rest. No more impressive triumph of delineation has been issued for a long time past, and there can be no doubt that Dorinda will win many more admirers than paid homage to her in the flesh. There is nothing very exciting about the plot, but it is so capably constructed as to fix the attention of the reader. The work gives us a clever study of various aspects of human nature, and the presentment is always fresh and attractive. *Barren Ground* ought, because of the healthiness of its tone and the charm of its fashioning, to enjoy a very wide circulation.

Times Literary Supplement [England], 9 July 1925, p. 462

A very powerful, melancholy story is *Barren Ground*, Miss Ellen Glasgow's new novel of Virginia. She takes you into a small hard-working community of people who wrest a poor living out of the wretched soil of Pedlar's Mill, somewhere in the bleaker and more thinly populated regions of Virginia, and one by one each figure that she calls into being takes on life and reality. She is extraordinarily able to make you feel these obscure little lives in their real and dramatic importance. She never insists that extreme hardship, poverty and preventable sickness are merely sordid, as is so often the case with the novelist who deals with the labourer on the land. Her characters do not illustrate a theory or a theme; they endure and enjoy life as men and women do.

Dorinda Oakley, whose story it mainly is, stands out with a kind of grandeur. She is a simple, ardent creature, on fire with youth and its vague expectations of something certain and splendid awaiting discovery. She loves and is betrayed, a common tale uncommonly presented. She hides her secret and goes off to New York, is injured in a street accident which destroys her hopes of a child, and meets, through the doctor who attends her, friends with whom she stays and works for two years. News of her father's illness takes her back to Pedlar's Mill, a sombre woman unable to be much more hurt by anything that life can do to her. She farms like a man, and takes care of her half-demented mother, impregnable to suggestions of love, without the slightest comprehension of the normal pleasures of girlhood. There is in her no longer any response to youth, and she can meet the man who has betrayed and jilted her with no ability to suffer or even to care that she cannot feel. When she is left solitary she (unaccountably to herself) marries the widower of an old friend, chiefly to care for his brood of children. Her life is one of service, of unremitting toil, and in that she finds her satisfaction. She utters no fine sentiments, but you feel that nature itself is consolation to her, inexpressive as she may be. There are no sentimental scenes, no relief. Miss Glasgow is stern; she makes no concessions. The result is an unusually impressive and fine book.

Brighton [England] *Gazette*, 10 July 1925, p. 4

One is apt to be suspicious of a book which introduces its heroine in a shawl and falling snow setting and its hero whose dark red hair, burnished to a copper glow, grows in a natural wave. One's suspicions here are all wrong. Miss Glasgow in *Barren Ground* gets clear of all superficialities and gives us in this new novel of hers in many ways an astounding work. She has given herself the job of writing a good book on sodden material. She does it deliberately, determined that the reader shall be spared nothing. She flings it in one's teeth that Dorinda is tall and plain. She is a woman—we part company with her white-haired—hardened and embittered by life whose highest ambitions only rise to cows. "To think that she who had never owned anything, should actually possess these adorable creatures!"—and, again we get her ruminating on bulls "with admiration and envy," thinking "I wonder if I shall ever own a creature like that." . . .

Miss Glasgow is a fine writer. She has achieved her end to a superlative degree. But her material is sodden through and through.

Punch [England], 169 (15 July 1925), 55

Creative work is the accepted outlet for a woman whose passion (legitimate or illegitimate) has met with disaster; but what makes Miss Ellen Glasgow's rehandling of this theme interesting is the masculinity of the work to which her heroine turns. Dorinda Oakley is the only daughter of a Virginian homestead—*Barren Ground*—on which thistles and broomsedge have won victory after victory over generation after generation of her ancestors. Dorinda's mother, early crossed both in love and religion, is an artist in toil for toil's sake; and Dorinda, revolted by a fanaticism which makes thrift "a tyrant, not a slave," determines that come what may she herself will escape from the land. Half inspired by this ambition and half by a mere girlish love for love in any guise, she engages herself by innocent ruses to a young city doctor on a visit to his dying father. But Jason Greylock is a paltry libertine who, having seduced his *fiancee*, allows himself to be bullied into marrying a former flame. Dorinda escapes to New York, her child is born and dies, and she herself is put in the way of a career and a happy marriage. But the call of the land is too strong, and she returns to Virginia, with modern methods in her head and adequate capital at her command, in time to take her father's place and succeed where he failed. The *minutiæ* of her task are particularly well described; in fact the design of the whole book reflects its agricultural *motif* by combining long horizons with an uncommon conscience for detail. I can imagine both factors proving wearisome to the pampered or jaded reader; but even the most pampered or jaded should be grateful for the vivacious characters, black and white, who occupy, so to speak, the middle distance.

"The Art of Miss Glasgow," Birmingham [England] Post, 17 July 1925, p. 3

The broad outlines of Miss Ellen Glasgow's new book, Barren Ground, recall in some particulars the theme of Life and Gabriella. A closer examination shows the similarity to be merely superficial. The texture of the story, though a trifle closely woven, is remarkably lucid; and in the better sense of the term, it satisfies. Miss Glasgow is perhaps meticulous as to detail, but her detail is never superfluous, and every word assists in the construction of atmosphere. The solidity thus attained is not merely stereoscopic. The scenes live, and the characters move in the dimension of time as surely as they are moved through space in the progress of the narrative. Dorinda actually ages as the story unfolds; and even were the reader not reminded of the toll exacted from her youth by the passing years, there would remain a vivid sense of the actual flow of time itself about this central character, and about each person in the story.

Character drawing is not merely a matter of consistency and we feel here that Dorinda Oakley and Jason Greylock are no dead bundles of attributes. Their personalities appear to evolve from within, and their final development is a reasonable product of the reaction between temperament and environment. The underlying *motif* of the book is enigmatic in the sense that the ultimate purpose of life itself remains an enigma. Dorinda pits life against love, winning an ostensible victory; but even in her last dismissal of romance—"I am thankful to have finished with all that"—may be discerned the note of courage rather than of conviction. Barren Ground is a story of great beauty and outstanding ability.

Archibald Henderson, "Soil and Soul," Saturday Review of Literature, 1 (18 July 1925), 907

Twenty-one years ago, when I first reviewed one of Miss Glasgow's novels, the characteristic word employed for The Deliverance was "epic." So gripped was I by the stark power and epic sweep of that work that it took more than three columns to say what I wanted to say....

When I encounter reviews of Barren Ground entitled "Realism Crosses the Potomac" or some such nonsense, I am staggered anew with the fortuity of fame. For more than a quarter of a century, Miss Glasgow has been writing novels informed with high seriousness, close and sincere studies of regional environment, "realistic" in the only true sense of the word, namely, the close reflection of the forms and nuances of real life in a specific geographic setting, heightened and illuminated through the selective processes of art. Almost at the outset of her career, Miss Glasgow had a sense of epic mass and realistic background. As the waving hemp fields of Kentucky in James Lane Allen's *The Reign of Law* soothe and humanize the spirit of the young free-lance of modern thought; as the great staple, Wheat, in Frank Norris's *The Pit*, looms ever larger until it takes on the lineaments of Fate; so the dark-green background of the Virginia tobacco fields supplies the resolving mood in the general harmony of Ellen Glasgow's *The Deliverance*....

Hitherto, Miss Glasgow has been animated by a worthy but somewhat restricted ideal for the writing of fiction. Dwelling in Richmond, that whispering chamber of sectional failure and a lost cause, she has turned her face, with resolute courage, toward the new day of economic and industrial rehabilitation for the South. Her novels have been less biographies of individual destiny than documents of sociological change. They are regional, as is the Sussex fiction of Thomas Hardy; local as are the novelistic studies of the Five Towns of Arnold Bennett. But, till now, they have not been universal. With *Barren Ground*, Miss Glasgow at once takes rank with the Hardy of *Tess*, the Zola of *La Terre*, the Hamsun of *Growth of the Soil*.

It is true that Miss Glasgow still finds sustenance for her fiction in the contrast between the social classes—between the Dorinda Oakley of plain origin and the Jason Greylock of aristocratic lineage. But this contrast is immaterial and essentially factitious. *Barren Ground* is a superb study of the evolution of an individual, the growth of character under the grinding stress of individual folly and economic pressure. At the head of this review are the words: Soil and Soul. In conquest of the soil, this glorious heroine saves her own soul alive. Besides the glamorous seductions of Morand, Margueritte, Arlen, the treatment by Miss Glasgow is artistically satisfying in its austerity and virginal restraint. Besides that sugary slave, Leona, in *Arrowsmith*, Dorinda is Spartan in courage, heroic in energy and will. She triumphs over Nature and Self with ruthless and iron determination, but in the end Life itself defeats her. She is Napoleonic in ironic consciousness and selfless force: "Could I be what I am, little one, cared I only for happiness?" ...

Surely *Barren Ground* is a great novel—great in austerity, great in art, great in humanity.

Eve, 22 July 1925

And so, when we read a romance of the simple folk of the soil like Ellen Glasgow's beautiful story, *Barren Ground*, we rather envy them the silence and the toil and the desolation of their surroundings. Gazing at the Ritz Hotel we, in a metaphorical sense, love to pull it down and gaze yearningly towards, well, let us say, the country in which this story is placed, the flat country of Virginia, where thousands of acres run wild with undergrowth and forests, and a "single cultivated corner is like a solitary island in some chaotic sea." I daresay that the people who live there are burning the pines and the broomsedge and building up in imagination a Ritz Hotel. Oh! why are the best things in life so often enjoyed by those who live just on the other side of the wall? But so it is too often. Therefore there is a most appealing sense of peacefulness in this story of men and women and their unceasing struggle to wrest a living from the resisting earth. They have learnt to ask so little from life, and in asking so little find a thousand moments of happiness which we could enjoy too were it not that we believe there is something ever so much more thrilling to be had if we wait a while. But it is a beautiful story, this story of a farm-bred girl whom, after some tragic years in New York, is forced to return to carry on her father's work on a lonely farmstead, and how at long last she eventually finds that peace which passeth all understanding.

O.C., Liverpool *Courier*, 23 July 1925, p. 4

Full of colour, character and philosophy is Ellen Glasgow's latest book, *Barren Ground*, which contains also a little of the atmosphere of Greek tragedy in its conflict of man and destiny. It is the story of a woman of character who, after one devastating emotional experience, is denied love and youth and devotes herself to the land, which ultimately brings her happiness in understanding.

Miss Glasgow's instinct for the dramatic combines well with her knowledge of humanity and strong feeling for essentials. Dorinda Oakley is a character one does not easily forget, a character not merely a personality, typical of man's struggle to fulfil himself though destiny denies him the gifts he demands. She dominates the book and yet is inseparable from her environment, her somber richness of beauty and austere sensitiveness seeming to emanate from the land itself.

The minor characters are excellently drawn with a perfection of detail, but it is the effortless grace of style and strength of insight that make *Barren Ground* so fine a book.

Merrogate [England] *Herald*, 23 July 1925

Barren Ground by Ellen Glasgow.—Here is a very vital new novel, a work of unusual and outstanding ability. Miss Glasgow is an artist, whose leisurely, spacious style may not appeal to the majority, but it has won her the devoted allegiance of the discriminating reader. *Barren Ground* is an odd, and, in some ways, eerie book; it is, in parts, unutterably sad, with the desperate melancholy of a wet autumn day, but, like an autumn day, it is laden with beauty. It is the life history of a Virginian woman, born in the '60s, when life was an appalling struggle for "the poor white" class, whose stark unhappiness and unending warfare with Nature the author has depicted with almost uncanny realism. We follow Dorinda through the fevered hours of the love interlude with Jason Greylock, with its appalling ecstasy and bitter aftermath; her fight with the land, and her ultimate victory over the barren acres, and her own temperament. We leave her triumphant and hasten to record our sincere admiration for a pen so fearless, a penetration so acute, and a style so rarely beautiful. Surely, this is the best novel that 1925 has given us.

Church of England Newspaper, 24 July 1925, p. 5

There can be no doubt as to the power and skill of Ellen Glasgow. She can write and not only write but carry with her the sympathetic feeling of her readers. We do not know where she comes from, but from the tales we have read we imagine that she is a Southern Stateswoman. But her work is singularly free from Americanese, as she has a great command of the very best English and the rhythm of her sentences is equal to the richness of her vocabulary.... Somehow as we read this tragic tale we seem to move in the atmosphere of a mind akin to that of George Eliot.

Lydia Languish, "Down on the Farm," *John O' London's Weekly* [London], 25 July 1925, p. 528

It must always be difficult for an author to decide where the detail necessary to the creation of atmosphere ceases and overelaboration steps in. This would seem to have been Miss Ellen Glasgow's difficulty in *Barren Ground*. The opening chapters are inclined to drag. One feels that one is faced with stiff reading, and whilst the spirit admires, the flesh suggests skipping. Let it be said at once that perseverance will be its own reward. There is an ever-growing fascination about this story of a woman's single-handed struggle with life in the wilds of Queen Elizabeth County, Virginia.

[...]

George B. Dutton, "The *Atlantic*'s Bookshelf," *Atlantic Monthly*, 136 (August 1925), 10

It is perhaps unfortunate that title and publisher's announcement combine with the sombre woodcut on the jacket to give the impression that *Barren Ground* is a Virginia specimen of the pastoral novel, twentieth-century style, exploiting tillers of the soil who are almost indistinguishable from their cattle, following with sordid gratification their lives of grunting drudgery relieved by bestial loves. 'Realism has crossed the Potomac,' the advertisement proclaims. However, realism is an elastic term. In truth Miss Glasgow does not ignore the narrowness and deprivations that condition existence on secluded, worn-out farms in the back districts of the Old Dominion. She has fashioned no sugary idyll. But shining through her account of sun-blackened fields and sagging houses and drooping workers is the genuinely beautiful story of Dorinda Oakley, who through disillusionment and misfortune learned to bend adverse circumstances to her indomitable purpose.

"No matter how hard it is, I've got to go through with it," Dorinda would mutter to herself as dream after dream crashed; until she came to see, in the words of the author, "that as long as she could rule her own mind, she was not afraid of the forces without." So from a girl in an orange-colored shawl, wistfully yearning for romance, she developed into a middle-aged woman who faced the future without, indeed, romantic expectancy, but with spiritual integrity and vision. Through intelligent effort the barren ground of human nature had been made productive.

Clearly this is not the record of a biological entity rooting and grubbing in instinctive fulfillment of racial destiny, but the history of what it may still be permissible to call a soul. Dorinda is the embodiment of a noble conception, and the narrative of her experiences is one of pith and movement. Realistic in the sense that it does not in general exclude the trivial or the ugly, it is founded on values and attains to a luminosity that are absent from most realistic fiction.

There are, to be sure, puzzling opaque

patches in the book. These are not, however, the result of devotion to fact, but, rather, unaccountable lapses into conventionality in the usually veracious record. It is as if suddenly the writer's imagination had flagged, her grasp on actuality had relaxed, and in desperation she had fastened upon the old reliable devices to bridge awkward situations. To transport a heroine to New York only to have her run over in a crowded street puts no strain upon credulity. To have her rescued by a surgeon whose unique skill saves her life, and whose generosity enables her to start the rehabilitation of her father's family, is an evasion of responsibility. Again, the stress laid upon Dorinda's material success distracts attention from her spiritual triumph. Alfalfa and butter are inadequate and superfluous symbols of the soul's victory. In short, the novel lacks complete integration.

Yet, when so much has been vouchsafed, complaint seems ungracious. It is more just to dwell upon excellences. Miss Glasgow has told a story of meagre lives and shown the possibility of inner enrichment and growth. She has traced the happenings of humdrum years and revealed their underlying significance. She has turned her back upon gold lace and shining swords and tender vows, and has found the true romance amid the dust and mud of a little Southern farm, in the heart of a girl who came to see the challenge to courage and the call to high adventure in the homely duties of life.

Checklist of Additional Reviews

Edward Allen Cleaton, "Miss Glasgow's Greatest Study of Life," Richmond *News Leader*, 15 April 1925, p. 8.

Ruth Snyder, "A Story of the New South," Huntington [West Virginia] *Advertiser*, 20 April 1925.

Virginia McCormick, Norfolk *Virginian Pilot*, 26 April 1925, sec. 1, p. 6.

Louise Collier Willcox, "Miss Glasgow's Novel," *New York Times Book Review*, 26 April 1925, p. 26 (letter to the editor).

"Try This Book This Week," New Orleans *States*, 26 April 1925, sec. 3, p. 4.

Edmund Fitzgerald, "A Woman's Pilgrimage from Romance to Reality," *Literary Digest International Book Review*, May 1925, 376, 378.

Stuart P. Sherman, "Edge of Romance," Minneapolis *Journal*, 3 May 1925 (reprinted from *New York Herald Tribune Books*, 9 April 1925, sec. 5, pp. 1–3).

John W. Crawford, "No Frailty in Fiction," New York *World*, 10 May 1925, sec. M, p. 4.

Charlotte *Observer*, 10 May 1925, p. 9.

Birmingham *Age Herald*, 10 May 1925, p. 10 (reprinted from Greensboro *Daily News*, 3 May 1925, sec. 2, p. 4).

R.D. Townsend, "Six Important Novels," *Outlook*, 140 (13 May 1925), 68.

S. Morgan-Powell, "A Conquest of Life," Montreal *Star*, 23 May 1925.

"Barren Ground," Louisville *Courier-Journal*, 31 May 1925.

"Fiction," *Booklist*, 21 (June 1925), 340.

Ida Wolffson, "Power Surges in *Barren Ground*," Forth Worth *Star-Telegram*, 14 June 1925.

Grant Overton, "Have You Read—?" *Collier's*, 75 (20 June 1925), 45.

Louise Collier Willcox, "Four Distinguished Novels," *Virginia Quarterly Review*, 1 (July 1925), 261–71.

Open Shelf, July 1925, p. 81.

Birmingham [England] *Gazette*, 2 July 1925, p. 4.

Anne Nicholas, Indianapolis *Star*, 5 July 1925, sec. 4, p. 32.

Louis J. McQuilland, *GK's Weekly* [England], 1 (11 July 1925), 381.

"New Novel," Inverness [Scotland] *Courier*, 14 July 1925, p. 3.

Methodist Recorder [England], 16 July 1925, p. 12.

"Soil Ennobles a Story," *Public Opinion* [England], 17 July 1925, p. 64 (excerpt from *Observer*, 5 July 1925, p. 4).

Aberdeen (Scotland) *Press and Journal*, 20 July 1925, p. 2.

G.G., "Ellen Glasgow, a Novelist," Holyoke [Massachusetts] *Transcript*, 28 July 1925, sec. 1, p. 6.

"Book Gossip," Beckenham [England] *Journal*, 1 August 1925, p. 4.

"A Remarkable Heroine," Nottingham [England] *Guardian*, 1 August 1925, p. 6.

Daily News [England], 10 August 1925.

"*Barren Ground* Magnificent Work," Manchester [New Hampshire] *Union*, 17 August 1925, p. 7.

"Briefer Mention," *Dial*, 79 (September 1925), 260.

Elizabeth Lay Green, *Reviewer*, 5 (October 1925), 118–19.

"Some of the Year's Best Fiction," *American Review of Reviews and World's Work*, 72 (December 1925), 667–8.

Nelson Antrium Crawford, "The American Farmer in Fact and Fiction," *Literary Digest International Book Review*, 4 (January 1926), 101.

THE ROMANTIC COMEDIANS

The Romantic Comedians

by
Ellen Glasgow

Published by
DOUBLEDAY, PAGE & CO.
GARDEN CITY, N. Y.
1926

A. Hamilton Gibbs, "Victorian Group Contrasted with One of Present Day in Attitude Toward Sex," *New York Evening Post Literary Review*, 11 September 1926, sec. 3, p. 4

What May Sinclair did for a Vicar in the *Cure of Souls* Ellen Glasgow does for a Judge in *The Romantic Comedians*, with this difference, that to the dissection of an elderly gentleman she has added the oldest French plot in the world, that of *le cocu*. At the hands of the French it has received treatment varying from simple filth to academic psychology, and it goes without saying that Miss Ellen Glasgow has subscribed to the latter method.

The Romantic Comedians is a study in contrasts, whose purpose is to show in the light of today the remnants of a group born in the eighteen sixties, emphasis being laid upon their attitude toward sex. The older group is represented first of all by the Judge who, having buried his devoted wife of thirty-six years' standing, is in that state of encroaching decrepitude when the last dying kicks of the old Adam obsess him to the exclusion of all else. His wealth purchases for him a young wife, a girl of twenty-three, a post-war girl to whom the Victorian shams are hateful and who insists on calling a spade a spade. She is allowed to retain enough Victorianism, however, to exclaim that if she doesn't find love she will die! And when she finds it she goes through an orgy of tears and despair before she runs away with it that would have done credit to any Cranford Miss. The others in the eighteen-sixty group consist of two women—one whose engagement to the Judge thirty-six years ago was broken off in a lovers' quarrel and who has remained in a state of arrested virginity ever since; the other the Judge's twin sister, who in her day stood for what the post-war girl does now, having thrown her bonnet over the mill and having triumphantly survived no less than four husbands in Europe and an apocryphal number of lovers. At the opening of the story she is enjoyably living upon her reputation.

Miss Glasgow's gently satirical picture of the older group is, of course, exactly paralleled in the younger one, and the comedy which Miss Glasgow wishes to show is that the present generation, despite a few differences of definition, fools itself in exactly the same way as the last.

It is all very light and amusing and extremely well written. But after *Barren Ground* it seems like a literary holiday. There is something completely unreal in the atmosphere of today as represented by the girl and the things she does. She is so much an anachronism that it is impossible to believe that the World War ever took place, and consequently it is equally impossible to convince oneself that the older group is still alive. Furthermore, it weakens immeasurably the point as to both generations being fundamentally the same.

Those aspects of the book are, however, secondary. The primary feature is the drawing of the Judge and it is for that that Miss Glasgow deserves praise. Unlike the French authors, she has not made him a figure of fun. She has made him rather a figure of tragedy. He is the eternal man, struggling unsuccessfully with his own nature, blundering pathetically along the way of life, accepting the second best only, because the best is always unattainable, always just beyond his reach if not beyond his vision. Those would-be noble lines, the offspring of deluded desire: "I am the master of my fate, the captain of my soul!" have no place in Miss Glasgow's philosophy. Her man is rightly a piece of driftwood in the sea of his own passions and her depiction of the learned Judge after a long and dignified career hoodwinking himself as naively as any inexperienced youth is a far more true conception than that of the poet.

It is unfortunate that the book lacks the perfecting balance of the modern half. Given the equally vivid presentation of the girl and her lover, it would have been an added leaf in Miss Glasgow's crown of bays.

Gerald W. Johnson, Baltimore *Evening Sun*, 11 September 1926, p. 6

To anyone capable of appreciating craftsmanship publication of a new novel by Ellen Glasgow is always an important event, but the technical competence of this writer never counted for more than in the book which Doubleday, Page & Co. brought out yesterday. *The Romantic Comedians*, indeed, is almost a novelists' novel. It is altogether a novel for highly civilized readers, for considerable knowledge of the world is requisite to any sort of comprehension of its excellence.

The thesis of the book is that adage in which so much of the accumulated wisdom of the race is compressed: "There is no fool like an old fool." Judge Honeywell is a gentleman of fine culture, a jurisconsult of distinction, an honest man and an idiot; but as to the characteristic last named, he endures no unenviable eminence, for so, in the last analysis, are we all. Judge Honeywell demonstrates his incompetence, which is spiritual rather than mental, by his inability to apprehend the reality that a man of 65 is definitely out of the realm of youth. He does not wish to be old, therefore he decides that he is not old, and the romantic comedy that results from that decision is the story.

The quality of the book is involved in the fact that it is a comedy. The judge's life is devastated, his vanity is shattered, his home is wrecked, in the ordinary parlance of novelists, his heart is broken. In the cage of ironic destiny he bruises himself against the bars in vain; but Miss Glasgow achieves the design of the Mikado to

Make each prisoner pent
Unwillingly represent
A source of innocent merriment,
Of innocent merriment.

Does it sound ghastly? Well, it isn't, really, except to schoolboy minds. Remember, this is comedy, not burlesque. It is comedy written by one of the coolest, clearest minds among the writers of the country. Miss Glasgow holds no brief for any of her characters. She is utterly aloof, utterly detached, interested only in the exact delineation of each successive actor upon her stage. This necessarily means that she is not antagonistic to any of her people. She is profoundly convinced that "men (and, she adds, women) have died and worms have eaten them, but not for love." It follows that romantic heartbreak is essentially amusing, but she recognizes that, like any other practical joke, it is not likely to amuse the victim.

She recognizes something more. It is brought out in the concluding paragraph of the book, when the old judge after his disastrous essay into the sort of amorous adventure that only youth is able to carry off successfully lies bedridden, beaten down, all but killed by inexorable reality, apparently a complete wreck, apparently done for. Then suddenly one realizes that it is April and that he is casting an appraising eye upon his comely nurse. With that the book ends.

It is a delicious finale of a hilarious comedy, but it is something more. Even in his idiocy the old boy is indomitable. After all, the best laid plans of mice and men as often as not are follies as grotesque as Judge Honeywell's love affairs, but the life of the spirit that will not fail as long as life shall last is not grotesque. Even in these silly mortals, whose tragedies are fantastic, whose agonies are absurd, there is a spark that Noah's flood cannot quench, a resistance that the engines of Destiny cannot break until the man himself is dead.

In admitting this Miss Glasgow has come closer to realism than all the woeful painters in India ink. It makes of her comedy high comedy, the sort that walks delicately upon the verge of tears.

Joseph Collins, "Ellen Glasgow's New Novel a Tragedy of Old Age," *New York Times Book Review*, 12 September 1926, sec. 3, p. 5

Miss Glasgow's new novel, *The Romantic Comedians* is the essence of the tragedy of old age. She has developed a theme rarely attacked by the novelist, and she has done it with such keen understanding and comprehensive psychology that her characters, acting without false gesture, follow logically their inevitable destiny and behave as real people would were they in similar predicaments and situations. The result is a fine story which leaves a taste of reality, of sincerity, of substantiality.

One of our delusions is that tragedies of love and moral upheavals generally belong to youth; old age is looked upon as a haven of rest, safely distant from mental earthquakes and sentimental chaos, as a period of calm after the storms of youth and adolescence. Physiologists have known for a long time that the heart is the ultima moriens in man, but novelists have yet to learn it. The sapient Hebrew prophets and historiographers knew it, but modern chroniclers of behavior have forgotten it. When King David was old and stricken in years and neither clothes nor food got him heat, the fair damsel Abishag was sought and found.

The pathos of old men is in the disproportion that exists between their love-hunger and their capacity to satisfy it. Though the desire to crack nuts does not desert a man after his teeth have fallen, he can transfer it to softer foods. But the need of love, the necessity of giving and receiving it, the indomitable impulse in man to pretend to himself that he has lost none of his capacity to commune with a beloved one, soul and body, that is not, and seemingly cannot be sublimated in old age. In some men, sometimes in the most far-seeing and judicious ones, it becomes an obsession no longer appeasable by bodily satisfaction.

That was Judge Honeywell's pathetic predicament. After more than thirty-five years of married life, the Judge was left a widower. His wife had been too perfect to be entertaining, too steeped in virtue to allow humor to enter their life, too intent on her husband's welfare to give heed to her own. Now that she was dead, devotion to her memory carried him to her grave every week that he might cover it with flowers.

[...]

Successful as Miss Glasgow has been with all the characters in the novel, her Judge is above praise for his human and plausible behavior. He is so realistic in substance that we seem to have known him in the flesh. He is in the pure tradition of the South, where he had his fullest development and his rankest growth, nourished by Southern sentimentality; he attempted to fight his inheritance, he refused to bow the head to emotional conventions, and he was set on finding his pleasure where less tradition-bound men find it: in the complete surrender to his instinct, far from his heritage of romance and idealism. It may be argued that the charm and irresistible attraction he found in Annabel showed that he was blind to reality, a slave to romance. Had he been truly an idealist, he would have reverted to Amanda, especially after Annabel's desertion of him and firm refusal ever to return to him. Fundamentally, the Judge was a man: he deluded himself into believing that Annabel's soul was pure and that he wanted her for her moral qualities; in reality, he thought her limbs were gracious and he loved to watch her undress. He may be the traditional Southern gentleman, but he is also the embodiment of all of Adam's descendants, and he is as quick to forsake "tradition" as a snake is its skin when it comes in conflict with his primitive urge. Amanda is the only typically Southern character in the book; her type was exceptional even in Queenborough, where her conduct excited comment and elicited praise given only to unusual feats: her gait was resolute, her tradition unshaken, but the type became extinct with her.

[...]

Where has the vaunted Southern sentimentality gone in this novel? The way it has gone in reality, beyond reach of time or of sighs, the way the traditional South is fast going. If Judge Honeywell had been the traditional Southerner, his sense of chivalry, his respect for virtue, and his admiration for Amanda's sentimentality would have made him turn to her, especially after Annabel's gesture. The old man in him would have been blind to the nurse's elusive charm and he would have required the more effective comfort of Amanda's presence. Indeed, it was tempting to bring the book to a close on such a note, it would have been in the true tradition of Southern novelists; but Miss Glasgow is a disciple of reality, anxious to depict life as she knows it to be, rather than as she might wish it to be, universal in her scope rather than limited in her appeal, and she could not make her Judge spoil his texture by reverting to Amanda, even the second time. That is where the strength and power of the book lay: Honeywell married to Amanda would have been no story at all, and a false gesture. It would have been slow death in a deadly atmosphere.

There are passages in *The Romantic Comedians* to which students of behavior will revert when they wish to understand the psychology of old men: one of them is the dream the Judge has after taking a thimbleful of old Bumgartner; the images that pass before his eyes, the desires that smile at him on their way to the clouds, the reaching out of his arms toward what he thought was half woman and half dream, and proved to be all woman, all these are told in great simplicity and powerful style. So is the slow but inevitable realization of Judge Honeywell's inadequacy to play up to Annabel: no one can read of his struggles, of his ineffective though willing and eager adjustment to her stride, of his giving up everything that had spelled happiness for him in order to make her happy, without a surge of sympathy toward him; Annabel was not worth it, perhaps; indeed she was selfish, self-centred, materialistic and romantic all at once, shallow and bent on getting her own way and catering to her own emotions. Leaving her at that is sufficient, she neither deserved nor needed our compassion, although Miss Glasgow seems anxious that we should like her. She stresses her qualities of fairness and her horror of shams of any sort, but it is difficult to believe that Annabel did not know her marriage was a sham when she contracted it. Neither remorse nor gratitude prompted her to different behavior toward her husband. The physical repugnance she experienced for him explains much; but Annabel was no angel: she had been in love, she had experienced physical amorous feelings, so she knew before she married the Judge that he was as incapable of thrilling her as Amanda was of thrilling him. It was the price she had to pay for luxury and a future; but she was not solvent and had no desire to be.

Women readers of *The Romantic Comedians* will wish to atone for Annabel's deceit; men will think they would have been wiser than the Judge. The laws of nature are not to be put down in black and white, and the desire of the moth for the star, of the night for the morrow, is not a poet's fancy; it is a reality which supersedes sentimentality and romance.

Epigrammatic in style, ironic in flavor, sustained in intensity, *The Romantic Comedians* makes us think of Joseph Conrad, of his homily and justification of youth; we think of "Youth! All youth! The silly, charming, beautiful youth," of the strength, the romance, the glamour of youth. What he has done for youth, in making us understand and love it, Miss Glasgow has done for old age in winning our sympathy for it and reminding us of its feebleness, sadness, drabness, inherent loneliness and pathetic tragedy.

Carl Van Vechten, "A Virginia Lady Dissects a Virginia Gentleman," *New York Herald Tribune Books*, 12 September 1926, p. 1

It will be with keen delight, I fancy, that Miss Glasgow's earlier admirers, and many new ones, will peruse the finely wrought pages of her latest book, so reasonably entitled *The Romantic Comedians*. It has been the convenient custom to divide the novels of this author into two groups: in the one she is described as serious realist, in the other as satirist. There is some justification for this arbitrary classification, although a careful reader will find abundance of irony in *Barren Ground* and sufficient realism in the treatment of *The Romantic Comedians*. Her new book, however, may fairly be put under this heading of social satire, and I meticulously refrain from prefixing the epithet gentle. High-spirited would be a more accurate adjective. There is even, on occasion, a touch of that deliberate and graceful malice which decorates the drawing-room conversation of a woman of the world. I may offer as an appropriate example the description of the attitude of the youth of Queenborough (Miss Glasgow's euphemism for Richmond) toward Edmonia Bredalbane, returned from Europe at a ripe sixty-five to rest on her laurels for gallantry. These young people "clustered about her," Miss Glasgow reports, "in candid pursuit of some esoteric wisdom of sex.... They treated her scarlet letter less as the badge of shame than as some foreign decoration for distinguished service."

This rare quality—rare, at least, in fiction writers—of malicious, feminine wit hovers over this volume as beneficently as the redolent bouquet of *fine champagne 1812* rises from the depths of a crystal goblet. Always feminist in her point of view, Miss Glasgow has observed that the male is the vainer sex, and she has taken a particular pleasure (a pleasure which any reader will share, even a man of sixty-five, for he will be too vain to confuse his own case with that of Judge Honeywell) in dissecting the insides of an elderly gentleman who believed himself capable of enlisting and holding the affections of a particularly high-strung girl of twenty-three, merely because she had entered the matrimonial state with him. The reader assists at the gradual disillusionment of this elderly gentleman. Nevertheless, although it is certainly not Miss Glasgow's intention to waste pity or sympathy on the ancient fellow, she is too much of an artist to be unjust to him. Romance, the confusion of passion with love, is the target of her ironic attack. She observes her wayward heroine with as keen an eye as that with which she regards her elderly gentleman. She has no illusions in regard to either of them. It is plain, however, that she would lead us to believe that the romantic conceit of masculine old age is at the same time sadder and more ridiculous than the romantic conceit of feminine youth.

There are, I fear, a few shocks in this book for those not yet acquainted with Miss Glasgow's honesty of purpose, already reflected in her previous novels, more especially for those who have grown up on the nightingale and "yes, massa" type of Southern fiction. To be sure, there are gardens and moonlight in *The Romantic Comedians*, the scent of lilies-of-the-valley, the shimmer of amethyst scarves over alabaster shoulders, but we are also informed that Southern gentlemen regard the copper arms of mulatto chamber-maids with amorous intensity—the expression of this obvious fact is almost a novelty in Nordic Southern fiction. Furthermore, we learn that even in Victorian days a lady might lose her virtue (I employ the word in its technical sense) several times in Paris without forfeiting caste in the eyes of the F. F. Vs. Moreover, the heroine of the tale takes leave of her ancient husband to satisfy her passionate desire for a young lover without the formality of demanding or even desiring a divorce. I have also noted how little inclined this author's Virginia characters are to read books. In this connection it must be admitted, however reluctantly, that Miss Glasgow may be considered an authority on the habits of Virginians.

If, indeed, Miss Glasgow continues to create these clarifying pictures of the characteristics of her native state, it will not be long before Virginians may be regarded as human beings (which, despite the novelists—one must, of course, except James Branch Cabell—a few of us have believed them to be all along) rather than as stilted puppets who, if they were men, held the somewhat vague ideal that the noblest form of human conduct was to behave like a Virginia gentleman and, if they were women, believed that to cling to a crinolined and unperfumed physical chastity (or to fidelity in marriage) was a Virginia lady's whole reason for existence. I daresay that Virginians will welcome this new light that is being thrown on their human aspects by a lady who loves Virginia sufficiently to have always made it her home. As for the outside world, it should, I think, be delighted by this witty, wise and delicious novel.

Hunter Stagg,
"*Romantic Comedians*:
Study of Modern Virginia
Society,"
Richmond *Times-Dispatch*,
19 September 1926,
sec. 3, p. 10

Miss Glasgow's new novel is about a widower of 65, who did not wish to marry the beautiful maiden of 58 who had waited for him, but quite naturally, being a man, preferred the vital young girl of 23 who hadn't. And so they were married, but I do not know that their story is intended as an argument against all marriages between elderly gentlemen and young girls. It is certainly, however, an argument against any elderly gentleman marrying a young girl like Annabel Upchurch.

For Annabel was temperamental and she saw in this state of being no cause for reserve, for all her sapiently helpless mother's fear that it would spoil her matrimonial prospects. Annabel was prone to fall in love, and she saw in this condition no subject for reticence for all the pain and embarrassment her confidences, as a jilted girl caused those of her elders who had spent their lives concerning similar tragedies. The most important thing in the world to Annabel was the way she felt, and the next most important thing was to spread as far as she could generous and exact accounts of the way she felt.

After that she recognized, with most of her generation, the supreme right of a feeling to be converted as soon as possible into action, regardless of the consequences to the feelings of others. To her the right to live was considerably more than a phrase, and inhibitions were a mere word. She was a very serious minded young person, this lovely, slight, lightly clad, madly dancing Annabel, and the things she was most serious about in her mind were, first, extracting the greatest amount of woe from her disappointment in love; and, second, enjoying to the fullest extent all the drama there was, in the discovery, through a new young man, that she had never loved before. What she was least serious about appeared to be her marriage, in the intervening blighted period, to the kind and wealthy old Judge Honeywell. Not that she wasn't kind to her husband.

It was just that he didn't seem to make much impression on her. He had done a great deal for her, and she was truly grateful, but—what was gratitude, what was consideration, what was conventionality, what indeed was anything when it became a question of doing right by the way one felt? From beginning to end Annabel took the greatest interest in, and had the greatest respect for the way she felt. And, for Annabel, to take an interest in a thing was to do something about it at once.

This newest heroine of Miss Glasgow's is a decided departure, but she takes rank immediately with the best of the long series of feminine portraits the Virginia author has given the world. Few writers have mingled such sympathetic understanding with unrelenting truth in dealing with this type of modern girl, few have presented so fairly and temperately the conditions which, seen as Miss Glasgow sees them, make it impossible to blame Annabel for the crude differences between herself and, say, Miss Amanda Lightfoot, whose conduct when jilted in her own youth was still admired by all and envied by none. Indeed there are more than one indications in the book that Miss Glasgow considers many of the differences to be all in favor of the modern girl.

So does the author seem to find many of the differences between the stately Miss Amanda and the judge's sister, Edmonia, wholly in favor of that disreputable woman, who had a vulgarity of speech—which was not a stranger to several of the best families, "and whose seeming improprieties were beginning to appear, in the light of newer valuations, as nothing less than strength of mind and character." This Edmonia, fat and gross after many indiscretions, more marriages, and much high living on the continent, is one of the most delightful of the many figures which Miss Glasgow has in this book skillfully used as ironic symbols to play, one upon the other, for the finer shading of her already exquisitely etched irony.

As for the judge, that poor dear, estimable old gentleman—well he convinces one that it was for no other reason than that Miss Glasgow possesses an uncomfortable [under]standing of men that Mr. Cabell called her a past mistress of parenthetical malice. *The Romantic Comedians*, in spite of the interest of the other characters, is after all entirely the judge's book, which is why one hates to say much of him in the short space of a review. Miss Glasgow has said so much and said it so subtly, so amusingly, and with such masterful artistry, that it would be a shame to offer a mangled summary of her portrait of this man. Although, *The Romantic Comedians*, as a study of conflicting characters, and also as a study of modern Virginian social life, is a book of deep penetration and large significance. It is also a promise, which many will welcome, that Miss Glasgow is going to give even more freedom in the future to that strong ironic vein which has always flavored her work. More power to it.

Henry Seidel Canby, "The Moth and the Flame," *Saturday Review of Literature*, 3 (25 September 1926), 133

There is still such a thing, thank heaven, as civilized novels which are neither stale nor dull. Amidst acrobatic experiments in syncopated narrative and sophisticated refinements of saying too much well, they do not get their due from the knowing ones of the bookish world who are too busy with adolescence or decadence to waste time in maturity. Yet they are still being written, and are likely to remain as the most satisfying replica of our culture. For no matter how jazzed the age or how incoherent the philosophy of a new time, the men and women who do more than drift giggling, weeping, or moaning upon the rapid current will be subjects for a narrative more solid than impressionism and more significant than a reporter's tale.

Yet to qualify for the civilized novel requires a good deal more than taste and control of the medium; in fact the merely cultivated novel is, and always has been, one of seven deadly bores of literature. The novelist must have everything of insight, fire, awareness, originality that the boldest experimenter or the wildest rhapsodist possesses, and be able to turn them all to the uses of interpretative art. This is not too weighty a preface to introduce so distinguished a novel as Miss Glasgow's *Romantic Comedians*.

I know that "distinguished" threatens to become one of those "reviewer's words" which carry a hint of exaggerated praise or perfunctory exaggeration, but I am using the word in its specific sense of successful differentiation. Miss Glasgow, whose last book had power without great distinction, has here taken that ancient situation, the old man's darling, and with ease and mounting strength of story lifted it out of Virginia, out of pathos, out of satire into a breathing portrait that is as modern as it is human.

The old have had a bad time of it in recent literature. No one takes them seriously; especially when they are passionate. "Wicked old men" and crusted or absurd old women have held the stage. It has been youth's fling in literature. What is choice in Miss Glasgow's novel is her equal grasp of the ironic pathos that waits upon both youth and age. *The Romantic Comedians* is indeed an old man's story, the story of Judge Honeywell, perfect product of Virginia Victorianism, but it is his story only because of his passion for his twenty-three year old wife, and her passion given elsewhere, her repugnance, her sacred egoism, her irony could have no better advocate and mouthpiece if the novel were dedicated to the frustration of youth. The judge has endured for thirty-six years "the double-edged bliss of a perfect marriage," he has put far behind him an earlier passion of his youth for Amanda, the perfect product of Virginia Victorianism in its feminine aspect, who waits for him now, still regretting, still hoping. But he seeks youth as Ponce de Leon the spring, humbly, rewarded for a thousand sacrifices by a single lovely emanation, and is frustrated and abases himself and still the intoxicant he cannot drink dazzles his judgment, sweeps everything but his principles aside.

John Farrar, "The Editor Recommends," *Bookman*, 64 (October 1926), 223

Ellen Glasgow is rapidly stealing May Sinclair's crown. *The Romantic Comedians* ... is one of the most difficult of stories to write: the love of a man over sixty for a girl slightly over twenty. Yet the gentle satire, the pungent wit, the amazing facility of this great artist, make it plausible and never disagreeable, unless, indeed, Miss Glasgow wishes it to be so. A great book. It is lighter in key than *Barren Ground*, yet its depth is the same. Every page has its quotable gem, sly observations of human frailty caught in unforgettable phrases. "Like most lawyers," she writes of her aged hero, "and all vestrymen, he was able to believe automatically quite a number of things which he knew were not true." I repeat, a great book!

"The Benefit of Malice," in "The Roving Critic," *Century Magazine*, 112 (October 1926), 764–5

In *The Romantic Comedians* by Ellen Glasgow, on the other hand, the atmosphere is as clear as a desert's. Gamaliel Honeywell, a learned Virginia judge, finds himself at sixty-five a widower, with love, not malaria, restless in his blood. There is a woman, Amanda Lightfoot, of suitable years, who has, after jilting him before his marriage, waited for him like a virgin Penelope. But the love he once felt for her has never grown up in its notions of what constitutes charm in a woman, and he courts and wins, thanks to his wealth, a disappointed girl of twenty-three. No novelist needs more than this situation to make a drama. Tragedy comes speedily to mind, and farce. Miss Glasgow has preferred to keep her action on the difficult level of ironic comedy. Her sense of justice increases the difficulty of the task. Judge Honeywell might be called an old fool, but Miss Glasgow does not call him that. She knows he has been made into what he is by the traditional nonsense of chivalry, the local habit of gentility, and the natural tendency of aging men who hanker too hopefully for their irrecoverable fires, to mistake for spontaneous desire what is only a sentimental reminiscence. And as she treats him justly, so does she treat Amanda, who prefers patience to experience, and the Judge's sister Edmonia, who has had far more experience than patience, and the young wife Annabel, who, without either patience or experience, understands what she wants and how to get it, for the simple reason that she has but one authentic impulse in her. All these are so expertly balanced in the action that the clash appears to be taking place in nature, almost without the interposition of any artist. The result is the more striking because Miss Glasgow has let loose in her latest novel, as she has never done before, the energy of her amused malice. Fortunately that malice is not a lightning which darkens in the intervals of its illumination. It is, rather, a scalpel, delicately cutting away what does not belong where it is or what has ceased to be useful. It is a sharp intelligence exhibiting passions which to the actors are confused but to the auditors are comprehensible. To do that both intelligence and art are necessary. *The Romantic Comedians* is, like most of Miss Glasgow's books, somewhat longer than it had to be, but it is the best of them all since *Virginia*, and in several respects is better than *Virginia* itself.

Harry Esty Dounce, "A Really Fine Novel by Ellen Glasgow," *New Yorker*, 2 (2 October 1926), 88–9

In Ellen Glasgow's *The Romantic Comedians*, this department does not see the "death-blow" to southern chivalry that others are seeing. Neither, we would wager, does Miss Glasgow, for Judge Honeywell is not southern chivalry, except incidentally. He is an old-school sentimental romantic, of a stamp by no means peculiar to the South; and although the antiquation of the sentiments he shares is one of Miss Glasgow's themes, her main one is the universal comedy, and tragedy, of the Evergreen Heart, as Shaw's John Underwear Tarleton would term it, when it beats in the breast of a scrupulous, strictly inhibited, aging gentleman.

What we do see in *The Romantic Comedians* is a really fine novel worth dozens of its author's *Barren Ground*, and we deny that our preference is due to a prejudice in favor of gentility. *Barren Ground* was ambitiously planned and rather majestically written, and therefore (or so this department will believe to its dying day) nearly all reviewers and critics played safe, acclaiming a Big Achievement, in the face of the fact that some parts were just bad and nine-tenths of the whole was tiresome.

Nothing is tiresome this time, and if anything is bad, it is a tendency they have once or twice to converse on stilts; but that doesn't grow serious. Every character is well understood, and gets due, and not excessive, sympathy; everything rings true, much is searching, much touching; the end in particular is too good to spoil it for you by describing it.

Joanne Rosamond Milner, "The Literary Lantern," Louisville *Courier-Journal*, 10 October 1926, sec. 3, p. 7

There is but one statement with which to start this pillar of cloud and that is a bit of solemn advice: Read Ellen Glasgow's *Romantic Comedians*. Stuart Sherman some time ago hailed Miss Glasgow as "the brainiest woman in the South," and went on to say that "the whole range of her fiction constitutes our broadest and most searchingly intelligent picture of the Southern scene and the emerging spirit of the new South." And this new South emerges with a vengeance in *The Romantic Comedians*! It is, we feel certain, the book which Miss Glasgow mentioned to us sometime back as a "romantic (or rather ironic) comedy of the modern South—the South of 1925." Different from most of this author's earlier work, it marks a victory in a new field—light, easy-moving, sly, satire. The romantic comedians were happiness hunters, holding to the illusion that love and happiness were the same thing. In her presentation of a 65 year-old lover and his 23 year-old bride, Miss Glasgow has plenty of opportunity to exercise her wit and irony. It is all great fun if the reader can just separate himself from the romantic tradition and sentimental maudlinism.

R. D. Townsend, "Three New Novels," *Outlook*, 144 (20 October 1926), 252–3

The fading of romance is rather a favorite theme in Miss Glasgow's novels. In her *Romantic Comedians* we find it approached partly from the satirical and partly from the sorrowful side. The dignified elderly Judge who is so ill-advised as to marry a charming young girl does in a measure win our sympathy, but we never forget that this is a case of "no fool like an old fool." His sister, who boasts of her four husbands, and enjoys the scandalous aroma that clings to her past, neither amuses nor edifies; she is there to stand for the gross conception of love as hilarity and indulgence. The sweet old maid who has loved the Judge all her life stands for the essentially unembodied romanticism of the old era. The young wife is the modern girl; she is not restrained from following the leading of passion despite her genuine gratitude to and regard for her elderly husband. Not one of the characters appeals to one as does Dorinda in *Barren Ground*, who picks up the threads of her life after the crash of her romance and becomes an efficient, friendly, useful citizen. *Barren Ground* was not scattering satire like this new story, but a fine study of courage and womanliness. For that reason it is the stronger and more wholesome book.

On the other hand, we find here glitter of epigram and cleverness. Of one lady we are told that "she is so noble that she creaks," of the sex in general that "the only trouble with perfect ladies is that they lie as perfectly as they behave." Men come off poorly—the Judge is a gentleman, the others are shadows. Of husbands we are told, "Every woman has to choose between a young husband who is seldom there when you want him and an elderly one who is always there when you don't want him." Of the Judge's once too gay but now elderly sister it is asserted that young people "treated her scarlet letter less as the badge of shame than as some foreign decoration for distinguished service." This last bitter touch indicates that the author, after all, may be at heart on the side of romantic sentiment rather than that of modern obstreperousness.

Christopher Morley, "The Bowling Green," *Saturday Review of Literature*, 3 (30 October 1926), 255

There can be no doubt in my mind that the two most exciting books I've read lately are Ellen Glasgow's *The Romantic Comedians* and William Bolitho's *Murder for Profit*. Miss Glasgow's novel is one of those phenomena curiously rare in America, a really witty book. We have in this country a huge putting-out of able books, smart books, buffoon books, conscientious books; even of charming, beautiful, and moving books. But that cruel and exquisite aroma known as wit is specially infrequent. There are half a dozen younger writers who are conscientiously supposed, by their publishers, to be the cream and bubble of mulled vinegar: it is odd to see how extraordinarily turbid and thick they appear alongside the acid elixir of Miss Glasgow's book. I must make my hard confession: I had always respected Miss Glasgow, and had believed her work to be important, meritorious, and worthy. But respectfulness is the dullest of all feelings and I discard it forever. I can see that she is adorable. Also it is something more than a witty book, it is wise and humane, written with full judgment and a skill as supple as dainty steel. It is perfectly crystallized without knots or strings. It contains also the most cunningly amusing "line" in recent fiction, which I should not dream of quoting.

Dorothea Lawrance Mann, "Ellen Glasgow: Citizen of the World," *Bookman*, 64 (November 1926), 265–71

[...]

Yet granting all the things which Ellen Glasgow has done to the southern gentleman—and indeed the pricks of her rapier must have left him in sore case!—she has surpassed herself in her new novel, *The Romantic Comedians*. It may not be her greatest novel, but I have a strong suspicion that it is her most brilliant. The swift passes of her rapier dazzle us and her irony is fathomless. Moreover the deadliest quality of her thrust comes from the fact that this time she has made her realism an international affair. Judge Honeywell may have acquired his manners in that state which found "the school for gentlemen" a prouder title than "the mother of presidents," but Judge Honeywell's propensity for finding springtime in his aging heart cannot be limited to time or place. Possibly nowhere except in romantic Virginia could an Amanda have cherished a hopeless passion for one man while so many equally eligible men were seeking to comfort her. Not in Virginia alone, however, do men of sixty refuse the suitable marriage with the woman who has waited faithfully for them. It is realistic and quite disillusioning that Judge Honeywell as a widower should look upon his loving Amanda as too old for marriage. "An object of respect was far from being the partner with whom you would prefer to dance." They do not make women like Amanda now, he reflects sadly, as he turns his eyes and heart to Annabel, one of those modern young girls "without corsets and without conversation."

Ellen Glasgow harries all these good Virginians with their smug little conceptions of life, for she is one of the few novelists of whom the psychologists heartily approve. She does not even respect our October judge whose love is all gentleness. What has gentleness to do with love, we find her reflecting scornfully, while the marriage fails and the incorrigibly gallant judge once more puts his lips to the intoxicating spring of youth!

Mary Ross, "Squirming Romantics," *Nation*, 123 (3 November 1926), 456–7

Manners, and their ethical equivalent, morals, are a pathetic witness of mankind's hope of certainty. "We will have an eternal verity," says the moralist. "Or at least rules of the game, by which all decent people abide," says the mannerist. So simple it would be if we could freeze a smooth crust over thought and action, across which to skate in premeditated ease. But woe to the skaters—for life, flowing on below the specious solidity, works a treacherous hole here and there; or the spring freshets come and all once more is confusion. From slapstick up the intellectual game of comedy is to catch the slothfully trusting spirit when it has been lulled to trust in some formula and show that life itself is nimbler, surer, tougher than our presumptuous expectations.

It is such a game that Miss Glasgow plays in *The Romantic Comedians*. Judge Gamaliel Bland Honeywell stands in the pale Easter sunlight at the grave of his Cordelia and feels a suspicious fluttering in his heart; behind him lie the sixty-five temperate, ordered years of living which have preserved his figure and his digestion; before him the wayward spring and Annabel with small heart-shaped face, pale gold freckles, and geranium mouth. And all about lies the simple sophistication of Queenborough, Virginia. It would be so suitable, Queenborough feels, if Judge Honeywell should console his widowed state, after a decent interval, with Miss Amanda Lightfoot, the passion of his youth, from whom he was parted by an absurd lovers' quarrel thirty-seven years ago. Miss Lightfoot, miraculously preserved in the regal splendor of a reigning belle, feels so herself in so far as a lady can feel at such a point. She has always worn blue and lavender, because they were Gamaliel's favorite colors before that silly misunderstanding cast him, on the rebound, into the arms of the virtuous Cordelia. But now, as Annabel discovers, Gamaliel's favorite colors are red and green. Suitability happens to be that last thing that will stir Judge Honeywell's heart this rebellious spring. He even cannot suppress the suspicion that when all is said, he hadn't wanted a perfect wife; he desires, contrary to both custom and reason, the things which are not good for him—the excitement of novelty, the ringing challenge of youth.

Judge Honeywell had put a fatal trust in suitability, and Amanda in faithfulness, and Annabel in passion. For Annabel of the direct younger generation is no less romantic than her faded elders, and Miss Glasgow spares none of the absurdities of her tragic renunciation of love after the defection of a youthful suitor; her resigned marriage to Judge Honeywell; and her impassioned and histrionic flight with the inevitable eligible young man, who comes by to rescue her from the position of an old man's folly. The joke is on them all—an essentially civilized, humane joke, which takes account of the fact that these are no automatons jerked hither and yonder by chance; no puppets of crude sex, but people forced to hold up their heads in the current of experience which rushes them along.

It is almost impossible to resist quoting from the smooth and sparkling pages in which Miss Glasgow turns her kind, amused gaze on one after another of the squirming romantics. Both dialogue and analysis are full of sentences that seem too good to be true, and yet are so truly a part of the fabric of the book—no mere wisecracks—that they can hardly be torn from their setting. The remarks of Judge Honeywell's loose and liberal sister Edmonia, for example.

It is this Edmonia, who followed her own realistic ways with head as well as heart, who alone seems able to get beyond the rose and purple mists of romanticism which have betrayed the rest. "You could have forgiven my committing a sin," she says to Gamaliel, "if you hadn't feared that I had committed a pleasure as well.... It wasn't my fault, it was my being able to get up again, that you couldn't forgive.... You know I always had what mother used to call a pleasure-loving mind, and I never approved of the sour kind of duty you pretend to enjoy. On the contrary, I've always believed that happiness, any kind of happiness that does not make someone else miserable, is meritorious."

The Romantic Comedians is a wise and witty book.

William Lyon Phelps, "When Crabbed Age Marries Blooming Youth," *Literary Digest International Book Review*, 4 November 1926, 749

The new novel by Ellen Glasgow might well be regarded as an illustration of a remark by Turgenev, "For every age love has its tortures." In *The Romantic Comedians* there is only one happy person—the author. The leading characters suffer from unsatisfied and repressed desires, but their extremity is the novelist's opportunity. Especially is this true of the hero, Judge Honeywell, sixty-five years old, a decorous and irreproachable widower, who quite naturally, tho idiotically, falls in love with a young girl, and, as a natural result, is happy neither with nor without her. The reader spends most of the 346 pages inside the Judge's mind, a smoldering inferno. Altho the Judge and his young wife and her mother and the Victorian virgin (still and always in love with him) are all miserable, the novelist is happy. Here is a subject made to her hand, and she thoroughly enjoys dealing with it, which she does in a manner both honest and artistic. Given these people and this environment, one feels that the results set forth here are inevitable.

Life is a serious and difficult game, and unfortunately is often played by fools, who not only play it badly, but are ignorant of the rules.

The tragedies of love might to a considerable extent be avoided by either of the following arrangements: Let every person in the world become and remain young, beautiful, graceful and alluring; or, allow only those persons to feel sentimental who are young and beautiful. I am surprized that no one has yet proposed that these propositions be incorporated in the United States Constitution.

It is as absurd for men and women who are old to fall in love with young people as it would be for them to play tennis with Mr. Lacoste, and they would be no more ridiculous in the latter predicament than in the former. There is only one way in which the former game can start, and Miss Glasgow, being well aware of the fact, as she is of many other facts, makes crabbed age and youth take that way. It is where age has cash and youth has none. For, as Elspeth wittily says in *The Conning Tower*, Ladies prefer Bonds.

You see, the scheme of things entire is not exactly in accord with the heart's desire. Two of our most prominent latter-day prophets, Mr. Shaw and Mr. Wells, have suggested improvements, which, if they could become facts, would make a novel like this untrue to life. Mr. Shaw would have every one born at the age of eighteen, indulge in kissing, petting, and so on, for three years, and get it all done and out of the way; then have the life of reason set in and last for seven or eight centuries. Mr. Wells would have all men and women reach a Utopia where they would rise completely above the discomforts caused by our present make-up, desire, jealousy, and other impedimenta. One difference between the two reformers is that Mr. Shaw knows that his scheme, like most reforms, is an impossible dream, whereas Mr. Wells, so skeptical in many ways, has the touching faith that his plan is actually coming off.

Each man in his time plays many parts; and, according to Ellen Glasgow, love is a romantic comedy. The spectator sees them all as comedians, as a swearing golfer in a bunker looks funny to a passer-by. One not an artist might conceivably regard players at golf or love or life with envy; but the novelist, May Sinclair or Ellen Glasgow, can and does take refuge in irony.

The Romantic Comedians is an excellent work of analysis and implied criticism; furthermore, it is definitely and strictly contemporary. Thus do persons act and talk in our time. Tho the novel is quite free from didacticism, that element being out of style, there is, as there is in all sincere works of art, a lesson for those who wish to profit by it. It is to cultivate the mind, the reason, the intelligence; for this is the only way to avoid the ever-present snares of self-deception. Schopenhauer said that love born of the will is an illusion, and the only escape is through the intellect, by means of that consciousness which he inconsistently said was the chief mistake of our being. His remedy was asceticism, for Schopenhauer was an ascetic—at his writing-desk.

Ellen Duvall, "The *Atlantic* Bookshelf," *Atlantic Monthly*, 138 (December 1926), 18

In *The Romantic Comedians* Miss Ellen Glasgow has written a very clever book whose title inevitably challenges a fleeting mental comparison with George Meredith's older work, *The Tragic Comedians*.

But in substance and treatment, in feeling for life, the two books are wholly unlike. In Meredith's rich novel the heroine feared to grasp life's thistle boldly enough, while the hero was too punctilious to snatch—hence timidity and pride made of them frustrated lovers. In Miss Glasgow's novel the chief character mistakes life's thistle for love's rose, and pays the usual penalty for mistakes.

To those that take their fiction with all seriousness—like Henry James, for instance, fiction may be divided into two classes—the fiction of power, that of the heart; the fiction of knowledge, that of the head. Miss Glasgow's present book, like Mrs. Wharton's work in general, belongs to the latter category: its appeal is rather to the intellect. And if humor be "the smile in the eyes of wisdom," then Miss Glasgow's wisdom lacks the smile. There is an edge to her wit; she does not wear it as Joan of Arc did her sword—sheathed. Her characters, admirably drawn and highly individual, are not "typical" of any part of the country, though the scene of the story is laid in Queenborough, presumably Richmond. Her people are gentlefolk with the limitations and advantages of Anglo-Saxon traditions, social position, customs, and conventions, together with certain church affiliations, at several of which the author aims the shafts of her wit, leaving others exempt. The women are particularly interesting, especially Mrs. Upchurch, "too wise ever to be original, too tactful ever to argue," a flatterer of men by instinct and habit; and the amusing old emotional swashbuckler Edmonia, who declares that "America is an anæmic nation, and the danger with national anæmia is that it runs to fanaticism in the brain," and who further avers that the "honey" of her attractions is due, not to her "actual virtues," but to her "legendary vices."

After the somewhat staccato wit and much worldly-wiseness—for there is an exquisite subtlety, and the same is not wisdom—of this book, one can only ask the favor of Miss Glasgow that she will follow it with a sequel giving the fortunes of Annabel and Birdsong in their pursuit of the will-o'-the-wisp, happiness. For Annabel, belonging to no particular section of the country, typical of a certain kind of present-day young person alike devoid of any sense of responsibility toward God or man—Annabel is quite a memorable picture. She is, however, represented as "honest," with "an inchoate sense of justice." But in the outcome of her destiny she fails to live up to this presentation.

"I won't take a man from any woman," she declares, before paying her significant visit to Amanda. But wouldn't it have been equally fair not to allow a woman to be taken from any man? Isn't it a poor rule that won't work both ways?

Miss Glasgow never fails to be interesting and suggestive, as she is here; but her earlier novel showed a kindlier feeling toward our common humanity.

Robert Herrick, "*The Romantic Comedians*," New Republic, 49 (8 December 1926), 91–3

Miss Glasgow's new story is less weighted with matter, less voluminous in detail, than some of her previous volumes, and therefore reveals more fully the ripening competence of her art. More than any American novelist now writing, with the possible exception of Mrs. Wharton, Miss Glasgow preserves the nice balance between craftsmanship and material. If she is less deft in expression than Mrs. Wharton—and at times she seems almost rotund and sententious—she has apparently exhausted less her vein. While with Mrs. Wharton it is now a remembered and sometimes stale world, Miss Glasgow has grown from book to book with that South she began with a full generation ago.

If Miss Glasgow knows her South and its people in and out in all their phases she is never content with mere presentation: she sees them always in relation to the larger world of contemporary ideas. Distinctly she is a novelist with ideas, even with a latent thesis, which latterly—in *Barren Ground* and *The Romantic Comedians*—emerges as a condemnation of the common illusion of personal happiness through romantic passion, so often substituted for the illusions of duty, ambition, pride. Specifically the theme of *The Romantic Comedians* is, in Mrs. Upchurch's words, "the disadvantages in man or woman of an incurably amorous habit of mind."

Judge Honeywell's belated amorousness fixed itself at sixty-five on the wispy Annabel, disastrously: his fate illustrates again the ancient adage of "no fool like an old fool," with a woman. The misfortunes of a disparity of ages in mating is no new subject. But the title drives home a larger theme, that of all romantic comedians at the eternal game of self-delusion and disillusionment. So far as the story sets forth the ironies and the follies of desire at odds with the power of fulfillment, it is on sure if well trodden ground—although it is safe to say that marriage between a Judge Honeywell and an Annabel would result disastrously without disparity in their ages, for he was a prig of a man and she an avid egotist of a girl. Physical revulsions and incompatibilities in sex are not always due to age discrepancies. But Miss Glasgow is not content with an ironic exploitation of another instance of May and November mating.

She pushes her thesis further into a general disapproval of the common human effort to gain happiness through love. That illusion has persisted, no more in literature than in life. Some emotional glamor to heighten the process of living seems to be a necessity of the human spirit, and the illusion of love between men and women is no more ridiculous than those other illusions of religion or ambition with which middle age is wont to console itself.

The Romantic Comedians proves nothing more novel or fundamental than that the Judge was an amorous and foolish old man. In fact he was too little romantic. A true romantic, he would have married the faithful Amanda without question, instead of the unreal Annabel, seeing her declining beauty through the radiance of his youthful love, thus creating a sustaining illusion for his old age. But not being truly romantic, he exhibited the pathological symptoms of the exhausted male, seeking the renewal of physical forces through the embraces of youth. This familiar pathological case Miss Glasgow has described exactly, decently—and cruelly, even to the grasp of old habits of creature comforts on that doleful last journey of disillusionment, where his arm chair, his fire, his home quite banish the image of the lost Annabel.

Mrs. Upchurch, somewhat younger than the Judge, has mastered what seems to her creator the true philosophy of disillusionment: she has a feline instinct for the minor creature comforts, without the disturbances of emotion. Comfort and the patter of daily routine are all that may be expected, after youth. Romance, passion, love are illusions warming only below forty. Beyond that emotional deadline only the mockery of dead desires is possible. Logical but untrue. Innumerable instances of happiness in love among the middle-aged and old prove that not only the desire, but also the capacity for the larger illusions persist beyond the imaginary deadline. There are failures as well as successes, after forty as before! The secret is wholly individual and elusive, as is the secret of all living. To deride the human effort for fulfillment through love, to establish age limits in emotion, is futile and undiscerning. Sentimentalists will always pay the price and true romantics win the prize, in age as in youth.

"New Books in Brief Review," *Independent*, 117 (11 December 1926), 681

In her latest novel, Miss Glasgow has left the *Barren Ground* which last she worked, to create another of those keenly ironical tales of Virginia ladies and gentlemen. Her theme is the old one of December and May in wedlock, but it is so embellished with a keen understanding of character and with a sly debunking of the conventional sentimentality toward Southern customs that it establishes its author even more surely as an authentic realist. Miss Glasgow does not depend upon any such crudities as the usual realist effects, but her very subtlety makes transparent the curtain of Southern conceits. Behind it, gentlemen and ladies are still gentlemen and ladies, but they have become more human for all that. *The Romantic Comedians* is one more evidence that Miss Glasgow deserves her place well in the forefront of American writers.

"Perennial Husband," *Time*, 8 (20 December 1926), 30

Judge Gamaliel Bland Honeywell—note his middle name—was jilted in the heat of his Southern-Victorian youth by queenly Amanda Lightfoot. On the rebound he married a dove-like Cordelia whose solicitude for his digestion during their 36 years together far surpassed her sublimation of his romantic tendencies—or, dare we say, his passions. They had no children. She modestly discouraged his tenderest husbanding. Hence it was not surprising that Gamaliel at chivalric 65, caught himself thinking, as he laid his fifty-second weekly wreath on Cordelia's grave, of other women—of Amanda the faithful, "so noble that she creaks," who had repented for her pride and never married; of nymphs and dryads on spring breezes and in dreams; even of a mulatto making a bed. Nor was it surprising that he progressed from elderly solicitude to queasy warmth for Annabel Upchurch, Cordelia's impecunious niece, aged 23. Annabel had no moral sense but a heart. The heart had been cracked by her first lover. She had winged eyebrows, cherubic curves and, like the Blonde that Gentlemen Preferred, she loved presents. So they were married and a romantic comedy was wound up when she ran off with the next passing youth and Gamaliel caught a chill running after her.

The portraiture has icy precision. Epigrams rattle like hail. Southern stuffiness—the scene is Queenborough, Va.—is snowed under by pretty drifts of poetic irony. It is engaging reading—but the wrong person wrote the book, overwrote it, if these generation-comparisons are to be taken seriously. Miss Glasgow is too merciless to make her Judge bearable; too doctrinaire to know what she means by Annabel. The best character is Gamaliel's twin sister, Edmonia, who lost her virtue young, married four times and loves to tell about it all.

Frederick P. Mayer, "Discussions of New Books," *Virginia Quarterly Review*, 3 (January 1927), 133–4

I should have liked to record my enthusiastic reception of Ellen Glasgow's *The Romantic Comedians*, for she is a woman, who, since her *Barren Ground*, makes you expect high accomplishments. I must confess, however, to a disappointment; I do not believe that satire is the happy field for a writer whose intense seriousness and vivid color of austerity in *Barren Ground* made that book a success. In The *Romantic Comedians*, there are, however, flashes of genius. There is first of all the description of place, the moody color of Miss Glasgow's pictures of the out-doors that make the book almost convincing despite the stiffness of its characterizations and the wooden quality in its plot. Moments like this make *The Romantic Comedians* worth all the time it takes to read it:

> Turning away, he went slowly indoors, and it seemed to him that he carried the inescapable burden of the April twilight within his heart.

Throughout the novel, lovely pictures of rooms and places color the story with authentic poetry.

The second quality I enjoyed was an occasional epigrammatic touch. If there had been more of it, the drag of tempo would possibly have escaped detection. At one place, the Judge tells his sister, "at your time of life, you might find something better to do than interfere with the private affairs of other people." Edmonia replies, "At our time of life, Gamaliel, there isn't much else that we can do."

Despite all this, the book seems to me self-conscious and uneasy. It is not convincing irony. It does not, for me, tear away the dusty vestiges of sentimentalized Southern life. It tells a story, using a highly specialized plot (with rather ugly implications if it were carried through as in *Barren Ground*) that says little about Southern romance or romantic illusion and says little about unhappy marriages, which it chose to discuss. Of course, it is easy to see that Ellen Glasgow picked her May-and-December plot to emphasize the folly of the shop-worn figures of Southern stories, but she does not achieve that primary result and hence misses any secondary result, as well. The situation, highly specialized, tends to make us say, "Well, of course, the Judge looks silly, and so do his ideals of conduct, but if he had been put in a real situation, he wouldn't seem ridiculous." That seems to me the primary fault in the satire. The second is somewhat different. I found the book dull; the situations and the character development seemed dragged out and tedious. The verve and intensity of *Barren Ground* nowhere rescued the Comedians from their unreality and from their dullness. *The Romantic Comedians* has back of it an observance and critical attitude towards the life Miss Glasgow knows that is heartening. She is doing something, even in *The Romantic Comedians*, that is worth doing. She deserves all our attention to whatever she may in the future have to say.

Times Literary Supplement [England], 10 March 1927, p. 161

In this modern version of the marriage of January and May, the part of January is taken by a retired Virginian judge, left a widower, after many years of placid, prosaic wedlock, at the age of sixty-five, and, as he believes, recapturing his youthful ardour in his infatuation for a beautiful girl of twenty-three, who accepts him partly for his wealth, partly on account of an unhappy love affair. For a time she enjoys touring Europe with him *en luxe*, and spending his money, but nothing can overcome her physical aversion, and on their return she elopes with a man of her own age. The judge makes one pathetic bid to hold her, and when this fails his flickering vitality fails with it, and he resigns himself to old age and its creature comforts. There is considerable subtlety in Miss Glasgow's handling of what can never be a very pleasing subject, and some shrewd wit also.

Checklist of Additional Reviews

Dorothy Foster Gilman, "The Virginian Romantic Comedians," Boston *Evening Transcript*, 18 September 1926, sec. 6, p. 3.

"Autumn Novels," *American Review of Reviews*, 74 (November 1926), 560.

Booklist, 23 (November 1926), 80.

Baird Leonard, "Life and Letters," *Life*, 88 (11 November 1926), 34–5.

Wisconsin Library Bulletin, 22 (December 1926), 333.

"Culling the Sweet and Bitter Fruits of Six Months' Fiction," *New York Times Book Review*, 5 December 1926, sec. 3, p. 5.

THEY STOOPED TO FOLLY

ELLEN GLASGOW

THEY STOOPED TO FOLLY

A Comedy of Morals

MCMXXIX
DOUBLEDAY, DORAN & COMPANY, INC.
GARDEN CITY, NEW YORK

"Stoopers to Folly," *Time*, 14 (29 July 1929), 39

Milly Burden became pregnant in a small Virginia town. Her lover, Martin Welding, a nervewracked U. S. soldier, had returned to France after the War. Yet Lawyer Littlepage, to whom Milly was secretary, forbore to dismiss her despite her flippancy, her sullen desire to live her own life regardless of the opinions of others. Furthermore Milly reminded Lawyer Littlepage of his daughter, Mary Victoria. Encouraged by softness, Milly confided her worry over Welding's nerves. In return, Lawyer Littlepage had Mary Victoria, who was in Europe, look Welding up.

This Mary did, so successfully and with such persistence and missionary zeal that the two returned from Europe as man and wife. Soon Mary Victoria was pregnant, too, but that did not prevent Welding from deserting her "to find a place where there are high mountains and snows that never melt and nothing else except loneliness." Mary Victoria remained with her father because "even though I have lost love, I may become a power for good in the life of my child." Milly went to New York on the trail of "something worth loving."

Other folly-stoopers in the story are Aunt Agatha, still mourning in a third-story back bedroom because she was "betrayed by a Southern gentleman who moved in the best circles but was married already"; and Mrs. Dalrymple, divorced for infidelity. She "looked as much like a king's mistress as if she had stepped straight out of profane history, had been obliged to seek moral climes more congenial in profligate Europe."

Author Glasgow, pride of the South, is a good stylist, competent, prolific, weakly satiric, with a high artistic reputation and more than a trace of sentiment.

Lewis Gannett, "Books and Other Things," New York *Herald Tribune*, August 1929, p. 8

Ellen Glasgow is so gay and gallant in her pessimism, so obviously a thoroughbred throughout her annihilation of every premise of thoroughbred society, so bubbling over with wit and epigram, that one may read *They Stooped to Folly* from cover to cover, chuckling at every page, without realizing how profoundly nihilistic a book it is.

Virginius Littlepage was born between generations. His father had been one of those Virginian gentlemen who found it "less embarrassing to commit adultery than to pronounce the word in the presence of a lady." But Virginius, while he would have been "wounded to have any woman imagine that he was deficient in a lower nature," and was titillated all his life by the lush beauty of Mrs. Dalrymple, never overcame his inhibitions. He never felt quite at home in the atmosphere of "tight thinking and loose living" into which he was born, and in his age he began to have a heretical suspicion that the ruined woman was an invention of man, a suspicion very corrosive to his inherited philosophy.

Victoria, his wife, was "endowed with every charm except the thrilling touch of human frailty." She never failed to smile in any crisis, and was instinctively far more decent than her philosophy should have permitted her to be. Whenever trouble arose, Victoria wanted to help. She failed, as her husband came to see, "to accept the greatest modern discovery, that nothing we do or say matters to the universe. She never lost the primitive belief that the cosmos was her audience." She was, in fact, in her little realm of Queenborough, rather like Gladstone, who talked to Queen Victoria as if she were Parliament.

[...]

Miss Glasgow destroys self-sacrificing love with a wit more acid than any denunciation could ever be. She leaves moral earnestness dissected into a horrible compound of sadistic egotism. She has pity for stumbling sinners, but no compassion for hypocrisy. She leaves one appalled by the revelations behind the question, so natural to the age of Bryan and Queen Victoria: "Oh, Marmaduke, what good can possibly come from finding out what ought not to be true?" Her only religion seems to be Milly's.

"Is anything sacred to you, Milly?" asked Mr. Littlepage.

"Truth would be, if I could find it. Truth that you could really believe in, not just shams and labels."

They Stooped to Folly stands out, unquestionably, head and breast and shoulders above the ruck of current fiction, both in the mellow luster of its style and in the civilized sharpness of its thinking. The story is scanty, but Virginius and Victoria, Mary Victoria and Milly and Marmaduke are all painfully living human beings. One knows them; one almost, but not quite, hates them; one ends by pitying them. They could not help being themselves. It is a book that will be read with joy and discussed and debated, and some of the epigrams that flood its pages in almost lush abundance are likely to become part of the American vocabulary.

Dorothy Foster Gilman, "Three Heroines Who Stooped to Folly," Boston *Evening Transcript*, 3 August 1929, sec. 6, p. 2

[...]

Is this story suitable material for Miss Glasgow's extremely sophisticated pen? She is far more interesting in the play of words and the notation of clever phrases than in bringing out the human values in the men and women she has created. When E. F. Benson writes a social comedy he invariably has the good taste to touch lightly, to occupy himself only with the gay banalities of people to whom life has no deep significance, at the moment when he chooses to have us meet them. Miss Glasgow has courage. She satirizes passionate affection, devotion, steadfastness of purpose, the pathos of old age, the overwhelming grief that comes to a girl whose child has died and who starts life anew deserted by her lover. She selects one by one the fundamentals of life and holds them up to ridicule. She allows Mrs. Littlepage and her friend Louisa the solace of an intimate and comforting friendship. Yet it is despite all Miss Glasgow's words merely a friendship on paper. Let one honest unspoiled emotion arise overnight and she plucks it out of the story as if it were a weed. Over and over again she analyzes the relationships between Virginius and Victoria, between their daughter and her literary husband, Martin Welding. When Mrs. Dalrymple begins to exercise again her familiar fascinations over the Southern attorney it is an affair of small consequence. Littlepage is punctilious, even in his tepid philanderings. One suspects that his daughter is capable of real suffering. She was extremely successful in Europe managing men in camps and relief stations. Her executive talents did not prepare her however for matrimony. The methods she found admirable in the Balkans failed completely with Martin. Yet Miss Glasgow never goes below the surface in explaining to us exactly why Martin suddenly left his wife a few weeks before their child was expected. Nor does she adequately account for the artist Marmaduke's quixotic devotion to Louisa. That romance with its illusions and implications deserves finer treatment.

Perhaps Miss Glasgow has been hampered in her work by a fear of sentimentality. Possibly she has an honest dread of being the author of a commonplace story of a small Southern town. Her bon mots about sex relationships are continuous and extremely amusing for the first two hundred pages. Then it seems as if the shafts of her wit begin to lose their accuracy. It is excellent drawing room entertainment, never even faintly redolent of the stable. Perhaps because of the author's good taste and discretion the bright flashes of humor go round and round in a somewhat circumscribed circle. Nevertheless, one ought not to quarrel with any author for good taste. The serious defect in Miss Glasgow's work is not related to her charm of style, to her fancy, or to her cultivated sense of the ridiculous. Her lack is more fundamental. It is a lack which is not likely to militate against her in the eyes of the many who enjoyed *The Romantic Comedians*. For them this new novel will provide a fare even more delectable. In that tale she exposed the follies and philanderings of an elderly Southern gentleman. She now displays for our edification a world filled with animated, well-mannered automatons who pay homage to all the non-essentials of life, possessing no emotions that are not trivial, whose moods of regret and bewilderment are but temporary vapors. Even Victoria's death hardly touches either her husband or her presumably devoted friend.

The scene between Louisa and the stricken husband two days after his wife's death is very typical of Miss Glasgow's talent and its limitation. It is as if the narrator were gazing at these two characters through a telescope. The distance between them and their creator is great, and their thoughts and feelings are reduced to a small emotional value. It is scarcely likely that Louisa, left alone with the task of disposing of the letters and personal belongings of her intimate friend, would have soliloquized so brilliantly yet abstractly upon the limitations of the great Victorian tradition. Any honest, loving friend, worn out with the agonies of bereavement and the final services at the cemetery, would have broken down and wept a dozen times that Sunday afternoon.

No tears are shed in this story unless they moisten the cheek at an hour when her bright eyes do not perceive them. Even poor Marmaduke, when he admits to his brother the reason why Louisa has never been willing to marry him, after a courtship of more than twenty-five years, speaks like a puppet.

Every emotional opportunity which Miss Glasgow happens upon she transforms into either a delicate farce or a conversational commentary surrounded by the atmosphere of a Frigidaire. Towards the last few paragraphs the reader has a hint of a rather austere philosophy. Milly Burden decides to start life anew in another city or town. She asks not for love, so she tells Mr. Littlepage, but for someone worth loving. Mary Victoria, walking in the garden, smiles when her father encourages her to hope for Martin's return. "Doesn't everything come back," she says with a sigh, "if you wait until you have stopped wanting it?"

Miss Glasgow has selected these two young women to voice her ultimate declarations. Despite all the mirth, all the wit and the infinite procession of brilliant epigrams, the author's own attitude towards life is only sincerely evoked in these final pages. This is perhaps the reason we feel a lack of warmth in the novel. Why should there be tenderness and loving kindness among human beings if they must all seek earnestly for someone worth loving? That in itself would prove a lifelong task. It would necessitate a perpetual pilgrimage by reason of its definition.

Added to that attitude of mind is Miss Glasgow's second affirmation in restraint of loving kindness and simple happiness. Believing, as one suspects she does, that what you really desire never comes until you no longer wish for it there seems no logical reason for taking the world at its own valuation. Mr. Littlepage has two sons but they are neglected by the author. His mind is not the mind of a Southern gentleman. It is Miss Glasgow's mind, shrewd, subtle and completely aware of all the futilities of life. She has evolved her own philosophy. Translated into characters which make fiction, it is depressing. If you share her conclusions about the world this novel will be delightful reading. Otherwise it will make you shiver a little, as if touched with the suggestion of an autumnal chill.

Amy Loveman, "When Men Betray," *Saturday Review of Literature*, 6 (3 August 1929), 19

Miss Glasgow in this "comedy of morals" has again proved her right to be regarded as perhaps the leading woman novelist of America. No one of our female writers has her wit, her ironical insight into the foibles of human nature, her ability to reduce to an epigram the findings of her penetrating insight. Few of the men writing our novels are her peers, and no one of them surpasses her in the beautiful precision of a style which conceals its artistry under its art. She has discernment and wisdom, a detachment which permits her to watch the human comedy with amusement, and a sympathy which while it takes nothing of incisiveness from her comment leaves it always without trace of bitterness. She is, in short a delectable novelist, one whose intelligence is always tempered by her humor, and whose humor is always in fee to her understanding.

This is not to say that *They Stooped to Folly* is a completely successful book. Curiously enough its faults lie chiefly in its failure adequately to realize its female characters. While Miss Glasgow has made her Mr. Littlepage walk the pages of her novel a Southern gentleman to the life, with both the defects and the merits of his virtues, with a faith in the standards of the past and a pathetic puzzlement as to the freedom of the present alike convincing and persuasive, she has drawn her Victoria and Mary Victoria, the mother good as involuntarily as the rose is fragrant, and the daughter wearing the patent of nobleness with conscious determination, too much to an ideal pattern. Where Mr. Littlepage speaks and moves with the accent and the gait of reality, his wife and daughter are born of the novelist's pen. Aunt Agatha, too, who stooped to folly in a day when to decline from the upright was to retire to unresenting self-effacement, Mrs. Dalrymple who sinned lightly and continued to bank heavily on her womanly charms, have something of lay figures about them. Milly alone, poor Milly, so imprudent in her love, so passionate in her despair, so exuberant in her liberation from the fetters of her infatuation, Milly alone of the women of the book is a vividly veracious figure. Completely of her day and her generation, she is at once the exemplar and the justification of youth in revolt against the despotism of facts and militant in its assertion of the right to happiness.

"The world," in the much quoted words of Horace Walpole, "is a comedy to those that think, a tragedy to those who feel." To the critical intelligence of an Ellen Glasgow there cannot be other than comedy in a situation such as that which involves her characters, in an order of existence which allows a Mary Victoria to claim justification on the highest moral grounds for her marriage to the lover she has been asked to retrieve for Milly, which makes the father who has attempted to enlist his daughter's services in behalf of his secretary the unwitting instrument of fresh misery for the girl he would have befriended, which shows the object of two women's devotion driven to desperation by surfeit of affection and cherishing. To the quick humanity of an Ellen Glasgow, however, there cannot but also be tragedy in the quagmire of human relationships, and it is the saving compassion of her reaction to the embroilments of circumstance which lends significance to her interpretation. Miss Glasgow's art is a circumscribed one, but within its limits it is admirable. It has charm, it has brilliance, and that indefinable distinction which to possess is to be of those who grace, not follow, literature. The savor of her writing lingers.

A[gnes W.] S[mith], "A Study in Scarlet," *New Yorker*, 5 (3 August 1929), 60–1

The idea around which Ellen Glasgow built her newest novel, *They Stooped to Folly*, is so amusing that you feel the author had nothing to do but let her pen run away with itself. Miss Glasgow entertains you with the spectacle of three generations of fallen women. They are none of your cheap fallen women, they are fallen Virginian ladies. Aunt Agatha, of the Victorian Era, is more of a fallen dumpling. You see her as an old lady, whose life has been consecrated to repentance, consoling herself with movies and banana sundæs. Mrs. Dalrymple, of the Edwardian Age, wears her scarlet letter jauntily; in fact, she rather makes much of it. Milly Burden, the modern girl, "sins naturally"; she also sins dully and unprofitably. She is honest, but she pays for her honesty by losing the romantic glow of Aunt Agatha's mistake, and the worldly consolation of Mrs. Dalrymple.

These three Magdalenes bring their troubles to Mr. Littlepage, a chivalrous southern gentleman. His heart bleeds for them, bleeds all the more profusely because his wife and daughter are such intelligent and flawless ladies. The daughter is a woman of the New South, Elsie Dinsmore's great-granddaughter, and Miss Glasgow damns her fervently and wittily.

For all its pert and saucy style, *They*

Stooped to Folly is a sagacious piece of writing. Miss Glasgow presents her Freudian cases with gaiety, restraint, and a touch of well-bred malice. You can hear her ironic laughter above the sound of the sobbing of her characters. She writes as if she had something true and important to say but, being a polite hostess, didn't want to be dull or boring about it.

Polly Daffron, "Ellen Glasgow's Latest Novel Is Mordant Comedy of Morals," Richmond *Times-Dispatch*, 4 August 1929, sec. 3, p. 14

Ellen Glasgow's new novel, *They Stooped to Folly*, just published by Doubleday Doran and selected as the literary guild book for August, is the story of three women who became "involved in those troubles that overtake women who are [more] generous than prudent." Presented as a "comedy of morals," it is more truly a comedy of persons, for Miss Glasgow has evolved numerous fascinating and vivid characters whose portraits she paints with delicate irony and rare skill.

Through the pince-nez of Virginius Littlepage, Virginia gentleman of Georgian appearance and Victorian mind, we view the realistic puppets of *They Stooped to Folly*. We meet Aunt Agatha, who was ruined not through a fall from virtue but because of Victorian psychology. Mrs. Dalrymple, who stumbled often and unwisely because of a fatal sex attraction. (In later years she would have preferred a moderate amount of card sense.) And Milly Burden, who fell gallantly and naturally, treating her fall casually as if it were her own affair.

In vivid contrast to the three who stooped to folly are Mrs. Littlepage, who was a good wife, but lacked piquancy; her daughter, Mary Victoria, of overwhelming goodness, but lacking her mother's redeeming wholesomeness, and Louisa Goddard, Victoria's bosom companion, an admirable spinster who would have made the reputation of any man she chose to marry.

For Mr. Littlepage one can only feel sympathy. There is poignant tragedy in the life of this aging aristocrat whose desires were ever unrealized because of his convictions. He craved Mrs. Dalrymple, but lacked the stamina to realize his romance. The restraint of home life palled, but his gentleman's code kept him housebound. He was as much a martyr to the gentleman's code as Aunt Agatha was a victim of a senescent psychology.

Throughout the book the dully righteous and the glamorously fallen women seem to war for attention and understanding. The fulsome charms of the luscious Mrs. Dalrymple make Victoria's virtuous assets pale. Mary Victoria, in her marriage and attempted dominance of Martin, Milly's lover, loses her father's sympathy and support.

Indeed the only victory of the "good women is Victoria's glorified postmortem place in her husband's affections." Then Virginius understood "that love was not loyalty; it was not loving kindness; it was not even tenderness. You might love a woman and yet deceive her; and might love a woman and yet betray her; you might love a woman and yet destroy her. You might do anything in love, he saw at last, with a pang of agony, but cease to remember."

To find adequate verbiage to praise the perfections of *They Stooped to Folly* is difficult. There are phrases of breath-taking beauty alongside of mordant irony and scintillating witticisms. There are so many quotable lines that a choice is practically impossible. There are ... but eulogisms fail.

They Stooped to Folly will, it seems safe to prophesy, establish more firmly Miss Glasgow as America's foremost woman novelist. And a P.S. must be appended in praise of the dedication, which is—

> To James Branch Cabell
> ... In Acknowledgment of Something About Eve ...
> This Book that Commemorates the Chivalry of Men.

Percy Hutchison, "Wit and Wisdom in a New Novel by Ellen Glasgow," New York Times Book Review, 4 August 1929, sec. 4, p. 2

It is significant that Ellen Glasgow has dedicated her new novel, They Stooped to Folly, to James Branch Cabell. The author of Jurgen is America's arch-ironist of morals and manners, and Miss Glasgow labels her work "A Comedy of Morals." But Miss Glasgow does not follow her mentor into his imaginary world, for she intends no such gigantic satire as Cabell has done, her purpose being to pillory her fellow-mortals, female and male. And Miss Glasgow also acknowledges indebtedness to another observer of human frailty, namely, Oliver Goldsmith, from whom she quotes the lines printed in every anthology:

> When lovely woman stoops to folly,
> And finds too late that men betray,
> What charm can soothe her melancholy?
> What art can wash her guilt away?

It will be noticed, however, that the American novelist does not go on to the stanza in which the poet gives as the only remedy a cessation of living. Not one of Miss Glasgow's lovely and frail women dies. So far, then, is the twentieth century from the eighteenth; Ellen Glasgow from Oliver Goldsmith.

The scene of They Stooped to Folly is a town in the American South which the author calls Queenborough. The time is the period immediately following the World War. And the persons of principal importance are Mr. Littlepage, a manufacturer of the South's new economic era, but whose family was deeply rooted in the old; Mr. Littlepage's wife, Victoria; and their daughter, Mary Victoria. The three ladies who stooped are Aunt Agatha, the Victorian; Mrs. Dalrymple, of the gay and naughty '90s; and Milly Burden, an entirely modern young miss, who rides triumphant on the phrase that her life is her own.

Thus Miss Glasgow's instructive and delectable fabrication becomes, as the author somewhere implies, "a study in sin." But in our opinion this able adept at the rapier-thrust would not like the phrase to be taken too seriously. If the ladies of her novel not merely stooped but plunged headlong from their perches, it was because man had placed them on perches too lofty. They became a little dizzy, that was all; and as they had not in the first place chosen or decreed the height of their ensconcement, they should not be too sharply blamed. Moreover, the book is specifically a "comedy"; which means that judgment is suspended. If there be a moral to the tale, if They Stooped to Folly is not merely a humorous survey of life but a criticism of life as well, the reader will discover it for himself. One will get from Miss Glasgow's book just what one brings to it, neither more nor less. To come to the book and one of the sinners:

> Mrs. Dalrymple, who had been blessed with sex attraction, but would have preferred, as she grew older, a moderate amount of card sense, or even a strong religious belief, could have enlightened Mr. Littlepage on the subjects of Europe and widowhood. Endowed with much energy and little temperament, she might have remained virtuous had her figure been less pronounced or the field of woman's activities more varied. But in the late '90s, when she had flourished and fallen, an immense feminine vitality was confined with the narrow range of a wasp-waist and the exacting ritual of being a lady. A deceptive bosom, which inspired hope in men, and a naturally kind heart, which hesitated to dispense disappointment, had been, if not the occasion, at least the original cause, of her frailty.

Mrs. Dalrymple obviously having had a husband as well as a lover, it may make for clarity, as well as further to display the dry-point of Miss Glasgow's delineation, to quote the author's words under those two heads.

> Before her fortunate second marriage, and even more fortunate widowhood, she was the heroine of a scandal that had shaken the canons of refined conduct to their solid foundation. While her husband, conforming to the dramatic style of the period, had promptly transfixed her by a divorce, her lover, a practical rather than a theoretical exponent of chivalry, had discreetly married a lady of sober views and impeccable conduct.

These two passages, which are all but Meredithian, certainly have few parallels in American fiction dealing with finite beings and not, as in Cabell, with purely imaginary entities. They are not, however, quite Meredithian. Ellen Glasgow has not the supreme genius of the author of *The Egoist* at playing around and about a subject without eventually demolishing it. Her caustic burns just a bit too deep, her rapier comes too near the slice of a saber; for it has, besides the sharp point, the cutting edge which that weapon should not possess. The feeling of the present writer is that perhaps the author of *They Stooped to Folly* tries to be a trifle overwitty, and that, had she penetrated more deeply to the heart of her story, had she developed her characters more fully, and worked out her plot more convincingly, she would have produced the truly masterly comedy of morals her novel falls just short of being.

Milly Burden's lover, slightly abnormal from birth, and rendered doubly so by his experience in the war (shell-shock has been a great boon to novelists), possessed, to judge from the lives he wrecked, some sort of supernatural power over women. So careful was Milly of his "happiness" that she did not inform him that she was to become a mother! But when he deserts her for a vagabond life in Paris she is frantic for his return and the revival of his love. And when Mary Victoria—after having labored with the Red Cross, and, apparently single-handed, rendered the Balkans unsafe for bacilli—marries Milly's recreant knight, and is deserted in turn, nothing will do for her but she must set out to find and recover the careless husband. There may be such men as Martin

Welding alive in the world. If so, there are probably hosts of other men who would like to acquire the secret of their philandering. But if they exist, they are unknown except to themselves and their women, and, perhaps, the psychiatrist; and the novelist who wishes to parade them through his pages has the duty laid on his shoulders of convincing the reader of the character's reality. In *They Stooped to Folly* this Martin Welding is not real, Mary Victoria is not real, Mr. Littlepage is nebulous, and Milly Burden is but a theorem. Mrs. Dalrymple alone lives.

It may be argued that comedy does not make the same demand for reality that tragedy makes, or that intermediate genre which the stage labels "drama," or merely "a play." But the fact remains that the great masters of the comedy of manners (or morals) who have chosen the novel for their medium, Thackeray, Meredith and Galsworthy, while they have permitted the irony to abate not a whit, have created persons as well as written epigrams. However, Miss Glasgow's shortcomings have been dwelt on not to indicate failure but to show how nearly she attains. If for nothing else, one will read, and probably reread, *They Stooped to Folly* for such lines as:

> Louisa had traveled far since the '80s, when spinsters, like husbands, preferred sweetness to light.

Although the year is not yet done, and there are torrents of novels on the Fall lists, it is safe to say that until there arises in this country a novelist who, like Galsworthy and Thackeray and Meredith, can combine the creation of full-bodied fictional characters with wit of observation, *They Stooped to Folly* will remain unsurpassed in any year in its chosen field of the comedy of manners. And when it is surpassed perhaps it will be by Ellen Glasgow herself. It is our guess that this is precisely what will take place. And until then *They Stooped to Folly* should remain the most delectable mingling of ironic wit and tolerance yet done on this side of the Atlantic.

Isabel Paterson, "Rue with a Difference," *New York Herald Tribune Books,* 4 August 1929, sec. 11, pp. 1, 5–6

[. . .]

. . . The really modern note of modern fiction is its conscious sociological slant; and the extraordinary experiments in style and form which we have seen are in the main attempts to create a special medium for the new material. Interesting and sometimes successful as they have proved, they are not indispensable. Ellen Glasgow makes the traditional method, with slight modifications, serve brilliantly in *They Stooped to Folly*, a study of the revolution in the moral code governing feminine conduct which has occurred within the span of one lifetime, or what is ordinarily reckoned as three generations. Three women stand, or rather fall, as examples.

The cycle of change is apprehended through the eyes of a Southern gentleman, Mr. Virginius Curle Littlepage, but with innumerable glinting sidelights from the minds of other persons concerned. . . .

[. . .]

This group dilemma Miss Glasgow has analyzed in the spirit of classic comedy. The breadth of her inquiry and the penetration of her wit are a constant delight. Innumerable epigrams tempt to quotation, and to choose one is to slight others as good. For a complete characterization, can this be excelled: "Her manner of reciting Browning as if she were trying so patiently to bring out the best in him, had been the attitude of Mary Victoria toward her husband." And for a note on the impact of impressionist art on the elder generation, there is Mrs. Littlepage's "suspicion, when she looked at Marmaduke's pictures, that every woman is purple under her clothes."

And how could a suppressed chapter of social history be more succinctly indicated, suppression and all, than by the brief colloquy between Mr. and Mrs. Littlepage, beginning with the remark of Virginius, in defense of Milly Burden: "The seduction of a woman does constitute some sort of claim on a decent man. When there has been a child the claim would appear to become stronger."

"Why, I thought you argued just the other way a few days ago about your uncle Mark?" Mrs. Littlepage said.

"But that," Mr. Littlepage explained, with legal punctilio, "was the case of a mulatto child."

In such restraint of statement is the secret of power. Among American women novelists Ellen Glasgow occupies a unique position. Her career has not only been synchronous with the "Southern renaissance" in letters; without her, it is easily credible that it would not have occurred in her time. She has been a liberating influence—a phrase which would puzzle the Mary Victorias, who confound influences with restrictions. Rejecting at the outset the romantic school of Southern fiction which had long since ceased to be adequate for any broad treatment of Southern life, she sharpened her pen on the toughest realities, until she had her material under control. In the process, her keen intelligence diverted her talent as a story-teller to propaganda for a while. But if she wrote "novels with a purpose," the purpose was to tell the truth. At the fullness of her powers she was seized with that "divine despair" which is the making of an artist. To the scientist, life is the series of phenomena out of which he educes natural laws; to the moralist, it is the conflict of appetite and aspiration which must be reconciled under a Divine Plan; to the artist, it is the chaos out of which he must create beauty. With this realization Miss Glasgow's purpose crystallized into a style. If she now works out a theme she is not primarily concerned to prove a point. Dealing with life, she makes the best of it by turning it to the uses of her art.

It took immense fortitude to sustain the part of a Southern lady of the Victorian period. Crinoline was not enough; they had to be made, like their best brocade gowns, of stuff that "would stand alone." Perhaps the cream of the jest, as Mr. Cabell might say, is that Miss Glasgow proved her breeding most completely in breaking with the tradition where it hampered her individual gift, while drawing upon it for the good manners which enabled her to make the break without becoming spectacular, and therefore ineffective. She stood upon her rights, and maintained them, in the best tradition of Virginia, the state of Washington and Jefferson.

Frances Lamont Robbins, "Novels by Three Women," *Outlook and Independent*, 152 (7 August 1929), 590–1

This week bears out what Rebecca West has said about the excellence of modern women novelists. One rarely meets at once three novels by women so varied and so excellent as these. Beside the poised and measured richness of these books, the usual feminine outpouring is the "harebrained chatter of irresponsible frivolity." Ellen Glasgow's book would stand out in any week or year; and the other two must be placed among the fine novels of the season. Each book is distinguished by some particular, and some particularly feminine quality: Susan Ertz's [*The Galaxy*] by its detail, Sarah Millin's [*The Fiddler*] by its emotional intensity, and Ellen Glasgow's by its honesty. For we maintain that honesty like hers is found only in women, unencumbered by the ideals which cling to the most disillusioned of males, unhampered by the nice requirements of chivalry.

[...]

They Stooped to Folly is ... satiric comedy of the first water. If not the richest, for she lacks tenderness, or the most profound, for her scope is limited, Ellen Glasgow is surely the most brilliant of American novelists. This piercing, pitiless comedy of morals is performed against the stage of modern Virginia. Being a southern novelist, Miss Glasgow understands the traditional villainy of War, and in *They Stooped to Folly*, the World War is the villain in whose horrid wake white porticos lie blackened and lovely gardens, bare. On the stage, three female figures stand as symbols: Aunt Agatha Littlepage, who was seduced fifty years ago, retired thereupon to the back-bedroom and emerged only when the War had healed her hurts with movies and ice-cream sodas: Mrs. Dalrymple, who fell in the Lily Langtry Nineties and continued to fall with all the grace of a king's mistress, but only in foreign parts, until the War sent her home to upset Mr. Littlepage: and Milly Burden, who had a war baby and didn't care who knew it and whom the Littlepages succored to their cost. Before these motionless symbolic figures, the actors in the play sidle and scramble, strut and prance, performing almost every small human antic and making almost every grand gesture. And with perfect and terrible detachment, Ellen Glasgow burnishes the antics and dulls the bright edges of the gestures to make a comedy of dazzling brilliance and exquisite balance.

Make no mistake about *They Stooped to Folly*. It is an amazing book, an exciting book, but an exhausting one. So much penetration, so much honesty, so much wit requires reading as well as writing. Reading it, one begins, presently, to start each new sentence hoping that it may be commonplace, to resent the cruelty of the galloping author who will not give the pedestrian reader's mind a breathing spell. As a reviewer, we dare not say it, but as a fellow reader we must confess that we enjoy *They Stooped to Folly* more in retrospect than in first experience. And that is a tribute which one cannot pay to very many books.

Fanny Butcher, "Ellen Glasgow Writes Satire of Older Notions," Chicago *Daily Tribune*, 10 August 1929, p. 7

Ellen Glasgow is one of our foremost satirical novelists. She was the first one to see in her native south material for fiction which combines reality and gentle satire. For years her reputation among critics as a brilliant and keen novelist mitigated against her popularity. Every one talked about her as if she were a movement instead of an individual who told an amusing story with unusual skill.

The world of readers, however, lately discovered for itself that a writer can be at the same time important and delightful. Her latest novel, *They Stooped to Folly*, has been chosen by the Literary Guild and had an advance of publication edition of 120,000.

They Stooped to Folly is the story of a southern gentleman and of five women who touched his life, three of whom stooped to folly and two of whom were so adamantinely good that even he could realize that goodness was perhaps on occasion a trifle boring.

The five were his wife, Victoria Littlepage, his daughter, Mary Victoria, poor Aunt Agatha, Amy Dalrymple and Milly Burden. Of Victoria Littlepage Mr. Littlepage thought: "After thirty years of married happiness he could still remind himself that Victoria was endowed with every charm, except the thrilling touch of human frailty. She was not only modest, which was usual in the nineties, but she was also beautiful which is unusual in any decade. In the beginning of their acquaintance he had gone even farther and ascribed to her intellect; but a few months of marriage had shown this to be merely one of the many illusions created by perfect features and a noble expression. To be invariably right was her single wifely failing. For Victoria, he sighed as he admitted it, was a genuinely good woman. The pity of it was that even the least exacting husband should so often desire something more piquant than goodness." (Incidentally that gives a flavor of Miss Glasgow's rich humor.)

Mary Victoria was not only good, but she made a business of it. She wasn't satisfied with war work, but had to go back after the war to do some more active good in the Balkans. She got herself a husband with the tactics of a pirate, but because she had saved his life she wore her halo like any good woman. How she "saved" him so thoroughly that she lost him is one of the most brilliant parts of the book. Miss Glasgow's understanding of that situation is real understanding, not mere amused observation.

Aunt Agatha, "Poor Aunt Agatha" as she was always called, was ruined in her youth and she had spent her whole life atoning. "Whether you realize it or not," Miss Glasgow writes, "being ruined is not a biological fact, but a state of mind. What really ruined poor Aunt Agatha—yes, and Mrs. Dalrymple, too—was not a fall from virtue, but Victorian psychology." Aunt Agatha was so old that there was no reason why she shouldn't go out alone to a movie now and then, but Victoria always had a secret feeling that there was something very reprehensible in the taste that Aunt Agatha had for ice cream sundæs, that it wasn't befitting in a fallen woman to have any carnal desires.

"Mrs. Dalrymple, from a provincial and pretty widow, had been transformed by Europe and her war record into a bright, hard woman of the world. She had been blessed with sex attraction, but she would have preferred, as she grew older, a moderate amount of card sense or even a strong religious belief."

And finally Milly "had fallen not heavily, like poor Miss Agatha, nor even lightly, like the slippery Mrs. Dalrymple, but quite naturally, as if it were her own private concern."

Mr. Virginius Littlepage's responsibilities and attractions for and to that galaxy of ladies is the theme of an amusing satirical picture of southern life, shot with tragedy, but never tragic, for the author's sense of the ludicrous always triumphs over fate's gaudiest movements.

Gerald W. Johnson, "Ellen Glasgow's Mailed Fist Inside a White Kid Glove," Baltimore *Evening Sun*, 10 August 1929, p. 6

Ellen Glasgow in her latest novel has adopted the practice of Anatole France. She is wrapping dynamite in curl-papers. *They Stooped to Folly* is witty, amusing, light as thistledown in appearance, but under the surface it is as grim and ruthless as a prohibition agent raiding the Y.M.C.A.

Ostensibly the theme of the book is the changing fashion in feminine sin. We are presented with three ladies, of three generations, each of whom stooped to folly according to the mode of her time. This is a brilliantly amusing skit, in which the author finds free play for her wit and her extraordinary gift of irony. It is a giddy, farcical, mildly scandalous story, done in the spirit of the better French ironists; it is like a more graceful and less raucous novel by Maurice Bedel.

But underneath this glittering whimsicality there is another novel, a 100 per cent American novel, without even a chemical trace of the Gallic spirit. The theme of this is the ghastliness of a person filled with moral certainty. The heroine of this secondary novel is a perfect woman, nobly planned, to warn, to counsel and command. She is a good influence in the world, an inspiration to men, the object of adoration to the multitude, with no motive in life except the highest and purest.

With this woman Miss Glasgow does not deal in the spirit of Anatole France, or Bedel, or any other Frenchman. Her model here is none other than that perfect flower of our civilization, that American of the Americans, the immortal and inimitable Carrie A. Nation. That is to say, Miss Glasgow walks into her heroine as Carrie walked into the saloons of Wichita, Kan., with an umbrella, a hatchet, a crowbar and an armful of cobblestones. And when she is through that heroine is as complete a wreck as ever was a joint in the Sunflower State after Carrie had been dragged, yelling, to jail.

As to the complete morality of this sort of work, one may cherish doubts, but it is impossible to cherish any doubt that it makes a gorgeous show. The terrific crash with which the perfect character goes down under the impact of a well-aimed brick is somehow music in the ears of sinful men. After all, the do-gooders, and especially the feminine do-gooders, are among the most dreadful apparitions ever encountered by anyone who has never had delirium tremens, and a slashing attack on one of them by a female heavyweight:

"cheers the heart of man
As rum and true religion."

In life, for all I know, Miss Glasgow may be practically imponderable; but in literature she is a heavyweight, all right, and what she hits once does not require to be smitten again. But one wonders a little if she has not overdone it in this work. *They Stooped to Folly* begins so airily and lightly that one is convinced that the play is to be another such delicate and delicious fantasia as *The Romantic Comedians*. This seems a somewhat inappropriate overture to a prize fight, no matter how grand and glorious. When the curtain rises to the music of flutes and violins one does not expect to see it come down on a chaos of shattered glass, fallen plaster and wrecked furniture.

However, this may be mere captious criticism. In *They Stooped to Folly* hypocrisy receives its due meed of giggles, and the chronic do-gooder gets an awful beating. It may be an ill-assorted program, but it is an absorbing one.

Harry Hansen, "The First Reader," Chicago *Daily News*, 12 August 1929, p. 12

Ellen Glasgow's new novel, *They Stooped to Folly*, is presented as "a comedy of morals." Primarily it is a study of attitudes, and of changing attitudes toward morals, done in this author's delightfully ironic style. The importance of Miss Glasgow's story is negligible compared to the way she tells it. Her writing reads like that cultured, epigrammatic conversation one always hopes to hear but never does.

The emphasis of the publisher's announcement is on three women who stooped to folly in various ways demanded by their times and temperaments, but the author has most in view her chief character, Mr. Virginius Littlepage, gentleman of Virginia, with whose cogitations and attitudes we are primarily concerned. Much attention is given to his wife, who becomes the foil for Miss Glasgow's choicest irony; the other characters fade in importance and are more talked about than talking....

Thus we get a very engaging view of what makes up the code of a gentleman. Mr. Littlepage, who was affected this way and that, never quite became a part of the changing world. He could understand, but he could not take part in the struggle. Like many another, he could find no horses on which his hidden desires might ride.

R.W.N., "Mature Comedy," Springfield [Massachusetts] *Sunday Union and Republican*, 25 August 1929, sec. E, p. 7

... Miss Glasgow's book, one begins to perceive, is not merely lively and interesting; it is dangerously vital, perhaps beyond the ability of censor to apprehend. It is ironic with the keenness and subtle implication of choice and incisive comedy—more richly matured even than *The Romantic Comedians* in comprehension and deft urbanity of human anatomizing. Untangled fiction can be as scientific in its method as science is when unentangled with preconceived purpose and immediate intent. *They Stooped to Folly* puts human animalculæ under its diamond lens to show each specimen "as is," and to let us recognize through the revelation a bit of the truth about the human nature that is the men and women of our acquaintance (except ourselves).

Clifton Fadiman, "Follies of Middle Age," *Nation*, 129 (28 August 1929), 225–6

To the art of Miss Glasgow's narrative, apart from her mental preoccupations, no one can remain insensible. The clarity of her prose and the ease of her wit are, if not unequaled, certainly not excelled in contemporary American writing. Neither the clarity nor the wit, true enough, is of the first order: for the clarity is the result of a well-arranged and harmonious rather than an impassioned mind; and the wit, too, while never merely linguistic, is rarely more than the social insight of the ordinary civilized man—but superbly phrased. Take, for example, the two or three sentences in which Marmaduke Littlepage sums up the "lesson" of the book: ". . . Being ruined is not a biological fact but a state of mind. It may sound paradoxical to any survivor of the nineteenth century, but Milly has proved to me that it is impossible to ruin a woman as long as she isn't aware of it. What really ruined poor Aunt Agatha—yes, and Mrs. Dalrymple, too—was not a fall from virtue but Victorian psychology."

Now, all this is so concise and elegant that one almost forgets to perceive that it is not subtle or original. Miss Glasgow's ironic insight, always genuine, always pleasing, reminds one of Rochefoucauld and the French epigrammatists: it is a perfect distillation of the advanced viewpoint of a given age. It is not idiosyncratic; in her wit we do not recognize the lineaments of a personality, but rather the distinctive features of an intelligent society.

This explains her mastery of the comedy of manners, a mastery more than amply redemonstrated by *They Stooped to Folly*, certainly the suavest and possibly the most penetrating of her novels. In it she deals with the changes the last hundred years have witnessed in the popular attitude toward feminine frailty. Considering the (superficially) ticklish nature of her subject, the book is a miracle of desensualization. Even Virginius's passing encounter with Mrs. Dalrymple is hardly more than touched by a breath of passion. The note of elegant, satiric social comedy is expertly sustained throughout, a fact which will allow most readers to emerge from the book with the same satisfactory feeling of sadly smiling tolerance for human weaknesses that is the key to Miss Glasgow's own temper.

I say "most readers," for I have a feeling that Miss Glasgow's appreciative and enthusiastic audience will be found largely among the youthfully middle-aged, those now in their thirties—those who are a part of Milly's rebellious and freedom-seeking generation. The contemporary "younger generation" will be forced to admire Miss Glasgow's serene art, but I think they will be unable to enter very violently into the problems which interest her. *They Stooped to Folly* will be to them a novel of distinctly post-war vintage, one which records, more elegantly and much more intelligently than other books, that excited revolt against convention with which the once younger Middle Western novelists are associated. To them, perhaps, the whole subject of virtue versus sex freedom will seem a little moldy and academic, and Miss Glasgow's novel merely a skilful re-exhuming of something which has been buried under the weight of innumerable novels and "thoughtful articles."

Miss Glasgow's sympathy is clearly with

Milly, her casually sinful rebellious heroine. She conceives Milly as a typical representative of modern youth, whereas the more reflective young Americans of today will probably have their patience sorely tried by Milly's repeated asseverations that she has "a right to her life" and "a right to be happy." They will see only too clearly that Milly has no such right, because she is not sufficiently intelligent or fore-sighted to make good her claim to freedom. They will realize that Milly is just as completely under the domination of the ideal of romantic and possessive love as poor Aunt Agatha was under that of womanly modesty; and that while she remains under this domination, she will be too weak to realize the freedom about which she so freely talks. The business of being "free," of course, is only incidentally a matter of throwing off shackles; it is largely concerned with assuming responsibilities and limiting rather than extending one's desires. Because a large number of young men and women are soberly realizing this fact, they are less excited than was Milly's generation by such shibboleths as "the right to live one's own life" and other romantic war cries. To them, therefore, *They Stooped to Folly* will seem a little out of date, although to their elder brothers and sisters it may appear as a moving record of the advanced morality of today.

H. L. Mencken, "Two Southern Novels," *American Mercury*, 18 (October 1929), 251–2

The South, politically, is in almost as sad a state as it was in the days of Reconstruction. Here and there, to be sure, a statesman of a certain elemental dignity hangs on, but almost always it will be found, on examining him closely, that his ears have been cut off, his gluteus maximus well paddled, and his insides filled with BB shot. Such mutilated survivors of a gentler day cannot last much longer; they are going out as Methodism comes in. In a few years I predict formally, Pat Harrison of Mississippi will find himself, relatively speaking, a publicist of lofty talents and sterling rectitude, no doubt to his own unaffected astonishment. For the morons are in the saddle down in that hot, lush, charming country, and they prepare to ride to Hell and back. The catastrophe that shamed and staggered the gentlemen of Virginia last November will be repeated often, and on a larger and larger scale. [*Editor's note*: Mencken supported Al Smith in the 1928 election, and he may be referring to Virginia's support for Herbert Hoover; all of its electoral votes were cast for Hoover.] In more than one State it is already impossible for a self-respecting man to get his nose into politics: the business of statecraft becomes a monopoly of pliant Jenkinses, with cotton-mill sweaters leading them by the nose and roaring ambassadors of Christ helping them with kicks *a posteriori*. Is Bishop Cannon destined to be crowned Emperor of the Confederacy? I doubt it, but only because too much decency lingers in him— a legacy of the days when, at ordination, he swore that he "groaned after perfection," and was as yet unseduced by games of chance. He will be upset soon or late by a greater and worse, combining all the gifts of Jonathan Edwards, Frank Hague, Anthony Comstock, Cole Blease, Mabel Walker Willebrandt, Wayne B. Wheeler and Al Capone. I look for this marvel confidently, and have grabbed a good seat in the gallery. It will be the greatest show since the Massacre of St. Bartholomew's.

Meanwhile, the intellectuals of the South take it out in satire, the immemorial refuge of the skeptic who has abandoned hope. It is a good sign, for the thing that the satire displaces is sentimentality, for years the dominant Southern curse. Even so recently as twenty years ago it was hard to imagine a Southerner (not obviously insane) poking fun at the South, but now, under the tutelage of Miss Ellen Glasgow and James Branch Cabell, they are all doing it, and some of the imbecilities that they expose, it must be confessed, are really most amusing. In *They Stooped to Folly* Miss Glasgow herself shows how neatly and effectively the thing may be done. Her theme is nothing less than the Southern attitude toward fornication—certainly a ticklish enough subject, even today; in the old days the barest mention of it would have covered the James river with blue flames. The action swirls around the bewildered soul of Mr. Virginius Curle Littlepage, a human bridge between the old Virginia and the new. Brought up during the Civil War *Katzenjammer,* with the Victorian domestic ethic in full blast about him, he saw his Aunt Agatha, for a trivial slip, exiled to the third floor back, and there doomed to drag out her years in sombre atonement. The next generation, his own, took a bold step toward antinomianism. The voluptuous Amy Paget, caught in indiscretion, was incarcerated in no such hoosegow. To the contrary, she went to Paris, acquired there the whitewash of a husband, buried him in Père Lachaise, and then came back to flaunt her sins and tempt poor Virginius himself. It is not Amy, however, who gives him the most painful cause to think, but his young stenographer, Milly Burden. She represents the new generation, wholly emancipated and completely appalling. She neither falls on the field, like Aunt Agatha, nor runs away, like Amy. Instead, she stands her ground, admits everything shamelessly, and defies anyone to do anything about it.

The fable, in its essence, is not Virginian; it might be laid in any State of this imperial realm, North, East, West or South. But Miss Glasgow is no mere storyteller. Her merit lies precisely in her skill at giving her tale a local investiture and a local significance. Her Virginius Littlepage is not simply an American staggered by a more or less familiar situation; he is a Virginian utterly demoralized and undone by a situation that, in the Virginias now dying so stertorously, remains unimaginable to a man of the right instincts. What makes the comedy is his effort to dispose of it in the traditional Southern manner—by encasing it in humane assumptions, by refusing to regard its more inconvenient facts, by waving it away with gallant and poetic gestures. The device used to work magnificently, but no more. We are in a new world. The Aunt Agathas of today, even in Virginia, refuse to climb the obliterating third-floor stair. They remain in the drawing-room, discussing the business as if it were a public question. Worse, they get a great deal of plausibility in what they say: it becomes increasingly difficult to think of effective answers to them. Thus poor Virginius swoons out of the picture, shocked and gasping. The human race, in its reproductive aspect, has become unintelligible to him. He has begun to distrust all women. He has even begun to fear for himself.

Miss Glasgow writes very skillfully. She knows how to manage situations and she has an eye for the trivialities which differentiate one man or woman from another. Her humor is not robust, but it is sly and never-failing. If she has a salient defect, it is that she sometimes yields a bit too easily to the lure of pretty phrases. Her dialogue could be a great deal more realistic than it is; only too often her characters simply make speeches to one another. They are usually amusing speeches, but that fact doesn't dispose of their stiffness. Rather too much of the story, it seems to me, is devoted to Milly and her Greenwichy rebellion. It is too typical of the age to need so much exposition. I'd like to have heard more about the discreet peccadilloes of Mrs. Dalrymple, *née* Paget, and a great deal more about the disaster of Aunt Agatha. In Aunt Agatha, indeed, there is plainly a whole book. It would be instructive to find out precisely how she got into her forlorn third-floor back, and what went on in her head during her long years of expiation there. That story would be worth the telling.

Kenneth B. Murdock, "Folly and the Ironist," *Virginia Quarterly Review,* 5 (October 1929), 596–600

Miss Glasgow's "Comedy of Morals" is circumscribed ostensibly by Queenborough, Virginia, where three women have "stooped to folly." Aunt Agatha atones by withering alone, "a ruin," until the War summons her to make pyjamas and to recapture a hint of life in a passion for banana sundæs and the movies. Amy Dalrymple finds in her later years no life except what she can capture in weary gropings for a new love affair. Milly Burden, a product of the present century, makes the shibboleth, "the right to be happy," her ideal, modifying it when happiness is denied by substituting pleasure for happiness and finally deserting it altogether to seek "something worth loving." Unlike the others she refuses to see herself as "fallen" and never admits that the biological fact in any way conditions her individual future. In theory all that matters is that her life is hers still; in practice she finds no balm more sovereign than Aunt Agatha's love for sweets, except in her final flight to what she fancies will be "freedom" in New York.

"When lovely woman stoops to folly" the traditional questions are "What charm can soothe her melancholy? What art can wash her guilt away?" Miss Glasgow does not answer, if, indeed she even asks. Given the situation a moralist or propagandist might load the dice. A little tampering might exalt the Victorian standard which makes Aunt Agatha what she is or might disguise Milly's half-fledged search for a philosophy as allegiance to a gospel. But Miss Glasgow, as comic ironist, is proof against temptations to lapse into a sociological study, content to light up the facets of the situation in the cool rays of her wit. Thus treated the stuff she works in, worn as it is by much use, offers bountiful resources for comedy. There is the contrast between Aunt Agatha's point of view and Milly's. There is the clash between the conduct of the two ladies who stooped and felt that stooping was a fall, and the conduct of one who refused to admit that she had even stooped. There is the sharp interplay of light and shade in the attitude of the Southern gentleman (who gets his full share of satire) and that of his wife, or sister, or daughter, facing the same set of facts. There are other characters to represent differing outlooks on the tangle, and each is made a peg to which is tied one of the interlaced threads of comedy.

Above all there is Virginius Littlepage, Southern gentleman, lawyer, idealist, bewildered by changing moral standards, by his own abortive yearnings toward lawless love, and most of all by his own mind, more advanced than his tongue, more drastic in its conclusions than his code should, he feels, permit. He, Milly, his wife, Victoria, and Mary Victoria, their daughter, who marries Milly's erstwhile lover in order to save him from himself, are the chief characters of the novel. There is, too, Louisa Goddard, loved vainly for years by the rebellious artist, Marmaduke, Virginius's brother, and all the time secretly loving Virginius herself, masking her secret under a most efficient exterior and a precise knowledge of the social history of ancient civilizations.

Most of the book is simply the record of Mr. Littlepage's response to the situation. He wavers in his opinions. He has both respect and affection for Milly. He loves his daughter but distrusts her motives in capturing another woman's lover, even though those motives are externally displayed in the colors of nobility. He advances toward Mrs. Dalrymple only to flee nervously on the eve of lawless delights, quite contentedly taking refuge at his own fireside. He is a figure of fullness and color. At times, to be sure, he seems to contain in himself too much. It is natural that there should be two or three men at war within him, but now and then he seems to achieve a detachment which brands him as for the moment merely the mouth-piece of Miss Glasgow. With him, we are told, "sophistication had never filtered through the interwoven wires of prejudice," but sometimes fundamental sophistication speaks in his voice without the slightest vibration of those wires. Then he sparkles but loses the hue of life.

The other characters seem less successful. They are usually sketched by a trait, a turn of mind, an experience, but do not desert the flat world of types. Each is set up less as a character in the full sense than as a beacon to mark a critical angle in the situation. Mrs. Dalrymple, though her physical charm is sharply presented, seldom comes out of the pages enough to stand alone. Mrs. Littlepage and Louisa are certainly thoroughly painted, but perhaps because theirs is the burden of being the protagonists of Queenborough's virtue, they seem often to be abstractions, embodiments of patterns of life, and slip all too easily into the lifelessness which Victoria's husband in his most discerning moments half recognized in her. They are too mildly tempered by baser motives to be credible; they rarely betray concretely the secret of their influence on Virginius and the others.

Mary Victoria, again, is but a sketch, though quite vivid enough to explain the reactions upon her husband. And, finally, Milly, upon a realization of whom the story depends for poignancy, is too faintly outlined. She has physical attractiveness, apparently; she is courageous and pathetic in her confidence in her rights in a world where, so far as this novel is concerned, neither she nor anyone else seems to be able to keep them; she is admirably incisive in her rejection of some stupidities and half-truths, but she remains remote. She loved Martin, but how? Why? It is difficult to catch her thinking. She is hard to believe in because she seems to put on ideas ready-made. Yet, if she was what we are told she was, she must have thought, and back of her courage there must have been some drama worth seeing.

If the book had no character but Mr. Littlepage, however, and if he were less well drawn than he is, it would still shine simply because of Miss Glasgow's mind and her artistry in words. The style, in its restraint and quick responsiveness to every phase of the theme, once more proves her quality. The epigrams tread upon each other's heels, and even though most of them are on subjects long ago worn bare by epigrammatists, they flash as brightly as though their themes were as new as the day. The wit, malicious, ironic, mocking, is of the sort that only the most fortunate artists can maintain. In it, not in any distinction of plot or characterization, lies the merit of the novel. "Poor Aunt

Agatha had been a carefully guarded ruin, and Victoria was aware that Southern gentlemen of the great tradition visited such ruins only by moonlight." "To reduce behaviour to a formula, however wanton, appeared miraculously to invest it with the dignity of an intellectual habitation and a name." Perhaps the feast is even too bountiful, and sometimes the wit falls too regularly into one or two forms. Curle Littlepage is "as safe as a Liberty Bond and almost as uninteresting." "Intemperate virtue is almost as disastrous in marriage as temperate vice." "His respect for her was as unenterprising as his respect for the Ten Commandments. . . . Her firm brown skin . . . looked not so much youthful in texture as impervious to age. . . . Her features wore an expression of faint surprise, as if the mysteries of Babylon had left her in a state of perpetual astonishment." The mould is too uniform, but no one would break it if to do so might spill its contents.

Superficially Queenborough and its people, no doubt, might appear as a finished product of a skillful cabinet-maker, like a fine old inlaid table top. Miss Glasgow has found the joint beneath the veneer, and has gently sliced it off. Into every weak spot in the inlay she has slipped her knife, until all that is left at last is a pile of neatly excised bits. Out of them curiously comes beauty. They reflect prismatically, as a flat surface could not. The clear flame of her wit kindles them to an incandescence which glows far into the world of men and women and glitters on the ironic complications of their dealings with life.

Churchman, 140 (5 October 1929), 17

There has been no little just complaint that modern writers of fiction who can draw characters one would find interesting to know are none too plentiful. That charge could not be sustained against Miss Glasgow by any reader of this, her latest novel. In addition to giving us men and women who are not machine-made, flat products of dabblers in writing, she has, through those characters, produced an impressive commentary on the conflicts, complications and contrasts inherent in the change from Victorian to present-day life and manners. Anyone with a spark of interest in human beings would delight to have the opportunity of meeting Mr. or Mrs. Littlepage, or Marmaduke or Molly or Mary Victoria or "poor Aunt Agatha," who move with the reality of flesh and blood, of brains and emotions, through the chapters of this novel. Here are the finest products of Virginian civilization of the Victorian period, carrying over into the present century, to be played upon by a world whose ideals and practices have been turned topsy-turvy by the Great War. One suspects that Miss Glasgow has written a novel not for today alone, but one which, generations hence, will be read as a graphic picture of the struggle for moral readjustment at a turning-point in American civilization.

John Hervey, "Sympathetic Art," *Saturday Review of Literature*, 12 October 1929, 268

I have before me, to use a somewhat shopworn phrase, the latest example of the contemporary novel of the species to which I have referred. It bears the title: *They Stooped to Folly*, in itself a masterpiece of best-selling selection, and is, all things considered, so almost perfect an example of the order to which it belongs that it well deserves the vast amount of appreciation which it has been receiving and to which these paragraphs are an unpretentious addition.

Experience in contemporary novel-reading has instructed most novel-readers, with little doubt, that the Proper Thing must begin with a seduction. But in the present case the fair author has, as it were, parlayed her one best bet, as the sporting fraternity would say, clear across the board, backing it straight, place, and show. For her point of departure is not one seduction, but three. These interesting events, moreover, cannot correctly be termed departures. For we never get away from them. Not for a moment. There are times in real life when such occurrences are forgotten, for the nonce at least. But never in this novel in which they have been embalmed and treasured up. They are placed in the center of the stage, directly under the spotlight, at the beginning of the show. They never budge from it. And they are the last thing in evidence as we close the book. Perhaps the contemporary novel reader never tires of seduction and its consequences. Perhaps, too, he—or even she—may. Even where the censorship has been benignant the memoirs of Casanova have had a much more restricted sale than many suppose.

Readers of those adventurous and almost intolerably prolonged chronicles, howbeit, will recall that their relator—their creator in the true sense, seeing that many of them are now believed to have been imaginary rather than authentic—fixes upon the page the lineaments of the seduced ones almost invariably with a "longing, lingering look behind." He felt for them an affection which, with few exceptions, he wishes also to evoke in the reader's breast. How many endearing epithets he finds for them, how many charming and ingratiating details he weaves into his narrative in the effort to persuade us that they were lovable! Which is one reason why their story still enthralls.

No such emotion, however, has glowed in the breast of the creator of the three heroines of *They Stooped to Folly*. On the contrary, she has for them a corrosive scorn and contumely. Taking each unfortunate in turn, she, as it were, strips her naked and exposes her to the jeers of the market-place. With a pen like that of Suetonius, pitilessly barbed, each in turn is flayed alive and placed quivering before us. Not only is this true of poor Aunt Agatha—it is just as true of the second and third members of the trinity. Of a different type and temper, seduction had with them very different sequels. But that makes no difference with their ultimate fate. Through the protective armor which they attempted to put on the merciless pen riddles them completely. There is no doubt in the world that they are contemptible and are limned so of set purpose.

However, while it is the seduced who get the worst of it, literally and otherwise, in this so-very-popular production—popular alike with the critics and the public, it is proclaimed—nobody gets the best of it. That is to say, the best of the author.

These characters, the book says very explicitly, may have fooled themselves, they may have fooled others, they might even fool us, the readers—but the author does not propose to let them. Not she. Always at our elbow with another damaging detail, sly innuendo, subtle disparagement, witty sneer, or civil leer, every page becomes in effect an indictment of the so-called human race. "What a shabby set they are!" the writer seems to say. "Wait a moment! Let me whisper you something more ignominious. They are really without extenuation. People are like that."

One closes the book marveling that throughout its length the writer has not betrayed a spark of genuine sympathy for a single one of its protagonists—for just at the moment when she seems about to do so, you may be sure that she is merely preparing some fresh stroke of derision. Ibsen, in one of his letters, describes how he kept a viper—dead, one supposes?—twined about his inkwell while writing one of his most envenomed arraignments of society. What, one wonders, did the author of *They Stooped to Folly*, festoon about hers while in the act of composition?

Meditating how completely the quality of mercy has been strained out of the volume, one recalls the great masters of the art of fiction and recalls also that they were of sympathy all compact. We remember the triumphant cry of Taine: "Balzac loves his Valérie!" when he was contrasting the author of the *Comédie Humaine* with Thackeray and the latter's unconcealed loathing of his Becky Sharpe. The great French critic, one of the most creative of all practitioners of his art, reproached the author of *Vanity Fair* for his lack of sympathy with his own heroine and bade us turn to the pages of the *Comédie* in order to discover how much greater were its portraitures. Becky, in comparison with the atrocious Marneffe woman, was an inoffensive creature—but Balzac places the latter before us with a sympathy which makes her live with an immortal virility; whereas Thackeray, lacking that sympathy, accompanies Becky with an unflagging *obbligato* of detraction.

All modern satirical novelists—at least all who write in English—nest in Thackeray, just as all novelists whatever, as Henry James has said, nest in Balzac. But Thackeray was not merely a satirist, though a very great one. He was also the man who was found convulsed with weeping when he had "killed the Colonel." *Sunt lacrymæ rerum* was, after all, true to Thackeray after his fashion and he paid his devoir to that truth from the greatness of his heart.... But we cannot conceive of the author of *They Stooped to Folly* indulging any such weakness. All her characters, as the youthful Joe Vance would have said, are hinsecks—and pearly drops for trampled worms are unspeakably Victorian.

So we are shown only one side of these poor beings. All are static and never dynamic, never for a moment truly human: as, not having been conceived in a humane spirit, they cannot be. All the literary skill that has been expended upon them cannot alter this condition.

Suppose—just suppose—that Aunt Agatha had been presented to us with the sympathy that her "case" really demanded. Not with any false sentimentality, but with a comprehending charity, whose aim was to show her in the round, not merely a figure, cleverly caricatured, upon what is in effect a flat surface. Aunt Agatha, done as she is in *eauforte*, vindictively etched and "bitten" with a bitter brilliance—suppose she had been bathed instead in the *ære perennius* of sympathetic understanding, that we had been allowed to walk around her and know her in her habit as she lived instead of as a puppet in a show of marionettes. What a poignant, what an unforgettable creation she might well have been!

[Here a discussion of Constance Fenimore Woolson's *For the Major* argues that Woolson showed more "sympathy" and "love" for her characters than Glasgow does.]

A novel is, after all, only a story: what the author, what the reader, makes of it. But in the end it remains either sincerity or a simulacrum. Either it is warm with life and suffused with humanity or it is something got-up and frigid, clever to the ultimate but unconvincing. *They Stooped to Folly* will plead in its own defense that it is merely a comedy of manners. But outside Thespis's own domain few things more veritably tragic than the lives of Aunt Agatha and her fellow-victims could well be imagined. Fate was indeed unkind to them, but their crowning misfortune has been the hatred of their own creator.

"Balzac loved his Valérie!".... [Ellipsis in original.] And by that sign he conquered.

B. E. Todd, "Fiction: The Hall of Laughter," *Spectator* [England], 143 (2 November 1929), 641

Miss Ellen Glasgow is cynical, too, but more consistently so than Mr. [Michael] Arlen [in *Babes in the Woods*], and her mirror also reflects greediness—not for little loves and glittering "gadgets" but for life itself. The mouths of her heroines droop at the corners and their hands are outstretched to take and to hold. Her new and very brilliant book which is sub-titled "A Comedy of Morals" has for its text the lines:

"When lovely woman stoops to folly,
And finds too late that men betray,
What charm can soothe her melancholy?
What art can wash her guilt away?"

All the American women in her book have been betrayed in one way or another, and each is trying to soothe herself. "Aunt Agatha," who fell in an age when Victorians did nothing to break the fall of any young lady, seeks comfort in her old age from cinemas and ice-cream sodas. Mrs. Burden, whose husband deserted her because he could not stand her incessant virtue, and whose daughter has been betrayed by a neurotic waster, consoles herself by grim acts of duty. Milly Burden still claims credit at the bank of life, but finds none since her lover stole away her gilt-edged illusions, when he married her employer's self-righteous daughter. Miss Glasgow's mirror is a very clear one: it stands in the hard light of day and no shadows blur its tortured reflections. She has once again proved herself an able craftswoman: as usual her work is exquisite.

Phoebe H. Gilkyson, "Ellen Glasgow," *Saturday Review of Literature*, 6 (23 November 1929), 467

To the Editor of *The Saturday Review*:[1]
SIR:
Miss Ellen Glasgow's new novel needs no defense; if it did, a regiment of sharper

pens than mine would mobilize at once. But that it should be used as text for Mr. Hervey's complaint of "modern" novelists is too delicious to pass without comment.

Miss Glasgow is "modern," to be sure, and has been so since she published her first novel, in her 'teens, about thirty years ago. Her modernity has consisted always of courageous, unprejudiced thinking, and of growth and progress as years passed. But that the author of *Barren Ground*, or *One Man in His Time*, or *The Builders*, should be condemned as frigid, sneering, pitiless, scornful, and so on, is absurd, nothing more. In her two most recent novels, from a list of eighteen, Miss Glasgow has entered the field of satire, and it is apparent that Mr. Hervey doesn't like satire. Very well; let him turn back to her earlier books: he will find therein romance, realism, and a sympathy that is free from sentimentalism. Only a true Southerner can write of the South without sentimentalism. If *The Romantic Comedians* and *They Stooped to Folly* seem flippant, after that, it is because the reader, unlike Miss Glasgow, hasn't the vitality left for laughter. Pity is all very well, and isn't absent from Miss Glasgow's books, but she has no reverence for supine submission to standards that sacrifice the female to the glory of the male, or to a hypocrisy that "finds it less embarrassing to commit adultery than to speak of it."

Hers isn't light laughter. Mr. Hervey is quite right in detecting the undercurrent of tragedy. The tragedy is there, as it always is in true irony. But most ironical of all, such tragedy as Aunt Agatha's was futile and unnecessary, and it is time for a courageous soul to jeer such penalties of "Southern chivalry" out of countenance. Count Keyserling has declared that Virginia has the only true culture of the United States, explaining that the people of no other community stand still long enough to appreciate leisure, beauty, or social intercourse. But it is true that no other section of the country—not even New England—is so hide-bound in its prejudices on the subject of women. We call Mr. Hervey's attention to the fact that the author doesn't "sneer" at Milly. Milly is a rebel; she bruises herself sulkily against tradition, but one prophesies that in the end, tradition will be worse bruised than Milly. She has pride, courage, and intelligence; the world needs her type and must eventually make place for her. No, one doesn't pity Milly, but one respects her.

We hold no brief for the synthetic cynicism of so many moderns. Stories of patient love and sacrifice will always hold their place in human hearts. But too much sweetness and light cloys and drugs the mind; wise, ruthless laughter is cleansing and stimulating. For such moderns as Miss Glasgow, let us be grateful.

1 In response to Hervey's review on pp. 315–17 of this book.

Louise Bogan, *New Republic*, 61 (4 December 1929), 50–1

It is difficult to trace the exact nature of the failure in Miss Glasgow's book. She writes competently and fully, and, in many instances, with real wit and intelligence. The problem in her latest novel is grievously misstated in its title, which places emphasis upon varying reactions to unfortunate love-affairs in women of different periods. As a matter of fact, her novel is chiefly concerned with the reactions of Mr. Virginius Littlepage, his wife, Victoria, and their daughter, Mary Victoria, members of an aristocratic family in a

"New Novels," *Times Literary Supplement* [England], 5 December 1929, p. 1026

"There are occasions, Marmaduke, when I should think twice before calling you a Southern gentleman," Mr. Littlepage said sternly to his raffish and more than middle-aged brother; and this curious observation—the statement of a serious American ideal—is in keeping with the old-fashioned air of Ellen Glasgow's new novel (*They Stooped to Folly*). The Southern ladies who stooped were four, each of them closely connected with good Mr. Littlepage: his Aunt Agatha, betrayed by a Southern gentleman called Colonel Somebody, "who moved in the best circles, but was married already," and left to languish as a lost soul with no resource but the theatre every afternoon; his secretary, Milly Burden, a war victim with a buried baby and a defiant post-War shamelessness; his old flame, Mrs. Dalrymple, and his daughter, Mary Victoria. The latter, certainly, married her neurotic War hero, but hers was the greatest folly of all. Her mind was furnished with nothing but the stoutest American ideals, reinforced concrete ideals; and a sickly young man whom she knew to be involved with another young woman seemed to her the most promising material on which she could get to work. Incidentally he was Milly Burden's lover, whom she as a post-War worker in troubled Europe had been commissioned to retrieve for the distressed secretary. Her method of carrying out this duty was to bring him back as her husband, thus upsetting a number of people, although her father's faith in her goodness and nobility remained unshaken. He changing Southern city, to the invasion of their lives by tough modern reality.

The aging Mr. Littlepage tries to ward off his sense of futility by rather feeble gestures toward lost romance, on the one hand, and a temperate appraisal of contemporary mixed values on the other. He bestows clandestine caresses on Mrs. Dalrymple, the light lady of the 90's, at the same time that he defends and protects Milly, the modern exemplar of lost virtue, even after his daughter has married Milly's former lover. Mrs. Littlepage tries to make vicarious amends to Aunt Agatha, who, in the 80's, was the victim of a guilty love, and to other such broken lives, by her charitable interest in Houses of Hope for female delinquents. Mary Victoria, having married her husband with the forcible intention of reforming him, ends by rushing after him as he flees, with a regrettable lack of decorum. Miss Glasgow has written down her true problem solidly but repetitiously. In her eagerness to point her case, the most subtle situations are driven through by phrases too general to be illuminating. The fallen ladies remain figurines—even Milly's revolt against becoming a "helpless victim of life" is somewhat unbelievable, after Miss Glasgow has made her cling with the utmost tenacity to the image of a worthless lover for seven years. Mr. and Mrs. Littlepage are most successfully treated: two "old children" afraid of any romanticism not of their particular brand. In order that anything really significant might come to such a puzzle of emotions freed or thwarted by changing convention, something more than a mere competent exploration of surfaces would be required. The surfaces must be ripped through. Miss Glasgow has tools for that more penetrating method, but she does not use them.

was called Virginius, and the mere sight of the opulent Mrs. Dalrymple, whom he had once kissed, made him forget sobriety and Southern deportment. But he did not actually stoop to folly.

The Littlepage family is presented with the skill and acumen to be looked for from Miss Glasgow. It is all quite interesting, but the most interesting thing about this book is the emergence of the fact that as time goes on the social importance of the late War is becoming greater in the United States than anywhere else. They are buying it up, incorporating it into their daily life, now that it has been over for eleven years, using the emotions and experiences of others as a child uses the paints in his paint-box. Every American family—in fiction—has been profoundly affected, and there is a rush of heroes to the publishers that is very gratifying. Miss Glasgow accepts this convention, but her stooping ladies would have been as engagingly foolish had they never sniffed the battlefields or heard a military band.

Checklist of Additional Reviews

Joanna Rosamond Milner, "The Literary Lantern," Louisville *Courier-Journal*, 4 August 1929, sec. 4, p. 2.

Frederic F. Van de Water, "Some Novels Have Plot and Some Have Not," New York *Evening Post*, 17 August 1929, sec. M, p. 6.

L.M., "Ellen Glasgow Satirizes Musty Moral Attitudes," Kansas City (Missouri) *Star*, 7 September 1929, p. 4.

Helen MacAfee, "Outstanding Novels in Brief Review," *Yale Review*, n.s. 19 (Autumn 1929), viii, x.

Booklist, 26 (November 1929), 70.

Open Shelf, December 1929, p. 157.

THE SHELTERED LIFE

THE SHELTERED LIFE

By
ELLEN GLASGOW

Doubleday, Doran & Company, Inc.
Garden City, New York
MCMXXXII

Dorothea Brande, "Four Novels of the Month," *Bookman*, 75 (August 1932), 405

As if to show that this grooming of girls for marriage to the end that they are wrecked as human beings is timeless and international comes Miss Ellen Glasgow's new book, *The Sheltered Life*.... As always, the South is Miss Glasgow's scene, and a belle of the nineties and a girl of today are her twin heroines. Under its quiet manner this novel is one more indictment of our attitude toward sex, for little Jenny Blair Archbald is shown in the opening pages as a child of imagination, courage, and decency. In the end she has foundered in a swamp of inertia, of obsession with the philandering husband of a woman she worships, of appalling clandestine intrigue which leads her to betray everyone she has cause to love. Such a miasma of sex arises from the pages of *The Sheltered Life* as many a piece of open erotica might envy, yet Miss Glasgow leads you into the bog step by step, like one under an evil enchantment.

This is, I should say, frankly a thesis book, and the thesis is one we have all heard *ad nauseam* these last twenty years: that no good comes to a society which allows passion and chivalry to be separated. This has been the theme of more than one of Miss Glasgow's earlier novels; it was the endless and elaborately illustrated theme of Evelyn Scott's recent *A Calendar of Sin*. Without any great effort one could give a score of titles, from the lists of the past two years, of other books on the same subject. Miss Glasgow's small canvas is extraordinarily effective; infinitely more so, to me, than Miss Scott's jumbled panorama of bad examples. Yet the suspicion creeps in, at the very moment of approving Miss Glasgow's entirely believable characters, her carefully worked out story of decay and death, that if the battle these crusaders are fighting so ardently is not already won they may as well lay aside their arms and rest; if, after all this belabouring, passion and chivalry will not strike hands and become allies, then it is because they are supernatural and immortal enemies and we cannot reconcile them.

Gerald W. Johnson, "Ex Libris," Baltimore *Evening Sun*, 13 August 1932, p. 4

Ellen Glasgow, of all people, has gone over and joined the horror-mongers! It is a fit occasion for wailing and lamentation, for with her defection goes the last hope of the literary South. As long as she held out there was one citadel of suavity, one fortress of calm reason, spiced with wit and softened with geniality, one saving remnant of a civilization that was civilized. But when she goes down, all is lost: Raw-Head-and-Bloody-Bones becomes the symbol of Dixie and William Faulkner triumphs over us.

Of course, even her surrender is distinguished. Being Ellen Glasgow, she could not join the bloody-minded in any other than a graceful, witty and magnificent way. Her new book is, from the technical standpoint, one of her best, which is equivalent to saying that it immediately takes rank with anything that America has produced, for she is unquestionably among the dozen most competent novelists this country has brought forth. Indeed, for sheer craftsmanship it is hard to think of any single volume that unquestionably takes rank above *The Romantic Comedians*.

But somehow the passion for goose flesh that seems to infect every really good *litterateur* below the Potomac has gotten into her blood. What on earth is the matter with the South, anyhow? Consider the apparitions that have arisen among the magnolias within the last few years—the primitives of Julia Peterkin, the morons and manic-depressives of Paul Green, the tortured illiterates of Thomas Wolfe, the perverts and degenerates of Faulkner—and name, if you can, a more appalling procession of madness and despair. Senator Lodge, with that suave Massachusetts insolence of which he was a past master, once referred to the South as a "shotgun civilization," but to refer to what Southern writers have been presenting of late as a shotgun civilization would be fulsome flattery. Killing—just plain, unadorned murder—has been familiar to every land and every clime since Cain rose against Abel in the field. But honest, wholesome homicide is utterly out of the fashion in modern Southern writing. What we have now is murder tricked out in gaudy habiliments, and rendered a thousand times more horrid by its gauds. . . .

This notice will have been written in vain if it fails to convey the impression that here is a book of high distinction, possessing in abundance merits that the great majority of novelists strive after "with groanings that may not be uttered" and strive after fruitlessly. But it will also have been written in vain if it fails to convey the impression that it is a book to which the reviewer objects intensely, objects violently, and would, if this were aught but a respectable family journal, object profanely. For excursions into psychopathology should be left to slighter talents than that of Ellen Glasgow. Let persons who are incapable of the delicate and difficult work of transferring the relatively sane to the printed page busy themselves with the coarser job of describing the completely goofy. Ellen Glasgow can delight us and enlighten us and on occasion enrapture us. It is with rage, then, not with admiration, that one observes her at the infinitely slighter business of making our flesh crawl.

Mark Lutz, "Miss Glasgow Paints Picture of Virginia Before World War," Richmond *News Leader*, 26 August 1932, p. 6

Miss Ellen Glasgow's new novel, *The Sheltered Life*, advance copies of which have been received in Richmond, deals with the paradox that beneath an outwardly calm exterior there may course the most turbulent of emotions. Her theme, developed with the distinguished writer's effortless brilliancy of craftsmanship and characterization, has reality and sincerity and beauty.

The scene is in the Virginia town of Queenborough, which may or may not be Richmond. The time is from 1906 to the beginning of the world war. And the men and women who are mostly involved in its action are Jenny Blair Archbald, a somewhat precocious girl, who grows into a premature womanhood only to carry catastrophe into the lives of others; Mrs. Birdsong, an anxious belle of the nineties; George Birdsong, the unworthy husband of the beauty, and General Archbald, a gallant of the Old South, who became what was expected of him by learning how to put an end to what he might have become....

Miss Glasgow has neither employed the stark realism of *Barren Ground* nor the romanticism of *The Battle-Ground* and earlier works in *The Sheltered Life*. Her style is nearer that of *The Romantic Comedians* and *They Stooped to Conquer*.

As a social study of a small group it is one of the foremost novels of the year. As a study of the nuances and subtleties of an age just past, it has claims to even greater consideration. Miss Glasgow's poise as an artist, her grasp of human strengths and weaknesses, goes to make *The Sheltered Life* among the most powerful of the Richmonder's ironic pieces of fiction.

William Soskin, "Reading and Writing," New York *Evening Post*, 24 August 1932, sec. 1, p. 9

The Russia of Andreyev and Tchekov may seem far removed, both in space and in time, from one of the most patrician of the United States—Virginia; but Miss Ellen Glasgow's new novel, *The Sheltered Life*, suggests a surprisingly close kinship between some of the gracefully decaying families near Richmond and those near the St. Petersburg of pre-Soviet days.

In *The Sheltered Life* Miss Glasgow gives us a cast of characters worthy of the most somber of Russian novelists—the pathologically violent Dostoyevsky being excluded, of course, from present consideration. What is more, Miss Glasgow has produced a novel worthy of comparison with some of the works in the mainstream of Russian fiction. She has accomplished that without for a moment losing the wit, the peculiar understanding of Southern *mores*, the broad irony and the grace that have brought her distinction as an American artist.

In a day when the great majority of competent American novelists have proclaimed their belief that they have nothing more to say in fiction, that the novel is an outworn form which must be superseded by some new pattern more closely related to machines, Communism, the Kentucky coal fields, the bonus army and the proletarian scene, it is refreshing to come upon a work whose very substance vindicates the novel and which refutes these hysterical gentlemen most convincingly.

Not that *The Sheltered Life* hides its head in the sand of some esthetic desert, carefully avoiding contamination in the social scene. On the contrary, Miss Glasgow's story of a group of Southerners upholding the traditions of a protected and leisurely class, while the entire world upon which their social position and their morality were built is cracking up beneath them, is shot through with an acute and wise perception of a changing order of things. It indulges, indeed, in a type of symbolism by which the stench of the factory districts and the new industrialism of the South begin to pervade the atmosphere of these old families.

The point is that Miss Glasgow has mastered the art of fiction too completely and too well to submerge her individuals, made up of a thousand personal impulses and intimate, human factors, in a dramatically chaotic and impossible social welter. As so many other of the novelists who are being claimed for Proletarianism, as Zola and Flaubert and the Russians did, Miss Glasgow makes the social body a conditioning background, a soil out of which her characters rise and to which they return—but they remain individuals, large, real, artistically free-willed, impulsive, glandularly whole individuals who can reflect Miss Glasgow's own wit and understanding brightly and clearly.

The chief trouble with the leading people of *The Sheltered Life* lies in their own insulation from reality, their own finicky and introverted conceptions of their world. Their imagination, bottled up inside, has become a "hothouse for sensation." They have looked upon the exotic plants, the sports and the mutations of botany which this imagination produced, and they have mistaken such growths for the everyday, healthy forest of their own soil.

[...]

All that, however, is more or less the obvious drama, the "action" of *The Sheltered Life*. The important and rich quality of the book lies in another direction. There we find a gallery of characters portrayed, with Miss Glasgow's characteristic energy, in broad but sure and telling strokes. At the head of the gallery we must place the aged General Archbald, aged eighty-three, a noble old man who, for all his eagle-like appearance, had about him the "far-inward gaze" of a man born out of his time, who could not think or feel as the people about him thought or felt. He, too, is a victim to appearances, for thirty years a good husband to a woman he married when he had an attack of honor.

In a remarkable chapter of the novel, entitled "The Deep Past," Miss Glasgow achieves for this man very much what V. Sackville-West did for the gracious old lady of *All Passion Spent*. We are given to see, through a retrospective and dreamlike soliloquy that shifts from the garden in which the General sits to the important fragments of memory, the accidental and significant images in the stream of time that has made his life, the essential conflicts and the ideals through which he has struggled. It is as though youth and man and olden philosopher were viewing the past and the present simultaneously—with Miss Glasgow present to lend the suggestive lyric touches and the imaginative color to the dream.

That reverie reveals the original nature, the poet's being of the old General, as it was diverted into a thousand extraneous and superficial paths. It provides the philosophic core of the novel. We come to know the one fleeting, defeated passion of the man's youth. Except for that passion "he had lived entirely on the shifting surface of facts. . . . Always he had fallen into the right pattern, but the center of that pattern was missing."

So with most of the people of this book. The patterns they cannot help. The center of the pattern they cannot find. They are people who must be dealt with keenly, clearly and tolerantly. No writer I know could give us the gentle but sharp and nice irony such a story requires better than does Miss Glasgow.

Lewis Gannett, "Lewis Gannett Keeps Up with New Publications," Charleston [West Virginia] *Mail*, 26 August 1932

Ellen Glasgow has the sharpest and most civilized wit of all present-day American writers, and her new novel, *The Sheltered Life*, which Doubleday, Doran publish today, is liberally spiced with it. "Mild, charming, implacable, with all the secret malice of destiny," is the way she describes her Cora Archbald; she herself is on the surface deceptively mild, always charming, and implacable in her conviction that destiny is malicious.

In *The Sheltered Life* we meet again the decaying gentility of that Queenborough which is so like Richmond, still sacrificing themselves to the art of saving appearances, still permitting dead sounds to doom every living voice; and at the end of this novel, in a whirling melodramatic finish, Miss Glasgow denies even to unpretending youth any hope of happiness. To attempt to be natural, she seems to suggest, is even more cruel than pretense.

But Ellen Glasgow hides her dark philosophy beneath a sparkling surface. Who else could turn so neatly a description of a woman desperately seeking to live up to the tradition of her own beauty? "Mrs. Birdsong was one of those celebrated beauties who, if they still exist, have ceased to be celebrated. Tall, slender, royal in carriage, hers was that perfect loveliness which made the hearts of old men flutter and miss a beat when she approached. Everything about her was flowing, and everything flowed divinely." Who else would write that one of the grand old ladies of Queenborough had such an air that she always somehow suggested a Confederate flag being carried through the rain to the inspiring music of a regimental band?

"Think what it must have cost her to keep up being an ideal for more than 20 years," said one of Eva Birdsong's younger admirers. "You may talk about keeping up socially, but it doesn't touch the effort of keeping up emotionally." Miss Glasgow constantly tosses off such sparkling bits of profound wisdom. Eva had idealized her husband, George, who loved her but found it hard to remain an ideal 24 hours in the day; and she carefully preserved her ideal self. So that when it was too late, Eva Birdsong warned young Jenny Blair, "Whatever you do, never risk all your happiness on a single chance. Always keep something back, if it is only a crumb. Always keep something back for a rainy day."

"Romantic women like Eva," the implacable daughter of General Archbald said, "make the mistake of measuring a man's love by his theories." Whereupon the general mused: "If women could begin to realize how little what a man thinks has to do with how he feels!" And George Birdsong, who was Eva's husband, remarked one day that he could bear it better if Eva would only stop smiling. At another time, in a bitter burst of revealing honesty, he told little Jenny Blair that "Women like to sit down with trouble as if it were knitting. But men are different. Men must get away or take a drink, one or the other." George took both escapes, and Eva pretended loyally to know nothing of either of them.

Fanny Butcher, "Ellen Glasgow Writes Novel of Old South," Chicago *Daily Tribune*, 27 August 1932, p. 11

The foremost feminine protagonist of the old regime (in its present form) in the old south, Ellen Glasgow, has just given us another of her memorable pictures of social order which is, like Boston, more of a state of mind than a geographical section.

The Sheltered Life portrays the old south—in its post-bellum manifestation—and has as its chief characters two men and two women whose lives have been "sheltered," the women's by the care of their men folk, the men's by force of circumstances and by a tacit acceptance of a man's right to his private life....

Ellen Glasgow has a genius for a certain gentle satire. There is nothing swashbuckling about it, nothing bitter, but there is, undeniably, a barb in the lightest of her humor. *The Sheltered Life* is as rich in satirical humor as anything she has ever written, although the book is, when the delicious petals of the artichoke are peeled away, bristly with tragedy at its core, a tragedy which only protects the more delectable core of the book—that love is, perhaps, despite its disappointments, its agonies, its bitterness, a living, vital force in some lives. . . .

The story of Gen. Archbald is an epic of "the sheltered life." A southern gentleman, always living up to the ideals imposed upon a southern gentleman, he retained, in some magic fashion, his belief in love. His own love had been but for a brief time and, so far as the world might have judged it, futile, with death closing the hymn of love before he had heard more than the first few bars of the pæan, but in the chapters in which as an old man he reviews his life Miss Glasgow has made of him an epic. . . .

Miss Glasgow could very easily have made her novel more of an entity technically, giving it the fluid quality which the greatest of fiction always has, a quality which makes the reader so conscious of the inevitability of its telling (in manner as well as in fact) that he is entirely unconscious of the author's method. *The Sheltered Life* is not so blessed. The reader hears the creaking of the technical machinery. But even occasional creaks cannot do more than momentarily divert the reader from the fact that *The Sheltered Life* is a memorable record of a social scheme—and a social psychology—most of it only a memory, and that, so far as intriguing stories go, it was like Eva Birdsong, beauty and undeniable allure.

Henry Seidel Canby, "Youth and Age," *Saturday Review of Literature*, 9 (27 August 1932), 63

A true confusion in values has been evident in some of the most vigorous of recent criticism of American writers. It results from reviewing a book, and especially a novel, as if the worth of the book were to be determined by the probable future of the character types. If the characters and the ideas about them belong to a régime of which the critic disapproves, then he condemns the book as old-fashioned or futile. He seems to forget that some of the greatest books in the world (the Dialogues of Plato for an example) have been written with a social reference to an era already past or passing when the author drew together his reflections. But if the Greece of Socrates was crumbling, the Greek idea lived on. Recent attacks on two such artists in our Victorian past as Mrs. Wharton and Miss Ellen Glasgow have sprung from this prevalent fallacy. Neither the age of innocence nor southern aristocracy seems useful to those who predicate a collectivist state. Hence the art suffers in their eyes because it is born of sympathies which they neither understand nor like. They call these books and these writers reactionary. The term is erroneous. The artist sees life as continuous, whole, and enduring, while reforms, reconstructions, and revolutions make their mark and pass.

Miss Glasgow deserves praise from those who are most often her detractors. She is one of the very few writers upon the old and the modern South who understands tradition, who comprehends the intricate values of the life of a "gentleman" or a "lady," and yet never writes sentiment when satire is called for, never perfumes the "bad smell" of decaying gentility, never neglects either the significance of surface or the contradictions of desire and act. She is a realist who deals by preference with material romantic in aspect, and to the admirable competence in narrative expression which the modern school of British novelists of manners have attained, she adds a ruthless analysis and a willingness to conclude with tragedy which they more and more seem to lack.

[...]

I am not sure that I have followed Miss Glasgow's program in this carefully studied novel, for the characters and the scene are realized with such intensity that one makes one's own stories about them. She divides her book into "The Age of Make-Believe," "The Deep Past," and "The Illusion," which would seem to represent a spiritual progress in the old General, concluding in a determination to hold fast what he found to have been vital in his past. I think that, like many another novelist, she has injected into her story an unnecessary metaphysics, and this would explain a fault (unusual with her), *longueurs* both in the meditations of the General and in the descriptions of Mrs. Birdsong, understandable as the pinning down of a thesis, but out of harmony with the sure and vivid narrative, the reticent and yet all revealing analysis, of Jenny Blair's adolescent passion, of George Birdsong's errant maleness, of the heroic jealousies of Mrs. Birdsong, of the pathological amorousness of Aunt Etta. The same thing happens when Jane Austen grows moral on the subject of imprudent affections or when George Meredith begins to scintillate on feminism.

But perhaps this fault in a book, the patina of which indicates a ripeness that disarms criticism, is more due to the difficulties of the subject. For it is really General Archbald's story, the story of an old man who looks on, and sees, but cannot act. Hence the action in the novel is an action of youth and middle age—here significant and abundant action leading into life, not away from it, and conducted with all the decorous but dramatic make-believe of gentility upon the very edge of disgrace and disaster. And by contrast it is difficult for the reader to step back, as he must do, into the mind of old age, the mind of the General, where runs the real current of ultimate reality in this story. For the rest are shadows, brilliant, moving shadows, like figures on the moving-picture screen, while in his thought and against his memories, the real, the legitimate state is set. Miss Glasgow should have helped us more, there is a defect in technique of the whole, though the parts of this novel are so admirable. A second reading would restore the balance, guide the reader (as perhaps even this criticism may help to do); and even in this distressing day of a moth's life for books, this is a novel which may get the double attention which ripe works deserve.

R[obert] M. C[oates], "Books," *New Yorker*, 8 (27 August 1932), 44

Miss Glasgow's *The Sheltered Life* ... I thought to be incomparably ... better [than Manuel Komroff's *A New York Tempest*] both in matter and in form. It is the story—cast in a style that hovers between the past and the present of the drama, which itself is laid in a time some thirty years ago—of a great beauty who, marrying, finds that her husband, though he loves her fiercely, is far too gay a dog ever to remain faithful to her. The tragedy, then, is basically that of woman under the Victorian standards of morality, and it is told with a sober dignity, a kind of musing eloquence, that I found very moving.

W. A. Martin, Buffalo *Evening News*, 27 August 1932, Saturday magazine section, p. 3

Ellen Glasgow's new novel, *The Sheltered Life*, puts her securely in the rank of the great novelists of all times. The feeling one has in reading it is, here is a book that I must keep and read again and again. In *The Sheltered Life* Miss Glasgow has reached the perfection of literary style towards which she has been working for years.

The movement of the story is slow. The process is mostly analytical. Her characters, people in Queenborough, Virginia, have their counterpart throughout the world. They have their inner lives, known mostly to themselves, and their outer lives by which they are known to the world.
[. . .]

Although *The Sheltered Life* is, for the most part, minutely analytical, it arouses in the reader a fever of excitement. It seems to us by far the most beautiful thing that Ellen Glasgow has done; and we rank Ellen Glasgow among the greatest novelists of all times.

Newark [New Jersey] *News*, 27 August 1932, p. 14

For most part Ellen Glasgow's *The Sheltered Life* is another masterpiece of acute observation and satiric expression, but towards the end Miss Glasgow deserts her usual quiet tone and closes in a shriek of starkest tragedy. Throughout the book she has been exhibiting, with pitiless truthfulness, the effect of a philandering husband's unfaithfulness on a wife whose beauty and patience surpass Griselda's. Yet the closing episode is not less a commentary on the shallowness of emotion of some women, and if Miss Glasgow intends any moral to be drawn from her entrancing narrative, it is the necessity of discipline and judgment on the part of women when sex-emotions are called into play.

As always in Miss Glasgow's work, the background is an amazingly convincing delineation of the Southern scene, with its sweet and its sour aspects. Perhaps the finest portrait in the book is that of old General Archbald.

Robert H. Willson, Chicago *Herald-Examiner*, 27 August 1932, p. 12

Here is a story-book, *The Sheltered Life*, by Ellen Glasgow, just published by Doubleday Doran. It will be known as a novel but it is something more than that. It is a fine example of the classic art of the story-teller.

It is a story of the new South and of

human nature that is old. The average person does not live by a plot so much as by accidental encounter with environment and a natural succession of events. There would be no plot in *The Sheltered Life* and the author was too much of an artist to invent one.

However, that does not dispose of drama. You will pursue a charming, delightful association with new acquaintances, all unsuspecting until you come up to a crashing finale, which will leave you astonished, smothered, harried, imaginatively wheeling through space like a misplaced asteroid.

Gen. (Confederate) Daniel Archbald, 83, is important, linking the old South, which may grow older but never dies, to the new. The time is 1906 to 1914. In this Archbald family are Jenny Blair, a very modern granddaughter; her widowed mother, Cora; a peculiar aunt, Etta; and a normal aunt, Isabella.

Of equal importance are the friends and neighbors, including Dr. Welch and Mr. and Mrs. George Birdsong, the Birdsong romance being that of the young singer who gave up an operatic career to marry a weak, witless and handsome husband, with the usual results.

Jenny Blair is a study in the childish, adolescent psychology of young girlhood and the perplexity of conflicts between roving modernities of thought and the safeties of the sheltered life. For an almost clairvoyant study of old age Miss Glasgow has outdone herself in the character of Gen. Archbald. Son of a hunting, drinking, slave-owning Virginia family, he has the soul of a poet and the poet's horror of all forms of cruelty. He finds himself too gentle to be harsh, even in word, and thus he presides as head of a woman-ridden household that gives him "nothing that he wants and everything that is good for him."

The Sheltered Life is a masterpiece of fine writing, an example in style and an intimate revelation of the comedy-drama of life.

J. Donald Adams, "Ellen Glasgow's Finest Novel," *New York Times Book Review*, 28 August 1932, sec. 5, pp. 1, 13

The poet in most of us dies young, and few writers, unless they give their lives to poetry, retain for long that capacity to see things for the first time which is poetry's essence. But there is an element of poetry in all art of a high order, and that holds as true for the novel as for any other form. It is present in the novels of Ellen Glasgow, along with those other qualities which are needed if a writer is to touch human lives with illumination. Time has not dulled the bright edge of Miss Glasgow's vision—she has kept the flame of poetry alive, while the years have brought a brighter lustre to those gifts which experience tends rather to improve than to blight. Wit, wisdom and art are all the beneficiaries of time, and in Miss Glasgow's work they have all steadily strengthened. This last book of hers, *The Sheltered Life*, is in many ways her best. Perhaps the chief reason for its excellence is its more complete fusion of these several qualities which distinguish her work. In the novels which preceded it the balance was less evenly held....

In this new novel there is not only a true marriage of wit and wisdom; there is a deeper sympathy, a more sensitive pity for the toils in which life enwraps her characters. It is, perhaps, the most truly tragic of Miss Glasgow's novels, and the most completely satisfying. Youth, maturity, age, as life enfolds these people in each of them, are plumbed with a line that runs deep and true. Happiness, real or illusory, the bitter and the sweet, are here commingled.

The Sheltered Life has for its setting that town of Queenborough, Va., which was the scene of *The Romantic Comedians*. The time stretches from about 1905 until the outbreak of the World War, and thus Miss Glasgow's characters bridge the gap between the old and ordered world and the impingement of a new, bringing with it altered values and fresh attitudes. Like a time thread through the novel runs the story of General Archbald, one of the most completely evoked of Miss Glasgow's admirable portraits of old gentlemen. Against his personality, against his memories interwoven through the narrative, are projected the lives of those younger people of his circle whose fortunes we are to follow....

That chapter of *The Sheltered Life* in which General Archbald reviews his life, "The Deep Past," has the exquisite beauty which readers of *The Forsyte Saga* will remember in the interlude called "Indian Summer of a Forsyte," but the burden of its thought is greater. There are passages in that chapter which Miss Glasgow has never equaled, and which one must needs go far to match.

[. . .]

The final pages rise to a dramatic and powerful climax. Mrs. Birdsong's health has been shattered, her beauty paled. George and Jenny Blair devotedly attend her; the atmosphere in which they move and meet is tense. This is the situation when Mrs. Birdsong, the forecast of death already in her face, looks at them out of the dusk in the library and sees George fold Jenny Blair in his arms. This scene, with its quivering intensity, and the tragic close which follows immediately afterward, leaving Jenny Blair crying in her grandfather's arms, "Oh, Grandfather, I didn't mean anything, I didn't mean anything in the world," together constitute one of the most memorable scenes in American fiction.

Miss Glasgow has brought to this book a wise tolerance for human weakness, not at all touched by sentimentality, though it is accompanied at times by flashes of that piercing and remorseless wit which she knows so well how to wield. But the wit is never corrosive, and the sting which it carries is washed away in the waters of compassion. It is the book of a woman who has learned not to expect too much of life, or of people, but who keeps still the love of life and love of her fellow-creatures. There lies Miss Glasgow's wisdom. Life tricks us, yes; it can deal with us cruelly, but we need not, if we have courage, "the only virtue that has a lasting quality," be destroyed.

With this book before us, there can be no challenge of Miss Glasgow's achievement as a serious artist. She won her way, rather slowly at first, to that recognition, but *The Sheltered Life* establishes her quality beyond a doubt.

Clyde Beck,
"Ellen Glasgow Surpasses Herself in a New Novel,"
Detroit *News*, 28 August 1932, arts section, p. 14

This is the Ellen Glasgow of *The Romantic Comedians* and *They Stooped to Folly*, but here she is found working in the atmosphere of great literature rather than in the confines of the psychological novel.

It is true, even in her past work, that she rarely fails to be explicit; but here she broadens out into art that makes individuals, situations and regions universal. The characters in this book are somehow compact and undeviating, for all the conflict within them; the situations are bold and clear cut; the realism is complete and satisfying; and beyond that the style takes on many times the classic and proverbial nature which is the form of timeless things. . . .

The high point of the novel as literature seems to me to be the second book, entitled "The Deep Past." Here, in the mirror of the old general's thoughts, the reader can look forward and back—back to the world of make-believe described in the first book, and forward to the illusion that is the lot of all, except the general, perhaps, at the end. We are not entitled, Miss Glasgow seems to say, to suppose that any rational view of life will solve it for us. The elements are too mixed in us to respond to a universal medicine. The end is illusion for all, except the very luckiest and strongest, who suppose they can have their way and the luckiest and the strongest are few in this world.

Miss Glasgow's locale is, as usual, Virginia; but it is a mistake to suppose that the region is essential, except in the way of tone and emphasis. The "sheltered life," the inability to face and solve issues, has always been common enough, North and South—and all over the world. Possibly it means nothing more than the normal protective impulse of the individual.

At any rate Miss Glasgow has given it a setting with all the elements of literary permanence; and though it is yet early to assess the extent of her powers, this book is without much doubt her most significant work in recent years.

Denver *Post*, 28 August 1932, p. 5

A book where very little occurs and yet which seems to illuminate the whole drama of living, is *The Sheltered Life*, by Ellen Glasgow, one of America's foremost women novelists and most sure and witty portrayer of her own south.

It is a difficult novel to discuss, because if one mentions its quietness, that seems to allow no quarter for the emotional dynamite which lies concealed thru the whole plot and whose fuses may be lit at any moment. But these fuses remain for the most part below the surface of practical vision and are not finally touched with a match. Two of them, however, are touched—the fuse that leads to the illusion of Mrs. Birdsong's beauty and the one to the illusion of Mr. Birdsong's fidelity. When these illusions, like dynamite sticks, explode, for Mrs. Birdsong, there is nervous collapse; for Mr. Birdsong, suicide. . . .

The novel is, in short, the subtle, sympathetic and admirably written delineation of a tragedy; the tragedy that lies inherent in life, if not in the outward battle of those who must struggle, at least in the inward emotional conflict of those who are sheltered; the tragedy of that inevitable drag-net of character and circumstance; but so cleverly and artistically done, that life seems, as it does to many of us an existence where nothing ever happens.

Walter Spearman, "Ellen Glasgow's Book Is of Sheltered Life," Charlotte *News*, 28 August 1932, sec. A, p. 8

What one means by that expression "civilized writer" may be seen in Ellen Glasgow's latest novel, *The Sheltered Life*. In her style is an urbanity, an intelligent understanding, a cultivated wit and a clearly expressed irony worthy of an Anatole France or a George Meredith.

Unlike those Southern writers who are particularly interested in portraying the sectional life around them, such as Julia Peterkin or Elizabeth Madox Roberts, Ellen Glasgow more closely resembles James Branch Cabell in her strict attention to style and her evocation of atmosphere....

Ellen Glasgow's skillful character analysis, her deft feeling for words and a certain poetic cast to her prose are fully as evident in this new novel as in her former ones. And with them is a mellowness of meditation that humanizes her sharp-edged irony without weakening its effect. If occasionally the brilliance of her writing tends to obscure the reality of her story, that is hardly a flaw to be too severely criticized....

Isabel Paterson, "Ellen Glasgow Recreates a Vanished World," *New York Herald Tribune Books*, 28 August 1932, sec. 10, pp. 1–2

The quality of life is continuous change with the illusion of permanence. Odd as it may sound, the Victorians did not know they were living in the Victorian era. They were living in the present, "the heirs of all the ages, in the foremost files of time." It is impossible for us now to conceive how our attitudes and ideas will appear to future generations, because they are a projection of our own thoughts, and we have no perspective on ourselves. The function of art is to provide that perspective. In *The Sheltered Life* Ellen Glasgow has taken three finite points out of the immediate past as a vantage ground for the survey of life itself. Here are three souls [Jenny Blair Archbald, General Archbald, Eva Birdsong] seized at the same chronological moment, but each of a different and representative age in his or her own life....

[. . .]

This antithesis of wisdom and power is exemplified in all three lives singly, and as they are set against each other. Jenny, in her prettiness and selfish innocence and ignorance, is the very channel of power, though she has no control over it. Personally she is trivial; but as a force, as youth, she smashes the world of her elders to bits. She is the instrument of death, even; for life continually breaks the molds of yesterday; and the breakage is death. Jenny wrought literal destruction, providing a terrific climax which must be left to the reader of the book to discover. And she was not making a facile excuse when she cried out in terror that she had not meant anything. She didn't need to mean it; she was it.

That is the virtue of Miss Glasgow's story; that the meaning is implicit in the characters. They are truly created, and their world with them. It is a world which vanished hardly twenty years ago; the war is usually thought to have made an end of it, but it was gone already. The war only made its disappearance evident, afforded a date in the calendar. It ended when women ceased to regard the home as their sole "sphere" and went out to see what kind of a world men inhabited.

This is perhaps Miss Glasgow's richest work, a summary of life by a woman who has observed acutely, felt and thought deeply, and wrought herself a technique adequate for the expression of her experience.

Sara Haardt, "The First Reader," Norfolk *Virginian Pilot*, 29 August 1932, sec. 1, p. 4

The latest book of Miss Glasgow—*The Sheltered Life*—was foreshadowed in *The Romantic Comedians*, where, in a style as brilliant as it was sensitive, she described a Southern gentlewoman and a Southern gentleman of the Victorian era and the tragedy that marked them in a land that owns tragedy only in the grand manner. Yet, beside Eva Birdsong in *The Sheltered Life*, Amanda Lightfoot in *The Romantic Comedians* pales to a mere shadow, and beside Old General Archbald, Judge Honeywell becomes a ghost minus a voice; as for Annabel Upchurch, the young heroine in *The Romantic Comedians* who would lead her own life at the cost of all others, she never experienced anything as poignant or as savage as the irony which pursues Jenny Blair Archbald, the general's young granddaughter, from her earliest childhood.

Miss Glasgow has given these later characters forms that allow her full imaginative liberty. Amanda Lightfoot, for all her queenly proportions, never overstepped the conventional ideal, and Judge Honeywell felt unequal to the task of rebellion once he had contracted a cold in his chest. But Eva Birdsong, though she is born and reared in the same tradition that throttled Amanda Lightfoot—the same Virginia town, in fact—is of different stuff. As Eva Howard she was called the Virginia Lily because of her beauty and her charm and her elegance:—"The social history of Queenborough was composed wherever she decided to live that history."

Her beauty, however, even in an age that worshipped beauty, was not the most remarkable or the most glamorous thing about her; she had a singing voice so pure in quality it might have won her a world conquest; she had intelligence and a presence that would have put to shame the professional beauties of London and Paris; she had strength and a jealous pride; above all, she had the courage of her emotions—she had, in a moment of incalculable rapture, eloped with George Birdsong, a charming, no-account, incurably polygamous soul, without giving her triumphs a thought, and she had taken his shotgun and killed him with her own hands when at last she could endure his infidelity no longer.

That, in brief, is Eva Birdsong's side of the story. We see her, mainly, through two pairs of adoring eyes—those of Old

General Archbald, whose devotion to her is inexhaustible even at 83, and those of Jenny Blair Archbald, a vivid little thing but as comic an egotist as Annabel Upchurch, whose love for George Birdsong inspires a deeper, if guilty, devotion to his wife. But, above all, we see her through the eyes of Miss Glasgow, and what Miss Glasgow sees is beyond any romantic convention; she sees plainly that Eva Birdsong, despite her overwhelming gifts, is lacking in the greatest gift of them all—a sense of humor—and that living with her, and her unattainable ideals, was something of a bore.

Furthermore, with that artistry which is at once sympathetic and as sharp as the thrust of a rapier, Miss Glasgow plainly shows that the boredom and the hypocrisy and the helpless reproach which ungulfed George Birdsong were not shattered by the crack of the gun.

There are Jenny Blair Archbald, who precipitated the situation with George Birdsong and who crumbles at the first realization of it; Old General Archbald, with only the empty dreams of his youth to console him; Etta, his homely old maid daughter, a hopeless neurotic who "had lost faith in men and found it difficult to be romantic about God"; Cora, his daughter-in-law, a good woman, adroit in handling the young and the old; John Welsh, a serious young physician, Eva Birdsong's cousin, who loves Jenny Blair, but who "harps upon the prose of living when she asks him for rhapsody"; and there is Eva Birdsong herself whose loveliness fades into pallor at the end.

Miss Glasgow has never written so brave a book; she reaches a superb level of drama and reality which she has never reached before. All through these pages she has poured out the tragic futility which lies at the root of Southern social history, and which is its justification and its power.

"What was the use?" demands Old General Archbald as he warms his withered flesh in the April sunshine. "Why couldn't the dead stay dead when one had put them away? . . . What was the meaning of it all? Why had passion strong enough to ruin his life forsaken him while he lived? Why had it left only . . . diminished shapes, performing conventional gestures in a medium that was not time—that was not eternity?"

"Womanhood Affronted," *Time*, 29 August 1932, 40

The Southern lady of the old school, helpless product of exaggerated chivalry and Victorian prudishness, may never in real life have been such a pathetic monster as Authoress Glasgow's heroine, but she was at least recognizably similar. This sad story of how a fading Virginia belle tried to taper off into normal old age may affront the shades of Southern colonels but should arouse only wondering pity from a differently complicated generation.

To the aristocracy of her Virginia town Mrs. Birdsong had become a legendary beauty long before she began to lose her looks. In the best tradition of famous belles she had married George, least eligible, most worthless of all her flocking beaux. George was a charmer, that goes without saying, but he was woman-crazy, could not even draw the color line. The situation was unfortunate but usual. Where Mrs. Birdsong deviated from the human to the holy was in refusing to do anything about it except by straining more & more to be George's ideal. Never natural when George was around, she never reproached him, always smiled, always pretended he was knight to her lady. Both of them had a terrible time but pretended to each other that everything was perfect. When little

Jenny Blair, daughter of her old friend the General, began to grow up and be attractive to George, he manfully resisted temptation as long as he could. Jenny Blair chose an unfortunate moment to throw herself into George's arms. Mrs. Birdsong saw them: for once her lacquer cracked. The result was shattering for George, disastrous for George's overworked ideal.

Authoress Glasgow writes of her Southerners as one having authority; through her velvety Southern glove she makes her iron fingers felt. Only the old General (who has not been successful with women) seems to have her full sympathy. She allows him several pretty speeches, some good ones: "When a man is young, every woman seems to be moving in his direction. When he is old, he realizes that they are all moving away."

Ellen Anderson Gholson Glasgow, born, raised and resident in Richmond, Va., hotbed of Southern tradition, decided she would not be a romantic, sentimental Southern belle-lettriste. She announced: "What the South needs now is—blood and irony." Plump, lively, slightly deaf, she finds life agreeable and amusing. Though she thought she could die of happiness if her first book was accepted, after her 17th was published she remarked: "I've never been happy and have not died." Authoress Glasgow lives in an old house in the heart of Richmond at No. 1 West Main Street, entertains there her friends James Branch Cabell, Mary Johnston, Joseph Hergesheimer, Hugh Walpole. She has never married.

Clifton Fadiman, "Ellen Glasgow's South," *New Republic*, 31 August 1932, 79

A few Southern novelists—T. S. Stribling, Fiswoode Tarleton, Fielding Burke—try to treat their native soil realistically. But those who command the greatest technical resources, such as Mr. Cabell, Miss Roberts and Julia Peterkin, fly to cloud-cuckoolands of fantasy and introspection, or substitute for the tragic problem of an enslaved race a set of Negroes who move unconvincingly between the two worlds of quaintness and melodrama. Among these Southern novelists, the position of Ellen Glasgow is not perhaps so easy to define. Her books, particularly those produced during the last six or seven years, show an intelligent if not a powerful grasp of certain historical Southern realities. She has traced with wit and first-hand intimacy the decay of the land-owning post-Civil War aristocracy and has exposed with a kind of suave mercilessness its intellectual poverty, its blindness, its feeble romanticism. As Southern novelists go, I suppose we should call her a realist.

Yet one should recollect that, like most of her peers, she leaves untouched that South which is important to us today. She laments with elegance and restraint, the harsh breath of an intrusive industrialism; but a natural allegiance to her own class (some of whose fetishes she is, as an insider, privileged to mock) blinds her to the obvious fact that the machine and the plantation are merely two forms of exploitation. To the bloody struggle which in the last thirty years has transformed the Southern laboring class into a race of peons she is of course anesthetic. Nor is there any indication that she is aware of the salient feature of Southern social and economic life—the continuation of black chattel slavery under the disguise of the industrial hire-and-fire system. It would be silly to ask of Miss Glasgow that she be conscious of these things; but it is surely of some importance, as she is considered a major American novelist, to define the limits of her interests.

Ellen Glasgow, employing wit, finesse and even a certain objectivity, reworks again and again a Southern past as dead as the political reputation of Andrew Mellon. Her latest book satirizes, with a mildness and a sympathy which its tragic finale cannot disguise, the genteel traditions of her own caste. The action takes place during the ten years before the War, the period in which the moral and economic degeneration of the old Southern upper-middle class proceeded most rapidly. With one aspect of this decay *The Sheltered Life* concerns itself—the emotional pretense (particularly in regard to sex), the false pride, the sentimental optimism which are the natural expressions of a defeated aristocracy. The point of the tale lies in the frustrated life of Eva Birdsong, a Southern belle of the Lily Langtry variety (combining both the physical and mental perfections of a really high-grade wax figure). To admire the qualities of Eva Birdsong is the main occupation of most of the other characters in the book. But they are a facade; behind them the real Eva suffers in silence for twenty years while her handsome husband gives protracted lessons in the Virginia tradition to a Negro washerwoman. The pretense is finally too much for Eva. She discovers Mr. Birdsong engaged in a final and inexcusable gallantry; goes completely out of her mind (making the shortest trip on record); and shoots him dead. So much for *The Sheltered Life.*

It seems to me that stories such as these, no matter how expertly written (and it should be said that *The Sheltered Life* is far inferior stylistically to *They Stooped to Folly*) can have at best only the value of historical novels. It is impossible to relate such a book to the modern consciousness, unless one is over fifty and interested in sentimentally reliving the emotional idiocies of the world of one's youth. There is nothing here—not a character, not a scene, not a situation, not a conflict—which retains freshness or vitality for us today. As exhumation *The Sheltered Life* takes a respectable place; more it would be hard to claim for it. All of which is not astonishing when one remembers Miss Glasgow's remark, made last October at the University of Virginia conference of Southern writers. Uttered in all honesty and sincerity, it illuminates her outlook and sets clear bounds to what may be expected of her by any reader fully alive to his own time. She said, "I find my sympathy shifting to that outcast from the machine civilization, the well bred person."

Mary Ellen Chase, "The Bookshelf," *Atlantic Monthly*, 150 (September 1932), 14

Ellen Glasgow in *The Sheltered Life* is interested not in psychological theories and ideas but in actualities, not in *why* her people act as they do but in *how* they act. And she has written very well an extraordinarily convincing and satisfying story. Laid in Virginia, in the town of Queenborough, the action, much of it mental, centers about the Archbald family, every member of which, from the old General to his granddaughter, Jenny Blair (the central figure), is so clearly drawn as to be unforgettable. Aunt Etta's repressions, Mrs. Birdsong's complexes, Cora Archbald's self-deception, the old General's thwarted yet splendid life, Jenny Blair's premature adolescence—all these exist, nay, *live* with no need of analysis or of psychological terms to bolster them up and rob them of their own vitality. Personally I find in this story of Miss Glasgow's her best work. It has power alike in its restrained pathos and in its equally restrained yet cruel irony; its treatment is as objective as that of Hardy, and yet, like Hardy, its author leaves us assured of her own sympathy through the rhythm of her phrases and through her fine choice of settings and details. Few tragic endings have been handled more admirably, so far as I know, in American fiction.

Emily Clark,
"*The Sheltered Life*—
Ellen Glasgow's New
High in Brilliance and
Satire,"
Philadelphia *Inquirer*,
3 September 1932, p. 7

In this latest book Ellen Glasgow has not let down the standard she set herself years ago—a standard unusual among her contemporaries—that each successive novel should be better than the preceding one. It is in greater degree a subtle record of the spirit, and in lesser degree a social satire than preceding Glasgow books. Last fall I heard Miss Glasgow say, at a meeting of Southern writers, that Southern literature must cease to be Southern and become universal. *The Sheltered Life* is unusual among Southern novels because it is universal.

This latest novel by Miss Glasgow is concerned with people who might have been born anywhere. It is laid in her Queenborough, which of course is Richmond, but happily her characters are not a result of any fixed social system. Nor is there a hero, heroine, or protagonist of any kind. This is a study of seven persons, varying in their importance to the story. Among them, old General Archbald alone can be liked. Two families live in one block of a section of their town almost socially deserted. Eva Birdsong, a woman with all the glamour of distinguished beauty (the sort of beauty which is no longer distinguished, if it exists, outside of Hollywood) is married to George Birdsong, a handsome mediocrity who has never made sufficient money to maintain a woman, holding the belief that she might have been another Langtry, as she should be maintained. In spite of this failure his wife continues under the spell of his physical fascination, and is content to live drably as long as she is able to hold even a part of his attention. George Birdsong is a brilliant study of a consistent sensualist, as brilliant a study, I believe, as has been made of this species.

The Archbald house nearby contains the old General; Mrs. Archbald, his widowed daughter-in-law, a horse-leech daughter to him since the early death of her husband, who conceals this fact by an unsurpassed talent for never speaking the truth; her daughter, Jenny Blair Archbald, eighteen at the ending of the book, with all baseless egotism of youth and all the "shallowness of innocence"; the General's daughters, Isabella, handsome and vital, jilted by her fiance for a trifling indiscretion, who later elopes with a handsome former carpenter to revenge herself when the wavering lover wants her back; and Etta, a born failure, repulsive to men and alarming to the women friends with whom she has tried to fill her life, when her thwarted nature finds occasional outlets in sadism.

General Archbald is the medium for Ellen Glasgow's personal tastes and ideas, and he is as lovable a person as has been created by even a romantic novelist. Reared by his grandfather, a typical Georgian sportsman, who loved to pursue "any animal that was able to flee," and a mother who supported his position, General Archbald remains to the end humane and skeptical, as Miss Glasgow herself is humane and skeptical. From the time when, a young boy, on his grandfather's estate in Virginia, he is overwhelmed by nausea at the sight of his first frightened buck at bay, and is smeared with the animal's blood by his grandfather as a punishment for being a milksop, until he is eighty-three in 1914, when the Austrian Archduke is murdered and the world goes up in flames, he remains humane and skeptical. He is a veteran of the Army of Northern Virginia. He "remembers the *Maine*." He also remembers that in his year spent in Germany at the close of his Oxford career, "kindness had been an attribute of the German people." And he remembers that the look of fear in hunted creatures is akin to the look of hatred. "In every war," he murmurs, "there is always a Belgium. I have heard it all before."

These seven persons make a story whose ending is perhaps Miss Glasgow's finest writing. *The Sheltered Life* is a novel of the first rank, of a brilliance, depth and beauty universal in their quality.

Stark Young,
"Deep South Notes, VI: At Sheltered Valley,"
New Republic, 72 (7 September 1932), 100–2

[...]

The Sheltered Life is told with less [than *They Stooped to Folly*] of what might be called affability, an affability that in Miss Glasgow's case is a combination of wit, a certain high, delicate reserve, unwilling, almost inherently unable, to make a public lay-out of the full meaning, and a fine courtesy that assumes in us an intelligence that knows when more is meant than the eye meets. The new book commands from the writer's self a more definite insistence on the content desired. There is, accordingly, in it, most of all in that section of the old man's deep past, a certain sadness of knowledge; but it is not a sad book. For that there is too much exercise of understanding—and the exercise of any faculty is a form of exhilaration—too much movement toward finality. And, though there is a curious, bright-edged clarity, functioning as if by nature's light, it is not cynical. From this gift for witty semblances and a protecting mask of brilliance and apparent ease—an ease and facility gaily or sternly summoned before she enters the presence of others—from this profound understanding and openness to truth, derives an underlying melancholy in Miss Glasgow's work. For a mind and temperament like this is too final and clear to overstress its message or drag out explanation, too sincere and passionate to wheedle, too distinguished to solicit a solemn, preachy attentiveness, and too well bred to exhibit the least suspicion of what must sometimes be a despair of being fully apprehended.

But if last night I slipped up to my room and took out *The Sheltered Life* with any idea of its being Southern—a pardonable platitude on my part, hankering for the apropos in the midst of this quiet, fragrance and old story at my cousin's house—if I said to myself I will read a Southern book in this Southern setting, I was headed for a fall. *The Sheltered Life* is not about the South at all. It is set in some Virginia town, which is the sort of community the author is at home in; and some of the traits and habits shown can be called Southern, if you choose, though they are mostly found all over the United States and out of it, among people of a certain class or, rather, who live on a certain plane. About the most you can say on this point is that these ways and traits, likely to be found anywhere besides the South, are at least not denied there. So much for me and my sentiment, then, getting badly left!

The old man, left behind by the years, is the real protagonist of the book; and all Ellen Glasgow's ultimate feeling about life is put into him. He represents the tragedy, wherever it appears, of the civilized man in a world that is not civilized. He has nothing to do with the Southern-colonel theme or anything like it, though he was in the Civil War—for that matter he had once lived on the Continent and in England and had fallen in love there with a married woman, who, because of a sick child, failed him in their planned elopement and in the end took her own life, "lost, vanished, destroyed by the fear for which he had loved her in the beginning!" As for the rest, the people all mean well, even the worst of them; they are not judged by the author with any laid-on precept and theory, but in the course given them; assigned to each of them is his judging destiny, exactly as to every actor in a drama, to use Plotinus' figure, is assigned his robe and crown, like a singer in a song. Even Mrs. Birdsong, the beauty, whom some may take as the central figure of the book, though she is by no means so, is not merely the Southern-belle theme. She is the symbol of the beauty motive in the Edwardian-Langtry epoch; and she flourished even more opulently in London, in the flesh and as the fashionable ideal, during that age of the beauty.

Even the title misled me, as I looked at it, settling comfortably into my pillows. *The Sheltered Life* might have meant something Southern, with a hint in it of Miss Glasgow's familiar irony, but it also turns out not to be Southern at all. The irony in it is profounder still and is not without its poignancy as well. This title implies no age or place. It implies the effort of one human being to stand between another and life. The tragedy in the story, a tragic crux that is long since age old, results from this fruitless endeavor and necessity to bend and shape the lives of the persons we love, not from selfishness alone—a far more superficial theme than Miss Glasgow's—but from the way personalities impinge on one another with the best motives or no motives, or from the sheer oneness of all human life together. Mrs. Birdsong demands of George, her husband, who worships her, a fidelity impossible to his nature, which takes him to other women at times, the mulatto woman Memoria, the public women of the streets and finally to the young girl in love with him, the old general's granddaughter. Her husband demands of Mrs. Birdsong the ideal she means to him; the girl herself, with that strange fatality of "vague wildness" and young, innocent desire, demands whatever it is she wants of George, of life, meaning all the time not "anything in the world." So they go, all with no intention to hurt another. And in a wider sense the same tragedy is being repeated out in the world. The World War was beginning and men were killing each other from the highest possible ideals. This is the final scope of the book's theme. The old man, his point of view, his thwarted strong body, saw the age pass him by. Not in the South especially, it was over the world that ideas, forms, were changing, the familiar order going, the beliefs and certainties. The shelter for men's lives, of religion, convention, social prejudice, was at the crumbling point, just as was the case with the little human figures in the story....

It is in old General Archbald, the pivotal character, that the high motive in *The Sheltered Life* appears, the motive of pity. In him are the usual old-age motives, as a matter of course, but it is the pity motive that makes him uniquely imagined, so far as I know, among novels. The great classic combination of pity and terror we have no longer with us, for terror, save only in imaginations of power, does not work strongly in our modern life. The pity that Miss Glasgow develops is not the slush sort, social-worker male arresting the horse beater or the lithographic *mater dolorosa* female theme, but a universal attribute fitted in this case to the masculinity of the character. General Archbald, born perhaps for a poet, filled with horror at the slaughter so dear to huntsmen, cultivated, sophisticated, experienced in the range of male living, has never done as he most willed.... All his character is based on imaginative pity; he has always been unable to hurt people or forget their happiness. And at length he has arrived at contemplation, the sense of a happy time still ahead of him, loving those he loved and loving life all the more because they were no longer necessary to him, not any person, not even life. The whole conception of this theme is deep and persuasive, lightly adult and finely written....

Dorothea Lawrance Mann, "The Meaning of the Sheltered Life," Boston *Evening Transcript*, 10 September 1932, book section, p. 2

[...]

Miss Glasgow has given us clearly the two sides of the picture of the sheltered life. There is Jenny Blair's side through which we observe the building up of the sheltered life, and there is Eva Birdsong's side where we perceive the effect of the sheltered life. Both are among the most vividly realized characters Miss Glasgow has ever drawn. Nowhere else in this country has so much emphasis been laid on women's beauty as it was in the old South. Eva Birdsong is the survivor of this old tradition. Deeply as he loves his granddaughter, General Archbald can never look at her without commenting to himself that the girls of today will never be of the type of Eva Birdsong, whose beauty was so great that it seemed sufficient cause for existence....

No novel by Miss Glasgow has been without its criticism of life. The sheltered life is pilloried here with all the vigor of her fighting spirit. We must watch that terrible, ghastly breaking of the woman who has been an ideal for more than twenty years. We must realize that even when she is about to go to the operating room Eva Birdsong feels that she must keep up the same picture for her husband to admire. In those later months when it becomes increasingly clear that Eva Birdsong will never be a well woman again we know that the deepest tragedy for her is not death, which she will welcome whenever it comes, but the fact that she can no longer be the beauty which men have admired, that she can no longer be that ideal which has commanded the deepest loyalty of her husband, no matter what smaller diversions have been his. More and more we realize that there is nothing remaining for this woman when she can no longer hold this position.

We must watch, too, what this sheltered life does to the young girl now grown nearly to womanhood. She is, we are reminded, at "the empty age" before the springs of character have filled up. More than that, however, we realize is the matter with Jenny Blair. All her childhood she has known nothing save possessive love and a stifling care. She is guarded on every side and all that is asked of her is that she grow, if not to beauty at least to prettiness, that she present the miracle of youth and innocence, and that finally she grow up to be someone's ideal. Yet because of this life she lives we watch her swept along into situations much beyond her experience and into a tragedy which would never have come to her had her interests been turned outward instead of being concentrated on her emotions. It is strange indeed to find this Jenny Blair turning out the villain of the story!

The sheltered life exists first of all perhaps because of possessive love and Miss Glasgow, with her lack of sentimentality, her stern grasping of essentials, sums up more graphically in this book than ever before what possessive love means. As General Archbald comments: "There is a freedom in not being loved too deeply, in not being thought of too often. Possessive love makes most of the complications and nearly all the unhappiness in the world." Miss Glasgow is curiously gentle—for her—in treating this man who is a survivor of an old tradition, who all his life has been fooled because of the necessity of living up to traditions, and of not failing people who love him more than he loves them, and who for years upon years has worshiped the ideal which Eva Birdsong represents, giving her a loyalty and an understanding which she fails to receive from younger men. There is beauty in this story and there is power, for Miss Glasgow is one of the few novelists who can take the stuff of life and make of it a lasting interpretation.

"Ellen Glasgow's Accomplished Novel of Southern Life," Springfield [Massachusetts] *Sunday Union and Republican*, 11 September 1932, sec. E, p. 7

... Ellen Glasgow is a novelist of repeatedly achieved variation. "Achieved" may not be the word. She discloses a variety that is natural to her outlook, mind, and art. Her art is not fecund, but re-creative; her out-look, extensive, expansive, and varied. So in her latest novel, *The Sheltered Life*, with its scene in the South, we find again a fresh subject-matter, and a differing examination of fresh aspects of this life that people live according to the conditions under which they are called to live it. . . .

So Miss Glasgow subtly, understandingly, and humanly gives us her observations of "the chaos that lies beneath the placid surface of sheltered lives." This is a fresh and sometimes poignant, sometimes humorous and sometimes ironic story of persons one will not forget, on whom a period stamped the impress of its particular standards.

Dorothy Van Doren, "Inquiry into Life," *Nation*, 135 (21 September 1932), 261

Whatever her place among them, Ellen Glasgow writes in the style of the best novelists. She belongs in the great tradition, and the difference between her and the rawer, bolder, keener spirits who are concerned with the contemporary scene is that they believe they know what life should be, and Miss Glasgow is merely trying to find out what it is.

That is what makes of *The Sheltered Life*, which is the story of yesterday in the South, something more than another *Age of Innocence*. Ending her tale with the first reverberations of the World War in August, 1914, Miss Glasgow has placed it in time far beyond wars or the insecurity of governments. She has described a lost world, the world of sheltered women and sheltering, if unfaithful, men; her Queenborough which may be only another name for the Richmond she knows so well, is as remote as the moon from the Europe of 1914–18, and the world of 1932. Her Mrs. Birdsong, whose whole career was to be a beauty, may exist no more. A set of manners which would make a man ask a woman to marry him simply because he had inadvertently spent half the night with her in a broken-down sleigh, although neither loved the other, and which would make her accept him and live with him as his wife for thirty years, may have vanished. But if this code of behavior is no longer observed, Miss Glasgow is by no means dependent on its existence for the wisdom and penetration of her observations about men and women. She holds this vanishing day in her hands and turns it around as carefully as if it were a ball of glass in which she could see the human heart. Who were these people, she asks? What did they think when they acted as they did? Out of what clay did they spring, and in what mold may they, with their inheritance and their traditions, eventually be cast?

This particular form of inquiry would, I believe, lift Miss Glasgow above the run of her contemporaries, even if she were not also gifted with wit and irony and with the ability to tell a well-ordered and moving story. Those furious young Don Quixotes who find in Willa Cather, for example, merely gentle piety about a lost age, would, if they were as honest as they are brave, be compelled to acknowledge more substance in Miss Glasgow. She it is who can say: "For one confirmed habit had not changed with the ages. Mankind was still calling human nature a system and trying vainly to put something else in its place." Or: "To be sure, as Jenny Blair was too apt to retort, we were living in the twentieth century, and ideas were modern. Modern, yes, but there had been modern ideas in every age, not excepting the long ages that were probably arboreal." Or: "First love is simply between two persons, you and your lover, and it changes as everything must that exists merely between two human beings. But last love has courage in it also; it has courage and finality, and facing the end and all the emptiness that is life." Courage to face the emptiness of life is a quality that only years can bring. The young scorn it, probably rightly. The old cannot explain or define it, nor do they always own it; but I should imagine that when they met this particular courage they would salute it with the highest honors.

It remains only to say that the men and women in *The Sheltered Life* are warm and living. Mrs. Birdsong, of the radiant eyes and the queenly carriage, who could finally not endure having been an ideal for forty years; George, her husband, who loved her, who knew he was not worthy of her little finger, and who was not able, therefore, to be faithful to her; General Archbald, who after eighty years had discovered that happiness was to be free from the tyranny of chance, to be released from wanting; Jenny Blair, a child, a young woman, whom the sheltered life did not quite cover, and yet who remained in it for first love which would be restrained neither for loyalty nor kindness—these and the other persons in her book Miss Glasgow has drawn fully and credibly. In creating them, she has contributed something to human experience, merely by saying, dispassionately and completely, what their experience was. That perhaps is all that should be asked of a novelist. And while novelists remain who can do it, to whatever degree, we need not be concerned about the future of this particular form of literary endeavor.

Howard Mumford Jones, "Battalions of Women," *Virginia Quarterly Review*, 8 (October 1932), 591–4

On the principle of setting a thief to catch a thief, literary destiny has set our women novelists the task of delineating the monstrous regiment of women. In *The Sheltered Life* a female battalion clings about General Archbald, and his granddaughter, Jenny Blair, brought up by indirections to find directions out, is the occasion of the ultimate tragedy. Two of Miss Cather's three stories in *Obscure Destinies* turn upon analogous situations. In one ("Neighbour Rosicky") the good Rosicky, despite medical warning, dies as a result of working his son's fields in an effort to create happiness for a city-bred daughter-in-law, and in the other ("Old Mrs. Harris") Grandmother Harris sacrifices her existence to a daughter brought up a southern belle. There are other female figures in these books, but it is curious to observe the cruel precision with which two distinguished American women novelists delineate the damage women do.

Miss Cather's volume will not greatly increase her reputation. "Neighbour Rosicky," it is true, a return to the earlier manner of *My Antonia*, is a charming genre picture of immigrant Bohemian farm life, gentle and penetrating and beautiful. But "Old Mrs. Harris," the longest of the three tales, seems to betray labor, and though Mrs. Harris herself is a remarkable creation, the other personages are not well-rounded. Miss Cather seems to have had difficulty with Mrs. Rosen, the Jewess who serves to interpret the story, and whose conversation does not ring true; and, what is more awkward, the story wavers between being a tale and being a short novel without quite satisfying the conditions of either genre. The third sketch, "Two Friends," is merely a slight essay.

Miss Glasgow's book, on the other hand, is rich and full, with those inimitable touches of wit and wisdom which only Miss Glasgow can give. Certain of its elements, to be sure, are familiar. In how many of her fictions have we met the Virginia old maid, blighted in youth by plainness or an unhappy love affair, and spending the rest of her futile existence in complainings which an indulgent family elaborately explain away! The southern mother, full of outward helplessness and inward competence, pretending that this is the best of all possible worlds, and laboriously bringing up her daughter in the same pink pretences—her we have met before. And the ageing Virginia gentleman, secretly regretful that southern chivalry has cost him the best years of his life, but gallantly carrying on—this, too, is a figure with which Miss Glasgow has made us familiar.

One notes also in the present volume the vestigial remnants of the sociological urge which produced Miss Glasgow's earlier fictions. The Archbald family lives in that part of Queenborough (let us pretend it is Queenborough) which is socially out at the elbows by reason of the industrialization of the city, symbolized in *The Sheltered Life* by an inelegant smell which the Archbalds attempt to ignore. Moreover, the flow of time in the book is across three wars which, like parallels of latitude, allow us to measure our progress through the social history of the South. (Once or twice, Miss Glasgow gleefully dares to call the first of these conflicts the Civil War.) But sociology in *The Sheltered Life* mainly hovers, an awkward ghost, in the background. Miss Glasgow's theme has latterly (and wisely) been human beings, not Humanity.

There remain four characters who really make the novel—Mr. and Mrs. Birdsong, Jenny Blair Archbald, and the dog, William. There have been various canines in modern fiction—who can forget Mr. Galsworthy?—but William, a polite and desponding setter, is a notable addition to the race. Mrs. Archbald, lacking penetration, commonly addressed him, we are told, as if he were a distinguished member of the Mongolian race, a happy touch which defines Mrs. Archbald's lack of penetration, and William. One regrets that William does not more frequently appear.

As for Jenny Blair, she is at once curiously and painfully true, and curiously elusive. Much of the story is seen through her eyes, and particularly when she is a little girl, this part of the narrative is superbly accurate. But the exigencies of the tale compel Miss Glasgow to abandon her point of view from time to time. In these sections Jenny Blair becomes merely a vague, youthful figure. Yet the exasperation which she arouses is proof of her reality, so that, if Miss Glasgow has not quite solved the technical problem of presentation in her case, we are compelled to admit the validity of the events which depend upon her character.

But the real triumph of *The Sheltered Life* is Mr. and Mrs. Birdsong, although, short of quoting huge sections of the book, one despairs of conveying the extraordinary vitality of a married pair hot for certainties in this our life. Beautiful and fragile, passionately in love with her weak-willed husband, insanely jealous, Eva Birdsong carries beauty like a curse. From the time we first hear of her to the time when, having seen Jenny Blair in her husband's arms, she kills him (and every one elaborately pretends it was an accident) she moves, a haunting figure, through a world which really has no place for her. Equally vital is George Birdsong, possibly an even greater artistic triumph. For George is more than an errant husband. As his wife is burdened with devotion, so he is burdened with vitality, and Miss Glasgow has succeeded in making his sexual aberrations inevitable, his weakness transparent, and his wife's adoration believable. Moreover, she has finely handled the episodes (beginning in childhood) through which Jenny Blair and George drift towards each other and to catastrophe. The theme of the book is sex, but sex in terms which make the usual run of novels portraying marital infidelity look like the scrawlings of crude little boys.

D.P., "Ellen Glasgow Exposes Pretense of the Nineties," Kansas City [Missouri] *Star*, 15 October 1932, p. 12

There is always a strong temptation to stick pins into the proud ladies and gentlemen of the '90s, to see if they are real. Ellen Glasgow does this, philosophically and sympathetically, in *The Sheltered Life*, rather with the attitude that although "this hurts me more than it does you," it must be done, in the interests of science. So the well-hidden sorrows of Eva Birdsong and General Archbald are dragged to the light for psychological airing, and the fallacy of the sheltered life of little Jenny Blair Archbald is exposed....

When Jenny Blair reaches 17, the soaring dream she has created is brought tumbling down by a shot. But even in tragedy she must keep up pretense, must keep a secret, as George Birdsong had taught her to do so long ago. To outsiders that shot must always have been an accident.

It must have given some solace to Eva Birdsong and to the general that, as their secrets were being revealed, the world in which they had lived was being destroyed by change. Everywhere the veils of pretense were being torn away; to reveal the open face of unashamed frankness.

For this new world, Ellen Glasgow has written a convincing argument. She has written it well, too, as is her habit. The book is full of beautiful similes, fluttering in the mind of Jenny Blair. They are the inarticulate ecstasies of childhood put into words. Even the pages that are little but neighborhood gossip are given charm by Miss Glasgow's skill.

The book carries forward the ridicule of Victorian moral hypocrisy expressed so forcefully in Miss Glasgow's previous work, *They Stooped to Folly*. It reinforces her position as foremost woman writer of the South.

Clare Armstrong, "New Books," *Catholic World*, 136 (November 1932), 247–8

Miss Glasgow's latest novel deals with the pre-War decade. The setting is Queenborough in her native state, Virginia, where two families, the Archbalds and the Birdsongs, continue the homes and traditions of a passing age. All is change around them, and the fetid smell of encroaching industry penetrates the fragrance of their garden inclosures.

In Grandfather Archbald, symbol of the past order which insured the sheltered life and himself its victim, Miss Glasgow gives a gentle portrait of old age, loosening its grasp on life's last gift—its memories. It is hard to really care much about anyone else in the Archbald family. Cora, the domestic pivot, manages the household and everyone in it adroitly and affectionately; her protective eyes ceaselessly sweep the horizon that no unseen enemy may threaten her stronghold, but in her very farsightedness she overlooks the battle on her doorstep; and with unimaginative solicitude, she becomes a tyrant rather than a refuge. Her daughter, Jenny Blair Archbald, is youth in the crude, reaching out for the promise of life with never a thought besides. She has an impulse where her heart should be. When the book closes she is eighteen, and her closing words are: "I didn't mean anything in the world!"

Miss Glasgow has not given us here, a love story; there is in fact a hollow lack of love in the book, though it drifts to its tragic conclusion on a strong current of passion, admiration, pretense, infatuation and other fluid substitutes for love.

There is much talk about the grand passion where George Birdsong is concerned, but it is obviously only a manner of speaking. George has the likeable traits as well as the limitations of a healthy hunting dog. He is affectionate and casual, likes to kill, and rapaciously devours everything that appeals to his sensual appetite. Nothing restrains him, not even the beautiful Eva for whom he would like to feel a loyal devotion. Eva is a form upon which her associates drape their illusions. The reader, free from the potency of her physical presence, sees a feeble pathetic woman, with frozen smile, struggling to support an intolerable burden of false ideals. That her governing emotions are pride and jealousy serves only to insure her final collapse.

Miss Glasgow has given us a fairly unpleasant, dreary theme for contemplation. It is as if she put these little Tom Thumb people under glass for laboratory scrutiny. Under the microscope they disclose magnified traits of ugliness. But we must not thereby be misled into peopling our world with such distortions. The sheltered life, in itself, need not produce them. Perhaps, if we shift our viewpoint and look into the sheltered life with Louis Hémon, with Willa Cather, we shall find that what Miss Glasgow's people need is not less shelter so much as more soul.

E. K. Brown, "Blood and Irony," *Canadian Forum*, 13 (November 1932), 64–5

Not excepting Pearl Buck's own *Sons*, this is the best American novel since *The Good Earth* and, what is perhaps higher praise, as good a novel as any Ellen Glasgow has written in her thirty-five years of authorship. It is good because of the visibility and human complexity of at least six characters, the simple naturalness of the story, the bittersweet elegance of the style and, above all, the delicate humanization of a social idea, the idea expressed in the title. Blood and irony, Ellen Glasgow said long ago, are what the literary treatment of the South most needs. In the meantime William Faulkner and Thomas Wolfe have given us novels in which blood flows as freely as on the hunting-field. Ellen Glasgow keeps blood flowing where it ought to flow, through the veins of warm-natured individuals, not out of their entrails or their noses. Branch Cabell has made the irony of life the cream of his jest; but the characters caressed by his irony are really as thin-blooded as Sara Orne Jewett's New England spinsters. Ellen Glasgow's irony is sharper, but she allows her characters to come to life, to take root in their drawing-rooms and gardens and in our minds, before she exposes them to her irony. She is a great novelist while Cabell is simply an elegant misanthropic essayist who has adopted the novel-form.

Queenborough (read Richmond) in 1906 and in 1914 is the subject of *The Sheltered Life*. The creed of the old South was still powerful in 'the good families' of which she writes. For women it prescribed a life of boredom conducive to the survival of beauty, chastity, and manners, and punctuated by semi-secret adulteries. For men there was hunting of foxes, deer, and women, with liquor and oratory as secondary satisfactions. The heroine's mother had found that 'one could bear any discomfort of body as long as one was not obliged to be independent in act,' and had wallowed happily in the sheltered life until she lost all sense of truth or value and took to lying for its intrinsic delightfulness. Her sister-in-law, a plain woman, had failed to ensnare a husband and, in a society where a spinster of 'good family' was a museum-piece, became a sexual neurotic at twenty-five. Worse still was the fate of Mrs. Birdsong, the kind of beauty about whom an earlier novelist would have written six hundred pages of sticky rapture. The nervous tension of her marriage to an ardent and unfaithful husband brought her to such exhaustion that at forty-two she longed for the quiet of death. 'Whatever you do, Jenny Blair,' Mrs. Birdsong pleads, 'never risk all your happiness on a single chance. Always keep something back if it is only a crumb.' But Southern women had nothing to keep back, not even a crumb of artistic or mystical or political zeal; in their sheltered lives they were as perfect examples as civilization has ever known of the hypertrophe of desire which, as Mill pointed out, was among the most tragic consequences of the subjection of women.

Not only is this novel an important study of an important theme; it is also a triumph of technique. The doings of Queenborough are reflected for us by two pairs of eyes, the eyes of Jenny Blair, nine years old when the novel opens, and of her seventy-five-year-old grandfather. One has escaped from the prison of social life and the tangles of personal relationships, and the other has not yet entered either. The ironic effect of the novel is assured by the choice of these two characters as the reflectors. If the novel has a serious flaw, it is in the character of young John Welch whose strident indignation at the foibles of the sheltered life is not a tenth as damaging as General Archbald's scornful pity. The general is one of Ellen Glasgow's most solid studies: he had adopted the wrong career, married the wrong woman, lived with the wrong people, but he had 'kept something back,' enough to fill his old age with thoughts and feelings so fine and so deep that he can utter them only in the long soliloquies which are as beautiful as anything written in our time.

Emily Newell Blair, "My Book of the Month—and Yours," *Good Housekeeping*, 95 (December 1932), 88, 152

If I were ever invited to join some group to choose *the* book of a week, or a month, or a year, I should most certainly have an attack of stage fright. But if any one were to ask me to name *my* book of this month I should not hesitate a moment. I should simply name the book that has given me the most pleasure: *The Sheltered Life* by Ellen Glasgow. And no matter how many others might prefer another book, my choice would still be this tenderly satirical account of how the ignorant innocence of a simple young girl furnished the fuse that set off an explosion in three lives.

It was to be expected that I would like this book. Hadn't I as a girl loved Jane Austen's delicious little satires on the English Georgians? And what Jane Austen did to their manners and morals, Miss Glasgow does to those of the Virginian Victorians. She sheds the gentle light of her irony upon them so that we see their code for what it is, a sentimental evasion of facts—and this, although she is too wise to ignore its values. How could she, when she has, as she once said to me, "seen Southern ladies ignore facts out of existence"?

Yet, as befits a writer living in a century when science is discovering (or claiming to discover) the explanations of human conduct, Miss Glasgow probes much deeper than Miss Austen did. She is at once more drastic in her handling of her characters and more understanding of them. Just as piquante as Miss Austen, she is more kind; it is the causes of their conduct, rather than her characters themselves, that she holds up to scorn.

[. . .]

I have said before and I say it again, that to me she is first among American fictional artists.

Take, for instance, her exposition of character: in the hands of some authors Jenny Blair would appear only as a selfish, stupid girl; Eva Birdsong as a silly, self-fooled, neurotic woman, and George as a sensual profligate. So they would see these people—such they would conceive to be their true, their real selves. But Miss Glasgow looks not only *at* her characters but through them and around them, and she sees that their ideals are also a part of them; she discovers other qualities—kindness, generosity, courage; she sees their charm, their graceful manners, their strivings—even Eva's beauty and "armour of gayety" have a value for her, and George's physical vigor and good intentions, and Jenny Blair's naive and wistful longings. And these things, too, she paints into their portraits. So we find them, as she does, lovable, attractive, with qualities to be admired even when their conduct meets our disapproval.

And then her style! If there was a word which was the antithesis of "vulgar," that would be the word to apply to it. But "elegant" is too pretentious, "chaste" too weak, "refined" too negative. Alas, there is no word to define that something which is to a style what perfect breeding is in man or woman.

This, then, is my book of the month!

Roland Nelson Harman, "Fool's Paradise," *Commonweal*, 17 (7 December 1932), 167

James Branch Cabell has emphasized how necessary the human race finds it to keep forever before itself some picture of a life more nearly perfect than that it is daily enduring. We are better off, he says, if we can believe that we are more important than we superficially seem and that somewhere else real happiness is to be had. Mr. Cabell does not think that the question as to whether the dreams are true is of great importance. It is on this point that Ellen Glasgow differs from Mr. Cabell, although the two are friends and admire each other's books. It makes a difference to her that very often there is no truth back of the dream. For, as a veracious chronicler of southern life, Ellen Glasgow knows that the shattering of a fool's paradise can be a deep tragedy.

Her latest novel, which is perhaps her best, describes just such a tragedy. One of its principal characters is Eva Birdsong, lovelier even than Mrs. Langtry, who has sacrificed everything for a man unworthy of her. Her awakening is terrible. Equally outstanding in the book is old General Archbald, who has dutifully put aside pleasure all his life, who has "made a good living by putting an end to himself." Around these figures the drama is constructed.

Ellen Glasgow might be called an imaginative realist, for she writes of contemporary life with an attempt to understand rather than to indict. Her style balances sympathy for individuals, never for systems, with irony that is the comment of reality on illusion. In *The Sheltered Life* her imagination and skill have produced a profound and beautiful drama that extends beyond its immediate scene.

Times Literary Supplement [England], 9 February 1933, p. 90

The scene of Ellen Glasgow's new novel *The Sheltered Life* . . . is laid in the Virginia with which she is thoroughly familiar, the lazy and attractive blacks making a background for the lazy and peculiarly conceited whites, waiting on them half in slavery still and punctuating their tragedies with childish laughter. In the town of Queenborough the two diehard families of Archbald and Birdsong refuse to move from their homes in the quarter that is rapidly deteriorating into an unsavoury slum. They have large houses and gardens and they pretend to ignore the smells and sounds that none the less intrude on their fastidious senses. Only the child, Jenny, questions the constant effort to ignore the present.

Jenny is the only young thing in old Mr. Archbald's life and the single mitigation of his lot, which is an existence hedged round by the acute watchfulness of three daughters who are determined he shall not marry again. Jenny's mother is a widow, Etta is one of those pre-Freudian invalids so useful in fiction, and Isabella is frustrated but makes her escape. Next door are the Birdsongs, Eva "as lovely as Lily Langtry" and George, her husband who trifles with other women, white and black. Miss Glasgow gently turns a handle and the old-fashioned panorama moves. There is no action, only the gradual growth and development of Jenny, who is not, if the truth must be told, acutely vital or intelligent although she is an improvement on her mother and aunts. At seventeen or so she falls a victim to George Birdsong's well-exercised charm and becomes involved in Eva's tragedy of waning health and looks and bitter jealousy. The climax is slow in coming, but it is very well staged, and, whatever Jenny's shock at George's "accident," the reader welcomes the definite destruction of all her shelters and pretences and the hope that she will now step out of stuffiness and grow up.

Checklist of Additional Reviews

Frank Daniel, "*The Sheltered Life*," *Atlanta Journal Magazine*, 21 August 1932, p. 18.

Harry Emerson Wildes, "Of Making Many Books—," Philadelphia *Public Ledger*, 24 August 1932, p. 9.

William Soskin, "Reading and Writing," New York *Evening Post*, 27 August 1932, sec. 1, p. 7.

Charles Hanson Towne, "A Number of Things," New York *American*, 27 August 1932, p. 11.

"The Chaos of Placid Lives," Boston *Herald*, 27 August 1932, p. 11.

Majl Ewing, "Novel Depicts Frustration in Southern Elite," Richmond *Times-Dispatch*, 28 August 1932, sec. 1, p. 12.

G.H.H., "Ellen Glasgow's Novel of the South," Wichita *Beacon*, 28

August 1932, magazine section, p. 2.
P.H., "Ellen Glasgow's Newest Novel: *The Sheltered Life* Has Her Usual Excellence," Providence *Journal*, 28 August 1932, sec. A, p. 10.
Rosamond Milner, "Civilized Realism," Louisville *Courier-Journal*, 28 August 1932, sec. 2, p. 7.
Durham *Herald Sun*, 28 August 1932.
Booklist, 29 (September 1932), 18.
Mary Ellen Chase, *Bookshelf*, September 1932, 14.
O.S.R., Cleveland *Bystander*, 1 September 1932, p. 29.
Helen MacAfee, "The Library of the Quarter: Outstanding Novels," *Yale Review*, n.s. 22 (Autumn 1932), viii.
Gertrude Springer, "But Life Breaks In," *Survey*, 68 (1 November 1932), 564.
Herschel Brickell, "Some Favorite Novels," *North American Review*, 235 (January 1933), 92.
Louise Maunsell Field, "The Modest Novelists," *North American Review*, 235 (January 1933), 63–9.

THE OLD DOMINION EDITION OF
THE WORKS OF ELLEN GLASGOW

The Old Dominion Edition
OF THE WORKS OF
ELLEN GLASGOW.

The Voice of the People.

Printed in GARDEN CITY, NEW YORK,
at the Country Life Press, 1933.
DOUBLEDAY,
DORAN
&
COMPANY, INC.

James Branch Cabell, "Two Sides of the Shielded," *New York Herald Tribune Books,* 20 April 1930, sec. 11, pp. 1, 6

A definitive collection of the works of Ellen Glasgow has very happily begun with the publishing of revised versions of four of her novels of Southern life, and with yet four other of her books announced for inclusion in this handsome Old Dominion Edition a little later in the year. The event is fortunate, if but as indicating a vague elementary justice to exist now and then even in literary affairs.

For the belatedness of Ellen Glasgow's general recognition as the foremost woman novelist of America seems nowadays quite extraordinary. She had been publishing for twenty-eight years with a considerable if varying meed of popular success.

Her vogue, even as a Southern writer, was distinctively third-rate, with Miss Mary Johnston and Mr. Henry Sydnor Harrison well in the lead. In fact, throughout these twenty-eight years Ellen Glasgow had published as if it were in the obscuring shadow of the famousness and the large sales of Mary Johnston. Ellen Glasgow was considered, if at all, in connection with Mary Johnston. Ellen Glasgow was that other Virginian woman who wrote books: and some of her books had in their season been fairly popular.

Thus matters stood until the appearance of her fifteenth novel, when *Barren Ground* was brought out, in the spring of 1925. Then alone did it occur to any one of any least importance—so far as I know—to appraise seriously the work of Ellen Glasgow by any æsthetic canons.

For *Barren Ground* was unmistakably the work of a very actual and a highly competent artist. Its sales, they tell me, were not enormous: but it got for Miss Glasgow that intelligent sort of consideration which she had prodigally earned without critical detection. Meanwhile she was publishing *The Romantic Comedians* and *They Stooped to Folly*, with an accompaniment of ever increasing plaudits now that the proper superlatives to apply to her were known by all the better-class reviewers.

The belatedness of this recognition, I repeat, seems nowadays extraordinary. Yet I think too there are to be found in the earlier work of Ellen Glasgow the influence of certain modes then current, each one of which made directly for the timely and popular appeal of the book at the date of its publication, and each of which, as literary fashions shifted, had tended to hide the book's real merits as a work of art. Those early books were very, very generously proportioned: the general bookbuying public is always favorably impressed by a visibly long book, if but upon the thrifty principle of getting your money's worth. When these books were written, the ghost of Thomas Nelson Page still haunted everybody's conception of the South, keening in Negro dialect over the Confederacy's fallen glories: yet another Sentimental Tommy had made familiar the canny dialect of Thrums; and many persons were reading the Wessex novels of Thomas Hardy with an admiration which appears inexplicable. In brief, these earlier stories of Southern life were written at a time when novels in dialect were prevailingly popular. Moreover, these books were written at a time when all American novels ended happily, just as a matter of course.

These things are trivial. These things are, in every case, extraneous to the main matter of the book wherein they occur.

355

Yet it was just these things, I think, which for so long a season had combined to make many of those earlier books by Ellen Glasgow appear, to the casual eye, somewhat stolid and wholesome looking, a great while after stolidity and wholesomeness had been expunged from the list of possible literary virtues. Today, of course, we know that Ellen Glasgow was never stolid, and that wholesome is precisely the last adjective which any patriotic Southerner would ever hurl at her. Today we recognize that in these superficial matters Ellen Glasgow conformed to the mode of her day very much as she then wore her beautiful bronze hair à la Pompadour. My point is merely that it was these things, I think, which delayed the recognition of Ellen Glasgow's preeminence.

My point is furthermore that in this new edition these very things have been remedied. I remark that both the occasional over-plus of length and the occasional superabundance of dialect have been attended to most dexterously. Miss Glasgow has proved an accomplished surgeon. She has amputated. She has lightened. It is as though she had blown dust from the pages. She has, in brief, improved matters wonderfully. And though her happy endings remain perforce unchanged yet when Maria Fletcher returns to the ex-convict "through the sunbeams," and when Dan and Betty "begin all over again, but this time together," it appears the course of wisdom to regard these ultimate sentences as an over-sweet liqueur at the end of a highly satisfactory banquet.

For the banquet is there. You have in the works of Ellen Glasgow something very like a complete social chronicle of the Piedmont section of the State of Virginia since the War Between the States, as this chronicle has been put together by a witty and observant woman, a poet in grain, who was not at any moment in her writing quite devoid of malice, nor of an all-understanding lyric tenderness either, and who was not through any tiniest half-moment deficient in a very consummate craftsmanship. What we have here, to my first finding, seemed a complete natural history of the Southern gentlewoman, with every attendant feature of her lair and general habitat most accurately rendered. But reflection showed the matter to be more pregnant than I had at the outset suspected; for the actual theme of Ellen Glasgow the theme which in her writing figures always, if not exactly as a relentless Frankenstein's monster, at least as a sort of ideational King Charles's head, I take to be The Tragedy of Everywoman, as it was lately enacted in the Southern States of America.

You will note that almost always, after finishing any book by Ellen Glasgow, what remains in memory is the depiction of one or another woman whose life was controlled and trammeled and distorted, if not actually wrecked, by the amenities and the higher ideals of Southern civilization. The odd part of this is that it so often seems a result unplanned by the author, and more often than not, a result which by no system of logic could result from the formal "story" of the book. It is merely that, from the first, Ellen Glasgow has depicted women, and in some sort all women, as the predestined victims of male chivalry. That is a creed, whether it be true or not, to which her faith has been given with a fervency no other creed has ever awakened in her inhumanly logical nature: it follows that whensoever she touches upon this creed, if but in passing, that fervor blazed. And the most tiny flash of it stays unforgettable.

I turn, for example, to the earliest written of the four books in hand. When all the story of *The Battle-Ground* is gone by, what I recall most clearly are the contented bustlings about of Bettie

Ambler and of Mrs. Lightfoot after being rescued from the pampered estate of well-to-do Southern gentlewomen by the realities of warfare. These ladies, as you may remember, when once they had been released from that sheltered exaltation, got a sort of picnicking delight out of the uncivil realities by which men were appalled. "But then the Major," as Mrs. Lightfoot observes, forgivingly, as to her husband, "is a romantic at heart, and he is still surprised when human nature acts like human nature." Thus clearly did Ellen Glasgow state her main complaint against men, as far back as in 1902. She has repeated it since, time and again, with accents which have steadily lessened in condonation.

Then, too, what remains in memory after *The Deliverance* has been finished is that incisively symbolic figure of Mrs. Blake, blind and forever imprisoned in an ancient tall chair—an heirloom, of course—and kept drugged with chivalrous lies. *Virginia* is, throughout, quite frankly an account of the futile antics of that shielded and stainless wife and mother who is indigenous to the post-prandial oratory of politically gifted Southrons. This story of Virginia Pendleton is, in short, the tragicomedy of the woman who conforms in all things to our best Southern notions of womanly perfection. There is no pressing need to inquire through what chance its leading character was christened Virginia. And lastly, *They Stooped to Folly* is the tragicomedy of the woman who conforms to one especial Southern gentleman's desires as a sexual animal rather than to the ideals of his sex as a whole. But the point is that, to Miss Glasgow's finding, the conformist and the nonconformist to men's chivalrous delusions about women are punished with equal severity. Where the one is drowned in reprobation; the other is stifled in mind and spirit, with in either case man's chivalry serving as the executioner.

I shall not further pursue this distressing theme. Yet I think of Angelica Blackburn in *The Builders*, inane and ruthless and secure upon that pedestal to which Southern chivalry has lifted the Southern lady; and of her elder, very near kinswoman, Angela Gay, in *The Miller of Old Church*, who has surrendered all rights and obligations in order to grasp more effectively at the privileges of an invalid Southern lady from whom must be hidden away all unpleasant happenings; and of Angela's sullen spinster sister, also, whose career as an artist has been denied her by the circumstances that "it was out of the question for a Virginia lady to go off by herself and paint perfectly nude people in a foreign city." I think of Dorinda Oakley, in *Barren Ground,* and of her life-long conflict with male notions as it was fought out in the Commonwealth of Virginia. I think of that fine desiccating flower of Southern womanhood, Amanda Lightfoot, in *The Romantic Comedians,*—who had herself not ever any need to think about anything, because all had been decided for her by the appropriate feelings of a lady and the Episcopal Church. I think of Gabriella Carr, in *Life and Gabriella,* who, after the hard years had taught her some little wisdom, ran away in a panic from the most faithful and the most chivalrous of Southern gentlemen because she simply could not stand being married to his delusions.

I think of all these luckless women, I repeat, and of yet other women whom Ellen Glasgow has created. And everywhere I find the problem: What is a woman to do before the toplofty notions entertained by the romantic male as concerns women? Is it best to conform to these notions, at the cost of a cankering dishonestness and of a futile pottering over ever-present small household tasks, or to ignore these notions, at the cost of a chilled and futile spinsterhood not over patiently endured by the casual charity of your nearer and less sympathetic relatives, or to rebel flatly against these insane notions by letting "human nature act like human nature," at the cost of acute discomfort and of ostracism and, in the end, of futility? Such is the problem which in its every solution involves futility. Such is the problem which, in our chivalrous Southland, Miss Glasgow has tacitly decreed to be the Tragedy of Everywoman—for all that she has found it a tragedy of the mixed Jacobean school, wherein the comic scenes are as plentiful as the sad ones, and it is the latter which she has recorded with the larger gusto.

No, I shall not further pursue this quite dreadful theme. For to me in particular this is an embarrassing theme. Ellen Glasgow and I are the contemporaneous products of as near the same environment as was ever accorded to any pair of novelists. From that environment she has built her Queenborough and I my Lichfield; yet no towns have civic regulations more widely various. In our shared environment she waited a sad long time, as I, for recognition. She, waiting, wrote her salty reams about chivalry, in the while that within a stone's throw I was sprinkling sugar upon the same topic. Yes, the coincidence and the contrast are odd. Yet I find the outcome of it all, in the shape of our various books, to be troubling. The outcome permits me not the least doubt that this over-logical woman must decree me also to be "a romantic at heart," and must thus dismiss all my toplofty and age-old notions serenely. The outcome would even seem to suggest that the one or the other of us may be wrong. Yet I prefer to interpret it as proving only that never while life lasts can the two sexes ever quite understand each other. This is perhaps a rule which holds always and everywhere. Ellen Glasgow and I have but attested between us that it very rigidly holds in our chivalrous Southland.

Moreover, I observe that when, after some twenty-eight years of writing within the limits which befitted a Southern gentlewoman (with disquieting overtones), Miss Glasgow departed from that seemingly discreet course by publishing, in *Barren Ground,* a quite unladylike book, she then attained for the first time a really appreciative and appreciable audience. I observe that when she more or less emulated the not unfamous old monk of Siberia, at the high cost of deriding the high tenets of our chivalrous Southland, in *The Romantic Comedians,* and yet again in *They Stooped to Folly,* then Ellen Glasgow became a major figure in American letters. As a loyal Southerner, I can but deduce with regret that the wages of sin may turn out to be art of a superb quality.

Stark Young, "Prefaces to Distinction," *New Republic*, 7 June 1933, 101–2

There will be reviews of these novels, evoked by their appearance in the attractive volumes of this unified edition of Miss Glasgow's work. The comment here will turn on the prefaces that the author has now, with the exception of *They Stooped to Folly,* written for each of them.

I have already mentioned elsewhere that affability—the only name I had for it at the time and I can find no better now—that characterizes Miss Glasgow's writing, an affability that consists of a certain reserve, arising partly from delicacy and breeding, partly, I should think, from an early sense of solitude. There is through this an unwillingness, doubtless an inability as well beyond a certain point, to lay on thick the implications or make a public spread of the full meaning. The willingness to insist on the content of her writing has in her later work grown with Miss Glasgow; certainly *The Sheltered Life* was more distinctly commanded in this respect. I have often been puzzled over the great popularity of her novels, and have come to think it rests on some central core of meaning and personal essence; for certainly there are many who, if they really took in the caustic insight, social satire and demolition scattered here and there, would be stung or incensed by it, and, on the other hand, many who, if they sensed the undercurrent of intensity and courage, would be deeply moved and unpopularly shaken. It should be interesting, therefore, with such a writer, to see what she has written in these prefaces, for which her success has provided an invitation, and distance, with its degrees of personal detachment, a fruitful perspective.

In the course of these prefaces, all of them but one running scarcely two pages, we can see the first movements of the young writer's mind, the will, for example, to leave the world of which John Esten Cooke spoke in the eighteen eighties in his book on Virginia, quoted by Miss Glasgow. If no great original genius has arisen, he says (leaving out Poe), many writers of attainments and merit have produced works that have instructed and improved their generation; which he considers better than amusing them, and from which he goes on to say that this literature has the distinct character of respecting good morals, good manners and of not offending delicacy or piety or trying to instill a belief in what ought not to be believed. As a young girl Miss Glasgow determined also, as she tells us—how briefly!—in the prefaces for *Barren Ground* and *The Romantic Comedians,* to write of the South not sentimentally, not as a conquered province, but as a part of the larger world—a remark that should be of use to critics of, for instance, *The Sheltered Life* in gauging the relation of the locale to the real purport of the novel. At that early period, too, something was dawning that looked forward to the time when, in the *Virginia* preface, she could say, for her heroine, taught by a Victorian academy the correct attitude of evasive idealism, prepared for the perils of the actuality, that "she was the perfect wife as man invented her and as he imagined her"; and that "the pathos of it was that she was not a weak character but a woman whose energy of soul, tradition and education had been deflected into a single emotional center"; that "she was an exquisite, if slightly fantastic, creation, and had the Victorian male been as pliant in nature, the moral experiment might have been pronounced a success."

The longest of the prefaces, and the most important, begins the volume of *The Miller of Old Church*. Its concern is first with tracing the course of literature in the South, and then with an attempt to clarify the relation of the present-day novelists and coming novelists of the South to their material. . . .

[. . .]

We have then a discussion of the new tendency in the South toward "Americanism." It is a careful treading over the ground of this theme, with the conclusion that there is no reason why "American novels, excellent or otherwise, should not be written; but they will be written by those novelists who are concerned more with the quality of excellence than with the characteristic of Americanism." . . .

In the shorter prefaces the indication, luminous and reticent, appears when Miss Glasgow is noting what are really the most exact perceptions with regard to her own growth or the nature of some work of hers. We have the recollection behind

359

Deliverance, of that visit with her mother at the old house, the room with the yellow ships and blue water on the wall, and of how later "this occasion flickered to life in my memory, and gradually, after the habit of ideas that have been long buried beneath clustering impressions," the figure of the heroine "gathered symbolic substance and power" . . . from that hour in which the two characters "walked from the Virginia tobacco fields into my mind, my imagination was steeped in a quality of light that I hesitate to call epic." In the preface for *The Battle Ground:* "If I dealt with romance it was because one cannot approach the Confederacy without touching the very heart of romantic tradition. It is the single occasion in American history, and one of the few occasions in the history of the world, when the conflict of actualities was profoundly romantic." Another preface: "If I might select one of my books for the double-edged blessing of immortality, that book would be, I think, '*Barren Ground*'" . . . "it became for me, while I was working upon it, almost a vehicle of liberation." The setting of the book . . . back to recollections of childhood . . . "the country as familiar as if the landscape unrolled both within and without" . . . "the saturation of my subject with the mood of sustained melancholy was effort-less and complete . . . time, like a mellow haze, had preserved the impressions unaltered. They were the lighter semblances folded over the heart of the book." [Ellipses in this paragraph are in the original review.]

Such revelations and comments, hesitant and brief, always distinguished, will be, I suppose, the best comment on the novels of Ellen Glasgow.

Meanwhile the novels remain as they remain, and Miss Glasgow, for all her purposed extension of the human field, remains, as should be the case with every writer, essentially of her own region; her bases are Southern. The deceiving exhilaration derives from the lively exercise of her faculties, the wit from the instinct to be amusing in company, the crackle and luster of the spirits from the inner notion of what one is when one enters a company. The smooth formalism of the surface in this writing is an element of decorum, not without its distant heritage from Jefferson's and Voltaire's eighteenth century; the modulation in stress and insistence is, out of an almost unconscious *amour propre,* to be taken for granted. To be clear is sometimes only to be inconsolable; to be gallant and polite is sometimes only to be solitary. Looking closely at many of the passages in these novels, you will find them made now, out of a kind of pride, antithetical or balanced into epigram, now brilliant, out of an exquisite courtesy. The not infrequently tart edges of the style very often will be discovered on examination to be essentially a reaction toward cruelty, which is a prevailing motif in Miss Glasgow's imagination, working there secretly from our immediate intuition. A prevailing mood is melancholy, but it is there only as implicit and tender, as if privately conveyed.

H. L. Mencken, "A Southern Skeptic," *American Mercury,* 29 (August 1933), 504–6

Some time ago, in the eminent *Nation,* Miss Glasgow printed an article under the title of "What I Believe." It might have served admirably as a general preface to the present edition of her novels, for it set forth plainly the origins and scope of the amiable skepticism that is at the bottom of all of them. That skepticism came in the first place out of the circumstances of what must have been an extremely lonely and unhappy childhood.

Here was a little girl of an almost morbidly sensitive and imaginative sort, set down in a Virginia that had been reduced by the fortunes of war to a kind of aching chaos, socially, politically and economically, and was trying desperately to fashion a new social order out of the black stumps and smouldering brands of the old. The easy way, obviously, was to seize upon a few simple principles, a set of bold and easy patterns, and give them, by a sort of acclamation, the authority of Sinai. But many of them, alas, would not work, and not a few of them were plainly false, so what issued out of the struggle was no more than a mass of gaudy artificialities, comforting to the simple but immensely unpleasant to the intelligent. Among the intelligent was the little Glasgow girl, a decorous pigtail down her back. She revolted against the blather, but had no philosophy to meet it. "I excelled only in imaginary adventures. . . . I saw painful sights. . . . The tragedy of life and the pathos which is worse than tragedy worked their way into my nerves."

Escape came at the hands of a teacher encountered in Richmond—a sort of miraculous accident. He recalls forcibly the bearded youth who, at the same time, was arousing and inflaming young Frank Harris in faraway Kansas. Dead at twenty-six, he yet managed in his short years to cover a vast area of reading, and, what is more important, a vast area of genuine thinking, centering on what was then called political economy, but running up hill and down dale in all directions. Miss Glasgow herself was but sixteen when she encountered this extraordinary pedagogue, but she was ripe for him, and when he presently passed out of her life and his own he left her with something closely resembling a philosophy. It is with her yet, and every one of her long series of books is informed by it. It is a kind of skepticism that is pungent without being harsh; at least two-thirds of it is simple tolerance. "I believe that the quality of belief is more important than the quantity, that the world could do very well with fewer and better beliefs, and that a reasonable doubt is the safety-valve of civilization."

One may applaud this platform without forgetting how seditious it must have seemed in the Virginia of thirty years ago. But Miss Glasgow, having once mounted it, did not budge an inch. Some day the history of her novels in her home-town must be written. They began as scandals of high voltage, and it was years before Richmond was ready to admit that there was anything in them save a violent enmity to the true, the good and the beautiful. As the news gradually oozed over the Potomac that they were regarded with high politeness in the North there was some reconsideration of this position, but it was not actually abandoned until comparatively recent years. To this day, indeed, Virginia is a bit uneasy about its most distinguished living daughter, and even her appearance in all the solemn panoply of Collected Works will probably leave her something of a suspicious character. For skepticism, save in a few walled towns, of which Richmond is surely not one, is still a kind of wickedness in the South. The thing most esteemed down there, whether by the hidalgos who weep for the lost Golden Age or by the peasants who sweat and pant for the New Jerusalem, is the will to believe.

Frankly, I do not blame the Virginians for stopping cautiously short of taking Miss Glasgow to their arms, and covering her with proud kisses. For the plain fact is that the whole canon of her works is little more or less than a magnificent *reductio ad absurdum* of their traditional metaphysic. Thrown among them, and essentially of them despite her struggle against the bond, she has had at them at close range, and only too many of her shots have hit them in almost pathologically tender places. In her gallery all of the salient figures of the Virginia zoölogy stalk about under glaring lights, and when she has done with them there is little left to know about them—and not too much that is made known is reassuring. She has, in brief, set herself the task of depicting a civilization in its last gasps, and though her people have their share of universality they are still intrinsically Virginians, and hardly imaginable outside their spooky rose-gardens and musty parlors. They remain so even when the spirit of progress seizes them, and they try to take on the ways and habits of mind of the outside world. Surely the polyandrous Edmonia Bredalbane, in *The Romantic Comedians,* seems, at first glance, to be anything but provincial. But that is only at first glance. Soon it appears that she is Virginian in every corpuscle, despite all her far rides on her witch's broomstick. One parts from her quite sure that this witch, precisely, could not have happened anywhere else on earth.

Miss Glasgow's Richmond colleague, Mr. Cabell, has gone in, at intervals, for the same pitiless illumination of the local scene. There are, indeed, obvious resemblances between *The Rivet in Grandfather's Neck* and the Glasgow novels, though there are also important differences. But Cabell has thus come to close quarters with his fellow Democrats only at longish intervals; for the most part he has contented himself with doing them, as it were, at second hand, in the form of mural figures in a gaseous Virginia of his own imagining. This transformation has improved their looks and augmented their store of ideas, but it has left a good many of them disquietingly un Virginian, or, at all events, Virginian only to specialists in the species. I daresay that Miss Glasgow herself reads the Cabell books with a kind of understanding denied to the rest of us. If so, she gets double value for her money, and both times it is high value. As for herself, she avoids the hazes of allegory. Her portraits may not be exactly photographs, but certainly there is a blistering realism in them, and as she herself hints in some of her prefaces of this *Old Dominion Edition* they were made, in many cases, from models who once actually breathed the Virginia air.

Her work shows no falling off with the years. Her latest books, on the whole, are her best, and most critics will probably agree with her in putting *Barren Ground* (1925) in first place. It took her a long while to reach its fine design, its impeccable surface, its general ease and certainty: when she wrote it her first book was already almost thirty years old. But her laborious apprenticeship was surely not wasted, for it gave her a professional assurance that is rare among American novelists, and to only too many of them apparently unattainable. There is no sign of the inspired amateur in her latest volumes; she knows precisely what she wants to do, and she does it with never-faltering skill. Her canvas is sometimes small, but within its limits she has thought out the lay and significance of every inch. Not many of her rivals know the novel-writing business as thoroughly as she does, or have brought to it so acute, so ingenious and so civilized a mind.

James Southall Wilson, "Ellen Glasgow's Novels," *Virginia Quarterly Review*, 9 (October 1933), 595–600

Under the chaperonage once of an old friend of his, I was listening to Sinclair Lewis chatting about American writers when in a banteringly argumentative way he declared that there was no American novelist who had written a good book after his second successful novel. I knew that he was just baiting me for the fun of the thing but I denied the statement—for the fun of the thing—with a vigor that sent him into shouts of merriment and the challenge: "Name two and I'll surrender." I named Cabell. As I had expected, he granted me Cabell, with the comment that "he didn't count because he was an exception to all rules." He accepted Willa Cather too, with a boyish ardour of admiration. Then I ventured the reckless generality that every one of Ellen Glasgow's novels was better than the one that came before it. I think he rallied me a bit for choosing three novelists born in Virginia, but in our general agreement and enthusiasm for her later novels we forgot the original wager in a ripplingly shifting argument as to whether *They Stooped to Folly*, which had just been published, is better than *The Romantic Comedians*, which had preceded it.

Now that Ellen Glasgow has crowned her own career with *The Sheltered Life*, a novel too good to win the Pulitzer prize, and her publishers have printed eight of the best of her other novels in the uniform *Old Dominion Edition*, it is easier to see, in re-reading consecutively her representative work, the development of one of the most significant novelists that America has had. I should modify a little the sweeping statement with which I sought to provoke Mr. Lewis to argument. Each of Ellen Glasgow's novels shows growth since the one before it; but I do not think that *The Deliverance* is as successful a novel as *The Battle-Ground* or *The Voice of the People*, which were earlier; and *Virginia* was her best novel until *Barren Ground w*as published. To my judgment, too, *The Romantic Comedians* represents most nearly the perfection of her art. *The Sheltered Life* is richer in variety and range, perhaps it has more depth of meaning. But *The Romantic Comedians* is perfect of its kind and (if we omit Meredith, whose novels are too sparkling and vividly individual to be without flaw) it is, of its kind, as far as I know, the only English novel of which that can be said. It is to the novel somewhat what *The Way of the World* is to the drama; but while Congreve wrote with a brilliance that Ellen Glasgow cannot equal, the flash of his wit lacks the contrasting background of wisdom in her novel. A compassionate sense of the tragedy of life gives an ironic flavor to her comedy of manners which makes its wit more biting, without turning bitter the kindliness of her tolerance.

In one of the prefaces which add an interest to the new edition of her novels, Miss Glasgow expresses the wish that she had waited until she was thirty before she published a novel. With a sense of the exquisite power of the later novels, one can understand the artistic sensitiveness that would give her that feeling; but for the America, not to speak of the Virginia, of their decade the four earlier novels can stand on their merits without concession for the early age of their author. They form a group, *The Voice of the People*, *The Battle-Ground*, *The Deliverance*, and *The Miller of Old Church*, that succeeds in the author's purpose, as no one else

363

could then have succeeded, in giving a social history of Virginia since the Civil War. That so young a woman should have seen the irony of the situation of the South torn between its loyalty to an old tradition and its hunger for the recuperative sustenance that was promised by industrialism, is in itself amazing, but it seems even more so to the critic who feels that in her younger books she herself showed a belief in some of the nostrums that the materialistic "progressives" had to offer. She sought an honest realism, and within the books that many people read for the brightness of their romantic coloring there was a wholesome ironic core; but that was an anachronistic idealism rather than a critical realism which made her view the effects of slavery and aristocracy in the old South in a spirit more akin to that of an abolitionist than of a philosophical historian. She was tolerant even in her salad days and as an analyst of a social tradition she was always keen but never sharp. She was as witty and almost as wise in those earlier writings as in her later ones, only the wit crackled more and shone less, and the wisdom was more "knowing" and less comprehending. She got her effects, and the interest with which the stories can be re-read after all these years without seeming at all literary museum pieces proves that she was a competent craftsman from the beginning. Yet her frame-work was somewhat set and formal, and her love of animals and desire to make certain characters sympathetic betrayed her into sentimental lapses which she must have been totally unconscious of; such as young girls saving a yellow dog from the ravaging pack at the risk of life, or taking rabbits out of traps and feeding them before setting them free.

She came of age as a novelist with the publication of *Virginia*. Except for a minor detail or two, such as Oliver Treadwell's giving all his money to a starving student in Germany because he is of more worth to the world, she is, to quote her own Uncle Ish, "no mo' un inspector er pussons den de Lord is"; she gives to each the fate that his character as formed by his acceptances and his choices has made for him. *Virginia* and *Barren Ground* stand together as two of the most honest realistic studies of American life so far written. *Barren Ground* is the most ambitious novel that Ellen Glasgow has written and she says that it is the one which she would select for "the double-edged blessing of immortality." The very theme, the triumph of "the spirit of fortitude over the sense of futility," forces critical comparison upon another plane from that of, let us say, *The Romantic Comedians*, which of its kind is matchless. One feels something of the effort that has made *Barren Ground* the powerful book that it is and one remembers other novels of the soil that are greater, but one understands why the story of Judge Honeywell flowed "into words with an effortless joy." She is not, to quote her own words, said of one of her characters, "maintaining throughout the struggle her manner of unconquerable irony"; she is letting her own creative mind play wittily upon the lives of people of the sort that she knows best and the novel grows like a day or a plant, to the very last line when "all the tender little leaves of April were whispering together."

Her three "comedies of manners" alone, *The Romantic Comedians*, *They Stooped to Folly*, and *The Sheltered Life*, place Ellen Glasgow among the three most important living American novelists. That, of course, is a dogmatic thing to say, but my dogmatism may prove as good as the next man's, and dogmatism offers one way of being emphatic. In these later books her technique has grown in artistry without having become self-conscious. Her style is less crisp and consciously clever and more flowing and rippling as though it threw up the sparkling wit and poetry and humor like spray from the force and depth of its own movement. She has the sophistication born of sympathetic experience and her wisdom has become an enveloping philosophy of life in which tolerance and understanding are blent, rather than flashes of insight into separate problems and individual characters. She is as clear-eyed now in viewing "this mass production of mediocrity" called "progress" or in satirizing "a popular young man without charm but as loud and bright and brisk as the New South," as she was, and is, in puncturing the "belief that a pretty sham has a more intimate relation to morality than has an ugly truth." The background of these novels of contemporary life is still the past, the Virginia in which the memory of a Saint Memin portrait could give a weak wife a feeling of superiority to her wealthy husband, and where a girl like Cynthia Blake "would have crucified her happiness with her own loyal hands rather than have dishonored by so much as an unspoken hope the high excellencies inscribed upon the tombstones of those mouldered dead." And for what she thinks the false idealisms left over from days that are dead, she does not "sweeten disapproval with tenderness"; but her themes are more elemental, of the eternal tragi-comedy of man and woman rather than of the spirit of commercial materialism that was born "from the ashes of a vanquished idealism."

From the beginning Ellen Glasgow realized, as Hardy did, that life must have its roots in time and place. She has written the social and spiritual history of Virginia from the period of the Civil War to the present and in this respect her work has an essential unity. She sets her scenes with her own ancestral furniture. Microphylla roses, syringa, and crape myrtles grow in her old gardens and pink oleanders stand in green tubs. Her heroines of the past wear a gardenia or a Jacqueminot rose in their hair. Paulownias and magnolias grow in the streets, deer-berries and black gum in the woods, and broomsedge in the fields. Her people speak in Virginia accents and pay homage to Virginia loyalties. So the stage must be set for all human comedy or tragedy. In the truth with which she has shown the elemental in man in the setting that she knows, she has achieved the universal. When she has forgotten to tell us how wrong slavery was, how the Civil War has given the poor white man his chance, how Victorian women were what men made them and the men the victims of their own creations, and remembered the eternal themes, by so much has she been the more universal in her appeal.

In the range in which she excels as a novelist, Miss Glasgow has a quality that is fine and will prove enduring. Her work is always sincere and understanding. She has beauty of expression and a store of poetic imagery from accurate observation. Her constructive skill is manifested by the sustained effects and cumulative interest of all her stories. Her insight into character is deep and her intellect is penetrating and wholesomely sophisticated. Her novels are not remarkable for range or variety of robust characterization nor for a spectacular power of creating memorable scenes. Her best scenes are quiet ones, marked by a subtle intensity. She writes in a spirit of friendly urbanity and gives to her pages a charm that is best suggested by the word, fragrance. Above all, her wit is forever fresh—with an epigrammatic tang that makes everything she writes delightful.

VEIN OF IRON

Vein of Iron

BY ELLEN GLASGOW

*"Effort, and expectation, and desire,
And something evermore about to be."*

HARCOURT, BRACE AND COMPANY
NEW YORK

Thyra Samter Winslow, "The First Reader," New York *World-Telegram*, 29 August 1935, p. 19

Vein of Iron, by Ellen Glasgow, is published today. That it will go immediately into the best-seller lists is inevitable. And this popularity reflects credit not on Miss Glasgow as much as it does on the reading public.

When a book as fine and as true and as thoughtful as *Vein of Iron* is given general acclaim—and I'd like to bet that it will be—it seems to me that literature is pretty safe here in America. I'm a little tired of authors "too good to be popular" and the idea that only shallow and tawdry books sell.

Vein of Iron is rich in emotion and understanding, with a profound feeling for the fullness of life in the past and the present. And those who love Ellen Glasgow need not be told that her prose is beautiful—I've never known it as lovely as in *Vein of Iron*.

The story is laid in the village of Ironside, in Shut In Valley, Virginia, and in the city of Queenborough. The most delightful as well as the most heartrending scenes are laid in Ironside.

In this village the Fincastles have lived since they took the land from the Indians. They were simple people and just, with duty and religion more important than happiness, but with happiness found in small things. They were poor—had always been poor—but they still lived in "the manse," and there was enough to eat. They managed to hold up their heads with dignity, with the idea of the South—"none better and few as good."

[. . .]

Vein of Iron is mostly Ada's story, her love for Ralph McBride—handsome, fascinating and yet weaker and more petulant and sullen than Ada, who nearly wrecks both of their lives, though it is tradition and pride and another woman which help in the wrecking. Their love rises to the heights, is thwarted by separation and by war. And they are united—never again to reach the heights but to make out, as most of us make out, by compromising with life.

William Soskin, "Faith and Hunger in Virginia Hills," San Francisco *Examiner*, 29 August 1935, p. 11

Ellen Glasgow is the literary pioneer who broke away from the gaudy, romantic traditions of the Southern novels. Now she rises above the heads of the young Southern futilitarians and calls for a simple quality of human fortitude.

Vein of Iron is the title of Miss Glasgow's new novel. It suggests in no uncertain terms that the contemporary browsers in the slums, the specialists in poor-white degradation and the novelists for whom miscegenation is the ultimate destiny of all characters have, all of them, a direct kinship with the older romantics Miss Glasgow spurned. Both species are built about backbones made of flabby jelly.

Miss Glasgow does not preach any polite Pollyanna creed. Her story of three generations of the Fincastle family in the Great Valley of Virginia plunges deep into the economic misery of our own godless days and knows the feel of acute hunger and the death of human hopes just as

Herschel Brickell, "Mood of *Vein of Iron*, a Book of Our Own Times, More Earnest than Author's 'Social Comedies,'" New York *Post*, 29 August 1935, p. 23

surely as do the most hard-mouthed of the Erskine Caldwells or the most blood-soaked of the Faulkners.

John Fincastle, the free-thinking philosopher of the story who puts his church behind him to write works repudiated and ignored by America and who comes to know the breadlines of the city as well as the poverty of his own village in the hills, is an example of the long-view man. In him there is intellectual loyalty. The heaven and hell within his own being makes him tower above the wasteland.

John's wife was an invalid, unsuited to the privations of mountain life and unable to match the sturdy courage of John's heroic mother. But the wife saw that she had to choose a way of life, even in her invalidism. She had to choose between high spirits and low spirits, and she "chose what I thought would be easier on others." A delicate but true branch in the vein of iron.

Most of the direct action in the story centers about the daughter, Ada. Ralph, the man she loves, is forced into marriage with another girl through a device which seems to me the weakest point of Miss Glasgow's story. Eventually they are reunited in marriage, only to know the disruption of the depression and the grinding horror of mass life in the city. If Miss Glasgow had built the meaning of their experience on more moving and more credible personal lives I think the book would attain majestic proportions. As it is, the novel remains a thoughtful and courageous work.

Ellen Glasgow's *Vein of Iron*, published today and sent to subscribers of the Book-of-the-Month Club as the September choice, is a striking departure from the mood of the author's three "social comedies" immediately preceding the present book.

With *The Romantic Comedians*, *They Stooped to Folly* and *The Sheltered Life*, particularly the last named, as witty as the other two and more profoundly wise, Miss Glasgow produced novels that have no equals in the whole range of American literature within their special province.

Vein of Iron more nearly resembles the Virginia novelist's earlier work in its earnestness and gravity. The intelligent and sensitive observer and recorder of life is likely to alternate between the two moods represented by the comedies and by the new work; at times even the relief of ironical laughter seems out of place.

Perhaps, since there is such a difference between *Vein of Iron* and *The Sheltered Life*, the latter as completely civilized a novel as has ever been written in this country, there is little point in making a comparison. I must say, however, that my own taste runs to the social comedies for the reason that they, of all the books Miss Glasgow has ever done, seem to me to give the fullest and most complete opportunity for the exercise of all her talents as a writer.

It may well be, however, that *Vein of Iron* will please more people than *The Sheltered Life*, because such delicate and subtle wit as is Miss Glasgow's is not always the most widely appreciated of qualities in good fiction. Moral earnestness is better liked and more generally understood, it seems to me.

The "vein of iron" that furnished the title for the novel is the Scotch-Irish strain in certain Virginians. The curious persistence of sturdy independence and unbreakable self-respect that is characteristic of this breed is a theme worthy of a first-rate novelist; it is both interesting in itself and also as a commentary upon the innate difference between human beings and the way in which they stand up to life.

Rooted in the past through its relation of some of the perils and trials the Scotch-Irish pioneers underwent and their almost incredible stubbornness in resisting disaster, the hard inner core of their beings appearing to be inviolate in any circumstances, the story comes on down to our own times.

Its modern setting, which gives Miss Glasgow a chance to comment upon so much of what has happened to this country within the last few strange and troubled years, will give it an added interest, the interest that is to be expected from some footnotes on our own follies. Miss Glasgow's gift for epigram finds abundant opportunity.

[. . .]

Miss Glasgow's striking ability to create character, to put flesh-and-blood people into her books, is strongly evident in *Vein of Iron* and one of its most distinguished features.

Her latest novel, then, has the great virtue of saying something, of presenting a belief and illustrating its workings and of performing the task with the skill of an accomplished and painstaking craftswoman.

Also, her career from the beginning shows how useful it is for a novelist to possess a brain, although the intellectual quality does not always appear to be necessary when one examines the careers of some of our distinguished fiction writers.

Miss Glasgow's brilliance of intellect explains, I think, why her work has followed a steady upward curve, exactly, as I have said before, the reverse of the production line of virtually all her contemporaries.

Heywood Broun, "It Seems to Me," New York *World-Telegram*, 30 August 1935, p. 17

Not long ago I expressed the opinion that all novels are too long, and I have no intention of retracting this opinion. Nevertheless, it just doesn't go for Ellen Glasgow's V*ein of Iron*.

If I hadn't read the book already, almost any of the very favorable reviews it has received would have frightened me away, since all the critics have insisted on its solemnity as well as its magnificence.

That seems to me a little misleading. While it is true that Miss Glasgow makes no effort to crack the quip, there is plenty of quiet humor in the tale she tells for all its tragic undertones.

Admittedly, *Vein of Iron* is old-fashioned in its technique and even more so in its point of view. It is a horse and buggy novel. The author seems to feel that rugged individualism has not yet run its race and that salvation must always remain strictly a personal achievement.

I do not believe these things, and, as a matter of fact, I suspect that maybe Miss Glasgow has become a trifle skeptical in spite of her protestations. She is such an excellent reporter of life that the very facts which she assembles war against her. The sacrifices which her folk make for crumbling traditions and for conventions which are properly outmoded show up palpably as futile.

Whether the author is willing to confess it or not, her theme is one of frustration. At least this is surely so of all the male folk in the book. Although Ellen Glasgow has never been numbered, as far as I know, among the disciples of feminism, *Vein of Iron* is, among other things, a tract in celebration of the fact that man is but a clinging oak who can survive only through the aid of some sturdy vine.

Grandmother Fincastle, for instance, bore many children, and she baked and sewed and went through the usual routine of those who hold that women's place is in the home, and yet she strides through the book like some Alexander seeking new worlds on which to impose her will.

The matriarch of the Fincastle family is by many leagues my favorite character in any novel which I have read in two years' time.

Perhaps my overreadiness to weep about the harsh lot of folk in fiction is not properly a part of any attempt at literary criticism. But I must record the fact that there is a scene in *Vein of Iron* in which Grandmother Fincastle marches in to assist in the birth of an unwanted baby and that these particular pages are as eloquent and moving as anything in modern fiction.

I came to this part of the book along about 3 o'clock in the morning—and recently I haven't been staying up past midnight even for poker games. Miss Ellen Glasgow by this time had slapped a full nelson and a toe-hold on my attention, and I watched the dawn come up as I swung into the final chapters.

I can hardly say that I read *Vein of Iron* at a single sitting. It is a book which is known in the trade as "a full-length novel." I didn't count all the words, but there must be something like a couple of hundred thousand. Even a pretty fast reader will find himself occupied for at least a week.

But the book is well organized and architecturally sound. There is no danger of getting lost in any maze, and so it is always possible to pick it up again after dinner or the necessity of working or any other tedious interruption takes you away. A good many characters are introduced, but not in a manner to confuse you.

Personally, I get mad at mass novels in which the chapters jump around from the castle of the Quentins to the hovel of the Sullivans and then back to the other side of the tracks again.

I have read novels in which some late chapter began, "John Slingo flicked the ashes from his cigar"—, and I was obliged to say to myself, "Who in hell is John Slingo?" And then it was necessary to turn all the way back to page 19, where he first appeared in his role of the forgotten secondary plot.

Vein of Iron has its single thread and follows it faithfully, patiently and with the motor always running. To me it is Miss Glasgow's best novel, and that puts it very close to the top in modern American fiction.

James Boyd, "Valor and Blind Courage," *Saturday Review of Literature*, 12 (31 August 1935), 5–6

Among a few people who were talking about books not long ago the question was raised why the American writer lacks, as we say of horses, staying power. Beginning with Mark Twain and coming down to a number of current names which the reader is at liberty to supply for himself, we said that a writer's career in this country consisted more often than not of a brilliant piece or two of early work and then diminuendo or eclipse. Many answers were given—it does not require a large literary gathering to supply many answers to any question—but one of the most interesting was that the American writer has no strongly held, consistent attitude toward life. At the beginning he or she writes out of fresh childhood memories and out of a childlike blind gusto for the world which carries the possessor triumphantly beyond the age where a man, if he is ever to do it, must begin to find himself, then ebbs and leaves him stranded and defenceless. As an exception, an example of the opposite, the name of Ellen Glasgow was brought in. Certainly she is one of the few well known American writers of today who has within her the principle of growth. Her earliest books, I imagine, were pretty modest ventures. I have not read them. But in her list of eighteen works of prose she has moved steadily forward to a position all the more deserved because it is hard-won. And I think that the basis of this movement lies in her point of view. It is not strikingly original, in fact its strength lies in its long ancestry, but it is held tenaciously, with wit, with tenderness, with shrewdness, and, above all, with passion. By virtue of it, all she does has momentum and direction. Each time she writes a book she puts her gradually increasing skill to the service of a long-held single aim. . . .

The method of presentation is characteristic. Miss Glasgow is a woman, a wise and strong one, and part of her strength has always been that she has no desire to write like anything else. We have then a woman's sense of values, the interest in the minutiæ of life, the comprehension and development of detail in apparent obliviousness of the relative importance of things. Miss Glasgow sometimes treats big moments with an almost scandalous casualness and turns to accumulate little moments with the unerring and happy instincts of a bee. This reversal of emphasis is accentuated perhaps by the fact that the ability to write live dialogue is the most uncertain of her gifts. At first glance this would seem to be a serious defect. This is the age of live dialogue, and by the term we do not mean dialogue which reproduces speech as it is, but something much more skillful, dialogue which produces the illusion that it is being spoken. In the hands of Hemingway the effect gained by extreme skill in selection, in timing, in hidden music, is very striking. With him old methods have been reversed: characters do not create dialogue, dialogue creates the characters. In this field technique can go no further. He is but one, if the chief, of many writers who have taught us to look for tension, speed, lightness, and a sense of immediate actuality in the novel's spoken word. It is therefore interesting to see how profoundly our emotions can be stirred, our attention held, by a novel which does not avail itself of this instrument and which, on top of that, most resolutely declines to capitalize the opportunities for drama.

[. . .]
... As you close the final page of *Vein of Iron*, whether you agree with all or any of its patterns, with all or any of its methods, you will recognize that you have had the experience of reading a work of wisdom and integrity, written with a single purpose by a woman with a single heart.

Fanny Butcher, "Hugh Walpole, Ellen Glasgow Score Again," Chicago *Daily Tribune*, 31 August 1935, p. 6

Ellen Glasgow has also turned from her customary mood and manner in *Vein of Iron*. It is southern in setting, but its problems, its characters, its psychology are in no sense sectional. It is a story of "character," of moral strength and spiritual courage, exemplified in the indomitable old grandmother who was iron overlaid with the gentleness of compassion, of the mother who was delicacy and physical and mental sensitiveness overlaid with iron, and of the grandchild—the real heroine of the book—who by her birth and her association combined the fine qualities of her forbears. . . .

The most interesting thing about *Vein of Iron* technically is, I think, the sense of impending tragedy with which the author suffuses the pages, without ever giving them any unnatural injection of calamity.

Mr. Walpole's pages [in *The Inquisitor*] are pricked black and blue with hints of tragedy and disaster. In Miss Glasgow's there is not one hint, from her, that life is hard and the living of it a task which only iron in the spirit makes bearable. But all the time the reader has that undeniable and at the same time tragic and beautiful fact impressed upon him.

There are pages of *Vein of Iron* which are poignantly touching, and in none of them is Miss Glasgow brilliantly satirical as she has previously been—in both those qualities it differs from most of her work.

Clifton Fadiman, "Books," *New Yorker*, 11 (31 August 1935), 57–9

Everything Ellen Glasgow most deeply believes about America, past and present, she has put into *Vein of Iron*, and she has inscribed her creed in a prose as measured and lucid as any now being written in this country. Depending upon when one was born, one will accept or remain apathetic to the moral values lying at the core of the book. But no one can deny the artistry that informs it and the fine gravity of the mind back of it. I do not know whether this is Miss Glasgow's best novel, but I do know that the sixty-seven pages composing the first section are as beautifully written as anything of hers I have happened to read. Only one of her qualities you will not find in *Vein of Iron*—the civilized wit which links her with the eighteenth rather than with the nineteenth century. *Vein of Iron* is devoid of satiric content and its subject matter is "weighty"; hence the wit has been strained out of it as an irrelevancy.

The story concerns the fortunes of the Fincastle family, descendants of early Scotch Presbyterian pioneers who settled in the Great Valley of Virginia, fought the Shawnees, worshipped a stern God sternly, held sacred learning in reverence, were proud of their moral fanaticism, and endured without complaint and even with a kind of tight-lipped pleasure untold hardships and disasters. They had, as Grandmother Fincastle (the pioneer link with the past) puts it, "character" and "strong blood." The manner in which the Covenanters' "vein of iron" reveals itself again in the characters of Ada Fincastle and her mother and father comprises the main thread of the book.

Ada should have married Ralph McBride, her childhood sweetheart. Ralph should have forged ahead and become the great lawyer for which his talents predisposed him. But one evening—this was in 1911—Ada quarrelled with Ralph because he had swallowed a few ounces of moonshine, and as a result Ralph married the wrong girl and Ada had to wait six years before she won her lover back. But he was no longer quite the same. The war had altered him, the crash was to deepen his bitterness. Through an apparently gray marriage, through poverty and hardship, Ada preserved her "vein of iron," created love and harmony out of seemingly impossible materials, and won through at the end to peace and contentment. Miss Glasgow believes in romantic love, the family, gentility, and the pioneer virtues of endurance and self-reliance. Those who argue that these values are at least questionable will point out that the "vein of iron," heroic as it is, is necessarily linked with a puritanism that tends to make people miserable, even if it does save their souls. As Ada says in despair after her misunderstanding with Ralph, "Why didn't Mother or Grandmother tell me that self-respect doesn't help you when you've lost happiness?" If the "vein of iron" hadn't been quite so heroic, Ada might have been told that men, the base creatures, are entitled to an occasional drink, and she would not have had to go through all the suffering of her middle years. It was this same "vein of iron" that afflicted poor Ada with pangs of conscience that she never should have had. (She made the error of bearing Ralph an illegitimate child and never forgot that Grandmother was put-out about it.)

But even if the basic morality of the book should puzzle you, as it does me, there remain fine characterizations— particularly of Ada's Emersonian father, with his countenance "that seemed to be cut out of light"—and many, many pages of careful and tranquil prose. My own preference is for Miss Glasgow in her vein of irony rather than in her vein of iron, but those to whom the traditional system of moral idealism still makes its appeal will find here a novel suited to their temperaments.

J. Donald Adams, "A New Novel by Ellen Glasgow," *New York Times Book Review*, 1 September 1935, sec. 6, pp. 1, 15

Effort, and expectation, and desire,
And something evermore about to be.

These lines, from Wordsworth's *Prelude*, are printed on the title-page of Miss Glasgow's new novel. They sum up, in a very few words, her essential attitude toward life. For although Miss Glasgow may justly be described as an ironist, any one who has read her thoughtfully must see that she wears her irony as a shield. It is her buckler against the tragedy of human experience. From all her best work one derives the conviction of her belief that unless we live with "effort, and expectation, and desire," we are mocked by life—we are betrayed by it unless we keep the sense of "something evermore to be." Every novelist as deeply intelligent as Ellen Glasgow must view the world with irony; but irony with nothing beyond it is defeat, and "courage," she once observed, "is the only lasting virtue."

That vein of iron runs through her most significant novels, of which this is one. I am inclined to regard it as her best, the fullest expression of her mature experience. Certainly it belongs in the group of her major work, with *Virginia* and *Barren Ground* and *The Sheltered Life*. In mood it is closest to *Barren Ground,* as it is also in setting. *Vein of Iron* is a story of the Scotch-Irish who settled the Great Valley of Virginia. It touches upon, but does not center about, the Tidewater people of whom she has chiefly written. The people of *Vein of Iron* are plainer folk—plain, but stubborn in their pride and rock-ribbed in their strength.

The story embraces three generations, with brief excursions into the deeper past, and its closing chapters concern the years through which we have just been living. In these concluding chapters Miss Glasgow faces bravely the disordered and disturbing world in which we live. With admirable compression and a searching sweep that little escapes, she telescopes all that we have watched and thought about and feared as the social fabric of our age has crumbled before our eyes. . . .

[. . .]

Miss Glasgow has always succeeded in bringing her novels to a strongly fibered and satisfying conclusion. Her books never peter away, just as her work in general has marched to increasingly higher levels. *Vein of Iron* gathers itself together magnificently, after a rather slowly paced but never uncertain beginning. Some readers may feel, as I did, that what is essential to the story in the opening childhood chapters might better have been introduced a bit further along, and they themselves omitted, so that the novel would begin with those excellently done reveries of the several Fincastles, etched with that same fine technique which distinguished the superb "Deep Past" section of *The Sheltered Life*. When one has said this, and added that Ralph comes alive very slowly (we know him well by the end), one has said about all that can be said by way of subtraction from a very fine achievement.

Vein of Iron definitely meets the test of first-rate fiction. It creates character in the round; it deepens and broadens our understanding of life. It rises to what I conceive to be an essential requirement if the novel is not merely to mark time or pass into a decline—it makes clear that realism of itself is not enough, that with the fact must go the vision, that the novelist must feel as well as see, that poetry in a wide sense is an integral part of the best fiction. The novel has never reached its highest levels as purely a social document; it never will. As Seán O'Faoláin wrote not long ago, the shadow of Defoe is too long over the novel in English; illumination does not lie along that path.

This novel is beautifully written. Ellen Glasgow has made herself, from inauspicious beginnings, one of the finest prose stylists of her time. There is in America no novelist, and few writers of any other description, who can vie with her in the felicitous phrase, carrying at its core sharply perceived truth or slowly garnered wisdom. She is, without a doubt, the most fruitfully thoughtful, as she is, upon occasion, the wittiest novelist that this country has yet produced. She has had her equals, if not her superiors, in the sheer technique of her craft, but I can think of none other in whose work is combined so many of the qualities which make for fiction that lives beyond its day. Though many have praised her, she has not yet received the full measure of recognition that is rightfully hers, but time unaided will make her place secure.

Frank S. Hopkins, "Ellen Glasgow's Newest Novel Hailed in State and Nation," Richmond *Times-Dispatch*, 1 September 1935, sec. 1, p. 9

[. . .]

Vein of Iron must not be interpreted as an unmitigated glorification of pioneer virtues. Miss Glasgow has enough wisdom to keep in mind the unnecessary cruelty and intolerance of frontier morality and in a quiet way she pokes a good bit of fun at the stern Presbyterianism of her rock-bound characters.

One has the feeling, however, that, living in the more easy-going present, she has a strong nostalgia for those bygone days of rugged simplicity and strength. She points out to us that happiness forged in the crucible of suffering is deep and abiding, and that character then had a grandeur which is rare today.

While the book is primarily past-minded, its insistence upon the necessity of character to happiness shows Miss Glasgow as a critic of the chaotic present with keen concern for the collapse of traditional values.

Regardless of the book's basic theme, however, it is a masterpiece of fiction writing. The characters are vividly presented, and the story is told with power and beauty. No one can read it without feeling once more the familiar mastery and magic of Miss Glasgow's pen.

"Ellen Glasgow's New Novel Is Far Cry from Genteel Tradition in Portrayal of Melancholy Years Since World War," Dallas *Morning News*, 1 September 1935, sec. 4, p. 2

Ellen Glasgow's new novel is not about the Virginia of the planters in those receding years when "the war" meant the Civil War, even though other wars had intervened; but it is a story of the Piedmont that deals especially with the World War and the melancholy years that have followed it.

The first scenes of the realistic drama show life in the hill village of Ironside, a community ruled by Scotch Presbyterians whose ethics was a churchliness that sometimes rose to the height of unadaptable and pugnacious idealism. The preacher Fincastle could give up his church for an idea, but he had little except the example of unbending martyrdom with which to guide those of less intelligence through the complex patterns of a changing age. . . .

Ellen Glasgow, who as a beginning novelist some thirty years ago, was clearly working in the romantic vein and who still owes a great deal to the genteel tradition, is by now pretty far from home. Once she made her stories end, "they lived happily ever afterward," but now she has her puppets caught, like Hardy's, in the web of destiny. Unrebuked her heroine taunts God for injustice and carelessness of mankind's suffering. The novelist maintains her own dignity and gentility and writes about love like a spinster, but as an artist she is herself very lonely in this era of scrambled ethics and uncharted transition. Doubtless she would like to escape from Queenborough and go back to Ironside with Ralph and Ada.

"Retreat to the Hills," *Time*, 26 (2 September 1935), 55–6

In the nine years since the Book-of-the-Month Club was founded, seven writers have had two novels chosen by it. Last week Ellen Glasgow moved into the exclusive company of Booth Tarkington, W. R. Burnett, Thames Williamson, Rosamond Lehmann, James Gould Cozzens, H. G. Wells and Vicki Baum—with an ambiguous, partly realistic, partly philosophical novel of three generations of Virginians, poor but cultivated folk who struggled to find some significance in the harrowing changes that swept their lives.

Ada Fincastle, sensitive, grey-eyed daughter of an unfrocked minister, inherited from her pioneer ancestors a stubborn courage that protected her from despair no matter what disasters engulfed her. Her memory of a poverty-oppressed childhood was a catalog of disappointments and perplexities. When she set her heart on a particular doll with real hair, her unworldly father, who wrote obscure books and corresponded with deep thinkers throughout the world, got her a cheaper one instead. And later, when she desperately needed help to save the man she loved, her father could only try to console her by repeating useless words of grave wisdom.

Strangely passive, Ada could think of no way to strike back when Janet Rowan, employing crude trickery and the threat of scandal, trapped Ralph McBride, who had planned to marry Ada. Ada waited, while Ralph's hatred of his wife had at last reached a point where he could understand why men sometimes murder women. He could not get a divorce, but before he went away to war he and Ada found happiness in a hideaway in the mountains. Left in the small, nosy village, facing her strict religious grandmother, the taunts of the children in the street, Ada bore Ralph's child. She moved to a Tidewater city, worked, learned to look with compassion on the struggles of her poor neighbors. Ralph returned and they were married but a deep strain of war-created fatigue and despondency sapped his ambition, created a reserve that Ada could not understand, sometimes led him close to disaster. Unemployment destroyed their modest comfort, spread ruin in the families around them. They retreated to the hills they had left, new pioneers planning to build another life on the wreckage of the old.

Born in Richmond in 1874, Ellen Glasgow published her first novel, *The Descendant*, in 1897, has published 19 volumes since then. Of medium height, brown-eyed, slightly deaf, she lives in an old house in the heart of Richmond, writes in a garden hidden behind high shrubs and a forbidding iron fence, entertains visiting celebrities, is described by her friend James Branch Cabell as a *grande dame* of a rare and almost extinct type. Although *The Romantic Comedians* and *They Stooped to Folly* are among her more popular works, critical opinion is that none of her novels has measured up to *Barren Ground*, published ten years ago.

Dorothy Van Doren, "Salvation from Within," *Nation*, 141 4 (September 1935), 277

As distinguished from those novelists who believe that a disorganized and unjust political system can be replaced by one which will offer to the individual the order and justice he needs and deserves, Miss Glasgow, fully recognizing the harsh illogic of the world today, presents a counter-theory of salvation of the individual by his own integrity and inner virtue. Her scene is the Great Valley of Virginia; her protagonists are the Fincastle family, chiefly exemplified by grandmother, son, and granddaughter, descendants from a line of pioneers who sought the first American frontier in the face of wild forest and wilder savages, and possessors of the iron that brought the earlier members of the family through the trials of establishing a nation. The story begins with ten-year-old Ada in the year 1900; it ends in 1932, with Ada and her sixteen-year-old son carrying on the Fincastle tradition, after years of privation, humiliation, and disappointment, through a World War, a decade of post-war recklessness, and the first four years of worldwide depression.

Miss Glasgow, in other words, has attempted to cover a large canvas in time and to touch the lives of most of the villagers of Ironside with the movement of the world for thirty years. Her Fincastles during that time have plenty of suffering on which to test the edge of their fortitude. Ada's first disappointment, the doll with real hair that she wanted and the doll with a china head that she got, is by no means her last. She lives to lose her lover to a slut, to watch her mother die of a lingering and painful illness, to bear her child in ignominy, to nurse her husband through war-engendered despair, to experience bitter poverty. But such is the bright strength of her spirit that she is as ready for a new life at forty as she might have been at ten, and has as much energy, resilience, and tenderness to undertake it. Nor is her inner fortitude Ada's only consolation; her two-day idyl on a mountain top, the happy first years of her marriage, the closeness of her family, the enduring love of her husband, these also sustain her. It is to Miss Glasgow's credit that her Ada, if she is firm, is not a prig; if she can bear sorrow, she can also experience joy; and she has her moments of rebellion.

Only the stubbornly doctrinaire will quarrel with a novelist for saving the world in his own way; and salvation by inner virtue may be as good a way as any other. Miss Glasgow is a writer of comedy; in comedy you may lift yourself by your own bootstraps, so long as you experience the ultimate lift. Ada was brought to peace and sufficient comfort at last by her own ardent endurance; her father by the consolations of philosophy; her grandmother by her unshakable confidence in the existence of God. For their friends the Hamblens, who perfectly exemplified the dignified and decorous tradition which the Fincastles—and through them, one may guess, Miss Glasgow—admired, dignity and decorum were not enough to keep them from disaster. When their small living was swept away in a bank crash, they could find no other way out than suicide. Perhaps the wild post-war generation, who discarded dignity for reckless pleasure and substituted for decorum a heartless irregularity, were right after all. Perhaps only those are saved by inner virtue who are born under a lucky star, or who are designed for the heroines of comedy. The less fortunate majority may require the world to move before they are relieved of their suffering.

Miss Glasgow's readers, of course, are not bound to resolve these problems. They can be content with a novel of more than average interest and intensity by a novelist with more than ordinary skill at creating characters who breathe and walk by themselves. They may complain that too many events are crowded into a book that nevertheless sometimes seems too long; they may object that disappointment suffered by a person in a story must not be too clearly suspected by the reader in advance. They will still be able to read a novel important not only for its description of contemporary life but for its recollections of one of the most moving aspects of the American past. That Virginia which Miss Glasgow knows so well she makes more clear with every book she writes; as it continues to be familiar, it will also be received with affectionate admiration.

Gerald W. Johnson, "World of Women," Baltimore *Evening Sun*, 7 September 1935, p. 8

In *Vein of Iron* Miss Ellen Glasgow has made a considerable addition to that very special world of her own creation, peopled by women and by lay-figures that, for lack of a better appellation, we are compelled to term men. Nowhere in this country is there a more competent portrait painter of the more contemptible varieties of the male half of the human race; but Ellen Glasgow has never pictured a complete man. Probably, she has never seen one, or has not recognized him; but this gap in her experience is what has prevented her from stepping out of the ranks of the fine novelists and occupying a place among the great ones.

Her latest book, *Vein of Iron,* is an admirable example of both the strength and the weakness of her work. The gallery of women it presents deserves unstinted praise; but the men are so obviously designed merely to create situations on which the personalities of the women may work that it is impossible to take them seriously. One is a philosopher, and we are told the greatest that America has produced; yet he possesses significance only because his almost imbecile incapacity to deal with life creates difficulties for the women of his family to overcome; otherwise he is quite without significance and of little importance. The fineness of his moral perceptions serves to emphasize the sordidness of the rest of the world, and he is used to give an exquisite, poetic end to the book; but he is an abstraction, not a man, and ought to bear some allegorical name—Mr. Greatheart, for instance.

Moreover, the whole plot hinges on an incident that will strike the average Southerner as psychologically incredible—submission to a shotgun wedding by a man who was not guilty as charged. Doubtless there are creatures who would endure this form of humiliation, but this was supposed to be a pretty good man; and it is quite beyond belief that any Southerner who was even half a man would understand that sort of thing unless he was undoubtedly guilty. Hence the novel has a wrong twist at a vital point; and all that follows is wrapped in an aura of unreality.

Once this caveat is entered, however, unfavorable criticism is ended. Grant that this is a world in which only the women are genuine personalities, and *Vein of Iron* instantly gains the status of a superb novel. Grandmother Fincastle is a creation of which any American novelist, living or dead, might be proud. Here is the genuine pioneer type—hard, narrow and ruthless, but with amazing strength, capable of amazing depths of tenderness, and endowed with a capacity for loyalty that can lift quite ordinary lives close to the sublime. Grandmother Fincastle is of a type which of late has found little favor in the role of heroine, namely, the authoritarian. But under the stress of adversity, the modern world is finding that there is much to be said for the personality that, having once yielded allegiance to an ideal, cannot be pried, or torn, or blasted away from it.

But Ellen Glasgow is not solely the psychologist. When she turns her hand to it, she is a magnificent reporter, as well. One feature that alone would lift *Vein of Iron* far out of the ruck of ordinary fiction is the splendid and terrible picture of the depression that it includes. Tons of statistical reports contain less truth about this visitation than the picture of Father Fincastle and Old Man Midkiff in the breadline. Here is the whole story, and all else is mere elaboration; this catastrophe, we are told in two or three blazing pages, ground the faces of the poor and broke the hearts of the fine. Knowing that, why bother with details? However, who knows that until he has been told, not in the language of the schools, but in symbols? Old Man Midkiff and Father Fincastle are the symbols; and he who has seen them has seen the depression.

Vein of Iron is in no sense a propagandistic novel, but none of the proletarian writers has been more effective, and few have been half as effective in driving home the conviction that he who stands idle in the presence of this horror is a traitor to his time.

It is striking, too, when viewed from another angle. Here is some of the most corrosive comment that has ever been made on the Jazz Age. Ellen Glasgow is not scandalized by the morals of the post-war generation, nor distressed by its frivolity, nor outraged by its flippancy; she is merely made slightly ill by its ugliness and stupidity. She passes it, not with hands thrown up, nor with head shaking, but with her nostrils pinched between thumb and forefinger.

For the rest, we have in *Vein of Iron* another exemplification of that supple, yet sinewy, style which long ago won for Miss Glasgow recognition as one of the most powerful as well as one of the most adroit of American novelists. The acute observation of earlier books is here, too, as well as the intellectual balance that gives to the Glasgow books the appearance of extraordinary clarity and sanity. Among feminists this should be the most popular of all this novelist's works; for Miss Glasgow's characteristic merits in it are as much accentuated as her characteristic weakness.

"Miss Glasgow's Achievements," Petersburg [Virginia] *Progress Index*, 8 September 1935, p. 4

The statement that a writer has published his or her nineteenth or twentieth novel is in itself not impressive except as indication of a physical achievement. With Miss Glasgow, whose *Vein of Iron* is just published, it is an entirely different story, for in all her long list—she began to publish at an early age—there is not one title which she might care to disclaim. Of course there has been the improvement which the reviewers label "growth," but Miss

Glasgow, it need not be said, started at a point far above that on which many careers end.

One of Virginia's needs is a history of her social and economic changes of the last three quarters of a century. Seemingly strange, perhaps, is the fact that the nearest approach to this is a shelf of Miss Glasgow's novels, for she has mirrored these changes far more accurately than could any scholar, however excellent his equipment might be. It would be unjust to emphasize the historical aspect and neglect to say that primarily her novels are works of art, quite as likely to be enjoyed by a European who knows little of Virginia and cares less as by the Virginian who finds on every page the deeds, thoughts, and speech of his neighbors. Miss Glasgow displays in her fine series of novels a knowledge and understanding of life which make for a realism far more authentic than any of the self-proclaimed literature of that school. Only the element of genius can explain how her novels are as local as a parish register and as universal as life itself.

Stark Young, "Ellen Glasgow's New Book," *New Republic*, 84 (11 September 1935), 133

At its core this last is, of all Miss Glasgow's novels, the most profound and serene. Compared, for instance, to *The Sheltered Life*, it is rather less open and fluent and more channeled and intense. As a whole, in fact, its line is as final and distinct as a myth-form or a legend. The theme of the book is implicit in the title. If I should ask the author what that theme is, she would, doubtless, be likely to say that it is best brought out in a question: What is it that has enabled human beings to endure life on the earth? One after another in *Vein of Iron* she has considered and interpreted these answers. Religion? Philosophy? Love? Simple human relationships? Or merely the character that is fortitude? What is the vein of iron that has enabled not only families, but races, nations, strains, to survive and even to forge, or weave, some continuing tradition?

In this novel the vein of iron is, immediately, the Scottish strain of fortitude that has come down from the earliest pioneers in the valley (the roots of the story derive from the Great Valley of Virginia, not the familiar Tidewater region of Miss Glasgow's previous work). But though the iron vein—that fortitude and character in the blood of these Scotch Presbyterian pioneers—is thus close at hand for us, the basic theme of the novel is something far less confined to any locality and far less limited to any racial temperament. By some chemistry of thought in the writer, these elements of predestination and courage in a harsh creed spread into a passion for finality and life. The motif of, for example, death is thereby magnificently employed. Of the chief characters we see one after another the three oldest die, the three deaths separate and varied in physical and spiritual detail. Each occasion is made to bear on the central theme of the book, and to express, also, the character of the person in both its earthly and its timeless aspect. This is accomplished with no sentimentality or softness; life remains life, death, death, and the scene that belongs to it is bitter, salty and exalted.

[. . .]

K. Ellingson, "When Realism Went South," Colorado Springs *Gazette Evening Telegraph*, 13 September 1935

[. . .]

When this latest Glasgow novel appeared reviewers immediately vied with one another in the splashing of superlatives. For a time it seemed that the literary periodicals had turned their columns over to the blurb writers. I read that *Vein of Iron* was by long odds the finest of Miss Glasgow's works, that it eclipsed even the best by Miss Cather and the venerable Wharton. Now I have changed my mind about the blurbists having taken over the book columns, for, having read *Vein of Iron*, I, too, would toss my hat into the air if I had one to toss.

This great novel is not, in my opinion, the best that Miss Glasgow has written, but it is equal to the best. I cannot perceive wherein it surpasses *Barren Ground*, but I believe it matches it in general excellence. Miss Glasgow's wit, her trenchant utterance, has suffered a little in the last 10 years, with the result that the irony in her latest novel is less subtle than in *Barren Ground*, but her powers of observation are sharper and her ability to evoke sympathy for the kind of men and women that we denounce in everyday life is greater than it ever was. The result is that a slight diminution of ironic wit is amply compensated for by increased perception and evocation of sympathy.

[. . .]

Against a background of the south from 1901 to the present time the story of that grand family of the Fincastles is unfolded. And in the unfolding of their story, in the meticulous revelation of their lives, Miss Glasgow brings us face to face with a question that she herself makes no attempt to answer in a general way: "What is the meaning of this struggle with life?" To this profoundly thoughtful and powerful writer, the question is one which each must answer for himself. She tells us what John Fincastle regarded as the meaning of life, what that meaning was to Ada, to Ada's mother and to old Granny Fincastle. Only in regard to Ralph did she fail to point out an individual point of view regarding life. That far she goes in dealing with the great question, but no farther. Yet one feels that she is constantly searching for a more extensive answer, that she has been searching for it with undiminished zeal since she began writing, 35 years ago. And one feels, too, that her long search has been guided always by hatred of sham, by compassion for the strong figures of life who march tragically on, besieged and battered for a while and solitary and lonely in the end.

Bernard Smith, "In the Genteel Tradition," *New Masses*, 16 (17 September 1935), 26–7

Miss Glasgow's list of published books has now reached the very impressive total of twenty, most of which are novels, all of them distinguished by meticulous craftsmanship and a fine feminine feeling for the more delicate shades of mood, the subtler aspects of character and all that in nature is most pleasing to the senses. With each succeeding novel she has further perfected her enviably sure, deft touch, until today it is indeed a rare reader who will not surrender, momentarily at least, to the pervasive compound of lovely color, the scent of flowers, refined yet rich emotion, nostalgia and Virginian idealism that is the peculiar distinction of her work. Not without cause has her position in the world of conventional belles letters become increasingly eminent and secure. If not America's first woman novelist, she is certainly, in the opinion of most reputable critics, of the company of such "immortals" as Willa Cather and Edith Wharton.

There are a few readers, however, who have always been impervious to her charms. Since I am one of them I will admit that I have never before been able to offer really cogent reasons to support my rather ungracious stubbornness. I felt only a vague uneasiness about the truth and importance of her pictures of life among the decaying aristocrats of her beloved Tidewater region. It seemed to me that they were embellished pictures, pictures distorted by too much sympathy, too much compassion to allow a realistic understanding of what lay beneath the decay and what the value was (to "civilization") of the grace and ritual and "culture" of these Southern ladies and gentlemen. I have been told that her pictures are true—factually as well as artistically—and that no one has ever so profoundly searched into the souls of these people as she has. Since I have never been south of Washington I have been willing, though a little reluctantly, to grant her the truth, but I have not been willing to grant her the value. Her work seemed to me to relate not at all to anything that I or any of my friends can consider significant or moving or even simply interesting in this country today.

I am pleased to be able to report that I can now sustain my point of view with somewhat more rational arguments. I have discovered that when the eminent Miss Glasgow comes down to the earth that most of us recognize, she is a great deal less than omniscient. In fact, I am tempted to go so far as to say that she really doesn't know what she's talking about. I discover, too, that she is not especially gifted with imagination and her beautiful poetic style fails to overwhelm me. She should never have written this novel. She should have confined herself to that rarefied sphere of existence inhabited by those whose blood is no paler blue than aquamarine or ice.

Vein of Iron is the story of several generations of Fincastles—a family descended from pioneers, Calvinist clergymen and Indian-fighters, who live in a valley in Virginia's mountain land. Around them are forests and old farms and tiny villages and beyond, the Blue Ridge and the Appalachians. Living now are these of the Fincastles: the inevitable Grandmother, a true descendant of pioneer stock, doughty, valiant, iron-willed; her son, a defrocked minister, agnostic, philosopher, dreamer; his wife, a daughter of the Tidewater nabobs, fragile, sweet, happy in spite of privation and pain; their daughter, a piece of the Grandmother, proud, indomitable, "single-hearted." I hope that I have been able to convey, in spite of absolute fidelity to Miss Glasgow's portraits, the triteness of these stock characters. I am tired of lusty grandmothers and incredulous of unworldly dreamers in the wilderness of Virginia who write five-volume works of metaphysics capable of being appreciated only by half a dozen scholars in Europe.

At any rate, the story is concerned chiefly with the love and marriage of the daughter, Ada. She grew up with and adored a youth named Ralph McBride, whose Irish paternity was doubtless responsible for "his charm and his amused, friendly manner," "his auburn head," and "his sudden smile that had a power over her heart." Unfortunately, just as they were about to become engaged, he was trapped into a marriage with a silly, spoiled, beautiful, but cunning young lady whose father was apparently the richest man in town. Ada despaired, yet the "vein of iron" in her—that singular heritage from the Fincastles of the frontier—enabled her to go on living and even to find some happiness. Eventually, Ralph divorces his wife, has a brief affair with Ada (of course, she becomes pregnant), and goes off to war. Of course, they marry when he returns, but, of course, he has returned from France embittered and grey. It would have helped a great deal at this point if Miss Glasgow had indicated that McBride's bitterness grew out of wisdom—out of a realization of the injustices that made possible the horrors of war. There is no such indication. There is no indication at all of the cause of his bitterness. He is just bitter.

They move to the city (Richmond?) where for a few years they prosper. The stock market crash in 1929 does not touch them, but the depression does. McBride's illness despoils them of their savings, ultimately he loses his job and then, together with their child and Ada's incredible father, they suffer poverty, humiliation and that miserable fear of tomorrow that only the proletarian can ever know. In the end, the father leaves them unobtrusively and goes back to their old mountain home to die. Ada and Ralph follow him and when they arrive they know that to settle once more on the land of her ancestors is their destiny and that they will find peace and contentment there without riches.

The story is obviously false from beginning to end. Its falseness is literary—a sequence of events which arise not out of the author's personal experience or knowledge, but out of a limited imagination engaged in creating a narrative concerning a way of life about which the author is ignorant. It results from accepting a poorly understood subject: the events conform to a pattern, each element of which may be convincing, but the composite romantic and even lurid. No situation seems wholly natural. Its logic is not that of reality but of literature and the reader is reminded at a hundred points of other novels, other stories, other scenes. It is not only the characters (all of whom are traditional types) that give this impression, but the actual incidents irrespective of the parts played in them by the personages of the story. The constancy of the childhood lover, the reversion to the pioneering strain, the pregnancy, the wartime disillusionment of Ralph, the cheerful patience of the self-sacrificing Ada, the finding of themselves in poverty, the return to the land of the forefathers—nothing is without a literary precedent, everything conditioned by the needs of romance instead of the demands of life.

Nor is that all that lends falseness to Miss Glasgow's novel. To a writer of her stature and her manifest gifts, one must concede without question that she has felt deeply the fate and suffering of her characters. But she has felt them remotely—in a realm of imagination that on the one hand has no contact with fact and on the other has not attained the level of genius. For example, the most poignant section of the book is that which deals with poverty, breadlines, illness and the grief of social rootlessness. With what timidity Miss Glasgow enters that fearful world of the poor. With what gentility she pictures the hungry and the desolate! How clean the air is, how pure the spirit, how pathetic! How unconvincing! Miss Glasgow is lost, just as she was lost when she touched on the war. She cannot write of things she does not know. When she does, even her style suffers. Its richness becomes then something very close to lushness.

But in justice to Miss Glasgow, I must add that that style, with its embroidery of wit and physical sensitiveness, makes her novel readable enough so that one may go through it without realizing that she has done a courageous thing in writing it at all. It is no light matter for a novelist as old as Miss Glasgow to adventure in foreign lands and with foreign themes. She has failed utterly, but let us respect her attempt. We know her now as a writer of definitely bounded talents, but at least we know her as a person of feeling and sincerity.

R. M. Gay, "Autumn Fiction," *Atlantic Monthly*, 156 (October 1935), 18–19

Ellen Glasgow's new novel, *Vein of Iron*, is the story of Ada Fincastle, between her little-girlhood and her middle age. It is a searching study of the force of a fine tradition in making bearable a life which would have defeated any woman less strong.

In the first great crisis of her life, when her lover, Ralph, is leaving her after a quarrel, "while she stood there and watched him cross the floor, it seemed to her that joy was slowly ebbing from her heart. Yet something stronger than joy, the vein of iron far down in her inmost being, in her secret self, could not yield, could not bend, could not be broken." This basic stanchness Ada inherited from her grandmother, a Scotch Presbyterian of the most unflinching orthodoxy, and her father, a philosopher and once a clergyman, who had been expelled from his church because of heterodoxy. Even her mother, the physically frail Mary Evelyn, for whom the hardships of genteel poverty were too severe, had her heroism too and her philosophy, expressed in the memorable sentence: "It is only in the heart that anything really happens"; and finally Aunt Meggie, "who in comfortable circumstances would have seemed only ordinary," never wavered in the principle of following the dictates of her heart. The consequence was that Ada lived through personal disaster and through the hysteria of the war and the frustrations of the post-war days, experiencing the extremes of sorrow and want, and yet could say to her husband at the end, "Oh, Ralph, we have been happy together!" and he could only reply, "Yes, we've had a poor life but we've been happy together."

In thus stressing the theme of the book, I have made it sound like a parable of contentment. It is true that any good novel is really a parable; but it is only in retrospect that one feels that Miss Glasgow has written an apologue, and one badly needed in our times. The theme, variously illustrated in the portrayal of Grandmother, Mr. Fincastle, and Aunt Meggie, who have integrated their lives by means of religion, philosophy, or love, and, antithetically, in the portrayal of Ralph, Janet, Minnie, who have never found any such integration, gives meaning to this story of the life of a family in the Great Valley of Virginia; but the story is extremely interesting on its own account. Told without the satire of some of the author's recent novels, even eschewing the wit for which she is so notable, *Vein of Iron* in the sobriety and sincerity of its narrative and portrayals, seems, if not Miss Glasgow's finest novel, her wisest.

M[argaret] C. M[eagher], "New Books," *Catholic World*, 142 (October 1935), 113–14

Miss Glasgow's latest novel spans three generations of the Scotch Presbyterian Fincastles. With technical mastery she projects the heroic fundamentalist grandmother, the heretical, freethinking son, John, and the modernist granddaughter, Ada, who shatters to bits the stout moral code of her ancestors. The background shifts from the old manse in the Valley of Virginia, ancestral home of the pioneer Fincastles, down to Queenborough, familiar ground to Miss Glasgow's readers. When the narrative restores Ada to the half ruined house in the Valley, the ancient homestead seems to function both as unifying factor and as symbolism.

The author gives chance its due share in our mortal predicaments, but she makes disaster spring from the flaw in character. Here it is Ralph McBride's fear of being unlike the herd and Ada's quick temper that beckon malign destiny and hand Ralph over to the foolish Janet. Without waiting for the Reno divorce-mill already in motion, the lovers act on the romantic belief that they "belong to each other." Ada, though reared in the strict Calvinist tradition, shows no trace of moral conflict. With jubilation, a true child of her era, 1901–1935, she plans a flight and yields triumphantly to her lover.

Some of the characterization is firm and consistent, the background and atmosphere show the author's magic, there are flashes of wit and moments of insight—all conveyed in a style of distinction. Nevertheless there is a basic flaw in the development of the theme of the story, the fortitude that binds the generations together with iron links and makes tradition. Ada, still unconscious of sinning against the moral code, returns in poverty with Ralph, "to lean back on" the dead Fincastles, who are "lending her their strength." This sounds the mystic note. But Ada's appeal is like that of a Catholic reciting the litany of the saints while denying the Incarnation or the Real Presence. The ancestors she invokes had practiced not only fortitude in material things, but the kind that involves the renunciation of forbidden fruit. Like the grandmother in the earlier chapters, they would repudiate Ada's romantic philosophy that love justifies itself. Miss Glasgow has shown herself an able critic on more than one occasion, both of twentieth century literature and the welter and chaos of modern society. Either she chooses to ignore this flaw or she has sold out to the moderns.

Frances C. Lamont Robbins, "The New Fall Fiction," *American Mercury*, 36 (October 1935), 244–5

Ten or twelve years ago, when there were questions as to what contribution the South would make to the renascence of American fiction, Ellen Glasgow said: "What the South needs now is blood and irony." She has, herself, given the South its most powerful, because its most intelligent irony; and in her new novel, she offers blood. Followed to its logical conclusion, the hopeless, denigrating attitude toward humanity which characterizes the contemporary school of fiction, would lead to the universal suicide of a race of worms. Miss Glasgow, in *Vein of Iron,* tapping the iron in her own soul, bears witness to man's kinship with God. Her Fincastles came from Scotland to the Valley of Virginia in Indian days, as leaders, pastors, scholars, rebels. Whether they lived by faith in pre-destination and a Presbyterian God, or by faith in free will and the God within themselves, they lived bravely and well. Circumstances had no final power over them. They bore unquestioning the burden of their own behavior. In *Vein of Iron*, the twentieth-century Fincastles are the indomitable grandmother; the scholarly humanist father, free thinker, then pacifist; the daughter, a modern woman except in her willingness to assume the responsibility for her acts, who lives through war, prosperity, and depression, a balanced, fearless spirit. The Fincastles can no more be broken and cast down than can "God's Mountain" which rises high behind their valley manse. The story, in its setting of contemporary life well understood, depends for interest upon no originality of plot. Its major characters are complemented and set-off by the secondary ones; the "tidewater" mother, whose sweet fragility endeared her to the stalwart Fincastles, people who lived in remarkable emotional independence and to whom the clinging, delicate woman must have seemed always a child; the young husband, broken on the modern wheel; the background characters who make of Valley town and Tidewater city a microcosmic world. The firm, warm quality of Miss Glasgow's prose has never shown to better advantage than in this fine novel.

A woman of controlled sensibility, who has never needed to take care lest she be romantic, Miss Glasgow has, in *Vein of Iron*, foregone the delights of iron for the joys of a larger sympathy. Where she has sometimes been merely clever, she is, here wise. She brings to her work that third element, rare in contemporary American fiction, which makes for permanence. In her, creative gift, and literary talent, too infrequently found together in our modern novelists, are supplemented by a truly cultivated mind. It is a thing that the pure poet, mouthpiece for emotions and wisdom beyond his own, can do without. But we have few pure poets among our novelists today, and I believe that the emptiness of their minds accounts for the shallowness and lack of resonance in their work. Deep calleth to deep.

Taken as a whole, Ellen Glasgow's work has a truth which goes beyond realism; though she is a realist, she never descends to the realistic. Her highly cultivated intelligence, perfectly aware of the implications of modern life, is not deceived by the current visions, either of a new earth or of a new heaven. Her firm belief in the vein of iron in man holds her interest fast to the greatest of subjects, the struggle of the individual against Fate.

James Southall Wilson, *Virginia Quarterly Review*, 11 (October 1935), 620–5

[. . .]

In integrating her novel [*Vein of Iron*] through the beliefs implicit in it, Miss Glasgow does not yield to the temptation to be unrealistic. The difference between her realistic practices and Mr. Stribling's might be suggested by recalling that her Queenborough, Ironside, and God's Mountain, are not the real names of those places upon the map, but that he stresses the actuality of Florence, Alabama, as the place he means. He hits at real evils by depicting an unrecognizable community that would be incredible to anyone who did not already believe in it: she creates a society of mixed good and evil that would be convincing to the imagination even if it did not win recognition through its fidelity to its original. Truth never shouts so loudly as its impersonators.

But in her *Vein of Iron* Ellen Glasgow has not lost her vein of irony. Fundamentally this is a humanitarian book evolving through its characters a philosophy of life. In it, with less wit than is usual to her, she yet pays her mocking respect to an America gone badly wrong, "with its watered psychology, its vermin-infected fiction, its sloppy minds that spill over." It is Richmond only as Richmond is typical that passes through the gambling period into the breadlines of depression. The social criticism conspicuous in almost every Glasgow novel is in this one brought down to the year of its publication.

John Chamberlain, *Current History*, October 1935, pp. vii, xii

The month abounded in fiction of more than average worth. There was Ellen Glasgow's *Vein of Iron*. The story of a Scotch-Irish girl who was born of pioneer stock in the Great Valley of Virginia, this novel is a ringing championship of "courage as the noblest virtue." Miss Glasgow, as always, commands her medium. She creates living characters; her prose is always pleasurable, even when she deliberately subdues her gift for epigram, as she has done here. My only objection to *Vein of Iron* is that it tries to tie courage to pioneering individualism, when it is obvious that courage can be an individual quality of any type of person, whether he be Daniel Boone, Trotsky or Gandhi. Conversely, one can have yellow frontiersmen, yellow communists or yellow pacifists.

Harold R. Walley, "The Book Worms Turn," *Ohio State Journal*, 2 October 1935, p. 6

If this column serves any useful purpose, it is to emphasize those books which the discerning reader must not miss. Once again I advise you of a novel of a very distinguished order. To read it is to live life more abundantly, to appreciate more richly the enduring impact of art upon experience. Certainly Ellen Glasgow has written no more substantial and mature novel than *Vein of Iron*. . . .

This is the story of a Virginia family during the past 35 years. The first Fincastles were a hardy breed who brought to Shut In Valley a stern religion to cope with a harsh life. From life they asked no quarter, even as they asked none from hostile Indians who stalked them. They were a heroic race, wrestling a spare living from the soil, building the stone manse as a family fortress, worshipping a grim Calvinistic God, and contented with the slender yield of a strenuous life.

There was a vein of iron in American pioneer stock. Despite mutations, it continued in John Fincastle, who lost his church because of his philosophical writings, and in his daughter Ada. Ada Fincastle grew up with poverty and disappointment. She learned early the difference between hope and fulfilment. In the members of her family she saw frustration transfigured to achievement. Her's was a clear vision, a determined spirit, and a stoic wisdom.

She lived to taste beauty and romance,

and to see both crushed. First in the sheltered valley of her youth, then in the economic chaos of a tidewater city, she learned the impassivity of life and man's callous cruelty to man. She learned to seize her happiness and to fight for existence in the midst of a toppling world and a bewildered humanity.

This is an uncompromising book. It has no illusion, and its restrained pity is tempered with a stoic irony. For this reason it is perhaps the most mature novel which has dealt with recent American life. In it is no jejune rebellion or naive faith in panaceas. To Miss Glasgow life is an unyielding medium, and he who would transform it to his heart's desire must labor mightily for a partial victory. And he must combat his fellow without and the demon within.

Some books are the signed testament of their creators. Others are the implication of a rich personality and philosophy. *Vein of Iron* is of the latter sort. In the rounded completeness of its character, the flow of life through its pages, its tactic weighing of values, it is a creation of amazing breadth and depth. This it is to live in America today, but to live with sharpened senses and mellowed wisdom. What Miss Glasgow has to say of protest, of counsel, of hope, is implicit, but it is also unmistakable. And it is inextricably woven into a novel of absorbing interest and distinguished creative artistry.

Anne Page Johns, "*Vein of Iron,*" *Junior League Magazine*, 22 (November 1935), 69–70

Fortitude, stoic and deathless, is the vein of iron struck by Ellen Glasgow for her new and most significant theme and title. In her study of this proud if comfortless virtue, the village of Ironside struggles through a pocket of the Alleghanies, just at the foot of "God's Mountain." Here, in 1900, living for each other in valiant sacrificial penury, were three generations of a strong Scotch-Irish family. But the Fincastles were not peasants. Besides the Old Manse, they had a notable heritage of pioneer piety and intellect, a certain unyielding spiritual fibre. . . .

Realism leavened with irony, but overlaying a quality deeper and more significant than either, is the fabric of this book. In the ascending importance of Miss Glasgow's twenty novels of the mid-south, *Vein of Iron* reaches a new level of modern craftsmanship. Like its people, the story lives, moves, solves its own purpose and pattern. Written with the same admirable subtlety and grace, immensely readable, it is less a novel of manners, more philosophical in spirit than its forerunners. To her near compatriots, Miss Glasgow's work holds the added charm of the undisguised, familiar scene interpreted for our delight in the artist's vivid terms.

Edith H. Walton, "The Book Parade," *Forum*, 94 (November 1935), 12

An affirmation of the will to live, of the refusal to accept defeat, is the theme of this long, fine novel. Miss Glasgow's Fincastles are people of sturdy stock, descended from a line of Scotch Presbyterian pioneers who settled in the Great Valley of Virginia. Ada Fincastle, the heroine of the book, inherits from her ancestors an invincible staunchness which carries her successfully through a very trying life. She is made of more enduring stuff than her husband, Ralph, whom she marries after long waiting and separation; and when the black tide of depression overtakes them in the Tidewater city of Queenborough, it is Ada who somehow keeps the family from going under. Like her vigorous old grandmother, like her frail mother, married to that idealistic ex-minister, John Fincastle, Ada feels that in spite of disaster her life has been a happy one. Miss Glasgow's accustomed wit and irony play no part in this novel, but *Vein of Iron* has a richness and warmth, an awareness of modern problems, a wise understanding which place it definitely with her very best work.

Dorothy Dunbar Bromley, "Solitude in Love Depicted by Novel," New York *World-Telegram*, 8 November 1935, p. 30

As good a way as any to cure the grip is to take to your bed and barricade yourself behind your favorite books. So it happens that today I'm in a mood to beat the drum for Ellen Glasgow's *Vein of Iron*, which hasn't yet had its full meed of praise in this woman's hall of fame.

While the reviewers have used dollar adjectives in praising this chef d'oeuvre of Miss Glasgow's, they may have scared off a few readers by their soft-spoken complaint that it lacks the author's usual wit and irony.

But *Vein of Iron* is not that kind of book. As its title suggests, it goes deep below the surface, revealing to you universal passions, joys and sufferings, almost as unforgettably as another woman writer, Sigrid Undset, does in her very great book, *Kristin Lavransdatter*.

[. . .]

Louise Maunsell Field, *North American Review*, 240 (December 1935), 546–9

[. . .]

The long novel is so thoughtful, so rich in wisdom and in understanding, so full of memorable scenes and yet more memorable individuals, it is difficult to decide what to choose for special comment. No more truthful, and consequently more heartbreaking description of the depression has yet appeared than that Miss Glasgow gives us in her account of what happened in Mulberry Street. On the other hand, it would be anything but easy to find a more beautiful treatment of love's ecstasy than the episode on the Indian trail. Miss Glasgow looks at life steadily, clearly and above all honestly, with a gaze undistorted by romanticism and undimmed by pessimism. There is sweetness and contentment and joy in existence as she sees it, as well as bitterness and disappointment and pain. Even Aunt Meggie, who had missed the love which enabled Mary Evelyn, despite poverty and frustration, to assert, "I have been happy," found delight in small, practical things; while John Fincastle, the "splendid failure," relished life as his forefathers had done, and as his daughter did—meeting it always with the same high courage.

"There's one thing they can't take from us, and that's fortitude," he declares, speaking for once as the mouthpiece of his creator. Contrasted with this work of beauty and power and clear vision, many of our best sellers seem things of mere tinsel and straw.

Robert Cantwell, "A Season's Run," *New Republic*, 85 (11 December 1935), 149–50

... But there are a few tendencies [in the season's creative writing] sufficiently well defined to permit of more general groupings. There is, first of all, the lamentable collapse of a number of those writers who, only a few years ago, were being hailed as the creators of masterpieces and the leaders of American culture—novelists of the type of Willa Cather, Ellen Glasgow, Elizabeth Madox Roberts, whose latest books have revealed their inability to deal with the emotional and practical problems of the contemporary world in even the most elementary terms. The works of Willa Cather have always seemed to me to have been taken more seriously by the critics than was absolutely necessary; but *Lucy Gayheart* is simply a maudlin book, peopled with stock characters who move through stock situations and who die, unexpectedly and accidentally, to bring the story to a ramshackle conclusion. At one point Miss Cather does attempt to face the modern Middle West—one of her characters is a banker who is presented as being ruthless with the farmers as a result of his disappointment in love—but after five of the six characters die he has a change of heart. Ellen Glasgow's *Vein of Iron* is a much more durable work; her people are more vital and varied and interesting, and they come up against problems—the War, unemployment—that force them to reach into the reserves of their experience and understanding for strength to keep going. But that—to keep going, even if it is in hopelessness and misery—is evidently all they want; and when at the last Miss Glasgow pictures her impoverished family retreating to the hills to start over, the vein of iron in them seems considerably less heroic and admirable than she tries to make it.

Seán O'Faoláin, "Fiction," *Spectator* [England], 156 (6 March 1936), 414

Heaven knows how many recipes there are for making a novel, but two frequently met today are illustrated by the first books on this list [*Show Down* by M. Escott and *Vein of Iron* by Ellen Glasgow]. The one is to take a lump of crude life and spatter it on the pages of a book, despising such literary conventions as movement to a crisis, balance of characters, contrapuntal incidents, sub-audible comment by author, carefully arranged suspense, sign-posts pointing to later developments, and so on. The other recipe reminds us of those trays of fine sand in which a modeller may faintly thumb out a design; these are the definitely literary books, and their faintness comes from a topical melancholy and is indicated by the subjective note and moodily contemplative music of the style.

It would be unjust, however, to suggest that Mr. Escott's novel is just a characteristic bit of Brutalism. It has, certainly, so much of Hemingway in it that Hemingway might well have written it; but though I do feel that *Farewell to Arms* is one of the grand books of our time, its grandness is essentially romantic, and there is nothing romantic about *Show Down;* it is more sincere, I think, than Hemingway ever is. . . .

Neither would it be fair to think too rigidly of Miss Ellen Glasgow's *Vein of Iron* as a novel of the second type—the type of which Mr. Escott's hero says:

> "I don't like things patted into a pattern and made to sound queer and bodiless. . . I'd rather have bad art bursting out of a man than good art being minced out into patterns. Slick and smooth and graceful. . . It's all this plastering over and smoothing things down that takes away from the feel of strength and effort."

For Miss Glasgow, though somewhat too sweet in her imagery and pensive over tragedy, would agree with Mr. Escott; indeed, thirty years ago, she was railing at the "evasive idealism" of the "modern novel." She writes here of the Great Valley of Virginia as she did in *Barren Ground,* centering her story about John and his daughter Ada, the last of the Fincastles, a staunch Scotch-Irish Presbyterian family who drove across the old Indian road from Pennsylvania to Virginia where for generations they worked as pastors of Ironside and built up a mountain parish. . . .

This is obviously a carefully patterned book, and as such its weakness is that it is a trifle too deliberately graceful. The history of the forbears of Ada Fincastle is, in truth, confusing and over-written. The style has too much of the sadness of the dying fall about it. The images are too mannered—*e.g.,* "Misery broke over her in a curved wave"; the washing on the line "swayed upward in the breeze, was puffed out in rosy billows, and covered in a single immense wave the whole field of vision"; a girl has "eyes like smothered flames under black lashes." The emotion is always likewise smothered into a sigh, and one fears that there is more than a little "goody-goodiness" in the general idealism. For all that a vein of iron does hold the softer material together, and it remains a book which might well be read by everyone—if there be any left—who thinks that America has no tradition of dignified and gallant living.

"Scottish Virginians,"
Times Literary Supplement [England],
7 March 1936, p. 201

How firm a foundation does Miss Ellen Glasgow lay on which to build the infinitely careful structure of her story about Scottish Virginians, which she calls *Vein of Iron*, a phrase that describes the outcrop of hard Presbyterian character in American soil. She takes her time to add detail to detail till we know the Fincastle forebears as well as the landscape round the manse and the furnishing of the old house itself.

John Fincastle was a deposed Scottish minister, a philosopher and a modernist in religion who had stood his trial for heresy and schism, so that his manse was merely a house with no attachment to a church. His mother, one of the fine, solid, selfless characters in a fine and conscientious age, retained her own orthodoxy and never ceased to mourn the misfortunes that had come upon them through her son's unfortunate beliefs, all of which she ascribed to "the influence of the British Museum, and to the sinister volumes (never would she have glanced into one of them) that he had bought at such sacrifices (he had gone without a greatcoat; he had even gone without food) when he was a student." John continued to read and philosophise throughout a dreamy and poverty-stricken life, and it is a vein of less than iron in Miss Glasgow's narrative that introduces the famous German professor, come all the way to Virginia to shake the hand of one of the world's known great thinkers.

His women-folk—mother, sister, wife and daughter—believed in him and cherished him; but they suffered bitterly enough from his renunciation of doctrine. Their battle with poverty makes the background of Ada's young life; the clash of old and new ideas in the household breeds in her a strange self-sufficiency and a clear mind. Her love affair with Ralph McBride, a stormy and uncheerful young man not without the power to charm and to attract devotion, is something of a long battle, too. Her story is in part tragic, but the deep feeling between her and Ralph cannot be wrecked, and is untouched by petty meanness. The book covers the past thirty-five years, glancing at the War as it affects this particular family, leaving the younger trio—Ada, her husband and son—struggling in the uncertain present. Miss Glasgow's work must always be taken seriously and read slowly. Her present novel can but add to her reputation for painting with fidelity and feeling a moving picture of human endeavour.

Randall Jarrell, *Southern Review*, 1 (April 1936), 397–401

A group of Scotch emigrants settled in Pennsylvania, then went south to Virginia; their minister was John Fincastle, called by his Presbyterian congregation the "Scholar Pioneer." He was something of a philosopher; his great-great-grandson, John Fincastle, was so much more of one that he was turned out of the ministry for heresy. When Miss Glasgow's book begins, in 1901, he is living in the Fincastles' old house, in a small Virginia town, Ironside. With him live Grandmother Fincastle, his wife, Mary Evelyn, his sister, Meggie, and his ten-year-old daughter, Ada. *Vein of Iron* is the story of this family.

If Miss Glasgow had been writing fifty or a hundred years ago, she would have given directly the history of Ironside and the Fincastles; today, she chooses to inform the reader obliquely. "Toward Life," the first part of the book, tells the story of one day in the child Ada's life. Different chapters are narrated from the points of view of Ada, Grandmother Fincastle, John Fincastle, Mary Evelyn, and Meggie Fincastle. The characters occupy themselves little with action or perception; their concern is recollection. They repeat with unvarying delight, the histories of their families, the names of their mothers, the events of their childhood—things familiar to them, no doubt, but things which the reader has to learn. If one were to begin a novel by making the hero almost drown, so that all his life might "flash before his eyes," the readers would feel that he had chosen a somewhat arbitrary mechanism of information; the reminiscences of Miss Glasgow's characters are almost as extensive, and they have not the excuse of being about to drown. Miss Glasgow selects for their reveries that form of presentation halfway between the modern novelist's version of James' stream of consciousness, and an earlier convention of the reporting of thought: that is, some of the character's thoughts are given in direct quotation, and some are told about indirectly, and, further to vary the texture of the mass, momentary sensory details are constantly thrown in. To handle this method satisfactorily, the writer must have sensibility of almost exaggerated delicacy so far as stylistic effects are concerned. Generally, the method handles the writer.

Telling a story from several points of view has its disadvantages and difficulties. For one thing, the characters' turns of thought, their styles of rumination, must be differentiated; in this, it seems, Miss Glasgow usually fails. What differences of content or elevation there are, are obscured by a certain regularity and heaviness of style. In the novel the little girl differs from the adults mainly in that she thinks in shorter sentences; one reviewer cites this as a notable example of Miss Glasgow's artistry.

Vein of Iron is, in short, what Ada did and what her father thought. It is unnecessary to do more than briefly summarize the course of the Fincastle family.

The story brings them down to the present time; in the last part, "The Dying Age," they move to the city, and Ada (who stands for a sort of pioneer courage and obstinacy) and her father (who adds to these qualities the detachment and skepticism of the philosopher) serve as norms against which Miss Glasgow can set up an industrialized urban life.

Miss Glasgow's attitude toward our time is uncompromising. Burke once said, you can't indict a whole people; such a thought would never enter Miss Glasgow's head. It would be difficult to exaggerate her dislike for the superficial qualities of our age. The next paragraph, of excerpts from Miss Glasgow's book, will give a good idea of both the matter and form of her indictment.

"Whatever could not feed the machine was discarded as rubbish . . . They were all alike, especially the women . . . like rows of shallow saucers slopping with idealism . . . A world that had mistaken sensation for happiness . . . Through sheets of rain a drunken man lurched against her as he tossed a pint flask into an alley . . . Drunken boys . . . sprawling . . . The rosy knees and red mockery of their lips . . . The wide insatiable mouth, painted red as a wound, and the flaunting bare knees above rolled stockings . . . Unreal and fantastic as a nightmare . . . Distraught, chaotic, grotesque, it was an age, she told herself, of cruelty without moral indignation, of catastrophe without courage . . . Could the human race, glutted with horrors of its own making, survive upon a material basis alone? . . . A strange country, with its watered psychology, its vermin-infested fiction, and its sloppy minds that spill over . . . There were still teas without tea, and motion-picture faces without a film, and endless gin-drinking, and hastily bitten-back hiccoughs, and stories just a little funnier that went just a little farther than last year, and much talk of prize fighting, which was Puritanically forbidden, and of fox-hunting, which was Cavalierly allowed, and ardent prophecies that the next legislature would permit horse racing and gambling and pari-mutuel betting . . ."

This hardly requires much comment. There is a troubling flavor of the tabloids about most of Miss Glasgow's judgments. Short skirts and rouge have for her the fascination of obscenity. What she says is very familiar, and very obviously said; she has given us her dislike pure, not bothering to make it over into art. A greater writer has said better:

Turning and turning in the widening gyre
The falcon cannot hear the falconer;
Things fall apart; the center cannot hold;
Mere anarchy is loosed upon the world
. . .

Possibly the last great German idealist, according to Miss Glasgow, said that the American people might some day realize that John Fincastle was their greatest thinker; writing about a great philosopher has its difficulties and its rewards. The smallest feather of so rare a bird should engage the reader. We are charmed to know that Kant liked "any music, just so it's loud and military," not because of the opinion but because it was the great Immanuel Kant who held it. But for this interest to attach to John Fincastle, we must feel that he *is* a great philosopher. To convince us, Miss Glasgow would have to be either a great philosopher or a great writer: that is, either give the philosophy itself, or else make a character whose acts and sayings are so entirely consistent and point so certainly in one direction, that they force us to believe in him unreservedly, and to feel that it is merely because it would take too long, and because we might not be able to understand it, that we are not given the philosophy as well as the philosopher.

Miss Glasgow is of course not interested in the first of these alternatives; the most definite thing she says about Fincastle's great book is that it was a "reconciliation between the will and the intellect." This has a familiar ring; a Kantian might say that the reconciliation has already been effected, a psychologist repeat, with some irony, the word *will*. Fincastle believes that "God is essence, not energy." It is hard to interpret the statement, and it reminds us too much of Santayana.

Miss Glasgow has not the professional's attitude toward philosophy, and so fails to give it to John Fincastle. (Quoting Miss Glasgow: "Philosophy is not a reform but a consolation . . . it is still what it has always been, the only infallible antidote to life." The function of philosophy is to—console! One assures Miss Glasgow that this is *not* what philosophy "has always been.") Philosophy for her is essentially ethics; she is decidedly what James called "tender-minded." If Miss Glasgow were aroused in the middle of the night by a burglar, who clapped a pistol to her head and demanded, "Name me a philosopher!" you can be certain it would not be Hume. John Fincastle occasionally says things worthy of himself; but his thoughts in general, his judgments about the "Dying Age," are not so much those dramatically proper to the character of a great philosopher as those that Miss Glasgow happens to have herself. His sayings too often make up in sententiousness for what they lack in logical acuteness. The reader believes in him as a religious thinker, a noble and sympathetic character—not, however, as a great philosopher.

Miss Glasgow's style may be called commonplace; she is fond of the most obvious and familiar rhetorical devices, and these are most evident in important scenes, scenes in which she depicts some irresistible emotion, some mystical rapture. In general, her style is a good, average, useful style, but when one compares it with a first-rate one, both its inadequacies and ornaments become obvious. This style is at its best in occasional very slight, very sensitive, discriminations, especially in similes designed to convey the effect of sense perceptions. Some of these are unusually successful: "The syllables were as empty as old wasps' nests . . . The row of sandstone slabs, as yellow as old teeth . . ."

Miss Glasgow is generally better in handling unpleasant scenes than in handling pleasant ones. In fact, it is surprising to see how much she depends upon shock as an æsthetic device; Miss Glasgow, in a review, once spoke with energetic despair of the methods and effects we associate with such Southern writers as Faulkner and Caldwell. Miss Glasgow is at times not so far removed from them as she might think.

One feels about *Vein of Iron* that it was intended to be a great book; the plan of the whole novel is very impressive; and yet the texture and details are too often commonplace, the words of the characters too often have the value of something overheard in the street or over the telephone—no more. Miss Glasgow has seen to the spirit, and let the letter take care of itself. Then too, Miss Glasgow comes to her work hardened, full of prejudice and presupposition.

Still, Miss Glasgow's book has considerable power. We readily believe in the characters as real people, in the story as something that really happened; some of the book, about the pioneers, about Grandmother Fincastle, about John Fincastle, will affect the reader unreservedly. Particularly affecting is such a scene as that in which Grandmother Fincastle comes to Ada, at the birth of her child.

Checklist of Additional Reviews

Wisconsin Library Bulletin, 31 (July–October 1935), 84.

Henry Seidel Canby, "*Vein of Iron,*" *Book-of-the-Month Club News,* August 1935.

Margaret Germond, "New Books at Random," Washington *Evening Star,* 28 August 1935, sec. A, p. 8.

W.K.R., "Written in Praise of Fortitude," *Christian Science Monitor Weekly Magazine Section,* 28 August 1935, p. 12.

Paul Donald, "Ellen Glasgow Writes Absorbing Chronicle of Family Life in Virginia," Richmond *News Leader,* 29 August 1935, p. 9.

Dorothea Lawrance Mann, "Ellen Glasgow in Her Own Virginia," Boston *Evening Transcript,* 31 August 1935, book section, p. 2.

"Among the Outstanding Books," *Literary Digest,* 120 (31 August 1935), 24.

Booklist, 32 (September 1935), 15.

Helen MacAfee, *Yale Review,* n.s. 25 (September 1935), viii.

Stanley E. Babb, "Ellen Glasgow's New Novel," Galveston *Daily News,* 1 September 1935, p. 9.

Dorothy Canfield, "Ellen Glasgow's Fine

Tribute to Courage," *New York Herald-Tribune Books*, 1 September 1935, sec. 7, pp. 1–2.

Eleanor Carroll Chilton, "Ellen Glasgow's New Book," Louisville *Courier-Journal*, 1 September 1935, sec. 2, p. 8.

"Ellen Glasgow's Novel of Changing Standards," Springfield [Massachusetts] *Sunday Union and Republican*, 1 September 1935, sec. E, p. 5.

E.M.C., "*Vein of Iron* Yields Riches in a Novel by Miss Glasgow," Kansas City [Missouri] *Star*, 7 September 1935.

Kenneth Horan, "Ellen Glasgow Tells Value of Strong Spirit," Chicago *Journal of Commerce*, 7 September 1935, p. 2.

"A Reassuring Novel of the Depression," Fort Worth *Star-Telegram*, 15 September 1935, sec. 2, p. 8.

M.G.P., "Powerful Novel of Modern America," Worcester [Massachusetts] *Telegram*, 6 October 1935, sec. 3, p. 7.

Gertrude Springer, "People with Fortitude," *Survey Graphic*, 24 (November 1935), 552.

John Chamberlain, "Books of the Times," New York *Times*, 15 November 1935, p. 19.

Wilbur L. Caswell, *Churchman*, 149 (15 December 1935), 18.

Herschel Brickell, "Our Free Press," *American Monthly Review of Reviews*, 93 (January 1936), 6.

THE VIRGINIA EDITION OF THE WORKS OF ELLEN GLASGOW

ELLEN GLASGOW

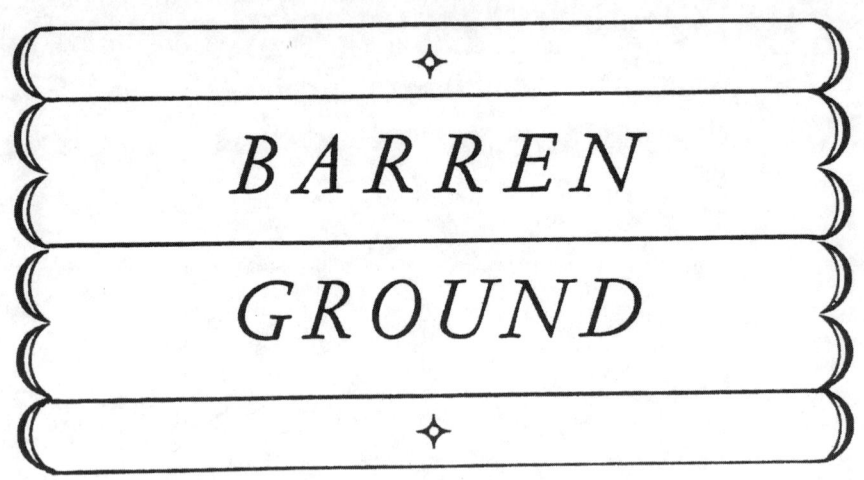

Volume I
⋄§ *VIRGINIA EDITION* ₰⋄

CHARLES SCRIBNER'S SONS
NEW YORK · 1938

Richmond *News Leader,* 21 January 1938, p. 8

The historian of American literature not less than the bibliophile will be grateful for the *Virginia Edition* of Miss Ellen Glasgow's later novels. As issued yesterday in a superb limited edition of 810 copies, printed from type, the first three novels of the edition are *Barren Ground, The Miller of Old Church* and *Vein of Iron.* Each of these has a preface in which, with all the candor of her nature, all the wisdom of her maturity and all the wit of her youth, Miss Glasgow explains why and how the book was written. These prefaces are superb. Each illuminates the particular novel, the development of the writer's profound art, and, in a wider sense, the trend of the noblest American writing of the post-war era. No better antidote for the rude and sordid clumsiness of a certain school of fiction can be found anywhere. To these prefaces we shall have occasion many times to refer, because they become on first reading a part of every man's intellectual treasure-house. For the moment, may we say that this edition shows, more than ever, how slovenly and inadequately the *cliché* of "realism" describes Miss Glasgow's works? In the finest, best sense, hers are novels of realism, but, as one runs over them in mind and sees them together in this dignified format, they seem above all to be novels *of courage.* That is one of many reasons we are proud that this is styled the *Virginia Edition.*

Howard Mumford Jones, "Ellen Glasgow, Witty, Wise and Civilized," *New York Herald Tribune Books,* 24 July 1938, sec. 9, pp. 1–2

Miss Glasgow is one of our wisest commentators as well as being one of the wittiest women of the day. It is true there are always those who do not recognize wit except as wisecracking or who cannot comprehend social comment unless it is sociological. There are few wisecracks in *They Stooped to Folly* or *The Romantic Comedians,* which are nevertheless products of the comic spirit, humanely malign. None of Miss Glasgow's novels is sociological *à la* Union Square. But wit in its true sense is the bright original well of her genius, and the twelve novels now reprinted are a unique social history of Virginia from 1850 to 1933, which the historian of manners and the economic interpreter will always have to consult.

One is glad that publishers have honored an author so great in her total achievement. Yet there is something humorous about reading Ellen Glasgow in the chilly glory of fine printing. The liveliest mind in Virginia is not yet ready for a typographical tomb. The tribute of beautiful format is richly deserved, but the implication that she is about to become the youngest daughter of the skies must be emphatically repudiated. A cheerful pessimist, she writes: "I feel younger at sixty than I felt at twenty when I was oppressed by my own and the world's sorrow."

The prefaces written for this edition place their author in the great line of English novelists and are likely to be the most important pronouncements upon novel writing since Conrad and Henry James. They are filled with golden wisdom which young novelists should ponder. Miss Glasgow has learned that "the subject, important as it is, possesses only a secondary value in fiction, and that the chief, the supreme merit lies in the vision of the artist, in the direct light of imagination." Though the novel cannot ignore time and space, "there must be a downward seeking into the stillness of vision, as well as an upward springing into the animation of the external world." The chief weakness of the contemporary novel is its contentment with the animation of the external world. . . .

Miss Glasgow has been governed by three principles: the novelist must wait between books for the well of the subconscious to fill; the novelist, though he live among the surfaces of accepted facts, must also live the "strangely valid life of the mind"; and the novelist "must preserve inviolate the inaccessible valley of revery into which he can descend." Incredibly remote from Marxian criticism and sociological fiction, these are utterances which a Thomas Mann could understand and approve.

The present edition includes those novels which best illustrate Virginian life. So far as I remember, Miss Glasgow is the only important American novelist to devote her mature powers to a single commonwealth; and it is a mark of her undeviating growth in beauty and wisdom that at no time in her fruitful career has she been in danger of falling into mere local color, regionalism, theory or sectional combativeness. It seems easy to remark that she has written of Virginia only when it was apropos of human life instead of writing of human life only when it was apropos of Virginia, but the verbal distinction points to the special place of Miss Glasgow in American literature.

The gulf which separates *The Descendant* (1897) and *Phases of an Inferior Planet* (1898) from *Barren Ground* (1925) is that between the ardent beginner and the mature artist, but it is instructive to note the themes which persist in her work. She has been haunted by heredity. The young novelist, suffering a severe case of evolutionary measles, accepted heredity in the Darwinian sense; the Virginian was inevitably interested in family. As a Virginian she has mirrored the distinction among good families, good people, poor whites and servants; as an evolutionist she believes that heredity is a profound force in character. In *Barren Ground* Dorinda succeeds because of a strain of innate fortitude in her inheritance; in *Vein of Iron* the Fincastles triumph for the same reason. If birth and breeding get the Amblers and the Lightfoots through *The Battle-Ground,* a tangle of biological traits gives us the melodrama of *The Deliverance,* the tragicomedy of *The Sheltered Life,* the intricate responsibilities of *The Miller of Old Church.*

This interest has limitations. Colored servants and Northerners have parents, but lack ancestry. It is inconceivable that any Virginia gentleman—even Christopher Blake in *The Deliverance* or George Birdsong in *The Sheltered Life*—can be wholly vile. For Fletcher, the overseer in *The Deliverance,* there is pity, since he is human; for George Birdsong there is a kind of forgiveness, since he is after all a Birdsong. This engaging weakness, least evident in *They Stooped to Folly,* is the only limitation upon the tolerant sympathy of this novelist.

The heroines of the earlier novels are young girls of artistic temperament compelled to adjust imaginative existence to harsh reality. The adjustment of inward life to outward reality is a second dominant theme in this admirable fiction. Miss Glasgow distinguishes the false imagination which becomes a sentimental refusal to acknowledge facts (on this she is more wittily merciless than anybody since Meredith) from that inward attainment of spiritual integrity which is the strength of Dorinda in *Barren Ground,* Betty Ambler in *The Battle-Ground,* and, oddly enough, Victoria in *They Stooped to Folly*—that astonishing invention of a proper wife who refuses to acknowledge an improper world. The same obedience to an inward law brings Nick Burr to death at the hands of a mob in *The Voice of the People* and sends John Fincastle on his mystic final journey in *Vein of Iron.* It is the special glory of Ellen Glasgow to have distinguished between the life of the spirit and the life of the subconscious mind; and though she employs the method of mental soliloquy, she has never mistaken psychoanalysis for spiritual strength.

In the truest sense of the word Miss Glasgow gives us a feminine reading of life. Politics, industry, agriculture, finance are only incidental to personal relationships. The business and bank accounts of her male characters do not interest her except as instruments for spiritual failure or achievement. She has sought no reform. She has viewed men mainly in relation to women, women in relation to men and to each other. She paints the friendships of men and women, but not the friendship of men and men. She judges character by its adequacy in the difficult business of love and family life, by its capacity for tolerance and an amused patience. Her young men are mostly uninspired, but she is invariably successful with children, simple people (wherein she recalls George Eliot) and the life of dogs.

But it is in her portraits of adult women that Miss Glasgow excels, and I venture to assert that her gallery of female characters surpasses in richness and variety almost any group of similar portraits in American fiction. The young wife, the matron, the deserted girl, the lady of damaged repute around whom linger the last enchantments of the middle ages, the female sentimentalist, the old maid, Victorian and belated—she has seen and studied these women with ironic patience and a sympathetic pen. Granted that she had rich material, that she came into artistic maturity in Virginia at precisely that moment when the old personalized society was passing into the industrial order, she has had the instinctive tact to seize upon this material and embody it in permanent form ere it disappeared. And she is equally successful with her old men who are, Tiresias-like, the embodiment of the highest wisdom of both sexes.

She is equally successful in presenting the flow of time—more so, I think, than with the spatial surroundings of her characters. The style moves, it is vibrant with light, it submerges plot and character in a pellucid river which as it flows carries the story, and the reader with the story, imperceptibly through time. For this purpose she has not needed any of the mechanisms hailed as discoveries by younger novelists, but like Trollope she possesses an intuitive sense of time as flow rather than as duration. The heroine begins perhaps as a young girl, she suffers a love disappointment or she marries, she has a child, and presently, almost without our knowing how, she has become middle-aged. And yet throughout the novel, did we but know it, some old man, a General Archbald or a John Fincastle, has perpetually reminded us that change is the only permanent law.

Despite the flattering success of some of her books, it has remained for European critics, not to forget a few discerning American ones, to see her greatness in its proper light. For hers has been a difficult position. The impatient North might have brushed her aside as another of those Southern novelists; and she has devoted forty years to chronicling existence in a state which regards conversation as a form of literature and literature as an inadequate substitute for conversation. Caught thus between two cultures, she has nevertheless won a public which has followed her with devotion, if not always with comprehension. Occasionally, it is true, one finds persons living in outer darkness who have not read her at all. A cultivated Bostonian, when I made some passing reference to Miss Glasgow, innocently inquired: "What has she written?" This can only be matched by the anecdote (doubtless apocryphal) of the wealthy Richmond lady who sent her servant to One West Main Street to borrow Ellen's latest book. Or perhaps it is better matched by the failure of the Pulitzer committee to discover that she exists. The ears of that body do not seem to be attuned to one of the few writers of civilized style yet living in the United States.

Henry Seidel Canby, "Ellen Glasgow: Ironic Tragedian," *Saturday Review of Literature*, 18 (10 September 1938), 3–4, 14

This dignified edition of the writings of Ellen Glasgow is a double gift to her admirers. It contains not only all her important novels to date, but also a remarkable series of prefaces, in which the author sets down for each of her novels what she has tried to do, how far in her own opinion she has failed, or succeeded, and why. Taken together they are an invaluable critique upon the art of fiction, by a major novelist who has always written upon themes of importance and with full consciousness of her responsibilities as a practising artist. Here is no surprised self-appreciation, but a confident, yet modest, analysis of achievement by a writer who is expert, professional, sincere, and with a critical judgment that permits detachment even in the intimacy of her own completed work. Creative writers are not always, or often, good critics. But when they possess the nicely balanced mind that permits self-study and self-knowledge, and particularly when they write of their own work, their criticism is likely to be a contribution to literary history.

In reviewing this Virginia edition, however, I do not intend to review these prefaces, except by occasional reference. To repeat Miss Glasgow's lucid analyses of her books would be an impertinence, since no one else will write so well of them; to differ from her estimates is usually to differ from her in taste rather than in opinion, so shrewd and just and unsparing of her faults has she been in these essays, which I hope will some day be published as a book.

But this set of her novels does offer an opportunity to re-estimate from a reader's viewpoint the work of Ellen Glasgow. Her reputation has had a curious history. A realist and an uncompromising artist, at first she shocked her native Virginia while quickly winning praise from critics of fiction. Later, when her art had matured, she won wide popular successes, while the professional critics, perhaps because of these successes, busied themselves with newer writers, often of not one-tenth her ability, whose rawer imaginations followed paths which she sometimes had opened, on into regions of human nature that were more sensational news than stories of gentlefolk who remained aristocrats even when they decayed. She has never had a Pulitzer prize—a fact for wonder when one looks through the now long list of awards in fiction for books with the enduring quality of *Barren Ground* or *The Sheltered Life*.

One reason why Miss Glasgow has had inadequate critical estimation is that she belongs to the great classical tradition of the novel. The great subject for the novel since its beginning in the eighteenth century has been manners, and when the novels have been also great these manners have been no superficies of behavior, but a code, a habitual philosophy of living according to which men and women proceed;—a philosophy, like all philosophies, sooner or later beaten upon, undercut, crumbled away by the insidious waves of new manners, new ideas, new codes in the making. It is a process with indefinite extensions toward the future as well as the past, yet it is subject to different accelerations. Our times, for example, have certainly been years of unusual rapidity of change. But the fact of changing codes has often been lost sight of in the more sensational results of change, and this again has certainly happened in recent years. The novel, reaching out through biology, psychology, economics, politics, most of all I think, ethics, has run like fire into regions little studied by the artist before—has become impressionistic, newsy, sociological. It has been read for scenes, dialogue, new types of character, information about depravity, about sexual intercourse, about crime, about psychological neuroses. Art has suffered, but the area of fiction has been happily enlarged.

Yet all this has no bearing whatsoever upon the value of what I have called the classic novel, organized about an idea, told usually to show what happens to the manners of a culture when that culture begins to rock and settle toward the past. Nor has it made any difference in the success of the classic novel with the general reader. In this country, not only Miss Glasgow, but also Mrs. Wharton, and Miss Cather—our three most eminent practitioners of the classic art of novel writing—have proved that the novelist does not have to be a journalist, or sociologist, or a psychologist, but only a master of narrative, in order to win success with stories where manners make or mar the man.

Miss Glasgow began, of course, with stories of the code of the old South at bay before the Industrial Revolution. She was a pioneer there, as any reader of mature age knows who remembers the sentimental heroics being published coincidentally with her first novels. She wrote also of the new South that had made this code an anachronism, but careful as are her studies of the rising poor white, she did her own class best, except in *Barren Ground*, that masterpiece of run-out fields and broom grass. Her clear mind understood the coarser material, as this book especially proved, but her heart was with the aristocrats. Like Jane Austen, she was most successful with those whose folly she exposed while loving them. And not only because they were her own people. The novel is not at its best with heroes and heroines in the accepted sense, who have the energy of success and make the plot, but with those others who are worked on by circumstance, who at the beginning of the story are already moulded, who oppose to life a principle or a prejudice or a set of loyalties, it makes no difference which, that life, like the incoming wave, has to attack, finding a contour and a fabric resisting the wave and destroyed by it. General Archbald, in *The Sheltered Life*, that old aristocrat wise from unhappiness, is a far more memorable figure than the farm boy turned speculator in the early novel called *Romance of a Plain Man*, who dominates the story, yet nearly wrecks himself on his own crude energies that cannot in a generation learn wisdom.

I would call attention to these early stories—such novels as *The Voice of the People* and *The Romance of a Plain Man*—because they seem to me to prove that Miss Glasgow is one of those novelists who begin with high and sound ideas which at first cannot be realized. No writer escapes from his own time, however radical he may seem to his contemporaries and to himself. It does not need Miss Glasgow's prefaces to these books to show that she knew in the first nineteen hundreds how divergent was her realism from current taste, and particularly that of the South. While there are in all her novels timeless characters, like General Archbald, who have prototypes in every period, even in her early books the current issue of a decaying chivalry and an unworkable code is drawn with the utmost clarity. One can love her Richmond, but never romanticize it, nor respect its virtues except as one respects memorials of a past. And yet in spite of their clairvoyant insight, these books when read today date themselves inescapably. The dialogue is often that exchange of clever sayings, with little depth and a high finish, which was so characteristic of the nineties. It is even possible to take out pages that sound like "The Dolly Dialogues," which every college writer then was imitating. The beautiful women, too, for all her frank honesty in describing the code by which they have lived, have an aura that suggests Thomas Nelson Page's heroines or the Gibson girls. She knew *what* they were, but she saw them as the age saw them, as no modern by any possibility could.

She suffered, of course, from a conflict between her brain and her eyes, or, more accurately, between her understanding and her sympathy, which was tinted, as sympathy always is, by the emotional colors of the time. Not even Samuel Butler, that great original, could escape this, and his posthumous novel, *The Way of All Flesh*, which used to be thought of as pre-Shavian, is now being pushed further back toward the Victorianism in the mode of which, in spite of its iconoclasm, it was written.

Fortunately, Miss Glasgow's later and better novels are not posthumous, but the fine fruits of a living woman, whose eye has kept its sharpness, whose hand has acquired extraordinary skill, and whose unchanging concept of manners develops freely in a time which has adjusted itself to realism.

If, leaving the theme of her books, which, after all, with an artist like Miss Glasgow, is almost incidental, I try to single out the essential quality of her work, I must call it a sense for tender and ironic tragedy. All three of these words are important. There is a tenderness in her comments on such characters as Mrs. Birdsong or Jenny Blair, or in the musings of General Archbald, or Mr. Littlepage in *They Stooped to Folly*, which is sharply different, more feminine and also different without reference to sex, from the more Olympian attitudes of a Thomas Hardy, or the sentiment of a Booth Tarkington, or the honest matter-of-factness of a Dreiser, or the hates and loves of a Sinclair Lewis. But this tenderness is always ironic. Ellen Glasgow has no illusions about life, though, being wiser than many of her younger contemporaries, she values illusions. The child Jenny Blair inspires a marvelous tenderness in all who love young life, and the firm grasp on self which makes personality, but her egoism is, ironically, both her charm and her final disgrace. Beauty in women is often absolute in Miss Glasgow's novels, yet it never attracts absolute virtues, except when life has already wrung out their virility. The very structure of society in her Queenborough is ironic in the extreme. Industry and the new code of material success are cheerfully destroying there a rotted culture, tearing down its gracious Georgian buildings, encouraging among the members of its society their weaknesses—drink and gambling and women—while making their virtues futile. Yet the result, already visible, is an ugly environment, and a restless discontent among the newcomers who do not know what to do with success. But Miss Glasgow's irony is always tender—God himself is made tenderly ironical in Miss Glasgow's novels, because she sees her world as always a departing and a becoming.

And she is a tragic writer, one of the few

in later American literature. I do not mean that *The Romantic Comedians* is not comedy, or that there is not rich comedy throughout all her novels. But in this brief survey I am seeking for her dominant quality—and that is tragic,—tragedy lurks behind even her comedy. Tragedy for her is not the American tragedy of a youth, ignoble at the beginning, and crushed by an ignoble society. Her tragedy also is classic. Its symbol is Aunt Matoaca in *The Romance of a Plain Man*, a woman of principle, whose conflict between the rights of women and the inviolability of her own class was resolved in a Spartan eccentricity, in which her virtues became the enemies of her friends. But Aunt Matoaca is heavily underlined. The tragedy which stirs Miss Glasgow's imagination is not eccentric; nor entirely unhappy. It is the tragedy of frustration—the waste of life through maladjustment of man to his environment and environment to its men. It is the poignant tragedy of nobility, cramped by prejudice, or of beauty gone wrong through inability to adjust to the real, or of a good philosophy without premises in existing experience.

Tragedies of all kinds are eternal in human history, but the choice of scene may determine their success as art. Miss Glasgow's choice, predetermined, of course, by her own experience, has been fortunate. Virginia, as she writes of it, has the advantage of wide contrasts in behavior, philosophy, and faith, which is a great help to the novel of manners. In Virginia, also, the old Colonial and Federal America came closer to meeting with vigor still present in one and energy abundant in the other, than elsewhere in the United States. Charleston kept its code but it decayed quietly. Boston and Philadelphia flowed, the one toward the intellectual life, the other toward quietism, so early in our history that the contrast between their old societies and the new industrial age was a different and less dramatic one when it came. New York was a traders' city from the beginning, with a traders' code adjustable to all weathers.

Like so many true novelists, Miss Glasgow's distinction is not to be found in her style. Her style is always adequate:—in her musings and commentaries it rises above adequacy to a beautiful excellence, in her dialogue sometimes falls below that of her peers in the art of fiction. Perhaps this may be due to the articulate but not highly literate mind of the South, or at least the feminine South, which she draws upon for her records. I find her Negroes' speech far racier and more personable and (I should say) better written than her whites'. But style is not the chief glory of a novel. Indeed a novel, unless it is a satire or a fantasy, does not exert the same pressure upon language as poetry, essay, or even history. There is inevitably and properly something familiar in the novel which asks for not too much consciousness of the word. Novels are seldom written about stylists, and style in the sense of beauty cannot always reside in their dialogue.

True style in a good novel colors, but no more than colors, with the author's temperament, the transcript from reality, and carefully avoids any elevation beyond the pitch of the daily life for which it is a medium. Miss Glasgow's work stands this test admirably. And style, in that larger sense, of harmonious construction, which conducts the reader unfailingly along the path of narrative which has been chosen as the author's way of telling a story, she long since mastered, and practices as well as any one living. Her novels move slowly, by comments on action, and musings after it, as much as by scenes and incidents, yet, as her popularity shows, she holds her readers by this difficult technique, which many more experimental novelists have attempted with only a few who will read them.

I nominate her as our best contemporary master of the tragic drama of significant manners. I nominate her as our tenderest realist of men (men more than women), and our most clear-eyed ironist, for since she is ironic only of the men and women she likes and admires, she never mixes her irony with the stronger but cruder brew of satire. I nominate her for the next American prize worthy of her, for it is certain that she must be numbered among the handful of painters, sculptors, and critics of our time in America, who would be approved both for their craftsmanship and their vision by connoisseurs in any age.

J. Donald Adams, "The Novels of Ellen Glasgow," *New York Times Book Review*, 18 December 1938, pp. 1, 14

The Prefaces which Miss Glasgow has provided for this collected edition of her work have a threefold value. They are, first of all, an illuminating commentary on the novels they introduce, and on the art of fiction itself; they present the fully matured point of view of one of the finest intelligences which has pursued that art in this country; and they reflect, as do the novels themselves, the complete integrity with which, for forty years, she has practiced her craft. Like Edith Wharton and Henry James, she has been gripped always by an overmastering interest in the technique of her art, and, with the exception of James himself, none of our novelists has provided us with a similar blueprint of his growth and attitude.

Growth has assuredly been hers. The history of American fiction, especially within the span of years covered by Miss Glasgow's work, is crowded with unfulfilled beginnings, with brilliant promise never brought to fruition. In spite of the fact that Ellen Glasgow belongs among the born novelists, her early work gave no clear indication of the stature she would eventually assume. One reason, perhaps, for the inadequate recognition which even up to now has been hers lies in the fact that her slowly ripening powers prolonged unduly her apprenticeship. Her growth, though steady, was so gradual that it was insufficiently perceived. As the Prefaces testify, she is herself fully aware of this slow development; she is indeed, an extraordinarily objective observer of her own completed work, and of the nineteen books she has written seven have been omitted from this edition.

The twelve novels here included are arranged, not in the order of their writing, but in three groups within which a chronological order is followed, according to the period covered in each novel. The first consists of three novels of the Virginia countryside (*Barren Ground, The Miller of Old Church* and *Vein of Iron*); the second, of three novels of the city (*The Sheltered Life, The Romantic Comedians* and *They Stooped to Folly*); and the third, of six novels (*The Battle-Ground, The Deliverance, Virginia, The Voice of the People, The Romance of a Plain Man* and *Life and Gabriella*), which constitute a social history of Virginia from 1850 to 1912, later supplemented by the six novels in the other groups.

As a young girl, revolting against the rosewater romances of the Old South which she had read *ad nauseam*, Miss Glasgow determined that she would write of Southern life from a realistic approach. She was the first writer so to do, and the first to include within her scope all the social classes of her region. She set for herself the task of reflecting in her novels a social structure in its entirety; and not a static picture, but one which was to take account of the forces of dissolution and change, a dynamic presentation of life evolving under the impact of time. As her work broadened and deepened, as her grasp of her material became surer, her novels transcended their regional and documentary character; their Virginian origin became an accident of birth; they became, essentially, a mature and wise reading of life, marked by those flashes of illumination which can be had from fiction only on its higher levels.

It was with *Virginia*, I think, written midway in her career, that Miss Glasgow definitely lifted herself to those higher levels. She was, briefly, to drop below them, but beginning again with *Barren Ground* in 1925, all that she has since published meets the test which she herself applies to the art of fiction––that it shall illuminate experience. *Virginia*, though she has in more recent years surpassed it several times, remains one of her best novels. It contains one of her most memorable scenes, handled with superb restraint and understanding—the meeting between Virginia and the mistress of her husband. There is the portrait of a lady of her time and place—and of that something which belongs to neither—which has not been excelled in the American novel. *Virginia*, too, marks for me the definite emergence of Miss Glasgow's style. Its irony was not yet full blown, its perfection of phrase not yet fully attained; but the firmness is there, the structure is forming—an unmistakable distinction is present.

Humor she has always had, although she has not always given it play. It was deliberately excluded from *Barren Ground*, which sustains a mood with greater intensity than any of her books. Time has sharpened the edge of her comic sense, and it is a long way from the pastoral comedy of *The Miller of Old Church* to the probing wit of *The Romantic Comedians* and *They Stooped to Folly*. But even when wit is in the ascendant, the comic sense in Ellen Glasgow never gives way completely before the tragic sense of life—how could it when she is so acutely aware of their close affinity—and, as she rightly observes of *The Romantic Comedians*, there is tragedy in the theme, "though it is tragedy running, like the 'divine things' of Nietzsche, 'on light feet.'" For, as one critic observed, "the story is the illusion of perpetual youth and Judge Honeywell is man eternal."

When I say that Miss Glasgow has the tragic sense of life, I am simply saying, of course, that she views life without illusions. That has been a main source of her strength as a novelist. She has learned not to expect too much of life or of people. For her, courage is the best and most lasting of the virtues, and those who have it, though they may be tricked and betrayed by life, remain undefeated. It is a virtue with which she has more frequently endowed her women than her men, and not unjustly, perhaps, as the sex more schooled in fortitude. It is the distinguishing trait of nearly all her most memorable women, beginning even with Betty Ambler of *The Battle-Ground*, down to its incarnate presence in Dorinda Oakley of *Barren Ground*. Even Mrs. Birdsong of *The Sheltered Life*, slipping through life without looking it in the face, has a muted sort of courage, which flares forth only in her last and tragic act.

Miss Glasgow's women, with few exceptions, are the realists, her men the poets and philosophers (speaking, to some degree, in a figurative sense), and that, putting the more primitive impulses aside, is coming pretty close to one of the essential differences between the sexes. Miss Glasgow sees men more clearly, I think, than any contemporary woman novelist, and her old gentlemen, with General Archbald of *The Sheltered Life* as perhaps her finest delineation, are one of her best contributions to the novel.

My own choice of Miss Glasgow's finest single achievement would lie between *Barren Ground* and *The Sheltered Life*. Both are technically outstanding, both are profound in their reading of life. In *Barren Ground* an unforgettable record of indomitable spirit comes to us solely through the transmitted experience of a single person, through whose sensibilities the entire narrative takes its course. *The Sheltered Life* is built up from two contrasting points of view. As Miss Glasgow herself explains, "Age and youth look on the same scenes, the same persons, the same events and occasions, the same tragedy in the end. Between these conflicting points of view the story flows on, as a stream flows in a narrow valley. Nothing happens that is not seen, on one side, through the steady gaze of the old man seeing life as it is, and, on the other side, by the troubled eyes of the young girl, seeing life as she would wish it to be." Out of this method emerges a deeply moving portrayal of eager anticipation of life on the part of youth, and philosophic acceptance of its reality on the part of age. These are books with timeless themes, without the least dependence on "trends" in the novel, nor is their setting of the slightest consequence; they are human experience illuminated through the art of fiction. And as such, their tenure of life should be long.

I wish that every beginning novelist in the United States might read these Prefaces and profit by their sanity and penetration. If the art of fiction is to go forward, if the younger realists are to grow beyond the merely transcriptive rendering of life which nearly all of our serious fiction is, they cannot afford to neglect such a rational and suggestive record of one novelist's growth.

Regarding the future of the novel, she recognizes that it must "at last turn either toward a more promising vista or into a blind alley," and although doubtful of the outcome, it is characteristic of her that she should close these Prefaces on a note of expectancy, even as regards the continuation of her own work. Life has been for her, she says somewhere in these pages, in spite of its disappointments and disillusionment, a continual "becoming," and so she can write that "because I have, in my time, accumulated resources of as yet untouched material, I may affirm, in conclusion, that this final preface is not a valediction to the past, but only the prelude to a new and more happy beginning."

Ellen Glasgow has not entombed herself in these handsome volumes. She lives and works still in the spirit of those lines from Wordsworth's *Prelude* with which she prefaced *Vein of Iron:*

Effort, and expectation, and desire,
And something evermore about to be.

Whatever may be added to this body of work, it stands now as likely to be one of the most enduring achievements in American fiction. Ellen Glasgow is of our best, and I hope that some day the Nobel Prize will bring her that wider recognition she has so richly deserved.

Checklist of Additional Reviews

Robert B., Munford, Jr., "12 of Miss Glasgow's Books Appear in Limited Edition," Richmond *News Leader*, 22 January 1938, p. 20.
Joseph Henry Jackson, "Notes on the Margin," San Francisco *Chronicle*, 12 March 1938.
"3 Glasgow Books Issued," Richmond *News Leader*, 28 April 1938, p. 2.
James Southall Wilson, "Ellen Glasgow: Ironic Idealist," *Virginia Quarterly Review*, 15 (Winter 1939), 121–6.

IN THIS OUR LIFE

In This Our Life

BY ELLEN GLASGOW

hb

HARCOURT, BRACE AND COMPANY
NEW YORK

Sterling North, "Freedom in Our Time," Chicago *Daily News*, 26 March 1941, p. 19

Ellen Glasgow begins to date. She still writes distinguished prose. She continues to depict believable characters. She can fashion a story with remarkable craftsmanship.

But the fact remains that her concepts are still in the artistic cul-de-sac which stopped so many of the famous writers of the 1920's.

Even when her characters have a "vein of iron" they are dangerously immature emotionally. But when, as in this novel, all but one have a vein of weakness and moral corruption, it becomes startlingly clear that Ellen Glasgow writes consistently of individuals who, male or female, married or unmarried, rich or poor, strong or weak, rakes or ascetics—are actually frustrated virgins.

These are hard words concerning the work of a distinguished writer. But they have the virtue of stating simply the flaw to be found in too many novels.

Obviously the continuous search for "freedom," which seems to be the motivation of every character in this book (like the "room-of-one's-own" motif which ran through so many novels in the 1920's) is the inability to adjust oneself to wife, husband or family. Sex, when mentioned, is in terms of romantic conquest, the "destructive" impulse, light flirtation, or something slightly ugly. Otherwise emotional energy is spent in acquiring a "vein of iron" or, as in this novel, selfish and trivial gratifications.

Asa Timberlake, the little man and gentle hero of this novel, is married to a professional invalid who makes the most of her heart trouble. The time is the present. The place a tidewater city in Virginia.

Asa and Lavinia have two daughters significantly named Roy and Stanley. They also have a son Andrew, who is of no importance to the story.

Roy has the "vein of iron" in this story. Stanley is the spoiled little wench who proceeds to ruin the life of almost every other character in the book including that of Roy, Roy's husband and her own fiancé.

All of the characters are people you have met—and for the most part disliked. Ellen Glasgow understands intimately their weaknesses without quite understanding their common weakness.

A great many people will enjoy this book—particularly those who consider themselves above the mine run of romantic fiction and do not recognize the formula in its more artistic disguise.

Lewis Gannett, "Books and Things," New York *Herald Tribune*, 27 March 1941, p. 21

Ellen Glasgow's wit is so sparkling that it obscures the fact that she is the most consistent pessimist among contemporary American writers. Her new novel, *In This Our Life*, ends with no hope and little integrity left to her cast of characters; but Miss Glasgow is so utterly without malice and without the ponderous apocalyptic gloom which envelops the pessimists among her juniors that the chuckling reader hardly notices that she has stripped love and life of meaning.

[. . .]

In This Our Life is perhaps a little bleaker than some of Ellen Glasgow's earlier novels, and it is less integrated. The moving sub-story of Parry, the half-white colored boy, is a thing apart, notable for its subtle understanding of the lack of understanding between Negro and white in a Southern community, but it is almost an interpolation. The wit sparkles as of yore, but sometimes the interior monologues seem almost a drag upon the story. Yet, when you have noted all its weaknesses, *In This Our Life* remains stamped, from beginning to end, with the personality and style of Ellen Glasgow, one of our major novelists.

Charles Poore, "Books of the Times," New York *Times*, 27 March 1941, p. 21

Ellen Glasgow, like George Bernard Shaw, enjoys setting her characters to talking and thinking incisively about what's wrong with the world. Unlike Shaw, she never lets them run on to really unconscionable lengths. But, like Shaw, again, she makes you listen to what she has to say through her skill in dramatic craftsmanship.

There is a brilliantly plotted situation at the center of her new novel, *In This Our Life*. Its skillful unfolding animates pages that might otherwise seem almost stiff with the astute philosophic commentary that is expressed sometimes in dialogue, sometimes in the impeccably syntactical thoughts of alert, ironic characters.

The dramatic situation concerns the Timberlakes, a shabby-genteel family living in a Southern city within a thousand miles, say, of Richmond. There are two daughters (Roy and Stanley); one 19, the other a little older; one troublingly attractive and enormously selfish, the other plainer and truer; one married and very much in love with her husband, the other engaged to be married and very much in love too: with her sister's husband, however, not with her own fiance.

Out of that situation comes a sudden elopement that leaves havoc and heartbreak in its wake, cancels a wedding, leads to a suicide, a new engagement between the two who are most wronged, the breaking up of that engagement, in turn, and further tragedy.

Always watching and analyzing that generation, Miss Glasgow creates an older one that disapproves (articulately and often epigrammatically) of the younger people's standards and yet finds none too many dependable certitudes of its own. I don't think you will consider their judgments lacking in severity. But they do not precisely spare themselves, either.

Not since Sinclair Lewis completed *The Prodigal Parents* has the younger generation of the moment (every generation was once the younger generation of a given moment in time) been vouchsafed a more drastic critique, perhaps, than it enjoys in Miss Glasgow's novel. Yet that is only one aspect of her wide-ranging commentary on the strange world of today.

In the last analysis, however, the young seem to elude her. We see clearly enough how they look to their elders. But somehow they blur, or have an air of speaking parts in a thesis when their own thoughts are introduced and when they are talking to each other. Moreover, though we are reminded that the Younger Generation of the early Nineteen Twenties (which holds the original patent on the designation) has grown rather elderly by now, its characteristics seem to haunt the commentary on the younger generation of the late Nineteen Thirties that is up for appraisal here.

Miss Glasgow's portraits of the older

characters are excellently drawn. First of all, there is Asa Timberlake, the father, disenchanted and ironic, bedraggled but unbeaten. He suggests, on occasion, a Southern Harry Pulham [narrator of John P. Marquand's *H.M. Pulham, Esquire*] with more perspicacity and fewer opportunities.

He is much put-upon, with an ailing, querulous wife, a constant fear of being tossed out of an inferior position in a business his father once commanded, and a family whose more spectacular discords have already been suggested. Asa has his own dream of escape from a loveless marriage. All he asks is to be in the country with Kate and the dogs. Yet even that is withheld. All burdens sooner or later fall upon him, and he also serves as the principal Greek chorus of the piece.

In Uncle William, a self-made man of fortune who keeps two of the Timberlakes on a kind of partial dole, Miss Glasgow has drawn a definitive picture of a pompous, pious, vigorous old humbug. Uncle William's fond partiality toward Stanley, the youngest daughter, has a fair share in implementing most of her disasters, first and last.

Miss Glasgow's superb mastery of form, exercised in every department of the novel, compels our attention even when we tend to grow ungratefully restless under the reiteration of characteristics already thoroughly established. In some instances she sets herself perhaps too easy problems. Craig, for example, is rather a cardboard specimen of the impractical young idealist filled with ill-digested notions for world-betterment. He is very easily toppled over. And of course he is toppled over, again and again and again. Parry, however, who has more white blood than black, and who faces brutal obstacles in his efforts at advancement, is a skillfully and subtly realized illustration of one of the dilemmas of the South.

The younger generation, as we said, comes in for a pretty thoroughgoing questioning in the course of the story. Modern youth, Asa thinks to himself with that wonderful epigrammatic conciseness that Miss Glasgow's characters often show in their thoughts—modern youth has no passion; it has only passions. And all the older characters contribute their share of similar verdicts. But the younger side also has its innings, and kind things are said about the young moderns from time to time.

The stream of philosophy and the stream of dramatic action flow side by side through the pages of *In This Our Life*. They come together to make a climactic scene in the grand manner, where every one's standards are put to the test.

The last word belongs to Asa, who comes out of it more creditably than any one else. In spite of everything, he still has hope. Not much to hope for, he seems to think, the way the world is going in this our life. But, still, hope.

Edward Skillin, Jr., "*In This Our Life*," *Commonweal*, 33 (28 March 1941), 579–80

The study of environment, which traces back to such writers as Howells, Crane and even Mark Twain, is perhaps the leading theme in American fiction of the past 20 years. Sherwood Anderson and Sinclair Lewis led the way with their well-documented studies of small towns and industrial cities, the hotel business, professional life, etc. Elmer Rice is the leading playwright to center all his energies on reproducing a slice of life, scientifically accurate in every detail. In such photographic studies characters are secondary; how many of Lewis's heroes or heroines can be said to be still remembered? Also of less import is the world of ideas, that rich source of inspiration for so many leading European novelists. Faithful reproduction based on painstaking research is uppermost.

Ellen Glasgow, on the other hand, with her interest in ideas, is closer to the European pattern. This is strikingly true of her latest book where philosophizing is so pronounced that hardly a domestic conversation takes place without embodying questions on the meaning of life or some important psychological observation. With characters in no way remarkable for their intellectual efforts set in a sleepy small town in the South, this is at times hardly credible. It is the one flaw in an otherwise remarkable work of art. And yet this is because the author has so much to say about the present.

*In This Our Lif*e is really a study of the effects of the lack of religious faith on two American generations. Nearly all the young people seem beset with a desperate, self-centered quest for happiness. Stanley, the younger daughter, is so beautiful that when she decides to run away with her sister's husband she sets in motion a series of events which ruins several lives. Her mother, who had become a chronic invalid so that everyone would wait on her hand and foot, is remarkably successful in getting constant attention. Uncle William represents the successful industrialist who achieved his power and wealth through enterprise and ruthlessness.

Injustice in America today is symbolized by the fate of Parry, a sensitive, intelligent, ambitious Negro boy, as well as by Stanley's intense and straightforward sister, Roy; both suffer deeply. Asa Timberlake, the hard-working, self-sacrificing father, has a life of drudgery broken only by occasional days with an understanding friend in the country. Perhaps his greatest sorrow is his inability to understand his children, even Roy, his favorite child.

The horrors and violence of war and revolution which figure so prominently in other leading best-sellers are missing in this book, but Miss Glasgow does not present a happy picture. Her criticism of modern American life is almost wholly negative, and it continually rings true. The only thing is that the Timberlake family, young and old, could hardly be considered as typical as undoubtedly they are meant to be. The constancy and strength of the sixty-year-old Asa provides the one positive element in a book, which I repeat, will be remembered not for its characters or a vivid *mise en scène*, but for its rich and stimulating succession of ideas.

H. O'N., Albany [New York] *Knickerbocker News*, 28 March 1941, sec. A, p. 19

Ellen Glasgow bares the very pattern of all life in this searching, sometimes searing, but never disillusioned story of a family, particularly of Asa Timberlake. The scene is Miss Glasgow's beloved South, but it is a South in modern transition, the old definitely crumbling into nothing, the new emerging, somewhat distorted, but a fundamental humanity preserving through the trials of the spirit attendant upon the new birth.

The Timberlakes were, as many families whether of the north or south, not completely happy, but living within a fairly well understood mold calculated to keep them out of mischief in the deeper sense, in their middle class existence. Asa had never been a success, and Lavinia, who married him as her last chance and whom he married partly because her uncle had a lot of money, found fault with him. There was no love between them.

Asa longed for freedom to go and live with Kate, who was a farmer's widow and who liked Asa and his love for dogs. But the family, particularly Roy and Stanley, Asa's two daughters, brought his half dreams of happiness to naught. Even when Uncle William seemed near death and the chance of freedom arose, come what might in the form of popular prejudice, an automobile accident in which Stanley's car figured, implicating a young Negro, spoiled the plans. And Roy, whose husband, Craig, was deeply affected by Stanley, was also driven to an act of desperation.

This novel appeals alike to the intellect and the emotions, showing how closely they are bound together under the smooth guidance of this novelist. To read the story is to forget everything until it is finished, because it is the realism that all of us must recognize, yet presented in a manner most of us wish we could accomplish ourselves in trying to find the same things Asa sought.

Howard Mumford Jones, "Product of the Tragic Muse,"
Saturday Review of Literature, 23 (29 March 1941), 5–6

[. . .]

In This Our Life is distinguished writing. I think the middle portion not as good as the other parts, I think the novel not quite of the calibre of either *Vein of Iron* or *Barren Ground*. But *In This Our Life* is not so much a work of fiction as it is a testament, a summary, a philosophy, a belief. The wisest woman in the South has written her commentary upon us, and we do not yet know how profound that commentary is. Beyond stoicism lies serenity, but beyond serenity lies mischief. Most of our novelists have not yet attained stoicism, and consequently have no comic sense.

There are a great many things in the life of Virginia which Miss Glasgow has ignored. She deals but little with the South Side, with the mill towns and the great ports and industrial centers, with the apple industry or coal mining or the railroad. She has written little or nothing about the "new Americans," her books being cognizant of but two races—the Anglo-Saxon and that portion of the Negro populace which comes under the classification of household servants. It is, however, impossible to reconstruct the economic structure of Elsinore from *Hamlet*, and I do not regard *Othello* as documentary sociological evidence about race relations in the island of Cyprus. The mocking mischief of the comic spirit, the insight of the tragic muse—their subject must ever be the ardors and endurances of humanity, not economic determinism or the yearbooks of the department of agriculture. The traditional culture of Virginia has sufficed for Miss Glasgow, as the traditional culture of the English country house sufficed for Miss Austen. Let others do the big bowwow strain.

American fiction has power, but it lacks finesse. Novelists burn with admirable zeal as they write their essays to do good, but they do not always pause to inquire what good is being done. The phantom of the Great American Novel still haunts the publishing houses, who look upon fiction as the modern epic. But the novel, said Fielding, is a comic epic in prose. It is a singular fact that our two most settled and continuing regions, Virginia and New England, should have brought forth the two contemporary novelists who have best understood what Fielding meant. Mr. Marquand and Miss Glasgow are, in the French sense, moralists. Unlike Mr. Marquand, Miss Glasgow has devoted herself to the social morality of a single state, so that, in the whole history of the American novel, there is no achievement quite like hers. Some call her a novelist of manners only. But in her view manners are but the outward and visible sign (often misleading) of an inward and spiritual grace.

Louis Kronenberger, "Family Feeling," *Nation*, 152 (29 March 1941), 382–3

Someone like myself, who knows little of Miss Glasgow's work, must be deceived by this book until he is very far along in it. It seems, until then, like the kind of fiction we long ago lost interest in. It seems like one of those studies of middle-class family life which we used to read at our ease in a pleasantly stable world—one of those traditional, tolerably accomplished novels with lifelike enough characters and situations, but with no real power to stir or stimulate us, and no ability to linger in our memory.

But as the book proceeds, it takes on edge, it takes on weight. Its form, to be sure, is so traditional as to be uninteresting. Its style, though sometimes witty, seems serviceable and fluent rather than anything more. Its characters enact too many similar scenes and go in for too many explanatory "reflections." All the same, these things date Miss Glasgow rather than delimit her. Before we have finished her book, things have happened which do not happen by accident. We have come to know its people; we have begun to see what middle-class families are like and what, aside from consanguinity, they are the products of. Most of all we have learned how Miss Glasgow, within a familiar form, works with a special insight; and not only cuts psychological corners, but blasts social rock and storms moral fortresses. Her book tells us something about human nature and human institutions alike—a very respectable day's work, to say the least.

Miss Glasgow's approach to the Timberlake family is largely through the eyes of Asa, the father—a man of sixty tied to an invalid wife he has never loved and to a job (with his wife's rich uncle) he has never succeeded at. Dutiful and kindly in his habits, he is yet skeptical and undeceived in his thinking. The one person in the family he really loves is his married daughter Roy, and never more than when Stanley, his other daughter, blasts Roy's happiness. In terms of plot the book tells of the trouble that Stanley, who is shallow and selfish, stirs up—first in jilting her fiancé to run off with Roy's husband Peter; then in driving Peter to suicide; again, in winning back her fiancé after he has become engaged to Roy; and finally, in getting a young Negro blamed for a reckless act of her own. But the incidents of the plot are important only for their effect on the characters, for what they reveal about "family feeling," and for what they expose of family life as a middle-class institution.

There are no villains in the story; only people; which is why Miss Glasgow's study of family feeling is the more damning. Family feeling is not enough to keep

Stanley from running away with her sister's husband. But on the other hand it is quite enough to make Stanley's relatives conspire to save her skin at the expense of sending an innocent young Negro to prison. It would be hard for two incidents to say more—morally speaking—about the family as a middle-class institution than these two do.

The whole book, in its modulated but merciless way, probes the social morality of the thousands of families that the Timberlakes, in their Tidewater city, represent. But Miss Glasgow comes to concepts by way of people, and her people react upon one another, in the end, as human beings. Stanley, petulant and irresistible and weak, reaching out hungrily for happiness, is not less real for being also a type; nor is Roy, proud of her strength and defiant in her courage, unreal for being a familiar species of "heroine." Asa, I think, is not so much a character as a set of values; through him Miss Glasgow is able to pass judgment on the others, and even on life. Nor is it only in his sympathy and skepticism and moral sensibility that Asa seems to speak for the author; he speaks just a little also—though not defensively—for the generation they both are part of. No study of a family can avoid being concerned with the conflict between generations.

Miss Glasgow is not only an adult novelist but, like very few others of her sex in America, an unsentimental one. She understands what is Southern about her people as she understands what is human about them; but though she shows sympathy, it never corrupts her judgment. Her art, I should think from my scant knowledge of it, has been overestimated, but not her astuteness. The people who could give her cards and spades on technique, or with the help of Hemingway sharpen her dialogue, or toss out whole pages from her book as wasteful or slow-moving, still could learn from her a good deal more than they could teach.

Clifton Fadiman, *New Yorker*, 17 (29 March 1941), 60–1

Ellen Glasgow's new work has all the moral stamina of her other books but little of their mitigating wit. There is an unexpected note of despondency in this long chronicle of defeat and disintegration in the South. The constant flashes or irony that made *The Sheltered Life* so delightful, without impairing its truth, are notably absent from *In This Our Life*. Miss Glasgow is never bitter, but she does not seem overhopeful, either. The effect of the book is an indictment of a segment of American life, not an indignant indictment but a brooding, compassionate one.

The centre of the rather loosely constructed story is Asa Timberlake, a failure at fifty-nine, a slave to his hypochondriac wife, resentfully dependent on his wife's rich uncle, William Fitzroy. There are two daughters, irritatingly named Roy and Stanley. Roy inherits her father's innate decency and adds to it a harsher spirit of independence; Stanley is the regulation Southern belle, childish, selfish, and pretty nauseating, if you ask me.

The family gets involved in a series of crises. Stanley steals Roy's husband; Roy falls half in love with Stanley's old fiancé; there's a suicide and a serious automobile accident. Under the impact of all this, the family, with the exception of stoic Asa, goes to pieces, and at the end we are confronted by a half-dozen lives that, if not ruined, are sadly overcast by the shadow of defeat.

Only Asa, Miss Glasgow's mouthpiece,

though he is a failure as breadwinner and husband, has the stoutness to meet the family crises with honesty and courage. Miss Glasgow wishes us to understand that his innate superiority comes from his quiet possession of an older tradition, a tradition the younger generation and even those of his own generation have abandoned. I think Miss Glasgow generalizes too sweepingly when she makes Asa reflect, "Life had defeated them. Oh, well, but after all, was it life? Or was this sense of puzzled failure nothing more than the despondent mood of an age that is finished?" I think, too, that she's rather hard on the young folks (with whom her hand is less sure; she seems to describe them from hearsay) when Asa says of one of them, "Like all the rest of us, like our world, our time, our code of living, he has no direction; he is incapable of any permanent motive."

I believe Miss Glasgow's case against "our world, our time, our code of living" is poorly argued. One must look elsewhere for the book's values: at her careful characterization of Asa, with his small, pitiful dream of freedom and his unheroic integrity; at her ruthless picture of modern marriage, for which apparently she has little admiration; at the satirical portrait of Lavinia, Asa's wife. Roy, too, a girl destroyed by her over-evaluation of love, will rank among Miss Glasgow's major creations.

The book is too long and rambling and suffers a sharp drop in intensity toward the end. It is needless to add that it is beautifully written, though more gravely, more heavily, than is Miss Glasgow's wont.

John Cournos, "This Week's Book: *In This Our Life*," Philadelphia *Bulletin*, 29 March 1941, sec. F, p. 1

Miss Ellen Glasgow is a novelist who grows from strength to strength. She has long since attained major stature as a writer of fiction, and in her new book, *In This Our Life,* she has outdone herself.

Its main theme is frustration, and the ways that human nature reacts to it in persons of various temperaments. Taking into consideration the high literary merit of the story, *In This Our Life* may be safely assigned to rubbing friendly shoulders with such masterpieces of realistic fiction as Thomas Hardy's *Jude the Obscure* and Edith Wharton's *Ethan Frome.*

Never was the conflict between the older and the younger generations so acute as it is today, and Miss Glasgow gives us a vivid picture of this conflict as it takes place in a southern family. Here is a cauldron of seething passion, brimming over with human nature in its tensest moods, with all the tragic under and overtones which owe their existence to such capricious fates as made old Greek drama famous.

Not that the roles played by Asa, Lavinia, Roy, Stanley, Peter, Craig, William and all the other memorable characters of this story are wholly dictated by external circumstance. Miss Glasgow is too good a novelist to yield the direction of the action to accident.

Rather is she imbued with the notion, also Greek, that "character is fate." So many things in life, as we all know, happen by chance; we also know what a devastating effect such chance happenings may have on certain people. If the people of Miss Glasgow's novel get more than their share of unhappiness, we are never once in doubt that it has all been inevitable from the start, seeing the kind of people they are, and, still more, the kind of inter-relation into which they are thrown.

[. . .]

Elizabeth Glasgow Howe, "Ellen Glasgow Interprets Life in Novel Certain to be Most Distinguished of Year," Boston *Evening Transcript*, 29 March 1941, sec. 5, p. 1

[. . .]

Her [Glasgow's] philosophy, as it gradually evolved, is firmly grounded in her conviction that it is character which gives meaning and direction to life. This mental attitude, though suggested in such early works as *The Voice of the People* and *The Battle-Ground,* has deepened with her maturer experience, until it has reached its finest expression in *In This Our Life.* Enlivened by her flashing wit, and pointed with delicate irony, the pattern of the tale gradually reveals itself. Each person fits into the scheme of the whole; each apparent accident contributes to the conclusion that character is indeed destiny. *In This Our Life* is the *Vanity Fair* of our civilization.

[. . .]

The brilliant, epigrammatic quality of Ellen Glasgow's style is always a delight. *In This Our Life* is the kind of book one would like to underline or read aloud so that others might share our pleasure in particularly penetrating or amusing expressions. A rich, powerful novel, it will leave the reading public with an added sense that its author fully merited her recent award of the Howells Medal "for eminence in creative literature." Creeds may die, and social orders pass away, but as long as man's fate depends on his own character development, he may with agony and travail work out a world "with all things new."

J. Donald Adams, "A New Novel by Ellen Glasgow," *New York Times Book Review*, 30 March 1941, sec. 6, p. 1

Without being topical, Miss Glasgow's new novel, her first in nearly six years, is in a very real way a book for our time. Back of it lies the sense of a period of confused and changing values, in which we move gropingly toward some end unforeseen. It is a story that deals, as Miss Glasgow's novels habitually do, with individual human relationships, for her interest has always been in the individual's reaction to life, not in the problems and conflicts of the group. Believing, as she does, that the novelist's primary concern is with character, she could not write otherwise.

In This Our Life is a book for our time because at its core is an attitude, or, better, a conviction, to which men and women today must hold if they are to live effectively in the world we face. Ours is a world in which the problems seem at times too great, the march of destructive forces too overpowering, the prospects of happy solution too dim. The conviction which animates this book, as it has animated a large part of Miss Glasgow's fiction, is that the only triumph over life lies in the refusal to accept defeat. She has, as an artist, consistently held to the tragic view of life, even when the comic spirit glinted through her pages, but she has never embraced a philosophy of despair.

It is a token of her strength as a novelist that she has always been able to find new forms into which to pour this conviction that lies at the heart of her work. And that is what she has done again in her latest work. She never retells a story with the aid of new extraneous details, and the people of whom she writes have always a life of their own. Never are they merely variants, as in the case of so many lesser writers, of figures that she has employed before.

The scene is again Queenborough, that Virginia Tidewater city which has provided the background for so much of Miss Glasgow's work. But as we all know by now, Miss Glasgow's province is not of Virginia, but of the world. If she has written the social history of the Old Dominion, she has written it in terms which have pertinence for the lives of men and women everywhere.

[. . .]

In Roy, summoning all her strength to meet the blows life has dealt her; in Asa, thwarted by circumstance and principle from achieving the freedom he craves; in Craig, the prey of his own emotions, Miss Glasgow has given us three of her best-drawn characters. We see them all in relation to that conviction which dominates Miss Glasgow's attitude toward life, and which she has never presented more forcefully than in this book. *In This Our Life* is a novel rich in human values. It is the work of a writer with the mind of a philosopher, stored with knowledge of human nature in its weakness and its strength, and those of her readers who prize not least of her qualities the epigrammatic flashes of perception which she so perfectly phrases will find them here in profusion. In Asa Timberlake's questioning wisdom Miss Glasgow has drawn bountifully from her own.

It has been a heartening experience for all who prize the novel as a form of art to observe the unwavering integrity of Miss Glasgow's devotion to that art. She has never compromised with her conception of what fiction, on its more ambitious levels, should be. And each new book, this one included, has added its cubit to her stature.

Evelyn Hart, "Ellen Glasgow Speaks in Quiet but Brilliant Tone," Dayton *News*, 30 March 1941, sec. 3, p. 9

Ellen Glasgow, silent for too long a time, speaks at last in her new novel with her usual quiet voice, quiet but strangely brilliant and clear, with a carrying force that should stretch from boundary to boundary and beyond. She has done here a magnificent job of presenting a generation—two generations, in fact—through close-ups of a family and a community, through examination of the state of mind of her characters, in a story that ends a few days before the outbreak of the current World War.

Miss Glasgow, finished stylist and keen student of human nature, has been one of the important contributors to the literature of the country during the last several decades and in this, as in her former novels, she reveals and strengthens her own philosophy that "character is destiny." Things don't just "happen" to the people in Miss Glasgow's stories—her characters, by virtue of their own inherent qualities of kindness, gentleness, avarice, selfishness, aggressiveness and what not, determine their own fate to a great degree. Environment, of course, and a few uncontrollable circumstances are taken into consideration, but for the most part it is the person's own temperament and viewpoint and personality that are important.

[. . .]

Miss Glasgow is a superb craftsman, building her story carefully, intensifying her characters and the clash between personalities, increasing page by page the reader's fascination and eagerness to find out the destiny of her very real people. Roy and Asa are the characters the reader cannot forget when the story ends—father and daughter faced with similar problems and tackling them with such different approaches. In the maze of free verse, stream-of-consciousness technique, blaring realism and literary nudity, it is refreshing and invigorating to find a novel well written about characters who are alive and struggling and questioning—as aren't we all.

"Ellen Glasgow's New Novel Ranks with America's Best," Hartford *Courant*, 30 March 1941, magazine section, p. 7

[. . .]

This is Miss Glasgow's most profound, thoughtful, and philosophical treatment of man's individual and eternal conflict with the desires, shadows, fears and darknesses that infest the soul and torment the spirit. It ranks with the finest in American fiction and has a quality that makes it timeless. While the publishers stress the fact that it deals with today, the story closing just as Europe is about to plunge into the abyss of total war, that is relatively unimportant. It does however add something to the reality of our understanding that there is a never ending conflict between things as they are and things as they should be. Neither Asa, the father, nor Roy, his daughter, ever were able to feel at home in this world nor did they have a high opinion of it. Only the hypochondriac mother and the utterly selfish and childishly egotistical daughter, Stanley, could even at times come to terms with it. For the rest, life needed changing, the universe needed changing, all the way from the election to human nature.

Paul Jordan Smith,
"What I Liked Last Week,"
Los Angeles *Times*, 30
March 1941, sec. 3, p. 6

[. . .]
America's most distinguished novelist, Miss Glasgow's understanding of human frailty, of those tragic spiritual conflicts that so often end in futility, has seldom revealed itself to better advantage. And as to the writing of this story it should be observed that the sentences of it are packed with thoughts within thoughts to provide more thoughts. Over these pages the reader will ponder and remember—and not forget. For here is gracious writing, wise and humorous and tender.

B[everley] L. B[ritton],
"Miss Glasgow Makes Departure,"
Richmond *Times-Dispatch*, 30 March 1941, sec. 4, p. 9

[. . .]
It is perhaps Miss Glasgow's ability to make her characters so vivid that is the book's outstanding feature; every one is completely alive, and the threads of each life are clear despite their sometimes violent intertwining. Through this aptness for characterization some scenes become almost unbearably intense; the conflict invariably is fully dramatized, yet never overdone. Stanley's character is drawn with almost merciless irony, but completely convincing; Roy, on the other hand, who, despite her modern convictions, is old-fashioned enough to find love highly important, emerges more slowly, as befits the ideal she represents.

But the reader is struck most forcibly with what may be a departure for Miss Glasgow in this book. Has she chosen merely to turn her satire on modern rather than old-style living, or has she come to believe that, despite its weaknesses (of which she has been the most consistent critic), the old way of life was better? There is much talk, in *In This Our Life*, of the thinning strain, the lack of moral fibre, in the youth of today. Is this merely the impartial novelist pointing out the good and bad in all ways of living, or does it represent an essentially altered point of view?

This reader inclines to the belief that the unfamiliar, and as yet unsettled, patterns of life with which Miss Glasgow deals is responsible for the seeming change. Whatever the answer, it only makes the book the more provocative. An absorbing story, it is filled with a great deal of quiet, calm wisdom, presented in a masterly prose that reveals intact and undiminished Miss Glasgow's power as an American novelist.

Malcolm Cowley,
"Miss Glasgow's 'Purgatorio,'"
New Republic, 104 (31 March 1941), 441–2

I have managed for the last fifteen years not to read any novels by Ellen Glasgow, and this in spite of her growing reputation. During those years, no other American novelist was praised so almost universally, exception being made for Willa Cather. No other American novelist—this time without exception—was published in two collected editions, of which the second was in twelve volumes printed from type, numbered and signed, with prefaces by the author. The trouble was that the twelve volumes looked a little forbidding on the library shelves, and that the praise by eminent critics sounded dutiful and pious. Just as Miss Cather's later novels suggest an architecturally flawless but empty and unheated cathedral, so Miss Glasgow's collected works—to judge by what the critics said—were an Episcopalian church where the best Virginia families worshiped, under the eyes of a conscientious, rather modernist rector.

And that impression was not dispelled by reading the first chapters of her latest novel. *In This Our Life* starts out as a sermon against the younger generation for its lack of standards, discipline and moral stamina. Although the sermon is delivered with a great deal of tired wisdom—the wisdom of not asking too much or expecting to get it, the wisdom of making compromises and yielding to necessity—it seems in the beginning no more than the familiar complaint of age against youth. "I don't see why they can't get along together, things weren't like that when we were young." Eve must have had such thoughts about Cain and Abel, just as Lavinia Timberlake has them about her own children. But slowly, as the story continues, one finds that Miss Glasgow is approaching it from a different angle and is dealing with a central problem of our time.

Her characters are the members of an impoverished Richmond family, each of whom has a different relationship to the standards by which Virginians used to live. Asa and Lavinia Timberlake, the father and the mother, are survivors of the older tradition: the father observes its forms, though he tells himself that he has ceased to believe in their meaning; the mother has solved the conflict between "ought to be" and "is" by living completely in her dreams. Both are dependent on the charity of Lavinia's uncle, a domineering capitalist dying of cancer (here the symbolism is unmistakable). Andrew Timberlake, the only son, is a completely unimaginative business man. The older daughter, Roy, lives by no standards except courage and personal honesty; the young sister, Stanley, has no standards whatever and thoughtlessly involves the family in a whole series of catastrophes. All the Timberlakes are portrayed with the understanding that Miss Glasgow has acquired by dealing with a single background for more than forty years. Instead of broadening her knowledge of people, she has chosen to deepen it.

Craig Fleming, a young lawyer who is jilted by Stanley and who later thinks he has fallen in love with Roy, is a character less convincing than the others, being presented completely from the outside, yet he is even more important as a symbol. He is a young man in whom the Virginia blood has run thin, a well meaning idealist always ready to devote himself to another cause or person, but without inner conviction. "I want to fight for something," he says, "but I don't know for what. When I look around me, I can't see a blessed thing worth fighting for." He wants to enlist in the Spanish army, but delays until the Loyalists have been defeated. Thinking of people like Craig, Asa Timberlake says—and here as elsewhere he seems to be speaking for the author—"The mistake with them, and with the whole of their extraordinary place in time, is that they have never really broken through the tight shell of their egoism. The world without them exists merely as an extension of the confusion and the thwarted longing of the world within." By now we begin to perceive that the story Miss Glasgow tells is something more than the conflict between generations or the decay of the old Virginia stock and pattern. On the scale of a single family with its rather commonplace disasters—a broken marriage, a suicide, an automobile accident—she is presenting a whole world in limbo, the helplessness of people engaged without guidance in a search for individual happiness. Lonely, they become fearful; fearful, they become rash and cruel and involve themselves in a common destruction.

That this is her real subject becomes evident in the last episode of the novel. At the end of August, 1939, the older daughter feels her whole world crashing around her. Having lost the husband to whom she was deeply attached—Stanley had stolen him—and having fallen in love with Craig Fleming only to learn that he too would always belong at heart to Stanley, she wanders into the street, knowing only that she must get away. Caught in a sudden rainstorm, she meets a young Englishman and goes home with him. Nothing improper happens, this being a novel by Ellen Glasgow; Roy merely sits in the living-room of a strange apartment and listens while the young man tells his story; but that story seems to illuminate her own tragedy. The Englishman is saying that he is lost and lonely, on the blank edge of insanity, and that now he is going off to war in the hope that his individual fears may be lost in the collective danger. At last he falls asleep, while Roy strokes his hair. When she leaves him, "It was the hour between dawn and day, when life had reached its lowest ebb, and the movements of the earth seem to pause."

That—if one may underline Miss Glasgow's meaning—is the hour of civilization with which she has been dealing in her novel. And she seems to be saying that not only the nameless young Englishman but all her characters and all her world are getting ready to plunge into destruction in order to escape their own will-lessness, their lack of direction and their sense of being continually driven back on themselves. . . .

Miss Glasgow in her latest book is neither parochial nor old-fashioned. One feels, however, that she has chosen rather decorous incidents and commonplace people to express her vision of despair and utter chaos. Though her purgatory is real, not much happens there; and it is as if we peeped out at it from behind the curtains of a Richmond parlor.

"Blood and Irony," *Time*, 31 March 1941, 72–4

"When I consider her as a person," wrote Novelist James Branch Cabell of his friend, Ellen Glasgow, "she arouses in me a dark suspicion." Cabell's suspicion is that Ellen Glasgow "is a gentlewoman as well as a genius in an era unfavorable to either. . . ." Ellen Glasgow has aroused even darker suspicions among U.S. readers. They have suspected that she is dull or highbrow, and have translated their suspicions into a considerable lack of interest. Some who have read her *Barren Ground*, without reading *They Stooped to Folly*, consider her a too stern daughter of the voice of God. Others who have read *The Romantic Comedians*, but not *Vein of Iron*, consider her a light-minded iconoclast from whose irony nothing is safe.

In 1938 the American Academy of Arts and Letters elected Novelist Glasgow to membership. But the Pulitzer Prize committee still has not recognized her existence. She had the misfortune to publish *Barren Ground* the same year that Sinclair Lewis published *Arrowsmith* which won the prize. In the next nine years the Pulitzer committee passed over three of her best books in favor of Bromfield's *Early Autumn,* La Farge's *Laughing Boy,* Stribling's *The Store.* Novelist Glasgow went right on writing, revising, perfecting the series of novels which she had projected at the beginning of the Century—"a social history of Virginia."

This week Ellen Glasgow, now 66, added *In This Our Life* to this impressive series. Not her greatest book, it is an interesting detail in the mural of her life work. She had been working on this detail since 1935, had revised it at least three times. It is not unusual for Novelist Glasgow to rewrite a single chapter 15 times.

Like most Glasgow novels, this one is laid in Queenborough, the imaginary Virginia town which she had made as much her literary province as Hardy made Wessex or Trollope Barsetshire. It is the story of the ineffectualness of a Southern aristocrat, Asa Timberlake, who has lost his money but not his manners. The Timberlake fortune had been invested in a cigaret factory. Now factory and fortune belonged to the Standard Tobacco Company. Asa still had a job with Standard, but he never knew for how long. His wife, plain-faced Lavinia, had stooped to marry him. Later she developed a heart ailment that enabled her to wield an invalid power that she had never known in healthier days. Asa's conscience is her slave. Sometimes he succeeds in sneaking off to spend Sunday with Kate Oliver on her river farm. His hope is that some day Uncle William will die and leave Lavinia a legacy. When that happened, Asa meant to leave and go to Kate. But when at last it did happen, it was already too late. Asa had begun to establish a protectorate over his daughter, Roy. "You will stand by me?" Roy asked. "I will, Roy, as long as you need me." "Looking up at the closed sky, once again

[Asa] had a vision of Kate and the harvested fields and the broad river. Still ahead, and within sight, but just out of reach, and always a little farther away, fading, but not ever disappearing, was freedom."

Nearly all the characters in the book are defeated. The weak ones are crushed. But Asa's defeat is a victory, for it implies that under his apparent ineffectualness there is something stronger than his daughter's brittle bravery. Like the Greek dramatists, Novelist Glasgow believes that men's characters are men's fate, and that tragedy is never in defeat but in surrender. "An honorable end," she is fond of saying, "is the one thing that cannot be taken from a man."

James Southall Wilson, "Ellen Glasgow: 1941," *Virginia Quarterly Review*, 17 (Spring 1941), 317–20

[. . .]

The story [of *In This Our Life*], which is so much a story of losing happiness through the pursuit of it, is so absorbing that the reader forgets how sharply the book is a criticism of this our life today in America; but the satire is there. And there too is the charm of Ellen Glasgow's witty prose, sparkling with epigram, circling at times about an emanation of a place or a mood like a flock of pigeons iridescent in the sun, or glowing occasionally with quiet restrained emotion. No philosophy runs, like a vein of iron, patently throughout the story. Even the satire is implicit, and, like one of her characters, the novelist is careful "to keep a discredited sense of values hidden," more or less, from her readers.

Tightly woven together, the threads of the narrative form a pattern that is the triumph of a practical artist's skill. Yet the skill is that of an intriguing storyteller, too; for the interest never flags as the tense situations rapidly dissolve and flow into resulting situations tenser and more moving. *In This Our Life* ought to prove for its season the most popular of all Ellen Glasgow's novels. It is easy to read; it has rapid movement; it has spice, and daring, and beauty of style; it has vivid characterization; it is a challenge to this generation and it raises questions to be pondered over for tomorrow. It may not be Ellen Glasgow's greatest novel, nor her wittiest, nor her wisest. To readers in general it may prove her most successful.

Robert Bridges said of the heroes of Shakespeare's tragedies that they were greater than their actions. Perhaps likewise all noble authors are greater than any of their books. Ellen Glasgow, even as a writer, is greater than any one of her novels. But her novels collectively are the measure of her genius. *In This Our Life* is worthy of "the great tradition" she has built.

Edwin Mims, "Social Drama of Frustration," Nashville *Banner*, 2 April 1941, sec. 2, p. 4

A good many years ago Walter Hines Page said to me: "Keep your eye on a young novelist whom I have just discovered in Richmond, Va. She is a thinker as well as an artist; she will go far." I followed his advice and have read with eagerness and admiration every one of her novels as they have appeared from time to time during the past forty years. It was no surprise to some of us when Miss Glasgow was recently awarded by the American Academy of Arts and Letters the Howells Prize for distinguished work in American fiction—an award that atones for her failure to receive the Pulitzer accolade from year to year. She has with patience and artistic conscience bided her time, refusing to follow the lure of publishers and the demands of the public.

Her latest novel cannot be adjudged properly without reference to her previous novels for it completes a cycle of historical backgrounds that begins with the period just before the Civil War and ends with the period just before the outbreak of the Second World War (1938–39). Read, not in the order in which they were published but in the light of periods which can now be distinguished clearly, they constitute a remarkable achievement, comparable to Balzac's representation of French social history. It need scarcely be said that Miss Glasgow has a style always distinguished, sometimes epigrammatic, sometimes lyrical, that she knows how to tell a story, how to delineate characters with a certain profound psychological insight, but above all she has the power to suggest through these media a social background, a social drama. She knows her Virginia, and indirectly the South. Unlike Willa Cather, her chief rival in American fiction, she has specialized in the life of one province—the Virginia of cities like Richmond and Norfolk, of rural sections, of the Valley. Descendants of the old aristocracy, the new blood of the middle and lower classes, Negroes of new as well as old types, the Scotch-Irish element, and, above all, women of every conceivable type—all these struggle with conservative and progressive forces as inevitable as fate.

Unlike Thomas Nelson Page, she has a critical instead of a romantic mind. Unlike the realists, or naturalists, of the most recent school of Southern fiction, she keeps a balance between the resolute facing of facts and a sane and reasonable idealism. Unlike Cabell, she does not escape from life, she meets and masters it.

In This Our Life is more realistic than any novel she has written, and therefore more depressing. Miss Glasgow's vein of irony, and her scorn for sentimentalism, for "evasive idealism," for superficial romance as opposed to actuality, have developed in the direction of cynicism and even downright pessimism. One hastens to add that the points of view of characters in this novel cannot be identified with those of the author; she is presenting, artistically, an era of disillusionment, of aimless drifting, of broken traditions, of restless discontent, of abandoned creeds and patterns of life, with seemingly nothing to take their places. . . .

[. . .]

Fanny Butcher, "Ellen Glasgow at Her Best in Novel of Dixie," Chicago *Tribune*, 2 April 1941, p. 21

Never in all of the finely wrought novels which have proved Ellen Glasgow one of our great creative artists has her special gift been more evident for delineating the subtleties of character conditioned by a way of life—the southern way of life. That she does it almost casually and in passing, by the merest suggestion, makes her genius the more exciting.

In This Our Life is a story of high emotional content that might have had any background and any protagonists and it would always have been tense and dramatic. It is the story of the overriding vanity and selfishness of a pretty girl who takes everything she wants—love, her sister's husband, even a life—and pays nothing. It is the story of a disillusioned, unhappy man who has tried vainly to make a good life for himself and his family and has found neither happiness nor decent consideration from them. It is the story of a girl who loved once with ecstasy, a second time with contentment, had both her loves torn up by their roots by her sister's hand, and still bore a brave front.

It is, incidentally, the story of a Negro boy who wanted an education and the tragedy which his desire brought him. But it is something more than the sum of these stories, for inherent in each character is the south. The spoiled sister would not have been selfish in exactly that way, the clear-eyed sister with the straight heart, the father, finely proud, the Negro boy with his white blood scourging him would not have acted as they did if any other sunshine and rain had brought them to bloom. The situations are universal emotionally, and the men and women have nothing local about them, but the characters are rooted in their own soil.

I felt that the final desperate gesture of the older sister was out of key, that the traditions in her blood would have made her desperate in some other way, but every other situation and act in the long, interest clutching tale seemed to me subtle and superb.

In This Our Life may well prove to be one of Miss Glasgow's and the season's best sellers.

"Illusory Goal of Freedom Is Theme for Ellen Glasgow," Pasadena *Star News*, 5 April 1941

Character is destiny, or fate. This is the theme implicit in Ellen Glasgow's many novels. There is no tragedy in being defeated: only in surrendering.

Asa Timberlake was a Southern aristocrat who had once been rich but now is poor. But whether rich or poor he always put great store by manners, which to him were the marks of a gentleman. Asa was a great one to toy with ideas; and one of his ideas was that he found more happiness with Kate Olliver than he found with Lavinia, his strait-laced, unimaginative wife.

Asa also had a conscience which was tethered to Lavinia. He had always hoped, or, at least he had hoped for many years, that when Uncle William died he would remember Lavinia in his will and leave her a sufficient sum so that she could be comfortably supported. That, he told himself, would release him from the obligation of providing for her, and he would then be free to live with Kate. But Time kept his dream at bay. "Still ahead, and within sight, but just out of reach, and always a little farther away, fading, but not ever disappearing, was freedom."

There are readers who may not regard *In This Our Life* as Miss Glasgow's most distinguished novel, but it is of the same rich texture as the earlier novels. Wit and wisdom are here as impressively arranged as in *Barren Ground, The Romantic Comedians* and *They Stooped to Folly*.

As a pioneer realist in American letters Miss Glasgow was leading the field more than 40 years ago. In 1897, when she was only 23 years old, she wrote her first novel, *The Descendant*, and shocked the natives by her daring handling of a theme that Virginians thought no properly brought-up Virginia girl should discuss.

Considering the body of her work, one is at a loss to understand why she has never been awarded the Pulitzer Prize. Perhaps the poo-bahs of Morningside Heights may yet convince themselves that they have given the award to less deserving recipients.

Claire Keefer, "Novel of the Week," Ottawa *Evening Journal*, 5 April 1941

In This Our Life by Ellen Glasgow, is another deeply-felt drama of modern tragedy. As ever this most distinguished American novelist is preoccupied with courage—that vein of iron that holds generations together, and does not recognize defeat even when overwhelmed by it. Because she has faith in an inherent soundness of the human race she brings to her latest novel the reassurance that something good must come even from this muddled present.

To Ellen Glasgow, Virginia is what the Black country of Wales is to Francis Brett Young, what Wessex was to Hardy and the Lake country to Walter Scott, for her novels have made this state peculiarly her own. As ever the scene is laid in the town of Queenborough where already the old aristocratic families are tinged with decay. In a flimsily built house at the other end of the town from the scene of his childhood Asa Timberlake lives with his invalid wife, Lavinia, who never ceases to remind him she married beneath her. They have two daughters, Stanley, the spoiled favorite and typical Southern Belle brought subtly up to date; and Roy, the hard, brittle, but honest, modern product.

[. . .]

That Ellen Glasgow with the exception of Willa Cather is America's finest living novelist there is surely no question at all. Her prestige goes unchallenged by any of the opposite sex and *In This Our Life* added to *The Sheltered Life* and *Vein of Iron* constitutes a saga of modern Virginia comparable to Galsworthy's *Forsyte Saga* of England.

Lee Berry, "World of Books," Pittsburgh *Post-Gazette*, 5 April 1941, sec. 1, p. 6

WISDOM: There's hardly a major novelist now practicing the art of fiction who hasn't at least one bad book to his or her credit. But in this respect (as in so many others) Ellen Glasgow occupies a unique position among her contemporaries. Since she first won a national reputation some 25 years ago she has never written a novel unworthy of her great talents.

In This Our Life, Miss Glasgow's first novel since *Vein of Iron,* offers the immediate stimulus for these remarks. Whether or not it marks an advance over her previous work is and will remain a matter of personal opinion. There can be no question, however, that in grace of style, depth of understanding and edge of irony it is worthy to stand beside anything Miss Glasgow has given us in the past.

The story, set in the Virginia Tidewater city of Queenborough, revolves around a series of crises in the life of a shabby-genteel family named Timberlake. Asa, approaching 60, is married to a querulous hypochondriac, a woman who had early learned that "a physical malady may be turned, by a prudent and far-sighted woman, into a moral support." Employed in a tobacco business that had once belonged to his grandfather, Asa has eked out a poor living for his wife and two daughters, supplemented by a sort of allowance from Uncle William, a rugged individualist who glories in the petty tyranny his wealth permits.

Of Asa's two daughters, one, Roy, is married to a young surgeon, while the other, Stanley, is about to marry Craig Fleming, a helpless weakling who can solve everyone's troubles but his own. When Stanley deserts her own fiancé and runs away with her sister's husband, she sets in motion a train of events which tests the spiritual fibre of every major character in the book. A sub-plot, involving an ambitious colored boy with white blood in his veins, casts a sharp and unforgettable light on one of the major problems of contemporary American life.

Although the play of Ellen Glasgow's wit lights up many of the book's 467 pages, *In This Our Life* is essentially a tragic novel. The problems it faces are the problems of the spirit, and the wisdom it offers is the wisdom of an artist who sees life in terms of a few eternal truths rather than in the specific hopes and fears of a single era or a single generation.

Because Miss Glasgow has always chosen to express herself through the medium of fiction, no discussion of her work, however brief, is complete without some mention of her superlative mastery of the novel form. Scrupulously avoiding all passing literary fads and fancies, she has always been content to tell a straight-forward story in terms of a few superbly realized characters, unfolding both story and characters in a prose style that is the wonder and envy of lesser writers.

Margaret Halsey, "Ellen Glasgow X-Rays Another Virginia Family," New York *Patriot and Morning Advertiser*, 6 April 1941

Ellen Glasgow is a scientist at heart. Miss Glasgow's new novel, *In This Our Life*, has an unassailable theme, flawlessly presented. The book is perfect. But it is not very warm. To say this is not to suggest that it ought to be warm. The statement is made only in an effort to convey the impeccable, laboratory-like quality of the author's view of life. Miss Glasgow's message is that you cannot live life on any better level than you are equipped to live it, and that is not a thought which people want to take home and nickname "Cuddles."

[. . .]

In This Our Life is the product of a stately and imposing talent—and a talent, moreover, which is implemented down to the last detail. Miss Glasgow's style matches her habit of thought. It would not be right to call it bare, but it is unornamented and Quakerish. This mathematical and uncolored quality pervades the whole book.

Miss Glasgow's emphasis is all on what is going on inside people, and she tells you only those things about what they look like or what their houses look like that is absolutely necessary for you to know. She seldom draws pictures. It is as if she had X-ray eyes and could not see any way but *through*. If she brings in a tree or a sofa, it is because those objects have some connection with what a character is thinking or feeling.

One is reminded, in contrast, of Miss Glasgow's contemporary, Willa Cather, who loves to draw pictures. Miss Glasgow's is the more studious and philosophical mind, but she is not so poetic or so comforting as Willa Cather. Her scenes are performed austerely on a bare stage. They are, however, masterly scenes. For pure unanswerableness, it is hard to beat $(a + b)^2 = a^2 + 2ab + b^2$.

Robert Clayton, "Contemporary Virginia Is the Background for a Typically Fine Novel by Ellen Glasgow," Chattanooga *Times*, 6 April 1941, sec. 4, p. 5

Starting with brilliant promise, the American writer often fails to mature. When this was discussed in an interesting controversy in *The New York Times Book Review* recently, it was pointed out that certain women writers are exceptions to this generalization. Willa Cather and Ellen Glasgow have consistently maintained a body of distinguished work.

Both these writers have produced books recently and Ellen Glasgow's is a still greater indication of the maturity of her art, of keeping pace with our troubled present with no loss of quality. *In This Our Life* is set in a tidewater Virginia city in 1938 and 1939; there are the war rumblings that made those years uncertain and depressing, and the book ends with a significant episode about an uprooted young Englishman on his way back home to fight.

But more topical still, this is a novel

about the most important thing in the world today, freedom. It does not lessen its importance that it is personal, individual freedom, as it would have to be with Miss Glasgow treating it. The core of the novel is, in miniature, the thing that is wrong with all of us, for freedom starts at home.

[...]

It is redundant to mention style in a Glasgow novel. The same unobtrusive perfection is here: The carefully laid scheme of slow characterization building to a fascinating situation; the epigrammatic wisdom, gentle, slightly satiric. Whatever theme is considered at the moment—the ruin of family fortunes, the hollowness of family feeling, the inevitability of character shaping one's fate—the comment is illuminating.

In This Our Life is one of Ellen Glasgow's best books. I like it better than any since *Barren Ground*. Roy Timberlake is a memorable girl to set beside Dorinda Oakley, and it is pleasant to have a man sympathetically presented as the central character. People have been grumbling that the Pulitzer or no other prize has been presented Miss Glasgow. The truth is she needs no awards. Her dozen novels are fame in themselves. They will be read as long as people want to know about life.

Rosamond Milner, "An Unsatisfactory Glasgow," Louisville *Courier-Journal*, 13 April 1941, magazine section, p. 15

In This Our Life is the first novel Ellen Glasgow has written in almost a half dozen years. Its theme is as old, as universal as the one Goethe sounded in a little poem that runs in part like this:

What is hope? A fleeting rainbow
Children follow through the wet;
'Tis not here, still yonder, yonder,
Never mortal found it yet.

Miss Glasgow writes of the young, in Virginia today, and emphasizes the line that divides them from the "lost" generation of our post-war world; they have hope and courage but not one conviction. She writes of the middle-aged and the old, who cling to hope with defeat stamped on their faces. She writes, without intensity, of the position of the Negro and leaves the almost white boy, Parry, slumped in failure before the fight, his hope dim. . . .

The story of Stanley, who is the most perfect characterization in the book, is its highest peak. The tragedy and ruin that follow in her wake, her own final ultimate of careless murder and cowardice that would have put the blame on Parry and that left every member of her family circle except her father ready to sacrifice the boy for her, is a rare, dramatic study of character and situation, perfectly convincing.

Miss Glasgow is a finished and penetrating writer to whom American literature owes a great deal. Her qualities are all present in this last book. But it is hard to see how it can be honestly ranked as an important one. It is even a little dull, now and then, because its material is not particularly fresh, its characters not always compelling enough to recharge it, and its theme not vital enough to bear the characters along in the current of any exciting idea. And just now we badly need a stronger note than the old one on which the book ends—that of the always fleeting rainbow of human hope as all that may beguile human suffering. . . .

Francis X. Connolly, "Insipid Liberalism Challenged in Great Prose," *America*, 65 (26 April 1941), 77–8

When Asa Timberlake, a shabby genteel Virginian, passed his boyhood house on his way from the tobacco factory to the suburban monstrosity which was his present home, he began to reflect upon the sterility and the stupidity of the modern world. The demolition of his old house seemed to him an appropriate symbol of the final defeat of a way of life. The grace, the courage, the beliefs, however naive, which had inspired the ladies and gentlemen of his boyhood seemed to have given way completely to the angular bad manners and the hard-boiled sentimentalism of the age of gasoline and cheap gadgets. Timberlake sighed, recalling his own loveless marriage and the impetuous nihilism of his daughters Roy and Stanley.

A presentiment of failure is the prelude to a tragically significant story. Stanley, beautiful, sullen and selfish, elopes with her brother-in-law, Peter Kingsmill. When this brilliant but brittle young doctor commits suicide, Stanley returns home to stir up more trouble. An innocent negro is held for a hit-and-run murder of which she is guilty. Roy, jilted again in favor of Stanley, gives herself to a scarfaced stranger she meets in a park. In the meantime Asa, humbled by poverty and outmaneuvered by his wife Lavinia, a tyrannical hypochondriac, putters throughout the book, his heart full of fumbling good will and prophecies of doom.

Within this framework, Miss Glasgow, who has no peer as a satirist, has presented her picture of contemporary civilization and her challenge to that insipid liberalism which has been so long regarded as an excuse for irresponsible conduct and sentimental thinking. No defender of the romantic Cavalier tradition, she admires even less the cult of the present and the fanatic futurism of parlor socialists. Like her mouthpiece, Asa Timberlake, she retains her respect for decency and character, even though she does not explicitly refer to the principles from which they originate. The self-pity of the present generation seems to her a warm and enervating bath of tears. Asa's children could not even survive the slow torture of boredom, much less the sudden violence of war and famine.

One may only suggest here the extent and quality of Miss Glasgow's achievement. *In This Our Life* is written on three different but mutually dependent levels of significance. It is first of all a family tragedy in which the younger people act out their lives with Asa as a sardonic chorus and Lavinia as an agitated mourner. Beyond this it is a penetrating study of frustrated men and women sick of life and scared of death. Roy, Asa, Uncle William Fitzroy, the greedy industrialist, and Craig Fleming, the soul-stale intellectual, are painfully clear and embarrassingly intimate. Miss Glasgow's criticism of society as a whole is a third element in the story. She is not as angry as Steinbeck or as bleak as Farrell, but she is even more merciless in her conclusion. In her view it is not the dust bowl of Oklahoma or the slums of Chicago or the corruption of the *bourgeoisie* that have got us down; our collapse, she thinks, begins and ends in the dry rot of character and in the puerility of thought which some fellow novelists share with her fictitious personalities.

Unlike other criticisms of American society, *In This Our Life* permits of a kind of personal catharsis. Where one is merely numbed by the animal world of the Joads and the Lesters, Miss Glasgow's book encourages one to think and gives us some permission to hope. She leaves her readers clinging to whatever principles and beliefs they possess and more than vaguely aware that the world of tomorrow may seem very old-fashioned to the survivors of the present crisis. Not only is *In This Our Life* therapeutic in its effect, but its language contains the brilliant metal of great literature.

Edward Weeks, "The Atlantic Bookshelf," *Atlantic Monthly*, 167 (May 1941)

Interesting to consider why the South has been so fertile in novelists over the past twenty-five years. A hasty list of those novelists born in or identified with the South in their maturity would include Willa Cather, James Boyd, Margaret Mitchell, William Faulkner, James Branch Cabell, Clifford Dowdey, DuBose Heyward, Erskine Caldwell, Stark Young, Elizabeth Madox Roberts, Pearl Buck, and Ellen Glasgow. What other quarter of the country can match that writing?

No one of these twelve writes a better prose than Ellen Glasgow. Her style is clear and smooth as amber. Her delineation of the Southern City (which might as well be Richmond), her pleasure in the back country, her sympathy for the Negro and the authenticity with which she follows his thought and dialect—these are accomplishments instantly recognized in her work. And beneath the surface one is aware of two forces which inform her fiction: first, her very Southern attachment to lost causes, and then the nobility of standard with which she reveres the past and scrutinizes the present. This is what I mean by the quality of Miss Glasgow's writing.

Asa Timberlake, the leading character in her new novel, *In This Our Life*, is a lost cause from start to finish. Like a spaniel, he enjoys rolling in the odor of decay. You are told at the outset that he, a relic of an old family, is a failure in his job and a misfit in his marriage; from that point the story revolves about his ability to save something from his personal defeat and to supply some order to the muddled careers of his children. Asa Timberlake's is a success story in reverse.

I shall be an evasive reader if I fail to report my dissatisfaction with certain aspects of this book. I miss in it any feeling of suspense, and I find myself wishing time and again that the author had written with more economy. Miss Glasgow stacks the cards against Asa—you know that from the start. Then—to make things worse—she deals the hands face up. Within the fifty first pages you have a pretty clear intimation of what's going to happen to Roy, to Stanley, and to Asa—and happen it does, with a minimum of mystification and a maximum of overemphasis. The inevitable ceases to be the inevitable—or any fun—in a novel if the author keeps reminding you of it at every turn. I am sure that some of this neon writing could have been avoided had Miss Glasgow been willing to condense her dialogues. They make the book a third longer than it need be, particularly those between Asa and his daughter Roy.

And is our modern world really as lugubrious as Asa sees it? Has all virtue died out of us? Are the oncoming as reckless and selfish as Stanley and Peter, as irresolute as Craig? Must the only well-adjusted person in the household be Minerva, the colored cook? Life was never as black and white as that. 'I'm damned tired of being sorry for people!' says Asa on page 84—which are my sentiments exactly as I close this novel! At least, such people as these.

B.M.K., "New Books," *Catholic World*, 153 (May 1941), 243–4

Miss Glasgow's book contains an even slighter but no less telling clue to what is wrong [than John P. Marquand's *H.M. Pulham, Esquire*], and in *In This Our Life* everything is desperately and catastrophically wrong. The scene is Tidewater Virginia and the story concerns the members of a once prosperous and socially prominent family, now fallen into impoverishment and moral decline. Again one figure stands out as representative of some sort of dimly apprehended moral order, the figure of Asa Timberlake, who has taken refuge in a shell of ironic amusement from the hardships of his lot, which include not only his genteel poverty, but his unloved and unlovable wife, Lavinia, and his daughters, Roy and Stanley. He suffers with Roy because of the tragedies brought about by her sister, a veritable demon of selfishness. But even Asa reaches a point where, as he puts it, he gets "fed up on pity." It is Uncle William who supplies the clue to all the wretchedness, which he says is due to the fact that the younger generation has no religion, but coming as it does from a consummate hypocrite this is no clue at all.

In This Our Life is a highly sensational, even melodramatic book, concerned, when all is said, with a problem that has engaged the minds of men throughout the centuries, the problem of human misery. It makes no attempt, however, to grapple with the problem, much less to suggest a solution, which is the only warrant for introducing the subject at all. The prevalence of suffering, the existence of evil are facts too obvious to require demonstration in a book. What is called for is a novelist capable of coping with those facts, of probing the depths of the human heart in terms of the heights from which it has declined, "damned with drink of immortality."

Lee E. Cannon, "Unending Quest," *Christian Century*, 58 (7 May 1941), 627–8

Miss Glasgow's novel probes deeply into modern life and finds little that is encouraging. The eternal human search for happiness is frustrated by the inability of the individual to free himself from the maze of illusion and the biological urge and act like a rational being. He is endlessly pursuing an ever fleeting object of desire. Freedom floats enticingly ahead, always in sight but just out of reach. For Miss Glasgow's characters are eleutheromaniacs, neither freeborn nor able to pay the great price of freedom.

With tolerant, kindly irony the novelist contemplates the scene and portrays the struggle with realistic insight. Her style skillfully conceals its painstaking artistry. Ellen Glasgow belongs to the best tradition of nineteenth century realism, and the honors that are now being bestowed upon her finally bear witness to the fact. She possesses that quality which the French call *sagesse*, plus a belief that "man has all that nature has, and more"; but she realizes that all too often the "more" fails to release itself from the web of the senses, and therein lies tragedy.

In This Our Life continues the series of Queenborough novels and brings us to the present day. The plot centers around Asa Timberlake and his family, and the analysis of the strains and tensions of family life is devastating. The generations have little understanding of one another or of themselves; the different members feel fettered and oppressed. Their search for freedom is unavailing because of their impotence to arrive at a clear comprehension of where they are or whither they want to go. The weaker seem to be living like parasites on the stronger, and the stronger through their very strength seem inevitably crushed because they resist. Miss Glasgow resents the injustice of this; she develops with an irony that verges on bitterness the quandary of the idealist caught in the flux of instincts and impulses, and feeling in despair that "there must be something to lean back upon if it's only a principle," some element of stability, despite the experience "that the shape of things returns again and again in the same pattern."

This volume is a shining example of first-rate fiction. It combines the work of the philosopher, the scientific observer and the artist. It reflects the flow of some of the main currents of modern thought, embodied understandingly in the depiction of the characters and presented with discriminating power and taste. It contributes to our knowledge and appreciation of life.

"What People Are," *Times Literary Supplement* [England], 8 November 1941, p. 553

Miss Ellen Glasgow is very much a woman novelist, one of the most accomplished in America, and this latest novel of hers exhibits to good effect her feminine sensitiveness and serious-mindedness, and on that account well deserves to be our First Choice this week. Her theme might fairly be described as, *tout court*, people. What people are, what they desire, what they do to one another, how they love, how they make themselves unhappy—all this is projected, with sharp feminine concentration, in the history of the Timberlake family in a city in Virginia round about the present time. There they are, these Timberlakes, exposed in an intense light, almost a glare, of emotional analysis, and in them and their fluctuations of feeling, of course, we recognize a good deal of ourselves. Asa, at sixty, the son of a tobacco magnate who had crashed in competition with the robber barons of American industry, is a confessed failure, a cogitative soul who wears a defensive mask of irony. Lavinia, his wife, whom he would hate if he let himself hate, is self-indulgent and querulous, an ageing woman with "the large loose mind and the comfortable waist of the hypochondriac," but also with odd moments of sagacity. Of their three children Andrew, who is married to Maggie, is commonplace and happy; Stanley, her mother's favourite, is gay, bewitching and egoistic; and Roy, her father's favourite, married to Peter, is tender, impulsive and sacrificial. The story is set in motion by Stanley's flight with Peter only a few days before she is due to marry Craig. That spells unhappiness for them all, especially Roy, Stanley and Peter do not get on. He commits suicide, she comes back home, Roy and Craig try rather desperately to fall in love with one another, and finally Stanley produces more unhappiness for everybody, and not least for Asa.

There are points, however, in which, in spite of its very real merits, Miss Glasgow's work misses fire. Delicately analytical though it is, *In This Our Life* is a little too like scores of other delicately analytical novels of recent years. It has extra graces of style; but, like those other novels, it seems to belong to a convention of fiction that is fast becoming exhausted. For individual psychology in the novel is no longer enough. The instrument that Henry James perfected, that matched the social outlook to Henry James's period, has since been adapted to the imaginative experience of a period of social disintegration, and the most striking result is evidenced in the anarchy of *Ulysses*, in which human personality is sealed off from nature, society and everything save its own subjectivism. That glorification of the individual consciousness, as we see now, marked the extreme limits of the protestant tradition of the novel. To turn back along the way the novel came is surely impossible. The unsatisfactory thing in Miss Glasgow's work is not, of course, that it makes much of character and personal relationships but that it comprehends hardly anything else. A hint that human beings function as individuals in society, yes; this, after all, is America to-day or just before the outbreak of war, and the sense of a dying or changing social order is implicit in Asa Timberlake's sorrowful meditations. But of those impersonal aspects of existence which alone give imaginative significance to the personal there is scarcely a trace.

Thus, despite all her skill and sympathy in analysis, Miss Glasgow seldom enlarges imagination in us. For one thing the intensity of her preoccupation with personal feeling comes very near the sentimental; most sentimental of all, perhaps, is her repeated emphasis that people can only help themselves in emotional difficulty, that salvation comes by one's own strength, that it is necessary to be hard and not sloppy. For another thing there is altogether too much nostalgia. And for a third thing the drifting stream-of-consciousness style, with its "he thought" and "she reminded herself," is no longer a tool in the service of naturalism. It is because Miss Glasgow is so gifted and sincere a novelist that criticism of this sort at this time is her due.

Harold Brighouse, "New Novels," Manchester [England] *Guardian*, 14 November 1941, p. 3

It seems to be shown by *In This Our Life* that extravagance of incident is not fatal to a novel well written and defended by a strong sense of character. The girl called Stanley, a lovely and ferocious egoist, eloped with her sister's husband Peter four days before she was to have married Craig, and within a year Peter committed suicide. Brought home by her doting father, Stanley wallowed in misdirected sympathy, released emotion by reckless driving, killed two people on the road, accused a young Negro chauffeur, and when this was disproved got off without trial through the influence of her rich great-uncle. And after all that Craig, engaged meantime to her sister, found himself still in love with her! This must be one of fiction's silliest sequences, yet the novel survives it. The subordinate Negro characters—the scene is Virginia—are real: and if emotions run riot it is a novel, in the American phrase, of social significance.

Clare Tullis, "New Novels," *Time and Tide* [England], 15 November 1941, pp. 999–1000

In This Our Life is a moralist's novel of which the subject, roughly speaking, is the "lack of direction" about "our time, our code of living." We don't feel quite like that at present but Miss Ellen Glasgow is concerned with a family in Virginia just before the war began and her book has many hard words for our "dying age." The family—patient father come down in the world, hypochondriacal mother, negligible, married son, two daughters—are used to illustrate her thesis. Asa, the father, while doing most of the moral work, plays also a Chorus-like part, brooding over Then and Now, the "general breaking-up of a pattern of life." Mind you his gloom has some justification, for his younger daughter devastates her family by going off with her sister's husband five days before her own wedding. Though a daughter like that would be disheartening Miss Glasgow should not have let Asa generalize quite so freely about youth from particular cases, for you can no more indict a whole generation than a nation (or can you? In view of some nations?). Unduly pessimistic though this seems to me, it is, of course, coming from this author, a thoughtful, sincere piece of work, distinguished by lucid writing and careful observation of character or the lack of it.

Edwin Muir, "New Novels," *Listener* [England], 20 November 1941, 702

In This Our Life, though it deals with a tragic theme, is temperate and cool in comparison. One feels in reading it at a more comfortable distance from life. Miss Glasgow's book is a dissection of the philosophy of the younger generation in a town in the Southern States of America. Her judgment of it is pronounced indirectly through the mouth of an elderly man, a man of character but a failure, who remembers the older tradition of endurance, ironical acceptance and honour, and is troubled by the short views of the younger people, their pursuit of pleasure, and their resolve to get what they can out of life as quickly as possible. Miss Glasgow is a writer of sensitive intelligence; but she tends to idealise the old tradition, and she does not convince us that it is a sufficient standard for judging the new, though she does expose with admirable skill the disastrous vulgarity of a philosophy of enjoyment supported neither by taste nor by intelligence.

There is probably a law of cause and effect in the divergences of moral taste between the generations, and Asa Timberlake, the ironical, elderly commentator on the follies of the young, was probably himself responsible for some of those follies, without knowing it. But to Miss Glasgow the older way of life is simply good on the whole, and the newer way of life simply bad on the whole. She simplifies the problem enormously; but having done so, she displays a great deal of subtlety in working it out. The consequences of the new philosophy are described with a remorseless imaginative sympathy. She never forgets that from a given set of premises a given set of consequences is bound to follow; and as these consequences are worked out in terms of human life, and end in disaster, the story is genuinely moving.

The thesis sometimes interferes with the dramatic effect, particularly in some of the dialogue, which states the general point of view of the characters too explicitly. Nevertheless, Miss Glasgow is a writer of exceptional discrimination, especially in the quality of conduct; she writes with a fine cold passion in a style whose precision gives an effect of wit; her technical control of her subject-matter is almost perfect; what she has to say could not have been said better. Behind the scrupulous justice of her diagnosis of the modern illness one feels that there is an initial unfairness; but to expect complete fairness in an account of contemporary life is perhaps to ask too much. At any rate she takes her age seriously.

Paula Snelling, "Ellen Glasgow and Her South," *North Georgia Review*, 6 (Winter 1941), 26–7

Ellen Glasgow is important historically because she began writing with critical realism at a time when her southern contemporaries adhered almost unanimously to the magnolia-and-massa creed. She is important to us today because she has kept abreast of the passing decades without losing perspective as so many younger writers have done. But she has not charged ahead to a vantage-point requisite for constructive leadership in an era of transition. Nor has she distilled the timeless from the temporal so that her writings would be of moment without regard for the calendar.

Her achievement is that she has applied to the southern scene the better technics of the traditional novel, and that her intelligence has enabled her to do the job with a thoroughness and acumen not surpassed by any writer who has taken our region as his province. For four decades she has recorded with sustained sensitiveness the surface functionings and incongruities of our life.

Yet, though Miss Glasgow's thesis (as proclaimed by her publishers) that character is destiny is discernible in every chronicle she has penned, her latest novel gives no more evidence than has appeared heretofore that its author possesses new or deep insight into the origins of character or its workings below the conscious level. She sees and shows that in troubled waters one individual has the strength to swim where another must sink; but she does not analyze the factors that make for strength or weakness, or does she probe deeply enough to find the roots of that ambivalence within the human soul whereby an individual (or a civilization) may dedicate its major efforts to its own destruction. Nor has she a surcharge of emotion and imagination which could take her inside diverse characters to illumine for us those acts not amenable to intellectual analysis.

It is as a novelist of manners that Ellen Glasgow must be judged, for it is here alone that her talents lift her to eminence. And thereby, however excellent her qualifications, she forfeits consideration in the high category to which her more enthusiastic reviewers—partly through looseness of critical standards, partly in belated penance for having failed save at intervals during her forty productive years to give the credit she unqualifiedly earned—would assign her. But within the realm of social satire she has had few peers in this country and century. Jane Austen occurs to mind as a novelist of analogous gifts and limitations with whom to classify her. Miss Glasgow would come off the better in the comparison were it not that tools are available today whereby a writer who falls short of genius may yet reach depths of understanding not readily attainable a century ago. By former standards, she has utilized well the exceptional talents she possesses; by the more exacting criteria required today, she is found wanting. . . .

Here [in *In This Our Life*] as always Miss Glasgow is concerned with problems of immediate and permanent significance. But she has not brought to her task the genius and vision required of its artists by a generation for whom old verities no longer suffice yet in whom new values have not come to focus.

Checklist of Additional Reviews

Robert B. Munford, Jr., "Miss Glasgow's New Novel Scheduled for March 27," Richmond *News Leader,* 9 January 1941, p. 8.

Esther Johnston, *Library Journal,* 66 (15 March 1941), 265.

Frank Daniel, "*In This Our Life,*" *Atlanta Journal Magazine,* 16 March 1941, magazine section, p. 12.

Howard Dutcher, "Personal Drama Is Presented in Novel," Richmond *News Leader,* 26 March 1941, p. 17.

May Lamberton Becker, "A Generation Not Lost but Running Away," *New York Herald Tribune Books,* 30 March 1941, sec. 9, p. 1.

M.D., "*In This Our Life* by Ellen Glasgow: Dramatic Novel Treats of the Strife Between the Young and the Older Generation, and the 'Philosophy of Life,'" Springfield [Massachusetts] *Republican,* 30 March 1941, sec. E, p. 7.

Wisconsin Library Bulletin, 37 (April 1941), 77.

Booklist, 37 (1 April 1941), 359.

Blair Fraser, "New World Symphony," Montreal *Gazette,* 5 April 1941, p. 6.

"A Family Divided," Baltimore *Morning Sun,* 6 April 1941, sec. 1, p. 10.

Dorothea P. Radin, "Fine Writing Lavished on Trivial Folk," Oakland *Tribune,* 6 April 1941, sec. B, p. 7.

G.O.K., "*In This Our Life,*" Santa Fe *New Mexican,* 6 April 1941, p. 3.

Helene Walker, "Brief Reviews of Late Books," Topeka *Daily Capital,* 6 April 1941, sec. C, p. 6.

Bookmark, 2 (May 1941), 13.

Elisabeth Cary Thompson, *Churchman,* 155 (15 June 1941), 20, 34.

Robert Littell, "Outstanding Novels: *In This Our Life,*" *Yale Review,* n.s. 30 (Summer 1941), x.

Howard Baker, "An Essay on Fiction with Examples," *Southern Review,* 7 (Autumn 1941), 405.

Glasgow [Scotland] *Herald,* 10 (October 1941).

Birmingham [England] *Post,* 11 October 1941.

A CERTAIN MEASURE

A Certain Measure

AN INTERPRETATION OF
PROSE FICTION

BY ELLEN GLASGOW

NEW YORK
HARCOURT, BRACE AND COMPANY

John Chamberlain, "Books of the Times," New York *Times,* 14 October 1943, p. 19

Ellen Glasgow has always gone her own way. As a young woman, growing up in a Virginia that still felt the need of clinging to pre–Civil War tradition, she set her face against the prevailing code of chivalrous sentimentality that was spoiling all Southern fiction. What the South needed, she told herself, was a literature of blood and irony in place of moonlight, wisteria, mint juleps and memories of Marse Robert, knight of the Confederacy. Modern realism, in America, is popularly supposed to have emerged and swept eastward from the flat lands of the Middle West. But Stuart Sherman observed back in the mid-Twenties that realism, in the person of Ellen Glasgow, "crossed the Potomac twenty-five years ago going north."

As a reader who knows only the later phases of Ellen Glasgow's work, I am not the most competent person in the world to judge *A Certain Measure*, which is a book made up of the collected prefaces to thirteen of Miss Glasgow's novels. But even though I know only four of the novels in question, I derived a great deal of satisfaction from Miss Glasgow's reflections on the art of her own fiction. Taken together, the thirteen prefaces constitute an amazingly well integrated philosophy of the novel. They also contain an urbane and wittily ironic commentary on manners and morals going back half a century and more.

Miss Glasgow broke long ago with Victorian tradition. But she is rather appalled at what she calls the "barbaric fallacy" of modern Southern letters, a fallacy which would have you believe that the States below the Mason and Dixon line are peopled almost entirely by half-wits, degenerates, paranoiacs, whole idiots, nymphomaniacs and rakehells. Miss Glasgow doesn't try to place herself in any hierarchy of Southern literature, but it is obvious from the context of her prefaces that she thinks Erskine Caldwell and Faulkner are false to life in one way as Thomas Nelson Page was false to it in another. To go from sentimentalism to barbarism, or vice versa, isn't Miss Glasgow's idea of progress. As a novelist of character, she can't appreciate the type of novelist who forgets that the standards of civilization demand a concern for people with sensitivity, reasonableness, free will and moral sense.

Like Balzac and Zola and other great Europeans of the nineteenth century, Ellen Glasgow has tried to make her individual novels fit into a grand scheme or design that embraces the understanding of a whole civilization and social movement. Her six "Novels of the Commonwealth," which begin with *The Battle-Ground* and end with *Life and Gabriella,* both dramatize and satirize the last stand of the Confederate tradition in Virginia and the rise of a clamorous "new" South, the South of a vital but ugly industrialism. I haven't read any of the "Novels of the Commonwealth," but Miss Glasgow's prefatory reflections on the art of determining just what is symbolic amid the welter of available detail should be pondered by all aspiring fiction writers regardless of the quality of Miss Glasgow's own stories.

The later Glasgow fiction is grouped as novels of the city and novels of the country. They fit into the broad canvas of Virginia life, but most of them have a philosophical significance that transcends time and place. *Barren Ground, Vein of Iron* and *In This Our Life,* all of which I happen to have read, deal with the ancient theme of fortitude. They are in Miss Glasgow's grim mode. But Ellen Glasgow's prose is a variable and flexible instrument. She prefers to link her narrative to the fortunes of a central figure, which means that each separate book must keep its tone. But this hasn't kept Ellen Glasgow from following up a grim book with one of wry and ironic comedy. And, as she herself points out in more than one of these prefaces, she varies the movement of her prose in any single book with a good deal of conscious art. The analogy to musical composition has occasionally been invoked by Miss Glasgow's critics, and she is happy to quote instances of the analogy.

If these collected prefaces constitute a long essay on the philosophy of fiction, they also add up to a fine piece of perceptive autobiography. Miss Glasgow's story of how she felt her way along to an understanding of what she wanted to do in fiction is a moving chapter in American cultural history. When she began writing she had no models, no teachers. Her decorous aunts and uncles and her conventional friends and cousins conspired against her. "If you must write," they said, "do write of Southern ladies and gentlemen." In her student days Miss Glasgow was particularly interested in science and economics. She read Adam Smith, Malthus, Mill and Darwin, and was deeply stirred by Henry George's *Progress and Poverty*. While she does not regret what she learned as a student, Miss Glasgow is now convinced "that a close and prolonged reading of science is an almost fatal exercise for an author who is trying to write better." She says it took a prolonged and "total" immersion in the centuries of sound English prose to restore her natural ear for rhythm and instinct for style.

Miss Glasgow speaks of envying Edith Wharton, who had a "friendly critic" to help her model the lump of her first work into a book. But the envy is probably misplaced. Having to feel her way along, Miss Glasgow may very well have escaped being ruined by the teachers of her day, most of whom espoused either a hothouse romanticism, a pale realism, or a heavy-handed imitation of Zola's naturalism. Teaching is not necessarily to be sneezed at, but it is the self-taught person who is least likely to be afflicted with what Max Schuster calls "hardening of the categories."

Harry Hansen, "The First Reader," New York *World-Telegram*, 14 October 1943, p. 23

It should put heart into young men and women who expect to write the novels of the future when an established novelist pays tribute to writing as an art and not as a device to attract customers. Bedeviled as they are by the ballyhoo for best sellers, unsettled by the big prices Hollywood pays indiscriminately for value and for junk, they sometimes wonder whether their teachers are superannuated when they ignore much current reading. They will be cheered by the publication of Ellen Glasgow's *A Certain Measure*, a book of essays about her work and her writing philosophy, in which she speaks, with the voice of maturity, of the eternal verities.

The novel in America has taken many forms, but the two main streams of expression remain unchanged; the classical, which distills the essence of life, and the romantic, or subjective, which is personal, naive and only occasionally representative. Miss Glasgow reveals her conviction that an author's mature work is based upon experience plus reflection on experience, and that reflection embraces the widest catholicity, drawing on what is seen and what lies half-obscured in the unconscious. After that comes the selectivity that distinguishes art from the amorphous mass, and that, in the case of Miss Glasgow, truly expresses the old saying that the style is the man.

Miss Glasgow's essays include the most discerning comment on the writer as artist since Willa Cather published *Not Under Forty* in 1936. Like the prefaces of Henry James, which were published as *The Art of the Novel,* they illuminate not merely one author but a whole writing attitude.

Like Miss Cather, Miss Glasgow practices a high art of selection. Her writing is disciplined in expression, balanced in narrative, exact in characterization and never strays from the theme. She has ideals of expression and form, but when writing detaches her mind from every literary formula. "Life and life alone is the power that controls the slowly evolving situation. If theory enters the act of creation, it is wrapped up in some unconscious assimilation of knowledge."

[. . .]

Jack Kilpatrick, "Miss Glasgow's New Book Is Work of a Craftsman," Richmond *News Leader,* 15 October 1943, p. 11

This is the book of a craftsman, wrought of the English language. For men with fine deep pleasure in style—in the wonderful neglected art of putting words together with clean precision—it is a book to read aloud, to keep close at hand.

For the 810 persons who secured the *Virginia Edition of the Works of Ellen Glasgow,* published by Scribner's five years ago, little review of this book is necessary. It consists of the 12 prefaces included in the limited edition, plus a new preface to *In This Our Life,* Miss Glasgow's Pulitzer prize–winning novel of 1941.

The 1938 prefaces have been rubbed and waxed and polished until the entire volume gleams like old mahogany. It is as nearly flawless as a group of essays can be.

[. . .]

This book contains hints that Miss Glasgow may be at work on a final novel to be named *Beyond Defeat.* She reveals that physicians permitted her to work only "15 minutes a day to half an hour" on *In This Our Life,* and one finds in her courageous closing sentences a fear that *Beyond Defeat* may never be finished. If not, Miss Glasgow's *A Certain Measure* will stand as a solid achievement to end her career. For sheer perfection in writing, few books will ever equal it.

Howard Mumford Jones, "The Regional Eminence of Ellen Glasgow," *Saturday Review of Literature,* 26 (16 October 1943), 20

Miss Glasgow's work is, I think, unique in American literature and perhaps unique in the history of English prose fiction. We have had, to be sure, writers like Trollope and Hardy who have exploited the imaginative possibilities latent in regions like Wessex and Barsetshire; we have had any quantity of "local color" and regional novelists since the days of the great Sir Walter; and we have had historical novelists who have stuck pretty closely to a particular area—one thinks of Cooper's various novels about the history of New York State or Mary Johnston's novels of Virginia. But none of these has made himself the artistic master of what one may call the historical sociology of a region in quite the fashion that Miss Glasgow has become the interpreter *par excellence* of life among the Virginians.

To be sure, Miss Glasgow's work is sharply limited. It is limited in time, in space, and in class. She writes no novel of colonial, revolutionary, or ante-bellum Virginia. Most of her fiction has had to do with the Tidewater country, with life in the Virginia cities; only occasionally has she strayed into the Great Valley or into the South Side. The existence of the coal-mining town, of drab little centers for distributing goods, of a great ocean port like Norfolk, or of the mill-town—these play but a small part in her novels. Her people, moreover, are "good" people, middle-class people, people from the decaying aristocracy, and a certain kind of Negro, mainly of the "servant" class. One would search her pages in vain for much trace of "immigrant" groups, Jewish merchants, the independent Negro farmer, the city proletariat, "aliens," and "Yankees." But Miss Glasgow as a novelist has a right to limit her field; she is not required to be a scientific sociologist, so that, within these limitations she has a right to claim that thirteen of her novels, taken together, constitute in the "freely interpretative form of fiction a social history of Virginia from the decade before the Confederacy" to the present time. No other state, so far as I can recall, has produced a major novelist who can make a similar claim.

For the most recent collected edition of these books Miss Glasgow wrote twelve autobiographical prefaces, here reprinted. To these is added a preface for *In This Our Life*, the book which finally convinced the Pulitzer Prize Committee that Miss Glasgow is a novelist of major importance. There is also a bibliography of critical articles about Miss Glasgow. Anyone sensitive to the present state and probable future of the art of novel-writing must recognize that these prefaces are pronouncements of the first importance.

One has to go back to the famous prefaces of Henry James for anything of like kind possessing an equal weight and dignity. Like Henry James Miss Glasgow recalls the imaginative origin of her books; dilates on the particular fashion in which each one seized upon her creative mind; comments upon the particular artistic form or method of each; indicates favorite characters or confesses to failure; and, à propos of the problem of each, lets drop golden opinions about the task and duty of novel-making. Unlike the Jamesian prefaces, these thirteen essays are held together by the common element of dealing not merely with novels but with novels that are themselves interlinked in a great historical series. Miss Glasgow's problem is not merely that of the figure in the carpet, in Jamesian parable; it is a problem of the figure in a succession of carpets, so to speak, each laid in the same sort of room. She is not merely a novelist; she is a novelist of Virginia.

But she is not a sociologist, or rather she is not merely a sociologist. The consequence is that the temptation to discuss the technique instead of the art of fiction is a temptation she avoids. It is conceivable, for example, in view of the extraordinary social changes in Virginia during the last hundred years, that Miss Glasgow might have dwelt upon the desirability of perfecting the trick of historical or sociological fiction. She might, from the vantage point of the 1940's, have decided that her novels should have been much more like *Middletown* and much less like *Middlemarch*. She might have lectured disciples and successors on how to do a series of sociologically accurate books about Michigan or Massachusetts.

But neither the young aspirant to fictional success, who is looking for some viable formula that will lead to royalties and Hollywood, nor the future Upton Sinclairs of the country will get much comfort from these prefaces. They deal, I repeat, with the art rather than with the talks about point of view not as if it were a magic formula to make all things easy but rather as if it were (what, indeed, it is) an organizing principle of imaginative creation. (See, in this connection, the preface to *The Sheltered Life.*) She talks about lapse of time, that most difficult of fictional problems, but she deals with it, not in the manner of the outward, mechanical tricks of Dos Passos (if Mr. Dos Passos will forgive me), but in the Shakespearian sense of time and the flow of time as being of the inward essence of literary creation. She discusses style as an outgrowth of vision, not as something consciously laid on from the outside. It is only in the explication of her character creations that she is not, in this sense, peculiarly illuminating, the reason being, I take it, that character is too immediate in her mind to permit the candid discussion she gives to environment and time.

All this may seem to be leading away from the concept of Miss Glasgow as a novelist of Virginia life. But we have been buying the art of fiction too cheaply in this country. The novel has become a sort of bastard art like opera. It is written both for the printing press and for the film. It has become a manufacture, a trade, a commercial obsession. Miss Glasgow has refused to consider herself less than an artist. She has not written of Virginia life but of human life in Virginia. She has taken two and three years to perfect a book, not because she wanted it to be sociologically accurate but because she wanted it to be artistically mature. And this sense of pace and dignity, this tacit assumption that the novel is a major work of art—these are the qualities she has brought to her interpretation of her immediate environment. Her prefaces are, therefore, a notable contribution both to the art of fiction and to the ways by which fiction, maturely conceived, can illuminate American life.

Joseph Wood Krutch, "A Novelist's Faith," *Nation*, 157 (16 October 1943), 442, 444

The United States, like all other civilized countries, has produced an enormous number of novelists—that is to say, persons who have written and published not one novel or two but many. The most obvious way to classify them is to make a division into the good and the bad; but this is not the only way, and it is not always or for all purposes the most significant way. Another very useful classification which may cut across the obvious one is made if we separate those who have from those who have not practiced their craft under the control of the assumption that novel writing is a unique art, with aims as well as methods peculiar to it. The latter may write for money, fun, or fame. They may also write to attack or defend some moral or political or social cause. But novel writing is for them one of the ways of achieving ends which may be also achieved in other ways. The former write novels to accomplish something which they feel would not be accomplished at all if novels were not written. It is not a question of art for art's sake—whatever that may mean. The novels may be written not for art's sake but in order, to take a phrase from the book at present under review, "to increase our understanding of life and heighten our consciousness." But the novelist, on this assumption, has a unique way of doing both these things.

Obviously one of Ellen Glasgow's claims to distinction is that she belongs to the rather small company of Americans who have persistently written novels on this assumption. The subtitle of the present volume—"An Interpretation of Prose Fiction"—is somewhat misleading. Actually it is not a treatise on the art of prose fiction but a collection of individual prefaces for an edition of her own novels. But because she has consistently been a certain kind of novelist these prefaces almost inevitably do become a defense of that general conception of the novelist's art to which she has been steadfastly loyal. For that reason also they give a meaning to her career.

Leave out of account the controlling faith, take what the merely hard-boiled would declare "the facts in the case," and that career might become the occasion for obvious irony. Here is a woman who began as a rebel against the genteel tradition and who ends, as rebels so often do, protesting against the rebelliousness of a new generation. As a young beginner she was convinced that Southern novelists did not tell the truth about Southern society. As the result of her early efforts one old lady told her sadly that if *she* had Miss Glasgow's talents she would devote them to proving that the South had been right; an elderly relative declared, "It is incredible that a well-brought-up Southern girl should even know what a bastard is"; a publisher suggested that she should try her hand at an "optimistic" novel. A little less than half a century later she is complaining that realism has often "degenerated into literary ruffianism" and that "nowadays, American novels are filled with illegitimate offspring, and New York is overcrowded with vociferous young radicals, just escaped from the South."

Now if she were actually saying no more than that while one bastard is necessary, too many of them—literal or figurative—are shocking, she would merely be furnishing an example to support the often-advanced proposition that all generations are alike in that each is convinced its elders did not go far enough and its younger contemporaries are going too far. But Miss Glasgow is interesting because she makes a good case for her contention that the essential difference is not merely a matter of far enough and too far. Though she can refer humorously to those present-day "Southern realists who are enjoying the more profitable disfavor of the present," and can protest that "the multitude of half-wits, and whole idiots, and nymphomaniacs, and paranoiacs, and rakehells in general that populate the modern literary South could flourish nowhere but in the weird pages of melodrama," what she is most importantly contending is that "the republic of letters" has "surrendered unconditionally to the amateur"—and by the amateur she means the novelist who may seek sensation on the one hand or earnestly propagate some moral or political doctrine on the other, who may even empty, with what he hopes is scientific objectivity, his notebooks into his novels, but who is not, in her sense, a novelist at all because he is not a writer who feels that novel writing is the result of a unique activity in the course of which reality as the individual sees it is recreated in a form from which his own deepest feeling toward it and judgment of it will emerge.

A review offers no opportunity to debate the validity of judgments implied or of æsthetic principles laid down. It does, however, permit the statement that Miss Glasgow's pages afford admirable occasion for such debate, as well as an admirable account of her own attitudes toward life and art. A large part of her work has been concerned with people living with a dying tradition, one which, in the novelist's opinion, both should and inevitably must die. Yet there is nothing in which she has believed more firmly than in the necessity of a tradition to a good life. Speaking of one of her novels she says: "My major theme is the conflict of human beings with human nature, of civilization with biology. In this constant warfare tragedy lies not in defeat but in surrender." Perhaps the fact that it was her fate to develop in a society where the only definable tradition was one already doomed to death is in part responsible for the evolution of her own dominant mood, which she describes thus: "Although a kind of cheerful pessimism lightly turning into ironic amusement, has hardened to fortitude, both my sympathy and my resentment are still as easily aroused as they ever were in the past. I have never lost the old irrational sense that, by some sinister fate, I had become in part responsible for the evils of a world which, like the Shropshire Lad, I had never made."

Clifton Fadiman, "Up from Thrillerdom—Ellen Glasgow," *New Yorker*, 19 (16 October 1943), 84–5

The history of Ellen Glasgow's reputation as a fiction writer exhibits the same irony that is so much a part of her fiction. She began as far back as 1897 (*The Descendant*) to tell the South what was wrong with it, at a time when the South (and the North, too, for that matter) was committed to historical romances written with a peppermint stick dipped in molasses. It was not until *Barren Ground* (1925) that her message began to penetrate, and even then praise came to her first from the industrial North instead of from her native South. Since 1925 she has been ranked among our major writers, though belatedly and with a gesture in which there is far too much formal respect and far too little recognition of her enduring literary qualities.

Now these qualities have been pointed out, with perfect tact and modesty, by Miss Glasgow herself, who demonstrates again that no critic can write about a novelist half so well as that novelist, provided he be also a critic. *A Certain Measure* contains the twelve prefaces written for the *Virginia Edition of the Works of Ellen Glasgow* (1938), revised for this volume and supplemented by a new preface to her most recent novel, *In This Our Life*. These thirteen essays tell us not only a great deal about Miss Glasgow's art but a great deal about literature in general and its place in American life since the beginning of this century.

From them it becomes clear that her work has an extraordinary coherence. Her thirteen important prose works in effect paint a living portrait of Southern manners from 1850 to 1939, accenting the most important single trend of the period, the rise of the middle class. For all her limitations (Miss Glasgow is not quite as anti-genteel as she would like to think she is), she has given us a solider, maturer, wiser, more inclusive view of Southern life than all the Faulkners and Caldwells put together, and in a prose that is pure and unaffected.

Certain of her prejudices will seem

strange to readers who were not born in the capital of the Confederacy. It is hard to know what to make of such a statement as "Nothing better or truer than 'Uncle Remus' has appeared in the whole field of American prose fiction," and the younger men and women may feel that she is far too hard on those writers of the Hemingway school whom she accuses of what she calls "the barbaric fallacy."

Hamilton Basso, "Ellen Glasgow's Literary Credo," *New York Times Book Review,* 17 October 1943, pp. 5, 37

The novels of Ellen Glasgow, to which the thirteen essays that make up this volume are intended as prefaces, are their own best celebration. And since their author here discusses them in detail, with more wit and penetration than has been shown by any of her critics, any specific consideration, volume by volume, has been made unnecessary. Now that Miss Glasgow has set out to explain how her novels came to be written, however, posing for our more intimate understanding the various problems each was intended to solve, it is perhaps necessary to glance briefly at their whole architecture in order to understand the creative hope that raised them up, and also to measure them against the expression of creative purpose—it can hardly be called a rule—that she here sets down.

While *A Certain Measure* is most conveniently described as a discussion of the art of fiction and one that will immediately take rank with the somewhat similar discourse of Henry James (similar, that is, in that James' critique also took the form of prefaces to his novels), it has for its most immediate concern not the literary method that is called fiction, or problems of technique, but the idea of fiction itself. The book, then, was not made for babes, nor for those whose chief concern is the market. Miss Glasgow has never cared two beans for commercial success. That it eventually came to her, along with the Pulitzer Prize, is one of those muffled paradoxes out of which she has distilled so much irony....

If this has an unfamiliar sound and falls curiously on our ears, it is because it is the sound that integrity makes. Whatever the verdict of that posterity which Miss Glasgow so emphatically distrusts, whatever the conspiracy of events, so much must surely be recognized—as must the auxiliary fact that no writer was ever more conscious of the writer's unique role and responsibility or sought more strictly to meet the demands of both. For while Miss Glasgow is not unaware of the other uses of fiction—the tale told for the tale's sake, the vessel shaped to hold philosophy—she has never veered from her belief that the chief end of the novel is to create life, "to intensify and interpret the daily processes of living," and, beyond that, as a secondary obligation, "to reflect, in a measure at least, the movement and tone of its age."

The novels Miss Glasgow discusses in this book range from *The Voice of the People,* published in 1900, to *In This Our Life,* published in 1941. How well, then, do they succeed in meeting the requirements of their author's definition: what life has been created and how much of an age's tone and movement do they reflect? Well, for one thing, they bring into being a whole panorama of life in the American South from 1850 to 1940, and, for another, they sum up the social experience of the South over the past one hundred years. And while it is perhaps true that no one of Miss Glasgow's novels may be called great—the word, as here understood, being one that can rightfully be applied only to such novelists as Tolstoy and Balzac—it is no less true that, as a sustained creative effort, their sum is the sum of greatness.

It is wrong, however, to think of Miss Glasgow as a "Southern" novelist. The adjective, with its implication of provincialism, has always done her a great injustice. For the theme with which she has concerned herself—the rise of the middle class as a dominant force in the life of the South—is likewise the major theme in the historical chronicle of life in America since the close of the Civil War.

It is somewhat surprising, in view of this, to find her basic purpose so rarely understood, to see the vain attempts to classify her when she so clearly defies classification, and to hear her being called a rebel and a satirist by those who have apparently never quite understood what she was rebelling against or trying to satirize. The prime concern of Ellen Glasgow, over and above everything else, has been with a conflict of standards and values.

[...]

The truth of the matter (need it be said?) is that Ellen Glasgow is one of the few members of that numerically small elite once described by her fellow-Virginian, Thomas Jefferson, as the natural aristocracy of talent and virtue. She has all her life been trying to oppose the dubious standards of a commercial era with the strictest standards of art—not for art's sake alone, though art in itself is highly important, but because the same values that make for greatness in art also make for greatness in living. Writing of the craft of fiction, she has written a notable essay on the craft of life. It is a privilege to be able to salute her in her own time.

P[aul] J[ordan] S[mith], "Novelist Critically Analyzes Own Books," Los Angeles *Times*, 17 October 1943, sec. 3, p. 4

In our opinion Miss Ellen Glasgow should long ago have been recognized by the committee which is engaged in awarding the Nobel Prize to distinguished literary artists. At least a dozen of her novels call for such recognition.

These hold elements not commonly found in American novels; that is to say hold at once certain distinguishing characteristics one seldom finds all together in any single novel—distinction of manner, clarity of thought, definiteness of aim; a profound knowledge of certain phases of American life and critical appreciation of changing social values. Perhaps those who now award prizes hesitate before writers who refuse to abandon reason for emotion and instinct.

When the novelist sets about making a critical estimate of his own work the result is seldom impressive. The efforts of Hardy and Meredith in this respect are not brilliant, however honest they may have been. But in this field Ellen Glasgow reveals a detachment that is little short of amazing. She is able to recapture here earlier moods, to restate her earlier objectives; she is able to criticize her books in relation to time and place. She recognizes immaturity where there was immaturity but does not try it by standards of present maturity.

Miss Glasgow examines 13 of her novels, tells why they were written, what they were intended to interpret, explains what the characters meant to her and what they were in their historical backgrounds; criticizes the manner (or, if you will, the style) of each of her books.

In so doing, of course, she discovers to her reader a great deal of her own personal and family history and all it is essential to know of her literary background.

Here then is the writer who in the late 90's, saw the South anæmic and sentimental and prescribed for its literature "blood and irony." In criticism as in fiction her work is rich and rewarding. To any young person of integrity bent upon being a novelist I should say, "Here is the best guide book I know for any American writer."

Carl Van Vechten, "Most Revealing Prefaces," *New York Herald Tribune Weekly Book Review*, 17 October 1943, sec. 8, p. 6

Ellen Glasgow has been writing through several generations of novelists and has watched most of them fade away into silence while she herself has become more and more artistically articulate. She has seen her work gathered up into two collected editions and is perhaps as certain of posthumous fame (she already enjoys the contemporary variety) as any novelist alive today. *A Certain Measure* is a collection of twelve prefaces she wrote for the Virginia edition of her novels, published by Scribner's in 1938. To these has been added the introduction to a later novel, *In This Our Life*.

Miss Glasgow enjoys the unique prerogative of the successful novelist to relive and outlive the past simultaneously. Now she feels her characters warmly, again she observes them objectively with a malicious wit. She renders them to us in as credible a form as any other contemporary creator of fiction has been able to do and she writes of a period and a locality with which she is entirely familiar, whether it be Queenborough (her location for Richmond) or the Virginia countryside. It is certainly no secret to readers of these prefaces in their original setting, and it should come as no surprise to any one else, that Miss Glasgow can summon up as much vitality and pleasurable content for this description of her method as she could for the novels. As prefaces, indeed, they are models of the form and, arranged here together in sequence, they come pretty close to establishing a course in how to write fiction.

Pretty close, perhaps, but Miss Glasgow would be the first (indeed, she says as much somewhere in these pages) to argue that no one person can teach another how to write. She suggests that the best thing to do in the circumstances, if you are a budding author, is to read everything on the subject you can lay your hands on and then to ignore all the advice and to go your own way. This, indubitably, was her own method, but I dare say many of the newer generation of writers may be able to avoid many pitfalls of the craft by familiarizing themselves with the fruits of this Virginia writer's rich experience.

Aside from all this, it is indeed a pleasure for any admirer of Miss Glasgow as an artist (and those who hitherto have not been readers of the novels may very well repair that omission if they encounter *A Certain Measure* first) to become acquainted with such an intimate analysis of what pains go into the making of fine fiction. From the day when as a young girl, Miss Glasgow wrote *The Descendent*, to the hour when she indited the final page of her latest novel, *In This Our Life*, her course has been a sure one. If she did not immediately strike her eventual powerful stride at least she began by strolling along the right road. As she sees it now, she developed slowly and did not reach the maximum of her creative strength until some time in the 1920's, but it could never be said of her that she was doing anything less than her contemporary best or that she was writing to please any one but her difficult self.

[...]

W.T. S[cott]., "Ellen Glasgow Surveys Her Virginian Novels," Providence *Sunday Journal*, (17 October 1943), sec. 6, p. 8

Five years ago Scribner's published in a limited edition, only 810 sets, Ellen Glasgow's twelve best novels about the State of Virginia. For that edition Miss Glasgow wrote a dozen pretty lengthy prefaces—"And I may confess that I have written so frankly in these prefaces only because I have borne always in mind the thought that this *Virginia Edition* is limited both in scope and in numbers"—which are now gathered into *A Certain Measure* with a thirteenth preface for her subsequent novel, *In This Our Life*.

The resultant book is not only a paraphrase of her fictional history of her State, and a commentary on those thirteen volumes; it is also to an extent an intellectual autobiography, a frequently revealing diagnosis of the Southern mind, and a rich plenty of discussion on the art of the novel. "I had not in the beginning, and I have not now, the slightest interest in fiction as a trade." . . . "The chief end of the novel, as indeed of all literature, I felt, was to increase our understanding of life and heighten our consciousness." . . . "I had come at last to perceive, after my long apprenticeship to veracity, that the truth of art and the truth of life are two different truths. In any case, I had wearied of external verisimilitude when it conflicted with the more valid evidence of the imagination." And as to achievement, (there is humility in this book but no mock modesty), the title phrase appears on the first page: "What honest craftsman, regardless alike of the appraisal of critics and the indulgence of readers, would squander a lifetime upon work that did not contain for him a certain measure of achievement?"—and on the last: "We find, in a certain measure, what we have to give, if not what we seek, both in the external world about us and in the more solitary life of the mind."

It is an important book. Its over-punctuated but admirable prose is instinct with wit and wisdom. First a rebel against the sentimental tradition of the South, now a rebel against the clinical realism of the Faulknerian style, Ellen Glasgow has gone her own way. It has been an honest way and *A Certain Measure* is its textbook.

Marian Sims, "Ellen Glasgow's Appraisal," Atlanta *Journal*, 17 October 1943, sec. C, p. 8

The twentieth century has been fortunate in having three great women writers, each of whom has chosen, in the main, to portray her own particular section of America: Edith Wharton, the East; Willa

Cather, the Middle West; Ellen Glasgow, the South. While Miss Glasgow's current book indicates that she has completed a program which was planned and begun 40 years ago, her readers can only hope that this is the end of a period rather than of a career.

A Certain Measure is much more than a dispassionate appraisal and documentation of the author's work. Miss Glasgow outlines her monumental plan for a social history of Virginia and traces the completion of that plan through 13 novels and almost four decades, but the book also is a credo and a summing-up; an illuminating interpretation of prose fiction by one of the most brilliant writers of our time.

Ellen Glasgow was the first of the Southern realists. ("What the South needs," she said once, "is blood and irony.") Even as a young girl she rebelled against the pallid sentimentality which continued to perpetuate in fiction—or to attempt without success to perpetuate—a tradition which existed only as a nostalgic concept in the minds of its survivors. Even as a girl she could smile when a Virginia lady urged her to write novels proving that the Confederacy was right, or when an elderly kinsman insisted severely that no well-brought-up Southern girl should even know what a bastard was. And as a pioneer in the field of realism; she is quick to disclaim kinship with the later school which, unjustifiably, adopted the designation as its own. "... I still failed," she confesses, "to see the necessity either of embalming maggots in literature or of keeping them alive on relief." Throughout her career she has held to her belief that, although the chief end of a novel is to create life, the truth of life and the truth of art are different truths.

For Ellen Glasgow is a genuine artist, with an artist's reverence for the tools of her craft and the apprenticeship it demands. She is bewildered (and her bewilderment is balm to one puzzled soul) "by the agility with which modern novelists spring up to discredit the art they have attempted to practice." Writers today, she observes, boast of having been pugilists, or ditch diggers, or stevedores; of having been everything but students of the art of writing. It is significant, perhaps, that while scores of these potential, peripatetic geniuses of both sexes have flashed and fizzled, Miss Glasgow has continued on her way, deaf to every voice but that of her own artistic integrity.

In a day when style is a forgotten virtue—when readers and critics alike seem to be tone-deaf—her faultless prose has the sound of unfamiliar music. It would be interesting and enlightening, I think, to read aloud from this book and then follow the reading with passages from many of the recent best-sellers. Or it may be that modern readers, like children who have known only jazz and swing, would be lost and irritated in the midst of outmoded harmonies.

A Certain Measure is a volume to be read carefully and savored; to be put aside, and read again.

John Selby, "'Virginia' Prefaces," Durham *Herald,* 17 October 1943

One might say that Ellen Glasgow is the one unchanging factor in American fiction today if it were not that the phrase makes Miss Glasgow out a standpatter—which she is not. The proof of the statement lies in a book she is publishing today.

This is *A Certain Measure,* and it is a collection of the prefaces Miss Glasgow wrote for the 1938 *Virginia Edition* of her work. There were 12 of these but the new book contains also the preface to *In This Our Life*, which was published later. The lot has been revised in the light of five more years of experience, and the fact that a wider public will have access to them is important. *The Virginia Edition* was limited to 810 sets.

Even though it is a negative statement, the kernel of the whole business lies in Miss Glasgow's often-reiterated statement that she "from the beginning had not the slightest interest in fiction as a trade." She began writing when women wrote pretty sticky romances, if they wrote at all. She matured as a writer in the days of huge magazine money for those willing to conform to the pattern. And now she is living in the midst of the raw and bleeding school, when realism is rampant and social consciousness is the foundation of a large amount of our fiction.

The prefaces, taken as a whole, show Miss Glasgow most at home in the social consciousness school, but with a difference. Her novels have been a social history of Virginia, one that begins a little over a decade before the War Between the States, and comes down to the present. She has consistently reflected in her writing the involved and changing pattern of Virginia life over this 90-year period, and she has consistently shown the pattern in the lives of her characters and their action rather than in torrents of words, turgid streams of consciousness, fake climaxes and monkeybusiness generally.

The wit and charm and sincerity of *A Certain Measure* is backed by an honest evaluation of her accomplishment. But it is amusing to see that some of the books with which she is not satisfied are still being used as school texts.

James Gray, "'Blood and Irony': Ellen Glasgow Tells How to Write a Novel," St. Paul *Pioneer-Press*, 18 October 1943, p. 8

Anyone who has ever permitted himself the delicious indiscretion of writing fiction must have been asked may times by infatuated but timorous beginners, "How do you start writing a novel?" In *A Certain Measure,* Ellen Glasgow tells, in brilliant and illuminating detail, how she came to embark upon each of the novels which make up the report of her life, the lives of her neighbors and the lives of their ancestors in the state of Virginia.

These discursive essays on literature and life were written first as prefaces to various reprints of Ellen Glasgow's books. They have been gathered together into a readable volume which belongs on that still far from crowded shelf devoted to the consideration of fiction as an art. Put it next to Mrs. Wharton's *The Craft of Fiction* and compare its witty, yet essentially sober, judgments with those contained in the prefaces of Henry James.

The enthralled beginner in writing may find stimulation in Ellen Glasgow's stories of how one of her novels came, firm and whole into her mind, when she recalled a story told to her in childhood by a "romantic lady" with "slightly mottled, and invincibly smiling features." Another novel took shape all in an instant when Ellen Glasgow walking with a friend passed by "a woman of later middle age who looked at us with eyes of a faded flower-like blue and the smile of a wistful Madonna" and her companion murmured:

"How lovely she must once have been!"

This talk of the springboards from which imagination takes off on its adventures is pleasant. It may nudge the fearful into the audacity needed to make a start. But Ellen Glasgow has much more important things to say about her craft, how, for example, she came to reject the nostalgic Southern tradition which devoted itself to a "mournful literature of commemoration"; how she undertook to bring to the writing of fiction a needed "blood and irony"; how she tried to feel her way all around the life she knew, expressing her discoveries, now in grim realistic novels of the poor and disinherited, now in comedies exposing the pomposity of romantic notions of social life; how, in brief, she taught herself to be an artist making her way along the lonely path that the conscientious must walk.

The difficulties which she faced as an artist were aggravated by the fact that her family had its own traditions and these rebuked her as a changeling for her desire to write. When her early books appeared, though they now seem to their author like highly romantic exercises, they were regarded by many, even among the genteel reviewers of the day, as observations which were quite improper on the tongue of a well-brought up young girl.

She had to struggle for her identity at the beginning and even in the middle of her career. There were always people about, and some of them were publishers, urging her to write "an optimistic novel of the Far West" or something in the vein of Henry James. Despite these shocks and the others which came to her when she found that writing men, gathered together, talked not of technique and themes but of the prices paid by the magazines, Ellen Glasgow persisted stubbornly in regarding fiction as an art and her own contributions to it as raw material which must be reworked three times before offering it to public view.

These essays have three levels of interest. On the first there is that of a craftsman's discussion of ways and means of creating effects. Every intelligent artist is preoccupied with the problems of technique because they are ones which he has had to solve, in solitude and pain, before he could get his work done. It is not Miss Glasgow's task to give fully illuminating lectures on the point of view; on the drama of the interior of the mind; on the relation of character to environment; or the obligation to make style suggest the temper and the pace of the story. But she does cast light, from her individual experience, on all of these matters and she analyzes her effects with insight.

The book may be read as autobiography describing not personal pleasures and crises but the growth of an attitude and the gradual development of the hardihood that makes it possible to survive for forty years as an artist.

Or it may be read simply as the lively comment of a shrewd and humorous woman about the life of our time. Ellen Glasgow, sixty when she wrote most of these prefaces but feeling younger she says than she did in her youth, is full of opinions on a variety of matters, all related to literature but having a wider application than can be found for them in the studio. Her South, she finds, is beginning to "coquet with alien ideas." It loves "noise, numbers, size, quantity..."; its "ambition is to be more Western than the West and more American than the whole of America." This she obviously regrets for it tends to spread vulgarity and produces the "barbaric fallacy" represented for her by the books of Erskine Caldwell and William Faulkner.

She has many quarrels and she states them with epigrammatic wit. One is with the cult of youth, wielding the weapons of the new sciences. "Pompous illiteracy," she writes, "escaped from some Freudian cage is in the middle and the voice of the amateur is the voice of authority."

Many a reader will wish to argue with Ellen Glasgow on every page. He may think her an opinionated and imperious person; but he will admire the strength out of which these convictions spring and the wit with which they are expressed.

Elizabeth Green, "Analysis of Her Own Work Given by Ellen Glasgow," Chicago *Sunday Tribune*, 24 October 1943, book section, p. 16

Here are 13 essays wearing the guise of "prefaces," but written as a block, not separately, some years after the books themselves. Together they represent the author's attempt to appraise her own work. If such an unusual and ambitious project falls a little short, the fault may be in the very nature of the undertaking.

A few of the topics reached for discussion via one preface or another (with rather slim connections) include: literature as art, the author's literary creed, the prospects for fiction in a new age, the romantic tradition as a blight upon southern literature, the lack of manner and manners in the current crop of authors, and social problems arising out of the Civil War.

Ellen Glasgow can, of course, speak with complete authority upon her own books, but in the other sections, tho the style is that of the competent craftsman, the content is neither new nor especially illuminating.

A[llen]. R. M[atthews]., "Ellen Glasgow Reveals Her Literary Credo," Richmond *Times-Dispatch,* 24 October 1943, sec. 4, p. 6

Miss Ellen Glasgow, Richmond author of many novels on life and manners in Virginia, here has written another brilliant book—nominally a criticism of all her previous work. Actually, *A Certain Measure* takes on the luster of a treatise on the honest pursuit of the art of fiction in general.

Miss Glasgow from the beginning has been a literary rebel. Born more than a decade after the War Between the States, when all its horrors had wiped out the old way of life of the South, she grew up to realize that in the place of actuality, most of the Southland had set up a fantastic dream of the past for worship.

The fiction of the South was just that—written words without basis in fact, a sentimentalized rush to the past. It became the Richmonder's ambition to put onto paper the South as it really existed, happy or unhappy, gentle or ruthless, but in any case caught in the conflict which the postwar changes had brought to the region.

"My single motive," she says of one book, "was to analyze the enduring fiber of human nature under the law of continuity and the sudden impetus of dramatic occurrences."

Her job was not an easy one. She was flying in the face of almost every tradition. Even her publisher urged her to concentrate on "popular" works—advice which she scorned.

[...]

In addition to her studies of her art, Miss Glasgow is revealing in her studies of herself and in her methods of approach to the problems of her work.

Beautifully written, her discussions of her work make her books cry aloud for rereading.

From the point of view of the reader or the writer, Miss Glasgow's book stands as a valuable addition to the works of criticism.

E.M.B., "Ellen Glasgow Sums Up," Springfield [Massachusetts] *Sunday Union and Republican*, 24 October 1943, sec. E, p. 7

Comparatively speaking, American literature is a young art. Its infancy, out of which it has but recently emerged, was a painful and unpleasantly self-conscious period, when only a few figures rose to stand against the sky for years to come. They were the courageous few who defied tradition not merely to enjoy the act of defiance but to discard the clumsiness or stupidities which cluttered up the past.

One of these is still, after many years of writing, one of America's most important novelists. She has just given American readers for all time a series of essays which, one realizes when the last page is turned, deal with most of the fiction which is our country's heritage and with much that is in the future. Ellen Glasgow, in *A Certain Measure,* purports to consider in retrospect only the novels from her own pen. Her wisdom, her "hindsight and foresight" combine to offer us a far wider picture.

Ellen Glasgow is, first and last, a student of social history. The field upon which she has concentrated her shrewd and compassionate attention is the South, or, to limit it more closely, the state of Virginia from 1850 to the present time. She has written seven novels which deal with Virginia, "the commonwealth," three which are concerned with the life of "the country" and four with the manners and morals of "the city." Her purpose, she says, was to "embrace those aspects of southern life with which I was acquainted ... to portray the different social orders, and especially the rise of the middle class as the dominant force in southern democracy." In the achievement of this staggering project, Miss Glasgow has built her own monument and, at the same time, erected a lasting magnificent memorial to the state she loved and understood so well.

The devoted reader of Miss Glasgow's novels will luxuriate over the generous gesture of welcome "backstage" which the author offers in *A Certain Measure.* Each step, and many of them took a daring which is not immediately recognized by the careless reader, is explained and justified before the next is taken.

As the novels are studied in chronological order, the growth of vision, the increasing sternness of the author's intent is clearly visible. Characters become doubly real as we see why they were inevitable. Plot and incident are heightened, seen against the steady light which illuminates them on these pages. Miss Glasgow, the surprising and even shocking young novelist of the 1890's, knew nothing about fear except the dread of failing to do what she must. Today she asserts her creed with undiminished courage, knowing that today's authors will consider it hopelessly "dated."

It is a good creed, many of us agree, and she who wrote by it so faithfully proved its value over and over again. "Though the chief end of the novel is to create life, there is a secondary obligation which demands that fiction shall, in a measure at least, reflect the movement and the tone of its age." It is an honest creed and the novels which were built upon it needed no tricks or violent outrages against decency to give them enduring life.

The serious student of the art of fiction will find abundant material in this book to read, mark and inwardly digest. If he has any desire to write of his own time with integrity he will learn much from the patient, tireless striving of the author. His idiom, his pace and his theme may be at wide variance from hers. He may scorn her as a traditionalist, but it would be hard, it seems to this reviewer, to regard her with anything but respect. If he is wise as well as ambitious he will mark the margins and dog-ear the pages of *A Certain Measure*.

Strangers to Miss Glasgow's novels and those who merely "read and run" will find these essays to be the revelation of an earnest spirit, a thoughtful mind, a sharp wit and a sympathetic heart. It is the opening of a book, of many books and of a busy life. In many ways it is the author's greatest and most endearing contribution to American letters.

Stark Young, "Beautiful Apologia," *New Republic*, 109 (25 October 1943), 588–91

In *A Certain Measure*, Miss Ellen Glasgow has brought together twelve prefaces from the *Virginia Edition* of her works, published by Charles Scribner's Sons. To these prefaces she has added yet another, that to her latest novel, *In This Our Life*. This is no place for a discussion of Miss Glasgow's achievements in fiction; there is scarcely room as it is in a brief space to do more than touch on a volume that is so rich and wide in scope and content. But it should be said that seeing the prefaces thus brought together in one mass does confirm the impression of the solidity and continuity of her many works, to emphasize the body of them. And critical comparative judgments aside, it could be said, I think, that we have had no other novelist who either would or could have written thus about his own work, a set of prefaces with such distinction, point, tact, wit and searching emotion. In these days, so vast and confused, when most books are at best only good material half-completed as literary medium, it is a notable experience to find a book so profoundly unified, so brilliantly quiet and proud and distinguished.

That would imply the poetic side of the matter, the loving use of wisdom that Dante meant, the constant movement from within outward that Miss Glasgow establishes in the course of this book, so that no matter what the subject page by page may be, the whole presents a startling and luminous freshness like great memories.

On the side of simple fact, these prefaces weave in and out of their fabric an elusive variety of content. There is a social history of Virginia, the South, and American life in general. There is the record of novel writing, its movements and fads and verities, during nearly half a century. There is the study of the position of women, of the lady and her decline, of the changing literary material for heroines. And finally there is the account of each novel as it was conceived or written— many of them, as she tells us about *The Deliverance*, flowered from a seed dropped carelessly in her mind when she was a child—and the moods, ideas, delights and agonies that went into their writing. This is perhaps the most notable element of the book, for we have here a remarkable combination of, on one hand, the writer's craft and practice, at times æsthetic principles on a grand scale and, on the other hand, of personal autobiography and experience. The blending of the two, where at times the æsthetic becomes personal and the personal becomes æsthetic, is at its best a consummate performance, at the same moment learned and poignant, homely, elevated and boldly technical.

[...]

No matter what her earliest intentions may have been as regards time, place and the society portrayed, it was inevitable that a writer of so strong a nature should end by dealing with her own part of the world, which is her native Virginia, with its implications, of course, of the great world of human society at large. This volume of prefaces is never more significant and absorbing than in those passages where Miss Glasgow records her relation to the South, its effect on her, its reaction to her works, and her judgments of Southern writers of this generation and earlier, taking them either as creative artists or in relation to the region from which they sprang.

In the midst of such reflections she would naturally come to the question as to why it was that the old South should have failed to produce great books when it produced great men in abundance. As soon as we turn from imaginative literature to the uses of imagination in life, we discover that the creative art of the South was not a substitute for experience but experience itself, circumscribed and intensified. From a forgotten episode, an attitude, or a gesture, in the yellowed pages of an old diary, passion will start out, alive and quivery, charged, we are almost persuaded, with the significance, if not the subtlety, of metaphysics. Belief vibrates around us, the air thickens; and we are transported to an age in which the supernatural, or what we feel to be supernatural, borrows validity from the worship that still enshrines it. The whole scheme of living in the South was founded upon an idea of civilization not the less abstract because it was expressed emotionally and rhetorically, but with little help from the written word. If literature was deficient in realities, life was full of what we may call, according to our habit of mind, exalted or evasive idealism. Life was lived so completely in the open and in action, yet with so bright a flame on this particular aspect of idealism, that the need was seldom felt of a retreat into shadows.

The comments on Southern writers of today fall here and there, with appropriate point, in one preface after another. Among these comments is one of many to be considered: "It would appear, then, that the balance of advantage lies with the present. Yet we cannot deny that, in spite of all we have gained in substance and in certainty of handling, we have left behind us, in the dark ages of faith and sentiment, that special faculty of pure narrative which makes fiction interesting."

A Certain Measure is a wide and humbling book, and for all its crackle and facade of style and protective wit, it is a tragic book.

Robert Molloy, "The Book of the Day," New York *Sun*, 27 October 1943, p. 22

[...]

Although she was a rebel against the "romantic" in Southern literature, Ellen Glasgow might fit Mr. [Jacques] Barzun's conception of a romanticist. She found a Southern literature full of "the formal, the false, the affected and the sentimental." Without any guide—in other words, starting from scratch as the romanticists had to do when the classic era expired—she broke new ground at the very beginning of a distinguished career. That career has been such a long one that it seems almost ungallant to mention its length.

In 1933 twelve of Miss Glasgow's novels were collected to form the *Virginia Edition* of her works. For each she wrote a separate preface. These, revised and with a thirteenth preface (for *In This Our Life*, which appeared in 1941) are published in a single volume, *A Certain Measure*. They form a novelist's confession of faith, a guide for critics and authors, and a delightful example of essay writing. It is not necessary to have read all the novels of Miss Glasgow to enjoy her remarks about them, her account of their conception, of the problems she faced in writing them. It is perhaps unnecessary to have read any. There is more than enough worldly and literary wisdom in these pieces to permit them to stand by themselves. I cannot imagine any one to whom fiction is something more than a means of passing time on a train who would not be interested and absorbed by them.

"Writer 'Goes Easy' In Self-Criticism," Pittsburgh *Press*, 31 October 1943

Can a writer honestly and detachedly criticize his own work? It's a nice point that has yet to be proved, and Ellen Glasgow's *Certain Measure* does not, alas, give us the clear affirmative we might have expected from one of her brilliant capabilities.

For a brilliant writer Ellen Glasgow undoubtedly is. Yet her novels have had faults which even the most casual critic might be permitted to mention. That's why it is disappointing to find that Miss Glasgow, in this book, which is a thoughtful consideration of her own past work, admits to no fault at all.

She, who is so sharply critical of the faults of the whole world in general, and other writers in particular, seems to lose that critical faculty when facing her own works.

A Certain Measure is not, at best, the type of book to find a wide audience. Those who do read it, from a deep interest in and even a love of Miss Glasgow's novels, are likely to regret it.

Harry Goldgar, "The Prefaces of Ellen Glasgow and the Practice of Fiction," Nashville *Tennessean*, 7 November 1943, sec. C, p. 5

For Miss Glasgow fiction is "experience illuminated" and the truth of fiction is truth of a different order from that of fact, but not a whit less important or less real. When she began to write, this verged on being a radical concept; today few novelists will disagree that the intentions of the novel are "to increase our understanding of life and heighten our consciousness." Disagreement comes instead with regard to the selection of material and the methods of illumination. Miss Glasgow chose ironic realism as her method, the rise of the middle class in our South as her subject matter.

These points Miss Glasgow clarifies early in her prefaces to the limited Virginia edition of her novels, now collected with a final preface to *In This Our Life*. But her primary subject is the tremendous difficulty of attaining artistic harmony between material and medium, and the ways of transcending it. She writes of her own problems with the just implication that they are common to all novelists; but her readers will see that they arise particularly from her revolutionary break with the Southern local color tradition and the necessity of working out the methods of realism for herself because there were no models. Much of the charm of the prefaces comes from the frankness of these technical discussions, more of it from some disarming autobiographical digressions and aphorisms.

One thing she never attempts: To tell anyone how to write a book. Nothing except the weather report, she says somewhere, is more unsafe to rely on than a theory of fiction. Yet she does, toward the end, reveal a threefold principle:

"1. Always wait between books for the springs to fill up and flow over.

"2. Always preserve, within a wild sanctuary, an inaccessible valley of reveries.

"3. Always . . . endeavor to touch life on every side; but keep the central vision of the mind, the inmost light, untouched and untouchable."

It is a spiritual rather than mechanical principle not surprising to receive from Ellen Glasgow. Informed by it, her prefaces become the record of an artist who has been dedicated to the craft of fiction for fifty years. They are a record of physical pain and mental anguish but of unflagging enthusiasm; of a revolutionist who outlived her revolt but refused to leave the field to mediocrity; above all of one who "became a novelist before I was old enough to resist, and . . . remained a novelist because no other enterprise in life has afforded me . . . equal contentment." Miss Glasgow is no longer young, and she is ill. But she has promised herself that, if her strength ever returns, she will write another novel and name it *Beyond Defeat*. Of course she will.

Robert Alterman, "Ellen Glasgow Scans Her Work and Methods," Dallas *Morning News*, 7 November 1943, sec. 4, p. 4

Ellen Glasgow has for long, and rightly, been considered one of America's important novelists. Her thirteen notable novels, satisfying and complete individually, form together a social history in fiction guise of Virginia from the decade before the Civil War down to the present. And now that she has reached—by her own confession—the autumn of her creative cycle, the time was right for an historical commentary on her own work and method.

It is this commentary that Miss Glasgow gives in her fine collection of essays, *A Certain Measure*. Written as autobiographical prefaces to her novels, the collected sequence allows the author to fulfill several aims concurrently: to trace the origins of her books and many characters in them; to present self-criticism of the form and method of each; to lend invaluable advice to aspiring writers as she discusses her own problems in novel-authoring; and to bring out hidden but dynamic forces of her own life that have heretofore not been noted, or at least not emphasized.

In achieving these varied purposes Miss Glasgow uses as a hinge to swing them on and bind them together one statement that is saved for the last sentence of the book, the statement that "we find, in a certain measure, what we have to give, if not what we seek, both in the external world about us and in the more solitary life of the mind." It is in this one line—which might stand as the title for the book—that she gives justification to her realistic approach to life, properly defines her field, and gives an insight into the very nature of her own being that brought about such a sharp break with literary traditions of the past.

[...]

So then, it is with *A Certain Measure* that Miss Glasgow, certainly an important literary figure considered in any light, is placed in her proper status. Told in the charming, lucid, sometimes brilliant, prose that characterizes her novels, this book of prefaces shows her as a significant factor along the highway of literary progress. For men of letters, the book is an important historical document; for working craftsmen in the field of literature, a fine handbook of method and style. The average reader will admire its graceful, distinguished writing; for all in general, *A Certain Measure* is, surely, the skilled and first-rate product of a skillful and genuine artist.

Hudson Strode, "A Book I Recommend," Atlanta *Journal*, 7 November 1943, sec. C, p. 10

As a sort of keystone to the arch of her distinguished achievement in fiction comes *A Certain Measure*, a brilliant book of criticism by Ellen Glasgow. It is delightful to read, profound and ironically witty at the same time. Its significance lies not only in the searching illumination it throws on the growth and the productions of the author herself, but because it is the best analysis of the creative process that has yet come from the pen of an American. For both the seasoned critic and the budding novelist *A Certain Measure* may well be like a discovered spring in a thirsty land—one that will retain its sweetness and bounty for a generation of writers yet unborn.

For Southerners this book should have an especial interest because of its pungent commentary on the social history of the region, with all its foibles and imponderable virtues. By many of America's foremost critics Miss Glasgow has for several years been recognized as Our First Lady of Literature. Now in the light of her latest volume, as one reviews the sum of her accomplishments in prose fiction, one might hope for the Nobel Prize to be offered her as a tangible laurel "for her services" to the art of letters.

Gilbert E. Govan, "Of Books and Writers," Chattanooga *Times*, 28 November 1943

... Although the prefaces which Ellen Glasgow wrote for a collected edition of her novels and which have been brought together in a single volume (*A Certain Measure*), discuss no other writer's work to any degree, nevertheless they are also about a portion of the development of literature in the United States by one of those who have made it. Miss Glasgow published her first book almost a half-century ago, and from that time to the present she has held a prominent place in our literature.

Frankly, I like her book better than any portion of the other, and it is more revealing than the whole. For Miss Glasgow is not only discussing the art of the novel, but the genesis, planning and direction of those she has written herself. What she tells us is not opinion, but fact. Though she admits she enjoys criticism—"That variable branch of literature shares with philosophy the favorite shelf in my library"—she uses it only for that purpose, "for I know also how very little their knowledge can help one in the actual writing of novels."

I have not read all Miss Glasgow's novels. There are some I haven't read for many years. Nevertheless, I was as interested in the prefaces to those as I was in the ones written for the books still fresh in my memory. These essays are enlightening as well as interesting. Through them run flashes of wisdom which illumine far more than the book under discussion or even the whole of Miss Glasgow's work. "Nothing, except the weather report or a general maxim of conduct, is so unsafe to rely upon as a theory of fiction," she says. "Every great novel has broken many conventions."

Nor is the art of the novel the only thing discussed by Miss Glasgow to the greater comprehension of her reader. There is good and wise comment upon Southern life and manners since 1850. In fact, I think this book will repay its reader's effort just about as well as any I have encountered lately.

[James] Branch Cabell, "As One Famous Virginia Author Sees Another—Cabell Reviews Glasgow's Volume of Prefaces," New York *Evening Post*, 2 December 1943, sec. B, p. 2

Somewhat as when Edward Gibbon had completed his *History of the Decline and Fall of the Roman Empire*, he then published his *Memoirs of My Life and Writings,* so now that Ellen Glasgow has finished her revised series of thirteen novels "which comprises, in the more freely interpretative form of fiction, a social history of Virginia," she has turned toward self-portrayal in *A Certain Measure.*

It has been observed (to round out the analogue) that "in the matter of style, Gibbon took a great deal more pains with himself than he did with the empire." Whereas each volume of the history except only the earliest, it may be remembered, was printed from his first draft, he wrote out for the memoirs a half-dozen pleasingly different versions before deciding upon the preferred disguise in which to make friends with posterity. His memoirs, in brief, were the more congenially and the more studiously composed of his two masterworks. And just so, *A Certain Measure* is, by long odds, the most zestfully done of all the many adroitly phrased books by Ellen Glasgow. I believe it, in fact, to be the best of her books.

Truly, in the production of an autobiography the historian has an advantage hitherto denied. It is the chief peril of an historian's work that his art must lead him to impersonate knowledge which he, or it may be even she, in mere point of fact and through no stint of endeavor, does not possess. Most precariously does this become true when the historian needs to make plain some special type of character or of emotion such as—perhaps on account of the involved artist's sex or race or rearing, or it may be through an unthrifty adhesion to continence and respectable living—the historian simply does not know anything whatever, except by report. I have heard mentioned hereabouts the word "intuition"; and I have made bold to regard the word as a quite possible synonym for "humbug." The historian, in his more vivid passages of impressive and subtle analysis, is compelled very often to fake his writing, through mere lack of omniscience.

Thus, during the composition of her social history of Virginia, "in the more freely interpretative form of fiction," Ellen Glasgow has been forced to depict, not only the actions, but the emotions, of several young men under the influence of love, and the retrospections, alike military and sociological and extra-marital, of a Confederate veteran—a passage which, quite rightly, she has chosen as containing some of her most representative prose. She has delineated also the resigned sentiments of a time-tamed husband toward his wife, the meditations of an illiterate Negress, and a father's partly impatient tenderness for his children. She, in brief, has needed (as a social historian) to deal introspectively with a large host of affairs which were no more comprehensible to Ellen Glasgow, through any vital experience, than was to Gibbon, let us say, the deplorably un-English temperament of the harlot-empress Theodora, or the moral standards of Mahomet, or the quaint zest with which quite a number of Early christians appeared to enter the arena. And yet to depict these alien mentalities was, in each case, a part of the writer's job which had to be discharged, in one way or another, through the aid of industry and of fancy, in default of knowledge.

In *A Certain Measure* this handicap has been removed with results brightly delightful. Ellen Glasgow here, for the first time, is free to speak in her own person and from her own point of view, as to herself and as to the books by which she will be remembered; as to human life in general; as to the Southern gentlewoman, and theories about novel-writing, and "the late confederacy," along with a bevy of pet philosophers ranging from John Stuart Mill to Stuart P. Sherman; and, in short, as to all her some-and-forty years of serene advancement, from being as modern as Thomas Hardy, at a period when modernity was hailed as fin de siècle, toward a more conservative state of grace, in the ghost-inhabited Elysium of our present-day American Academy of Arts and Letters.

Her intellectual self-record is thus made an oddly chameleon-like volume, by turns frank, or seductive, or arrogant, or self-contradictory, or rich with wisdom—being, when the need arises, as bare as Euclid, as diffuse as Mrs. Franklin D. Roosevelt, or as neatly burnished as a carved fragment from Pater—but at every moment the book remains pleasingly human. It is, in brief, all Ellen Glasgow just for this once only very moderately diluted by histrionics. You may, as you read, agree, or you may disagree, or you perhaps may foam at the mouth; but you will go on reading. *A certain Measure* thus composes a unique and a most stimulating epilogue to an enterprise without any exact parallel in American letters.

—For I think that Ellen Glasgow's large panorama of our Virginian life as a whole, throughout the course of four generations, displays an inventiveness such as appears hardly, if at all, inferior to that which throughout Gibbon's great history goads the Reverend H. H. Milman (at the bottom of about every third page) into a chronic frenzy of corrective footnotes. I believe that by means of her luminous prose our Tidewater Virginia has bee interpreted, from well-nigh every conceivable angle, in the light of humor, and of sound knowledge, and of a loving if not always underisive sympathy, for the benefit of any such possible posterity as may yet outlive the combined labors of ballistics and patriotism. And it follows that I do not applaud the result as being fiction of the first quality. My point instead is that, when viewed collectively, the work of Ellen Glasgow is far more important than fiction. It is history of the first quality.

Just so do I think that in *A Certain Measure* she has produced an autobiography of the first quality. And this, I can but repeat, is a bifold distinction which I believe to be shared by Ellen Glasgow with but one other known writer of English, along with her initials.

J.M. Lalley, "Posting The Books," Washington *Post*, 6 December 1943, p. 10

This is a collection of the prefaces that Miss Glasgow wrote for the special and limited edition of her principal novels, published five or six years ago by Scribner and sold by subscription. As presented here in a single volume, these papers offer something which is, as far as I know, unique—an important author's critical study of her own work. But it is also a confession of her artistic faith; and for Miss Glasgow, the art of the novelist has been something pretty close to a religion, since, as she says, it is only her life as a writer that has had reality to her.

The interest and value of the book lie in what it reveals of the intellectual and spiritual processes of a serious and self-conscious artist, as such. It is as full and as honest as such a revelation could well be; Miss Glasgow does her best to describe for us the psychological gestation and parturition of her novels, to tell us what parts observation, inheritance, reading, reverie and memory have played in the creation of each. And though she tells us very little, almost nothing, of her extraprofessional life, and nothing of her own emotional attitudes to persons or events, her confession has an almost embarrassing candor, such as is scarcely to be found in the frankest autobiographies. Miss Glasgow herself mentions in one place "the feeling of outraged reserve" that she has in writing about her books; and though she ascribes it to another reason, it must be to some extent because her books are, as she says, products of the deepest and most intimate part of herself.

Miss Glasgow is a novelist by vocation, in the stricter sense of the word. It was the life to which she believes herself to have been called by her nature and character, as other women have felt themselves called to the marriage-bed or to the cloister, and to which she has dedicated herself with that wholeness of purpose, of which perhaps only women—though certainly not all women—are capable. There is in the story of her artistic development, as she reveals it here, no point of crisis, no decisive accident which determined that she should be a writer and not something else. If Scott began to write novels because his lameness cheated him of a life of action, if Cooper began to write them merely to prove he could better another man's work, or Thackeray because he had lost his money and had failed at art, or Dickens because a publisher needed a printed text to put around another man's illustrations, or Trollope because it was more congenial and profitable than working in the postoffice, Miss Glasgow began writing them because it was the natural thing for her to do. "The truth is that I began being a novelist as naturally as I began talking or walking, so early that I cannot remember when the impulse first seized me."

To her work as a novelist Miss Glasgow could bring, besides the sense of vocation and an absolute devotion, a subtle sensibility and a strong, ironic intelligence. Because she was intelligent she could perceive, what so many have not perceived, how important it is for a novelist, especially a novelist primarily concerned with the influence of a rapidly changing society on manners and character, to have a philosophic viewpoint. She read widely in metaphysics and in the history of ideas and presently worked out, as she says, "a philosophy based on evolution," and evidently strongly influenced for a time by Darwin and Huxley; but in one of the prefaces she echoes Heraclitus, declaring in so many words that change is the only reality. Apparently, then, the function of the novelist is to observe the flux, to remember and out of his memory and meditation to epitomize the effects of the transition on the little world of his own characters. Because Miss Glasgow is both intelligent and sensitive she understood the primary importance of style to the art of the novelist, and how a style must be capable of being modified to suit not only character and situation, but also to suit the many possible angles from which they may be experienced. But she also understands that knowledge thus acquired is of value to the novelist only after it has been gathered into the deep wells of the subliminal self.

In all this we can find the secret of Miss Glasgow's great powers and of her one great and, I fear, fatal limitation. While conceiving human nature as perpetual flux, she has endeavored to find a point of rest where the artist can remain conscious of the flux, but be himself unaffected by it, where the novel can concern itself wholly with social change yet remain unchanged in its nature and function. Yet Miss Glasgow belongs to a line of novelists, including Henry James and Edith Wharton, who have themselves altered the function of the novelist from one of mere story telling and entertainment to one of satire and social criticism. And having herself cultivated irony at the sacrifice of passion, she is mildly outraged by those new novelists, those illiterates escaped from some Freudian cave, as she calls them, who have sacrificed both passion and irony to mere excitement and sensation or to scientific or political polemic, or to self-exhibition. She has, in fine, taken the novel more seriously than it ever deserved to be taken—not as a phenomenal aspect of the larger entity of literature, but as an entity and an end in itself.

Oliver Kirkpatrick, "*A Certain Measure*," Bronxville [New York] *Review-Press*, 22 December 1943

Few writers are able to read their earliest work without real distaste. Even those who do so would hesitate to write a critical survey of it. Ellen Glasgow has done just that in her new book *A Certain Measure* without false modesty and has produced a book of critical writing on her work from the first novel to the latest that is full of wise observations and penetrating thoughts on the art of fiction which every writer will find invaluable.

From her earliest beginnings she revolted against the magnolia-scented literature which was then the fashion among southern writers. For these romanticists everything about the South was romantic, and their novels were almost completely divorced from the realities of life. This was to the taste of the Southerners themselves who lived in a perpetual dream of the past.

To break with tradition and write of life as it was actually instead of what the Southerners wished it to be must have required courage. Miss Glasgow is merely casual in the references she makes to the opposition she must have faced not only from the people she was writing of but also from the critics. This is not surprising since all her work is imbued with a spirit of tolerance and with sympathetic understanding of human beings.

In addition she has that innate sense of good taste which another writer besides herself, Somerset Maugham, insists is fundamental to a distinguished style. Her writing has all the graciousness of the South whose environment and cultural background produced Miss Glasgow, and none of its unpleasing features. She communicates with the same ease and grace of manner that marks people of good breeding.

Miss Glasgow is what is known as a writer's writer, someone whom one practicing the profession of letters himself will enjoy with keener delight even than the lay reader. The processes by which she wrestled with and subdued the bogeys which every writer knows so well are a positive contribution to the art of writing. Her contemporaries can gain much from her, but she will have done most by having written a book which will always be an essential part of the best in critical writing.

Maxwell Geismar, "A Too Certain Measure," *Yale Review*, n.s. 33 (Winter 1944), 364-6

A Certain Measure has the interest of a literary puzzle as well as of literary criticism. With *The Voice of the People* in 1900, Ellen Glasgow sprang, like Minerva, from Virginia's brow; and for the last forty years she has been a thorn in the side of our critics. Is she the precursor of a notable resurgence or the heir to the genteel tradition—the ancestor of Thomas Wolfe or the rather eccentric literary aunt, say, of Robert Penn Warren? Has she told us just how short a Virginian gentlewoman must fall, or just how far a major American writer can go?

As an advocate of the comic spirit, Miss Glasgow must appreciate, too, the ironies of circumstance that have contributed to her predicament. *A Certain Measure* is a collection of Miss Glasgow's prefaces for the *Virginia Edition* of her books. Her own summary of her work shows clearly how she has been out of step, not only in the eyes of literary historians but in the perspectives of history. From *The Romance of a Plain Man* in 1909 to *Barren Ground* in 1925 she was a realist in an epoch of sentimental classicism; and she became a classicist in our own period of savage and almost paranoiac realism. It is only lately, as the trend of the times has turned from its prophetic stress on the primitive and irrational—and the pleasant E. M. Forster revival is one symptom of this change—that Miss Glasgow has met her period. Or I should say, that her period has met Miss Glasgow; for of the two she may seem the more solid.

On vital points *A Certain Measure* gives evidence of this stability. In terms of her work as a whole, Miss Glasgow is better informed, bolder, more flexible and acute than one might imagine from any section of her work. If there is a certain undertone here of a writer who feels an undeserved as well as a natural isolation, she has maintained her balance in the midst of her irritation. Miss Glasgow, in fact, is one of the few moderns whose fits of spleen achieve the dignity of the grand style. And this serenity was not always easy to gain. There were the environmental difficulties of becoming a lady novelist in a Virginian society that adored the lady and the novelist (of a certain order) but not the combination. Beyond these, there were even more intense personal difficulties: delicate health, the lack of any formal education, all the constraints of that Southern sheltered life through which the young Ellen Glasgow had to break.

And when the later novels, like *Vein of Iron*, came to rest on the classical trait of fortitude, Ellen Glasgow was merely preaching what she had been practising. In her own way she had turned these personal and cultural limitations to her advantage; and she had fallen back on the one tradition that a writer can never do without, and never has to be without. *A Certain Measure* tells us just how completely Miss Glasgow's life and temperament—her learning, feeling, and wit—are bound up with her integrity as an artist; her single-hearted and lifelong devotion to her craft. Nor is this a finicky devotion: witness her fondness for that bald chronicler of womanhood, Defoe.

But saying all this, I must add that Miss Glasgow still remains a disturbing figure for the critic to evaluate. What is the matter, after all, with *A Certain Measure*—and what is the missing element in Miss Glasgow's achievement that *A Certain Measure* brings to our attention? Reading this meticulous, beautifully articulated, and slender volume, one is stuck at once by the perfection to which Miss Glasgow has brought her art—and one begins to feel, at last, the limitations imposed by that perfection. Miss Glasgow, for example, will certainly never commit the errors—of taste, of commerce, of experience—that mark William Faulkner's work (and by sheer implication Faulkner looms up in these pages as a sort of Southern Gorgon). But neither can she give us the truths of Faulkner, or his often just as compelling fictions.

As in Miss Glasgow's sober chronicles like *Barren Ground* the final line—the uncertain and disquieting line—that will really show her characters is the line that is never crossed, so the "comedy of manners" in *They Stooped to Folly* is perhaps her highest achievement. But one may still point with pride to *A Certain Measure* as an example of an artistic consciousness that is rare in our imperfect American age and literary tradition; even while one must choose, in this case, the age and the tradition.

Lee E. Cannon, "Harvest of the Years," *Christian Century*, 61 (5 January 1944), 16

This book is a collection of essays, written by one of our wisest and shrewdest contemporary American novelists, as prefaces to the difference volumes of the Virginia edition of her works. They present not only a brilliant exposition of Miss Glasgow's theories of the art of fiction, but they give us also a clearer insight into the life of the artist and the way in which she develops her characters and plots from her direct and indirect experience of life. Her lucid explanations may not be of great value to the creative writer, but for the student of literature and reader of fiction they cast an illuminating ray. They are seasoned with, penetrating comments on literature in general and enriched with significant autobiographical details.

The author is one of our authentic realists, a seeker after truth, but one who has eschewed the lurid and sensational, who recognizes her own limitations and abilities with dignity, modesty and sincerity, but who believes in the importance of her work as an attempt to create life and to reflect the movement and tone of her age. One of her most salient traits is her affinity for the comic spirit that broods indulgently over the folly of our overheated activities and smiles with faint, amused irony, although keenly sensitive to the tragic meaning of existence.

Miss Glasgow has taken as her especial province the cultural and social history of Virginia from about 1850 to the present day, but her novels cover a much wider field than the Old Dominion. There is nothing provincial about them. They offer a sympathetic and tolerant picture, objective and ironically restrained, of human nature in its strength, weaknesses and foibles. Now with detachment and candor the author explains the inception of the successive novels, interprets her purpose and methods, and judges dispassionately her achievement. The effect on the reader is profound. Here he can follow the processes of artistic creation and see how fragments of actuality are transmuted by the creative imagination into entities of reality. The skilled and reflective writer lifts transient humanity from "the flux and reflux of material disintegration" into an invisible empire and gives it a garment of permanence.

The genuine novelist needs to be a composite of scientist, philosopher and artist, and Miss Glasgow has succeeded in blending these three. She reveals a sensitive, objective manner of observation, an intuitive understanding of human motives and a power of restrained synthesis and beautiful rhythmic expression.

The author's intention, she tells us, has been to show the "rise of the middle class as the dominant force in southern democracy," and she has documented her work both from history and from experience. She has also read widely in the history of literature and in criticism and she tells us of various literary and philosophical influences that have affected her work; but, best of all, she has introduced us to her own philosophy of art. Like Heine, Miss Glasgow has been a brave soldier in the warfare of humanity. She well says: "I have tried to take the longer view. I have put my faith in ideas; I have examined life, not from a remote angle of vision, but in the flesh, and with the pulse of the living. Always I have attempted, it may be unsuccessfully, to condense the results of experience and insight into a settled philosophy. To the imaginative artist, emotions, and even ideas, may be inconsistent in relation to art, but the truths of philosophy must, in a certain measure, be confirmed by the intellect."

This reviewer wants to express a deep feeling of gratitude to the author of these essays. He recommends them without reservations, and hopes that some inquiring spirit may be led through them to a better acquaintance with his American artist.

Benjamin De Casseres, "The March of Events," New York *Mirror*, 11 February 1944, p. 22

Ellen Glasgow, American novelist, of Richmond, Va., never took orders from the public or her publishers. She is an *artist*. A literary artist is one who obeys the voice of the inner self without regard to what the critics have said or are going to say and without any thought as to whether the book will sell or whether it will ever be published. Before you read the novels of Ellen Glasgow—if you have not already given yourself that delight—you should read *A Certain Measure*, which are introductory essays to her thirteen books of fiction, the masterpiece of which, to me, is *The Romantic Comedians,* although I have not read her complete works. All her scenes are Virginian, but so great a delineator of character is Miss Glasgow and so penetrating is her irony that her men and women have the universal touch. We who love *literature* (which is the art of enclosing great ideas in beautiful prose or poetry) salute Miss Glasgow and what may be her valedictory.

James Southall Wilson, "The Novelist as Artist," *Virginia Quarterly Review,* 20 (Spring 1944), 315–20

Nevertheless, there are arts, and the novel is one of them." I do not think that Ellen Glasgow would agree with me that the conception of the novel as a form of art originated in America with Nathaniel Hawthorne and was most completely adhered to by Henry James. If, as again Miss Glasgow says, "the republic of letters surrendered unconditionally to the cult of the amateur," some of the noblest figures in fiction of the nineteenth century, and a few of the twentieth, have represented the novelist as artist. To name them settles the argument. Joseph Conrad, Robert Louis Stevenson, Thomas Hardy, Meredith, Willa Cather, James Stephens, and Walter de la Mare. Is the list to be extended with George Moore, John Galsworthy, and, shall we say, Edith Wharton? They have in common, I think, the attitude of an artist working in a certain medium to achieve a work of art. I should agree with Miss Glasgow that Daniel Defoe was the first great novelist and that Fielding is the greatest English novelist, but I think that great artists as they were, they did not think of the novel as a form of art. The art was in the way the thing was done rather than the thing in itself and its form. To Defoe the art was in writing so that readers would feel that Moll Flanders would have thought and written so. Fielding talked of Aristotle and the laws of drama but his art was the art of great writing and great creation. It is the conscious thought of the form, the book as a whole, that makes a difference in Hawthorne's work—or Ellen Glasgow's. Not that this approach is necessary to a good novelist. She is right seemingly in thinking that it is unfashionable "to regard a work of fiction as a form of art." She herself says, "All that is required indeed for the novel . . . are three characters, two passions, and one point of view." And Fielding had all "the elemental properties which make great novels wherever they are written," which Miss Glasgow enumerates,—"power, passion, pity, ecstasy and anguish, hope and despair." But Fielding did not work as a painter fitting his design to his canvas. Conrad did, and Henry James. And in the prefaces to her own novels, which collected, with the title, *A Certain Measure*, constitute genuinely, as the subtitle implies, "an interpretation of prose fiction," Ellen Glasgow demonstrates that she, too, is the novelist as artist. "Only as a form of art has fiction ever concerned me," she affirms and elsewhere completes the affirmation, "And, from my unimportant point of view, only a form of art appears in a certain measure to be worthy of the dedicated service of forty years."

Unlike the conception of the hero—and the author—of *Tono-Bungay*, Ellen Glasgow's ideas of the novel are austere rather than comprehensive. "The true novel," she says, eliminating the run of the mill in a parenthesis, "is, like pure poetry, an act of birth, not a device or an invention." There is no phrase that she uses of fiction oftener in her prefaces than one with the word "art" in it, but the creative power as evinced in characters and style is what she discusses most. "The art of fiction has remained the most accurate mirror of different stages in the pilgrimage of humanity," is her tribute to the novel as a form; but her idea of what a novel must do is suggested by two sentences which I bring together: "The power to create life is the staple of fiction" and the chief end of the novel is "to increase our understanding of life and heighten our consciousness."

[. . .]

Since each of the chapters of *A Certain Measure* was written as a preface to one of the Glasgow novels the most rewarding phase of these essays is the discussion of the novels by their author. Not before in American literature has a literary artist of critical acumen discussed so intimately and at such length the creative processes and conscious aims that gave form to the novels. Each novel has its own story. Some were the result of careful planning and devoted labor. *The Descendant*, her first novel, was begun when she was eighteen and then put aside for several years. *The Voice of the People* grew "from an effortless and inherited knowledge," and *The Romantic Comedians* "bubbled over with an effortless joy."

Miss Glasgow suggests that from the beginning her novels formed themselves within her imagination in terms of the novel's own organic principles, but she makes it clear that her later novels were written with a more conscious interest in technique. She had learned that "the supreme merit lies in the vision of the artist" and she understood a theory of realism in fiction from the beginning of her authorship; but the understanding of "a single, or at least a restricted, point of view" came to her more gradually. She marks the development of a new awareness in her art with the writing of *Barren Ground* when she found herself able "to orient herself anew" and to respond "to a fresh and, apparently, a different, creative impulse." She illustrates with rare objectivity for a creative artist some of the ways in which she has employed reverie in prose, the past and present coexistent in time and time itself "as a subjective medium." She explains the purpose of the rhythms in certain of the novels and the patterns used in others. *Vein of Iron* is woven of sound and in the very beginning moves swiftly "to the patter of running feet." *The Sheltered Life* is "shot through with scents and colours." *They Stooped to Folly* is characterized by "laughing animation" and *The Romantic Comedians* is "composed of rippling lights."

Not always has Miss Glasgow found the understanding from her readers, including the critics, that she desired. Though from the beginning she wrote with a use of that "cutting edge of truth that we call irony," she was to learn that "in print, one must be brutally obvious if one wishes not to be misunderstood."

Especially she felt that *In This Our life* was not taken, as she meant it, as "an analysis in fiction of the modern temper," "a dissolving moment in time" "between an age that is slipping out and an age that is hastening in." She intended that Asa's refusal to surrender should be felt to be "one of those rare defeats that are victories."

A Certain Measure, like Somerset Maugham's *The Summing Up*, is the noblest type of autobiography that a novelist can write. It is worthy of the novels that it helps us understand. And if there be ironies implicit as well as expressed in this distinguished volume, it may serve to quote part of a sentence said of one of her novels and so to let the lady herself have the last word, "The sting of its irony lies in the point of its truth."

Checklist of Additional Reviews

Open Shelf, October 1943, p. 18.
Emily Whitehurst, "Fiction Art, Social Order Discussed by Glasgow," Memphis *Commercial Appeal*, 10 October 1943, sec. 4, p. 10.
John Selby, "Ellen Glasgow Writes Evaluation of Herself," Asheville [North Carolina] *Times*, 10 October 1943, sec. A, p. 6 (reprinted under various titles in the following newspapers: Asbury Park [New Jersey] *Press*, 10 October 1943; Charlotte *Observer*, 17 October 1943 sec. 3, p. 7; Columbus [Ohio] *Evening Dispatch*, 17 October 1943, p. 2E; Houston *Post*, 17 October 1943, Magazine section, p. 4; Pittsburgh *Post-Gazette*, 18 October

1943; Raleigh *Times,* 18 October 1943; New Haven *Register,* 24 October 1943; Columbia [South Carolina] *State,* 24 October 1943, sec. B, p. 4; Rochester [New York] *Democrat-Chronicle,* 24 October 1943).

John Selby, "Author of the Week," Wilmington [Delaware] *News,* 11 October 1943.

Clinton [Connecticut] *Recorder,* 14 October 1943.

Guilford [Connecticut] *Times,* 14 October 1943.

Joseph Henry Jackson, "Bookman's Notebook," San Francisco *Chronicle,* 14 October 1943.

Lansdale [Pennsylvania] *North Penn Reporter,* 19 October 1943.

[Douglas Southall Freeman,], Richmond *News Leader,* 22 October 1943, p. 12.

Latimer, Watson, "Ellen Glasgow," Columbus [Georgia] *Sun Ledger,* 24 October 1943, p. 5.

Cue, 30 October 1943.

"On the Road to Lasting Fame," Boston *Post,* 31 October 1943.

Marjory Stoneman Douglas, "Book Notes," Miami *Herald,* 31 October 1943, sec. C, p. 8.

Book Review Digest, November 1943.

Wisconsin Library Bulletin, 39 (November 1943), 143.

W.K.R., "A Novelist of the South Reviews Her Career," *Christian Science Monitor,* 6 November 1943, p. 13.

N.H.C., "A Clear Mirror of Dixie," Kansas City [Missouri] *Star,* 6 November 1943.

Booklist, 40 (15 November 1943), 90.

Gertrude R. B. Richards, "Ellen Glasgow Prefaces Her Novels of Virginia," Boston *Herald,* 17 November 1943, p. 13.

Caroline B. Sherman, "What's New in Fiction and Popular Non-fiction," *Southern Literary Messenger,* November–December 1943, p. 539.

Edward Weeks, "*A Certain Measure,*" *Atlantic Monthly,* 172 (December 1943), 139.

Katherine Woods, "*A Certain Measure,*" *Tomorrow,* 3 (December 1943), pp. 50-1.

Harry Sylvester, "More Books of the Week," *Commonweal,* 39 (3 December 1943), 185.

Margarette Smethurst, "Woman Novelist Reviews Her Works," Raleigh *News-Observer,* 26 December 1943.

W. T. Scott, Providence *Journal,* 2 January 1944, Sec. 6, p. 8.

Gastonia [North Carolina] *Gazette,* 15 January 1944.

Index

A., G., 55
Aberdeen [Scotland] *Press and Journal*, 269
Academy, xix, 27–8, 45, 47, 127–8
Academy and Literature, 64–5, 67, 91
Adams, J. Donald, xvi, xxxii,xxxiv, xxxv, 331–2, 375–7, 408–10, 421–2
Albany [New York] *Knickerbocker News*, 416–17
Albany [New York] *Knickerbocker Press*, 199
Alterman, Robert, 465
America, 434–5
American Mercury, 259, 310–12, 360–2, 387–8
American Monthly Review of Reviews, 116, 129, 398
American Review of Reviews, 41, 292
American Review of Reviews and World's Work, 269
Appleton's Booklovers Magazine, 116
Armstrong, Clare, 347–8
Asbury Park *Press*, 475
Asheville [North Carolina] *Times*, 475
Athenæum, xviii, xx, xxiv, xxv, 22, 65, 95, 112, 125–6, 153, 168, 188, 205
Atlanta *Journal*, 455–6, 465–6
Atlanta Journal Magazine, 254, 351, 441
Atlantic Monthly, xxx, xxxii, 31, 48–9, 94–5, 143, 172, 188, 267–8, 287–8, 338–9, 386, 435–6, 476

B., E.M., 460–1
Babb, Stanley E., 397
Baker, Howard, 441
Baltimore *Evening Sun*, xxix, xxx, xxxiv, 182–3, 228–9, 274–5, 307–8, 323–4, 380–1
Baltimore *Morning Sun*, 441
Baltimore *News*, 157, 211–12
Baltimore *Sun*, xxvii, 83–4, 107, 202–3, 245–6
Bangs, John Kendrick, xvii, 19
Basso, Hamilton, xxxvi, 452–3
Beck, Clyde, 332–3
Beckenham [England] *Journal*, 269
Becker, May Lamberton, 441
Bellman, 165–6
Berry, Lee, 431
Birmingham [Alabama] *Age Herald*, 268
Birmingham [England] *Gazette*, 269

Birmingham [England] *Post*, 264, 441
Blair, Emily Newell, 349–50
Bogan, Louise, 318–19
Book Buyer, xviii, 11–12, 13, 39–40, 67, 75
Book News, xx, 59
Book News Monthly, xxv, 47–8, 87–8, 116, 129, 144, 163
Book-of-the-Month Club News, 397
Book Review Digest, 476
Booklist, 129, 143, 154, 172, 188, 205, 223, 268, 292, 320, 352, 397, 441, 476
Bookman [London], xxvii, 49–50, 93–4, 205, 216–17, 281, 323
Bookman [New York], xvii, xviii, xxi, xxiii, xxiv, xxv, 5, 29–31, 43, 60, 90–1, 116, 125, 144, 148–9, 168–9, 184–5, 233, 284–5
Bookmark, 441
Bookshelf, 352
Boston *Evening Transcript*, xvii, xix, xx, xxiii, xxiv, xxv, xxvii, xxviii, 5, 23–5, 31, 50, 61, 71, 73–5, 80–1, 96, 116, 122–3, 135–6, 152, 158, 188, 205, 210, 249–50, 292, 296–8, 342–3, 397, 421
Boston *Herald*, 196–7, 351, 476
Boston *Post*, 476
Boston *Transcript*, 191–2
Boston *Traveller*, 205
Boyd, James, xxxiii, 373–4
Boynton, H. W., xxiii, xxiv, 125, 204, 249
Brande, Dorothea, 323
Brickell, Herschel, xvi, 352, 370–1, 398
Bridges, Robert, xviii, 20–1
Brighouse, Harold, 438–9
Brighton [England] *Gazette*, 263
British Weekly, 65–6
B[ritton], B[everley] L., 424
Brock, H. I., xxviii, 246–9
Bromley, Dorothy Dunbar, 391
Bronxville [New York] *Review-Press*, 470
Brooklyn *Daily Eagle*, xviii, 26–7, 50, 116, 120, 188
Brooklyn *Eagle*, 205
Broun, Heywood, xxxiv, 371–2
Brown, E. K., xxxii, 348–9
Buffalo *Evening News*, 330
Butcher, Fanny, xxxii, xxxiii, xxxv, 306–7, 327–8, 374, 429

C., E.M., 398
C., L., 186–7
C., N.H., 476
C., O., 266
Cabell, Isa Carrington, 165–6
Cabell, James Branch, xxviii, xxxii, xxxv–xxxvi, 254–7, 355–8, 467–8
Canadian Forum, xxxii, 348–9
Canby, Henry Seidel, xvi, xxxii, xxxiv, 212–13, 280–1, 328–9, 397, 404–8
Canfield, Dorothy, 397
Cannon, Lee E., 436–7, 472–3
Cantwell, Robert, 392
Carnegie Library of Pittsburgh *Monthly Bulletin*, 188
Carson, Norma Bright, 129
Caswell, Wilbur L., 398
Catholic World, 259, 347–8, 387, 436
Century Magazine, 281–2
Chamberlain, John, 389, 445–6
Chamberlayne, Lewis Parke, xxv, 170–1, 398
Chap-Book, xviii, 4
Charleston [West Virginia] *Mail*, 326–7
Charlotte *Daily Observer*, 154, 188, 268
Charlotte *News*, 334
Charlotte *Observer*, 475
Chase, Mary Ellen, xxxii, 338–9, 352
Chattanooga *Times*, 432–3, 466
Chicago *Continent*, 202
Chicago *Daily News*, 308, 413
Chicago *Daily Tribune*, xxxii, xxxiii, 205, 306–7, 327–8, 374
Chicago *Evening Post*, xxiv, 133–4
Chicago *Herald-Examiner*, xxxii, 330–1
Chicago *Journal of Commerce*, 398
Chicago *Record-Herald*, 75
Chicago *Sunday Tribune*, 459
Chicago *Tribune*, xxxv, 180, 429
Chilton, Eleanor Carroll, 398
Christian Century, 436–7, 472–3
Christian Science Monitor, 476
Christian Science Monitor Weekly Magazine Section, 397
Church of England Newspaper, 266–7
Churchman, 314, 398, 441
Cincinnati *Enquirer*, 205
Cincinnati *Times-Star*, 205
Clark, Emily, 228–9, 245–6, 339–40
Clayton, Robert, 422–3
Cleaton, Edward Allen, 268
Cleveland *Bystander*, 352
Cleveland *Plain Dealer*, 223, 250
Clinton [Connecticut] *Recorder*, 476
Cloud, Virginia Woodward, 157
C[oates], R[obert] M., 329–30
Collier's, 268
Collins, Joseph, xxvii, xxviii, 232–3, 239–41, 275–7

Colorado Springs *Gazette Evening Telegraph*, 383
Columbia [South Carolina] *State*, 476
Columbus [Georgia] *Sun Ledger*, 476
Columbus [Ohio] *Dispatch*, 203–4, 475
Commonweal, 350–1, 415–16, 476
Connolly, Francis X., 434–5
Cooper, Frederic Tabor, 144, 148–9, 168–9
Cournos, John, 420–1
Cowley, Malcolm, 204–5, 424–6
Crawford, John W., 268
Crawford, Nelson Antrium, 269
Critic, xviii, 7–8, 13, 28–9, 66–7, 75, 96, 112–13
Cue, 476
Current History, 389
Current Literature, xx, 50, 58–9, 88–90, 116, 144, 154
Current Opinion, 172

D., M., 441
Daffron, Polly, 300–1
Daily News [England], 269
Dallas *Morning News*, xxvii, 377–8, 465
Dallas *News*, 200–1
Daniel, Frank, 351, 441
Dayton *News*, 422–3
De Casseres, Benjamin, xxxvi, 473
Denver *Post*, 333
Des Moines *Capital*, xxvi, 181
Detroit *Free Press*, 205
Detroit *News*, 332–3
Dial, xviii, xx, xxi, xxii, xxiii, xxvi, 7, 17, 44–5, 62–3, 86–7, 110, 125, 151, 185, 202, 269
Donald, Paul, 397
Douglas, Marjory Stoneman, 476
Dounce, Harry Esty, xxx, 282–3
Droch, *see* Bridges, Robert
Dunbar, Olivia Howard, 112–13
Durham *Herald*, 456–7
Durham *Herald Sun*, 352
Dutcher, Howard, 441
Dutton, George B., 267–8
Duvall, Ellen, xxx, 287–8

East Anglian *Daily Times* [England], 262
Edgett, Edwin Francis, xxiv, xxv, xxviii, 135–6, 158, 188, 210, 249–50
El Paso *Times*, 223
Ellingson, K., 383
Englishman [India], 220
Eve, 265–6
Everybody's Magazine, xxi, 94
Ewing, Majl, 351

Fadiman, Clifton, xxxi, xxxiv, xxxv, 309–10, 337–8, 374–5, 419–20, 451–2
Farrar, John, 281

Field, Louise Maunsell, 160–1, 223, 352, 391–2
Fitzgerald, Edmund, 268
Follett, Wilson, 188
Fort Worth *Star-Telegram*, 268, 398
Forum, 50, 136–7, 391
Fraser, Blair, 441
Freeman, Douglas Southall, 476

G., F.A., 205
G., G., 269
Galveston *Daily News*, 397
Gannett, Lewis, 295–6, 326–7, 413–14
Garland, Hamlin, xviii, 11–12
Gastonia [North Carolina] *Gazette*, 476
Gay, R. M., 386
Geismar, Maxwell, 471–2
Germond, Margaret, 397
Gibbs, A. Hamilton, 257–8, 273–4
Gilkyson, Phoebe H., 317–18
Gilman, Dorothy Foster, 292, 296–8
GK's Weekly, 269
Glasgow [Scotland] *Herald*, 441
Goldgar, Harry, 464
Good Housekeeping, 260–1, 349–50
Goodman, Eckert, 88–90
Gould, Gerald, 217
Govan, Gilbert E., 466
Gray, James, 457–9
Green, Elizabeth Lay, 269, 459
Greensboro *Daily News*, 223, 231–2, 235, 253–4, 268
Guilford [Connecticut] *Times*, 476

H., G.H., 351
H., P., 352
Haardt, Sara, xvi, 335–6
Hackett, Francis, xvi, xxiv, 133–4
Hale, Edward E., xxvi, 185
Halsey, Margaret, xxxiii, xxxv, 432
Hamilton, Mary Agnes, 218–20
Hansen, Harry, 308, 446–7
Harman, Roland Nelson, 350–1
Harper's Bazar, xviii, 8–10
Harper's Magazine, xvii, xviii, 3, 19
Hart, Evelyn, 422–3
Hartford *Courant*, 423
Hartford *Daily Courant*, 116
Henderson, Archibald, xxi, xxviii, 95–6, 264–5
Herrick, Christine Terhune, 13
Herrick, Robert, 288–90
Hervey, John, xxx, 315–17
Hibbard, Addison, 253–4
Holyoke [Massachusetts] *Transcript*, 269
Hopkins, Frank S., 377
Hopkins, Jessie, 254
Horan, Kenneth, 398
Houston *Post*, 205, 475
Hovey, Carl, 60

How to Know the Books, 96
Howe, Elizabeth Glasgow, 421
Hoyt, Eleanor, xxi, 84
Hubbell, Jay B., xxvii, 200–1
Huntington [West Virginia] *Advertiser*, 268
Hutchison, Percy, xxx, 301–3
Hutton, Laurence, xvii, 3

Illustrated London News, 66
Independent, xviii, xxiv, xxv, 10, 21, 42, 61–2, 88, 107–8, 123–4, 142–3, 152–3, 184, 290
Indianapolis *News*, 260
Indianapolis *Star*, 269
Inverness [Scotland] *Courier*, 269

J., M.F., 39–40
Jackson, Joseph Henry, 410, 476
Jarrell, Randall, xxxiv, 394–7
Jerrold, Walter, 216–17
John O' London's Weekly, 235, 267
Johns, Anne Page, 390
Johnson, Gerald W., xxix, xxx, xxxiv, 274–5, 307–8, 323–4, 380–1
Johnston, Esther, 441
Jones, Howard Mumford, xvi, xxxiv, xxxv, xxxvi, 345–6, 401–4, 417–18, 447–9
Junior League Magazine, 390

K., B.M., 436
K., G.O., 441
Kansas City [Missouri] *Star*, 320, 347, 398, 476
Keefer, Claire, 430–1
Kelly, Florence Finch, 184–5
Kerfoot, J. B., 127
Kilpatrick, Jack, xxxvi, 447
Kirkpatrick, Oliver, 470
Knickerbocker News, 416–17
Kronenberger, Louis, xxxv, 418–19
Krutch, Joseph Wood, xxxvi, 449–51

Ladies' Home Journal, 67
Lady [England], 224
Lalley, J. M., 468–70
Lamp, xxi, 84
Languish, Lydia, 267
Lansdale [Pennsylvania] *North Penn Reporter*, 476
Leonard, Baird, 292
Library Journal, 441
Life, xviii, 20–1, 127, 231, 292
Listener [England], xxxv, 439–40
Literary Digest, xxii, xxvi, xxvii, 13, 50, 67, 85, 110–11, 144, 149, 170, 213–15, 397
Literary Digest International Book Review, 268, 269, 286–7
Literary World, xviii, 7, 22–3
Literature, 29
Littell, Robert, 441

Little Rock *Gazette*, 223
Liverpool [England] *Courier*, 266
London *Daily News*, xxvii, 217–18
London *Daily Telegraph*, 223
London *Morning Post*, xxvii, 216
London *Sunday Times*, 63
London *Weekly Sun and Sunday Sun*, 21–2
Los Angeles *Times*, 181, 201–2, 424, 453–4
Louisville *Courier-Journal*, xx, xxi, xxvii, 12–13, 31, 35–7, 53–4, 79, 116, 121, 140–1, 188, 215, 268, 283, 320, 352, 398, 433
Loveman, Amy, xxxi, 298–9
Lowrie, Rebecca, 228
Lutz, Mark, 324–5

M., L., 320
Mabie, Hamilton Wright, xx, 62, 67
MacAfee, Helen, 320, 352, 397
McCormick, Virginia T., 259, 268
McQuilland, Louis J., 269
Madras [India] *Mail*, 224
Manchester [England] *Guardian*, 438–9
Manchester [New Hampshire] *Union*, 269
Mann, Dorothea Lawrance, 284–5, 342–3, 397
Marcosson, Issac F., xvii, xxiii, 35–7, 119–20
Marsh, Edwin Clark, xxi, 90–1
Martin, W. A., 330
M[atthews], A[llen] R., 459–60
Mayer, Frederick P., xxx, 291
M[eagher], M[argaret] C., 387
Memphis *Commercial Appeal*, 475
Mencken, H. L., xvi, xxiv, xxv, xxvi, xxviii, xxxiii, 141, 153, 169, 187, 259, 310–12, 360–2
Merrogate [England] *Herald*, 266
Methodist Recorder [England], 269
Miami *Herald*, 476
Milner, Joanna Rosamond, 283, 320, 352, 433
Mims, Edwin, xxiii, xxxv, 126–7, 428–9
Minneapolis *Journal*, 268
Molloy, Robert, 463
Montreal *Gazette*, 441
Montreal *Star*, 199–200, 268
Morgan-Powell, S., 199–200, 268
Morley, Christopher, xxx, 284
Moss, Mary, 116
Muir, Edwin, xxxv, 439–50
Munford, Robert B., Jr., 410, 499
Murdock, Kenneth B., 312–14

N., R.W., 223, 308–9,
Nashville *Banner*, xxxv, 428–9
Nashville *Tennessean*, 464
Nation, xx–xxi, xxiii, xxiv, xxv, xxvi, xxviii, xxx, xxxii, xxxv, xxxvi, 29, 42, 55–6, 72–3, 92, 121–2, 140, 150–1, 164, 182, 222, 254–7, 285–6, 309–10, 344–5, 379–80, 418–19, 449–51

New Haven *Register*, 476
New Masses, xxxiv, 383–6
New Orleans *Daily Picayne*, 41–2
New Orleans *States*, 268
New Republic, xxxi, xxxii, xxxiv, xxxvi, 186–7, 204–5, 250–2, 288–90, 318–19, 337–8, 340–2, 358–60, 392, 424–6, 461–3
New York *American*, 351
New York *Daily Tribune*, 129, 137–8, 147–8
New York *Evening Post*, xxxv–xxxvi, 104–5, 228, 273–4, 320, 325–6, 351, 467–8
New York Evening Post Literary Review, 212–13, 257–8
New York *Herald*, xxvii, 198–9
New York *Herald Tribune*, xxx, 295–6, 413–14
New York Herald Tribune Books, xxviii, xxxi, xxxii, xxxiv, xxxv, 241–5, 277–8, 303–4, 334–5, 355–8, 398, 401–4, 441
New York *Mirror*, xxxvi, 473
New York *Patriot and Morning Advertiser*, xxxiii, 432
New York *Post*, 82–3, 188, 370–1
New York *Sun*, xxviii, 158–9, 239–41, 463
New York *Times*, 160–1, 398, 414–15, 445–6
New York Times Book Review, xxv, xxvii, xxviii, xxx, xxxii, xxxiv, xxxv, xxxvii, 37–9, 171–2, 227, 232–3, 246–9, 268, 275–7, 292, 301–3, 331–2, 375–7, 408–10, 421–2, 452–3
New York Times Book Review and Magazine, 212
New York Times Review of Books, 176–8, 194–6
New York Times Saturday Review of Books, xxiii, xxiv, xxv, xxvi, 56–8, 81–2, 100–2, 116, 119–20, 129, 138–9, 144, 147, 149–50
New York Times Saturday Review of Books and Art, xviii, xix, xx, xxi, 5, 17–19, 44, 50, 71–2
New York *Tribune*, xxvi, 178–80, 209–10, 229–31
New York Tribune Illustrated Supplement, 43–4
New York Tribune Sunday Illustrated Supplement, 85–6
New York *World*, 205, 235, 268
New York *World-Telegram*, xxxiv, 369, 371–2, 391, 446–7
New Yorker, xxviii, xxx, xxxiv, xxxv, 253, 282–3, 299–300, 329–30, 374–5, 419–20, 451–2
Newark *News*, xxxii, 330
Nicholas, Anne, 269
Norfolk *Virginian Pilot*, 268, 335–6
North, Sterling, 413
North American Review, xxiii, xxv, 114, 124, 139, 151–2, 166–8, 352, 391–2
North Georgia Review, 440–1
Northern Whig [England], 221

Nottingham [England] *Guardian*, 269

Oakland *Tribune*, 441
Observer [England], 261–2, 269
O'Fáolain, Seán, 393
Ohio State Journal, 389–90
O'N., H., 416
Open Shelf, 223, 269, 320, 475
Ormond, John Raper, 96
Orvis, Mary B., 260
Ottawa *Evening Journal*, 430–1
Outlook, xx, xxiii, 3, 31, 62, 86, 111–12, 124, 137, 152, 166, 205, 235, 268, 283–4
Outlook and Independent, 305
Overton, Grant, 268

P., D., 347
P., M.G., 398
P., T., 21–2
P., V., 191–2
Pasadena *Star-News*, 223, 430
Paterson, Isabel, xxxi, 303–4, 334–5
Payne, William Morton, xx, xxi, xxii, xxiii, 7, 17, 44–5, 62–3, 86–7, 110, 125, 151
Peattie, Elia W., 205
Petersburg [Virginia] *Progress-Index*, 381–2
Phelps, William Lyon, 286–7
Philadelphia *Bulletin*, 420–1
Philadelphia *Evening Ledger*, xxxvii, 220–1
Philadelphia *Inquirer*, 196, 339–40
Philadelphia *North American*, 205
Philadelphia *Press*, xxvii, 192–3
Philadelphia *Public Ledger*, 205, 351
Philadelphia *Record*, 224
Pittsburgh *Dispatch*, 205
Pittsburgh *Gazette*, 102
Pittsburgh *Post-Gazette*, 431, 475
Pittsburgh *Press*, 105–6, 463
Planet [London], 143
Poore, Charles, 414–15
Preston, H. W., 94–5
Providence *Journal*, 249, 352, 476
Providence *Sunday Journal*, 455
Public Opinion [England], 269
Publishers' Weekly, 175–6, 223, 235
Punch, 263–4

R., O.S., 352
R., W.K., 397, 476
Radin, Dorothea P., 441
Raleigh *News-Observer*, 476
Raleigh *Times*, 476
Reader, 108–10
Reed, F. Dana, 116, 120
Reely, Mary Katherine, 175–6
Referee, 235
Review of Reviews and World's Work, 96, 144, 172, 188

Reviewer, 223, 269
Rice, M. Gordon Pryor, 100–2
Rice, Mrs. M. Gordon Pryor, 81–2
Richards, Gertrude R. B., 476
Richmond *Dispatch*, 13
Richmond *News Leader*, xxxiv, xxxvi, 268, 324–5, 397, 401, 410, 441, 447, 476
Richmond *Times*, xix, 23–5, 35, 55
Richmond *Times-Dispatch*, xxiii, xxv, 79–80, 99–100, 134–5, 147, 161–3, 235, 279–80, 300–1, 351, 377, 424, 459–60
Robbins, Frances C. Lamont, 305, 387–8
Rochester [New York] *Chronicle Democrat*, 223, 476
Rogers, Cameron, xxviii, 252–3
Ross, Mary, xxx, 285–6

S., R.E., 212
St. James Gazette [England], 50
St. Louis *Globe Democrat*, x, xvii, 193
St. Louis *Post-Dispatch*, 205
St. Louis *Republic*, 205
St. Paul *Pioneer-Press*, 457–9
Salt Lake City *Herald*, xxvii, 180, 197–8
San Francisco *Argonaut*, 108
San Francisco *Chronicle*, 410, 476
San Francisco *Examiner*, 369–70
Santa Fe *New Mexican*, 441
Saturday Review [London], xxiii, 50, 67, 113–14, 128–9, 141–2, 187–8, 217
Saturday Review of Literature, xxvii, xxx, xxxi, xxxii, xxxiii, xxxiv, xxxv, xxxvi, 264–5, 280–1, 284, 298–9, 315–18, 328–9, 373–4, 404–8, 417–18, 447–9
Scott, W. T., 455, 476
Seibel, George, 102
Selby, John, 456–7, 475, 476
Sewanee Review, xxi, xxv, 95–6, 170–1
Shanghai *Times*, 220
Sherman, Caroline B., 476
Sherman, Stuart P., xxviii, 241–5, 268
Shipman, Carolyn, 96
Sims, Marian, 455–6
Skillin, Edward, Jr., 415–16
Smart Set, xxviii, xxix, xxxiii, 141, 153, 169, 187
Smethurst, Margarette, 476
S[mith], A[gnes W.], 299–300
Smith, Bernard, xxxiv, 383–6
Smith, Paul Jordan, 424, 453–4
Snelling, Paula, 440–1
Snyder, Ruth, 268
Soskin, William, 325–6, 351, 369–70
South Atlantic Quarterly, xxiv, 96, 114–16, 126–7, 169–70
Southern Literary Messenger, 476
Southern Review, xxxiv, 394–7, 441
Spearman, Walter, 334

Spectator, xix, xx, 45–6, 63–4, 92, 113, 126, 142, 172, 188, 235, 317, 393
Springer, Gertrude, 352, 398
Springfield [Massachusetts] *Republican*, 164, 188, 205, 223, 234, 441
Springfield [Massachusetts] *Sun Republican*, 103–4
Springfield [Massachusetts] *Sunday Union and Republican*, 308–9, 343, 398, 460–1
Springfield [Massachusetts] *Union*, 205
Stagg, Hunter, 209–10, 223, 229–31, 279–80
Stapp, Emilie Blackmore, xxvi, 181
Steele, Erskine, 114–16
Strode, Hudson, 465–6
Survey, 352
Survey Graphic, 398
Sussex [England] *Daily News*, 216
Sylvester, Harry, 476

Thompson, Elisabeth Cary, 441
Tid Bits [England], 224
Tillinghast, Philip, 136–7
Time, xxviii, xxx, 258, 290–1, 295, 336–7, 378, 426–7
Time and Tide [England], 218–20
Times Literary Supplement [London], xxi, xxviii, 92–3, 129, 154, 172, 196, 215, 234, 262–3, 292, 319–20, 351, 394, 437–8
Todd, B. E., 317
Tomorrow, 476
Topeka *Daily Capital*, 441
Town Topics, 96, 223
Towne, Charles Hanson, 351
Townsend, R. D., 268, 283–4
Truth [England], 223
Tullis, Clare, 439
Tyler, Alice M., 116

V., E.A.U., 35
V., R.W., 47–8
Van de Water, Frederic F., 320
Van Doren, Carl, 222, 250–2
Van Doren, Dorothy, xxxii, 344–5, 379–80
Van Vechten, Carl, xvi, xxx, 277–8, 454–5

Virginia Quarterly Review, xxx, xxxii, xxxv, 268, 291, 312–14, 345–6, 360–5, 388–9, 410, 427–8, 473–5
Vorpe, W. G., 223

Waco *News*, 261
Walker, Helene, 441
Walley, Harold R., 389–90
Walton, Edith H., 391
Warwick, Diana, 231
Washington *Evening Star*, 102–3, 397
Washington *Post*, 467–80
Watson, James Sibley, Jr., 202
Watson, Latimer, 476
Weekly Review, 204
Weeks, Edward, 435–6, 476
Wellford, Clarence, xviii, 8–10
Wells, Benjamin W., 50
Whitehurst, Emily, 475
Wichita *Beacon*, 351
Wildes, Harry Emerson, 351
Willcox, Louise Collier, xxiii, 96, 114, 124, 205, 233, 268
Willson, Robert H., 330–1
Wilmington [Delaware] *News*, 476
Wilson, James Southall, xxxii, xxxv, 363–5, 388–9, 410, 427–8, 473–5
Winn, Jane Frances, 193
Winslow, Thyra Samter, 369
Wisconsin Library Bulletin, 188, 223, 292, 397, 441, 476
Wolffson, Ida, 268
Wood, Gladys Wright, 261
Woods, Katherine, 476
Worcester [Massachusetts] *Telegram*, 398
World's Work, xx, xxviii, 50, 73, 252–3
Wright, Ralph, 217–18

Yale Review, 320, 352, 397, 441
Yorkshire [England] *Post*, xxviii, 222–3
Young, Gordon Ray, 181
Young, Stark, xvi, xxxi, xxxii–xxxiii, xxxiv, xxxvi, 340–2, 358–60, 382, 461–2